THE ROUTLEDGE COMPANION TO MANAGEMENT AND WORKPLACE SPIRITUALITY

The Routledge Companion to Management and Workplace Spirituality provides readers with a broad, cutting-edge overview of the discipline of management spirituality and religion (MSR).

Marques has gathered leading scholars from around the world who share their insights and research on important topics such as linking spirituality and religion, cultural influences on workplace spirituality, mindfulness, and managing spiritually averse people. The volume also covers each of the major religions from both East and West, as well as leadership and spirituality, and issues related to linking spirituality to ethics, sustainability, and corporate social responsibility.

This volume will prove invaluable to any student or researcher looking for a comprehensive survey of the field of MSR.

Joan Marques serves as Dean and Professor of Management at Woodbury University, USA. Her research focuses on workplace spirituality, ethics, and leadership. She has published extensively, including the books *Business and Buddhism*, *Leadership*, and *Ethical Leadership*, all published by Routledge.

ROUTLEDGE COMPANIONS IN BUSINESS, MANAGEMENT AND ACCOUNTING

Routledge Companions in Business, Management and Accounting are prestige reference works providing an overview of a whole subject area or sub-discipline. These books survey the state of the discipline including emerging and cutting edge areas. Providing a comprehensive, up to date, definitive work of reference, Routledge Companions can be cited as an authoritative source on the subject.

A key aspect of these Routledge Companions is their international scope and relevance. Edited by an array of highly regarded scholars, these volumes also benefit from teams of contributors which reflect an international range of perspectives.

Individually, Routledge Companions in Business, Management and Accounting provide an impactful one-stop-shop resource for each theme covered. Collectively, they represent a comprehensive learning and research resource for researchers, postgraduate students and practitioners.

Published titles in this series include:

The Routledge Companion to Organizational Change
Edited by David M. Boje, Bernard Burnes and John Hassard

The Routledge Companion to Cost Management
Edited by Falconer Mitchell, Hanne Nørreklit and Morten Jakobsen

The Routledge Companion to Digital Consumption
Edited by Russell W. Belk and Rosa Llamas

The Routledge Companion to Identity and Consumption
Edited by Ayalla A. Ruvio and Russell W. Belk

The Routledge Companion to Management and Workplace Spirituality
Edited by Joan Marques

For more information about this series, please visit: www.routledge.com/Routledge-Companions-in-Business-Management-and-Accounting/book-series/RCBMA

THE ROUTLEDGE COMPANION TO MANAGEMENT AND WORKPLACE SPIRITUALITY

Edited by Joan Marques

Routledge
Taylor & Francis Group
NEW YORK AND LONDON

First published 2019
by Routledge
605 Third Avenue, New York, NY 10017

and by Routledge
4 Park Square, Milton Park, Abingdon, Oxon OX14 4RN

First issued in paperback 2023

Routledge is an imprint of the Taylor & Francis Group, an informa business

Publisher's Note
The publisher has gone to great lengths to ensure the quality of this reprint but points out that some imperfections in the original copies may be apparent.

Library of Congress Cataloging-in-Publication Data
A catalog record for this title has been requested

ISBN 13: 978-1-138-49918-8 (hbk)
ISBN 13: 978-1-03-265307-5 (pbk)
ISBN 13: 978-1-351-01511-0 (ebk)

DOI: 10.4324/9781351015110

Typeset in Bembo
by Wearset Ltd, Boldon, Tyne and Wear

CONTENTS

CONTRIBUTORS

Princess Anifowose is an early researcher and currently works as a research assistant of the OB/HR department at the Lagos Business School. She has her first degree in Economics from Babcock University, Nigeria, and a Master's degree in International Business Management from Griffith College Dublin. She is passionate about Leadership, Sustainability, Social Innovation, and talent management. She is especially interested in research concerning a particular group of individuals that lie hidden within most organizations—championing and increasing organizational awareness of society's problems. These Intrapreneurs ("rebels for good" as she calls them), are the focus of her upcoming doctoral research. Before assuming her present assistantship position at Lagos Business School, she gained research experience at the Enterprise Development Centre, where she helped shaped the dreams of many entrepreneurs, especially women. She later volunteered with the Christopher Kolade Research Centre for Leadership and Ethics (CRLE), located at LBS.

Duysal Aşkun, PhD, frequently conducts research in the areas of organizational behavior and spirituality. Her articles have been published in highly reputable journals such as *Management Research Review*, *European Management Review*, and *Journal of Business Ethics*. She has been a co-editor of two books on Spirituality, and has authored two books in the areas of Industrial and Organizational Psychology and Spiritual Psychology. She is the co-author of the article "How do we demonstrate Oneness as a Behavior? Operationalizing Oneness through Scale Measurement" published in *Journal of Spirituality in Mental Health*. This is the first measure about "Oneness behaviors" as a result of the 4-year-long study. She is also the author of the self-help book *Your First Step to Re-create your Life in Oneness: Awareness* with a pen name "Kayla Wholey." Currently, she serves as an adjunct faculty at Fordham University-Gabelli School of Business and New York City College of Technology-CUNY.

Puneet Bindlish, PhD, is an academic and a consultant working in the area of Integrative Intelligence for organizations globally facing VUCA (Volatility, Uncertainty, Complexity, and Ambiguity) challenges. He is a faculty in the Department of Humanistics Studies with the Indian Institute of Technology, Banaras Hindu University IIT(BHU), Varanasi (India), and is the co-founder of the concept of Integrative Intelligence. He is a well published researcher and author with rich research, consulting, and entrepreneurial experience across sectors like health care, telecoms, technology, banking and insurance, education, sports, and public governance. He is well traveled with diverse cross-cultural exposure through consulting, research, and teaching engagements across Europe, North America, and Asia (Indian citizen). His current research interests lie in designing and implementation of integratively intelligent self-managed organizations.

Sylvia W. Burgess, PhD, is a Senior Partner with One Step at a Time Consulting, LLC providing services for leadership training and development. She has over 18 years of experience in teaching, facilitation, curriculum design, leadership development, community engagement, cultural competency, diversity and inclusion, team building, and conflict resolution. She is a published author in the areas of spiritual capital and community engagement. She received BA in Speech and Language Pathology and MPA from University of North Carolina Greensboro. She earned a PhD in Leadership Studies from North Carolina A&T State University. She has proven leadership and senior management experience in business, operational management, and training and with the Center for Creative Leadership. She has served as an adjunct professor at North Carolina A&T State University in the Leadership Studies doctoral program. She is a native North Carolinian and resides in Greensboro, North Carolina with her daughter, Avigayil.

Subhasis Chakrabarti is a Vedanta philosophy teacher at the Vedanta Institute Kolkata, India. He graduated from the Vedanta Academy, Malavli, India, with a diploma in Vedanta philosophy. His diverse research interests range from Western and Indian Philosophy to Neurobiology and Consciousness Studies. He holds a MBBS from the University of Kolkata, India.

Dylan Cooper, PhD, is an Assistant Professor of Management in the MVS School of Business and Economics of California State University Channel Islands. He has published in the *Journal of Behavioral Decision Making* and the *International Journal of Conflict Management*. His current research addresses advice taking within organizations and selection issues related to counterproductive work behavior.

Cheryl De Ciantis, PhD, is co-founder of Kairios, an independent human development research and practice group. She is co-author of the Kairios Values Perspectives theory and survey; and of *What's Important: Understanding and Working with Values Perspectives* (2014). She served as Senior Faculty and Director of the European Campus of the Center for Creative Leadership in Brussels, and has consulted extensively in public, private, and educational institutions and across business sectors, working as a coach, team and leadership development designer and facilitator, and organizational mentor specializing in creating and documenting in-depth, experiential creative/reflective learning and development methodologies and outcomes. An artist, writer, and storyteller, she obtained her Doctorate in Mythological Studies and Depth Psychology from Pacifica Graduate Institute, which houses the Joseph Campbell Library and Archive, where she initiated her research into the intersection of art, technology, and culture. She lives with her work and life partner, Dr. Kenton Hyatt, in Tucson, Arizona.

Debra J. Dean, PhD, is affiliated with Regent University as an adjunct professor. She is also President & CEO of Dean Business Consulting. Recent notable conference participation includes The Faith at Work Summit, Academy of Management MSR Consortium Planning, Academic Oasis, OPEX Week: Business Transformation World Summit, and the Regent University Roundtable. Latest research efforts include the following: (a) Integration of Christian Values in the Workplace: An examination of employee engagement, job satisfaction, and organizational commitment, (b) Religion and Spirituality in the Workplace: A quantitative evaluation of job satisfaction and organizational commitment, and (c) A Correlation Study of Employee Engagement and Servant Leadership. She received the 2018 Outstanding Reviewer award for the Management, Spirituality, and Religion (MSR) community, she was nominated as one of three top operational excellence leaders with OPEX, and was nominated as a top female leader within her previous global workplace.

Eric B. Dent, PhD, serves as Professor and Uncommon Friends Endowed Chair in Ethics at Florida Gulf Coast University. He is committed to an interdisciplinary research agenda and has publications in journals of leadership, consulting, philosophy, workplace spirituality, science, history, communications, psychology, education, and others. He has been honored for his teaching, scholarship, and service including two best paper awards at the Academy of Management Conference and North Carolina's highest designation of appreciation for distinguished volunteer service bestowed by the governor. He has served in many capacities in academia, ranging from Faculty Senate Chair to Business School Dean. He is a consultant to Fortune 500, government, and non-profit organizations as well as an invited speaker to national audiences. Prior to earning his PhD, he served as a corporate vice-president in the financial services industry. He began his career as a computer scientist with IBM.

Satinder Dhiman, PhD, EdD, serves as Associate Dean, Chair, and Director of the MBA Program and Professor of Management at Woodbury University's School of Business, Burbank, California. He teaches courses pertaining to ethical leadership, sustainability, organizational behavior and strategy, and spirituality in the workplace in the MBA program. Author, translator, co-author, and co-editor of 25 books, his most recent books include *Holistic Leadership* (2017) and *Gandhi and Leadership* (2015). He is the Editor-in-Chief of two major reference works: *The Palgrave Handbook of Workplace Spirituality and Fulfillment* (2018) and the Springer *Handbook of Engaged Sustainability* (2018). Recipient of several national and international professional honors, he is also the winner of the Steve Allen Excellence in Education Award and the prestigious ACBSP International Teacher of the Year Award. He is the founding director of a Wellbeing Consultancy, Foreverfulfilled.com. He has also completed advanced Executive Leadership programs at Harvard, Stanford, and Wharton.

Timothy Ewest, PhD, Associate Professor of Management, and MBA program director, has worked in higher education since 2002 teaching management, leadership, ethics, corporate social responsibility, and stewardship. His research interests include issues surrounding the integration of faith at work, and prosocial leadership. He has published journal articles and books on prosocial leadership and faith at work. He has also been invited as an editor for academic journals. Besides his duties at Houston Baptist University, has worked as a Visiting Research Collaborator with David Miller at Princeton University's Faith & Work Initiative and as a member of the United Nations Think Thanks on Responsible Management. He holds a Master's Degree in Theology from Wheaton College, a Master's degree in Theology from Regent University, an MBA from George Fox University, is an ordained minister in the Christian and Missionary Alliance, and holds a DMgnt from George Fox University.

Jean-Claude Garcia-Zamor, PhD, is a Professor of Public Policy and Administration at Florida International University in Miami, Florida. He has held a variety of senior positions in major international organizations. He served as Controller of the Inter-American Development Bank, Senior Specialist in Public Administration at the Organization of American States, and

President of the International Development Group, Inc., a 25-member Washington-based international consulting firm. He has also worked in Latin America and in Africa as a consultant for the World Bank, the United Nations, and the United States Agency for International Development. He is the author of seven books, has edited or co-edited six others and contributed chapters to numerous other books. He has also published extensively on issues of development administration, organizational behavior, comparative public administration, and ethics and government. His most recent book, *Ethical Dilemmas of Migration: Moral Challenges to Policymakers* was published by Springer Publishers in March 2018.

Dirk Geldenhuys, DADMIN, is a full Professor in Industrial and Organisational Psychology at the University of South Africa and chaired the department for 6 years. He is a registered Industrial Psychologist and Master HR Practitioner with lifelong honorary membership of the Society for Industrial and Organisational Psychology of South Africa. He was trained in and obtained more than 20 years' experience in Systems-Psychodynamics, Appreciative Inquiry, Socio Constructionism and for the past 5 years in Organizational Neuroscience. He teaches coaching on Masters' level and acts as promotor for doctoral and master students. In his private capacity he is involved in Organizational Development and coaches to individuals and groups on all organizational levels, across industries.

Ginger Grant, PhD, is the Associate Dean of Applied Research and Innovation at Humber College in Toronto, Canada and a Visiting Professor at the Copenhagen Business School in Denmark. As an Innovation Researcher and Academic Entrepreneur and Activist, her passion is creativity in business—the design, development, and implementation of narrative game plans that transform corporate culture, and drive employee engagement and high-performance teams for competitive advantage. She has held senior leadership positions and consulted in a variety of fields including engineering, telecommunications, education, transportation, government, law, software development, gaming, and the creative industries. She is a popular international conference speaker.

Céleste Grimard, PhD, is a full professor with the School of Management at the University of Quebec in Montreal. She publishes widely in the areas of burnout, bullying, emotions, and leadership. She has published numerous articles in peer review journals and book chapters, as well as several books on leadership, civility at work, civility in the classroom, managerial competencies, and employee effectiveness. She is a member of the editorial board of several journals including, among others, the *Journal of Managerial Psychology*, and *Team Performance Management*. She is a board member of the Association for Business Simulations and Experiential Learning.

William A. Guillory, PhD, is an authority on personal and organizational transformation. He has published more than 12 books on this subject including *Realizations*, *How to Become a Total Failure*, *Spirituality in the Workplace*, *Living Without Fear*, and the *Guides*. His most recent series is the Pleiadian Trilogy: *The Pleiadians*; *The Hunt for the Billionaire Club*; and *The Consortium*. Prior to founding the consulting firm Innovations International Inc., he was a chemical physicist of international renown, publishing more than 100 papers on the application of lasers in chemistry. He has facilitated leadership seminars for more than 400 organizations throughout the world. In addition, he has led retreats globally in personal and spiritual transformation through the Center for Creativity and Inquiry; where he is Executive Director.

Kira Haensel is a second-year student in the PhD Program in Public Affairs at Florida International University. She obtained her Bachelor of Arts in Public Administration from

Westfaelische-Wilhelms University in Muenster, Germany, as well as a Bachelor of Science in European Public Administration from the University of Twente in the Netherlands. She earned her Master of Arts in Latin American and Caribbean Studies with a focus on Public Administration from Florida International University. Her research interests are in Leadership Styles and Executive Personalities, Leadership in Crisis Situations, Leadership and Group Behavior.

Giles Hutchins is a pioneering practitioner and senior advisor at the forefront of the [r]evolution in organizational and leadership consciousness and developmental approaches that enhance personal, organizational, and systemic agility and vitality. He is author of several leadership and organizational development papers, and the books *The Nature of Business* (2012), *The Illusion of Separation* (2014), *Future Fit* (2016). Over the last 25 years he has been an international Management Consultant and Head of Practice with KPMG, and Global Sustainability Director for Atos, a technology multinational. He has advised organizations across the world, and across all sectors, has been interviewed by the BBC and advises a number of forward-thinking academies. He contributes to international business school research, runs deep-dive transformation Learning Journeys, is Chair of the Future Fit Leadership Academy is co-founder of Regenerators, co-founder of Biomimicry for Creative Innovation, and an executive coach to senior leaders.

Susanna Kislenko is a doctoral student in the Organizational Behaviour department at IESE Business School in Barcelona, Spain. Her research interests lie at the intersection of leadership and entrepreneurship, with a focus on founder identity and motivation. Prior to pursuing doctoral studies, she spent 12 years in the non-profit sector in Canada, holding a number of leadership roles in social service organizations. During this time, she received a scholarship from the Harvard Business School Alumni Club of Toronto to complete the "Strategic Management in Non-Profit Organizations" executive training program at Harvard Business School. Her academic work has been presented at a number of academic conferences, including Strategic Management Society (SMS) and European Group for Organizational Studies (EGOS) and she has co-authored two book chapters, a teaching case, and a journal article in the sphere of social entrepreneurship. She has also been a dedicated yoga practitioner for the last 19 years and a hatha yoga instructor for 14 years.

Wanda Krause, PhD, is faculty at Royal Roads University in the School of Leadership and MA in Global Leadership, and runs Krause Consulting at www.wandakrause.com. Her PhD is in politics with a focus on organizational development, where she evaluated the impacts of women's participation in their initiatives on civil society development in international settings. She has lived in six countries and taught and consulted in several as well. She has contributed to, written, and edited five books as award winning and international bestselling author: *When You're DONE Expecting: A Collection of Heartfelt Stories from Mothers all Across the Globe*; *Spiritual Activism: Keys for Personal and Political Success*; *Civil Society and Women Activists in the Middle East*; *Citizenship, Security and Democracy: Muslim Engagement with the West*; and *Women in Civil Society: The State, Islamism, and Networks in the UAE*; as well, she has contributed several journal papers and book chapters.

Sukumarakurup Krishnakumar (Kumar), PhD, is an Associate Professor of Management at the Keck Graduate Institute, Claremont, California. He completed his PhD in Management from Virginia Tech. He has been teaching Organizational Behavior and Leadership for over a decade. His current research interests are spirituality at work, workplace socio-emotional abilities, mindfulness, and prosocial behaviors. He has published articles in the *Emotion, Personality* *and Social Psychology Bulletin*, *Journal of Psychology: Interdisciplinary and Applied*, *Journal of Managerial Psychology*, *Journal of Management, Spirituality, and Religion*, and *Motivation and Emotion*. His research has led to the development of an ability-based test of Work-Emotional Intelligence. Additionally, he also investigates the role of emotions and emotional intelligence in prosocial behaviors such as gift giving and happiness.

Bekir Emre Kurtulmuş is Assistant Professor at Kuwait College of Science and Technology, Kuwait. Having previously studied at Cardiff Metropolitan University, UK, he has published several chapters and articles on international outlets. His current research involves institutional theory, the dark side of leadership, personality, and the strategic decision-making process.

Joan Marques, PhD, EdD, serves as Dean and Professor of Management at Woodbury University's School of Business, in Burbank, CA. Her research interests pertain to Awakened Leadership, Buddhist Psychology in Management, and Workplace Spirituality. Her works have been widely published and cited in both academic and popular venues. She has written more than 150 scholarly articles, and has (co)authored more than 20 books, among which, *Ethical Leadership, Progress with a Moral Compass* (Routledge, 2017); *Leadership, Finding Balance Between Acceptance and Ambition* (Routledge, 2016), *Leadership Today: Practices for Personal and Professional Performance* (with Satinder Dhiman; Springer, 2016); *Spirituality and Sustainability: New Horizons and Exemplary Approaches* (with Satinder Dhiman; Springer, 2016); *Business and Buddhism* (Routledge, 2015); and *Leadership and Mindful Behavior: Action, Wakefulness, and Business* (Palgrave Macmillan, 2014).

Karen Martin-Jones, PhD, affiliated with this project because of her passion and work with intergenerational leadership. Much of her research has revolved around the impact of technology and generational differences and its implications on instruction. She is the CEO and Founder of Leaders Emerging Around a Purpose, LLC (LEAP) where she works with high risk, high needs high school students to develop leaders who can effectively change the culture and climate of their schools through peer mentoring, civic and community involvement, and a host of other strategies to help them successfully lead and navigate high school and beyond. In addition, she teaches teacher candidates how to effectively use and implement technology as a tool for engagement and instruction. She has also taught a myriad of educational and computer science courses.

Claude-Hélène Mayer, PhD, is an Adjunct Professor (PD) at the Europa Universität Viadrina in Frankfurt (Oder), Germany and a Senior Research Associate at Rhodes University, Grahamstown, South Africa. She holds Master's degrees in Crime Science, Investigation and Intelligence (MSc) and in Cultural Anthropology (Magister Artium), a Doctorate in Cultural Anthropology, a PhD in Psychology and a PhD in Management. The Venia Legendi is in Psychology with focus on Work, Organizational and Cultural Psychology. She has published numerous monographs, text collections, accredited journal articles, and special issues on transcultural mental health and salutogenesis in transcultural management, shame in cultural and organizational contexts, transcultural conflict management and mediation, women in leadership, psychobiography, workplace spirituality, and faith development.

Peter McGhee, PhD, is a senior lecturer in the Faculty of Business, Economics and Law at Auckland University of Technology in New Zealand. Prior to that he was an analyst and operations manager in the financial services industry. His research interests include spirituality in the workplace, business ethics, corporate social responsibility, and sustainability. He is currently supervising PhD and Master's students in the areas of ethical leadership, spirituality and emotional intelligence, and diversity.

David W. Miller, PhD, is on the faculty of Princeton University, Director of the Princeton University Faith & Work Initiative, and scholar of the "faith at work" movement. He has taught at the Yale School of Management and the Yale Divinity School and was the founding Executive Director of the Yale Center for Faith & Culture. Prior to academia he was a senior executive in international business for 16 years. He is a Senior Fellow at The Trinity Forum, and frequent speaker at gatherings of business leaders, corporate events, and academic conferences. His views are often cited in the media, including in the *New York Times, Wall Street Journal, Fortune* magazine, radio, and the major television networks. He is also the author of *God at Work: The History and Promise of the Faith at Work Movement* (Oxford University Press, 2007).

Andrew Morris, PhD, is the former chair of the Martin V. Smith School of Business and Economics and a Professor of Management at California State University Channel Islands. He received his PhD in Organizational Behavior and International Business from the University of South Carolina. He has published a number of papers and book chapters on emotional labor but his current research interests include leader humility and pedagogical applications of positive organizational scholarship.

Matthew Mudford is a management consultant who holds a number of governance roles across his passions, Māori, sport, and art. Having completed his honors dissertation under the supervision of Dr. Chellie Spiller in 2016 at the University of Auckland Business School, he has since gone into the business world to further explore his interests in business and management. He lives in Auckland with his partner Millie and is supported by his whanau; Lenis, Danielle, Simone, Andrea, James, Luke, Tyrone, Madden, and Maia.

Sharda Nandram, PhD, is Consultant, Psychologist, Economist, and Professor at Nyenrode Business University, Banasthali University, Co-founder Praan Group. Her focus is Organizational Design, Integrative Intelligence for Entrepreneurs and Organizations globally facing VUCA (Volatile, Uncertain, Complex, and Ambiguous). She has over three decades of academic, consulting and entrepreneurial experience across health care, accountancy, banking and insurance, public government, education, and sports sectors. She has a diverse cross-cultural exposure: born in Suriname, is resident of the Netherlands, and third generation of Indian origin. Her consulting, research, and teaching engagements are across Europe and Asia Pacific. Her current research interests lie in design and implementation of integratively intelligent self-managed organizations.

Kemi Ogunyemi, PhD, is the Director of the Christopher Kolade Centre for Research in Leadership and Ethics at Lagos Business School (LBS), Nigeria. She holds an LLB degree from University of Ibadan, Nigeria; an LLM from University of Strathclyde, UK; and MBA and PhD degrees from Pan-Atlantic University, Nigeria. She leads sessions on business ethics, managerial anthropology, self-leadership, and sustainability management at LBS and is Academic Director for the Senior Management Programme. Her consulting and research interests include personal ethos, organizational culture, responsible leadership, sustainability, and work–life ethic. She has authored over 30 articles, case studies and book chapters and the book *Responsible Management: Understanding Human Nature, Ethics and Sustainability*. She also edited the series "Teaching Ethics

Across the Management Curriculum." She worked as director and mentor in projects of Women's Board (ECS) before joining LBS. She is affiliated to ABEN, BEN-Africa, EBEN, and ISBEE, and co-developed the UNGC-PRME Anti-Corruption Toolkit.

Eugene Ohu, PhD, is a senior lecturer and full-time faculty in the department of Organizational Behaviour/Human Resource Management at the Lagos Business School (LBS), Nigeria. His areas of teaching and research include leadership with a moral compass, conceptualized as virtues; human–computer interactions; work–life balance; mindfulness; cross-cultural management and communication. He also explores workplace spirituality as a resource for individual and organizational development. Some of his publications include, "When Work-Family Conflict Hits Home: Parental Work–Family Conflict and Child Health" (with C. Spitzmueller, J. Zhang, C. L. Thomas, A. Osezua, and J. Yu), accepted for publication in the *Journal of Occupational Health Psychology* (2018); "Mindfulness and Stress Reduction: Managing Workplace Stress" (with E. Laguda and K. Ogunyemi), published in *The Palgrave Handbook of Workplace Spirituality and Fulfillment* (2018); and "Mindfulness and Ethical Consumption" (with K. Ogunyemi) in *Encyclopedia of the UN Sustainable Development Goals: Good Health and Well-Being* (in press).

Edwina Pio, PhD, a Fulbright alumna, is New Zealand's first Professor of Diversity, and University Director of Diversity at the Auckland University of Technology, Aotearoa/New Zealand. Her research encompasses the intersections of work, ethnicity, indigenous studies, religion, and pedagogy. A thought leader, recipient of a Duke of Edinburgh Fellowship and widely published, her book *Sari: Indian Women at Work in New Zealand* was released by Sir John Key, former Prime Minister of New Zealand. Her work is published in journals such as the *British Journal of Management, Higher Education, Human Relations, Journal of Business Ethics, Gender, Work and Organization, Asia Pacific Journal of Management, Academy of Management Learning and Education,* and *Journal of Management Inquiry*. She has received national and international media attention for her role as an ethnic minority researcher who unfurls both positive narratives and epistemic fault lines emblematic of restrictive and inspiring covenants in organizations, education, and society.

Joanna Rowe lectures in Business Ethics and Corporate Governance at Hochschule Fresenius, University of Applied Sciences, in Hamburg, Germany. Having qualified as a mediator at the University of Hamburg, she currently pursues research interests in alternative dispute resolution in the intercultural context as well as in Positive Psychology. A graduate in Modern Languages from Gonville and Caius College, Cambridge, she worked in international book publishing and digital media for 10 years before turning to research and education. Prior to her lectureship she supported research teams at the Department of Organization and Management at the School of Business, Economics and Social Sciences, University of Hamburg, with publications in a wide range of international journals. She has also practiced Vipassana mediation from a very young age.

Jeffon Seely is a senior consultant, transformational speaker, and workshop facilitator. He is a highly recognized leading resource in the field of Diversity and Inclusion, Millennials, Mindfulness, and Leadership. Although rather young, a Millennial, he has had his own consulting firm for more than 10 years, specializing in programs involving mindfulness, meditation, and the evolving role of Millennials and the 2020 Generation. He has assisted major corporations, nonprofit organizations, and government and academic institutions with innovative strategies to integrate mindfulness and the evolving generations into management and leadership roles. He has facilitated diversity, inclusion, empowerment, mindfulness, meditation, generations, and engagement training courses to all levels of organizations across several industries. He also presents transformational speeches to audiences through keynotes, leadership seminars, retreats, and open forums.

Cynthia Sherman, PhD, is an Assistant Professor of Management at the Martin V. Smith School of Business and Economics at California State University Channel Islands (CI). She is also the Director of the Entrepreneurship and Small Business Institute at CI, building relationships and opportunities for students and community members throughout Ventura and Los Angeles counties. Her research interests are in the areas of entrepreneurial motivation, meaningfulness, mindset, and spirituality. She also teaches and researches in the social entrepreneurship field. Her work has been published in peer-reviewed journals such as the *Journal of Small Business and Entrepreneurship*, the *International Journal of Organizational Analysis*, and the *Journal of Management, Spirituality and Religion*.

Nikhil Somaru is a tech entrepreneur based in Durban, South Africa, who practices Vedanta philosophy, one of India's ancient wisdom traditions. He holds a diploma in Vedanta philosophy from Vedanta Academy, Malavli, India. He dropped out of engineering college to independently pursue his interest in technology and philosophy. He also volunteers as a Vedanta teacher at the Vedanta Institute South Africa.

Chellie Spiller, PhD, is a professor at the University of Waikato Management School. She speaks locally and internationally on wayfinding leadership, authentic leadership, leadership and decision-making, and how businesses can create sustainable wealth and wellbeing. She is co-author of a book on traditional Polynesian navigation, *Wayfinding Leadership: Groundbreaking Wisdom for Developing Leaders* (2015) with Hoturoa Barclay-Kerr and John Panoho. Wayfinding Leadership has catalyzed a new approach to leadership development that is growing fast and programs are currently being taught in a variety of domains such as Air New Zealand's middle management training, Global Women's Breakthrough Leadership course, the judiciary, the health sector and across Maori communities. In 2013 she co-edited a book with Professor Donna Ladkin entitled *Reflections on Authentic Leadership: Concepts, Coalescences and Clashes* (Edward Elgar Publishing), which was nominated in the top ten leadership books of 2013. She also co-edited the volume *Indigenous Spiritualities at Work* with Dr. Rachel Wolfgramm.

Anke Turner, PhD, is a full Professor of International Management at Hochschule Fresenius, University of Applied Sciences, in Hamburg, Germany. Her research interest is in exploring worldviews, values, and understanding of a "good life" in Europe ("the West"), Asia, and Africa, and their impact on entrepreneurship, organizations, and work life. She completed a 3-year residential Vedanta philosophy course at the Vedanta Academy in Malavli, India. In her career prior to becoming a researcher and educator, she worked for more than 10 years in the financial services industry with internationally operating institutions. She completed an MBA at the University of San Francisco, USA, as a Fulbright scholar and received her doctoral degree in Economics and Social Sciences from the University of Hamburg, Germany.

Isaac Wanasika, PhD, is an Associate Professor of Management at the University of Northern Colorado (UNCO). He holds a PhD with a concentration in Strategy from New Mexico State University (NMSU). He has served in various corporate and consulting roles, including the US State Department. His latest book, *Snapshots of Great Leadership* (2nd ed.), was recently published by Routledge. He is the Associate Editor for the *International Journal of Business and Emerging Markets*. His research has been published in the *Journal of World Business*, *Journal of Managerial Issues*, and other journals and book chapters. His work has been presented at national and international business conferences including the Academy of Management. His research interests include strategic leadership, organizational efficiency, new institutional theory, and base-of-the-pyramid strategies. He has received excellence awards for teaching and research at NMSU and UNCO respectively.

Rachel Wolfgramm, PhD, is a Senior Lecturer at the University of Auckland Business School, New Zealand. She combines an interdisciplinary approach to research with over three decades of practice-based experience covering sustainability, leadership, business ethics, identity, consumer behavior, and Māori and Indigenous development. She has published research in peer-reviewed journals, books, and technical reports and contributes regularly to international conferences, symposia, wānanga, and workshops engaging public, private, and creative sectors. She is currently Principal Investigator of a research project examining Māori Leadership and Decision-Making. The team is studying how Māori leaders generate and enact leadership to generate wealth and advance wellbeing.

Jody A. Worley, PhD, is an associate professor in the Department of Human Relations at the University of Oklahoma, USA. His primary research interests include organizational behavior (e.g., work engagement, work–family integration, and workplace diversity), and community psychology (e.g., quality of life issues for children and minorities). His publications within the past year have included book chapters on "Visionary Leadership in Team-oriented Settings," and "Hope as a Coping Resource for Caregiver Resilience and Well-being," as well as refereed journal articles on "Leading with Soft Skills," and "Performance Measurement Indicators in the Healthcare Industry."

INTRODUCTION

Joan Marques

This companion aims to serve as an important reference work in managing workplace spirituality. It specifically highlights spiritual performance in work environments, but begins at the roots: within the self. The first part of this work is therefore created with the intention to help readers understand that a spiritual approach is not something that should be instigated externally (even though encouraging factors and people can be helpful), but that should primarily start within. A spiritual person is one that is also responsible, among many other things, so this personal focus as an entry point is important to place matters within the right perspective.

In this work we focus on helping readers understand the correlation between management and workplace spirituality, underscoring the continuously increasing need for a spiritual mindset in work environments, and further elevating the topic into a mainstream phenomenon rather than one that is ethereal and too soft for work environments. To that end, this book highlights the relationship between spirituality and religion, aiming to clarify that these two phenomena are sometimes considered related, but don't necessarily have to be that way.

A collaborative effort of 42 contributing authors from ten countries (in six continents), including 11 US states, this companion embodies a true global effort in uniting perspectives and models toward increased awareness on workplace spirituality and its many advantages for our collective wellbeing.

Reviewing the comprehensive structure of this companion, we can summarize the five parts as follows:

Part I, which consists of six chapters, approaches *spirituality as a phenomenon that is first and foremost of a personal nature.*

- In Chapter 1, Dr. Joan Marques explains that workplace spirituality should not be limited to buy-in from top management. It can be applied by any person in a work environment. A spiritual approach could positively affect others through a ripple effect, whereby any worker with the right intentions could gear his or her immediate work environment toward enhanced spiritual performance.
- In Chapter 2, Dr. Satinder Dhiman immerses into the role of self-knowledge in life and leadership. Self-knowledge is the hallmark of all authentic leaders, since it helps those in leadership positions to lead from their true self. He describes leadership as a voyage of inner discovery, with self-knowledge as the key to leading from within.

- In Chapter 3, Dr. William A. Guillory underscores that spirituality is a phenomenon, which is dynamically changing as we ascend to more expanded levels of existence—and in different forms. He describes inner exploration as an in-depth examination of our personal consciousness.
- In Chapter 4, Jeffon Seely invites us to take an honest look at what is happening within ourselves when aiming to manage spirituality from a personal perspective. He encourages us to consider what steps we can take to recognize that we are not at the mercy of our thoughts but are that which empowers our thoughts: if we are able to look up at the conscious mind without attaching to any particular thought, we can create a space of freedom, almost as if we are looking up at our thoughts from our heart center.
- In Chapter 5, Dr. Kemi Ogunyemi describes spirituality as a universal human experience, referring to the way we seek and express meaning and purpose and the way we experience our connectedness to self, others, nature, and to the significant or sacred. She stresses that spiritual employees do not see pay alone as important, and points out that organizations also have an increasing interest in this phenomenon because of the benefits—both economic and beyond the economics—that it offers especially with regard to increasing ethical and responsible behavior.
- In Chapter 6, Drs. Andrew Morris, Céleste Grimard, Cynthia Sherman, and Dylan Cooper first describe key elements of intelligent failure and subsequently suggest that recognizing and rewarding intelligent failure can positively influence organizational outcomes. They explain that the benefits of intelligent failure can be further enhanced if organizations build a "spirituality of imperfection" into their cultures, whereby imperfection and mistakes are perceived not as limitations but as an inherent part of our humanness.

Part II, which encompasses four chapters, expands the perspective of *spirituality in the realms of religion and culture.*

- In Chapter 7, Drs. Timothy Ewest and David W. Miller provide a meta perspective of how historical collective cultural assumptions and the ensuing social forces they create have led to the assumed bifurcation of the sacred-spiritual from the material world. This has resulted in a perceived separation between the sacred-spiritual and material world, which has affected the ways in which individuals, and specifically scholars, have theoretically separated religion and spirituality.
- In Chapter 8, Dr. Eric B. Dent analyzes some starting axioms of a number of common religions such as atheist objectivism, Christianity, secular humanism, Buddhism, and Hinduism. He subsequently proposes that the MSR (Management, Spirituality and Religion) community elevate the scholarship to MSR 2.0, a markedly "upgraded" literature that would include definitional clarity and explicit starting axioms.
- In Chapter 9, Drs. Edwina Pio and Peter McGhee invite us to walk through the Christian traditions that influence workplace spirituality and management. They summarize spirituality as viewed through two major Christian traditions, Catholic and Protestant, focusing on two women and two men in each of these traditions and presenting the fabric of spirituality and work through portraying their lives.
- In Chapter 10, Susanna Kislenko explores how yogic principles influence leadership behavior and approaches. Using a combination of semi-structured personal interviews with individuals at the intersection of yoga and leadership, she finds that yoga influences leadership in three primary ways: by transforming leadership into a humble service, by allowing leaders to display their humanity through example, and by encouraging leaders to tune in within themselves for better decision-making.

Part III covers six chapters, and focuses on *conscious foundations of spirituality*.

- In Chapter 11, Dr. Joan Marques presents a strategy to build meaning and inclusion in the workplace by turning inward and engaging in a six-step process of insight-focused contemplations, which could enhance the quality of life at work for us and our colleagues. She refers to these six mindsets as, general awareness, specific awareness, holistic view, learning stance, interconnectedness, and void.
- In Chapter 12, Drs. Cheryl De Ciantis and Ginger Grant stress that disengagement in the workplace is high and that it is necessary to find the roots both of individual and collective sense of purpose. They posit that we arrive at a spiritual aspect of leadership through two pathways: (1) self-knowledge of values and unleashing of personal creativity through individuation, and (2) participating in values-based phronetic dialogue that synergizes the creative instinct for the good of a community.
- In Chapter 13, Dr. Claude-Hélène Mayer and Dirk Geldenhuys present an overview of workplace spirituality and wellness with regard to an organizational neuroscientific perspective. They argue that organizational neuroscience offers the possibility of synthesizing the constructs with specific implications for leadership and managerial practices, and discuss how spirituality can be applied in organizational settings with the aim of enhancing wellness.
- In Chapter 14, Dr. Duysal Aşkun emphasizes the necessity and significance of oneness for our inner and outer lives including organizations and societies. Understanding and cultivating oneness, she feels, would be incomplete if we do not consider the intra- and interpersonal underpinnings. She affirms that making oneness a reality for organizations could carve out the true essence of us humans.
- In Chapter 15, Dr. Isaac Wanasika describes the state of Emotional Intelligence (EI) in the modern work environment. He underlines the importance of EI at the workplace, and the significance of EI in the changing work environment. He also examines the impact of national culture on EI, along with different aspects of work that relate to EI.
- In Chapter 16, Dr. Debra J. Dean delves into the concept of spirituality to explain what it is and what it is not. She explains why spirituality is important and how one can make it useful in one's own life or in one's workplace. She shares her finding that the application of workplace spirituality in a secular organization is possible, reflecting on some important lessons learned.

Part IV comprises six chapters, and evaluates the correlation between *leadership and spirituality*.

- In Chapter 17, Dr. Eugene Ohu and Princess Anifowose elucidate that both leaders and followers in any endeavor are essential to the attainment of the set goal. They include within that scope the need to adhere to a moral compass. They propose virtues as both the coins and the compass guiding the behavior of all parties involved. Following Aristotle, they offer the four cardinal virtues as the guide and measure of the virtues, and hence the qualifier of moral direction.
- In Chapter 18, Dr. Chellie Spiller, Matthew Mudford, and Dr. Rachel Wolfgramm explore *mana* and leadership. *Mana* provides spiritual agency to take up respectful, right, and loving action in the world. We can learn much about the role *mana* plays in leadership, as part of a greater wisdom that views the world as connected by interlacing principles, such as respect, reciprocity, care, family, and guardianship.
- In Chapter 19, Dr. Sukumarakurup Krishnakumar reviews the domain of spiritual leadership and presents a model of Spiritual Leadership that involves emotional abilities and influence

processes. The crux of this theory focuses on: (1) how spirituality facilitates the expression and regulation of positive emotions from the leader's perspective; (2) how a leader's interactions with followers are enhanced by his or her spirituality, leading to prosocial influence processes; and (3) how prosocial outcomes are produced by the integrated use of spirituality and emotional abilities.

- In Chapter 20, Dr. Debra J. Dean lays out her research endeavor in exploring two main instruments to empirically test spirituality at work and contribute to the three most promising theoretical approaches to date. The research found that altruistic love, sense of community, and meaningful work significantly predicted job satisfaction, with altruistic love as the sole predictor of organizational commitment.
- In Chapter 21, Dr. Jody A. Worley highlights the role of empathy in the professional workplace by presenting evidence for internal and external benefits to a company when empathy is embraced and practiced as an integral part of the organizational climate. He describes the ways that empathy contributes to the professional workplace with a specific focus on internal contributions of empathy for workplace communication, collaboration, performance, and leadership.
- In Chapter 22, Dr. Wanda Krause delineates how we can learn to lead in times of increasing cultural diversity. She offers insights into creating wellbeing for all and harnessing the strengths of diversity in the workplace, which leads to greater performance.

Part V, the final part, consists of eight chapters and reviews ways of *treading a spiritual path toward stakeholders*.

- In Chapter 23, Dr. Timothy Ewest explores the connections between sustainability, ethics, and spirituality, arguing that if there are innate universal characteristics to human nature, they may provide a constraint to unethical behavior as well as a means to guide human behavior. He illustrates the polarities of the understandings and theories of human nature, and considers how prosocial research may act as a means to build a case for the connection between spirituality, sustainability, and ethics.
- In Chapter 24, Kira Haensel and Dr. Jean-Claude Garcia-Zamor take a closer look at spiritual leadership as a leadership style for managers in public administration, and investigate in what way spiritual leadership could be a fitting model for these leaders, as well as the distinct features from the private sector that require further development of public sector leadership.
- In Chapter 25, Dr. Anke Turner, Subhasis Chakrabarti, Joanna Rowe, and Nikhil Somaru recommend stakeholder theory as a guideline for managers that fosters responsible interaction with their direct and indirect stakeholders. This theory aligns the interests of a wider range of stakeholder groups in a unified endeavor for value creation. Considering today's environment of constant change and volatile conditions, they introduce Vedanta, an ancient Indian wisdom. Wisdom in Vedanta is attained through spiritual practice, which aims at the individual development of the personality, from selfishness to unselfishness to selflessness.
- In Chapter 26, Drs. Sylvia W. Burgess and Karen Martin-Jones introduce spiritual capital as an asset that every individual possesses and chooses to use in various ways. They focus on understanding the meaning and importance of spiritual capital as a means of sustainability for those in leadership roles. They underscore the necessity for leaders to understand the importance of spirituality and the role that it plays in assisting us in working together, building trust in our relationships and our fundamental wholeness as individuals.

- In Chapter 27, Drs. Sharda Nandram and Puneet Bindlish focus on the relevance of the ancient philosophy of yoga in the development of social entrepreneurship as a manifestation of sustainable welfare (*Shubh Laabh*). They thereby propose the eight limbs based on Ashtaanga Yoga as possible steps of knowledge creation and paths of discovering and following human aspirations.
- In Chapter 28, Dr. Bekir Emre Kurtulmuş reminds us that ethical challenges within organizations have become more prominent than ever. He refers to workplace spirituality as an increasingly accepted way to address this issue. Workplace spirituality, asserts Kurtulmuş, can be the source of organizational values and norms from which the ethical climate can be drawn.
- In Chapter 29, Giles Hutchins points out that contemporary leaders require a "new-norm" in their leadership capacity. To embody this new-norm we need a shift in worldview and consciousness: one that deals with root causes while simultaneously dealing with downstream effects. Hutchins points out that the way we lead and respond, while creating the conditions for others in our organizations to better lead and respond, directly influences the future-fitness of our organizations.
- In Chapter 30, Dr. Joan Marques focuses on the discontentment that lives among many people about their (work)life, and the way this affects other areas of our lives. In exploring what most of us are actually looking for, she provides a simple answer: loving-kindness, which can be attained through higher consciousness. Some of the rewards she presents for practicing loving-kindness are understanding, compassion, support, respect, and the will to help create a world where there is a greater sense of "Us" and a reduced sense of "I."

This comprehensive view on workplace spirituality will hopefully find its way to the collection of each current and future leader and scholar who aims to engage in performance that will improve the quality of life, not only for our human fellow earthlings, but for all that share this unique vessel of ours, which has thus far not been matched by any other in the vast universe.

With wishes for increased insights and ongoing wellness.

PART I

Managing Spirituality from a Personal Stance

1

UNDERSTANDING THE RIPPLE EFFECT OF SPIRITUAL BEHAVIOR

Joan Marques

The Spiritual Workplace: Reality or Not?

A major question that keeps arising when we consider the topic of spirituality in the workplace is how this trend could be possible in a world where the average organizational environment seems to lean more toward toxic than toward healthy. Over the past decades, several authors have dedicated studies and articles to this quandary. For instance, in a 2015 article, Giorgi, Shoss, and Leon-Perez stressed that the combination of high job demands and low job control remain to be the most critical threats to employee wellbeing. Ten years prior to that article, Heard (2005) had arrived at a similar conclusion and placed a price tag on this problem by asserting that *workplace* stress cost American business $3 billion way back in the 1990s, and that figure has continued to rise. Even earlier, Mor Barak and Levin had warned that a lack of feeling included formed the foundation of many workforce members to become dissatisfied and alienated. "Many workers lack a sense of inclusion, which is a key component in wanting to remain at a place of employment" (Mor Barak & Levin, 2002, p. 133).

On top of the stressful atmosphere that seems to have become more rule than exception in the fast-paced performance arena called "Corporate America," it also seems that establishing a spiritual workplace could be seen as practically impossible when one is not a member of top management. During the past decades we conducted several business organizational workshops and higher education courses on the topic of spirit at work, and we discovered that the recurring query was, "how can you establish or promote spirituality at work if you are not a member of top management?" This question is therefore one that requires a deeper look into the phenomenon of spirituality in the workplace and what is needed to make it work. Schutte (2016) rightfully remarks that spirituality in the workplace is a much-disputed inquiry field. Since spirituality in the workplace remains a discussion topic among various theorists—some consider it impossible without the involvement of religion, while others strongly reject the incorporation of the "R" word when talking spirituality—a clear reference to what is meant in this particular chapter seems to be necessary. So far, there are a few decent definitions toward this phenomenon we can refer to. Due to its comprehensiveness, and the fact that it results from the author of this chapter's own research, we will use the following definition for workplace spirituality in this chapter:

> Spirituality in the workplace is an experience of interconnectedness and trust among those involved in a work process, engendered by individual goodwill; leading to the

> collective creation of a motivational organizational culture, epitomized by reciprocity and solidarity; and resulting in enhanced overall performance, which is ultimately translated in lasting organizational excellence.
>
> *(Marques, 2005, p. 283)*

To the attentive reader it may become clear that, in the above perception, spirituality is kept separate from the realm of religion. It is perceived as the higher awareness that drives human beings to do well. It entails realizations of being interconnected to all other living beings, showing respect to everyone and everything that currently lives and breathes, or once did, and recognizing that there is more to life than our physical state of existing, or that which is visible to us. Spirituality in the workplace is, therefore, as presented in the above definition, the awareness that interconnectedness, respect, and recognition are not limited to ourselves and our private environment, but are also very much applicable to all those with whom we work on a regular or incidental basis, in such a way that these qualities can lead to more than mere enhanced enjoyable workplace circumstances, but to increased return on investments as well. It is therefore essential that the experience of performing our duties should be one that is rewarding to all involved, hence, providing ourselves and those we deal with in the workplace with feelings of trust, belonging, meaning, and fulfillment in all areas that we consider important toward the quality of our lives.

Nevertheless, the perfect picture painted in the paragraphs above refrains from providing insight into the possible establishment and successful performance of spirituality in the workplace when one is positioned in the middle or lower echelons of the organization. In most literature thus far, spirituality at work has been seen as a tendency that could only be successfully implemented if initiated by the organization's leaders. Williams, Randolph-Seng, Hayek, Haden, and Atinc (2017), for instance, perceive a clear link between workplace spirituality and servant leadership, affirming that servant leaders may have a greater impact on their followers by exhibiting authenticity and sincerity (key attributes of political skill) in their care for their followers' wellbeing. Kubicek (2005) refers to Emotional Intelligence (EQ), and Spiritual Intelligence (SQ) as intrinsic contemporary leadership concepts. In a review of Hicks' book *Religion and the Workplace: Pluralism, Spirituality, Leadership*, Wiles (2005) discussed an enumeration of essential components, such as "(1) tolerance, respect, and acceptance of other religious and spiritual traditions; (2) promoting a pluralistic, non-coercive, and non-degrading working environment; and (3) discussion of religious and spiritual harmony in the workplace" (p. 195) as prominent leadership strategies toward increased spirit at work. Terms such as "spiritual leadership" (Wolf, 2004), "awakened leadership" (Marques, 2010), "moral leadership" (Thompson, 2004), "authentic leadership" (Beagrie, 2005), and "ethical leadership" (Brown, Trevino, & Harrison, 2005), are just some of the many ways in which the implementation of a spiritual mindset in the workplace has been proclaimed as being a leadership responsibility. In order to present a possible perspective on how to implement spirit at work regardless of one's position in an organization, it may be prudent to first elaborate on the various aspects involved in spirituality in the workplace, as stated by various authors, and underscored through qualitative research by the author of this chapter: internal, integrated, and external.

Internal, Integrated, and External Aspects

A few decades ago, Burack (1999) identified three main pillars for the spiritual workplace—internal, external, and integrated—which he divided into four different but highly interrelated outcomes (p. 280):

1. "Leadership and the organization: demonstrated concern for employees, respect for others, consistency of actions and demonstrated acumen."
2. "Employees: conscientious (e.g. quality, cooperation) continuing skill and knowledge advancement, adaptability and high sustained performances."
3. "External (strategic constituents)—quality, consistency, environmentally aware, and a responsible community member."
4. "Mutual—trust and shared responsibilities for joint benefits."

Points 1 and 3 could be considered the external manifestations of a spiritual workplace from a worker's perspective: although point 1 is actually an internal organizational factor, it is still an external one for the individual at stake. Point 2 explains some of the internal drivers for a spiritual worker, and point 4 refers to the integrated factor: the interrelation between all parties involved.

It was even longer ago that Neck and Milliman (1994) referred to the critical interrelation between internal and external aspects in the work environment by exclaiming that constructive thought patterns can lead to an enhanced perception and greater sense of spirituality in work. These authors asserted that workers who manage to upgrade their internal verbalizations to a level of awareness, transforming their mindset from negative to positive, will be able to enhance the spirituality of their work. Introducing the term Thought Self Leadership (TSL), Neck and Milliman further explained, "with the positive application of TSL, workers will learn to establish a better report with their external reality in the workplace" (p. 9).

Walters and Fenson (2002) called for a skillful balance between workers' "internal and external world" (para. 6) to avoid conflict with others and within one's self, which can lead to stress and all of its fall outs.

Internal Aspects

The importance of the *internal* aspect can also be concluded from statements such as one made by Cash, Gray, and Rood (2000), that spirituality looks inward to an awareness of universal values; by Naimon, Mullins, and Osatuke (2013), who underscored that people with a high internal locus of control find more gratification in their work; by DeCenzo and Robbins (1998), who stated that "an individual's performance is a function of his or her ability to do his or her job, and his or her willingness to do it" (p. 99); by Goforth (2001), who exclaimed, "everybody has a need for something bigger in life than just making money and going to work" (p. k-2); by Barrett (1999), who asserted, "spiritual needs are met when our work aligns with our passion and has meaning for us or we feel we are able to make a difference through our ideas or by being of service to others" (p. 31); by Covey (1989) who concluded, "the spiritual dimension is your core, your center, your commitment to your value system" (p. 292); and by Terez (1999), who affirmed, "virtually all people have a driving desire to make a difference" (p. 19).

Through these and other citations in the abundance of existing literature, a wide variety of internal qualities that nourish the spiritual mindset in a workplace can be distinguished. Some of these qualities are *ethics* (Ayoun, Rowe, & Yassine, 2015; Mitroff & Denton,1999; Weston, 2002); *truth* (Naidoo, 2014; Covey, 1989; Wheatley, 2002); *belief* (Gunther, 2001; Lerner, 2000; Lewis & Geroy, 2000; McCoy, 2001; Morris, 1997; Neal, 2000; Wheatley, 2002); *respect* (Burack, 1999; Drucker, 1995; Heider, 1985; Kaye, 1996; Mitroff & Denton, 1999; Pierce, 2002; Rosner, 2001; Wickens, 2001); and *trust* (Burack, 1999; Green, 2000; Lerner, 2000; Levering, 1988; Mitroff & Denton, 1999).

In order to establish a listing of common themes in a spiritual workplace, along with the establishment of a workable definition for this phenomenon, the author of this chapter conducted two phenomenological studies between 2003 and 2012. The studies entailed in-depth interviews with pre-identified business executives. Criterion sampling was initially applied, followed by snowball sampling after initial participant identification. Answers from all participants were transcribed and horizonalized, after which overlapping was eliminated. Common themes were clustered and verified through the application of interrater reliability, a solidification measurement thus far rarely used in qualitative studies. Interrater reliability was 66.67%. This study produced the following listing of internal acts of a spiritually converted worker: honesty, synthesizing, committed, caring to achieve completely and accurately, seeking the truth, self-motivated, more open, receptive to new ideas from the organization, seeking ways to make additional contributions or improvements the organization would benefit from, devoid of excessive ego, loving to do what he or she is doing, guarding him- or herself from letting time restrict the quality of his or her performance, and more motivated to do things right.

Integrated Aspects

The significance of the *integrated* aspect can be derived from statements such as Pierce's (2002) insight that authentic spirituality of work does two things: (1) "it raises the practitioner's awareness of the presence of the spiritual in the work itself" (p. 37), and (2) "this raised awareness changes the way practitioners of this spirituality work and relate to others in the workplace" (p. 37).

Some phenomena in specialized literature that pertain to the importance of an integrated approach in a spiritual workplace are *understanding* (Ashmos & Duchon, 2000; Covey, 2002; Freshman, 1999; Lerner, 2000; Turner, 1999; Wheatley, 2002); *openness* (Mitroff & Denton, 1999); *team orientation* (Covey, 1989; Drucker, 1995; Green, 2000; Kaye, 1996; Terez, 1999); *giving* (Green, 2000; Vadermark, 2001); and *acceptance* (Ashmos & Duchon, 2000; Turner, 1999; Vadermark, 2001; Wheatley, 2002).

In the two phenomenological studies, the following corresponding listing of integrated acts of a spiritually converted worker surfaced: understanding the importance of the work; understanding objectives and their value; drawing on the strengths of colleagues; respecting the environment; and being a good listener.

External Aspects

The relevance of the *external* aspect in spirituality at work can also be extracted from statements such as Ashmos and Duchon's (2000) introduction of the Spirituality Movement in which they argued that "organizations that have long been viewed as rational systems are considering making room for the spiritual dimension, a dimension that has less to do with rules and order and more to do with meaning, purpose, and a sense of community" (p. 134), and Burack's (1999) referral to people-centered management, which entailed phenomena such as "recognition of the worth and value of people, desire to create high integrity work climates, and establishing a foundation of trust, faith, justice, respect and love" (p. 280).

The external aspect is further emphasized by multiple other statements such as "work is a spiritual journey for many of us, although we talk about it in different ways" (Kahnweiler & Otte, 1997, p. 171); "there is increasing evidence that a major transformation is occurring in many organizations" (Ashmos & Duchon, 2000, p. 138); "some companies are looking to bring a little spirit into the workplace" (Hein, 1999, p. 6); "every organization has a spirituality, whether it realizes it or not" (Weston, 2002, p. 30); and "the real difference between success and failure in a corporation can be very often traced to the question of how well the organization brings out the great energies and talents of its people" (Barrett, 1999, p. 30).

Some traits mentioned in spirituality at work related literature that underscore the external effects in a spiritual workplace are *creativity* (Ashmos & Duchon, 2000; Barrett, 1999; Chappel, 1993; Covey, 2002; Dorsey, 1998; Fox, 1995; Heider, 1985; Laabs, 1995; Lerner, 2000; McCoy, 2001; McDonald, 1999; Morris, 1997; Turner, 1999; Vadermark, 2001); *diversity* (DeCenzo & Robbins, 1998; Hicks, 2002); a sense of *peace* (Mitroff & Denton, 1999; Wheatley, 2002); and *harmony* (Heider, 1985).

The earlier mentioned phenomenological studies resulted in the following corresponding external acts of a spiritually converted worker: performing as a servant leader, a mentor, and a giver; being kind, motivating, and direct; providing quality; applying fairness; seeking to understand others; hard-working; expecting openness; being aware of the place of his or her contributions toward the success of the organization, and therefore also, getting fulfillment out of giving and helping others to get better in that organization; encouraging creativity; and encouraging other people to reduce the barriers that prevent new things from happening.

Transforming the Workplace into a Spiritual One

Based on the above distinctions, we can conclude that the first step toward a positive transformation of the workplace will have to happen at the internal level: within the individuals involved in the process. It may be a generally accepted fact that such internal changes, and thus, enhanced spiritual awareness, will work out more effectively, rapidly, and profoundly for the entire organization when they happen within individuals in higher positions of the organizational hierarchy. Yet, they can also occur within workers at lower levels, with moderate to high levels of success, depending on these individuals' personal rapport with co-workers. Before reviewing the effectiveness levels of transforming the workplace as an attempt executed by lower- and mid-level workers in a workplace, a brief review of some possible reasons that predominantly cause a non-spiritual workplace to alter into a spiritual one are appropriate.

Based on the findings of the phenomenological studies, it can be stated that the organizational reasons that could influence the transformation from a workplace that previously did not consciously attempt to nurture spirituality and the human spirit to one that now does, can be classified into two main causes:

1. Organizational-experiential, in which it may occur that unfavorable company developments (deterioration of morale, productivity, efficiency) call for reconsideration of the organizational rules of existence.
2. Leadership-experiential, in which the transformation can be instigated by a change in leadership perspectives, an unforeseen tragic event involving the leader, or the leader's desire to attract good people (workers and customers) to the business, and thus enhance the quality of life in the work environment.

The personal reasons that could influence the transformation from an employee who does not consciously attempt to nurture spirituality and the human spirit to one that does can be classified into two main causes:

1. Internal, whereby the transformation is mainly a consequence of a personal change (which can cause the employee to become spiritual without working in a spiritual environment).

Table 1.1 Organizational and Leadership Experiential Circumstances That Can Lead to the Application of a More Spiritual Approach in the Workplace

Organizational Circumstances		*Personal Circumstances*	
Organizational-Experiential:	*Leadership-Experiential:*	*Internal:*	*External:*
• Unfavorable company developments (deterioration of morale, productivity, efficiency) that call for reconsideration of the organizational rules of existence.	• A change in leadership perspectives. • An unforeseen tragic event. • The will to attract good people (workers and customers) to the business. • The leader's will to change: to enhance the quality of life in the work environment.	• A personal change, which can cause the employee to become spiritual without working in a spiritual environment. • A raised level of consciousness. • Confrontation with a life-changing problem. • Change of habits. • Change of lifestyle (getting married and starting to raise children: wanting to lead by example). • Desire for inner-peace and self-satisfaction • Aversion of a competitive environment. • The will to feel better about one's self, work, colleagues, and society. • Aversion of a heavy-handed hierarchical structure.	• As a result of a converted company culture. • Through positive influences from others. • The will to be involved in a ground-breaking organization. • Openness to new ideas and a new way of thinking.

However, the change in that employee can lead to spiritual influence of the work environment. Some of the internal reasons to transform such an employee are: a raised level of consciousness; the confrontation with a life-changing problem; a change of habits; a change of lifestyle (for instance, getting married, starting to raise children, and therefore wanting to lead by example); a general desire for inner-peace and self-satisfaction; a developed aversion of a competitive environment; a newly obtained will to feel better about one's self, work, colleagues, and society; or the aversion of a heavy-handed hierarchical structure.

2. External, whereby the transformation is mainly a consequence of a converted company culture (which can drive the employee to the realization that he or she can only continue to perform well in this setting if he or she adapts to the conversion). Some of the ways that this can happen are: obtaining positive influences from colleagues; the will to be involved in a successful, ground-breaking organization; receptivity to new ideas and a new way of thinking.

Table 1.1 represents the organizational and leadership experiential circumstances that can lead to the application of a more spiritual approach in the workplace.

The Ripple Effect

Although—as mentioned earlier—it is easier accomplished in cases of employees at higher levels in the workplace, the establishment of a spiritual transformation in a workplace could be possible for workers at various levels of the organization. It may take longer and require more perseverance, but, gradually, any worker with the right intentions could gear his or her immediate work environment toward enhanced spiritual performance in the sense as is interpreted in this chapter. An appropriate reminder at this point may be that religion should definitely be kept out of the picture, particularly in environments where representatives from various cultures, backgrounds, and religious convictions are employed.

To initiate the mindset of how one can establish or promote spirituality at work if one is not a member of top management, the following research outcomes may make sense: the author of this chapter conducted an additional study between 2010 and 2015 among working MBA students in university courses, all between the ages of 25 and 55 years, and predominantly employed in midlevel positions in a variety of industries. In this longitudinal research, one of the questions asked was, "How do you think your current work environment could be transformed into a more spiritual one?" From the broad variety of answers given to this question, the following two were selected as good examples to express the essence of this query:

1. "Through daily interaction and making trust building a part of our jobs. And through listening, and then applying, in order to more fully engage the crews."

The here-above posted statement is a typical illustration of how all layers of the organization can work toward a more spiritual environment. Trust building is not a thing that can be directed by management: it has to grow among workers in their interactions with each other. The latter part of the above statement, "listening and then applying in order to more fully engage the crews" may initially sound like a typical management responsibility, but it can also be executed at the peer level.

2. "By people helping each other out more often."

This statement, the shortest and most simply worded of all in the study, could be considered the most direct strategy toward establishing a more spiritual workplace without necessarily having to wait for management interference: if workers decide to be more positive and helpful toward one another, the seed of workplace spirituality will be planted, and the nurturing process can begin.

Whatever a worker's reasons may be for an internal transformation into a more spiritual person, his or her acts into the workplace, along with his or her increased awareness of interconnectedness and reciprocity, will lead to a greater level of empathy. Figure 1.1 demonstrates how the ripple effect that enhances quality of life in- and outside the work environment can be established regardless of one's position in the organization. The ripple demonstrates the following:

1. An individual gets confronted with internal reasons for enhanced spiritual performance: a transformation happens, and an increase in willingness to connect is ignited. This is the internal aspect of establishing spirit at work.
2. The now more spiritually attuned worker vigorously, and hopefully ultimately also successfully, connects with colleagues in order to enhance mutuality and reciprocity. This worker does so by demonstrating an enhanced level of empathy, which, in most cases, triggers a similar response in return. Here is where the integrated aspects start coming into play.
3. Due to the spiritual worker's encouraging behavior, co-workers will become positively influenced, reflect on their behaviors as well, and increasingly engage into team performance, which is expressed in increased support, elevated trust, and enhanced understanding. These factors, too, represent integrated aspects of establishing spirit at work.
4. Ultimately, all or most workers within the positively affected department will demonstrate a greater degree of responsibility and ownership, as well as awareness of the bigger picture, and, through their increased team behavior, will generate greater output and, hence, better organizational performance (external aspects), which will, in the right environment and

Figure 1.1 The Ripple Effect

under the right leadership, be translated to the workers in the form of increased job satisfaction. Increased job satisfaction, in turn, will further elevate the internal motives for the individual to remain a spiritual worker.

It is important to note that an individual, who is satisfied with his or her work environment, will generally be less stressed outside the workplace as well. Overall, this person will have a greater sense of wellbeing, and an enhanced desire to make others (at work and outside) share in his or her contentment.

Final Note

A final essential note should be in place here: some workplaces are just not susceptible yet toward spiritual transformation. The spiritual worker has to realize that. Not all workplaces will be adaptive toward conversion. In such cases, when no amount of effort sorts any positive effect, the spiritual worker should realize that exiting this toxic workplace is not a manifestation of weakness, but rather a demonstration of courage to move on to better spiritual harbors. Work environments are worldwide undergoing tremendous changes and therefore experience great uncertainty in these days. A spiritual worker, although responsible toward dependents, takes appropriate measures toward responsible behavior, yet tries not to lose his or her belief that, ultimately, things will turn out right: for him or her, and all who are involved.

References

Ashmos, D. P., & Duchon, D. (2000). Spirituality at work: A conceptualization and measure. *Journal of Management Inquiry, 9*(2), 134–145.

Ayoun, B., Rowe, L., & Yassine, F. (2015). Is workplace spirituality associated with business ethics? *International Journal of Contemporary Hospitality Management, 27*(5), 938–957.

Barrett, R. (1999). Why the future belongs to value added companies. *Journal for Quality and Participation, 22*(1), 30–35.

Beagrie, S. (2005). How to ... be an authentic leader. *Personnel Today*, 31.

Brown, M., Trevino, L., & Harrison, D. (2005). Ethical leadership: A social learning perspective for construct development and testing. *Organizational Behavior and Human Development Processes, 97*(2), 117.

Burack, E. (1999). Spirituality in the workplace. *Journal of Organizational Change Management, 12*(4), 280.

Cash, K., Gray, G., & Rood, S. (2000). A framework for accommodating religion and spirituality in the workplace/Executive commentary. *Academy of Management Executive, 14*(3), 124–134.

Chappel, T. (1993). *The Soul of a Business*. New York: Bantam Books.

Covey, S. (1989). *The Seven Habits of Highly Effective People*. New York: Simon & Schuster.

Covey, S. (2002). Free the spirits within. *Director, 55*(8), 43.

DeCenzo, D. A., & Robbins, S. P. (1998). *Human Resource Management* (6th ed.). San Diego, CA: Wiley.

Dorsey, D. (1998). The new spirit of work. *Fast Company, 16*, 224–232.

Drucker, P. (1995). *Managing in a Time of Great Change*. New York: Truman Talley Books/Plume.

Fox, M. (1995). *The Reinvention of Work: A New Vision of Livelihood for Our Time*. New York: HarperOne. Retrieved from www.newvision-psychic.com/bookshelf/reinventwork.html.

Freshman, B. (1999). An exploratory analysis of definitions and applications of spirituality in the workplace. *Journal of Organizational Change Management, 12*(4), 318.

Giorgi, G., Shoss, M. K., & Leon-Perez, J. M. (2015). Going beyond workplace stressors: Economic crisis and perceived employability in relation to psychological distress and job dissatisfaction. *International Journal of Stress Management, 22*(2), 137–158.

Goforth, C. (2001, October 7). Spirituality enters the office: A growing number of business executives are acting on the conviction that faith has a purpose in the workplace. *Ottawa Citizen*, k-2.

Green, T. (2000). Three steps to motivating employees. *HRMagazine, 45*(11), 155–158.

Gunther, M. (2001). God & business. *Fortune, 144*(1), 58–80.

Heard, M. (2005). Not your father's CPA firm! *Journal of Accountancy, 200*(3), 94.

Heider, J. (1985). *The Tao of Leadership: Lao Tzu's Tao Te Ching Adapted for a New Age.* Atlanta, GA: Humanics Limited.
Hein, K. (1999). A little spirit at work. *Incentive, 173*(2), 6.
Hicks, D. (2002). Spiritual and religious diversity in the workplace: Implications for leadership. *Leadership Quarterly, 13*(4), 379–396.
Hicks, D. A. (2003). *Religion and the Workplace: Pluralism, Spirituality, Leadership.* Cambridge, UK: Cambridge University Press.
Kahnweiler, W., & Otte, F. (1997). In search of the soul of HRD. *Human Resource Development Quarterly, 8*(2), 171–181.
Kaye, L. (1996). *Zen at Work.* New York: Three Rivers Press.
Kubicek, M. (2005). Meaningful management. *Training Magazine*, 10–11.
Laabs, J. (1995). Balancing spirituality and work. *Personnel Journal, 74*(9), 60.
Lerner, M. (2000). *Spirit Matters: Global Healing and the Wisdom of the Soul.* Charlottesville, VA: Hampton Roads Publishing Company, Inc.
Levering, R. (1988). *A Great Place to Work: What Makes Some Employers so Good (and Most so Bad).* New York: Random House, Inc.
Lewis, J., & Geroy, G. (2000). Employee spirituality in the workplace: A cross-cultural view for the management of spiritual employees. *Journal of Management Education, 24*(5), 682–694.
McCoy, B. (2001). CRE perspective: Living beyond the boundaries. *Real Estate Issues, 26*(2), 47–50.
McDonald, M. (1999, May 3). Shush: The guy in the cubicle is meditating. *Business & Technology.*
Marques, J. (2005). Socializing a capitalistic world: Redefining the bottom line. *Journal of American Academy of Business, Cambridge,* 7(1), 283–287.
Marques, J. F. (2010). Awakened leaders: Born or made? *Leadership and Organization Development Journal, 31*(4), 307–323.
Mitroff, I., & Denton, E. (1999). *A Spiritual Audit of Corporate America: A Hard Look at Spirituality, Religion, and Values in the Workplace* (1st ed.). San Francisco, CA: Jossey-Bass Publishers.
Mor Barak, M. E., & Levin, A. (2002). Outside of the corporate mainstream and excluded from the work community: A study of diversity, job satisfaction and well-being. *Community, Work and Family, 5*(2), 133–157.
Morris, T. (1997). *If Aristotle Ran General Motors.* New York: Henry Holt & Company, Inc.
Naidoo, M. (2014). The potential of spiritual leadership in workplace spirituality. *Koers: Bulletin for Christian Scholarship, 79*(2), 1–8.
Naimon, E. C., Mullins, M. E., & Osatuke, K. (2013). The effects of personality and spirituality on workplace incivility perceptions. *Journal of Management, Spirituality & Religion, 10*(1), 91–110.
Neal, J. (2000). Work as service to the divine: Giving our gifts selflessly and with joy. *American Behavioral Scientist, 43*(8), 1316–1333.
Neck, C., & Milliman, J. (1994). Thought self-leadership: Finding spiritual fulfillment in organizational life. *Journal of Managerial Psychology, 9*(6), 9.
Pierce, G. (2002). Don't be a Dilbert. *U.S. Catholic, 67*(9), 36–37.
Rosner, B. (2001). Is there room for the soul at work? *Workforce, 80*(2), 82–83.
Schutte, P. W. (2016). Workplace spirituality: A tool or a trend? *Hervormde Teologiese Studies, 72*(4), 1–5.
Terez, T. (1999). Meaningful work. *Executive Excellence, 16*(2), 19–20.
Thompson, L. (2004). Moral leadership in a postmodern world. *Journal of Leadership and Organizational Studies, 11*(1), 27–39.
Turner, J. (1999). Spirituality in the workplace. *CA Magazine, 132*(10), 41–42.
Vadermark, M. (2001). Seven spiritual laws. *Executive Excellence, 18*(9), 11.
Walters, J., & Fenson, S. (2002, March 9). *Authenticity in the Workplace.* Retrieved from www.spiritualsisters.com/ivyseal.htm.
Weston, S. (2002). Faith at work. *New Zealand Management, 49*(3), 28–30.
Wheatley, M. (2002). Spiritual leadership. *Executive Excellence, 19*(9), 5–6.
Wickens, B. (2001). Our changing life. *Maclean's, 114*(51), 24–26.
Wiles, B. (2005). Religion and the workplace: Pluralism, spirituality and leadership. *Journal of Interdisciplinary Studies, 17*(1/2), 195–196.
Williams, W. J., Randolph-Seng, B., Hayek, M., Haden, S. P., & Atinc, G. (2017). Servant leadership and followership creativity: The influence of workplace spirituality and political skill. *Leadership and Organization Development Journal, 38*(2), 178–193.
Wolf, E. (2004). Spiritual leadership: A new model. *Healthcare Executive, 19*(2), 22–26.

2

OPERATING FROM OUR AUTHENTIC SELF

Understanding Who We Truly Are

Satinder Dhiman

Introduction

"Leadership's First Commandment: *Know Thyself* … No tool can help a leader who lacks self-knowledge" (*Harvard Business Review* editorial, December, 2001).

This chapter explores the role of Self-knowledge in life and leadership. Self-awareness is now considered to be a foundational leadership competency (Goleman, 2004). Self-knowledge is the hallmark of all authentic leaders (Bennis, 2009; George, 2015), since it helps those in leadership positions to lead from their true self. In its wake, it bestows the gift of genuine humility, paving the way for selfless service and, finally, for servant leadership. The chapter underscores the value of humility as a prerequisite to, and consequence of, Self-knowledge. As leaders, when we are in touch with our deeper authentic self, we are also able to connect with the authentic self of others. In the final reckoning, Self-knowledge is the harbinger of the True, the Beautiful, and the Good in our life and work—the hallmarks of fulfillment and flourishing.

Self-knowledge deals with who and what we truly are. It is the ever-present awareness of our own being. Self-knowledge is not a journey of *becoming*; it is a state of *being*. It is a journey from unreal "me" to the real "I." The chapter briefly introduces the philosophy of Advaita Vedānta, as enunciated in the earliest Indian wisdom texts called Upaniṣads and the Bhagavad Gītā. Using teaching stories and illustrative vignettes, this chapter provides clear pointers to the present day leaders in their quest for personal and organizational wellbeing.

This chapter takes as axiomatic that leadership is voyage of *inner discovery* and that Self-knowledge is the key to leading from *within*. This journey begins with *knowing* oneself and culminates in *living* one's deepest values at the personal, team, and organizational level (Dhiman, 2015, 2017). As the following story (as narrated by Wallace, 2005) illustrates, without Self-knowledge one can overlook one's essential reality, even when completely *immersed* in it.

What the Hell Is Water?

There were these two young fishes swimming along, and they happen to meet an older fish swimming the other way, who nods at them and says, "Morning, guys, how's the water?"

And the two young fish swim on for a bit, and then eventually one of them looks over at the other and says, "What the hell is water?"

It is said that physical pain in life is unavoidable while much emotional suffering is optional. This chapter makes the felicitous assumption that true Self-knowledge can ameliorate most of our optional suffering and pave the way to lasting fulfillment. Therefore, it makes the plea that one needs to know oneself.

The Bhagavad Gītā and Upaniṣads: The Earliest Sources of Self-Knowledge

The Bhagavad Gītā holds a special place in the world's sacred and philosophical literature and has wielded an enduring influence on the spirit of humankind. According to a preeminent modern Sanskrit scholar, J. A. B. van Buitenen, "No other Sanskrit text approaches the Bhagavad Gītā in the influence it has exerted in the West." L. Basham (cited in Bolle, 1979, p. 224) and other Sanskrit scholars agree that the significance of the Bhagavad Gītā in India is comparable to that of the New Testament in Western civilization. Noting its widespread appeal and popularity, Minor (1986, p. 5), a modern exegetical commentator, states that the Bhagavad Gītā has become "the most translated text after the Bible." Count Hermann Keyserling (cited in Durant, 1930, p. 6), a German philosopher, hailed it as "perhaps the most beautiful work of the literature of the world." Steve Jobs' credo "Actualize yourself" seems to have come directly from the Bhagavad Gītā's philosophy of Self-realization. Peter Senge, one of the preeminent management thinkers of our time, has quoted the Gītā in two of his celebrated books, *The Fifth Discipline* and *Presence*. Gandhi regarded the Gītā as his "spiritual dictionary" and referred to it daily for seeking advice on life and leadership (Dhiman, 2015).

Although there are 108 Upaniṣads that are extant, out of these 10 Upaniṣads are considered more important because the great commentator, Ādi Śaṇkara, wrote elaborate commentaries on these: Bṛhadāraṇyaka Upaniṣad; Chāndogya Upaniṣad; Māṇḍūkya Upaniṣad; Kena Upaniṣad; Kaṭha Upaniṣad; Muṇḍaka Upaniṣad; Aitareya Upaniṣad; Taittirīya Upaniṣad; Praśna Upaniṣad; and Īśa Upaniṣad (see Gambhirananda, 1991). Once a seeker, so the story goes (Tejomayananda, n.d.), approached a Mahātmā ("a great soul") and asked: "Revered Sir, how many Upaniṣads do I have to study to know myself?" The Mahātmā replied with a question: "How many mirrors do you need to look at yourself?!"

The Need and Importance of Self-Knowledge

The importance of Self-knowledge can hardly be overemphasized. All wisdom traditions of the world have upheld the importance of Self-knowledge as a prelude to every pursuit of happiness and fulfillment. Its need has been rightly extolled in various wisdom texts of the world. It is s aid that, "one who knows oneself knows God" (see the Islamic *Hadith*: "*man 'arafa nafsahu faqad 'arafa Rabbahu*"). "Know yourself and you shall then know God," says a modern Indian saint, Śri Ramakrishna (cited in Satprakashananda, 1964, p. 232). An important Indian wisdom text, Muṇḍakan Upaniṣad 3.2.9 (Gambhirananda, 1991), goes a step further: "Who knows Brahman becomes Brahman" (**ब्रह्म वेद ब्रह्मैव भवति**: *brahma veda brahmaiva bhavati*)!

The Bhagavad Gītā, the Hindu wisdom text par excellence, describes it as "That which is to be known and by knowing which immortality is reached" (*… yaj jñātvāmṛtam aśnute …* **यत् ज्ञात्वामृतम् अश्नुते** BG 13.12; see Gambhirananda, 2001). In order to retain some flavor of the original, the chapter presents some Sanskrit terms and phrases in transliteration, using diacritics according to the International Alphabet of Sanskrit Transliteration (IAST) convention. For example, a small bar drawn over a word (e.g., "ā") indicates elongated sound: as "a" in the word "park." All translations are the author's, unless otherwise stated.

The Upaniṣads (Gambhirananda, 1991), the primary Hindu treatises on Self-knowledge, extol that "there is nothing higher than the attainment of the Self" (*ātmalābhānna paraṁ vidyate*: आत्मलाभान्न परं विद्यते); that "the knower of Self reaches the Supreme Felicity" (*Brahmavidāpnoti param* ‖ ब्रह्मविदाप्नोति परम्:‖ Taittirīya Upaniṣad 2.1.1); that "Self-knowledge is the harbinger of liberation while living" (Brahma-Sūtra Bhashya 1.1.12; see Panoli, 2011); and that "the knower of Self crosses over sorrow" (*Tarati śokam ātmavit*: तरति शोकम् आत्मवित्: Chāndogya Upaniṣad 7.1.3). The Kena Upaniṣad warns, "By not knowing the True Self, one is at a great loss" (*na cedihāvedīnmahatī vinaṣṭ*: न चेदिहावेदीन्महती विनष्टि: Kena Upaniṣad 2.5).

Similarly, in the Greek wisdom tradition, Socrates succinctly framed it as the highest principle of wisdom to "Know Thyself." *Gnōthi seautón* ("Know Thyself") is an ancient Greek aphorism and one of the two most famous Delphic maxims, the other being "nothing in excess." He did not mince words when he said, "The unexamined life is not worth living" (Plato, *Apology*, 38a; see Cooper & Grube, 2002). However, Socrates has left no self-help manual for us beyond such pithy dicta. His student, Plato, points out that "the essence of knowledge is Self-knowledge" (Plato, *Phaedrus*, 230a; see Cooper & Grube, 2002).

The following story demonstrates the power of knowledge (Paramarthananda, n.d.):

A certain billboard pictured a dog and a cat looking at each other.

The ferocious dog was trying to pounce at the cat, yet the cat seemed unperturbed and even amused, sitting quietly in front of the dog.

The caption simply read: The Power of Knowledge!

The dog was on a leash. The cat was aware of this fact.

This knowledge gave the cat the freedom to enjoy the moment with great peace of mind.

Such is the power of knowledge! If mere knowledge of our surroundings confers such security, imagine what level of security Self-knowledge can engender. This, then, is the true fulfillment of the Delphic Oracle (*gnothi seauton*): get to know yourself!

The following tale (cited in Bowling, 2000, p. 91; see Cashman, 2001, p. 31) further illustrates this point succinctly:

Just as the Great Revolution was getting under way in Russia, a rabbi on his way to the synagogue was stopped at gunpoint by a soldier. With his rifle pointed directly at the rabbi, the soldier said in a gruff voice, "Who are you, and what are you doing here?"

The rabbi replied with a question of his own: "How much do they pay you for doing this job?"

The soldier replied, "Twenty kopecks.

Then the rabbi said, "I will pay you twenty-five kopecks if every day you stop me right here and ask me those two questions."

If a leader knows the answer to those two questions, "Who are you?" and "What are you doing here?" all else will follow in good time and good measure. These two fundamental questions capture the essence of Self-knowledge and personal meaning and mastery and furnish the necessary foundation for the development of purpose-driven leadership. It must be noted that discovering one's highest purpose in life presupposes Self-knowledge and self-understanding.

Bennis (2009, p. 52), a noted leadership expert, provides the following four lessons/rules for facilitating Self-knowledge: "One: You are your own best teacher. Two: Accept responsibility. Blame no one. Three: You can learn anything you want to learn. Four: True understanding comes from reflecting on your experiences." Self-knowledge is not a matter of knowing something new; it is a matter of removing false notions about the self. It is a matter of *re*-cognition of who we truly are. *Self-knowledge is not a journey; it is a home-coming.* Socrates, however, did not care to elaborate precisely on how to go about this search. One common pitfall here is to take Socrates' injunction to know thyself to mean to know oneself intellectually or emotionally. The quest for Self-knowledge, however, has nothing to do with what is popularly known as self-improvement or spiritual betterment. As Krishnamurti (1954) eloquently puts it: "We are talking of something entirely different, not of self-improvement, but cessation of the [separate] self."

Those in the know have repeatedly pointed out that one has to know oneself in the very depth of one's being, exactly as one really is, with diligence and without any masks whatsoever. And this requires some serious work on oneself that calls for self-insight, sincerity, courage, patience, and discernment. It seems that the faculty of self-awareness serves as both the cause and effect of Self-knowledge. Self-knowledge is born of self-reflection and blossoms as a certain unmistakable quality of self-awareness that accompanies and pervades everything one does—a sort of glow that illuminates all our activities. This condition is often referred to as the faculty of mindfulness.

Seeker Is the Sought

"What you seek is so near you that there is no place for a way" (Nisargadatta Maharaj; cited in Frydman, 2012, p. 196).

While what we seek keeps on changing, the seeker in us continues to be the same. Self-knowledge reveals the radical fact that the *seeker is the sought*. One sage says, "What one is searching *for* is what one is searching *with*." The following traditional tale (cited in Mādhavānanda, 1934/2008, pp. 83–84) illustrates the point splendidly by highlighting both the predicament of self-ignorance and a way to end it.

The Missing Tenth Man

Ten monks crossed a river, and one of them counted their number to see if everyone had safely crossed. To their dismay, one was found missing. Then everyone took their turn at counting, but the result was the same. So they began to lament, when a kind passer-by inquired what it was all about.

On being told what had happened, he readily understood the situation, and asked one of them to count again. When he stopped at nine, the passer-by said to him, "You are the tenth man." This he repeated with the rest of them. Then they saw their mistake and went away happy. Everyone had left himself out in the counting!

This story highlights that the uniqueness of Self-knowledge lies in the fact that, unlike all other forms of knowledge, it does not entail any new acquisition of information. It only involves freedom from Self-ignorance. Like the tenth man in the story, gaining the essential Self means *realizing* our mistake of self-forgetfulness or Self-ignorance. The Self, like the tenth man in the story, appears initially to be not known through ignorance, but subsequently becomes known through knowledge. From an absolute standpoint, again—like the tenth man in the story—the essential Self was never lost to begin with and is ever-attained.

Sri Ramana Maharshi underscores this point succinctly in the following important passage (cited in Rajeswarananda, 2000, p. 111; Venkataramiah, 2013, p. 134):

> There is no greater mystery than this, that we keep seeking reality though in fact we are reality. We think that there is something hiding reality and that this must be destroyed before reality is gained. How ridiculous! A day will dawn when you will laugh at all your past efforts. That which will be the day you laugh is also here and now.

Strictly speaking, we cannot objectively *know* our Self because we *are* the Self. *The seeker is already the sought!* We are the knowing self—the pure awareness—the subject; and the knowing *subject*, by definition, can never become the *object* of knowledge. Wheeler (2012) clarifies this important point that "you *are* what you are seeking," succinctly:

> Trying to focus on your true nature is something like looking for your eyes, when the whole time you are looking through them. If you try to focus on your being or aware presence, you will be trying to turn it into an object. Since you are not an object, you will be looking in vain. Just see this point and pause. Being-awareness is here in all of its immediacy and clarity. *That* is it. Why should you try to focus on it, when you *are* it? See the false concept and the error contained in it. Your being is not to be obtained. It is pointed to as a present fact.
>
> *(p. 31, emphasis in the original)*

The Self seems *as though* veiled currently due to certain inhibiting factors, primarily, ignorance. This ignorance does not denote any lack of information or knowledge in any general sense. The ignorance that is referred to here is actually Self-ignorance, the ignorance or unawareness of our essential nature. The entire quest of fulfillment therefore is of the nature of awakening, a journey of recognition without distance from *here* to *here*. The following story (a traditional Sufi tale, transcribed by the author) splendidly underscores the paradox of missing our reality, while riding on it, metaphorically speaking.

Lost Donkey?

A man bought four donkeys and rode home on one of them.
When he reached home, his wife came out to greet him.
While sitting on one donkey, he started counting and found he had only three donkeys.
He said to his wife that he was missing one donkey!
His wife asked him, "How many donkeys did you buy?
He said, "I bought four, but now I only see three."
His wife smiled and said: "I see five!"

The man in the story is Mulla Nasruddin Hodja, a populist philosopher, and a consummate jester. He is known to poke fun at our common incongruities, using himself as an example. Our search for the Self may be "likened" to looking for the fourth donkey in the story: We have been at it all along, so to speak, yet failing to recognize it while comfortably riding on it! Paradoxically, avers De Mello (1988, p. 97), "Wisdom tends to grow in proportion to one's awareness of one's ignorance."

Attainment of the ever-attained Self, therefore, essentially means letting go of our false notions about what we take ourselves to be; that is, a limited body–mind–senses complex subject to mortality and unhappiness. It is about chipping away, so to speak, the fabricated edifice of the false "I," the imposter ego, posing itself to be the real Self. This special understanding requires subtle discernment to reclaim our true heritage. And this requires *knowledge*, not any special effort or *action*. We just have to *know* ourselves as we truly are.

Self-Knowledge: An Already Accomplished Fact

The only thing that is self-evident and ever-present is the Self—the *felt* awareness of our *being* or *presence*. Everything else becomes evident through the Self which is of the nature of pure awareness or Consciousness. Sri Ramana Maharshi explains succinctly:

> "I exist" is the only permanent, self-evident experience of everyone. Nothing else is so self-evident (*pratyaksha*) as "I am". What people call "self-evident" *viz.*, the experience they get through the senses, is far from self-evident. The Self alone is that. *Pratyaksha* is another name for the Self. So, to do Self-analysis and be "I am" is the only thing to do. "*I am*" is reality. I am *this* or *that* is unreal.
>
> *(Cited in Mudaliar, 2000, p. 182, emphasis added)*

Our whole existential experience can be reduced to two basic entities: "I" and "not-I." There is this "I" and everything else is "not-I." "I" refers to "I-am," the conscious principle, the "locus" of all experience and every emotion and thought. When Moses saw the blazing light of God on Mount Sinai, and, in awe, asked for God's name, we are told, the Light responded: "YHWH"—"I am That I am." Sri Ramana Maharshi used to say that the whole Vedānta is contained in the two Biblical statements: "I am that I AM" and "Be still and know that I am God" (see Venkataramiah, 2013, p. 320; Frydman, 2003). "I am" remains the most unique, the most exclusive, singular epithet to refer to oneself, as if partaking the Divine Reality.

This is also evident how pronouns work in all languages. The second and third person pronouns, You, They, He, She, It can be used to refer to any person or thing. But the first person pronoun, "I" can only be used to refer to one and only one person—namely, "you." Sri Ramana Maharshi has frequently emphasized this point in his writings: "It is only after the first personal pronoun arises that the second and third personal pronouns appear. Without the first person, the second and third persons cannot exist" (Godman, n.d.). There is only one person that is referred to when anyone refers to himself or herself as "I am." There is only one person in the whole creation that is like you, and that is you. You are the sole actor/director of your life's drama. It is a one act play, a monolog. And it is so for every single person! It has been rightly observed: "Remember, you are a completely unique and distinct person. Just like everyone else."

Little wonder, we have transitioned from a "me-culture" to "*selfie*-culture." Ever wonder about the secret of Apple's success. Apple Inc. chose their logo very well, all the way: first at the dawn of creation, it was the apple that was offered by Eve to Adam. Perhaps the same apple fell on Newton's head, knocking out all knowledge so that gravity can get in. And we are told that "an apple a day keeps the doctor away." Apple Inc. names its products ingeniously: *i*mac, *i*pod, *i*phone, *i*pad. Notice the prominence given to the "I." Hence, their success.

If Self-knowledge is a self-evident fact, how come we are told, as in the opening quote, that to know one's own self is the most difficult thing? How do we reconcile these two divergent viewpoints—that Self-knowledge is the most difficult thing and that Self-knowledge is the most naturally self-evident and an already accomplished fact? If Self-knowledge is an already accomplished fact, we may ask, why do we need all these reminders such as "Know Thyself" (Socrates)? If by its very nature the Self is the most self-evident fact, why do we need any teaching at all to know ourselves? The sages point out that although we know ourselves in a general way—we are *conscious* that we exist—we do not know our true nature.

It can be explained in this manner: "I am" is a self-evident fact. "Who am I" is a *discovery*. And this discovery needs a specialized means to proceed. It is because even if we have eyes, we still need a mirror to see our face. Vedānta—the science of truth about our existence—acts as a mirror to reveal "who am I." I know *I am*, but I do not know that *I am Brahman*. Vedānta says you are not the limited "body–mind–senses" complex that you take yourself to be. You are whole, limitless Consciousness. Know yourself to be so and be happy. Whenever we feel sorrowful, we are missing something; for, all sorrow is born of some sense of limitation—physical or psychological. All seeking essentially involves a desire to be free from limitations. We are all seeking *puraṇatvam*, the fullness of our being. Vedānta says you are already *puraṇa*, whole and complete: reclaim your true status—as limitless Consciousness—and be free.

Self-Knowledge *Is* Self-Realization

In the Vedāntic scheme of things, there is no difference between Self-knowledge and Self-Realization, for, to *know* the Self is to *realize* the Self. As Afdal al-Din Kashani (*c.* CE 12th century) puts it succinctly, "To know oneself is to know the everlasting reality that is Consciousness, and to *know* it is to *be* it" (cited in Chittick, 1988, p. 288). When one *knows* that the fire burns, one does not have to put one's hand in the fire to *realize* this fact. Put differently, in the realm of Self-knowledge, *knowing is being and being is knowing*. Unlike things that are separated from us by time and space—for which we have to do something to attain them—Self-knowledge does not involve doing something new or attaining something afresh. It is only a matter of re-cognizing, re-discovering an already existing fact: "the achievement of that which is already achieved, *prāpatasya prāpati*" (Dayananda, 2009, p. 39).

In Indian philosophy, enlightenment is spoken of as Self-Realization, the attainment of the Supreme Self. However, it is important to understand the exact sense in which the word "realization" is used. Sri Ramana Maharshi (cited in Mudaliar, 2000, p. 181), the great Indian sage, clarifies (emphasis added):

> We loosely talk of Self-Realization, for lack of a better term. But how can one realize or make real that which alone is real? All we need to do is to give up our habit of regarding as real that which is unreal. All religious practices are meant solely to help us do this. *When we stop regarding the unreal as real, then reality alone will remain, and we will be that.*

Vedānta takes it as axiomatic that "the highest aim of religion is … Self-knowledge" (Giri, 1984, p. 6). It is a science of reality and that the knowledge of the Self and the knowledge of the Ultimate Reality are identical (Iyer, 1930/1991, 1969/2006; Kulkarni, 1990). Ādī Śaṇkara, the great Advaita philosopher, urges that "you must realize absolutely that the *Ātman* [the Self] is Brahman [the All-Self]" (Prabhavananda and Isherwood, 1975, p. 70). In Indian philosophy, Self-knowledge signifies the knowledge that our true Self and the true nature of Reality are identical. This understanding first requires knowing what is real. Vedānta defines reality as that which does not change.

Vedānta states that the Witnessing Consciousness, which lies within everyone that perceives all changing phenomena, is the only unchanging reality (Satchidanandendra, 1989; Iyer, 1930/1991; Kulkarni, 1990; Schepetin, 2018). Everything else that is constantly changing is a mere appearance in Pure Consciousness. This Pure Consciousness is the *observer* of all that is changing. The Observer is the inmost Self (*pratyagātmā*) of all beings. Vedānta declares that You *are* the Self (Chāndogya Upaniṣad 6.8.7; Gambhirananda, 1991)—the unchanging Witnessing Consciousness that perceives the changes in the body–mind–senses, the three states (waking, dream, and deep sleep), and the phenomenal world. This is the Self or Ātman of Vedānta. Śrī Śaṅkara in his commentary to Brahma-Sutra 1.1.6 states that "what is meant by the word 'Self' is one's own nature" (Panoli, 2011, p. 75).

This unchanging pervasive Consciousness is the Absolute Reality and is called Brahman in its universal aspect. The same universal Consciousness is experienced as the Self in all beings and is called Ātman. There is an absolute identity of Brahman and Ātman, for Reality is One, without a second (Gambhirananda, 1991; Chāndogya Upaniṣad 6.2.1).

Parking the Ego at the Door: Key to Authentic Leadership

Self-knowledge helps us to be humble by highlighting the oneness and interdependence of all life. One of the most important pre-conditions for the spiritual quest is humility. Only humble leaders can serve a cause higher than themselves. Defining the process of becoming a leader in terms of authenticity and self-mastery, Bennis (2011) equates it with becoming yourself, which is not as simple as it sounds. He provides a succinct characterization of exemplary leadership in an interview to *Fast Company*:

> The process of becoming a leader is, if not identical, certainly similar to the process of becoming a fully integrated human being. It's got to do with authenticity, it's got to do with candor, it's got to do with the fact that one cannot truly lead unless one is an expert in self-management.

Leadership qualities, Bennis maintains, can only emerge from an "integrated self." Howard Schultz, the founder and chairman of the Starbucks chain of coffee shops, says that Bennis once told him that to become a great leader you have to develop "your ability to leave your own ego at the door, and to recognize the skills and traits that you need in order to build a world-class organization" (cited in Hindle, 2008, p. 218).

This goes on to show that humility is an essential ingredient of effective leadership. Jim Collins, the author of *Good to Great,* fully concurs and regards *compelling humility* to be one of the two hallmarks of level 5 leaders, the other being *fierce professional will* (Collins, 2001).

Bill George, the exemplary former head of Medtronic, who popularized the concept of authentic leadership, includes humility along with purpose, transparency, and integrity to define authentic leaders (George, 2015). Humility is also a pre-condition for serving others for without it, even service could be but an inflation of ego. Therefore, in learning as in leading, humility constitutes the key ingredient of living a profoundly significant life.

A story is told about Frank Lloyd Wright, the famous architect, who was once testifying in court for his friend. While taking oath, he is reported to have said, "My name is Frank Lloyd Wright, the greatest architect on the planet!" Later when his friend questioned him about his exaggerated sense of self-importance, Frank Lloyd Wright maintained, "I was under oath to tell the truth!" The human ego is always good at finding new avenues of manifesting itself, especially under the covert cover of humility. Such are the ways of the master magician—"our skin-encapsulated ego"—the socially induced hallucination of a separate self, to use a phrase coined by Aldous Huxley. Huxley (cited in Horowitz & Palmer, 1999, p. 291) calls self-centeredness "the fundamental human disability." Without fully overcoming this pervasive disability, there is no "psychological freedom" and the progress on the path of authentic life and leadership is at best doubtful.

What is Humility?

Most people often tend to confuse humility with false modesty. We all have been guilty of this at one time or another. We have a tendency to devalue what we have done under the pretense of humility. In fact, refusing to accept genuine appreciation is often a cover for seeking more praise from others. That is perhaps why true humility is very hard to come by.

Humility does not necessarily mean to think of oneself as insignificant, timid, or worthless. As someone rightly observed, "Humility is not thinking less of yourself, it's thinking of yourself less." (This quote is often misattributed to C. S. Lewis. According to the C. S. Lewis foundation, this quote belongs to the category of misattributed quotes and is *not* by C. S. Lewis. See www.cslewis.org/aboutus/faq/quotes-misattributed/.) In fact, humility signifies utter sincerity with oneself, requiring one to think of one's abilities as no greater, and no lesser, than they really are. Humble people know what they can and cannot do. They take note of both their gifts and their limitations in a realistic manner. True humility is definitely not about self-deprecation.

We are taught to think of pride is a good thing, whereas humility is the absence of pride. Pride has meaning only when comparing others to yourself. By comparing ourselves to others, we learn to play the ubiquitous game of "one-upmanship." A humble person does not base his or her self-worth on how s/he stacks up to others. She is content to make her honest contribution without raising a flag. Thus, such a person feels no need to play the game of one-upmanship.

No Humility: Only Different Shades of Pride!

Many wiser souls, somewhat jaded with cynicism, have pointed out that there is no humility; only, different shades of pride. We recall an interesting remark by a colleague: "Enough of me talking about myself. Tell me what you think of me!" Real humility is very hard virtue to cultivate. More often than not, humility may be a cover for subtle pride. In his classic *Autobiography*, Ben Franklin tells us how he embarked upon a rather ambitious regimen of cultivating various life virtues such as temperance, silence, order, frugality, sincerity, justice, and humility. He has noted that although a seemingly simple quality, humility is the most difficult virtue to cultivate because by the time one gets to master it, one becomes proud of it!

The following Sufi story highlights the dangers of self-conceit and the need to stay humble in all pursuits. The Sufi—one who is *not*—narrates the story as follows:

> ...and my third Master was a small child. I entered into a town once and a small child was bringing a candle, a lit candle, hiding it in his hands. He was going to the mosque to put the candle there. In the lighter vein, I asked the boy, "Have you lit the candle yourself?" He said, "Yes, sir." And I asked, jokingly, "Since you saw the light coming when you lit the candle, can you tell me from where the light came?" The boy became serious first and then laughed and blew out the candle, and said, "Now you have seen the light going, where has it gone? You tell me!" My ego was crushed, and my whole knowledge was shattered. And that moment I felt my own foolhardiness. Since then I dropped all pretense to knowledgeability.
>
> *(A traditional Sufi tale, author unknown)*

The teachings about compassion and humility find their closest parallel in the naturalistic philosophy of Taoism. Lao Tzu calls them "three treasures." They first occur in Chapter 67, which is also entitled "Three Treasures," of Chinese classic *Tao Te Ching* which Lin Yutang says contains "*Laotse's most beautiful teachings*" (Yutang, 1946/1976, p. 292, emphasis added). In Lao Tzu's view, nature arms with humility those it would not see destroyed: an axe first falls on the tallest tree. There is a poem by Chuang Tzu transliterated by Thomas Merton which beautifully underscores the value of the virtue of humility as follows:

> If a man is crossing a river and an empty boat collides with his own skiff, even though he be a bad-tempered man he will not become very angry. But if he sees a man in the boat, he will shout at him to steer clear.
>
> If the shout is not heard, he will shout again, and yet again, and begin cursing. And all because there is somebody in the boat.
>
> Yet if the boat were empty, he would not be shouting, and not angry. If you can empty your own boat crossing the river of the world, no one will oppose you, no one will seek to harm you . . .
> . . . Such is the perfect man:
> . . . His boat is empty.
>
> *(Merton, 1965, pp. 114–115)*

Spiritual Costs of Selfishness?

The psychological costs of self-centeredness are well documented in positive psychology literature, such as greater psychological distress (anxiety and depression), poor physical health (lower immune system and increased risk of cardiovascular diseases) and compromised personal and social relationship, and lack of emotional clarity. The biggest cost of selfishness, from a spiritual standpoint, is that it prevents the development of a subtle sense of discrimination and thus forestalls our growth on the path of Self-knowledge and spirituality. Being self-centered, the selfish person is not able to "perceive" the universal dimension of reality. If one is preoccupied with the small "s" of the "self" in oneself, one is not able to see the big "S" of the "Self" in all, which is the goal of all true spirituality. That is why all spiritual traditions enjoin performing selfless service and giving to charity to purify the mind and to heal the body and spirit.

A Case in Point: A Rare Story!

Last year, this author spent some time in an *āshram* (monastery) in the state of Gujarat, India. A gentleman came to visit us, who happened to be an architect by profession. He narrated a story about a wealthy person as told by one of his Indian friends who is now a famous cardiologist in Bombay. During his medical studies in the US, this cardiologist was working with another eminent US cardiologist. This US cardiologist was famous for having a very high success rate with his heart patients. Almost all the patients he would treat would get better, except in the case of a certain wealthy businessman.

The businessman did not get better at all after the prescribed treatment. This puzzled the US cardiologist. He thought long and hard about the case and could not find any loophole in his treatment. Something was interfering in the path of recovery and this famous US cardiologist could not figure out what it was.

Wanting to give it a last try, he asked the rich businessman if he could send a team of two doctors to stay at his home for the next three weeks to observe his lifestyle. They wanted to rule out all possibilities of what might be interfering with the cure. The rich businessman readily agreed. After all, he wanted to get better.

So, two young medical doctors were sent to this person's home to observe him 24 × 7. The now famous cardiologist from Bombay, who is narrating his firsthand experience to his architect friend, was one of the two doctors that was sent to the rich person's home to observe his living habits.

They observed and observed but could not find any unusual behavior on the part of the rich man that could be the contributing factor to the heart disease or preventing the cure. One day, they noticed something that strange about this businessman. He was talking to someone on the phone and whenever the question of money came up, he got very agitated. He was very very rich and getting more or less money would not have affected his wealth at all. Yet anytime he talked to someone about money, he got very agitated. Bingo! That was perhaps the clue they were looking for.

The two medical doctors reported it back to the main cardiologist who was attending the case. A meeting was arranged with the rich person and he was counseled not to get agitated about money since the amount of money he already had was so much that having more money or less money would make absolutely no difference to him. The businessman saw the value of the diagnosis.

In order to counter his habit of stinginess, the doctor prescribed him to give certain compulsory donations to the charities of his choice every week. After 3 months of this treatment consisting of giving mandatory donations, the businessman was 75% cured!

The cardiologist still wondered why the businessman was not cured 100%. Did they overlook something? Therefore, the same team of young doctors was sent back to the rich person's home for further observation. The prescription of mandatory donations continued. Since the donation treatment benefitted the patient, its frequency was increased. Now the businessman was to give compulsory donations every other day.

This time, the doctors noticed something else that was interesting. Every time this businessman gave donations, he felt a high sense of pride and superiority. This was reported back to the main cardiologist.

This behavior was analyzed and it was determined that this attitude of haughtiness was what was interfering with the complete cure.

It was recommended that the business person should feel himself lucky while giving the donations. In all true charity, it is the giver that should be humbled. After all, there are no sacrifices, only opportunities to serve.

The businessman followed the treatment for the next 3 months and was completely cured!

There are many morals to this story. For one, our health is not a mere physical phenomenon; it has a psychological and spiritual basis. If we want to heal the patient—not just the disease—we should look at the totality of the circumstances attending the case. Second, self-centeredness is the cause of much of our stress and suffering.

Humility: The Touchstone of Great Leadership

Humility is the cause and consequence of true learning, for nothing can go in a full vessel. Humility is indeed the touchstone of great leadership. A tree with fruits bends. Humility is also a precondition for serving others for without it, even service could be but an inflation of ego. Lack of humility leads to cluelessness and cluelessness quickly leads to a leader's derailment and demise. Humble leaders are great contributors. True humility is more like self-forgetfulness than false modesty—it means *emptying* ourselves of the false pride and pretense.

It has been said that the function of leadership is to produce more leaders, not more followers. What is the alchemy of producing more leaders? Most of the time, it is about leading from behind. In his autobiography entitled *Long Walk to Freedom*, Nelson Mandela equated a great leader to a shepherd: "A leader … is like a shepherd. He stays behind the flock, letting the most nimble go out ahead, whereupon the others follow, not realizing that all along they are being directed from behind" (1995, p. 22).

Elsewhere Mandela (cited in Lizza, 2011) states that "It is better to lead from behind and to put others in front, especially when you celebrate victory when nice things occur. You take the front line when there is danger. Then people will appreciate your leadership." Within the short compass of these two quotes, Mandela encapsulates the leadership lessons he learnt having spent 10,000 days in jail over a period of 50 years of struggle (1944–1994) for ending bondage. Leading from behind is a leadership style whose time has come. It is style which puts followers in the forefront of leadership line. However, it requires supreme humility.

Does humility mean low self-regard? To be humble does not mean to have a low opinion of oneself, it is to have an accurate opinion of oneself, says the psychologist Robert Emmons. Emmons (2009, p. 171) describes humility as the "realistic appraisal of one's strengths and weaknesses—neither overestimating them nor underestimating them." True humility is a matter of right perspective.

Is humility the most important quality to cultivate in life and leadership? Humility is unquestionably the most essential requirement when it comes to learning: without being humble, one cannot learn at all. And both history and current research testify that the best leaders are humble. In their *Harvard Business Review* study, Prime and Salib (2014) clarify that humble leaders should not be mistaken for weak ones for it takes tremendous courage to practice humility. These authors cite Google's SVP of People Operations, Lazlo Bock, who says humility is one of the traits he's looking for in new hires. Based on their current research and ongoing study of leadership development practices at Rockwell Automation, Prime and Salib (2014) share the following practices to garner a humble, inclusive leadership style:

- *Engage in dialogue, not debates.* Engaging in dialogue is good way to practice humility. When people debate to sway others to win them to their viewpoint, they miss out on the opportunity to learn about *other* points of view. When leaders are humble enough to suspend their own agendas and beliefs, they are not only enhance their own learning but they validate followers' unique perspectives.
- *Embrace uncertainty.* When leaders humbly admit that they don't have all the answers, they create space for others to step forward and offer solutions. They also engender a sense of interdependence. Followers understand that the best bet is to rely on each other to work through complex, ill-defined problems.
- *Role model being a "follower."* Inclusive leaders empower *others* to lead. By reversing roles, leaders not only facilitate employees' development but they model the act of taking a different perspective, something that is so critical to working effectively in diverse teams.

Inclusive leaders are humble enough to admit that they do not have all the answers and that the present day problems are too complex for any one person to tackle them single-handedly. Doing so, they garner the wisdom of the followers and allow them to come up with shared solutions. Humble leaders have the humility and wisdom to learn from those who have less power than them. Dan Cable in his April 2018 *Harvard Business Review* article entitled,

"How Humble Leadership Really Works," underscores the value of humility in servant leadership as follows:

> To put it bluntly, servant-leaders have the humility, courage, and insight to admit that they can benefit from the expertise of others who have less power than them. They actively seek the ideas and unique contributions of the employees that they serve. This is how servant leaders create a culture of learning, and an atmosphere that encourages followers to become the very best they can.

Concluding Thoughts

"It is enigmatic that man with all his pretensions to knowledge does not know himself. Nay, he knows himself wrong" (Satprakashananda, 1964, p. 232).

When asked what was the most difficult thing, Thales, a pre-Socratic Greek philosopher, mathematician, replied, "*To know thyself.*" There is no wealth equal to Self-knowledge in the whole creation. Its glory is such that it makes people walk away from the much coveted kingdoms. The Buddha is a case in point. He was a prince. He gave it up all to discover the truth of his existence. Today he is revered not because he was a *king-to-be*, but because he renounced the transient kinghood *without* and discovered the eternal kingdom *within*. What he found has inspired billions ever since.

To know the Self is to realize that there is nothing "personal" about it—in the sense of "myself" or "yourself." Since the true Self is at-one-with the Absolute Reality, to know the Self is to realize our oneness with all that is. Self-knowledge confers upon us the wisdom to see all existence as the expression of our very own Self and spontaneously act for the well-being of all beings. Selfless love and compassion naturally flow out of this understanding of unity and oneness of all life. This is the flowering of Self-knowledge in life and leadership.

References

Bennis, W. (2009). *On Becoming a Leader* (4th ed.). New York: Basic Books.

Bennis, W. (2011, December 26). Have the requirements for being a good leader changed? Interview: Fast Company: Leadership Hall of Fame (F. Company, Interviewer).

Bolle, K. (1979). *The Bhagavadgītā: A New Translation*. Berkeley: University of California Press.

Bowling, J. C. (2000). *Grace-Full Leadership*. Kansas City, MO: Beacon Hills Press.

Buitenen, J. (Ed. and Trans.). (1981). *The Bhagavad Gītā in the Mahābhārata: A Bilingual Edition*. Chicago: University of Chicago Press.

Cable, D. (2018, April). How humble leadership really works. *Harvard Business Review*.

Cashman, K. (2001). *Leadership from the Inside Out*. Provo, UT: Executive Excellence Publishing.

Chittick, W. (1988). *BĀBĀ AFŻAL-AL-DĪN*. Encyclopaedia Iranica, III, Fasc. 3, pp. 285–291. Retrieved from www.iranicaonline.org/articles/baba-afzal-al-din.

Collins, J. (2001). *Good to Great: Why Some Companies Make the Leap … and Others Don't*. New York: HarperBusiness.

Cooper, J. M., & Grube, G. (Eds.). (2002). *Plato: Five Dialogues: Euthyphro, Apology, Crito, Meno, Phaedo (Hackett Classics)* (2nd ed.). New York: Hackett Publishing Company, Inc.

Dayananda, S. (2009). *Introduction to Vedanta: Understanding the Fundamental Problem*. New Delhi: Vision Books Pvt. Ltd.

De Mello, A. (1988). *One Minute Wisdom*. New York: Doubleday.

Dhiman, S. (2015). *Gandhi and Leadership: New Horizons in Exemplary Leadership*. New York: Palgrave Macmillan.

Dhiman, S. (2017). *Holistic Leadership: A New Paradigm for Today's Leaders*. New York: Palgrave Macmillan.

Durant, W. (1930). *The Case for India*. New York: Simon & Schuster.

Emmons, R. A. (2009). *The Psychology of Ultimate Concerns: Motivation and Spirituality in Personality*. New York: Guilford Press.

Franklin, B. (1996). *The Autobiography of Benjamin Franklin*. New York: Dover Publications.

Frydman, M. (Compiler). (2003). *Maharshi's Gospel: The Teachings of Sri Ramana*. Tiruvannamalai: Sri Ramanasaramam.

Frydman, M. (Trans.). (2012). *I am That: Conversations with Sri Nisargadatta Maharaj* (2nd ed.). Durham, NC: Acorn Press.

Gambhirananda, S. (Trans.). (1991). *Eight Upanishads with the Commentary of Sankaracharya, Vol. 1 & 2*. Calcutta: Advaita Ashrama.

Gambhirananda, S. (2001). *Bhagavad Gita with the Commentary of Sri Shankaracharya*. Calcutta: Advaita Ashrama.

George, B. (2015). *Discover Your True North* (Expanded and Updated ed.). San Francisco: Jossey-Bass.

Giri, Y. (1984). *The Holy Science*. Los Angeles: Self-Realization Fellowship.

Godman, D. (n.d.). *Who Am I?* Retrieved from www.davidgodman.org/gen2/p/ramana/who-am-i/who-am-i.html.

Goleman, D. (2004, January). What makes a leader. *Harvard Business Review*, 12.

Hindle, T. (2008). *Guide to Management Ideas and Gurus (The Economist)*. London: Profile Books Ltd.

Horowitz, M., & Palmer, C. (Eds.). (1999). *Moksha: Aldous Huxley's Classic Writings on Psychedelics and the Visionary Experience*. New York: Park Street Press.

Iyer, K. (1930/1991). *Vedanta or the Science of Reality*. Bangalore: Adhyatma Prakasha Karayala.

Iyer, K. (1969/2006). *Collected Works of K. A. Krishnaswamy Iyer*. Holenarasipur: Adhyatma Prakash Karyalaya.

Krishnamurti, J. (1954). *Krishnamurti's Talks in India 1954 (Verbatim Report)*. Banaras. Retrieved from www.jkrishnamurti.org.

Kulkarni, D. (1990). *Guide-lines to Shaṅkara-Vedānta*. Bangalore: Adhyatma Prakash Karyalaya.

Lizza, R. (2011, April 26). *Leading from Behind*. Retrieved from www.newyorker.com/news/news-desk/leading-from-behind.

Mādhavānanda, S. (Trans.). (1934/2008). *The Bṛhadāraṇyaka Upaniṣad with the Commentary of Śaṅkarācārya*. Mayavati, Almora, Himalayas: Advaita Ashrama.

Mandela, N. (1995). *Long Walk to Freedom: The Autobiography of Nelson Mandela*. New York: Back Bay Books.

Merton, T. (1965). *The Way of Chuang Tzu*. New York: Penguin New Directions Books.

Minor, R. N. (Ed.). (1986). *Modern Indian Interpreters of the Bhagavad Gītā*. Albany: State University of New York Press.

Mudaliar, D. (2000). *Day by Day with Bhagavan*. Tiruvannamalai: Sri Ramanasaramam.

Panoli, V. (Trans.). (2011). *Prasthanathraya, Volume VI: Bramasutra*. Kozhikode, Keralam, India: Mathrubhumi Printing & Publishing Co. Ltd.

Paramarthananda, S. (n.d.). Essence of Vedanta [Recorded by S. Paramarthananda]. Coimbatore, Tamil Nadu, India.

Prabhavananda, S., & Isherwood, C. (Trans.). (1975). *Shankara's Crest-jewel of Discrimination: Vedanta*. Hollywood, CA: Vedanta Press.

Prime, J., & Salib, E. (2014, May). The best leaders are humble leaders. *Harvard Business Review*.

Rajeswarananda, S. (Ed.). (2000). *Thus Spake Ramana*. Tiruvannamalai: Sri Ramanasramama.

Satprakashananda, S. (1964). *Methods of Knowledge: According to Advaita Vedanta*. London: George Allen & Unwin Ltd.

Satchidanandendra, S. (1989). *Method of Vedanta: A Critical Account of Advaita Tradition* (A. Alston, Trans.). London: Kegan Paul International Limited.

Schepetin, I. (2018). The traditional method by which a Guru enlightens the student. *Les Cahiers Aditi*.

Senge, P. (2006). *The Fifth Discipline: The Art & Practice of the Learning Organization* (rev. and updated ed.). New York: Doubleday.

Senge, P., Scharmer, C. O., Jaworsk, J., & Flowers, B. S. (2008). *Presence: Human Purpose and the Field of the Future* (Reprint ed.). New York: Crown Business.

Tejomayananda, S. (n.d.). Discourses on Brahm-Sūtras, No. 1.

Venkataramiah, M. (2013). *Talks with Ramana Maharshi*. Tiruvannamalai: Sri Ramanasramam.

Wallace, D. F. (2005). Commencement Speech at Kenyon College. Gambier, Ohio, USA.

Wheeler, J. (2012). *Full Stop! The Gateway to Present Perfection*. Salisbury, UK: Non-duality Press.

Yutang, L. (1946/1976). *The Wisdom of Lao Tzu*. New York: Modern Library.

3

MANAGING SPIRITUALITY FROM A PERSONAL PERSPECTIVE

William A. Guillory

Defining Spirituality

Spirituality is a state of being which is sourced from within—beyond what we have been programmed to believe and value; both genetically and environmentally. Spirituality is the inner source of wisdom that is reflected in values and behaviors which are both humanistic and performance-oriented. These values include empathy, compassion, humility, passion, empowerment, and love; as well as inspiration, creativity, and imagination. One of the most profound expressions of spirituality is religion. Spirituality is source and religion is a human expression which compatibly embraces believers, non-believers, and those who are unaffiliated. Other expressions of spirituality include meditation, prayer, Yoga, and simply treating others with dignity and respect.

Most of all, spirituality is not a single state of being. It dynamically changes as an individual ascends to more expanded levels of existence—and in different forms. We use descriptions and words to describe how a spiritual experience has transformed our thinking and behaviors. Keeping in mind the words of the famous East Indian philosopher, Jiddu Krishnamurti, … what lies beyond cannot be put into words because, "the word is not the thing"…. Or the Polish–American scientist and philosopher, Alfred Korzybski, who remarked, "the map is not the territory." Both individuals expressing the view that we use these concepts and models to guide our conversation about a spiritual experience, not to imply that we are describing reality. The closest we come to reality is the experience and the subsequent way our personal consciousness is irreversibly altered.

For example, transforming from the dominant state of human existence on Earth, survival to compatibility, is to become more spiritual. A consciousness of survival is dominantly characterized by:

1. Scarcity
2. Win/lose
3. Competition
4. Separateness, and
5. Polarization.

Based upon power being associated with information; the collection, organization, and interpretation of data. These characteristics dominantly, but not totally, comprise the context of human existence on Earth. Within the framework of this paradigm, technology is developed with the intent of increasing the potential for acquiring and storing, processing, and retrieving information. In essence, this context of operation allows unlimited access to data, facts, and discoveries for the advancement of science, technology, medicine, economics, and every form of human interest and activity. It also allows planet-wide distribution on the Internet. The intent of one's activity is reflected by how information is used and the result it produces.

For example, information can be applied to characterizing, tracking, and programming individuals in a national or global society, as well as used for weaponry and security. In more advanced ways, it is applied to the development of androids, cyborgs, and the continuing advancement of artificial intelligence (AI). In essence, the applications of technological advancement are no more or less spiritual, in use, than the consciousness which drives it. In a dominantly survival-based society the characteristics above determine the intent of the applications. The question which arises from a personal perspective is "how much do we each participate consistent with a context of survival and how dominant is it in our personal and professional life?"

In contrast, a consciousness of compatibility is dominantly characterized by:

1. Respect
2. Equality
3. Interdependence
4. Collaboration, and
5. Freedom.

Based upon power being associated with knowledge; the creative transformation of information into knowledge. These characteristics are commonly judged as more spiritual than those of the survival paradigm, listed above, based on the observation of greater individual and collective harmony, understanding, and physical and mental wellbeing. The result of a transformation from survival to compatibility in consciousness is the following dominant paradigm for human existence:

The Seven Principles of Social Equality

1. All humans are *worthy* by virtue of their existence—no human should be exalted as superior to others.
2. All humans have an *inherent* right to be fed, clothed, and sheltered—with the support of others where necessary.
3. All humans have an *inherent* right to be educated to learn both physical survival and global adaptation.
4. All humans have an *inherent* right to freely explore and express their spiritual values through creativity, innovation, and/or any other form of human understanding, compassion, and love.
5. All humans have an *inherent* right to explore consciousness for the continual acquisition of wisdom.
6. All humans have an *inherent* right to religious expressions that provide spiritual growth in concert with the wellbeing of all humanity.
7. All humans have an *inherent* personal and collective responsibility to preserve a planetary social, physical, and spiritual environment for their continued existence.

This paradigm is available to anyone who chooses to adopt it as a context for living as a human being; or even a spiritual being having a human experience. In order to achieve this way of being and behaving requires the most critical element for spiritual growth—*inner exploration*. As a species, we appear to be deathly afraid of inner exploration, but totally enamored with outer exploration—even to the extent of physical injury or death, e.g., extreme sports or space travel!

Inner Exploration

Inner exploration is the in-depth examination of one's personal consciousness (mind) with the same enthusiasm and commitment as one uses for learning and applying new and existing computer software applications. Human mastery of outer-space exploration far exceeds the knowledge and wisdom that are necessary to constructively manage the technology which has been invented. This process is sometimes referred to as *self-mastery*.

A dedicated exploration of self-mastery begins with the awareness that every interaction experienced that results in a counterproductive feeling or emotion is feedback that an opportunity exists for learning and resolution. Resolution is synonymous with a *realization* (Guillory, 1984). A realization is typically the permanent invalidation of a programmed belief, and even sometimes a value held by some groups, such as the belief of the superiority of an individual relative to another by racial distinctions.

The steps involved in such an examination are the sequence outlined for Emotional Intelligence (Walton, 2002), when there is the experience of an unconscious perception which has the potential or reality for conflict:

1. Become aware of the feelings and emotions you are experiencing—stress, tension, pain, which translates into fear, anger, or sadness.
2. Focus inwardly on that place in your body rather than on the external event or person—inward focus reduces stress and creates a time interval for self-reflection and evaluation.
3. In this time interval, ask yourself: "Is this conflict about the external event/person or my own programming? Or, possibly both?"
4. If the answer is *Yes* to internal programming, then you can control a detrimental reaction—and exercise choice involving a personally appropriate response.
5. When you experience relief and possibly personal transformation, ask yourself: "What did I learn about that conflict that will help me to respond more appropriately in the future?"

One of the most constructive processes of engaging inner exploration is the proactive process of learning through interactive, experiential workshops and/or informal coaching; particularly, where those practices are led by a skilled facilitator. The greatest progress, in terms of inner exploration, is usually realized from a variety of personally chosen modalities, such as Zen, Tai chi, meditation, workshops, reading, gardening, support groups, close friendships, etc. Particularly, when the same level of commitment of an individual involving his or her long-term physical health is also applied to his or her mental health.

In the process, the serious practitioner of mental health soon discovers the iceberg model of in-depth analysis. That is, the true source of one's motivations is programmed at the subliminal levels of one's personal consciousness.

In such cases, there are two approaches one might employ for resolution: (1) the assistance of a skilled individual who knows how to facilitate this level of exploration; and/or (2) direct actions that have the potential to *provoke* and ultimately *unearth* the source of an ongoing problem, without ever knowing what it is through analysis. The challenging (behavioral) provocation is sufficient to create a *constructive head-on collision* between the two individuals and their unconscious programming.

For example, if an individual has difficulty working with a female in a leadership or management role because of an unknown subliminal perception, one of the most direct means of resolution is to work together on an important project. When they *inevitably* experience conflict in the process, they jointly agree to "dialogue" through the perceived difficulty—commonly assisted by a coach/facilitator. This dialogue is an integral part of the process. As they begin a shared exchange, spontaneous perceptions and beliefs will begin to emerge from a hidden part of the iceberg. Not surprisingly, the breakthrough perception or realization is commonly a perception or insecurity they share in common! It takes both contributing individuals to create and maintain an ongoing conflict. Obviously, this approach requires a commitment to resolution by *both* individuals, since they soon realize they are navigating the unchartered waters of their unconsciousness. The emphasis here is that such an approach is a *process*, not an *event*. The result is a transformation in their relationship and incredible personal growth from an individual perspective. These results are confirmed by the expressions of understanding, acceptance, and contribution to each other's success.

The ultimate resolution to this challenge—inner exploration—is finding a way to have the general public value equally, physical *and* mental health from K-1 through high school as a source of a healthy, functional individual—as well as a healthy functioning society.

It was suggested previously that spirituality is not a single level of being, but comprises several, if not many, levels, depending on the courage of the individual for inner exploration; each expanded level involving more humane states of functioning. In the next section, we will explore what these states might be and how they influence our thinking and behaviors as human beings.

Horizontal and Vertical Transformations

Figure 3.1 is a diagram of ascending levels of consciousness. The lowest level is the *bodymind domain* driven by survival. The common emotion experienced by this level of functioning is fear. Hence, there is a great emphasis on the application of technology for personal, national, and international security systems, as well as private weapons for self-protection from each other. Our behaviors with each other are strongly influenced by *fear* of each other, more than the outside world. In essence, fear is the companion emotion of survival—both perceived and real.

The circles within each level represent rings of consciousness—the total intelligence, knowledge, and wisdom of an individual or a group within that domain of functioning. In essence, the size of the ring is in direct proportion to an individual's reality *and* his or her openness for learning. ΔC represents the expansion in consciousness of an individual or a group as a result of a challenging, growth-producing event, such as the resolution of an individual's ordinary conflicts, misunderstandings, and occasional confrontations. A *node of transformation* represents the challenging event.

The greater the ring size, the greater an individual's mastery of that domain of operation. ΔC events represent *ordinary* acts of transformation. Whereas transformation between levels involves a paradigm shift which reorders significantly an individual's being, thinking, and behaving. These are referred to as vertical transformations and those within a level are referred to as horizontal transformations. Vertical transformation or transcendence (to even higher levels of consciousness) are typically the result of an *existential crisis*—a crisis which redefines an individual's reality about purpose, meaning, and values.

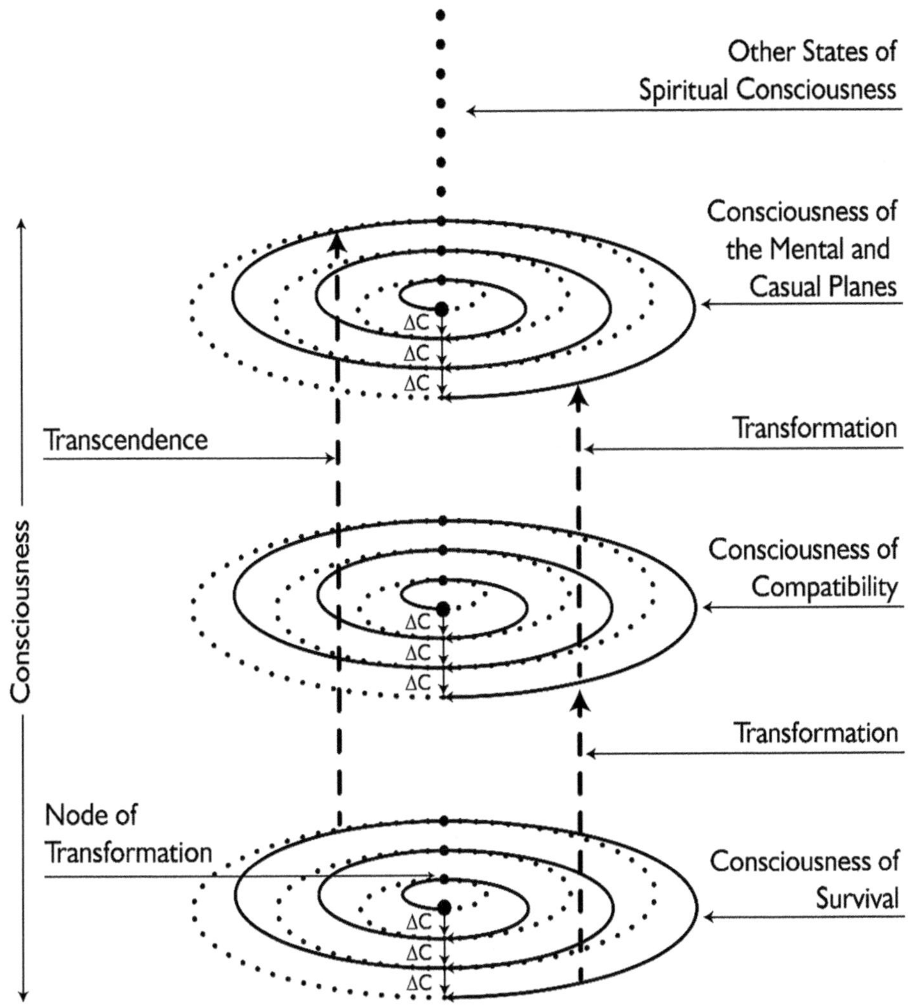

Figure 3.1 Ascending Levels of Consciousness

Vertical transformations are commonly triggered by *extraordinary* events, such as separation and/or divorce, death of a relative or friend, a car crash, or a life-surviving heart attack or illness. Vertical transformations also commonly occur among individuals who practice personal growth, as a way of life. *Personal growth is probably the most effective preventative way of ensuring one's health and longevity, along with preventative medicine.* In essence, the greater elimination of the source of personal conflicts—large and small—the more *resilient* an individual becomes. We define resilience as the ability to *respond* constructively to adversity (Reivich & Shatté, 2003). This ability is primarily forged during childhood by the way we learn to respond/react to life events. The vertical transformation we have discussed thus far is the shift from survival to compatibility—which is accompanied by greater understanding, empathy, and compassion for others—and gradually becomes a permanent (spiritual) way of being.

The transformation from Compatibility to the Mental-Casual Coupled Plane is shown as an ascending stage of spirituality. The Mental Plane represents the mastery of the accurate interpretation of interpersonal events as a threat or a non-threat to one's physical survival. It is the result of dedicated personal growth. The same as one would be committed to his or her physical wellbeing, through diet, weight-control, exercise, and overall lifestyle. The Casual Plane is mastery of the appropriate accompanying emotional response consistent with the accurate interpretation of an interpersonal event. Examples include *happiness* at a wedding, *empathy* for someone's loss, *joy* for one's success, and *elation* for one's resiliency. Mastery of this coupled level is the activities involved in Mindfulness—an in-depth understanding, empathy, and compassion for oneself and others (Watt, 2012).

Finally, we have noted other expanded spiritual states of existence beyond the Mental-Casual Plane. These levels are commonly experienced either in the meditative or sleep state, or through closed-eye imagery exercise. These experiences are generally employed for transforming and expanding further one's human reality through in-depth consciousness exploration.

Spirituality and Channeling

Channeling is simply the transition from one state of consciousness to another—typically from a more limited state to one which allows greater freedom, imagination, and exploration. Upon return from the channeled metaphysical experience, the realization is usually expressed as a book, insight, new invention, design idea, painting, or whatever form is consistent with an individual's passion. The expression could be as simple as being more humane with respect to differences. Figure 3.2 illustrates the transition from the bodymind domain to the metaphysical domain. The bodymind domain is governed by the laws of physics and the measurable concrete world. The metaphysical domain refers to those levels or states of consciousness corresponding

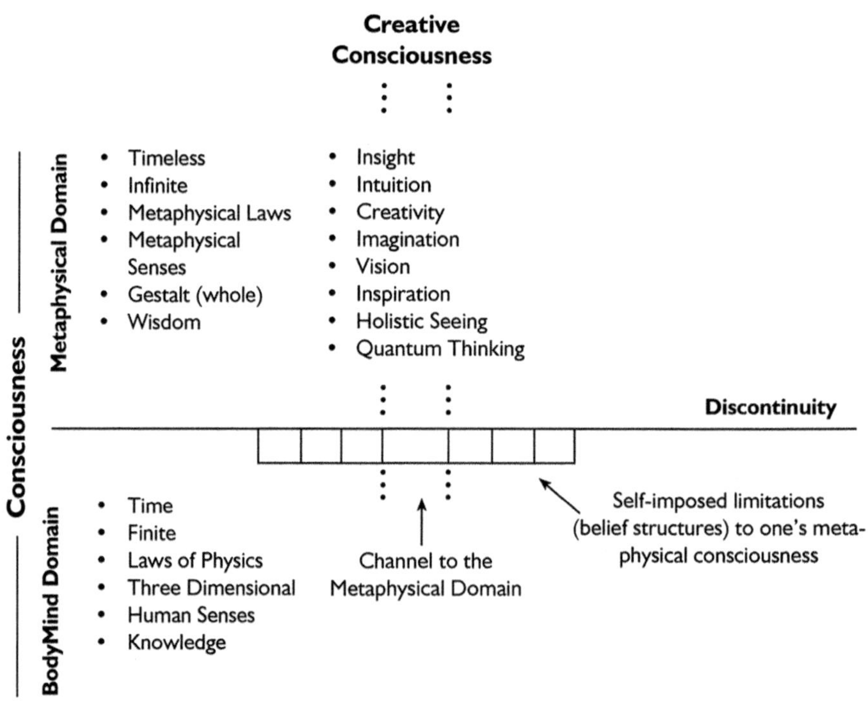

Figure 3.2 Domains of Consciousness

to the descriptors listed. Since Consciousness is infinite in capacity, there are states and domains beyond one's imagination and comprehension, represented by the dots. In truth most of us visit the metaphysical world on a nightly basis every time we dream—for rest, recovery, and problem solving as well as exploration. Whether we remember or not is irrelevant, since these processes are essential for our continued healthy existence.

The discontinuity which separates these two realms of consciousness is typical of an individual who *has not* created a natural channel through in-depth personal growth, or more commonly through personal trauma. The blocks below the line represent self-limiting beliefs an individual possesses, such as, "I don't believe … in metaphysics, or telepathy, or clairvoyance, or anything which might invalidate the infinite barrier one has erected to prevent this type of inner exploration or confrontation."

These blocks also represent the belief structures which are the nodes in Figure 3.1 that are used for the systematic process of consciousness expansion by the horizontal transformations we discussed. When one's ring size produces a highly self-aware individual with a natural aspiration for inner exploration, a spontaneous breakthrough occurs as a result of a "defining event." The rupture is usually permanent and leads to unlimited exploration, usually by conscious choice.

Besides the fun of exploration, every voyage to the other world automatically begins to create an expanded ring of consciousness—beyond compatibility or even more expanded states. This new ring begins to create an alternate reality within which that individual begins to also function, simultaneously!

In truth, most humans access the metaphysical realm on a regular basis whenever they are creative, innovative, imaginative, or inspired. Or, more likely, the state accesses them, in stressful situations, and then shuts down at the completion of the spontaneous-looking event. This is a common experience for artists, writers, actors, scientists, clergy, and others who experience *periods* of creativity and inspiration. For more daring individuals of inner exploration, they learn to *request* such experiences, which lead to the unlimited exploration of consciousness. Thus, visitations or spiritual experiences to other realms of consciousness may include conversations with spirit guides, paradigm creation, astral travel, visitation to other universes, spiritual oneness, and many other spiritual experiences, limited only by one's imagination or interest.

The crucial point of this discussion is that as a result of such experiences, the individual becomes more understanding of the shortcomings of others, open to possibilities, compassionate of human suffering, passionate about human experience and the opportunity to influence the wellbeing of others; and most of all, a much less desire for material possessions or symbols of success. This is an example of an *existential shift* in values that was referred to above. Eventually, the channel to the spiritual realm becomes so wide that it no longer exists. The result is a totally *integrated* or *actualized* individual which Maslow (n.d.) pointed to, at the time he created his hierarchy of needs.

Ten Ways to Integrate Spirituality in Your Life

1. First and foremost, embrace personal growth as life's opportunity for acquiring greater wisdom.
2. When you experience personal (or workplace) conflict, reflect inwardly for the source of your reactive emotion(s)—discover your unmet expectation as the key to discovering the source (Emotional Intelligence).
3. Compare your personal values with the major activities in your life. If the two are significantly out of alignment, attempt to understand and resolve the disparity.

4. Commit to one or two personal growth activities per month, e.g., self-help books or discs, seminars or workshops, local support groups, or simple meditation or self-reflection, etc.
5. Create a personal development program that enhances your career development plan, e.g., seminars on relationships, communication, leadership, teamwork, diversity, and creativity.
6. Adopt a personally appropriate spiritual practice that connects you to your inner wisdom, e.g., Yoga, meditation, prayer, Zen, visualization, dream journaling, etc.
7. Take 10 minutes each morning and afternoon to center yourself with respect to workplace and life's activities.
8. Become aware if you waste your personal or organization's resources (without permission), e.g., food, water, electricity, pencils, paper, fax, copies, phone time, work time on personal matters—your personal integrity.
9. Be more compassionate and non-judgmental of the shortcomings of others. (Remember, a person who is angry is a person in pain.)
10. Practice ways of contributing to others or your community with no expected recognition, reward, or profit in return.

References

Guillory, W. A. (1984). *Realizations: Personal Empowerment Through Self-Awareness.* Salt Lake City, UT: Innovations Publishing.

Maslow, A. (n.d.). *Maslow's Hierarchy of Needs.* Retrieved from https//en.wikipedia.org/wiki/Maslow%27s_of_needs.

Reivich, K., & Shatté, A. (2003). *The Resilience Factor.* Montclair, NJ: Bright and Happy Books.

Walton, D. (2002). *Emotional Intelligence.* New York: MJF Books fine Communications.

Watt, T. (2012). *Mindfulness: A Practical Guide.* New York: MJF Books Fine Communications.

4

SPIRITUALITY

A Personal Exploration

Jeffon Seely

Spirituality: A Personal Exploration

As we begin to ask ourselves, "How can I manage spirituality from a personal perspective?" we have to take an honest look at what is happening within ourselves. The easiest place for us to start is observing what is taking place within our mind, our consciousness. It has been said that if we are unable to shift our thoughts, it will be difficult to shift any area of our lives. This is what many people refer to as walking the pathway of mindfulness.

We are always filling our minds with something. For most of us, instead of being aware and attentive of what we are filling our minds with, we are filling our minds full of mess. If we keep filling our minds with garbage, eventually our thoughts will stink.

Our thoughts act as the building blocks that flow forth and direct our choices, often habitual, and ultimately our actions. These three keys, thoughts, choices, and actions, are always under our control and act as the paintbrushes we use each day to color the blank canvas we might call this moment.

The question becomes: what steps can we take to recognize that we are not at the mercy of our thoughts but are that which empowers our thoughts? A few empowering ideas we can bring into the forefront of our consciousness to reveal the potential within us and assist in the creation of our reality are as follows:

- If I continue to think the same thoughts for the next 12 months that I've thought the last 12 months, where will I be one year from today?
- If everyone I know were to think the same thoughts that I think on a day-to-day basis would I like to be surrounded by these people?
- If someone was asked to take a journey through the deep recesses of my mind and heart and was asked to keep a journal of what they saw taking place within myself for the next 6 months, would they come back and let everyone know that my mind reflected one of peace, compassion, positivity, possibility, and equality … or would they even come back at all?

These questions cause us to become conscious of our thinking, *thinking about our thinking*. These questions also allow us to find pockets of freedom between the thoughts we think and the part of us which does the thinking.

So often, we are looking to the outside world, exploring books, seeking mentors or guides to help reveal more of who and what we believe we are, completely unaware that what the majority of us are seeking is that which is within us and allows us to do the seeking. From this point of awareness, we come to understand that the thoughts flowing through our mind are creations of our own consciousness. We have the ability to focus on the thoughts that bring about peace, respect, and compassion, just as much as we have the ability to focus on thoughts that are of the opposite. If we are willing to honor this internal freedom that is available to us all, we are at the doorway of transformation.

A Space of Freedom

While we cannot control the events that occur in the world or take place around us, we are always in control of the way we respond to these situations. We often allow the external world to dictate our inner peace, thus are always at the mercy of what is happening "out there." As the thinker of our experience, if we are willing to interpret the external world without allowing the events outside ourselves to determine our inner worth, peace is always within reach. It is similar to a deep anchor in the ocean, centering a boat among large waves in the middle of the storm, feeling the effects around it but centered from within. A simple analogy to explain this is to imagine you are lying on your back, looking up at the clouds on a warm summer day. You feel the breeze gently brushing against your skin, seeing a few puffy clouds floating across a clear blue sky. You do not attach to any one particular cloud, instead lie peacefully, simply observing what is taking place above you. If a large storm cloud were to appear, you wouldn't jump up and walk beneath it as it continues on its path.

So it is with our thoughts. If you are able to look up at the conscious mind, simply observing the thoughts that grace your experience, not attaching to any particular thought just letting them flow as you would do the clouds, it is from this state that you create a space of freedom, almost as if you are looking up at your thoughts from your heart center. When a dark thought enters into your mind, you have a choice as to whether you will follow that thought or just let it pass. If you are willing to connect to the moment, honestly looking at your thoughts, and directing your focus, attention, and awareness to the thoughts that bring the most peace to yourself and the world, eventually, your choices, emotions, and actions will follow.

No one can jump within you and think your thoughts for you, though the opinions of others, the television and peers can tell you how to think, you are the thinker of your experience.

This is your space of freedom.

How to Create this Mental Space

Scientific studies have shown that the average human takes 25,000 breaths each day. That is over 9.1 million breaths a year. If we sleep on an average of 8 hours a day, roughly 2920 hours a year which is nearly three million breaths, that means, we still have 6.1 million breaths while we are awake, moving and being. This makes us ask the question, are we even aware of these breaths we are taking throughout our day?

The reason this question is so important is because by being mindful of the breath we breathe, it connects us to this space of freedom within. It reminds us that as with each breath, we have the ability to be attentive and direct each thought moment to moment.

The breath is the first way to find this space of freedom to consciously empower our thoughts, emotions, choices, actions, and energy to whatever ends we desire.

In addition to the breath, there is one more naturally occurring phenomenon that takes place internally that can help us tap into this space. This is our heartbeat. Studies have shown that the average person has roughly 100,000 heartbeats a day which totals 36.5 million heartbeats each year. Again, if we are asleep nearly 2920 hours a year, that means 12.1 million of those heartbeats occur when we are asleep. This leaves 24.4 million heartbeats that occur when we are awake each year. Most people don't recognize their heartbeat unless they are walking up a steep flight of stairs. However, if we are willing to be mindful of the heart beating within us, connecting to the beats moment to moment, this allows us to connect to this space of freedom. Because our hearts can only beat in this moment, it helps us remember that our thoughts can occur only at this moment as well.

Therefore, the second way to connect to this space of freedom is to recognize, appreciate, and honor each beat of our heart. Not just feeling the physical heartbeat but moving into a deeper introspection of recognizing the part of us that is beating our heart. For this is the same part of us that breathes our breath, enables our blood to flow, cells to divide, and atoms to thrive.

All occurring in this moment. All providing us with life.

Spirituality from a Personal Perspective

The essential element of this approach is to understand that no one can do this for you but you. Books can help to open doorways within our minds, religious settings can help open doorways within our hearts, but we must be willing to walk down that corridor toward the unknown, becoming an astronaut of inner space.

Spirituality from a personal perspective does not only mean what is occurring within ourselves, however, it requires us to embrace our interdependence with the planet beneath us, the sun above us, the air flowing through us, the people around us as well as the life within us. Each step we take is an interaction with the earth below, each breath we take is a connection with the cosmos above, each fruit and vegetable we consume brings the sun within us, ultimately deepening our connection to this intricate web of life.

This challenges us to embrace responsibility, accountability, and empowerment for the reality we have assisted in creating for ourselves. To he or she who can rule their mind, heart, and spirit, the universe is their playground, to he or she who is unwilling to rule their mind, heart, and spirit, often see themselves as a victim to the "cruel" world they find themselves in.

This leads us to the idea that world peace is impossible without inner peace. Creating a world of compatibility, ascending from a state of survival, is something that must be done on an individual level. The answers that we seek, the solutions to our problems, equity, justice, and unity is not found in some ancient script or at the bottom of a baptism tub. The answers that we seek are contained within you and me.

Are We Willing to Do Our Part?

If the answer is yes, then we must take the next step. This step requires us to bring this state of peace and awareness out from within ourselves and into the external world. It challenges us to look at the way we show up each day and includes the unconscious perceptions we carry with us, the words we choose to speak, and the footprint we leave on the planet. To deepen our understanding of what an outer expression of mindfulness is we must reflect on the impact we have on people and environments we find ourselves in.

To start this process we have to look at the behaviors and actions we show up with on a daily basis. It is a natural progression, from internal awareness to outer awareness, because the behaviors, actions, and results we experience are brought to life by that which occurs inside ourselves.

Therefore, if we are unwilling to recognize what is taking place internally, we'll never be able to consciously direct how we show up outwardly. Now that we have that out of the way, let's look at this a little bit deeper.

Outer Reflections

In the same way that a large rock dropped in the middle of a still lake will create ripples that eventually reach the shore, so it is with the way we interact with others and gently shake the world. Our words, actions, and interactions with others send these ripples out into the world, whether consciously or unconsciously. The first layer of this ripple can be observed when we examine our closest relationships. These are the people we spend the most time around. Unfortunately, for so many, we often take these people for granted: surface level conversations, being there but not fully being there, engaging with them but not at a level where we are brought to life. This is caused by not fully valuing the present moment we are sharing with one another or recognizing that each interaction is a "sacred" experience that will never happen that exact way again.

How have you chosen to show up with these people in your life? It may be your loved ones, children, partner, or great friends. Have you really been there or just been there?

An idea to think about which effortlessly helps us be more mindful is to remember that this life you are living right now is a one-time thing. There are no do-overs, unless we talk about reincarnation, but that would have to be another multiple volume book.

These same ideas and questions mentioned above can be asked about the second layer of the ripple that reaches our outermost relationships. These typically consist of co-workers, neighbors, or the individuals we are familiar with but are not in our innermost circle. The third layer of the ripple flows into our communities, our cities, states, and ultimately the world.

As we look at all of these areas we must ask, how am I impacting all of these layers? To find the answer, we have to look at the center that causes the ripple: ourselves.

Outward Expression

The way we communicate is one of the main ways that ripples are created. We can see there are three levels of communication when we look at the Subliminal Communication Model developed by Innovations International.

The first layer of this model is verbal. These are the words we choose to say that act as seeds that are deposited into the minds and hearts of others. Verbal communication, however, is the

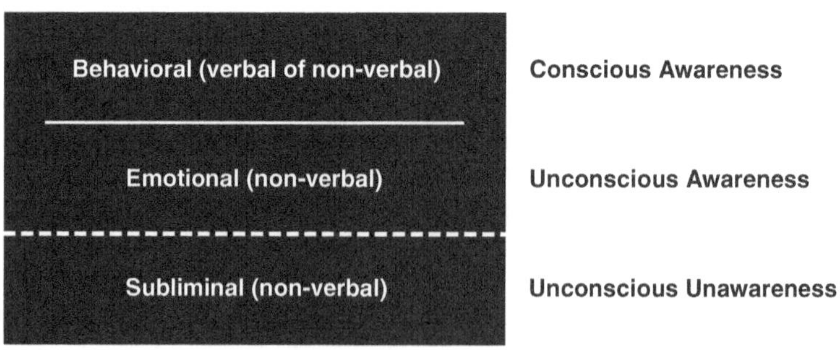

Figure 4.1 Subliminal Communication Model

least powerful of the three but is the level that we are most conscious of. The second level is emotional communication and the third, which is the most powerful, is subliminal. Both of these latter two levels cause us to step into the unconscious realm in ourselves. They explore the bottom two layers of this model we have to explore our intent, our unconscious perceptions, and the emotions that we allow to dominate our day.

As we take the steps to be mindful about the way we choose to think about the world and people around us, mindful of the thoughts we give our power to, attentive of how those thoughts fuel our emotions, words, and the way we carry ourselves, we then see the tools for transformation are found within.

Mindfulness and awareness both internally and externally are ultimately your responsibility.

5
SPIRITUALITY, RESPONSIBILITY, AND INTEGRITY

Kemi Ogunyemi

Introduction

Spirituality, responsibility, and integrity are terms that are very closely interconnected and rely on one another for a deepened understanding. Spirituality has been defined in a variety of ways—as the image in humanity of a spiritual creator by virtue of which human beings derive dignity and, consequently, are called to solidarity and subsidiarity, and to work for the common good of all humans (Sison, Ferrero, & Guitian, 2016), or as the non-material component of human beings (Fagley & Adler, 2012; Miller, 2007; Cash & Gray, 2000; Mitroff & Denton, 1999a; McCormick, 1994) by which they make choices, as a unifying element that characterizes the human being (Staude, 2005), or as a connection with "a divine, spiritual, or some other transcendent reference point, knowable or mysterious" (Ciulla, Knights, Mabey, & Tomkins, 2018, p. 7).

Responsibility flows from the spiritual capacity to choose (Ogunyemi, 2013), since a power to make choices means that the chooser is accountable for those choices and should answer for them, while integrity is a sign that the spiritual and material dimensions of the human being in question are operating harmoniously for the person's fulfillment, in line with the "transcendent reference point" and for the common good. If being spiritual is thus acknowledged as a foundational notion for describing human beings, then the need to preserve integrity and live with responsibility have their roots in that foundation. This chapter attempts to review extant literature on these three concepts and highlight their interconnectedness. In the process, much work showing that spirituality brings economic benefits to the organization is highlighted, but it is important to note that this is not always the case and that there are sound reasons to foster spirituality in organizations other than the economic (Brophy, 2015).

Spirituality

The word "spiritual" is of Latin origin, from the root word "spiritus" which roughly translates to a life-giving principle of an entity (Liu, 2007). This implies that the spirit animates the human being—gives life to the body—and spirituality would be the condition of having that life. It is through spirituality, that life-giving action of the spirit, that the different aspects of human life—physical, emotional, professional, and intellectual—are integrated, says Staude (2005). Going beyond this to add an external perspective, Torrance (1994) highlighted that it is through spirituality that the person continuously engages with others and transcends self. The consciousness of being "part of something bigger than themselves" is particularly important for business leaders (Ciulla et al., 2018, p. 4). Staude focuses on the internal cohesion and harmony while Torrance dwells on external transcendence. It is interesting to note that spirituality is distinct from religion—according to Karakas (2010), the difference lies in spirituality being personal yet universal and therefore non-denominational but rather common to all human beings, whereas religion tends to be institutionalized and to have specific ways of organization and traditions to which groups of human beings adhere. A number of other scholars support this basis for distinction (Klenke, 2003; Gupta, Kumar, & Singh, 2014; Bielefeldta & Canney, 2016), while others regard religion as one of the expressions of spirituality (Litonjua, 2016; Sison et al., 2016). As a component of spirituality, most religions call for selflessness and concern for the common good in the use of individual talents and skills (Bielefeldta & Canney, 2016).

Sison et al. (2016) point out three human capabilities that the ancient Greeks found to bear witness to human spirituality—the human being inherently experiences a capacity to transcend the material world with the mind in order to reach non-material concepts (abstraction); to choose what to do and to become (freedom); and to judge choices as good or bad (conscience). These last two evidences of spirituality are closely related to the concepts of responsibility (free choices) and integrity (conscience). This is why spiritual leaders would be expected to be "more 'homo moralis' rather than 'homo economicus'" (Vasconcelos, 2015, p. 195)—people who consciously chose to practice integrity, care about others, and take responsibility for their choices.

The growing interest in spirituality is evident in corporations, corporate meeting rooms, and the business world as well. For example, a growing number of organizations, including large corporations such as Intel, Coca-Cola, and Boeing, are reported to have incorporated spirituality in their workplaces, strategies, or cultures (Burack, 1999; Konz & Ryan, 1999). Popular spiritual practices have included holding Bible study sessions, Quran recitation periods, forming voluntary prayer groups, forming interfaith dialogue groups, organizing reflection sessions, offering meditation exercises, and organizing end of the year prayer sessions by government organizations. To account for the growing interest, Imel (1998) points to the decline in traditional networks of support, such as the family, which forces people to question the location of meaning, hope, and inspiration for what they will do in this world, and how they will make their living. Using this idea as a foundation, Jurkiewicz and Giacalone (2004) described the integrative role of spirituality in workplace as a basic need for employees' personal growth due to the declining role of families, neighborhoods, and other societal main players.

Among the spiritual values common to people everywhere, Brophy (2015) lists compassion, interconnectedness, human dignity, profundity, and transcendence. For Chawla (2014), agreeing with Jurkiewicz and Giacalone (2004), there are 10—benevolence, generativity, humanism, *integrity*, justice, mutuality, receptivity, respect, *responsibility*, and trust. Two of the 10 are the focus of this chapter.

Responsibility and Spirituality

As spirituality entails connectedness to the other(s), it enhances the sense that one owes a duty toward them, can influence them for good, or is needed to do good to them (Bielefeldta & Canney, 2016). This connectedness, at times combined with compassion, thus heightens the tendency to take responsibility for the way one's actions may affect others as well as leads to an awareness of the need for altruistic behavior. The spiritual person would try not to harm others as well as positively do good to them. Such a person is likely to create the processes and systems around him or her with the same outlook. Testimonies from MBA students demonstrate that a deepened understanding of human spirituality changes the person's orientation in such a way as to enhance a sense of responsibility and an understanding of the need for ethical behavior (Ogunyemi, 2013).

Translating this to an organization where spirituality is fostered, the level of responsible behavior would also be enhanced. For example, an organization that is high on spirituality should be more likely to pay workers fairly and promptly and to provide them with good working conditions as well as respect their work–life balance. Leaders that are driven by spiritual values also tend to both practice and promote responsible behavior (Lecourt & Pauchant, 2011; Ogunyemi, 2013).

With regard to the responsibility of the organization toward external stakeholders, Karakas (2007) identified that some corporations incorporate spirituality into their strategies within the framework of corporate social responsibility. At the macro level, a successful market system requires the ethical and responsible operation of markets and this ethos informs the responsible corporate organization (Klein, 2007).

Integrity and Spirituality

Klein (2007) suggested that any social system fails when human relations break down and that, therefore, a successful economic system depends on the integrity of its actors. Integrity is primarily a spiritual value (Chawla, 2014; Lee, Lovelace, & Manz, 2014), like many other core values that even organizations that say they are not spiritual profess to have. Wong (2003) highlighted this connection of integrity with spirituality when he used it to describe what happens when spirituality pervades a workplace—employees subscribe to intrinsic values greater than titles, positions, and material resources; employees show integrity, love, honesty, kindness, and respect; and employees take responsibility for their actions and the social and environmental impact of these on external stakeholders. It is not surprising, then, that when spirituality is embraced or at least accepted as part of a person's workplace identity, it is easier for the person to act with moral integrity when faced by ethical dilemmas and when in various conflicts of interest situations.

According to Comer and Vega (2011), employees experience flow, as an expression of their spirituality, when they act with integrity, from which we can surmise that integrity and spirituality are mutually enhancing. A person who acts with integrity reinforces his or her spirituality, while a person who acknowledges his or her spirituality and allows it to inform workplace activity finds it easier to behave with integrity and preserve moral uprightness. In fact, Cavanagh and Bandsuch (2002) go so far as to suggest that it is only when integrity is practiced in the organization as shown in the virtues and ethical actions of the persons in it that that organization can lay claim to authentic workplace spirituality, thereby making a check for integrity a way to evaluate spirituality.

Influence of Workplace Spirituality on Business Organizations

McGhee and Grant (2008) have inferred that since the beginning of the 20th century, there has been an increasing focus on the spirit, spirituality, and spiritual phenomena, and as this focus shifted to the modern workplace, there have been numerous articles and books, both popular and academic, written to champion the role of spirituality in improving organizations, markets, and economies. At the same time, some businesses still see no place for spirituality in the workplace and deliberately exclude it (Brophy, 2015). Yet, many scholars, for example Thompson (2000), suggest that organizations that encourage workplace spirituality improve in performance and profitability. As though responding to a question as to how this could work in practice, Burack (1999) suggests that fostering spirituality and allowing free expression of spirituality at work enables employees to feel complete and authentic at work which leads to a high degree of personal fulfillment and morale; and this in turn results in increased organizational performance. Pawar (2009) also reported a strong association between personal spirituality in the workplace and positive work attitudes such as job satisfaction, job involvement, and organizational commitment.

Again, Krishnakumar and Nick (2002) found that the encouragement of spirituality in the workplace can lead to benefits in the areas of creativity, process improvement, customer service, honesty and trust, personal fulfillment, and commitment, which will ultimately lead to increased organizational performance. It seems then that workplace spirituality is good for business. Providing a possible reason why this is so, McGhee and Grant (2008) were of the opinion that spiritual people confer their work and the workplace with the quality of connection to something greater than the material world and thus bring their spirituality into the workplace. Through this workplace spirituality, work becomes part of a bigger picture, as employees see their workplace involvement as a calling and not merely a means to an end. Within this sense of calling, they are able to incorporate the values of responsibility and integrity into their work and this is what stimulates the growth, individually and collectively, of associated values beneficial to the organization. Some of the associated values are already mentioned above—innovativeness, creativity, customer service, honesty, trust, commitment. As the awareness of the importance and benefits of spirituality for organizations has grown, it has gained in appreciation as an asset: Cash and Gray (2000) observe American corporations have moved toward a more value-expressive philosophy and tolerant culture in response to employees' requests for spiritual connection and sense of community. Following Lips-Wiersma's (2002) argument that employees fully expressing their spirituality can benefit their organizations through creativity, intuition, cohesiveness of vision, and purpose, and improved community building, this would prove to be a win–win move for any organization engaging in it.

Influence of Workplace Spirituality on Organizational Responsibility and Integrity

In studies of workplace spirituality, the organization as a community of human beings appears to be the definitional unit adopted by most scholars. Thus, in his effort to conceptualize workplace spirituality, Ruppel and Harrington (2001) considered it as an attitude of sharing and a sense of togetherness with one another within one's department as well as in the organization. This reflects the idea of human solidarity noted above as evoked by the nature of spirituality as calling for respect for human dignity and for an interest in the common good. Similarly, with a focus on how people feel and what they subjectively experience, Giacalone and Jurkiewicz (2004) defined workplace spirituality as the framework of organizational values evidenced in the culture that promotes employees' experience of transcendence through the work process and facilitates their sense of being connected in a way that provides feelings of compassion and joy. Again, there is an implication of solidarity in the notion of connectedness in a way that entails compassion and joy. Alternatively, Ashmos and Duchon (2000) defined workplace spirituality as the recognition of an inner life that nourishes and is nourished by meaningful work that takes place in the context of community. This approach gives prominence to the individual flourishing of the members of the community—subjectively (inner life) and objectively (meaningful work). Thus, according to Vasconcelos (2015, p. 189), people are called through workplace spirituality to work on "replacing the self as the source of ultimate concern with family, community, humanity, and divinity."

Given the foregoing, it becomes clear that the power of spirituality to reduce economic crimes and workplace deviant behavior cannot be overemphasized—people actually become more confident and engage in more ethical behavior (Vasconcelos, 2015). Waddock (2006) argues corporate scandals usually have resulted from self-centeredness, greed, egoism, and selfish passion instead of caring for others. People who do not care about others are more likely to act with disregard for the good of other people around them and for the common good, thus leading not only to big scandals but a cumulative negative effect coming from internal corporate misbehavior such as theft (time and other resources), insider trading, receiving of bribes, and other kinds of misconduct. Specifically, Chawla's (2014) study claims that this applies to salespeople's ethical behavior both among themselves and as representatives of the organization. Due to its nature and the values embedded in it, spirituality strengthens the individual against such traits as those described by Waddock (2006)—self-centeredness, greed, egoism, and selfish passion. Thus, Oakley and Cocking (2001) recognized the role of spirituality as promoting self-regulation in the working environment; they asserted that a person's spirituality, characterized by the degree to which they engage in and live out self-transcendence, interconnectedness, a sense of purpose, and a belief in an ultimate being, constitutes a personal constraint on unethical behavior.

The effect of spirituality on the promotion of ethical behavior in work environments continues being estimated with varied research approaches. When studying the relationship between the spirituality and ethical behavior in the workplace, Ashmos and Duchon (2000) saw spirituality as a transformative source of meaning, purpose, and a sense of community, which would lead to heightened sense of responsibility and higher levels of integrity as well. Perhaps because of this, Mitroff and Denton (1999b) believed that workplace spirituality entails the effort to derive a kind of consistency or alignment between one's core beliefs and the values of one's organization.

Gottlieb, Kelloway, and Barham (1998) stressed that workplace spirituality has enhanced the level of consideration for stakeholders other than the shareholders. In particular, the employees' work–life balance is better where there is scope for spirituality in the organization—the organization tries to integrate business needs with those of employees. In the process, managers have been discovering and experimenting with new ways and methods to help employees balance work and family through flexible work arrangements that allow for spiritual expression.

Researchers have also been able to demonstrate the possibility that spirituality in the workplace could foster teamwork among employees in an organization, again because they are likely to act more responsibly in the fulfillment of their team roles and team members that have integrity are valued and trusted. Daniel (2010) found that that workplace spirituality is a central variable in developing the culture of trust, inclusion, and innovation within various workplaces. In further support, McGhee and Grant (2008) stressed that spiritual people experience the object of spirituality via their desire to overcome the egotistical self to develop authentic relationships with others, with creation, and with their ultimate concern, and as they strive to find meaning and purpose in their life. This again entails acting responsibly and with integrity. Garcia-Zamor (2003) in turn stated that spirituality provides employees with a sense of community and connectedness which in turn increases their commitment, belongingness, and effectiveness. Older research in this line (by Kriger & Hanson, 1999) had already revealed that trust is crucial in forming a sound basis for commitment and that spirituality increases commitment by establishing a climate of trust in the workplace. This is clearly good for the organization.

Workplace Spirituality and Spiritual Capital

According to Zymonik and Dobrowolska (2015), for at least three decades, spiritual capital has been considered in organizations and management studies as the fourth capital in an organization, asides material, human (intellectual), and social capital. King and Roeser (2009) also found that spirituality, apart from being central to the lives of a majority of the people across the world, strongly influences the workplaces as well. It (spiritual capital) has been identified as one of the key indicators for achieving behavior that is responsible and with integrity in a business organization.

In general, spiritual and religious practices, beliefs, networks, and institutions have a measurable impact on individuals, communities, and societies, and this impact cascades into a workplace to constitute its spiritual capital and operate as an asset to the organization (O'Sullivan & Flanegan, 2008). In some exceptional cases, workplace spirituality can be overdone (Vasconcelos, 2015), as could happen, for example, if some employees took advantage of the organization by neglecting their work ostensibly for the sake of observing some spiritual practice(s) or could be a caricature, where it exists in an external way side by side with negative values such as injustice, ethical misbehavior, intolerance, divisiveness and discrimination, and lack of respect for human dignity (Cavanagh & Bandsuch, 2002).

One way to ascertain true spirituality is the virtue test proposed by Cavanagh and Bandsuch (2002). They submit that:

> *A spirituality that enables a person to develop good moral habits (or virtue) is appropriate for the workplace.* If a spirituality leads to the cooperation and motivation derived from good moral habits and virtue in a person, then that spirituality can be judged as appropriate. When a spirituality enables a person to develop good moral habits, this provides a benchmark or a positive test for the appropriateness of that spirituality.
>
> *(Italics in original)*

In other words, spirituality that does not help a person to develop integrity and responsibility in the workplace is questionable.

An Important Caveat—Intrinsic Reasons

Brophy (2015) points out the danger of organizations having an instrumental approach to workplace spirituality—seeing its benefits as a driver of employee responsibility and integrity as a tool to enhance performance and profitability rather than being rooted in a real interest in employees being responsible and having integrity. Organizations that instrumentalize spirituality in this way are those who adopt it as a means rather than as an end (Vasconcelos, 2015). As employees spend most of their lives in the workplace (Vasconcelos, 2015), any organization that wishes to be ethical and humanistic should exhibit integrity and responsibility by caring for their employees and the environment in which they function and not just the money they make.

Two reasons (among others) are proffered by Brophy (2015) as to why organizations should promote spirituality—(1) to respect the freedom of their employees as an integral value; and (2) to provide an environment in which employees flourish. This latter could be considered one of the points at which the fields of workplace spirituality and the humanistic management converge. It is a fact that workplaces can be toxic and destructive—they "are not benign" (Vasconcelos, 2015, p. 184) and they can be an arena of suffering for some employees. The responsibility to minimize the likelihood of such situations devolves on the stakeholders that have greater power. Another intrinsic reason is that spirituality increases individual resilience, as it sustains the person through successes and failures and enables him or her to manage the complexities of life including in the workplace.

Conclusion and Future Research Directions

The sense of connection that spirituality in the workplace fosters in employees helps them find greater meaningfulness in their work and leads them to self-demand in terms of integrity and responsible behavior. They are therefore more likely to engage in ethical behavior and to put in their best at work. An organization that realizes this would benefit greatly from promoting workplace spirituality. However, the reasons for promoting it should not only be the economic benefits of the spiritual capital thus generated. For the organization itself to act with integrity and responsibly, it should also prioritize and respect the employees' freedom and show concern for their wellbeing which includes acknowledging their spiritual dimension and respecting it.

Having attempted to look at the interconnectedness of spirituality, responsibility, and integrity in the workplace in this chapter, the following areas are suggested for future researchers: instrumental and intrinsic approaches to building organizational spiritual capital; impact on employees of an instrumental approach to workplace spirituality; the effect of spirituality in leadership on organizational growth and organizational health; and the mechanisms by which spirituality supports ethonomics, inclusion and intercultural empathy, and sustainability.

References

Ashmos, D. P., & Duchon, D. (2000). Spirituality at work: A conceptualization and measure. *Journal of Management Inquiry, 9*(2), 134–145.

Bielefeldta, A. R., & Canney, N. E. (2016). Relationships between religion, spirituality, and socially responsible engineering. *Engineering Studies, 8*(1), 66–90.

Brophy, M. (2015). Spirituality incorporated: Including convergent spiritual values in business. *Journal of Business Ethics, 132*, 779–794.

Burack, E. (1999). Spirituality in the workplace. *Journal of Organizational Change Management, 12*(4), 280–291.

Cash, K. C., & Gray, G. R. (2000). A framework for accommodating religion and spirituality in the workplace. *Academy of Management Executive, 14*(3), 124–133.

Cavanagh, G. F., & Bandsuch, M. R. (2002). Virtue as a benchmark for spirituality in business. *Journal of Business Ethics, 38*, 109–117.

Chawla, V. (2014). The effect of workplace spirituality on salespeople's organisational deviant behaviours: Research propositions and practical implications. *Journal of Business and Industrial Marketing, 29*(3), 199–208.

Ciulla, J. B., Knights, D., Mabey, C., & Tomkins, L. (2018). Philosophical contributions to leadership ethics. *Business Ethics Quarterly, 28*(1), 1–14.

Comer, D. R., & Vega, G. (2011). The relationship between the personal ethical threshold and workplace spirituality. *Journal of Management, Spirituality and Religion, 8*(1), 23–40.

Daniel, J. L. (2010). The effect of workplace spirituality on team effectiveness. *Journal of Management Development, 29*(5), 442–456.

Fagley, N. S., & Adler, M. G. (2012). Appreciation: A spiritual path to finding value and meaning in the workplace. *Journal of Management, Spirituality and Religion, 9*(2), 167–187.

Garcia-Zamor, J. (2003). Workplace spirituality and organizational performance. *Public Administration Review, 63*(3), 355–363.

Giacalone, R. A., & Jurkiewicz, C. L. (2004). *Handbook of Workplace Spirituality and Organizational Performance*. New York: M. E. Sharpe.

Gottlieb, B. H., Kelloway, E. K., & Barham, E. (1998). *Flexible Work Arrangements: Managing the Work–Family Boundary*. Chichester, UK: Wiley.

Gupta, M., Kumar, V., & Singh, M. (2014). Creating satisfied employees through workplace spirituality: A study of the private insurance sector in Punjab (India). *Journal of Business Ethics, 122*(1), 79–88.

Harrington, W. J., Preziosi, R. C., & Gooden, D. J. (2001). Perceptions of workplace spirituality among professionals and executives. *Employee Responsibilities and Rights Journal, 13*(3), 155–163.

Imel, S. (1998). Spirituality in the workplace. *ERIC Trends and Issues Alerts.* Retrieved from http://ericave.org, ERIC Clearinghouse on Adult, Career, and Vocational Education, ED 420789.

Jurkiewicz, C. L., & Giacalone, R. A. (2004). A values framework for measuring the impact of workplace spirituality on organizational performance. *Journal of Business Ethics, 49*(2), 129–142.

Karakas, F. (2007). The twenty–first century leader: Social artist, spiritual visionary, and cultural innovator. *Global Business and Organizational Excellence, 26*(3), 44–50.

Karakas, F. (2010). Spirituality and performance in organisations: A literature review. *Journal of Business Ethics, 94*(1), 89–106.

King, P. E., & Roeser, R. W. (2009). Religion and spirituality in adolescent development. In R. M. Lerner & L. Steinberg (Eds.), *Individual Bases of Adolescent Development.* Vol. 1 of the *Handbook of Adolescent Psychology* (3rd ed.). Hoboken, NJ: John Wiley & Sons, 435–478.

Klein, N. (2007). *The Shock Doctrine: The Rise of Disaster Capitalism.* New York: Metropolitan Books.

Klenke, K. (2003). The S factor in leadership education, practice and research. *Journal of Education for Business, 79*(1), 56–60.

Konz, G. N. P., & Ryan, F. X. (1999). Maintaining an organizational spirituality: No easy task. *Journal of Organizational Change Management, 12*(3), 200–210.

Kriger, M., & Hanson, B. (1999). A value-based paradigm for creating truly healthy organizations. *Journal of Organizational Change Management, 12*(4), 302–317.

Krishnakumar, S., & Neck, C. P. (2002). The "what", "why" and "how" of spirituality in the workplace. *Journal of Managerial Psychology, 17*(3), 153–164.

Lecourt, V., & Pauchant, T. C. (2011). Ignatian spirituality and management: A Study of "Ignatian Executives." *Journal of International Business Ethics, 4*(1), 18–27.

Lee, S., Lovelace, K. J., & Manz, C. C. (2014). Serving with spirit: An integrative model of workplace spirituality within service organizations. *Journal of Management, Spirituality and Religion, 11*(1), 45–64.

Lips-Wiersma, M. (2002). The influence of spiritual "mean-making" on career behavior. *Journal of Management Development, 21*(7), 497–520.

Litonjua, M. D. (2016). Spiritual, but not religious: Untangling a seeming paradox. *International Review of Modern Sociology, 42*(1), 21–55.

Liu, A. (2007, 2008, 2010). 4Capital and Performance. RM Institute. Retrieved from www.researchmethods.org/4capital.htm.

McCormick, D. W. (1994). Spirituality and management. *Journal of Managerial Psychology, 9*(6), 5–8.

McGhee, P., & Grant, P. (2008, January). Spirituality and ethical behaviour in the workplace: Wishful thinking or authentic reality. *Electronic Journal of Business Ethics and Organization Studies, 13.*

Miller, D. W. (2007). *God at Work: The History and Promise of the Faith at Work Movement.* Oxford: Oxford University Press.

Mitroff, I., & Denton, E. A. (1999a). A study of spirituality in the workplace. *Sloan Management Review, 40*(4), 83–94.

Mitroff, I., & Denton, E. A. (1999b). *A Spiritual Audit of Corporate America: A Hard Look at Spirituality, Religion, and Values.* San Francisco: Jossey-Bass.

Oakley, J., & Cocking, D. (2001). *Virtue Ethics and Professional Roles.* Cambridge: Cambridge University Press.

Ogunyemi, K. (2013). *Responsible Management: Understanding Human Nature, Ethics, and Sustainability.* New York: Business Expert Press.

O'Sullivan, M., & Flanegan B. (Eds.). (2008). *Spiritual Capital: Spirituality in Practice in Christian Perspective.* Farnham, UK: Ashgate.

Pawar, B. A. (2009). Individual spirituality, workplace spirituality and work attitudes: An empirical test of direct and interaction effects. *Leadership and Organization Development, 30*(8), 759–777.

Ruppel, C. P., & Harrington, S. J. (2001). Spreading knowledge through intranets: An analysis of the organizational culture leading to intranet adoption and use. *IEEE Transactions on Professional Communications, 44*(1), 37.

Sison, A. J. G., Ferrero, I., & Guitian, G. (2016). Human dignity and the dignity of work: Insights from Catholic social teaching. *Business Ethics Quarterly, 26*(4), 503–528.

Staude, J. R. (2005). Spirituality as spiritual practice. *Journal of Gerontological Social Work, 45*(3), 249–269.

Thompson, W. D. (2000). Can you train people to be spiritual? *Training and Development, 54*(12), 18–19.
Torrance, R. M. (1994). *The Spiritual Quest: Transcendence in Myth, Religion and Science*. Berkeley: University of California Press.
Vasconcelos, A. F. (2015). The spiritually-based organization: A theoretical review and its potential role in the third millennium. *Cadernos EBAPE.BR, 13*(1), 183–205.
Waddock, S. (2006). What will it take to create a tipping point for corporate responsibility? In M. Epstein & K. O. Hanson (Eds.), *The Accountable Corporation*. Greenfield, CT: Praeger, 75–96.
Wong, P. T. P. (2003). Spirituality and meaning at work. *Positive Living Newsletter*. Retrieved from www.meaning.ca/archives/presidents_columns/pres_col_sep_2003_meaning-at-work.htm.
Zymonik, Z., & Dobrowolska, A. (2015). Spiritual capital as the fourth capital in a TQM organization. *Journal of Management and Finance, 13*(2), 147–155.

6

A SPIRITUALITY OF IMPERFECTION

Recognizing and Rewarding Intelligent Failure[1]

Andrew Morris, Céleste Grimard, Dylan Cooper, and Cynthia Sherman

Success does not consist in never making mistakes but in never making the same one a second time.

(George Bernard Shaw)

It's not the note you play that's the wrong note—it's the note you play afterwards that makes it right or wrong.

(Miles Davis)

There are only two mistakes one can make along the road to truth: not going all the way, and not starting.

(Buddha (or as Yogi Berra might put it—when you come to a fork in the road, take it))

Introduction

A recent *New York Times* editorial (Reische, 2017) lamented the fact that modern technology was taking away the ability of students to make mistakes (stupid or otherwise) without life-long consequences. Implied was the notion that youth (age) should be given more room to experiment, to try foolish things, to make mistakes, and to not let these mistakes become "scarlet letters" that forever brand individuals as failures. However, in living hyperactive public lives through social media, college students are trying on concepts, ideas, and beliefs that may carry long-term repercussions. This is neither fair nor helpful for creating life-long learners. Without room to fail, youth may succumb to a version of perfectionism that harms their capacity for learning and creativity, both now and in the future.

What is true for youth might also be true for organizational leaders: "When driven by the fear of failure, leaders are unable to take reasonable risks. They limit themselves to tried and proven pathways" (Sanborn, 2015, p. 1). Organizational leaders face a rapidly changing business environment in increasingly complex organizations. As demands to make effective and profitable decisions increase and as the stakes rise, leaders confront intense pressures to make wise and intelligent choices. Yet, failure and mistakes are likely in uncertain and complex environments; indeed, they are inevitable (Tversky & Kahneman, 1974). Since mistakes can cost people their jobs and organizations their viability, leaders may be tempted to choose options that are adequate but not optimal. Perpetual satisficing grows into a pathway to mediocracy. As such, a central challenge of leaders is motivating themselves and others to take appropriate risks. The key to doing so is to recognize and reward *intelligent* failure, as argued by Sitkin (1992), Bock (2015), Edmondson (2011), and others. For example, Bock (2015) considers Google's ability to encourage and reward calculated risk tasking to have been critical to its success. Simply put, Google rewards both process and outcomes and, in so doing, has created a culture that encourages risk-taking. Similarly, within a few high tech companies the phase "Fail Fast, Fail Cheap, Move On" has become a slogan for how the company approaches new product development.

This chapter applies the concept of the "spirituality of imperfection" to helping employees and leaders grow more comfortable with learning from failure. This conceptualization of spirituality invites readers to accept imperfection and failure not as limitations but as a path toward being more fully human. In the sections below, we explore the concept of *intelligent* failure and how it differs from *failure*. In describing the benefits of intelligent failure, we provide examples from organizations that are designing for intelligent failure. We then ground this idea of intelligent failure in a framework of the spirituality of imperfection. Finally, we explore how companies can begin to build cultures that make intelligent failure more likely.

Intelligent Failure

The term "intelligent failure" was coined by Duke University professor of management Sim Sitkin (1992). According to Sitkin (p. 243), intelligent failures have five characteristics:

> (1) they result from thoughtfully planned actions that (2) have uncertain outcomes and (3) are of modest scale, (4) are executed and responded to with alacrity, and (5) take place in domains that are familiar enough to permit effective learning.

A critical difference between intelligent failure and *bad* failure is the extent to which the individual or organization learned something as a result of the failure. All failures are not created equal; failures that provide valuable information are inherently more helpful than failures that do not. As such, managers should not overlook mistakes and praise or reward those who are incompetent, sloppy, inaccurate, or imprecise. Intelligent failure is not like T-ball where every child gets a trophy.

In his examination of learning from failure, Sitkin (1992) concludes that a successful learning culture must accept that intelligent failures are an important component of learning. Numerous factors drive organizational failure. For example, organizational failure may occur as a result of employee deviance or inattention, poor leadership, poor processes, excessive process complexity, and environmental uncertainty (Pfeffer & Sutton, 1999). Such failures are particularly *bad* when they involve routine processes with predictable outcomes (Sitkin, 1992); in other words, when they could have easily been prevented. On the other hand, *good* failures occur with complex processes and high uncertainty. Such failures represent intelligent failures, because they can help an organization learn what works and what does not work. The discovery of drugs, a trial and error process that is capital intensive, lengthy, and fraught with the possibility of failure, is an appropriate example of intelligent failure. It is only through high-throughput screening and multiple clinical trials that variants are eliminated and new medicines are created (Warren, 2011).

In her highly engaging article, "Strategies for learning from failure," Amy Edmondson (2011) developed a spectrum of failures ranging from the worst to the intelligent. The worst (*bad*) failures are preventable failures in predictable operations. As Edmondson (p. 51) states:

> They usually involve deviations from spec in the closely defined processes of high-volume or routine operations in manufacturing and services. With proper training and support, employees can follow those processes consistently. When they do not, deviance, inattention, or lack of ability is usually the reason. But in such cases, the causes can be readily identified and solutions developed.

For example, while examining eggs for defects and cleanliness, an egg processing plant employee may be distracted by a loud sound behind the conveyor belt and, as a result, allow eggs coated in contaminants to be included on the processing line.

Next on Edmondson's (2011) spectrum are unavoidable failures in complex systems. These situations are characterized by novelty, non-routine processes, and extenuating circumstances. Some job contexts in which these types of failures may occur include healthcare professionals in hospital emergency rooms, soldiers in battle, and teachers in their first classrooms. Even if workers follow best practices for safety and risk management, small process failures may occur. Often, disasters are caused by a series of small failures that occur within a short period or occur in a particular sequence. To prevent disasters, workers need to feel they will be supported—not stigmatized—when they report small failures with equipment, systems, or procedures while it is possible to address and correct them, rather than waiting until a true crisis—or disaster—occurs.

Lastly, Edmondson identifies what she refers to as intelligent failures at the frontier. These failures occur within the context of innovative research (biotechnology, aerospace, etc.). Edmondson (2011, p. 53) considers these to be *good* failures that occur in environments where "answers are not knowable in advance because this exact situation hasn't been encountered before and perhaps never will be again." Intelligent failures are to be expected in companies working to create a new vaccine or build a new type of aircraft or vehicle. In these situations, good work involves good experimentation, and it is always hoped that the failures produced by good experimentation will be quick and decisive. If this is the case, the failures will prevent the organization from sinking more time, money, and other resources into unproductive work.

Benefits of Failure

Accepting failure and learning from it is easier said than done. Failure is anathema: we are afraid of it, we avoid it, and we penalize it (Dahlin, Chuang, & Roulet, 2018; Pfeffer & Sutton, 1999). Indeed, people spend enormous amounts of time and energy and employ any number of biases and heuristics (Tversky & Kahneman, 1974) to avoid admitting failure. Few people want to stand up in front of a group, no matter how big or small, and admit that they made a mistake.

Part of the problem is that failure is seen as a waste of time, money, or other resources. Another part is that people fear being labeled as lacking in judgment or incompetent and, thus, putting their careers in jeopardy. Thus, organizational members may be loath to ask for information and advice. Theory on information networks and advice seeking posits that the perceived social costs of asking for assistance play an important role in determining who is asked for help (Borgatti & Cross, 2003; Nebus, 2006), and that many organizational members resist seeking advice altogether due to fears of appearing incompetent, incurring social debts, or otherwise losing social status (Blau, 1955; Lee, 2002). For example, in two experiments, participants expected others to see them as less competent if they asked for advice in either a work-related vignette or an experimental task and, consequently, refrained from doing so when they believed that others' perceptions would affect their outcomes (Brooks, Gino, & Schweitzer, 2015). Field studies have similarly found that organizational members seek advice from higher status others and avoid seeking advice from lower status others, which the researchers attribute to concerns related to sacrificing social position and expending social capital (Agneessens & Wittek, 2012; Lazega, Mounier, Snijders, & Tubaro, 2012). These fears represent a substantial barrier to building a culture that supports intelligent failure, because unwillingness to seek information and advice reduces the ability to learn when things go wrong, locking organizations into bad failure. Yet, we can learn much from failure (Lehrer, 2009). Weick and Sutcliffe (2015) suggest that a closer look at failure reveals that repeated failing could have positive consequences, especially at the individual level. Navy SEALS, for example, redefine failure as an opportunity to identify a weakness, to learn, and to grow. There may be several mechanisms that produce these positive consequences. Frequent failing could trigger regular sense making and increased skill in doing so. In addition, frequent failing may trigger experiences with closure: people who fail to learn the lessons of closure are vulnerable when bad experiences occur. Their feeling is one of, "I can't handle this, it will never end, and I've got to escape it." In their research, Weick and Sutcliffe (2015) found that SEALS react differently to instances of failure. Their thinking appears to be: "I'm afraid of failure because I didn't prepare well. I'm not afraid of failure if I did the best I could … and learned from it." Finally, frequent failing could also change the character of individual SEALS through a mechanism referred to as "the continuity of experience." Every experience enacted and undergone modifies the one who acts. In SEALS training, every experience of failing happens to a slightly "different" person. It is not just durable traits that matter in dealing with failure. It is also "who" encounters that second, third, and fourth failure. The SEALS in Weick and Sutcliffe's study demonstrated that they can be both attentive to failure but not become immobilized by the potential repercussions of failing (or succeeding).

Aside from enabling individuals to grow as human beings and to become more competent, intelligent failure helps organizations move toward improved future performance (Edmondson, 2011). This is especially likely when new situations are encountered and established procedures or approaches do not work. In these cases, experimentation and intelligent failure are essential for organizations to learn and become more resilient. "Where success can foster decreased search and attention, increased complacency, risk-aversion, and maladaptive homogeneity, modest levels of failure can promote a willingness to take risks and foster resilience-enhancing experimentation" (Sitkin, 1992, p. 237). Thus, failures can signal the existence of problems to be resolved, motivate organizations to adapt and stimulate action, increase openness to taking risks, and increase organizational flexibility in their responses to their environments (Sitkin, 1992).

A Spirituality of Imperfection

Spirituality has been defined as a search for meaning and connection to others (Mitroff & Denton, 1999), and spirituality at work implies workers engaging in tasks that help to create meaning in their lives and connection with community (Ashmos & Duchon, 2000). Several recent studies have demonstrated the positive impact that spirituality can have on businesses and business leaders. For example, Singh, Corner, and Pavlovich (2016) found that spirituality (defined as an awareness of a greater force or power beyond the individual self) affected entrepreneurs' experience of venture failure. In essence, they found that spirituality helped entrepreneurs better manage failure, and, somewhat surprisingly, venture failure helped deepen their spirituality. A number of authors have also examined the role that workplace spirituality may have on learning in the workplace (Gatling, 2015; Howard, 2002). The relationship appears to be a positive one such that workplace spirituality is positively associated with learning.

The nature of personal spirituality is paradox, and the core paradox that underlies spirituality is a haunting sense of incompleteness—of somehow being unfinished. In many ways, this paradox and its resulting expression lies at the heart of Maslow's (1943) conceptualization of the need for self-actualization. Maslow conceived of self-actualization as an ongoing, never-ending process of realizing our potential through peak experiences. Similarly ongoing and open-ended, spirituality is more at home with questions than answers, and we discover it not by being told what to do but by engaging in creating meaning for ourselves. The ancient Greeks first used the concept of "spiritual" to distinguish and contrast between material and non-material things. In other words, spirituality was originally considered to be beyond the material, beyond possession, beyond the confines of the self. One experienced it but could not see, touch, possess, or command it. Indeed, the Greeks thought of spirituality as always being beyond our control. Spiritual growth involves becoming more *complete* and finding a fit between the self and one's reality outside self. It is not interested in explanations and techniques but rather a vision for living that celebrates experience and choice. Spiritual growth involves finding individual answers to the question, "How am I to live—usefully and in completion?" Thus it is not exclusive, dogmatic, or authority driven but open minded and questioning.

The term "spirituality of imperfection" was created by Seelaus (1998) in reference to St. Teresa of Avila who faced numerous challenges in her life and learned to accept herself as imperfect but, nevertheless, *worthy*. As Clarke (1976, p. 174) suggests,

> Her lack of illusions in regard to what it is to be human, allows her to come to such freedom that she can assign her imperfections no more importance than they deserve. She awakens to the truth that God is not concerned about the limitations of being human, but about love.

Thus, Seelaus proposes that a spirituality of imperfection:

> is not "anything goes" or "what you see is what you get." Rather, it is the simple admission that, in spite of our best efforts, we all fall short. But as long as the heart is intent on loving, our failures are not the issue.

Kurtz and Ketcham (1992) develop this notion of the spirituality of imperfection in their book of this title. In their book, they quote Francis T. Vincent, Jr., a former Major League Baseball Commissioner who says:

> Baseball teaches us, or has taught most of us, how to deal with failure. We learn at a very young age that failure is the norm in baseball and, precisely because we have failed, we hold in high regard those who fail less often—those who hit safely in one out of three chances and become star players (.333 average). I also find it fascinating that baseball, alone in sport, considers errors to be part of the game, part of its rigorous truth.

Like baseball, a spirituality of imperfection teaches us that failure is indeed the norm in life: errors are part of life's "rigorous truth." A spirituality of imperfection involves seeing ourselves as we really are and then discovering that it is only within our imperfections that we can find the peace and serenity that is available to us. In other words, a spirituality of imperfection does not offer a set of rules or an ideology claiming a greater truth, but rather it presents a vision celebrating experience and choice (Kurtz & Ketcham, 1992). It recognizes that our imperfection, mistakes, and failures can be a wound that permits growth and development to occur, and that to deny imperfection is to disown oneself, for to be human is to be imperfect. A spirituality of imperfection is rooted and revealed by uncertainties, inadequacies, helplessness, and a lack of control. It offers a context and suggests a way of living in which we endure our imperfections and use them to teach us. It suggests that our successes can be our failures and our failures our successes if we learn and grow from them. Or, as the Buddha teaches, our spirituality flowers when we understand that something is awry, that something is wrong with us.

A spirituality of imperfection begins as a cry for help but it develops as a way of living with our humanness. It urges us to accept imperfections as imperfections because this acceptance is necessary if we are to develop a vision of life and a way of living that can be endured and lived creatively. Thus, a spirituality of imperfection helps us understand that there are no guarantees in life, and life must be lived as *life* not as a goal. We must neither lose heart when things go badly nor become cocky when things go well since our failures and imperfections assure us that we must continue to toil and struggle. In paradox, the struggle itself develops our virtue and lets us know that we are spiritually alive.

Rohr (2011) suggests that too many of us spend too much of our lives seeking answers to questions like, "What makes me significant?" or "How can I support myself?" From this perspective, success is defined as material gain. Rohr argues that it is only when we begin to pay attention to our failures, especially the invaluable lessons that they hold, and seek integrity within the task we do that we move into a more complete life. He writes (p. 76),

> Failure and suffering are the great equalizers and levelers among humans.... There is a strange and even wonderful communion in real human pain, actually much more than in joy, which is often manufactured and passing. In one sense, failure's effects are not passing, and the pain of falling short is less commonly manufactured ... if we are lucky many of us discover in times of such falling the Great Divine Gaze, the ultimate I-Thou relationship.

Thus, a spirituality of imperfection is well illustrated by the analogy of the sinner being closer to the divine than the saint. Each time we fail (sin), we cut a string connecting us to the divine. But the divine ties it up again making a knot, thereby bringing us just a little closer. Each failure makes the string a bit shorter, and each knot draws us closer and closer (Stuart, 2013). Development of a spirituality of imperfection is a search for reality, for honesty, for true speaking and true thinking. It is to reject self-deception and to live a more examined and conscious life. It is to begin to see ourselves as we are: mixed up, incomplete, limited, and flawed.

At the individual level, practicing a spirituality of imperfection is likely to enhance individual humility. Accepting imperfection allows us to see our shortcomings and, in so doing, allows us to ask for help, which is a key dimension of leader humility (Morris, Brotheridge, & Urbanski, 2005). Interestingly, research by Owens and Hekman (2016) indicate that a leader's humility can enhance team performance by creating an emergent "spirit" that enhances psychological safety which allows the team to strive to achieve its highest potential. And, more broadly, humility was a core characteristic of level 5 leaders, the most effective leaders in Collins' (2001) research of 1400 Fortune 500 companies.

How to Develop Intelligent Failure

Given the foregoing discussion, we should encourage organizational leaders to create cultures that allow for intelligent failure through the development of a spirituality of imperfection. In their review of the opportunities, motivation, and ability to learn from failure, Dahlin et al. (2018) suggest that the keys to improved learning from failure are psychological safety and non-hierarchical environments with good communication and coordination within and between organizational parts. Simply put, leaders and organizations with a punitive attitude toward failure learn less from failures (intelligent or otherwise) because organizational members consider the cost of reporting failure to be too high. In this section, we explore how organizational leaders can create organizational cultures that promote psychological safety and failure reporting.

Researchers suggest there are specific ways to design an organization so that the organization and its members are more likely to experience intelligent failure (Bock, 2015; McGrath, 2011; Sitkin, 1992). First, they propose that actions be carefully planned and that success and failure be defined upfront so that if things go wrong, they will have a better understanding of the underlying causes. Second, failures should be managed quickly so that very little time elapses between outcomes and their interpretation. Third, formal mechanisms should be developed to share what was learned. The organization should develop ways to quickly, honestly, and completely disseminate information. These "After Action Reports" capture intent of the activity, what happened, why it happened, what was learned, and how the next activity will incorporate the new data.

These actions are particularly important when the activity is complex and uncertain. Dahlin et al. (2018) report that complex problems provide greater opportunities to learn since they appear to trigger faster and more efficient learning. Specifically, complex problems offer more venues for learning and counteract simplified cause and effect analyses. Evidence suggests that organizations often blame individual operators rather than try to find true failure causes. The tendency to play the "blame game" creates a hostile work environment in which individuals are looking not for answers but only to avoid being associated with failure. Thus, complexity may diminish non-reporting since it is not possible to blame a single person or department for a complex problem. As such, by recognizing and becoming conscious that complex problems are just that (complex), incorporating a spirituality of imperfection into organizational processes can overcome the problems of non-reporting and blaming. Moreover, a spirituality of imperfection may help to create a culture where everyone involved in a process understands that learning only occurs when employees feel empowered to report problems truthfully and trust that responsible managers will conduct proper analyses to determine the true causes of failure. Further, an organization that embraces a spirituality of imperfection is more likely to set realistic expectations and create accountability standards that are accepted and perceived as fair (Groysberg, Lee, Price, & Cheng, 2018).

Also, a spirituality of imperfection can encourage intelligent failure by creating a work culture in which seeking help and advice is the norm. We propose that organizations that introduce a spirituality of imperfection will be better at learning than other organizations since information sharing plays an important role in learning from failure (Edmondson, Bohmer, & Pisano, 2001). Such exchanges allow organizational members to learn both from their own failures and the failures of others (Dahlin et al., 2018). In particular, asking for information, advice, and help before acting allows one to gain insights from others' failures, while asking for the same in post-mortem events promotes learning from one's own failures (Ellis & Davidi, 2005). Applying the insights gained from such information exchange may help to transform bad failure into intelligent failure.

Furthermore, a spirituality of imperfection may increase advice and information seeking. Most clearly, embracing the reality of our own imperfection points out the value of seeking assistance from others: if we do not expect ourselves to have all the answers, others' input appears more valuable. Embracing imperfection can also reduce the perceived social costs of seeking advice. When organizational members do not require themselves to present a façade of perfection, the personal shame of appearing incompetent due to asking for advice is likely reduced. When the organizational culture includes an acceptance of imperfection, both in oneself and one's co-workers, the social threat of information and advice seeking is further diminished, because organizational members can reasonably expect that the social costs imposed by others will be smaller. A spirituality of failure, then, may both increase the perceived value and reduce the perceived costs of seeking advice from others, leading to increased sharing of information and advice within the organization.

Conclusion

In this chapter, we argued that different levels of failure could be experienced in the workplace. Some are a matter of training, attention, and focus. Others are more personal and require us to reassess our emotions, traits, and abilities to see if our behavior matches our values. We suggested that intelligent failure is characterized by the ability to learn from failures, and we posited that a spirituality of imperfection engenders the belief that failure is part of what makes us human. A spirituality of imperfection suggests that, as humans, we all make mistakes, and these mistakes are a chance for us to learn and grow. Having empathy for others starts with having empathy for ourselves. Thus, the ability to learn from our failures may be contingent on the degree to which we have developed a spirituality of imperfection. Indeed, Kurtz and Ketcham (1992) argued that, at the individual level, individuals who cultivate a spirituality of imperfection are less prone to conceit and self-sufficiency since the approach demands self-awareness and allows help seeking.

Although intelligent failure is beneficial to organizations, organizational members are often hesitant to seek information and advice because of the perceived social costs of doing so.

Table 6.1 Examining Organizational Practices

1. To what extent do organizational members tend to engage in *satisficing* (i.e., making adequate rather than optimal decisions)?
2. On a scale of 1 to 10, what are the organization's risk taking tendencies? What should they be?
3. In examining key events and incidents in the past five years, to what degree were organizational members rewarded or punished for taking risks? For making mistakes?
4. To what extent does it seem that failures are repeated? Covered up? Characterized by a search for scapegoats?
5. To what extent do managers have the tendency to overlook incompetent, sloppy, inaccurate, or imprecise work?
6. How much training and support are offered to enable organizational members to follow organizational processes and procedures?
7. How much support is offered to organizational members who make mistakes?
8. To what extent is individual growth valued? Are organizational members allowed to be a *work in progress* or is perfection expected?
9. What mechanisms exist that encourage organizational members to ask for help and guidance?
10. What processes does the organization have in place to learn from its failures? Formal after-the-fact review processes?

A spirituality of imperfection, at both individual and organizational levels, lowers those costs and, consequently, spurs advice and information seeking. Unsurprisingly, the likely outcomes of a spirituality of imperfection, that is psychological safety, non-blaming, and tolerance for errors, both lower the costs of advice seeking and increase learning from failure (Edmondson, 1996; Edmondson & Lei, 2014; Keith & Frese, 2005; Khatri, Brown, & Hicks, 2009; Tjosvold, Yu, & Hui 2004).

In summary, organizational leaders need to reflect on the extent to which their organization's culture supports and encourages intelligent failures. The questions posed in Table 6.1 may be a good starting point for this reflection. If indeed, as Cameron (2008) suggests, organizational culture can be changed with deliberate managerial action, then their answers to these questions may reveal where to focus their attention and efforts.

Note

1. It is important to note that the focus of this chapter is extending the conversation around spirituality and intelligent failure at the organizational level. At the individual level, there is already a considerable and growing literature on engaging in spiritual growth, dealing with failures, developing humility, and their impact on individual outcomes.

References

Agneessens, F., & Wittek, R. (2012). Where do intra-organizational advice relations come from? The role of informal status and social capital in social exchange. *Social Networks, 34*(3), 333–345.

Ashmos, D. P., & Duchon, D. (2000). Spirituality at work: A conceptualization and measure. *Journal of Management Inquiry, 9*(2), 134–145.

Blau, P. M. (1955). *The Dynamics of Bureaucracy: A Study of Interpersonal Relations in Two Government Agencies.* Chicago: University of Chicago Press.

Bock, L. (2015). *Work Rules! Insights from Inside Google that Will Transform How You Live and Lead.* New York: Hachette.

Borgatti, S. P., & Cross, R. (2003). A relational view of information seeking and learning in social networks. *Management Science, 49*(4), 432–445.

Brooks, A. W., Gino, F., & Schweitzer, M. E. (2015). Smart people ask for (my) advice: Seeking advice boosts perceptions of competence. *Management Science, 61*(6), 1421–1435.

Cameron, K. (2008). A process for changing organizational culture. In T. G. Cummings (Ed.), *Handbook of Organizational Development.* Thousand Oaks, CA: Sage, 429–445.

Clarke, J. (1976). *Story of a Soul.* Washington, DC: ICS Publications.

Collins, J. C. (2001). *Good to Great: Why Some Companies Make the Leap … and Others Don't.* London: Random House.

Dahlin, K. B., Chuang, Y-T., & Roulet, T. J. (2018). Opportunity, motivation, and ability to learn from failures and errors: Review, synthesis, and ways to move forward. *Academy of Management Annals, 12*(1), 252–277.

Edmondson, A. C. (1996). Learning from mistakes is easier said than done: Group and organizational influences on the detection and correction of human error. *Journal of Applied Behavioral Science, 32*(1), 5–28.

Edmondson, A. (2011). Strategies for learning from failure. *Harvard Business Review, 89*(4), 49–55.

Edmondson, A. C., Bohmer, R. M., & Pisano, G. P. (2001). Disrupted routines: Team learning and new technology implementation in hospitals. *Administrative Science Quarterly, 46*(4), 685–716.

Edmondson, A. C., & Lei, Z. (2014). Psychological safety: The history, renaissance, and future of an interpersonal construct. *Annual Review of Organizational Psychology and Organizational Behavior, 1*(1), 23–43.

Ellis, S., & Davidi, I. (2005). After-event reviews: Drawing lessons from successful and failed experience. *Journal of Applied Psychology, 90*(5), 857–871.

Gatling, A. (2015). A causal model for integrating workplace spirituality into hospitality organizational transformation. *Journal of Human Resources in Hospitality and Tourism, 14*(2), 177–194.

Groysberg, B., Lee, J., Price, J., & Cheng, J. (2018). The leader's guide to corporate culture. *Harvard Business Review, 96*(1), 45–57.

Howard, S. (2002). A spiritual perspective on learning in the workplace. *Journal of Managerial Psychology, 17*(3), 230–242.

Keith, N., & Frese, M. (2005). Self-regulation in error management training: Emotion control and metacognition as mediators of performance effects. *Journal of Applied Psychology, 90*(4), 677–691.

Khatri, N., Brown, G. D., & Hicks, L. L. (2009). From a blame culture to a just culture in health care. *Health Care Management Review, 34*(4), 312–322.

Kurtz, E., & Ketcham, K. (1992). *The Spirituality of Imperfection: Storytelling and the Search for Meaning*. New York: Bantam.

Lazega, E., Mounier, L., Snijders, T., & Tubaro, P. (2012). Norms, status and the dynamics of advice networks: A case study. *Social Networks, 34*(3), 323–332.

Lee, F. (2002). The social costs of seeking help. *Journal of Applied Behavioral Science, 38*(1), 17–35.

Lehrer, J. (2009). Accept defeat: The neuroscience of screwing up. *Wired*. Retrieved from www.wired.com/2009/12/fail_accept_defeat/.

McGrath, R. (2011). Failing by design. *Harvard Business Review, 89*(4), 77–83.

Maslow, A. (1943). A theory of human motivation. *Psychological Review, 50*(4), 370–396.

Mitroff, I. I., & Denton, E. A. (1999). *A Spiritual Audit of Corporate America: A Hard look at Spirituality, Religion, and Values in the Workplace*. San Francisco: Jossey Bass.

Morris, J., Brotheridge, C., & Urbanski, J. (2005). Bringing humility to leadership: Antecedents and consequences of leader humility. *Human Relations, 58*(10), 1323–1350.

Nebus, J. (2006). Building collegial information networks: A theory of advice network generation. *Academy of Management Review, 31*(3), 615–637.

Owens, B., & Hekman, D. (2016). How does leader humility influence team performance? Exploring the mechanisms of contagion and collective promotion focus. *Academy of Management, 59*(3), 1088–1111.

Pfeffer, J., & Sutton, R. (1999). *The Knowing-Doing Gap: How Smart Companies Turn Knowledge into Action*. Boston: Harvard Business Press.

Reische, J. (2017). The importance of dumb mistakes in college. *New York Times*. Retrieved from www.nytimes.com/2017/12/09/opinion/sunday/dumb-mistakes-college.html.

Rohr, R. (2011). *Falling Upward: A Spirituality for the Two Halves of Life*. New York: Jossey-Bass.

Sanborn, M. (2015). Why leaders fail. *Thought, 11*(15).

Seelaus, V. (1998). Thérèse. Spirituality of imperfection: Finding strength in weakness. Retrieved from http://carmelitesofeldridge.org/vilma5.html.

Singh, S., Corner, P., & Pavlovich, K. (2016). Spirituality and entrepreneurial failure. *Journal of Management, Spirituality and Religion, 13*(1), 24–49.

Sitkin, S. (1992). Learning through failure: The strategy of small losses. *Research in Organizational Behavior, 14*, 231–266.

Stuart, T. (2013). The knot of forgiveness. Retrieved from http://tomstuart.org/2013/01/23/the-knot-of-forgiveness/.

Tjosvold, D., Yu, Z. Y., & Hui, C. (2004). Team learning from mistakes: The contribution of cooperative goals and problem-solving. *Journal of Management Studies, 41*(7), 1223–1245.

Tversky, A., & Kahneman, D. (1974). Judgment under uncertainty: Heuristics and biases. *Science, 185*(4157), 1124–1131.

Warren, J. (2011). Drug discovery: Lessons from evolution. *British Journal of Clinical Pharmacology, 71*(4), 497–503.

Weick, K. E., & Sutcliffe, K. M. (2015). *Managing the Unexpected: Sustained Performance in a Complex World*. New York: Wiley & Sons.

PART II

Spirituality, Religion, and Culture

7

LINKING SPIRITUALITY TO RELIGION

Timothy Ewest and David W. Miller

Introduction

The ability to forsake the sacred/spiritual life was not always an option, nor was the presumed bifurcation between spirituality and religion. Sheldrake (1992) suggested that religion and spirituality may not always need to be deliberately linked and the schism that developed between the two was a result of advances in human knowledge, guided by historical-cultural events that changed perceptions of the transcendent.

This chapter reviews the historical origins, mainly Occidental, that created the divide between the sacred-spiritual and the empirical world as depicted by Taylor (2008). The goal of this chapter is to provide a meta perspective of how historical collective cultural assumptions and the ensuing social forces they create have led to the assumed bifurcation of the sacred-spiritual from the material world. This has resulted in a perceived separation between the sacred-spiritual and empirical world, which has affected the ways in which individuals, and specifically scholars, have theoretically separated religion and spirituality. The chapter challenges this distinction, drawing on social science research that suggests a connection and broad interdimensionality between religion and spirituality.

Origins of the Divide between the Sacred-Spiritual

Social forces, "that being an element of society that has the capability of causing change or influencing people" (Dominelli, 2004, p. 15), often provide a larger meta meaning and provide a theoretical context for analysis. Specific phenomena are frequently driven by large scale social events, values, and processes; although not typically acknowledged or detected by societies, organizations, and individuals (Rosenberg, 2015). Social forces frequently act as a motivational impetus for organizations and individuals, even if these individuals and organizations are alienated from each other. Social forces are also detected after the fact, when considering historical movements and ideals, and are believed to be factual understandings since they are based on historical events and accepted values (Eliade, 2013). While not every single individual participates in or is engaged by the social force, when societies, organizations, and individuals are driven by social forces they collectively act as a group mind (Durkheim, 1994). To detect social forces and the meta meaning which is directing and motivating societal action, one needs to trace significant historical events and corresponding values.

Charles Taylor (2008) traces the three historical developments that led to the bifurcation between the sacred-spiritual and the material world, thus creating or legitimizing a divide between religion and spirituality. Taylor's research considered the historical record and found that earlier worldviews did not recognize any separation between the sacred-spiritual and the material worlds, nor the nuancing of religion and spirituality. Rather, it is only in our modern or present worldview when humans began viewing the world with a different framework, creating deep divides within human perception regarding the sacred-spiritual and material world.

Taylor (2008) argues that the understanding of the sacred-spiritual for the classic or medieval individual did not have any consideration of not believing in the transcendent or God(s), which today is the denotation of secular. For the medieval individual the material world was traced by the divine, where angels moved the forces of nature and physical illness was a curse from God (or the gods) (Smith, 2014). Something was only considered secular when a person ascribed or made attributions to an event within the material world to a god who was not believed to have caused the event, or to a divinity that was not the most recognized dominate deity. But, generally, no one believed there was not a direct connection between the sacred-spiritual and the material world; it simply was not an option.

In this era individuals could have either a nascent or mature belief and practice system, but regardless of religious adherence to what was acknowledged as the most commonly accepted belief(s), they did had have high levels of religiosity regarding practices and the institution (Taylor, 2008; Conybeare, 2014). Some have suggested that ancient religions, including during the medieval era, had little if any awareness regarding creeds, or systemized beliefs and thus the focus was mostly on practices and institutions (Howe, 2004). The result, Taylor suggests, is that no one saw a division between the sacred-spiritual and the material world; it simply was not an option as a worldview for individuals until the Enlightenment.

Taylor (2008) notes the second perspective came from Enlightenment era thinking which promoted rationality and reason as a means to understand reality, and challenged existing largely unsystemized beliefs and church-inspired traditional practices. In doing so a neutral space or areligious space was created that was rationally oriented and thus "disenchanted" the world (Taylor, 2008; Inglehart & Norris, 2004). This occurred because considerations of the sacred-spiritual are difficult and in some cases impossible to validate empirically having their own logics. The preference then during this era, was for an areligious space as a means to avoid enchanted notions which interfere with a rational understanding of the material world and corresponding modernization (Berger, 1969). As Enlightenment thought progressed, other scientific contributors to the Enlightenment questioned the preeminence of reason, such as Freud who suggested the ego as primary or inceptive (Mack, 2010). The theoretical assumptions coming out of this period were that reason is ultimate and only it can provide a practical and accurate understanding of the world, whereas religion is reframed as myth. Yet, when reason was applied to understand the human condition it was problematic: the human dynamic may be more enigmatic. Clifford Geertz (1973, p. 111) refers to this perspective as the "scientific perspective," echoing Taylor's observation that the Enlightenment placed reason above other forms of knowledge.

Finally, Taylor (2008) suggests the emerging modern trend emerging out the Enlightenment, and holding to many of the same assumptions, adds an additional nuance wherein not believing in any transcendent elements to life is not contested, and is but one option among many choices. Here, the perspective harkens back to Feuerbach (2004) who suggested all of humanity's sacred-spiritual beliefs and practices are only a projection of human need onto the heavens, and should be demythologized to be understood as human values. This perspective is the natural extension of the Enlightenment emphasis on creating an areligious space, extending the idea to a preferable worldview devoid of the sacred-spiritual and places this as an acceptable personal rational perspective.

The result is that today there is a continued emphasis on and prioritization of reason and the belief of the enigmatic human, and acceptance of no need for transcendent beliefs. These assumptions have created a theoretical context with a plethora of definitions and research regarding the sacred-spiritual. For the individual, these present conditions have delegitimized the sacred-spiritual space, and created a crisis for those who associate with the sacred-spiritual space and use it for forming their personal values and identity (Emmons, 2003). Further, there is no academic consensus within existing scholarship regarding the definitions of spirituality or religion (Nongbri, 2013), making any suggestion of finding connections between the two appear untenable. Moreover, definitions regarding the sacred-spiritual have a tendency to relate to a presupposition which articulates one of the aforementioned historical perspectives. The primary intent of this chapter is to use Taylor's (2008) distinctions to provide a historically based narrative to explain at a meta level the theoretical presumptions that are in use and a social force within each era.

Taylor's First Definition of Sacred

Theoretical perspectives and ensuing definitions regarding the sacred-spiritual, specifically referring to religion and spirituality, suggest that segregation of life from the sacred-spiritual to be impossible. Thus any definition for spirituality or religion must integrate aspects of spirituality and religion which have no (secular or non-religious?) alternative. Moreover, any definition would be suggestive of using religion or spirituality as an interpretive lens to provide the material world with sacred-spiritual personal or community meanings, with no avenue to provide meaning without informing the sacred-spiritual. The beliefs may or may not be systematized, and refer largely to organizational edicts and practices. Moreover, there is a subtle or overt belief that communities, organizations, and individuals are flourishing or ethical when they adhere to, are confined by, or follow traditional community beliefs and practices.

For example, scholars have identified this space by suggesting it is "a God-oriented spirituality where thought and practice are premised in theologies, either broadly or narrowly conceived" (Spilka, 1993). This view suggests that religion is not a single individual's perspective, but is shared by a community, and thus spirituality is the individual expression of the individual's adherence to the transcendent as represented by the group.

Taylor's Second Definition of Sacred

Theoretical perspectives and ensuing definitions regarding the sacred-spiritual, specifically referring to religion and spirituality, suggest the possibility of separation of the material world from the sacred-spiritual. Here, reason is championed because it disenchants the material world of unexamined practices and unsystemized beliefs. Therefore, definitions regarding religion and spirituality are sensitive to the separation between the sacred-spiritual and the "real" or material world. These theoretical perspectives take positions which are apologetic, arguing one is justified over and against the other, clearly segregating the sacred-spiritual from the material.

In this perspective there are two interpretative lenses, the sacred-spiritual and the material world (secular), with the latter being relegated as an areligious space. Finally, there is a belief that communities and organizations must intentionally choose for themselves one of the two perspectives, with publicly held and government organizations primarily being in the areligious (secular) space (Meyer & Moors, 2005). Within designated secular or areligious spaces, individuals who adhere to the sacred-spiritual are asked to bifurcate themselves, practicing and processing their sacred-spiritual self in the proper context, that being outside designated areligious spaces. Yet, individual's values are subjective and enigmatic, and they are given a special dispensation from the scientific perspective.

For example, Inglehart and Norris, (2004) trace the sacred-spiritual and secular as two social forces that have corresponding human and national values which drive and determine behaviors. Weick (1995) observed that people who adhere to the sacred-spiritual have their own sense making regarding the person. Emmons (2003) posits that individuals are affected by the enlightenment period in contemporary society, wherein those who seek identity from the sacred-spiritual realm may struggle with having part of their identity marginalized. And, while religion and spirituality is still recognized to be a steady, if not increasing, force in most global communities (Casanova, 2011; Nandy, 2007), organizations and some government public entities endorse and demand the areligious space, indicating that while the spiritual life may not be retreating from society, it can be marginalized in organizational life (Wilson, 1982; Ashforth & Vaidyanath, 2002; King 2007). Berger (1969) observes that there is a preference for an areligious space in societies and organizations to avoid enchanted notions, which interfere with modernization which is driven by rational thought on the material world.

Taylor's Third Definition of Sacred

Here theoretical perspectives and ensuing definitions regarding the sacred-spiritual, referring to religion and spirituality, are much like the above, except with more emphasis on apologetics. The areligious space is understood as humane, or the ultimate teleological expression of human biology and these corresponding human values can be explained through the sciences (e.g., neuroscience). Therefore, definitions regarding the sacred-spiritual are either suggestive of illuminating how sacred-spiritual beliefs and practices should actually be understood as human values or biological proclivities. Sacred-spiritual communities or individuals which hold beliefs and practices that are not clearly reasonable and/or use myth or religious sense-making to explain the material world, are regarded as being locked in mythology, or not relevant to the furthering of the real human potential.

For example, arguably the best known popular advocate of this position is Sam Harris (2005), who argues

> Clearly, it is time we learned to meet our emotional needs without embracing those transitions in every human life that demand profundity—birth, marriage, death—without lying to ourselves about the nature of reality. Only then will the practice of raising our children to believe that they are Christian, Muslim, or Jesus be widely recognized as the ludicrous obscenity that it is. And, only then will we stand a chance of healing the deepest and most dangerous factures of our world.
>
> *(p. 88)*

Harris's (2005) dogmatic position against all religion is one logical complement of a new scientific culture, which considers reality to be confined to the observable. However, religious individuals use their belief in God, and not just reason alone, to make sense of the world around them (Weick, 1995).

The result is that people who hold sacred-spiritual beliefs are left with an alternative way to interpret or make sense of the world around, specifically using the teaching, revelatory insights, and traditions which outline expectations of the sacred-spiritual on their lives, and provide meaning in everyday events (Geertz, 1973).

Multidimensionality of Religion and Spirituality

Three contextual considerations are central to linking spirituality to religion, although largely concerning Occidental religion. The first is the existence of the present social force, dictating bifurcation of the sacred-spiritual from the material world. This acts as the generally accepted modern scientific perspective or paradigm. Specifically, coming out of the Enlightenment, is the assumption that the material world may be objective, but the individual is subjective and amorphous. Academic disciplines align research methodologies and operationalize definitions to fit these specific theoretical assumptions determined the present social force, or apologetically if the assumptions are based on a bygone era.

Second, Schmidt-Wilk, Heaton, and Steingard (2000) posit the struggle over operational consensus is partially due to the amorphous nature of spirituality; the definition is owned by various disciplines. But the final and primary challenge in tracing the connections or linkages between religion and spirituality is that both terms are attempting to delineate and codify a phenomenon that is existential (Vess, Arndt, Cox, Routledge, & Goldenberg, 2009), phenomenological (James, 1995), and, most importantly, multidimensional (Masters et al., 2009).

For example, The Brief Multidimensional Measure of Religiousness/Spirituality (BMMRS), exploratory factor analysis has seven factors. The first of which accounts for 42.08% of the variance, the next two factors each account for 6% and 6.53% of the variance, and the remaining four variables account for 2.95%, 3.19%, 3.78%, and 3.19% of the variance respectively (Masters et al., 2009). Another example comes from, Ashmos and Duchon (2000) who reported similar results with the Spirituality at Work Scale (SWS). The first two factors contribute 36.40% of the variance and the remaining five factors contribute only 5.86%, 5.37%, 4.40%, 3.38%, and 3.14% of the variance. Masters et al. (2009) citing Piedmont, Mapa, and Williams (2006) suggest that shared variance in variables within social science research concerning the sacred-spiritual is suggestive of multidimensionality, indicating the nature of religion and spirituality has overlapping facets, thus also appearing to have underlying a unified construct.

Therefore, finding commonalities between the religion and spirituality should not come as a revelation. Hill and colleagues (2000), took an exhaustive survey of vetted psychological research in the field of psychology of religion, an academic field that is robust, unlike the nascent, although emerging field of Management Spirituality and Religion interest group within the Academy of Management. Hill et al.'s survey of extant research found five connections between religion and spirituality. See Table 7.1.

Table 7.1 Research Connections Between Religion and Spirituality

1. Religion and spirituality (R/S) develop across a lifespan, occurring at every age throughout a person's life, wherein a person's religious and spiritual concerns are evident, within various cultures and within persons who have no religious training (p. 53).
2. R/S are inherently social-psychological phenomena, which means that they are expressed or are influenced by groups, and the groups' codes and norms which can be rooted in religious expectations (p. 54).
3. R/S are related to cognitive phenomena, involving commitments and different and complex thoughts. R/S thinking can be unique, having its own sets of reason and sense making.
4. R/S are related to affect and emotion, both the fervant commitment in ritual, and aspects of mindfullness.
5. R/S are tied to biological or endemic aspects of our humanity, either in evolutionary biological or thestic teleological perspectives, suggeting R/S are endemic to what it means to be human.

Source: Adapted from Hill et al. (2000, pp. 53–54).

The bifurcation of the sacred-spiritual and the material world as traced by Taylor (2008), suggests that the bifurcation is an accommodation to theoretical positions, social forces, which changed the existing assumptions or meta narrative within each era. The modern theoretical position has created a bifurcation between religion and spirituality, which social science research suggests is a false dichotomy.

Conclusion

This chapter reviewed the historical origins, mainly Occidental, that created the divide of the sacred-spiritual, with the empirical world as depicted by Taylor (2008). The goal of this chapter was to provide a meta perspective of how historical collective cultural assumptions and social forces, have led to the bifurcation of the sacred-spiritual from the material world and has resulted in a perceived separation between the sacred-spiritual and empirical world. This perceived separation has affected the ways in which individuals, and specifically scholars have separated religion and spirituality. The chapter concludes by delineating how social science research suggests a connection and broad interdimensionality between religion and spirituality.

The present theoretical context development, which has championed reason, but allowed for the human to remain enigmatic, may not be scientifically accurate. Ironically, research has suggested that reason does not play a central role for humans; however, there are a number of other motivators, including, emotions (Eisenberg, 1986) intuitions (Haidt, 2001), spirituality (Cowan, 2005), and religion (Ewest, 2015; Vitell, 2009). Research is suggesting that the human condition may be multivariate steaming from various experiences, but other research also challenges the researcher to consider the role of the transcendent.

Mark Chaves (1994) suggests religiosity may not be created by experiences, but instead it is possible that religion can be an inseparable aspect of our humanity and this is awakened within us when we experience the transcendent (God). For most, the tension between the scientific perspective and religious perspective means people of faith have to struggle with a gradual shift from a world where religion was central, to one that values disinterested secular observation.

References

Ashforth, B., & Vaidyanath, D. (2002). Work organizations as secular religions. *Journal of Management Inquiry, 11*(4), 359–370.

Ashmos, D. P., & Duchon, D. (2000). Spirituality at work: A conceptualization and measure. *Journal of Management Inquiry, 9*(2), 134–145.

Berger, P. L. (1969). *The Sacred Canopy: Elements of a Sociological Theory of Religion*. Garden City, NY. Doubleday.

Casanova, J. (2011). *Public Religions in the Modern World*. Chicago: University of Chicago Press.

Chaves, M. (1994). Secularization as declining religious authority. *Social forces, 72*(3), 749–774.

Conybeare, C. (2014). The city of Augustine: On the interpretation of Civitas. In C. Harrison, C. Humfress, & I. Sandwell (Eds.), *Being Christian in Late Antiquity: A Festschrift for Gillian Clark*. Oxford, UK: Oxford University Press, 138–155.

Cowan, D. A. (2005). Translating spiritual intelligence into leadership competencies. *Journal of Management, Spirituality and Religion, 2*(1), 3–38.

Dominelli, L. (2004). *Social Work: Theory and Practice for a Changing Profession*. Cambridge, UK: Polity Press.

Durkheim, É. (1994). *Durkheim on Religion*. W. S. F. Pickering (Ed.). Atlanta: Scholars Press, (59–73).

Eisenberg, D., & McLachlan, A. D. (1986). Solvation energy in protein folding and binding. *Nature, 319*(6050), 199–203.

Eliade, M. (2013). *The Quest: History and Meaning in Religion*. Chicago: University of Chicago Press.

Emmons, R. (2003). *The Psychology of Ultimate Concerns: Motivation and Spirituality in Personality*. New York: Guilford Press.

Ewest, T. (2015). The relationship between transformational leadership practices and global social responsibility. *Journal of Leadership Studies, 9*(1), 19–29.

Feuerbach, L. (2004). *The Essence of Christianity*. New York: Barnes & Noble Publishing.

Geertz, C. (1973). *The Interpretation of Cultures*. New York: Basic Books.

Haidt, J. (2001). The emotional dog and its rational tail: A social intuitionist approach to moral judgment. *Psychological Review, 108*(4), 814.

Harris, S. (2005). *The End of Faith: Religion, Terror, and the Future of Reason*. New York: W. W. Norton & Company.

Hill, P. C., Pargament, K. I., Hood, R. W., McCullough Jr, M. E., Swyers, J. P., Larson, D. B., & Zinnbauer, B. J. (2000). Conceptualizing religion and spirituality: Points of commonality, points of departure. *Journal for the Theory of Social Behaviour, 30*(1), 51–77.

Howe, L. (2004). Late medieval Christianity, Balinese Hinduism, and the doctrinal mode of religiosity. *Ritual and memory*, 135–154.

Inglehart, R., & Norris, P. (2004). *Sacred and Secular: Religion and Politics Worldwide*. Cambridge, UK: Cambridge University Press.

James, G. A. (1995). *Interpreting Religion: The Phenomenological Approaches of Pierre Daniël Chantepie de la Saussaye, W. Brede Kristensen, and Gerardus van der Leeuw*. Washington, DC: Catholic University of America Press.

Mack, M. (2010). *Spinoza and the Specters of Modernity: The Hidden Enlightenment of Diversity from Spinoza to Freud*. New York: Bloomsbury Publishing.

Masters, K. S., Carey, K. B., Maisto, S. A., Caldwell, P. E., Wolfe, T. V., Hackney, H. L., France, C.R., & Himawan, L. (2009). Psychometric examination of the brief multidimensional measure of religiousness/spirituality among college students. *International Journal for the Psychology of Religion, 19*(2), 106–120.

Meyer, B., & Moors, A. (Eds.). (2005). *Religion, Media, and the Public Sphere*. Bloomington: Indiana University Press.

Nandy, A. (2007). Closing the debate on secularism: A personal statement. In A. D. Needham & R. S. Rajan (Eds.), *The Crisis of Secularism in India*. Durham, NC: Duke University Press, 107–117.

Nongbri, B. (2013). *Before Religion*. New Haven, CT: Yale University Press.

Piedmont, R. L., Mapa, A. T., & Williams, J. E. (2006). A factor analysis of the Fetzer/NIA Brief Multidimensional Measure of Religiousness/Spirituality (MMRS). *Research in the Social Scientific Study of Religion, 17*, 177.

Rosenberg, A. (2015). *Philosophy of Social Science*. Chicago: Westview Press.

Schmidt-Wilk, J., Heaton, D. P., & Steingard, D. (2000). Higher education for higher consciousness: Maharishi University of Management as a model for spirituality in management education. *Journal of Management Education, 24*(10), 580–611.

Sheldrake, P. (1992). *Spirituality and History: Questions of Interpretation and Method*. New York: Crossroads.

Smith, J. K. (2014). *How (Not) to be Secular: Reading Charles Taylor*. Grand Rapids, MI: Wm. B. Eerdmans.

Spilka, B. (1993, August). Spirituality: Problems and directions in operationalizing a fuzzy concept. In Annual Meeting of the American Psychological Association, Toronto, Canada.

Taylor, C. (2008). *A Secular Age*. Cambridge, MA: Belknap Press of Harvard University Press.

Vess, M., Arndt, J., Cox, C. R., Routledge, C., & Goldenberg, J. L. (2009). Exploring the existential function of religion: The effect of religious fundamentalism and mortality salience on faith-based medical refusals. *Journal of Personality and Social Psychology, 97*(2), 334.

Vitell, S. J. (2009). The role of religiosity in business and consumer ethics: A review of the literature. *Journal of Business Ethics, 90*(2), 155–167.

Weick, K. E. (1995). *Sensemaking in Organizations*. Thousand Oaks, CA: Sage.

Wilson, B. R. (1982). *Religion in Sociological Perspective*. Oxford, UK; Oxford University Press.

8

MSR 2.0

Spirituality Plus Religion

Eric B. Dent

MSR 2.0: Spirituality Plus Religion

Someone reading the Management, Spirituality, and Religion (MSR) literature for the first time would readily conclude that spirituality is a "good" thing and that religion is a "bad" thing. The most widely quoted source in MSR is Mitroff and Denton (1999) and they report that their respondents say "[religion] divides more than it unites. It is more exclusive than inclusive. Religion is more concerned with perpetuating itself than with helping humankind. Spirituality on the other hand, is personal" (p. 48).[1]

Religion often has the negative connotations of being "parental," "authoritarian," and "requiring unconscious obedience" while spirituality is "self-managed, adult, self-directed, and conscious development" (Mohamed, Hassan, & Wisnieski, 2001). Zaidman, Goldstein-Gidoni, and Nehemya (2009) write "Unlike institutionalized religion, which looks outward and is anchored in formal rites and scriptures, spirituality is inwardly directed and is concerned with deeper motivations and with existential moments in the life course" (p. 617). Other sources suggest that religion has no place in the workplace (Delbecq, 2009) and that religion is not required for context in defining spirituality and its relationship to the workplace (Dehler & Welsh, 1994). Even the esteemed Dalai Lama (1999, p. 22) has been quoted as saying

> Religion I take to be concerned with faith in the claims of one faith tradition or another, an aspect of which is the acceptance of some form of heaven or nirvana. Connected with this are religious teachings or dogma, ritual prayer, and so on. Spirituality I take to be concerned with those qualities of the human spirit—such as love and compassion, patience, tolerance, forgiveness, contentment, a sense of responsibility, a sense of harmony—which bring happiness to both self and others.

These statements are typical, not extreme, within the MSR literature. In a review of the MSR literature to that point in time, Dent, Higgins, and Wharff (2005) found that only 29% of the articles directly linked spirituality and religion and only 43% of the articles that mentioned both spirituality and religion linked them. As Taylor (2009) noted, "many within the management and organization studies community insist that religion and spirituality are and must be empirically and conceptually separate" and that "religion, it is *almost* needless to say, is the bad sibling in this relationship" (p. 336).

From this sketch one could conclude that religion is divisive, more concerned with perpetuation than humanity, authoritarian, requiring unconscious obedience, outward and anchored in formal rites and scriptures, concerned with faith in the claims of one faith tradition, connected with dogma, and has no place in the workplace.

Hicks (2002) made another interesting observation about the MSR literature. He notes that there is broad consensus that MSR scholars avow that employees should be able to "bring their whole selves to work" (Mitroff, 2003, p. 376) but often a few pages later in the same article, the author will decry any religious expression in the workplace (Mitroff, 2003, p. 378). In the case of Mitroff, to his credit, he admitted his own internal inconsistency, but decided to press on maintaining the inconsistency rather than attempting to resolve it.

For purposes here, the final relevant observation about the MSR literature is to note the wide variety of definitions of spirituality and religion. In a recent article, Tackney, Chappell, and Sato (2017) described "the most enduring challenge" of the field as "the spirituality—religion juxtaposition" (p. 144).

The purpose of this chapter is to point out some "muck" that the MSR literature is mired in and to suggest that the explication of starting axioms will allow the field to take a quantum leap forward to "MSR 2.0." This muck consists of conceptual difficulties such as dichotomizing religion and spirituality, employing too many idiosyncratic definitions of workplace spirituality and terms within, and allowing papers that include philosophical inconsistencies in important concepts. Tackney et al. (2017, p. 247) summarized these difficulties as

> (a) delineating and operationalizing the key terms of religion, spirituality and workplace spirituality; (b) acknowledging the work to date in the MSR corpus around definitions of these terms, and (c) being explicit about how ontological and epistemological assumptions inform our methods.[2]

Having already discussed some aspects of the "muck," the chapter will then introduce a standard definition of religion and show how it is essentially synonymous with a belief system. Such belief systems all have starting axioms that cannot be deduced from within themselves. Consequently, a leverage point for the MSR literature will be the identification and explication of starting axioms. The next section of the chapter will illustrate, in some detail, the starting axioms of five selected religions or philosophies. The chapter will conclude with a discussion of how the MSR literature can advance to the next stage in a lifecycle of academic literature.

Religion Defined

There may be occasions when it makes sense to develop a context-specific definition. For example, one person may define *God* a certain way and another person a different way. *Religion*, however, is a universally used term with a standard, dictionary definition. Such a definition should be used unless the author has a good reason for developing an idiosyncratic definition. Consider, then, *The American Heritage Dictionary of the English Language*'s definition of *religion*:

> a set of beliefs concerning the cause, nature, and purpose of the universe, especially when considered as the creation of a superhuman agency or agencies, usually involving devotional and ritual observances, and often containing a moral code governing the conduct of human affairs.
>
> *(2006, p. 630)*

Someone's religion may be different from a so-called "organized" religion. When many people hear the term "religion," they automatically translate that to "organized religion" meaning one of the major organized religions of the world—Hinduism, Islam, Judaism, Christianity, and so forth. There is clearly nothing in the definition of "religion" that necessitates membership in an organized religion. One's religion, then, is one's "set of beliefs concerning the cause, nature, and purpose of the universe" (*The American Heritage Dictionary of the English Language*, 2006). Rather than frame a discussion in terms of a religion/spirituality dichotomy, it may be more fruitful to consider an individual's or group's "set of beliefs."

The Nature of Belief Systems

Hofstadter (1979) is perhaps the most popular of many to illustrate Gödel's famous incompleteness theorem and prove that, in any belief system, some elements of the system cannot be derived from other parts of the system. In other words, every philosophy or belief statement contains starting propositions that cannot be proven and are taken on "faith." Such starting premises may be true, false, accurate, inaccurate, realistic, or unrealistic, but such a judgment cannot be made using other components of the belief system. An excellent example of an unproven starting axiom is provided by Lewontin (1997, p. 29).

> We take the side of science in spite of the patent absurdity of some of its constructs, in spite of its failure to fulfill many of its extravagant promises of health and life, in spite of the tolerance of the scientific community for unsubstantiated just-so stories, because we have a prior commitment, a commitment to materialism. It is not that the methods and institutions of science somehow compel us to accept a material explanation of the phenomenal world, but, on the contrary, that we are forced by our *a priori* adherence to material causes to create an apparatus of investigation and a set of concepts that produce material explanations, no matter how counterintuitive, no matter how mystifying to the uninitiated. Moreover, that materialism is absolute, for we cannot allow a Divine Foot in the door.

Lewontin makes clear in this quote that the "religion" of atheism makes an a priori commitment, a "leap of faith," if you will, in materialism. So, one of the starting premises for atheism is the belief that all phenomena have material causes. As he points out, there is nothing within atheism which can lead to this conclusion. All philosophies, belief systems, religions have such a priori commitments.

Knowing what one's a priori commitments are may be a non-trivial task. Keller (2008) points out that one of the best ways of surfacing such commitments is by examining one's doubts, which tend to be more readily apparent. For example if a woman from an organized religion claims "there is only one true path to salvation" and a man denies that claim, he has revealed an a priori commitment. He has demonstrated belief in multiple paths to salvation. This belief, however, cannot be derived from within a philosophy so he is accepting it as an act of faith.

Starting Axioms

As noted above, all religions, belief systems, philosophies, worldviews, narrative identities, or whatever other descriptor is used, assume starting axioms that cannot be justified from within the system of belief. In one sense, the starting axioms are what people place "blind faith" in. In many cases, starting axioms cannot be validated to those who choose not to accept the starting axiom or premise. For example, all of the religions discussed in this chapter assume that reality is intelligible. However, none can derive that assumption from within its belief system. Each takes it as a matter of "blind faith."

Every human being holds starting premises. Every person operates using a religion or philosophy whether it is consciously chosen, or not. Many people have attempted to escape this predicament. For example, someone may say "No religion is better than any other. Each is simply a different path to the same destination." This very statement, though, represents a starting axiom. Likewise, several of the examples above from the MSR literature imply that the world would be a better place without doctrine or dogma. This claim, itself, is dogmatic or doctrinal. As Keller (2008, p. 12) notes, "skeptics believe that *any* exclusive claims to a superior knowledge of spiritual reality cannot be true." This objection, of course, is itself an exclusive claim.

Others believe they have escaped "blind faith" by devoting themselves to science. Like any other religion, philosophy, or belief system, however, science has starting axioms that are accepted on "blind faith." As Haught (2008, p. 45) notes, "Exactly what are the independent scientific experiments, we might ask, that could provide 'evidence' for the hypothesis that all true knowledge must be based on the paradigm of scientific inquiry?" Science makes a number of starting assumptions such as that all explanations are purely natural, that the universe has no purpose, that various phenomena, such as the speed of light, have remained constant throughout history, and that truth is worth seeking.

The next section explores some starting axioms of a number of common religions or philosophies such as atheist objectivism, Christianity, secular humanism, Buddhism, and Hinduism. The five offered here are selected merely for illustrative purposes. There are at least dozens of sets of starting axioms practiced by large numbers of people. Even within broad collections of starting axioms such as Hinduism or secular humanism, there is a range of additional starting axioms, or a group of proponents who may not accept an axiom listed below. Every effort has been made to ensure that what follows is the essence of the religion or worldview, the smallest number of axioms adhered to by most proponents. For example, adherents to each of these religions or belief systems have validated these starting assumptions. At one level, there may be as many different religions as there are people, because people make starting assumptions about so many different phenomena. This chapter arbitrarily includes five different religions that all have a large following. A similar analysis could be done with any type of belief system.

Atheist Objectivism

Atheist objectivism as embodied in Ayn Rand's work is included because her book, *Atlas Shrugged* (1957/2005) is listed as the second most influential book for American readers (first is the Bible) (McGrath, 2007). Thirty years after her death her work is receiving increasing attention, particularly as the US federal government directs a higher percentage of the overall economy.

To Rand's credit, she was more specific in laying out the foundational elements of her philosophy than many other philosophers have been (Dent, Parnell, & Carraher, 2018). Rand also makes clear that she understands that all belief systems make a priori commitments. She has written,

> An axiomatic concept is the identification of a primary fact of reality, which cannot be analyzed, i.e., reduced to other facts or broken into component parts. It is implicit in

> all facts and in all knowledge. It is the fundamentally given and directly perceived or experienced, which requires no proof or explanation, but on which all proofs and explanations rest.
>
> *(1990, p. 73)*

Rand has identified three axiomatic concepts—existence, identity, and consciousness. What is real exists. Reality is existence. "Consciousness is the faculty of awareness—the faculty of perceiving that which exists" (Rand, 1990, p. 37). Consciousness consists of the neurological processes in the brain which allow people to have a sensation. For the purposes of this chapter, the primary aspects of Rand's philosophy are nicely encapsulated in a statement quoted at length:

> At a sales conference at Random House, preceding the publication of Atlas Shrugged, one of the book salesmen asked me whether I could present the essence of my philosophy while standing on one foot. I did as follows:
>
> 1. Metaphysics: Objective Reality
> 2. Epistemology: Reason
> 3. Ethics: Self-interest
> 4. Politics: Capitalism.
>
> If you want this translated into simple language, it would read: 1. "Nature, to be commanded, must be obeyed" or "Wishing won't make it so." 2. "You can't eat your cake and have it, too." 3. "Man is an end in himself." 4. "Give me liberty or give me death." ...
>
> My philosophy, Objectivism, holds that:
>
> 1. Reality exists as an objective absolute—facts are facts, independent of man's feelings, wishes, hopes, or fears.
> 2. Reason (the faculty which identifies and integrates the material provided by man's senses) is man's only means of perceiving reality, his only source of knowledge, his only guide to action, and his basic means of survival.
> 3. Man—every man—is an end in himself, not the means to the ends of others. He must exist for his own sake, neither sacrificing himself to others nor sacrificing others to himself. The pursuit of his own rational self-interest and of his own happiness is the highest moral purpose of his life.
> 4. The ideal political-economic system is laissez-faire capitalism.... The government acts only as a policeman that protects man's rights; it uses physical force only in retaliation and only against those who initiate its use, ... In a system of full capitalism, there should be (but, historically, has not yet been) a complete separation of state and economics, in the same way and for the same reasons as the separation of state and church.
>
> *(Rand, 1962, p. 35)*

Some have argued that aside from Aristotle, Plato, and Kant, Rand is the only person to have offered a complete philosophy (Locke, 2007). As will be seen in the next section, others would include Christianity in this list (Schaeffer, 1976/2005).

Christianity

As with many religions, Christianity has had a long history and many people have written about it, so in some ways, it is difficult to encapsulate. For this chapter, anything referred to as Christian will have a base in the Bible and will hold to what are considered "essentials." As Keller (2008) notes, all Christians accept the great ecumenical creeds of Christianity but no Christian believes *only* these things. Such creeds include:

- God in three persons or essences (commonly labeled Father, Son, and Holy Spirit or Creator, Redeemer, and Sustainer) created the world.
- Humanity has fallen into sin and both good and sinful tendencies are within each person.
- God became incarnate in the person of Jesus of Nazareth to allow sinful people to have a personal relationship with God.
- In his death and resurrection Jesus made possible salvation for everyone so they can elect to be received by grace.
- Jesus established the church, his people, as the vehicle through which he continues his mission of rescue, reconciliation, and salvation.
- Finally, "that at the end of time Jesus will return to renew the heavens and the earth, removing all evil, injustice, sin, and death from the world" (Keller, 2008, p. 117).

This panoramic view of history together with other scriptural passages results in several axiomatic statements including:

- Every human being has innate dignity: "So God created man in His own image" (Genesis 1:27).
- Each person's character is of great importance: "Man looks at the outward appearance but the Lord looks at the heart" (I Samuel 16:7).
- God loves people and consistently acts in their long-term best interests.
- Human beings are fallible and will often make decisions not in their long-term best interest.
- Humankind is responsible for taking care of the planet and its life.
- People should stand against injustice wherever it is found: "Hate evil, and love good and establish justice" (Amos 5:15).
- The goal for Christians is to strive for perfection. "Be perfect as the Father in heaven is perfect" (Matthew 5:48).
- The source of knowledge is revelation in Scripture and in creation. "For since the creation of the world God's invisible qualities—his eternal power and divine nature—have been clearly seen, being understood from what has been made" (Romans 1:20).

Logically flowing from these starting principles are notions of private property, working and prospering from one's work, investment and risk-taking (the Parable of the Talents). Moreover, Christianity condemns laziness (Proverbs 12) and certainly doesn't advocate socialism ("For to everyone who has shall *more* be given, and he shall have an abundance" (Matthew 25:14–30 and Luke 19:12–27)). As Yang (2000, p. 259) notes, "the Scriptures neither argue against self-interest nor disparage prosperity. Christianity advocates a form of egoism, which … merely means the pursuit of an individual's 'good.'"

Secular Humanism/Scientific Naturalism/Atheism

Perhaps, one "benefit" to organized religions is that most keep track of their members and any foundational documents are well known. These characteristics are less clear with secular humanism, although its adherents represent a small but growing body of individuals in the world. Although many people may not be accustomed to thinking of secular humanism as a religion, over 50 years ago it was identified as such in the decision in the United States Supreme Court case *Torcaso* v. *Watkins* (1961). Two organizations who are providing structure for secular humanism are the International Humanist and Ethical Union (IHEU) and the Council for Secular Humanism (CSH). At the 50th anniversary World Humanist Congress in 2002 the IHEU unanimously passed the Amsterdam Declaration, a delineation of the fundamental principles of modern humanism that they have declared to be the official statement of World Humanism. One of the key differences between this type of atheism and Objectivist atheism is that the former will frequently believe that truth is relative, although this difference is not specifically explicated in the statement of secular humanism, below. According to the Amsterdam Declaration of 2002 ("Amsterdam Declaration 2002," n.d.), the fundamentals of modern humanism are:

1. Humanism is ethical. It affirms the worth, dignity and autonomy of the individual and the right of every human being to the greatest possible freedom compatible with the rights of others. Humanists have a duty of care to all of humanity including future generations. Humanists believe that morality is an intrinsic part of human nature based on understanding and a concern for others, needing no external sanction.
2. Humanism is rational. It seeks to use science creatively, not destructively. Humanists believe that the solutions to the world's problems lie in human thought and action rather than divine intervention.... Science gives us the means but human values must propose the ends.
3. Humanism supports democracy and human rights...
4. Humanism insists that personal liberty must be combined with social responsibility.... Humanism is undogmatic, imposing no creed upon its adherents...
5. Humanism is a response to the widespread demand for an alternative to dogmatic religion.... Humanism recognizes that reliable knowledge of the world and ourselves arises through a continuing process. of observation, evaluation and revision.
6. Humanism values artistic creativity and imagination and recognizes the transforming power of art...
7. Humanism is a lifestance aiming at the maximum possible fulfilment...

It is interesting to see, within a statement that is essentially a creed, the statement that no creed is imposed upon adherents. This is an example of the importance of clarity around starting assumptions. The next religion discussed, Buddhism, is noteworthy for never extolling an explicit creed.

Buddhism

"Life is suffering—escape it," (Jones, 1931, p. 80) says Buddhism. The central teaching of the Buddha (which means "Awakened One") is that life is difficult and painful, just by its nature (the First Noble Truth). Suffering occurs when people grasp after anything other than what is (the Second Noble Truth). This assumption is squarely in opposition with atheist objectivism, for example, which assumes that striving is one of life's greatest virtues. Buddhism teaches that the way to remove suffering is to stop the need for grasping and striving. A popular form of

Buddhist practice today is mindfulness (Scherer & Waistell, 2018), which is the first of the Seven Factors of Enlightenment.

Although Buddhism makes a number of underlying assumptions, it may be an incomplete philosophy because the Buddha believed that several questions are unanswerable, and among these questions are those that philosophers see as the cornerstone of any philosophy. The Buddha, for example, taught that whether the world is finite is an unanswerable question and that people should not bother to speculate on unanswerable questions.

Buddhism is perhaps best known for its psychological assumptions. The notion of consciousness is central to Buddhism. Consciousness is seen as a construct that is ageless, essentially existing outside time. The human body interacts with consciousness but does not generate it. In fact, Buddhism teaches that, in contrast to Descartes' great claim (I think, therefore, I am), the self "is actually a figment of the imagination" (Prothero, 2010, p. 179).

There is a universal unconscious and turning awareness to it fosters freedom and understanding. Consciousness connects all human beings. In fact, Buddhism contends that all things are connected and that there are no distinctions between worldly and spiritual problems. Compassion is at the core of the human experience and it arises when people connect their consciousnesses with all things (Kornfield, 2008). Buddhism considers states of consciousness to be far more important than external circumstances. What people visualize changes their bodies and their consciousnesses. Buddhists are encouraged to visualize wisdom, love, and generosity and to avoid grasping, aversion, and delusion.

Other important assumptions of Buddhism are that experience trumps belief (Prothero, 2010), that the universe is "made of stories, not atoms" (Kornfield, 2008, p. 138), that the whole world of earth, plants, animals, and humans is holy, and that all human beings have inner nobility and beauty.

Although Buddhism is on the decline worldwide, its adherents are increasing in the West, partly because some see Buddhism as most consistent with science. Capra's (1975) book *The Tao of Physics* popularized the notion that the two fields shared notions such as nonduality, and described quantum mechanics in terms consistent with Buddhism. Buddhists, for example, suggest that consciousness has both a sky-like function and a particle-like function (Kornfield, 2008, p. 39).

Hinduism

Of the great religions of the world, Hinduism is the oldest (Prothero, 2010) and, perhaps, the most complex. It has the third largest number of adherents, approximately 900 million or about 15% of the world's population. Hinduism does not have a "unified system of belief encoded in declaration of faith or a creed" (Flood, 1996, p. 14) but rather is "what Hindus do and think, and what Hindus do and think is almost everything under the sun" (Prothero, 2010, p. 135).

Hindus see the primary human problem as *samsara*, a perpetual cycle of life, death, and rebirth. Consequently, the status and condition of one's birth circumstances are not a matter of fate, but are determined by the good and bad actions taken in a prior life. The end of this cycle is *moksha*, which means *release*, a liberation from the unsatisfactory state of *samsara*. Some describe this experience as merging with the Impersonal, while others see it as the joining of an individual soul with a personal God. Other Hindu assumptions are that the aims of life are *dharma*—personal duty, ethical behavior; *kama*—sensual pleasure; and, *artha*—power and wealth. Hinduism's complexity and diversity is expressed in the various pathways to achieve these goals. The organized religion of Hinduism has no hierarchy providing a leadership structure and no shared creed.

Hindus do mostly share various other assumptions such as that of *karma*, the moral law of cause and effect. At the root of Hindu thinking is the expectation that every action has a consequence, and that the actor will ultimately, in this life or another one, experience the consequence of that action. Hindus engage in good works with the expectation that these will accumulate and result in a more fortunate circumstance at the next rebirth. Hindus also incorporate *yogas* (paths or practices) although these vary considerably depending on the type of Hinduism practiced. The term *yoga* is itself one of the six orthodox schools of Hindu philosophy.

Hindus have sacred texts including the Vedas, the Brahmanas, the Aranyakas, and the Upanishads. Many Westerners are familiar with another sacred text, the Bhaghavad Gita, which is a small portion of the Mahabharata. Hinduism is also filled with gods, the most prominent of whom is the elephant-headed Ganesha, who is revered as the remover of obstacles. Other gods include Agni (the god of fire and the acceptor of sacrifices) and Indra (the god of war, storms, and rainfall).

As noted below, many scholars claim that most religions are essentially the same. Such a claim may arise from that fact that many religions emphasize ethical action, for example. What becomes significant, then, is the priority given to that prescription in one religion compared with others. In the case of Hinduism, "doing your duty does take precedence over knowing your dogma, and right ritual (orthopraxy) is more important than right doctrine (orthodoxy)" (Prothero, 2010, p. 157). Consequently, in Hinduism, story and ritual are integrated and elevated in importance over doctrine, which is quite different from the priority in Judaism or Christianity.

Axioms Should Be Explicit

These brief sketches will not be acceptable to the adherents of any of these religions. Each religion is much more complex than what can be portrayed succinctly here. Still, this overview has demonstrated the wide range of starting axioms in operation among those who believe each religion. Prothero (2010, p. 1) notes that

> at least since … the 1960s, it has been fashionable to affirm that all religions are beautiful and all are true. This claim, which reaches back to *All Religions Are One* (1795) by the English poet, printmaker, and prophet William Blake, is as odd as it is intriguing.… Yet scholars continue to claim that religious rivals such as Hinduism and Islam, Judaism and Christianity are, by some miracle of the imagination, essentially the same.

Many of the starting axioms conflict with each other, so it simply cannot be the case that both are true. For example, secular humanism assumes that the universe was created without any purpose or intelligence, while Christianity assumes that the universe was created for a purpose by intelligence. Objective atheism assumes that human striving is, perhaps, the noblest of all human actions. Buddhism, on the other hand, assumes that human striving is the cause of suffering.

The role of scholars, in particular, should be to continue to explore starting axioms and determine which are "true." (That is a starting axiom for this author.) Scholars also have a responsibility to make explicit what is implicit. Popular sources may allow writings to be published that don't make definitions clear or that include surface-level analyses, but academic scholarship must dig deeper. In the case of the spirituality/religion dichotomy, scholars need to "dig" to the level of the starting axioms and make explicit their own assumptions in writing. Scholars must also insist that published statements adhere to generally accepted criteria for comparison by nearly all belief systems and scholars. Popper (1968), for example, argues for internal consistency and empirical adequacy as uncontroversial criteria. In the case of internal consistency, researchers would rule out, for example, philosophical assumptions such as "there is no absolute truth" because it is a statement offered as an absolute truth, and is, consequently, self-defeating. Empirical adequacy suggests that any data collected pertaining to a starting axiom or underlying assumption should be consistent with that axiom or assumption. For example, if someone held that belief that "people will commit more crimes during difficult economic times," that belief is not consistent with data about crime in the United States through 2010 (Vicini, 2010). The US Federal Bureau of Investigation (FBI) reported a 2.8% drop in crimes against property in the first six months of 2010 (when economic times were much worse than usual). There could be other explanations for why these data don't match the underlying assumption, but the burden would be on the person holding the assumption to provide evidence for why the assumption is still valid.

MSR 2.0

Kuhn (1970) has noted that chaos is a "precondition for the emergence of novel theories" (p. 77) and the foundational concepts for the study of MSR are certainly in that seminal, chaotic phase in which, for example, workplace spirituality can be defined as disparately as "a framework of organizational values" (Giacalone & Jurkiewicz, 2003, p. 13) and as wonder, play, ignorance, spontaneity, joy, imagination, celebration, discernment, insight, and creativity (Mason, 1994). Kuhn's (1970) second edition also included the important addition of a postscript where he introduces the disciplinary matrix that helps define a field in terms of its symbolic generalizations, shared commitments to beliefs, values, and exemplars.

I propose that for MSR to experience the "emergence of novel theories" (Kuhn, 1970, p. 77), the field must push toward greater shared commitments. However, to this point, there are few shared commitments because each author is free to simply stake out positions such as "spirituality is good and religion is bad" or "all spiritual paths lead to the same destination" or "there is only one true God." If authors would go beyond staking out a position and also make explicit the underlying assumption of that position, the field would be able to more easily compare commitments and determine which are more trustworthy than others. That would allow what could be called MSR 2.0.

The "2.0" moniker has been employed to connote the next version, the quantum leap of improvement over what has come before (simple "upgrades" are labeled as 2.1, 2.15, etc.). A quick Google search reveals everything from Gov 2.0 to Classroom 2.0. Perhaps, the most well known of these 2.0 labels is Web 2.0 which was coined by O'Reilly (2005) and incorporates the social media experience into the use of the world wide web. MSR 2.0 would mean that each author would make explicit the underlying assumptions of his work, and going beyond defining how he uses terms such as *religion* and *spirituality* to revealing starting axioms. Idiosyncratic definitions should be strongly discouraged, and, if by necessity they are employed, they must be appropriately validated. For example, Zaidman et al. (2009, p. 617) include an implicit definition of *religion* that "is not concerned with deeper motivations and with existential moments in the life course." It is really incumbent on these authors to justify a definition that is at such great odds with the vast majority of practitioners of organized religions. The broader field of Management still has this problem with terms such as *communication*, *quality*, and *leadership* being employed liberally without definition and validation in many articles.

In considering the state of a field such as MSR, visualize a continuum with one pole labeled "without readily accepted core definitions" and the other pole, "widely accepted core definitions." If various fields were placed along this continuum, it is likely that the more stagnant fields are at the polar ends. In the first case, the published works often read as editorials. At the other end of the spectrum, there are few places to "push the envelope." The ideal position is somewhere between the poles where there are common definitions on essential terms, but enough variance elsewhere to allow for multiple and fresh perspectives. This illustration is analogous to what chaos theory offers, that there is an "edge of chaos" (Dent, 2003) that is the "zone of creative adaptability" (Lewin & Regine, 2000) that lies between stability and chaos. At the moment, the MSR field, in terms of chaos theory, would be considered in chaos.

MSR 2.0 would also mean providing better evidence for claims made in articles and books. Mitroff and Denton (1999, p. 48) write that "religion is more concerned with perpetuating itself than with helping humankind." Such a statement is inconsistent with centuries of data throughout most of the world. As noted in the previous paragraph, it would be helpful to know how these authors define *religion* in this sentence, but assuming they are referring to the major, organized religions of the world, consider the most widely practiced, Christianity, and its role in the United States over the past two centuries. Because of its starting axiom that God revealed Himself in nature, Christianity has been the primary religion promoting science and innovation (Stark, 2005). The Christian church was the primary motivation behind the end to slavery. The Christian church established nearly every college and university founded before 1900. The Christian church founded nearly all of the long-serving benevolence organizations including the American Red Cross, the YMCA, and the Salvation Army. MSR scholars need to provide evidence for important claims in their works or they run the risk of being seen as introducing their own biases and ideologies (which may be appropriate if they are made explicit).

MSR 2.0 also means studying what is real rather than what is supposed. Meta analyses, such as Dent et al. (2005), have shown that the MSR literature lacked empirical studies, although the number of such studies has certainly increased since 2005. Yet, many of the articles published at this stage of the field's development are abstract, conceptual, and theoretical. That may be appropriate for this point in time, but will need to change as the field matures. As Giacalone (2010) noted in his editorial upon assuming the editorship of *Journal of Management, Spirituality and Religion*, "approaches that were acceptable even five years ago become inappropriate due to advances in the field of study" (p. 3). The MSR community of scholars should consider employing the techniques of the evidence-based management (EBM) "movement." EBM approaches began in medicine but got visibility in Management with the publication of *Hard Facts, Dangerous Half-Truths, and Total Nonsense: Profiting from Evidence-Based Management* by Pfeffer and Sutton (2006). Recent work using an EBM perspective has raised serious concerns about some of the most well-read books in management such as *In Search of Excellence* by Peters and Waterman and *Built to Last* by Collins and Porras. It is reasonable to assume that similar critiques of well-read MSR sources will likely question the methodology and decisions of those sources. The Academy of Management began sessions specifically designated as evidenced-based at its conference in 2010. EBM approaches should be especially attractive to the MSR community because they do not insist upon a logical positivist approach, but simply require evidence in whatever form most makes sense. But, there must be evidence of some form.

This chapter has intended to be persuasive in suggesting that everyone operates with a belief system that contains unproven starting axioms. If the term *religion* has been overly provocative, paradigm (Schwartz & Ogilvy, 1979), *weltanschauung* (Slife & Williams, 1995), narrative identity, worldview (Dent, 1999), philosophy, or related terms can be substituted. The main point is to surface and realize that a

> view of the world and human nature informs everyone's life. Everyone lives and operates out of some narrative identity, whether it is thought out and reflected upon or not. All who say "You ought to do this" or "You shouldn't do that" reason out of such an implicit moral and religious position.
>
> *(Keller, 2008, p. 15)*

It is the "ought to do" and the "shouldn't do" beliefs that need to be included even when spirituality, for example, is discussed.

Consider two examples of making explicit a religion or worldview, Gaia Spirituality and Alcoholics Anonymous (AA). Both claim to be spiritual, but not religious. The essential elements of the Gaia Spirituality religion can be readily surfaced. These practitioners believe the earth is "a living being, our ultimate mother, and not to do all we can to preserve and protect her is not only criminally ungrateful, but terminally stupid" ("Gaia Spirituality," n.d.). Using Keller's (2008) criteria for explicating a religious position by looking for what "you ought to do" or "you ought not to do," the website makes these positions clear. Those who inquire if they are a good fit for Gaia spirituality are asked, "Do you care for yourself?" (Do you strive to consume only clean, pure, non-genetically modified food?) "Are you working on your mental and emotional health?" "Do you participate in the life of your community?" (Are you active—and an activist—in the political life of your city, state, nation, and world?) "Are you comfortable working closely with diverse kinds of people—diverse racially, nationally, sexually, etc.?" "Do you care for your mother Earth?" "Do you honor the feminine face of the Divine as well as the masculine?" (Do you honor the solar, lunar, and terrestrial cycles of the natural world)? It is not difficult to see quickly that there are several starting axioms that comprise the religion of Gaia Spirituality.

Likewise, if one views the AA website or its foundational documents such as "A Brief Guide to Alcoholic Anonymous" the following starting axioms jump out—there is a power greater than humans; an individual can turn her or his will over to that power; making amends to people wronged helps maintain sobriety; prayer and meditation improve conscious contact with God (the power); God has a will and people should want to learn it and enact it.

Finally, in the spirit of "walking the talk," I would like to make perfectly clear some of the foundational assumptions of this chapter. Please note that the topic of this chapter has been how MSR research has been conducted, rather than a topic such as spirituality, so these foundational assumptions will be quite different from an article about religion, spirituality, mindfulness, and so forth. Some key assumptions I have made throughout the chapter are that truth is knowable and it is the job of scholars and researchers to investigate and reveal truth (such a statement appears in the founding mission of many universities, such as Harvard University), that clarity in definitions leads to greater understanding, that claims should be substantiated with evidence of some sort, and that the field of MSR will advance more effectively and quickly if researchers surface the underlying assumptions and starting axioms of their investigations.

Notes

1. Note that respondents were asked "What are the main *differences* between religion and spirituality for you?" (p. 191, italics added) but were not asked a comparable question about similarities between spirituality and religion. Moreover, the questionnaire also asked people to rate *religion* and *spirituality*, separately on a 1–7 scale with the polar ends being—tolerant/intolerant, close-minded/open-minded, inclusive/exclusive, and so forth. Consequently, it isn't clear if this "finding" is a result of the methodology employed or a true difference in the respondents.

2. Interestingly, they seem not to have followed their own advice because they didn't make explicit their own ontological and epistemological assumptions about definitions of "religion" and "spirituality." They essentially forced a delineation between religion and spirituality citing Ashmos and Duchon (2000) who merely "conceptualized" a difference. They then also cited the Dalai Lama, as I do here. This forced delineation, though, would be completely foreign to most of the Muslim faith, for example. So, in being clear about their ontological and epistemological assumptions, these authors should make clear that they have "chosen" this delineation, although others could equally legitimately choose otherwise.

References

American Heritage Dictionary of the English Language. (4th ed.). (2006). Boston: Houghton Mifflin.

Amsterdam Declaration (2002). (n.d.). Retrieved from www.iheu.org/adamdecl.htm.

Ashmos, D., & Duchon, D. (2000). Spirituality at work: A conceptualization and measure. *Journal of Management Inquiry, 9*(2), 134–145.

Capra, F. (1975). *The Tao of Physics: An Exploration of the Parallels between Modern Physics and Eastern Mysticism*. Berkeley, CA: Shambhala Publications.

Collins, J. C., & Porras, J. I. (1994). Built to Last : Successful Habits of Visionary Companies. New York: HarperBusiness.

Dalai Lama XIV. (1999). *Ethics for the New Millennium*. New York: Putnam.

Dehler, G., & Welsh, M. (1994). Spirituality and organizational transformation: Implications for the new management paradigm. *Journal of Managerial Psychology, 19*(6), 17–26.

Delbecq, A. L. (2009). Spirituality and business: One scholar's perspective. *Journal of Management, Spirituality, and Religion, 6*(1), 3–13.

Dent, E. B. (1999). Complexity science: A worldview shift. *Emergence: A Journal of Complexity Issues in Organizations and Management, 1*(4), 5–19.

Dent, E. B. (2003). The complexity science organizational development practitioner. *Organizational Development Journal, 21*(2), 84–88.

Dent, E. B., Higgins, M. E., & Wharff, D. M. (2005). Spirituality and leadership: An empirical review of definitions, distinctions, and embedded assumptions. *Leadership Quarterly, 16*(5), 625–653.

Dent, E. B., Parnell, J. A., & Carraher, S. (2018). Developing an instrument to measure objectivism. *Journal of Ayn Rand Studies, 18*(1), 1–23.

Flood, G. D. (1996). *An Introduction to Hinduism*. New York: Cambridge University Press.

Gaia Spirituality. (n.d.). Retrieved from www.gaia-spirituality.org/inquiry.html.

Giacalone, R. A. (2010). *JMSR*: Where are we now: Where are we going? *Journal of Management, Spirituality and Religion,* 7(1), 3–6.

Giacalone, R. A., & Jurkiewicz, C. L. (2003). *Handbook of Workplace Spirituality and Organizational Performance*. Armonk, NY: M. E. Sharpe.

Haught, J. F. (2008). *God and the New Atheism: A Critical Response to Dawkins, Harris, and Hitchens*. Louisville, KY: Westminster John Knox Press.

Hicks, D. (2002). Spiritual and religious diversity in the workplace: Implications for leadership. *Leadership Quarterly, 13*, 379–396.

Hofstadter, D. (1979). *Gõdel, Escher, Bach: An Eternal Golden Braid*. New York: Basic Books.

Jones, E. S. (1931). *The Christ of the Mount*. New York: Abingdon Press.

Keller, T. (2008). *The Reason for God*. New York: Dutton.

Kornfield, J. (2008). *The Wise Heart: A Guide to the Universal Teachings of Buddhist Psychology*. New York: Bantam Dell.

Kuhn, T. S. (1970). *The Structure of Scientific Revolutions* (2nd ed.). Chicago: University of Chicago Press.

Lewin, R., & Regine, B. (2000). *The Soul at Work: Listen … Respond … Let Go*. New York: Simon & Schuster.

Lewontin, R. (1997). Billions and billions of demons. *New York Review of Books, 44*(1), 28–32.

Locke, E. A. (2007). Wisdom: Objectivism as the proper philosophy for living on Earth. In E. H. Kessler & J. R. Bailey (Eds.), *Handbook of Organizational and Managerial Wisdom*. Los Angeles: Sage Publications, 477–504.

McGrath, C. (2007, September 13). Ayn Rand. *New York Times*. Retrieved from http://topics.nytimes.com/topics/reference/timestopics/people/r/ayn_rand/index.html.

Mason, E. S. (1994). Symbolism in managerial decision making. *Journal of Managerial Psychology, 9*(6), 27–35.

Mitroff, I. I. (2003). Do not promote religion under the guise of spirituality. *Organization, 10*(2), 375–382.

Mitroff, I. I., & Denton, E. A. (1999). *A Spiritual Audit of Corporate America: A Hard Look at Spirituality, Religion, and Values in the Workplace.* San Francisco: Jossey-Bass Publishers.

Mohamed, A., Hassan, A., & Wisnieski, J. (2001). Spirituality in the workplace: A literature review. *Global Competitiveness, 9*(1), 644–651.

O'Reilly, T. (2005). What is Web 2.0: Design patterns and business models for the next generation of software. Retrieved from www.oreillynet.com/pub/a/oreilly/tim/news/2005/09/30/what-is-web-20.html.

Peters, T. J., & Waterman, R. H., Jr. (1982). *In Search of Excellence: Lessons from America's Best-run Companies.* New York: Harper & Row.

Pfeffer, J., & Sutton, R. I. (2006). *Hard Facts, Dangerous Half-truths, and Total Nonsense: Profiting from Evidence-based Management.* Boston: Harvard Business School Press.

Popper, K. R. (1968). *The Logic of Scientific Discovery.* New York: Harper & Row.

Prothero, S. (2010). *God is Not One.* New York: HarperCollins Publisher.

Rand, A. (1962, August). Introducing objectivism. *Objectivist Newsletter.*

Rand, A. (1990). *Introduction to Objectivist Epistemology* (Expanded 2nd ed.). Eds. H. Binswanger & L. Peikoff. New York: Meridian.

Rand, A. (1957/2005). *Atlas Shrugged* (Centennial ed.). New York: Dutton, 2005.

Schaeffer, F. A. (1976/2005). *How should We then Live?* Wheaton, IL: Crossway Books.

Scherer, B., & Waistell, J. (2018). Incorporating mindfulness: Questioning capitalism. *Journal of Management, Spirituality and Religion, 15*(2), 123–140.

Schwartz, P., & Ogilvy, J. (1979). *The Emergent Paradigm: Changing Patterns of Thought and Belief.* Menlo Park, CA: SRI International.

Slife, B. D., & Williams, R. N. (1995). *What's Behind the Research: Discovering Hidden Assumptions in the Behavioral Sciences.* Thousand Oaks, CA: Sage Publications, Inc.

Stark, R. (2005). *The Victory of Reason: How Christianity Led to Freedom, Capitalism, and Western Success.* New York: Random House.

Tackney, C. T., Chappell, S. F., & Sato, T. (2017). MSR founders narrative and content analysis of scholarly papers: 2000–2015. *Journal of Management, Spirituality and Religion, 14*(2), 135–159.

Taylor, D. (1999). *The Myth of Certainty: The Reflective Christian and the Risk of Commitment.* Downers Grove, IL: InterVarsity Press.

Torcaso v. *Watkins*, 367 U.S. 488 (1961).

Vicini, J. (2010, December 20). U.S. crime down in 2010, FBI reports. Retrieved from www.reuters.com/article/idUSTRE6BJ3D520101220.

Yang, M. B. (2000). *Reconsidering Ayn Rand.* Enumclaw, WA: WinePress Publishing.

Zaidman, N., Goldstein-Gidoni, O., & Nehemya, I. (2009). From temples to organizations: The introduction and packaging of spirituality. *Organization, 16*(4), 597–621.

9

SPIRITUALITY AND RELIGION AT WORK

Christian Traditions in Action

Edwina Pio and Peter McGhee

A Christian View of Spirituality

Authors often claim that spirituality is a Christian term (Carson, 1994). However, while the words "spirit" (Greek [Gk.] *pneúma*) and "spiritual" (Gk. *pneúmatikos*) appear in the New Testament, the word "spirituality" is not a biblical word. According to Principe (2000), spirituality comes from the Latin word *spiritualitas*, a neologism which combines the Latin noun *spiritus* (spirit) and the adjective *spiritualis* (spiritual). Moreover, Principe states there is no evidence of the word "spirituality" being used prior to CE 5th century, when in a letter historically credited to St. Jerome, the author urges the recipient to "*Age ut in spiritualitate proficias*" (Latin [Lat.] So act as to advance in spirituality). However, if the Latin word *spiritualitas* reflects New Testament understandings, and if the first recoded use of this word urged a life lived according to the Spirit, then the New Testament's use of *pneúma* and *pneúmatikos* stands behind early Christian views of spirituality.

Ideas about the Spirit developed from the Old Testament reflection on the breath or *ruach* of God (Hildebrandt, 1995), and were further advanced by St. Paul in the New Testament where the Spirit was linked almost immediately to the risen Christ (Romans 8:9–11; 1 Corinthians 6:17; 2 Corinthians 13:13; Galatians 4:6, 5:25; and Philippians 2:1). St. Paul also used the adjective "spiritual" for outworkings of the Spirit (Romans 7:14, 1 Corinthians 12:1; Ephesians 1:3, 5:19; Colossians 1:9). And, most importantly, he compared a spiritual person (Biblical Gk. *pneúmatikos anthrōpos*) with a carnal person (Biblical Gk. *psychikos anthrōpos*) (1 Corinthians 2:6–15). From these verses, and others, we infer that a "spiritual person" is one whose life "is under the influence of, or is a manifestation of, the Spirit of God" (Sheldrake, 1992, p. 22). The "worldly person," on the other hand, opposes the workings of the Spirit in his or her life (Fee, 1994). This opposition, for St. Paul, was not between the spiritual and the physical, but between living two different ways. A dualistic contrast is not part of a Christian understanding of the human person or of created reality in general and hence there is no justification for the denial of flesh or a rejection of materiality (Sheldrake, 2000). In a nutshell, for Christians, spirituality is the exercise of the Holy Spirit in our everyday lives, including the workplace. It is about imaging God to the world and the world back to God (McGhee & Habets, 2018).

The Christian Tradition and Work

Tradition (Biblical Gk. *Paradosis*, or Lat. *traditio*), means the revelation made by God and delivered by him to his faithful people through the mouth of his prophets and apostles. It does not mean something "handed down" but something "handed over." The tradition was at first called "apostolic," because it was delivered by the apostles to the Churches they founded, and later also "ecclesiastic" because delivered again in each generation by the Church's teachers to the people. Its substance was held to consist of the central facts and beliefs crystalized in the creeds of the great orthodox bishops (D'Lima, 2018, 7 April). From the beginning of the 3rd century, the tradition was sometimes expressly identified with the Gospel record contained in Scripture. The occasional references in early Christian literature to an "unwritten tradition" left by the apostles appear to relate not to the body of information independent of Scripture, but to the evidence of primitive Christian institutions and customs which confirms scriptural teaching (D'Lima, 2018, 7 April). In a more modern sense, tradition means the continuous stream of explanation and elucidation of the primitive faith, illustrating the way in which Christianity has been presented and understood in past ages (Cross & Livingstone, 2005).

Within this tradition, Christians have long considered the spiritual nature of work. Initially, the emphasis was on the ascetic; work was both a means for, and a constraint to, a higher spiritual life. For example, Clement of Alexandria (*c.* CE 150 to *c.* CE 215) wanted Christians to be "ever labouring at some good and divine work" while at the same time, not being "busy about many things, bending downwards and fettered in the toils of this world" (Volf, 2001, p. 72). The author of the Epistle of Barnabas (*c.* CE 400) saw work as a means to "ransom thy sins" (Volf, 2001, p. 72). In the 6th century, St. Benedict developed a Rule, which codified work norms for monasteries. For instance, he wrote that, "Idleness is an enemy of the soul. Therefore, the brothers should be occupied according to schedule in either manual labour or holy reading" (Jensen, 2006, p. 31). For Benedict, work was seen "as a spiritual exercise and discipline, a penitential practice" (Volf, 2001, p. 73). Later, Thomas Aquinas, in his 13th century *Summa Theologica*, argued work was important because "without which human beings would not be apt for contemplation" (Volf, 2001, p. 70).

The Bible values work and people who work (Meeks, 1989). Its focus is summarized concisely by Jensen (2006), who notes that in Genesis 1:1, God molds creation into existence, thus making His work the source of all that is. At the same time, Genesis points to the importance of human work, as a response to God (Genesis 2:15). The Old Testament, Jensen argues, recognizes the communal dimensions of work; it protects the land and the vulnerable from profiteering and greed (Leviticus 19:9–10). The Sabbath prevents work from becoming an endless drudgery, while cultivating mindfulness about God's work (Exodus 23:10–11). And the Jubilee rules set strict limits to work and the profits from work (Leviticus 25:10). When Israel fails to keep these requirements, the prophets reprimand them (Amos 5:11).

For Jensen, similar attitudes are found in the New Testament. Jesus criticizes those that work at the expense of others (Luke. 6:24–25, 11:46–47). His parables are often set within a work context (Matthew 13:3–8, 13:33; Luke 15:3–7), and that work often changes as it is drawn toward the work of Jesus. Moreover, many of Jesus' parables (Matthew 20:1–16) offer an alternative conception of the value of work:

> it is not in its result or the length of time one has been engaged in work, rather, its value is that *people* are doing the work. In the upside-down values of the reign of God, those without paid work are valued as much as those who begin the work at the crack of dawn.
>
> *(Jensen, 2006, p. 25)*

This alternative conception does not mean people should stop working; indeed, in the life of the early church many remained in secular vocations (Acts 16:14, 18:13). Rather, the New Testament argues that work is valued, not for what it is, but because the doers of work belong to Christ. Ultimately, such work will continue in the afterlife (Revelations 21:6).

The Catholic Tradition

Tradition is not really a manmade reality; it is part of the gift of God, like the word of God that is given to us, it is also the interpreting of the word of God, which is a gift of God (D'Lima, 2018, 20 April). For the Catholic tradition, the Church is the community in which tradition is recognized and authenticated. In time, and because of polemics, tradition was pitted against Scripture, Scripture being seen by Protestants as God's word couched in a written language, whereas tradition was seen as man-made and created by the Church (D'Lima, 2018, 7 April). For Catholics, however, tradition means the ensemble of creed, code, cult, and community, as well as the magisterial teaching as put down in Councils or taught by the Pope (e.g., dogma, doctrine), and the practices of devotion that are man-made.

In recent times, two key Papal encyclicals have developed the relationship between spirituality and work further. The first of these, *Rerum Novarum* (Worker's Charter, 1891), considered the plight of the working class in light of expanding technology, urbanization, and industrialization (Cosden, 2005). This encyclical shifted the historical focus on the soul to include a person's social context (including work) as being important for their spiritual wellbeing. In 1981, Pope John Paul II published the encyclical *Laborem Exercens* (On Human Work). Written on the 90th anniversary of *Rerum Novarum*, this encyclical builds on Pope Leo XXIII's earlier work, while at the same time offering new insights. Cosden describes three key ideas that emerge from this letter. First, work is a means to an end, both for physical and spiritual needs. Second, work has social power; it unites people and builds community. It is in such community, that our humanity is maintained and developed. Finally, work is a fundamental aspect of humanity's existence, and as such is linked with what it means to be created in the image of God. By working, human beings are participating in the activity of the Creator; they image God back to himself.

Next we present two modern exemplars of the Catholic tradition, and seek to reflect their lives and their teachings to workplace spirituality.

Mother Teresa (1910–1997)

Mother Teresa is a figure who devoted selfless acts to aid the poorest of the poor. Her views on spirituality were exemplified by her praxis-in-action illustrated through her work. Of her long life of 87 years, she devoted countless acts of selflessness and support toward those who need it the most (Anthony, 2016), thus epitomizing a Christian tradition of service through the impetus of spirituality. Born in Skopje, Macedonia, 1910, Agnes Bojaxhiu was brought up by her two parents, Nikollë and Dranafile Bojaxhiu. After the tragic death of her father when she was 8 years old, Agnes turned to the Holy Spirit for support and guidance. At the age of 18, she left her mother, home, and country to join the Sisters of Loreto in Calcutta, India. From this point onwards her journey was to assist, support, and provide for individuals who were the poorest of the poor, through exercising spirituality in her daily work.

Established in 1950 by Mother Teresa, the Missionaries of Charity initially comprised 12 devoted members. Of these members, several were Mother Teresa's previous students from her days of teaching at St. Mary's High school in Calcutta. Residing in a small, abandoned building, the Missionaries of Charity adapted a parallel lifestyle to the living conditions of their poor neighbors. This notion was an act of sharing the same suffering in order to develop a greater understanding and thus a deep determination to help India's poorest of the poor. In the context of modern work this can be translated as managers/senior leaders going back to basics to truly understand the lived experience of their employees and then creating policies and actions which focus on community wellbeing. Missionaries were bound to a strict work schedule of 18 hours, 6 days a week, providing to the community, with disregard of age and religion. The Missionaries of Charity was later renamed Nirmal Hirday, "Pure Heart," reflecting their compassion and acceptance to those who were homeless, suffering from leprosy, unable to afford food, had no access to drinking water, medical care, or basic education (Ćwiękała-Lewis, 2015). In 2015, there were 4500 Sisters of Charity serving in over 600 locations in 123 countries globally. Mother Teresa also opened a Children's House, solely providing for unwanted babies left at the Mission's doorstep and abandoned children who lived on the streets of Calcutta.

Mother Teresa noted that people have been smothered by possessions, the love of money, and the things money can buy (Serge, Chenard, & Senechal, 2013). Work, she asserted, must have a purpose beyond money, in order to manifest the workings of the Spirit. Interestingly, Mother Teresa argued that it is not just about helping the community, but also about physically sharing their suffering. An example of this was her initially feeding her 12 members of the Missionaries of Charity plain rice as a staple diet for their main meals. Mother Teresa initially struggled to gain the trust of the people of Calcutta. The surrounding community believed her selfless deeds were merely an act to convert individuals to Catholicism. However, over time, the people of Calcutta found that this was not her intention. Mother Teresa did not discriminate individuals of different religions but welcomed them with open arms. During her lifetime, Mother Teresa was awarded with internationally recognized honors, for example, the Key to the City from the New York Mayor Edward Koch in 1985, the Jewel of India, symbolic of the nation's highest honor, and the Nobel Peace Prize (Brind'Amour, 2007).

Clad in a simple white sari with a blue border, she inspired millions with her fierce will, deep devotion to God, and relentless pursuit for doing good. The white symbolizes peace and charity, reflecting the underlying purpose of those who wear it. The blue bands are representative of the three vows her nuns must take; poverty, obedience, and dedicating their services to the poorest of the poor (Williams, 2002). She believed that "peace begins with a smile" and "if you can't feed a hundred people then just feed one" (Pio, Kilpatrick, & LeFevre, 2017), thus displaying how every person, irrespective of their status at work and in life, can live out the divine plan in their lives.

Pope Francis (1936…)

Bishop of the slums, Jesuit, Pope of surprises, Pope of paradox, radical Pope, the Great Reformer … Jorge Mario Bergoglio was born to Italian immigrants in lower middle class Buenos Aires barrio of Flores in Argentina (Ivereigh, 2014; Vallely, 2013/2015). He knew his four grandparents and their wisdom helped him develop a moral, cultural, managerial, and religious reservoir. On March 13, 2013, Bergoglio became the 266th pope of the Roman Catholic Church, the first non-European in more than a millennium, the first from the Jesuit religious order, and the first to take the name Francis. The name Francis is drawn from the 13th century mendicant St. Francis, known as the saint of the poor, a man of peace and poverty, who loved and protected creation. Bergoglio, when asked in the conclave of cardinals, if he accepted the vote to become pope, replied not with the traditional "Accepto" but the words: "I am a great sinner, trusting in the mercy and patience of God in suffering, I accept" (Stanford, 2014). Such humility and simplicity in the service of the world is a cornerstone of Christian spirituality.

Pope Francis, with amazing speed, has become a rock star through using 21st century technology for a 1st century role, through his emphasis on humility, prayer, mercy, and grounding himself in his pastoral role with merriment, while rejecting the pomp and privileges of his office. He broke with centuries of tradition, when instead of living in the Apostolic Palace he chose to live in a simply furnished room in the Vatican guesthouse. He visited a juvenile detention center and cleaned the feet of the inmates, including two Muslim women, for the Holy Thursday ceremony, bucking tradition, as the usual practice is to wash the feet of priests. He believes that the church has locked itself up in small things and small minded rules. The Pope through his actions and life seeks to engage with the messiness of humanity, and this is a clarion call for how persons can engage with spirituality in their everyday lives. The Pope does this through a *kairos* of mercy, and asks that we show mercy in renewing and revitalizing the church, and affirming human dignity with generous practical action (Francis, 2014; Ivereigh, 2014).

The Pope emphasizes that the Lord never tires of forgiving and individuals can ask for grace to ask for forgiveness, for God forgives with a caress not a decree. He focuses on the centrality of mercy. The word mercy derives from *misericordis* which means opening one's heart to wretchedness, and the Pope insists that we can all be part of the solution of our complex world where millions suffer under political oppression, are hungry, lacking in nourishment, and living in poverty. In his apostolic exhortation *Evangelii Gaudium*—the joy of the gospel—he exhorts every person to be a missionary disciple, for each one can make the world a better place through living our faith and our actions. In like manner, he challenged bishops to walk among the people to be pastors and remember the smell of the sheep. He has refocused emphasis on the healing mission of the church. Unlike his recent predecessors who were professors of theology, Francis is a former janitor, nightclub bouncer, chemical technician, and literature teacher (Chua-Eoan & Dias, 2013). He says the church must work "to eliminate the structural causes of poverty" and adds that while "the Pope loves everyone, rich and poor alike … he is obliged in the name of Christ to remind all that the rich must help, respect and promote the poor" (Chua-Eoan & Dias, 2013, p. 2). The five words that have come to define both the promise and the limits of Francis' papacy came in the form of a question: "Who am I to judge?" Francis begins, ends, and dots his day with prayer. He reminds his followers that there are three obstacles which may prevent spirituality in action and these are wealth, vanity, and pride. His inspirational leadership style is one of role modeling with a focus on core competencies and care for the vulnerable. He believes that business is a noble profession, but it must lead people to God (Gregg, 2017; Whaples, 2017).

His papal style can be construed as emanating in some measure from the spiritual exercises of the founder of the Jesuit order, Ignatius of Loyola. Executives who practice the spiritual exercises of the Jesuit founder Ignatius of Loyola, termed Ignatian executives by Lecourt and Pauchant (2011), exhibit leadership attitudes influenced by spiritual values which in turn influence organizations. There are six important categories of this spiritual practice and management in organization: decision-making, human resource management, the organizational mission, social responsibility, career development, and the meaning of work. Furthermore, these executives seek to mesh their work with those who suffer various forms of disadvantage such as racial discrimination or those with disabilities, and they see profits as a means to doing good for the community. Thus, wholeness, knowledge, and social justice are key to finding God in all things as epitomized in these Ignatian practices (Woods, 2015).

Pope Francis also embraces complexity and acknowledges the risk of a church obsessed with its own rights and righteousness which could wound rather than heal. For this, and many other actions:

> In a very short time, a vast, global, ecumenical audience has shown a hunger to follow him. For pulling the papacy out of the palace and into the streets, for committing the world's largest church to confronting its deepest needs and for balancing judgment with mercy, Pope Francis is TIME's 2013 Person of the Year.
>
> *(Gibbs, 2013)*

The Protestant Tradition

In 1517, a German monk called Martin Luther published his "Ninety-five Theses" and inflamed a spark that would become the Protestant Reformation. The main themes of the Reformation were the purification of the church and the idea that the Bible, not church tradition, should be the only source of authority. Apart from these, Luther, and his fellow reformers (e.g., Ulrich Zwingli and John Calvin), railed against the notion that only the clerical class had a spiritual calling, and that only church work had value (Volf, 2001). Countering this view, the reformers argued that all work was spiritual, and that all believers had a calling. Luther, for example, believed that all Christians had a spiritual and a worldly vocation. The spiritual call was internal to the believer; it was God's call on their life. The external call was to serve God in the world through one's work (Jensen, 2006). For Luther, there were two calls but both came from the same source, the Spirit of God.

An early convert to Luther's ideas, John Calvin applied them all to human conduct. He wrote:

> We are consecrated and dedicated to God, and therefore, should not henceforth think, speak, design, or act, without a view to His glory … Let this, then, be the first step, to abandon ourselves, and devote the whole energy of our minds to the service of God.
>
> *(1560, III.vii–1)*

For Calvin, every human action (including work) has value because God calls us to it, by his Spirit, in order that we might glorify Him. Developments in the 17th and 18th century saw a narrowing of this broad definition to two main aspects: duty and occupation (Stevens, 1999). Callings became "a means of serving God and sustaining God's world through supporting oneself, family and commonwealth" (p. 77). At this point, ideas of religion, work, and lifestyle began to merge. Ultimately, this perspective became the bridge between ancient views of work and our modern understanding most clearly identified in Max Weber's (1905/1976) Protestant Work Ethic.

Despite this, the core idea of being called by the Spirt of God to our work, which images God to the world and back to Himself, has remained consistent in much of Protestant thought (Cosden, 2005). Next, we discuss two exemplars of modern Protestant thought on spirituality and religion at work: Dorothy Sayers and Miroslav Volf.

Dorothy Sayers (1893–1957)

Dorothy Sayers was the daughter of an Anglican clergyman. She was born and raised in Oxford, England and studied at Oxford University where she gained a first class honors degree in modern languages. She was a well-known author of detective novels in an age where woman did not publish in this genre (Galli & Olsen, 2000). She also established her reputation as a religious writer with a series of plays (e.g., *The Zeal of thy House, The Man Born to be a King*). And from 1940 she published several works containing studies, lectures, and essays on theological topics.

These writings, as in her plays, provided fresh and penetrating insights into the meaning of Christianity in the modern world (Cross & Livingstone, 2005).

Her deliberations on work came primarily from a lecture called *Why Work*, later published in a book called *Creed or Chaos*. In this essay, Sayers (1949/2011) compares work with the act of divine creation; we are to view it as:

> A way of life in which the nature of humanity [*sic*] finds its proper exercise and delight and so fulfils itself to the glory of God. That it should, in fact, be thought of as a creative activity undertaken for the love of the work itself; and that human beings [*sic*], made in God's image, should make things, as God makes them, for the sake of doing well a thing that is well worth doing.
>
> *(p. 15)*

By elevating human beings to the status of creator, Sayers portrays human work as participating in the creation via the Holy Spirit. Thus, as a creative activity, work acquires a new dignity that makes it a proper inquiry in its own right. This should lead us to "ask of an enterprise, not, will it pay?" but rather, "is it good?" and of ourselves, not "what do we make?" but rather, "what is our work worth?" (p. 18). From this idea, three propositions arise.

First, work is not simply about making money to live but, rather, it is something one does to be fully human, to reflect the image of God. According to Sayers (1949/2011), we find "spiritual, mental, and bodily satisfaction, and the medium in which we offer ourselves to God" (p. 18). Failure to view work thus confuses means with ends, and alienates us from our labor. Second, work is a vocation, whether it be secular or not. Our labors "serve God, and the work itself must be accepted and respected as the medium of divine creation" (p. 21). Consequently, work that is contemptible, soul destroying, or harmful, that is, work unreflective of God's image within us, is unacceptable. Moreover, because our labors serve God, "Christian work is good work well done" (p. 23). If we focus on the demands of our work, then this is a guarantee that divine ends will also be met and met well (Breclaw, 1993). Finally, Sayers (1949/2011) claims, "the worker's first duty is to serve the work" (p. 24). By serving the work, we put God before ourselves. When we serve the community first, we make human beings the measure of all things. By putting the work first, we ensure our hearts are fully in it, thus producing "good work." Work that "is not good serves neither God nor the community; it only serves Mammon" (p. 25). Such a focus also ensures our sense of debt is not to others; rather the work becomes our reward. Consequently, we are less likely to falsify our work to please others. If we take these ideas as foundational, then several implications transpire for Christians in modern workplaces.

The gap between the sacred and secular is non-existent. Christians "are uniquely equipped and have a duty to provide a new and proper attitude towards work, informed by theological beliefs regarding human nature and God's purpose for humanity" (Miller, 2011, p. 10). Building on ideas from the Reformation, Sayers argues work is a holy calling from God, who uses it to build His kingdom (Harrison, 2004). We have the potential to take ordinary work that may be neutral in its content and purpose, and imbue it with meaning and value through the Spirit of God that resides within, and works through, each of us.

A Christian's reward comes from the satisfaction of doing the task well; this is their divine act of creation. Payment need only be enough to ensure that the work continues, and for a reasonable living standard (Harrison, 2004). Valuing work thus, minimizes the appeal of dehumanizing and degrading jobs, even if they pay well. Moreover, if we do the work for which God gifts us, then we reduce the problem of cheap labor, and of pursuing the highest paid occupations, since neither are conducive to growing God's kingdom. Admittedly, as Miller (2011) notes, this may not always be possible in developing countries and lower socio-economic contexts. However, if these ideas were implemented, then such contexts may become redundant.

Regarding work as a pleasure and privilege means Christians change their attitude toward leisure. Instead of viewing leisure as the best part of life, and trying to get through the working week as quickly as possible, we "should look on our leisure as the period of changed rhythm that refreshes us for the delightful purpose of getting on with our work" (Sayers, 1949/2011, p. 20). This shift in perspective ensures that we fight to make our work good. As Sayers writes, "there would be protests and strikes—not only about pay and conditions, but about the quality of the work demanded and the honesty, beauty and usefulness of the goods produced" (p. 21). Rather than regarding work as something to avoid, Christians are to give it primacy, to make it the end of our being. If we love our created work, then we display love for God who created all things through the Son and by the Spirit—including us (Harrison, 2004).

Miroslav Volf (1956…)

Miroslav Volf was born in Osijek, Croatia, which was then part of the Socialist Federal Republic of Yugoslavia. As a consequence of living through the Balkan war in the 1990s, he forged a theology of forgiveness and non-violence (Short, 2005), about which he has written several books. Perhaps his best known work, *Exclusion & Embrace*, was written in response to a question posed to him, "But can you embrace the cetniks [the Serbian fighters who killed Croatian woman and children during the war]?" (Volf, 1996, p. 9). Other areas of theological focus have included the nature of Christian community, the public role of faith, and human work. Educated in Croatia, the United States, and Germany, Volf has doctoral and post-doctoral degrees from the University of Tübingen in Germany. He is currently the Director of the Yale Center for Faith and Culture at Yale University and considered "one of the most celebrated theologians of our day" (Williams, 2005, p. 9).

Volf (2001) argues that the Protestant idea of calling (or vocation) needs revamping in modern society. He offers several reasons for this. Calling tends to emphasize the individual at the expense of the community, while also endorsing the status quo thereby tying people to menial work and unfulfilling jobs, especially in developing economies. Moreover, in modern organizations, there are significant challenges in balancing one's internal and external call; often the need for security, status, and wealth override a person's spiritual inclinations. Finally, there is difficulty adapting the concept to the social mobility of modern societies, where regular job change and dual occupations are common.

Volf's solution is that of the "new creation" whereby our work contributes, via the Spirit, to God's eschatological transformation. In other words, our labors co-participate with God in the redemption of the world. How does the Spirit accomplish this? He gifts (*charisms*) us the ability to work in ways that exhibit the values (i.e., the fruits of the Spirit—love, joy, peace, patience, kindness, goodness, faithfulness, gentleness, and self-control) of God's new creation. This means certain principles guide our actions in "structuring the reality of human work" (p. 81); principles reflective of these values, and reflective of what God ultimately desires for His world.

What difference does Volf's (2001) approach make? First, it clarifies the notion of calling. All Christians have the same call from the Father, through the Son, and by the Spirit to participate in God's redemptive plan. Work is not ideological, but rather is a spiritual partnership with God on "the project of the new creation" (p. 116). Second, this approach ensures individuals can change jobs. Switching roles does not infer a lack of faith; rather it is a new way of living out one's spiritual call. Such variation does not create uncertainty as Luther argued (Jensen, 2006), nor does it encourage laziness as the Puritans feared (Weber, 1905/1976). What we do is not important, rather the person who works receives a call to which his or her talents (*charisms*) make an adequate response feasible.

Perhaps most importantly, Volf's (2001) approach helps evaluate "good work." He argues in this present world, some forms of work are not part of God's plan for His new creation. Work not influenced by the Spirit (i.e., work unreflective of spiritual values such as peace, love, joy, kindness, patience, and so on), is work that does not cooperate with God and, therefore, is of little value from a Christian perspective. Rather, Volf writes, such labors interact with the evil powers that scheme to ruin God's good design. For example, using sweatshop labor does not reflect the values of the Spirit, and it does not collaborate with God to make the world a better place. Contrast this with work done in the Spirit—the Bible describes this as precious and eternal (cf. 1 Corinthians 3:12–15).

Along similar lines, we can gauge "meaningful work." From a Christian perspective, work that participates in God's new creation is always meaningful, even if at the time it does not seem apparent, because it provides the building blocks for God's eschatological *transformatio mundi* (Volf, 2001). Conversely, work contra the Spirit is often dehumanizing and destructive of creation, and ultimately meaningless, since it does not participate in God's plan for the world. For example, work that damages the environment disproportionately is unlikely to be meaningful from a Christian viewpoint because it destroys God's good creation, and does not anticipate what is to come.

Volf (2001) claims that as Christians, we live in the era of the Spirit. We are the first fruits of this new era, given gifts to work with God in the restoration of the world. Instead of a functional view of work, Christians determine that good and meaningful work contributes to the flourishing of others, and anticipates and reflects what is to come, a creation in perfect communion with God. Such a perspective should, in principle, reduce any sense of alienation Christians feel in their work, while minimizing the exploitation of others for instrumental ends. Correspondingly, it should encourage personal autonomy and development of individuals, while re-appropriating the communal dimension of work. In practice, this might include such things as caring for the marginalized, manufacturing in sustainable ways, avoiding cheap labor, paying a living wage, and largely operating in ways that honor God, the environment, and human beings.

Managerial Implications

What do these two related Christian traditions (Catholic and Protestant) tell managers about modern work? And how do these four dissimilar individuals (a saint, a pope, an author, and a theologian) enlighten us as to how Christian spirituality might be applied in modern organizations? Below are several implications for managers.

For Christians, work is a spiritual gift from God, and thus should be directed back to Him; it is an important means of imaging God back to himself (McGhee & Habets, 2018). Managerial emphasis on the substantive ensures work becomes the practice and nurturance of God's gifts, rather than a more functional box ticking and meeting profit targets exercise (Jensen, 2006). Many Christians want to excel at work because they view it as a calling, not just a job, and see it as a means of blessing (or thanking) God. Thus, their labor is its own reward (Sayers, 1949/2011). Managers who legitimize Christians in exercising their Spirit-led talents freely and fully are likely to reap significant benefits. For instance, evidence suggests that religiosity/spirituality augments employee wellbeing (Arnetz et al., 2013; Crawford, Hubbard, Lonis-Shumate, & O'Neill, 2009; Kolodinsky, Giacalone, & Jurkiewicz, 2008; Tejeda, 2015) and enhances decision-making (Fernando, Dharmage, & Almeida, 2007; McGhee & Grant, 2017; Phipps, 2012).

The Spirit of God is the source of all life (Moltmann, 1997). God's willingness to share His Spirit with us should underpin our own sharing and interdependence with others (Jensen, 2006). When work is hoarded or owned exclusively by others, workers can experience alienation from their labors and/or exploitation at the hands of the rich and powerful (Volf, 2001). Managers responding to the divine life within them, by contrast, should do everything they can to avoid such outcomes. How might this be achieved? Jensen (2006) suggests three ways. First, spread ownership across all workers, and/or amplify workers' voices in management decisions. In doing so, workers are not merely valued for utilitarian ends, but are grounded in who they are and whose they are, for all belong to God. Second, move away from conflictual strategies in the workplace. Instead of the zero-sum game that characterizes much of management–employee engagement, focus on abundance and sharing. The Spirit demonstrates that when good work is shared, then the bounty increases. After all, both management and employees want the same thing, "the creation of good products and services; the maintenance of a decent standard of living that comes, in part from good labor; and the continued ecological sustainability of work practices" (p. 103). Finally, reject the hyper-specialization of workers that results from a focus on efficiency at any cost. Any system that values ends over people is idolatrous since it violates the principle of respecting workers for who they are and for whose they are. Several methods such as job enrichment, job rotation, increased training and development, and increased worker autonomy and co-determination can all reduce such "Taylorism" (Prujit, 2000).

Individuals such as Mother Teresa and Pope Francis, who personify a lived, and fully engaged, spirituality with the world can inspire all Christians, as well as those from other faith traditions, to respect and love the marginalized, the outcast, the hungry, the poor, and the oppressed. Indeed, such behavior was incarnate in, and modeled by, Jesus Christ, who came to save the lost, to set the captives free, and to empower the last, while humbling the first. Global market capitalism, while improving the living standards of many, has led to widespread inequality between the haves and the have nots (Moe-Lobeda, 2002; Volf, 2001). Such disparity, whether it be wealth, gender, or ethnicity, contributes to many adverse economic and social outcomes (Wilkinson & Pickett, 2010). Managers who emulate the Christian tradition can display a praxis-in-action through working for the flourishing of both the organization and the community.

At an operational level, this means enhancing diversity, improving compensation structures for the least well off, reversing the use of contingent workers, and resisting the overall increase in employment insecurity (Riaz, 2015). At a strategic level, this involves transforming the dominant schema of organizations from that of technocratic egocentrism (Gull & Doh, 2004), to: (1) a deeply held shared compassion for human and non-human stakeholders (including the environment); (2) a value system built around openness, transparency, and service; (3) a focus on humility that recognizes all good gifts come from God and are to be distributed fairly; and (4) a long-term perspective that partakes in and hopes for the renewal of creation (Walsh & Keesmat, 2004). At a societal level, this necessitates reflecting on how products and/or services might contribute to economic deprivation. For instance, subprime mortgages did not reduce inequality, instead they kept families in financial lack through high interest rates and eventual foreclosures (Mahmud, 2012).

Finally, Christian spirituality surpasses the dual vision inherited from Greeks, augmented by René Descartes, and so prevalent in our modern organizational worldview (Giacalone, 2004), that the spiritual and physical are opposed realities. The Spirit of Christ makes the transcendent immanent; God is here and now, there is no insuperable abyss. Thus, our primary identity as Christians connects us with our material reality. Indeed our flourishing is inextricably tied to the flourishing of the earth. Pope Francis (2015), in a recent encyclical, "On care for our common home," articulates a similar idea. He argues that the "human environment and the natural environment deteriorate together; we cannot adequately combat environmental degradation unless we attend to causes related to human and social degradation" (p. 33). Contrary to popular belief, Christianity does not present a license for humanity to exploit nature. Instead it offers a moral foundation for environmental stewardship, upholds the intrinsic value of nature, and provides hope for the future. Thus, Christian managers should think of business, society, and nature as interconnected, and act in ways that enhance this system so that all life can flourish.

Conclusion

Throughout Christian history, work has been viewed both as a curse and as a means of fulfillment. In every age, work has been unavoidable, even if the topic has not held the explicit attention of most Christian theologians. Our experience of work at times reflects our estrangement from God, and at other times reproduces our communion with the Creator. Although work is a necessity, it is also a gift of creativity, of communion, and of co-creation with God (Jensen, 2006). When our work responds to that gift, we catch a glimpse of good and great work in action. While Christians often vary in their theology and practice, when it comes to work they all share a deep longing for the Spirit of God to be among people, and in their labors, as together they redeem creation and show God's love to the world.

References

Arnetz, B. B., Ventimiglia, M., Beech, P., DeMarinis, V., Lökk, J., & Arnetz, J. E. (2013). Spiritual values and practices in the workplace and employee stress and mental well-being. *Journal of Management, Spirituality and Religion, 10*(3), 271–281.

Anthony, C. (2016). The spirituality of Mother Teresa. *Australasian Catholic Record, 93*(4), 469–477.

Breclaw, K. E. (1993). Homo faber reconsidered: Two Thomastic reflections on work. *Thomist: A Speculative Quarterly Review, 57*(4), 579–607.

Brind'Amour, K. (2007). Mother Teresa (1910–1997). Retrieved from https://embryo.asu.edu/pages/mother-teresa-1910-1997.

Calvin, J. (1560). *Institutes of the Christian Religion* (H. Beveridge, Trans. 1845). Edinburgh: Calvin Translation Society.

Carson, D. A. (1994). When is spirituality spiritual? Reflections on some problems of definitions. *Journal of the Evangelical Theological Society, 37*(3), 381–394.

Chua-Eoan, H., & Dias, E. (2013). Pope Francis: The people's pope. Retrieved from http://poy.time.com/2013/12/11/person-of-the-year-pope-francis-the-peoples-pope/.

Cosden, D. (2005). *Theology of Work: Work & the New Creation.* Eugene, OR: Wipf & Stock.

Crawford, A., Hubbard, S. S., Lonis-Shumate, S. R., & O'Neill, M. (2009). Workplace spirituality and employee attitudes within the lodging environment. *Journal of Human Resources in Hospitality and Tourism, 8*(1), 64–81.

Cross, F. L., & Livingstone, E. A. (Eds.). (2005). *The Oxford Dictionary of the Christian Church* (3rd ed.). Oxford: Oxford University Press.

Ćwiękała-Lewis, K. J. (2015). Mother Teresa: Nurse and woman healer. *Polish Nursing, 58*(4), 430–432.

D'Lima, E. (2018, 7 April). The Catholic tradition. *Personal Correspondence.*

D'Lima, E. (2018, 20 April). Conversations with theologian Dr. Errol d'Lima. *Personal Correspondence.*

Fee, G. D. (1994). *God's Empowering Presence.* Peabody, MA: Hendrickson.

Fernando, M., Dharmage, S., & Almeida, S. (2007). Ethical ideologies of senior Australian managers: An empirical study. *Journal of Business Ethics, 82*(1), 145–156.

Francis, P. (2014). *The Church of Mercy.* London: Longman & Todd.

Francis Pope, I. (2015). *Laudato Si'.* Retrieved from http://w2.vatican.va/content/francesco/en/encyclicals/documents/papa-francesco_20150524_enciclica-laudato-si.html.

Galli, M., & Olsen, T. (2000). *Christians Everyone should Know.* Nashville, TN: Holman Bible Publishers.

Giacalone, R. A. (2004). A transcendent business education for the 21st century. *Academy of Management Learning and Education, 3*(4), 415–420.

Gibbs, N. (2013, December 11). Pope Francis: The choice. Retrieved from http://poy.time.com/2013/12/11/pope-francis-the-choice/?iid=poy-article-featured-content-widget.
Gregg, S. (2017). Understanding Pope Francis. *Independent Review, 21*(3), 361–374.
Gull, G. A., & Doh, J. (2004). The "transmutation" of the organization: Towards a more spiritual workplace. *Journal of Management Inquiry, 13*(2), 128–139.
Harrison, W. H. (2004). Loving the creation, loving the Creator: Dorothy L. Sayer's theology of work. *Anglican Theological Review, 86*(2), 239–257.
Hildebrandt, W. (1995). *An Old Testament Theology of the Spirit of God.* Peabody, MA: Hendrickson.
Ivereigh, A. (2014). *The Great Reformer: Francis and the Making of a Radical Pope.* London: Allen & Unwin.
Jensen, D. H. (2006). *Responsive Labor.* Louisville, KY: Westminster John Knox Press.
Kolodinsky, R. W., Giacalone, R. A., & Jurkiewicz, C. L. (2008). Workplace values and outcomes: Exploring personal, organizational and interactive workplace spirituality. *Journal of Business Ethics, 81*(2), 465–480.
Lecourt, V., & Pauchant, T. (2011). Ignatian spirituality & management: A study of Ignatian executives. *Journal of International Business Ethics, 4*(1), 18–27.
McGhee, P. K., & Grant, P. (2017). The transcendent influence of spirituality on ethical action in organizations. *Journal of Management, Spirituality and Religion, 14*(2), 160–178.
McGhee, P. K., & Habets, M. (2018). Priests of creation, mediators of order: Taking God to work. In T. Ewest (Ed.), *Faith and Work: Christian Perspectives, Research and Insights into the Movement.* Charlotte, NC: IAP, 77–96.
Mahmud, T. (2012). Debt and discipline. *American Quarterly, 64*(3), 469–494.
Meeks, M. D. (1989). *God the Economist.* Minneapolis, MN: Fortress Press.
Miller, D. W. (2011). Foreword. In D. Sayers, *Why Work?* McLean, VA: Trinity Forum, 3–14.
Moe-Lobeda, C. D. (2002). *Healing a Broken World: Globalization & God.* Minneapolis, MN: Fortress Press.
Moltmann, J. (1997). *The Source of Life* Minneapolis, MN: Augsburg Press.
Phipps, K. A. (2012). Spirituality and strategic leadership: The influence of spiritual beliefs on strategic decision making. *Journal of Business Ethics, 106*(2), 177–189.
Pio, E., Kilpatrick, R., & LeFevre, M. (2017). Navratna—the nine gems: Illuminating enablers, barriers and vignettes of South Asian women leaders. *South Asian Journal of Business Studies, 6*(3), 1–17.
Principe, W. (2000). Toward defining spirituality. In K. J. Collins (Ed.), *Exploring Christian Spirituality.* Grand Rapids, MI: Baker Book House, 43–59.
Prujit, H. (2000). Repainting, modifying, smashing Taylorism. *Journal of Organizational Change Management, 13*(5), 439–451.
Riaz, S. (2015). Bringing inequality back in: The economic inequality footprint of management and organizational practices. *Human Relations, 68*(7), 1085–1097.
Sayers, D. (1949/2011). *Why Work?* McLean, VA: Trinity Forum.
Serge, L., Chenard, G., & Senechal, C. (2013). The dark sides of Mother Teresa. *Studies in Religion-Sciences Religieuses, 42*(3), 319–345.
Sheldrake, P. (1992). *Spirituality and History: Questions of Interpretation and Method.* New York: Crossroads.
Sheldrake, P. (2000). What is spirituality? In K. J. Collins (Ed.), *Exploring Christian Spirituality: An Ecumenical Reader.* Grand Rapids, MI: Baker Books.
Short, R. (2005). *God's Advocates: Christian Thinkers in Conversation.* Grand Rapids, MI: Eerdmans.
Stanford, P. (2014). *Pope Francis Anniversary.* Retrieved from www.telegraph.co.uk/news/worldnews/the-pope/10678510/Pope-Francis-anniversary-Ive-done-things-well.-Ive-done-things-wrong.html.
Stevens, R. P. (1999). *The Other Six Days: Vocation, Work, and Ministry in Biblical Perspective.* Grand Rapids, MI: Eerdmans.
Tejeda, M. J. (2015). Exploring the supportive effects of spiritual well-being on job satisfaction given adverse work conditions. *Journal of Business Ethics, 131*(1), 173–181.
Vallely, P. (2013/2015). *Pope Francis Untying the Knots: The Struggle for the Soul of Catholicism* (rev. and expanded with nine new chapters). London: Bloomsbury.
Volf, M. (1996). *Exclusion & Embrace.* Nashville, TN: Abingdon Press.
Volf, M. (2001). *Work in the Spirit: Toward a Theology of Work.* London: Oxford University Press.
Walsh, B. J., & Keesmat, S. C. (2004). *Colossians Remixed: Subverting the Empire.* Downers Grove, IL: IVP Academic.
Weber, M. (1905/1976). *The Protestant Ethic & the Spirit of Capitalism* (2nd ed.). London: George Allen & Unwin.
Whaples, R. (2017). The economics of Pope Francis. *Independent Review, 21*(3), 325–345.

Wilkinson, R., & Pickett, K. (2010). *The Spirit Level: Why Greater Equality makes Societies Stronger.* London: Bloomsbury.

Williams, P. (2002). *Mother Teresa.* Indianapolis, IN: Alpha Books.

Williams, R. (2005). Foreword. In M. Volf (Ed.), *Free of Charge: Giving and Forgiving in a Culture Stripped of Grace.* Grand Rapids, MI: Zondervan, 9–10.

Woods, J. (2015). Conversations with Jesuit Dean Rev. James Woods. *Personal Correspondence.*

10

AT THE INTERSECTION OF YOGA AND LEADERSHIP

Humility as a Practice

Susanna Kislenko

> When an individual has achieved complete understanding of her true self, she will no longer be disturbed by the distracting influences within and around her.
>
> *(The Yoga Sutras of Patanjali)*

> Yoga is a journey and so is leadership. And yoga has its own different lineages, different schools of yoga, different traditions who have their own pathway. And leadership is also a journey. And I would hope that leadership would be a journey to a deeper understanding of oneself in the world ... my leadership journey is also a spiritual journey ... it's about wholeness and oneness.
>
> *(Interviewee #13)*

Introduction

The dissemination of yoga across the world, from East to West has been rapid since it was first brought to the West in the 1960s through celebrities like the Beatles, inspired by the teachings of Maharishi Mahesh, the father of transcendental meditation (Feuerstein, 2006). Up until the middle of the 20th century, yoga and its philosophies were not much known or studied outside South East Asia, with the practice originating in India itself. The word *yoga* means "union" in the ancient language of Sanskrit and in its purest sense is a mental, rather than a physical practice. It was only once the practice and traditions of yoga were brought to the West that the physical postures known as *asanas* and the breath component, *pranayama*, were brought to light (Olsen, 2014). The first wave of people bridging East and West practices and making yogic principles palatable for the global masses included B. K. S. Iyengar, whose texts remain the center of yoga teacher training programs around the world (Feuerstein, 2006). Although much of the widespread dissemination of yoga and yogic principles to the West took place in the latter part of the 20th century, this holistic practice owes its origins to sages and practitioners that lived over 5000 years ago (Samuel, 2008). Patanjali, an Indian sage from the second century BC, wrote *The Yoga Sutras* to explain how to live a life in balance (Adhia, Nagendra, & Mahadevan, 2010) and it is these sutras that guide yoga practice around the world today.

In a similar way, the study of leadership and its principles can be traced back to ancient philosophers in the East, back to sixth century BC with Lao Tzu, and in the West with Machiavelli and Plato (Bass & Bass, 2009). Leadership, however, did not become a true discipline of its own until the mid-1940s. Today, leadership remains one of the most debated and heated topics in business academia and beyond. In the context of this project, a distinction is made between leader development—an expansion of individual capacity toward leadership effectiveness—and leadership development, which is focused on the aggregate leadership capacity of an organization (Day, 2017). As the focus of this study is the change within the individual themselves as the result of a yogic practice, it is leader development that is the topic of interest. Although leadership was initially thought to be trait-based and stemming from genetic predispositions, current thinking on leader development shows that a great deal of leadership capabilities can be taught and learned (Day & Sin, 2011; Day & Dragoni, 2015; Day, 2017; Hammond, Clapp-Smith, & Palanski, 2017).

This chapter is focused on weaving the philosophical underpinnings of yoga and leadership, universally accepted concepts and practices in an effort to understand the way in which yoga influences leaders, leadership as a whole, and leader development in particular. As explained within the sections that follow, the findings of this study point to the significant influence of yoga on leader development, primarily centered on elements of humble service, being human by example, and tuning in through the practice of presence.

Yoga Practice and Leader Development

Much of the existing literature that brings together yoga and leadership originates in South East Asia. Specifically, there have been a number of attempts to prove and test the assertion of James McGregor Burns that "transformational leaders raise followers to higher levels of morality" (Mulla & Krishnan, 2012, p. 85). In the South East Asian context, this is evaluated through the lens of karma yoga. As it is explained,

> the word "karma" comes from the Sanskrit root *kri*, which means, "doing, affairs or activity" and includes all actions that a person performs, whether they are of body, speech or mind. The word "yoga" comes from the Sanskrit root *yuj*, which means "to join".
>
> *(Mulla & Krishnan, 2012, p. 31)*

Karma yoga is further interpreted as "made up of two dimensions: a sense of obligation or duty towards others and an absence of desire for rewards" (Mulla & Krishnan, p. 33). The literature from mostly India and Sri Lanka has found that there is, in fact, a relationship between yoga (karma yoga in particular) and transformational leadership specifically (Narayanan & Krishnan, 2003; Mulla & Krishnan, 2008; 2009; 2012; Satpathy, 2013).

As noted by Bass,

> Superior leadership performance—transformational leadership—occurs when leaders broaden and elevate the interests of their employees, when they generate awareness and acceptance of the purposes and mission of the group, and when they stir their employees to look beyond their own self-interest for the good of the group.
>
> *(1991, p. 21)*

One of the few studies that has merged yoga and leadership outside South East Asia looked at the effect of yoga on the potential of entrepreneurship traits being cultivated within university students (Marques, Ferreira, Rodrigues, & Ferreira, 2011). The study concluded that yoga contributes to the encouragement of typically accepted entrepreneurial traits such as autonomy, creativity, self-control, and self-esteem (Marques et al., 2011). These were also confirmed as being more general leadership traits, based on evolutionary understandings of leaders (Van Vugt, 2006).

Methodology and Case Selection

Using best practices for qualitative methods design (Golden-Biddle & Locke, 2007; Pratt, 2008; 2009) when the topic itself is understudied or in its nascent stages (Yin, 2013) such as the topic in question, this is an inductive study using semi-structured interviews. To support the way in which yoga might influence leadership, 14 semi-structured interviews were conducted with individuals who live and work at the intersection of yoga and leadership, either as yoga teachers who teach leaders or executive leaders (in the non-profit, for-profit, or public spheres) who are practicing yoga regularly. The interviews were conducted between January 2015 and July 2016 with individuals residing in Canada, Spain, Germany, and the US (a full list of interviewees appears in the Appendix to this chapter). An interview protocol was developed and used as a guide during each interview, adjusting as necessary based on the particular nature of the conversation (Miles & Huberman, 1994; Yin, 2013).

All interviews were transcribed by the author, aligned with best practices of staying close to the data (Yin, 2013) comprising a total of 87 transcripted pages at a cumulated length of 7 hours and 24 minutes. A personal meditation journal of one of the interviewees was also used to supplement the interviews themselves. All interviews were conducted either in person or over Skype and took place in either English or Spanish, depending on the language the interviewee was more comfortable using.

Findings

Using the Gioia methodology for data analysis (Gioia Corley, & Hamilton, 2013), the data collected provided the following aggregate dimensions: humble service, human by example, and tuning in. Figure 10.1 illustrates the data structure, capturing first order concepts, second order themes, and the aggregate dimensions in question.

Humble Service

A number of the interviewees highlighted the way in which a steady yoga practice supports the release or transcendence of the ego and thereby the promotion of humility within the leadership process. This idea was closely intertwined with seeing beyond oneself as an individual leader and supporting the growth of the collective as well as the larger concept of being of service. As one leader who is a long-term yoga practitioner explained,

> the fact that it's the kind of practice that requires you to let go of your ego, I find that very interesting because that's something that I struggle with a little bit. So it kind of puts me in my place and reminds me about how much I have to grow.
>
> *(Interviewee #1)*

This was a common sentiment among the various leaders interviewed. One long-term political and non-profit leader explained the particular leadership approach from a service-oriented perspective,

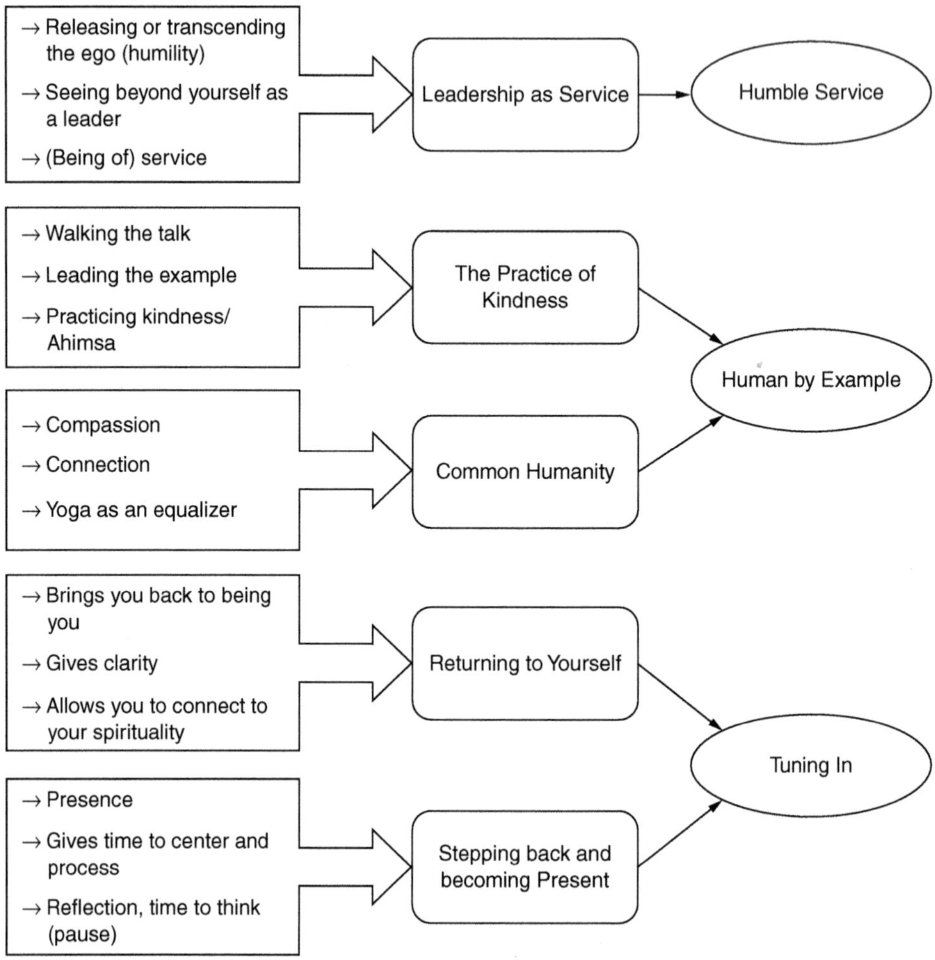

Figure 10.1 Data Structure for the Influence of Yoga Practice on Leader Development

> I try to lead by letting people actually do it themselves. Just pulling them back to make sure that they are in sync with the goal we have agreed to. What I try to do is inspire. I try to show an example and live that so that it's real, it's not just words. I try to let people have their part of it and figure out their own answers themselves.
>
> *(Interviewee #2)*

The leaders interviewed had common views about the perspective that having a regular yoga practice provided, one that forces an immediacy of internal questions associated with the way in which the individual defines themselves in their leadership role and, as a consequence, what type of leadership style and behavior this leads to. A leadership consultant who is also a yoga practitioner explained it this way,

> Also, the focus of attention being above or beyond themselves, beyond the ego which also links back to leadership. So what's your impact and how do you lead. From what

> center do you lead? Do you lead from the center here in your mind, do you lead from your egoistic center or from a holistic center?
>
> *(Interviewee #7)*

The nature of the yogic approach is as a form of service and this requires a release or a transcendence of the ego in that,

> if you can detach your own ego, you can actually unlock potentially what you didn't know was there.
>
> *(Interviewee #1)*

Human by Example

Beyond the transcendence of the ego, much of the discussion of the way in which a yoga practice affects leader development was centered on walking the walk, leading by example, and the practice of kindness, which is action-oriented and is known by the word "ahimsa" in yogic understandings (Interviews 3, 7, 8, 11). Intertwined with the practice of kindness, many of the interviewees described yoga's ability to bring people together in a common understanding of the human experience, comprising compassion and connection. Yoga, in many instances, was referred to as an equalizer that inspired the understanding of a common humanity. A long-term yoga teacher and practitioner explained it this way,

> I try to walk the talk as much as I talk about it. So just by acting in the class in a true yogic way of having non-judgement, having compassion, love emulating, you know just that we're all connected in an incredibly spiritual way.
>
> *(Interviewee #5)*

When discussing the benefits of his yoga practice, one interviewee explained,

> Anything that has to do with duality is I find not what I get in yoga. I find yoga is about coming together. Mind, body, spirit. It's you, in the company of other people, all doing the same thing. It's very empowering. Yoga is … a great equalizer.
>
> *(Interviewee #2)*

A long-term yoga practitioner and executive leader in the non-profit sector explained that,

> it's realizing that you are permitted to get to know somebody on a different level. And that is part and parcel of working with people. And if you are moving an organization along, you're leading an organization, that can't be done in absence of the knowledge and connections with the people that you work with. It just simply can't.
>
> *(Interviewee #1)*

Yoga seems to allow people the opportunity to find a common ground and this seeps into the manner of leadership of the practitioner,

> So not only compassion for others, but compassion for yourself. So I really learned that through yoga … just having great compassion for people. And I think that that really has helped me in all of my businesses dealings. Just being, you know, compassionate

> and open and understanding and understanding others in a way that I have never understood others before. Because I have a great compassion for them. No judgement. That's been, I think, one of the biggest things that yoga has given … truly. The compassion and the connection. Connection to people. We are all connected. And it doesn't matter if we're presidents or if we're, you know, custodians, we're all the same. And we can all learn a lot from each other and be more … just have lots of compassion for each other.
>
> …So you can see how helpful that would be to leadership. Just understanding the human condition on a much deeper level.
>
> *(Interviewee #5)*

Tuning In

In essence, yoga has been found to provide clarity, bringing the individual back to themselves and allowing all human beings to connect with our spiritual core. In order to truly return to oneself, there is a need to step back and become present, which gives one a chance to pause and reflect as well as to center and process the situation at hand, a skill that is invaluable for leaders especially in the context of decision-making.

One long-term executive leader simply stated,

> It gives you time to yourself in a physical, spiritual combination that eases some of the pressures of leadership. That you're not actually thinking about it. It brings you back to being you.
>
> *(Interviewee #2)*

This sentiment was echoed by a yoga teacher who often teaches leaders:

> I think that's what this is all about. Becoming present so that you can really experience the moment so that you can really do the best work.
>
> *(Interviewee #3)*

A leadership consultant who is an avid practitioner herself explained the principles or presence and centering as being two of the primary contributions of a yogic practice toward the benefit of leaders:

> And do you know what? It's the presence. I think the highest thing has been the presence. Cause it's not something I talk about. It's something people experience and they find themselves there. Through that. It allows them to connect with who they are. With who they are and at intimate levels where they wouldn't have gone otherwise or they wouldn't have experienced before. I think that's the highest impact of yoga in my work.
>
> And that has to do with centering. With finding your center and acting from there. Which links back to mindfulness, which links back to how you, what impact you have and what vibration do you send? And therefore, what vibration do you receive back when you act from that state of being. How much more capable you are to deal with issues, external issues, when you act from that point. Clarity of mind, perspective.
>
> *(Interviewee #7)*

From the leader development perspective, the benefit of the centering and presencing is associated with making decisions, one of the primary leadership tasks (Antonakis & Day, 2017);

> that I think yoga helps you in a way exercise your mind because you get into this very calm and centered place.
>
> When you are using your mind to make these difficult decisions all the time, you know you don't have really time to think. Maybe exercising the mind is the wrong way of putting it. Maybe it's resting it, I don't know. It does help you I think.
>
> It does help you I think become a better decision maker. The process of, sort of, reaching that calm place allows your brain to get used to achieving some clarity.
>
> *(Interviewee #2)*

In her experience of practicing yoga for nearly two decades and being in leadership roles for much of that time, one of the interviewees shared that yoga,

> helps center me and to allow me the time to process things. I don't think that leaders typically have enough time to process what's around them and it forces me to take that time. And I usually almost … like if I go into a practice stressed out and bursting with some big items that are on my mind, I always come out of that practice in a much better place, much more prepared to deal with something. The situation has been processed, even without really thinking about it too much. I've just emotionally gotten my head around it and I'm in a much better place to deal with it. It has that mechanism of slowing you down.
>
> *(Interviewee #1)*

Through stillness comes a sense of clarity, a way of being able to connect to our voice within.

> the all-knowing guru that lives inside of each of us. That if we just spend time reflecting on that, the answers come to you. So sometimes if you are looking for answers everywhere else, you have to take a moment and just focus on the guru within, the answers are revealed. So yoga has a very interesting and magical way of dealing with things. And it's a humble practice. It doesn't claim to have these amazing benefits, but somehow it does.
>
> *(Interviewee #1)*

A long-term executive leader in the for-profit sector who discovered yoga more recently described the change that occurred and the way her yoga practice came to influence many aspects of her life,

> I think it brought a certain level of calmness into my life. My professional life was very hectic. It was very dynamic. Constantly changing situations. Dealing with fires a lot. People situations. Business situations. All kinds of challenges and I became calmer after I started doing yoga because I think on some deep level, this ability to calm down and to relax mentally, I brought it back with me to work.
>
> And it became easier not to react right away, not to jump. Not to hectically look for solutions, but rather calm down and take my time. Perhaps to breathe and then to truly take a look at the situation in being more calms and almost becoming more

> philosophical about situations. And I think that definitely it was noticed by people who work with me and I was even asked, "Are you doing yoga?" You are calmer.
>
> *(Interviewee #6)*

Presence and a sense of calmness that comes as a result of being in tune with oneself was mentioned often when discussing the influence of yoga on leadership practices.

> One is being present. In the moment. I think that is very important and there's few times in my life that I've enjoyed that outside of my practice where I remembered to be completely present in the moment, not thinking too far ahead and not thinking too far behind. And remembering, quite frankly, the only moment that you can change is the moment that you're in. You don't have any influence over the past and you don't have any influence over the future that is real or tangible.
>
> *(Interviewee #1)*

Another long-term leader stated that he sees "yoga as an important part of being able to connect to myself and to sort of a calm place." He further explained,

> That's just how I see it. It just took me to being calm. Instead of everything sort of being ups and downs, it felt more like I was on … when I was on doing yoga and now in my professional work it feels more like I'm on a path. A river.
>
> You know, I still have to maybe paddle and enter the flow, but there's a flow. Instead of being at the intersection of three rivers in the midst of big boils and big waves.
>
> *(Interviewee #2)*

Conclusion and Further Reflection

Over recent decades, the topic of humility has begun to surface within the study of leadership and effective leader traits (Collins, 2001; Nielsen, Marrone, & Slay, 2010; Owens & Hekman, 2012). It is a trait that has made its way into leader development literature (Antonakis & Day, 2017) but as yet more on the periphery of the practice. In many ways, "leader humility is still viewed as a rare personality trait that somewhat mysteriously produces favorable organizational outcomes" (Owens and Hekman, 2012, p. 787). In addition to being mysterious in its effects, humility also appears elusive in terms of how to achieve it.

Connecting humility with ideas of being able to see beyond oneself and the release of the ego, this study has shown that yoga is one path toward humble leadership. When combined with yoga's ability to allow the leader to connect with themselves, become present and narrow in on the common human experience, yoga provides a valuable form of support for traditional methods of leader development. Moreover, yoga promotes the idea of leadership as service and being kind as a form of displayed leadership behavior that aligns with finding an element of humility in the practice of leadership, just as within the practice of yoga. A number of the long-term leaders interviewed who found yoga later in their careers expressed a common sentiment,

> From my perspective now, I don't think it's possible to overestimate the positive connection between the practice of yoga and success as a leader.
>
> *(Interviewee #2)*

Appendix

Table 10.A.1 Interviews

Interviewee	*Location*	*Description*	*Practicing Yoga in Years*
1.	Canada	Long-term non-profit executive	18
2.	Canada	Former political leader/current non-profit executive	2
3.	Canada	Yoga teacher/social worker/teaches leaders	14
4.	Canada	Musician and activist	1.5
5.	Canada	Long-time yoga practitioner and yoga teacher	20
6.	USA	Former long-term executive in the for-profit sector	3
7.	Spain	Yoga practitioner and leadership coach	1.5
8.	Spain	Yoga teacher/manager of a large gym and studio	20
9.	USA	Long-term yoga teacher who teaches leaders	12
10.	USA	Long-term yoga teacher who teaches leaders	20
11.	Canada	Long-term yoga practitioner and leadership expert	22
12.	Spain	CEO of large health company	15
13.	Canada	Long-term yoga practitioner and writer/activist	17
14.	Germany/India	Yoga teacher/clothing designer who teaches leaders	5–6

References

Adhia, H., Nagendra, H. R., & Mahadevan, B. (2010). Impact of adoption of yoga way of life on the emotional intelligence of managers. *IIMB Management Review, 22*(1), 32–41.

Antonakis, J., & Day, D. V. (Eds.). (2017). *The Nature of Leadership*. Thousand Oaks, CA: Sage Publications.

Bass, Bernard M. (1991). From transactional to transformational leadership: Learning to share the vision. *Organizational Dynamics, 18*(3), 19–31.

Bass, B. M., & Bass, R. (2009). *The Bass Handbook of Leadership: Theory, Research, and Managerial Applications*. New York: Simon & Schuster.

Collins, J. C. (2001). *Good to Great: Why Some Companies Make the Leap and Others Don't*. New York: Random House.

Day, D. V. (2017). The nature of leadership development. In J. Antonakis & D. V. Day (Eds.), *The Nature of Leadership*. Thousand Oaks, CA: Sage Publications, 108–140.

Day, D. V., & Dragoni, L. (2015). Leadership development: An outcome-oriented review based on time and levels of analyses. *Annual Review of Organizational Psychology and Organizational Behavior, 2*(1), 133–156.

Day, D. V., & Sin, H. P. (2011). Longitudinal tests of an integrative model of leader development: Charting and understanding developmental trajectories. *Leadership Quarterly, 22*(3), 545–560.

Feuerstein, G. (2006). A short history of yoga. Retrieved from www.traditionalyogastudies.com/articles_short_history.html.

Gioia, D. A., Corley, K. G., & Hamilton, A. L. (2013). Seeking qualitative rigor in inductive research: Notes on the Gioia methodology. *Organizational Research Methods, 16*(1), 15–31.

Golden-Biddle, K., & Locke, K. (2007). *Composing Qualitative Research*. Thousand Oaks, CA: Sage.

Hammond, M., Clapp-Smith, R., & Palanski, M. (2017). Beyond (just) the workplace: A theory of leader development across multiple domains. *Academy of Management Review, 42*(3), 481–498.

Marques, C. S., Ferreira, J., Rodrigues, R. G., & Ferreira, M. (2011). The contribution of yoga to the entrepreneurial potential of university students: A SEM approach. *International Entrepreneurship and Management Journal,* 7(2), 255–278.

Miles, M. B., & Huberman, A. M. (1994). *Qualitative Data Analysis: A Sourcebook*. Beverly Hills, CA: Sage Publications.

Mulla, Z., & Krishnan, V. (2009). Do transformational leaders raise followers to higher levels of morality? Validating James MacGregor Burns. Hypothesis in the India Context Using Karma-Yoga, presented at

Annual Conference for the Administrative Sciences Association of Canada (ASAC), June 2009, Niagara Falls, Canada.

Mulla, Z. R., & Krishnan, V. R. (2012). Transformational leadership and karma-yoga: Enhancing followers' duty-orientation and indifference to rewards. *Psychology and Developing Societies, 24*(1), 85–117.

Narayanan, J., & Krishnan, V. R. (2003). Impact of Sattva and Rajas Gunas on transformational leadership and karma yoga. *Journal of Indian Psychology, 21*(2), 1–11.

Nielsen, R., Marrone, J. A., & Slay, H. S. (2010). A new look at humility: Exploring the humility concept and its role in socialized charismatic leadership. *Journal of Leadership and Organizational Studies, 17*(1), 33–43.

Olsen, P. E. (2014). Namaste: How yoga can inform leadership education. *Journal of Leadership Education, 13*(1), 116–125.

Owens, B., & Hekman, D. (2012). Modeling how to grow: An inductive examination of humble leader behaviors, contingencies and outcomes. *Academy of Management Journal, 55*(4), 787–818.

Pratt, M. G. (2008). Fitting oval pegs into round holes: Tensions in evaluating and publishing qualitative research in top-tier North American journals. *Organizational Research Methods, 11*(3), 481–509.

Pratt, M. G. (2009). From the editors: For the lack of a boilerplate: Tips on writing up (and reviewing) qualitative research. *Academy of Management Journal, 52*(5), 856–862.

Samuel, G. (2008). *The Origins of Yoga and Tantra: Indic Religions to the Thirteenth Century*. Cambridge, UK: Cambridge University Press.

Van Vugt, M. (2006). Evolutionary origins of leadership and followership. *Personality and Social Psychology Review, 10*(4), 354–371.

Yin, R. K. (2013). *Case Study Research: Design and Methods*. Thousand Oaks, CA: Sage Publications.

PART III

Conscious Foundations of Spirituality

11

TURNING INWARD TO CONNECT OUTWARD

Paving a Motivational Path in Today's Workplace

Joan Marques

Where Did All the Meaning Go?

One of the most enduring concerns in contemporary workplaces is lack of meaning, closely followed by lack of engagement. This notion has been stated on multiple forums in the past decade or more. Singer (2011) notes, "A large percentage of employees admit to being unhappy with and psychologically disengaged from their jobs" (p. 12). The enduring nature of this problem becomes apparent through the consistency with which it has recurred in various sources over the past decade or more. In 1999, Mitroff and Denton already noted that workforce members no longer want to pigeonhole their emotions and feelings. "The search for meaning, purpose, wholeness, and integration is a constant, never-ending task" (p. xv). Tablan (2015) underscored this stance as follows: "Meaningful work is both an economic and a moral issue. It is closely associated with motivation and is a significant aspect of employee satisfaction" (p. 291) Elaborating on workforce members' desire to find meaning at work, Mitroff and Denton asserted, "They especially want to be acknowledged as whole persons in the workplace, where they spend the majority of their waking time" (1999, pp. xv–xvi). Sheep (2006) stresses that now, more than in the early 20th century, workforce members feel that they should not be considered a mere set of hands to do the work, but rather whole persons with feelings and emotions like all others, and Lips-Wiersma and Morris (2009) reaffirm that "The interest in meaningful work has significantly increased over the last two decades" (p. 491). Regarding the lack of engagement, Williams (2010) posits that human resource (HR) professionals have detected an increase in grievance reports, filed on grounds of bullying and harassment in the workplace, and warns that this pattern lies at the foundation of a decline in employee engagement.

Three Seasoned Motivation Theories

The above statements support the notion that the two problems mentioned at the beginning of this chapter—lack of meaning and lack of engagement—often go hand in hand. Workforce members frequently link their sense of meaning to the atmosphere in their workplace, which is predominantly determined by the connections they have with supervisors and colleagues. In workplaces where there is a close sense of togetherness and collaboration, there will be less dissatisfaction, even if the work itself is not very inspiring. Singer (2011) refers to the large number of psychological job studies that keep stressing the importance of employee involvement, as it conveys a sense of caring about their wellbeing, and fulfills their need of ownership. This leads to the notion that part of employees' idea of "meaning" at work is derived from their sense of belonging. The realization that emotions and feelings about work and the work environment are important contributors in the sense of job satisfaction has also been a regular topic of attention. Wärna, Lindholm, and Eriksson (2007), for instance, conducted a study on personal virtues to health and a sense of meaning at work, and listed "the virtues of pride, generosity, love and honesty as important in working life" (p. 191).

Both of the issues discussed here present elements of some seasoned motivational theories, such as Maslow's Hierarchy of Needs, McGregor's Theory Y, and Herzberg's Motivation–Hygiene Theory.

Maslow's theory, arguably the best known of these three, discusses the aspiration of human beings to attain self-actualized states (Udechukwu, 2009). Udechukwu clarifies that Maslow identified five basic needs that motivate humans. Ranked in the order they surface, the needs are: (1) physiological, (2) safety, (3) love or belongingness, (4) esteem, and (5) self-actualization. Maslow's critical notion in presenting his theory was that an unmet need may create an impetus to seek it, yet, once a need is satisfied, it no longer serves as a motivator, and therefore no longer drives behavior. This, then, is how higher order needs become the next level of motivating forces (Udechukwu, 2009).

McGregor's Theory Y, as McDonald (2010) summarizes its essence, "advocates that employees are ambitious, innovative and capable of self-motivation and self-control, provided managers create the right conditions (environment) and incentives (rewards)" (p. 634). Clem and Mujtaba (2010) expand on McGregor's full theory, which actually consists of two dimensions: X and Y. They first explain Theory X: "Theory X simply states that workers are inherently lazy and need a great amount of oversight to make them productive" (p. 5). Subsequently, Clem and Mujtaba (2010) address theory Y: "Theory Y is just the opposite, stating that employees want to work and will perform their jobs and that managers should make sure workers have the resources necessary to achieve organizational goals" (p. 5). Clem and Mujtaba conclude that Theory Y is more widely accepted as a management theory, due to its constructive nature and its ability to streamline the organization's goals and those of its employees. The author of this chapter frequently explains McGregor's theories X and Y in connection with one another and clarifies that they are actually self-fulfilling prophecies: a manager who approaches his or her subordinates as if they are lazy and unreliable sends out a negative message, and will usually not find his or her employees to be proactive and driven. A manager, who communicates and behaves as if he or she trusts and relies upon subordinates, has a much better chance to receive the encouraged or envisioned attitude.

Herzberg's Motivation–Hygiene theory distinguishes between environmental factors such as the workspace and co-workers—the "hygiene factors"—and internal perceptions such as meaning extracted from the work itself—the "motivators." Herzberg's hypothesis is that the hygiene factors are responsible for the absence of dissatisfaction, while the motivators are responsible for the sense of satisfaction in a worker. Sachau (2007) summarizes Herzberg's motivation hygiene theory as follows: "Herzberg challenged basic assumptions about what satisfies and motivates employees by claiming that pay contributes little to job satisfaction, all employees need to grow psychologically, and interpersonal relations are more likely to lead to dissatisfaction than satisfaction" (p. 378). Sachau also makes the interesting observation that Herzberg's theory has been considered controversial and unsubstantial, and almost declared dead, but that current positive psychology research brings to the surface a number of findings that are highly consistent with Herzberg's disparaged Motivation–Hygiene theory. Sachau therefore suggests to resurrect this theory, not in its micro-concept, but as a meta-theory that helps to explain, for instance, why more money matters as a motivator to a person in poverty, but not to a person who has his or her basic needs met. Herzberg's general advice to HR managers was to go easy on the hygiene factors, among which salary and other extrinsic rewards, so that workers' minimal needs in that regard are met, but mainly focus on the motivators, which involve intrinsic rewards such as a sense of meaning with the work one does, because these motivators will ensure longitudinal gratification.

As indicated by Sachau, Herzberg has a point there, because today's massive cluster of knowledge workers is looking at a much higher rate for meaning in what they do than ever before. This trend, while not tested through research, could be explained as follows: there is a greater disconnect between contemporary work, especially in countries such as the US, and its end results. Due to the service focus of the majority of jobs in this country, and the shift toward a knowledge based economy, we oftentimes don't see what our daily efforts ultimately lead to, as opposed to those who directly create something that they can see or feel. In other words: our system has progressed to greater service orientation and less manufacturing, and, while our rational mind may understand that, we are still human beings with a desire to witness the fruits of our labor and rejoice in that.

Udechukwu (2009) compares Maslow's hierarchy of needs theory with Herzberg's theory and draws the conclusion that Herzberg's work describes satisfaction horizontally, which resulted in a distinction between satisfaction and no satisfaction.

> Herzberg suggested that if an employee experiences a low level of job satisfaction, it does necessarily imply that the employee is dissatisfied.... Equally, if an employee experiences a low level of job dissatisfaction, it does not imply that the employee is satisfied.
>
> *(p. 79)*

Udechukwu subsequently concludes that Maslow chose to describe the phenomenon of satisfaction vertically, which created a more rigid picture of "met or unmet, strictly satisfied or not satisfied" (p. 79).

Regardless of how the theories of Maslow and Herzberg are perceived, however, the message ultimately coincides: more money only serves as a motivator when that need has not yet sufficiently been met, but stops being a driving force once it is satisfied. Perceived this way, both Maslow and Herzberg basically draw the same conclusion. Where Maslow refers to the basic needs (physiological and safety), Herzberg refers to hygiene factors (income, environment, the work itself); and both stress that when these needs are fulfilled, it is no use to multiply them indefinitely, as they will not increase the level of satisfaction. Providing these factors will only ensure no dissatisfaction, according to Herzberg's theory. However, the higher level needs in Maslow's hierarchy (sense of belonging, esteem, and self-actualization needs) are very compatible with Herzberg's motivators, which, according to his theory, are the real sources of satisfaction (intrinsic rewards, such as achievement, recognition, the work itself, responsibility, advancement, and growth). This, then, proves the coherence in both theories, even though one theorist reviewed the sequence vertically (Maslow), while the other (Herzberg) reviewed them horizontally.

Dealing with Loss of Meaning and a Sense of Disengagement

Based on the above discussion of the established motivational theories, it becomes apparent that the problem of today's workforce, lack of meaning and a sense of disengagement, lies in the higher level needs section of Maslow's hierarchy, which equals the motivators in Herzberg's theory: the absence of intrinsic rewards. There are numerous ways to approach this problem. In a review of Daniel Pink's 2006 book *A Whole New Mind*, Camplin (2011) praises Pink's ideas about the transition humanity seems to be going through, from excessive left hemisphere (of the brain) thinking, to a more balanced approach in which right hemisphere finally obtains a more prominent function. Further citing Pink's work, Camplin (2011) explains, "The left hemisphere of the brain is sequential, literal, functional, textual and analytic.... Left-brain thinking dominated education, feeding workers to the 'hardheaded organizations' during the Information Age (e.g., computer programmers)" (p. 43). The right hemisphere of the brain is the part that focuses on aesthetic, metaphorical, contextual, simultaneous, and synthetic issues. It is where the artistic and creative elements get encouraged, and it is also the side that has been grossly undervalued all through the 20th century when the industrial era was at its height. It is Pink's conviction that we are now shifting from the Information to the Conceptual Age, where creativity, empathy, and the ability to see the big picture, increasingly matter. Intrinsic motivation will finally be recognized as an honorable driving motive, and the erroneous notion of ever more money and other factors that have been saturated as needs, will finally fade (Camplin, 2011).

When therefore the sense of meaning is still suffering from a change in general working conditions in contemporary workplaces, as became apparent in recent decades, and we additionally have to deal with excessive and enduring aggression from co-workers, a negative cycle emerges. Seeing this cycle increases our understanding as to why we face such high percentages of unhappy workforce members who don't have a solid notion about ways to improve their circumstances. Considering, on top of everything, the strong individualistic environment in which we perform, where everyone has been programmed to fight for his or her own progress, where things change continuously, and where there is no real job security, the picture becomes painfully clear: we start feeling disconnected from our work, our colleagues, and even our own sense of gratification.

Moving Toward a Solution

Our current generation of workforce members is not only suffering from the disadvantages of a volatile workplace. There are many advantages that have emerged in the past decades as well. One of these advantages is the increased access to other cultures and, therefore, alternative ways to solve problems. With the abundance of information that can be accessed through the Internet, either through formal channels such as news, educational, and governmental sources, or through informal channels such as self-promotional and social networks, a multitude of strategies are being presented to those who are seeking for gratification, and the average human awareness level is on the rise. This was already clear near the end of the previous century, when Alexander (1998) delineated that the dynamic shifts in information availability and networking options, along with workforce challenges, demanded new problem solving skills, a sharper focus on core competencies, and increased cross-cultural awareness and interpersonal skills.

In the next section, two possible ways in which workforce members can recapture their sense of meaning will be discussed: (1) exploring the entrepreneurial route, and (2) adjusting the attitude toward the current workplace.

Exploring the Entrepreneurial Route

The entrepreneurial experience should not be limited to those who start their own business. Baines, Bull, and Woolrych (2010) point out that this is the narrow definition. Entrepreneurial behavior can also be exerted by workforce members who want to take more ownership over their daily experiences. It is known that entrepreneurs have a greater internal locus of control. That means that they take more responsibility for their actions, and first seek fault within themselves for everything that goes wrong. Entrepreneurship today is seen as the act of recognizing and pursuing opportunities, creating value, and bringing innovative change. People who think entrepreneurially engage in constructive networking, take responsible risks, and are proactive (Baines et al., 2010).

When referring to the entrepreneurial route, as done here, there are two interpretations possible. One can fulfill the most basic implementation of entrepreneurial thinking by actually deciding to exit the corporate workplace and starting a business or nonprofit in which he or she sets his or her own rules and creates his or her own performance environment. The advantage of doing this is that one can decide how he or she wants to develop the business, what size to maintain, what direction to get into, and the like. In doing so, one eliminates having to deal with difficult co-workers, because one becomes the owner of the business, and therefore hires whomever he or she prefers.

The other option is to implement the broader, contemporary interpretation of entrepreneurship, by remaining in the corporate work environment, but shifting one's paradigm toward entrepreneurial thinking. In this case one can swiftly and without any outward changes adopt the mindset of being a supplier of services to one's employer. By taking this stance, one elevates his or her perspective of the workplace to one of equality. Suddenly there is no self-pitying employee anymore, but an equal partner who can decide whether he or she wants to maintain this work relationship or not. In his book *The Brand You 50*, Peters (1999) encourages his audience to shift their mindset into seeing themselves as CEOs of "Me, Inc." and transform themselves into a brand. It is this very personal paradigm shift that can help workforce members to start seeing problems as opportunities for growth and learning, and convert their victimized mindset into an equal one. By adopting this mindset, one might find him- or herself acquiring a greater sense of responsibility over his or her performance, and a decreased concern with what "difficult" co-workers have to say.

Attitudinal Adjustment at Work

While the adoption of the entrepreneurial mindset within the corporate environment also entails an attitude adjustment, it touches on a different, more aggressive plane than the one to be discussed next. The attitude adjustment discussed in this section is one that grows from a devoted effort toward adopting a wisdom mentality, where one engages in deep reasoning, and then realizes the impermanence of everything. Thus far, the awareness of impermanence has mostly been interpreted in light of insecurity at work as Pfeffer (2003, p. 29), for instance, asserts:

> The loss during the past 10 years of security in employment, as both business and government downsize, merge, use temporary employees, subcontract, and outsource their services and production overseas, has left behind workplaces characterized by fear, pressure, and *impermanence*, with employees who are less loyal, less committed, angrier, and more disaffected.

The view of impermanence that emerges in this particular attitudinal adjustment is from a much greater magnitude. A more expansive picture of life and its capriciousness becomes manifest and the small things no longer instigate enduring negativity. All of this ties in with the awareness of impermanence that Thich (2007, pp. 8–9) refers to when he states:

> Impermanence … refers to the transient nature of all things. From moment to moment, all things in this world, including human life, mountains, rivers, political systems, are in constant transformation. This is called impermanence in each moment. Everything passes through a period of birth, maturity, transformation, and destruction.

Through this expanded awareness, one develops a sense of empathy for all co-workers, as one now also understands the greater connection that exists with his or her co-workers. This expanded awareness also leads to the understanding that it is no use to take things personally, because one can never understand fully what other people's motives are behind their actions. In workplaces particularly, we often deal with behavior that is difficult to digest. As Vasconcelos (2010) states it: "It is not uncommon for workers to face unfriendly relationships, new and further assignments, poor organizational climate, and aggressive bosses, in their workplaces. This contributes to an unhealthy organizational frame in the 21st century" (p. 369). Schein (1992) presents the analogy of an iceberg when reviewing organizational cultures: about 90% of it is invisible beneath the surface, so it can be easily misinterpreted. It is, however, not only the organization's culture that could be compared to an iceberg: its members could too. Co-workers also have histories of experiences and perceptions that are invisible to their environment, yet very influential in the ways they behave and perceive matters. People often act in response to the fears and preconceived notions they are dealing with, which may affect their behavior toward certain co-workers who may remind them of these past troubles. By realizing that people usually have problems with their own mental baggage rather than with others, and that they just substitute their issues in the person or group that most resembles them, one can develop a greater level of willingness to collaborate, even with the most difficult co-worker.

Turning Inward to Understand Interbeing

An attitude change is not implemented easily. Attitudes usually change when a change of perspectives occurs. However, it usually requires a transfixing experience, either on the extreme high end or the extreme low end, in a person's life to change his or her perspectives. In their review of four possible paths toward creating a spiritual workplace, Kinjerski and Skrypnek (2008) refer to this phenomenon as "The path of transformative events" (p. 324), which they explain as "a process that had occurred in response to a crisis or a spiritual awakening" (p. 324). In their book *True North*, George and Sims (2007) refer to these transformative events as crucibles, just as Bennis and Thomas (2002) labeled them earlier. A crucible is an experience that tests an individual to his or her limits. "It can be triggered by events such as confronting a difficult situation at work, receiving critical feedback, or losing your job" (George & Sims, 2007, p. 46). The difficult situation can also be instigated from outside the work realm, such as loss of a dear one, divorce, or illness. In a 2004 study on workplace spirituality by the author of this chapter, a number of business executives also considered the positive end of life changing events, and mentioned new responsibilities such as marriage, the birth of one's child, or other memorable developments such as recovery from a distressing illness, or the realization of a long awaited dream, for instance.

Many great leaders of today have experienced their share of crucibles before becoming the empathetic leaders they now are.

There are, however, less dramatic ways to acquire a change of attitude, leading to reduction or elimination of the problem with co-workers: through turning inward and getting in touch with the source of wisdom inside. Leonard and Biberman (2007) support the notion that the process of getting in touch with our spiritual side or exploring other dimensions of reality could be referred to as a shift to a different state of consciousness. This process is initiated and maintained in different ways by different people. Fry (2003) suggests practices such as spending time in nature, prayer, meditation, reading inspirational literature, yoga, shamanistic practices, and writing journals. Marques, Biberman, and Dhiman (2010, p. 23) postulate that specifically meditation is making prominent inroads as a vehicle toward greater awareness. They affirm,

> As the exposure to alternative ways of performing increases, receptiveness to alternative ways expands, and practices that were previously considered pure Eastern or Western become global. Meditation is one of those expanding practices. Though applied by selected groups in the Western world for centuries, meditation is increasingly accepted in Western environments, particularly now that the realization sinks in that meditation does not necessarily have anything to do with renouncing one's faith for another.

Leonard and Biberman (2007) mention several other Eastern energy practices such as tai chi, chi gong and martial arts, and yoga, and confirm that the intention of all these exercises is to increase one's "self-awareness, emotional self-awareness, positive self-assessment, and self-esteem" (p. 943). The methods used to realize the process of turning inward are multiple but, if conducted properly, they can all lead to one overarching change: the awareness that troubled co-workers should not be a source of irritation and fear, but of compassion. Ross (1997) shared the advantage of being in touch with one's spiritual dimension through an example of nurses, who become better able to relate and respond to spiritual needs of their clients. Marques et al. (2010) conducted a workshop in which they applied the concept of individual meditation, followed by group meditation, to find out whether synergy could be attained in problem solving, and found that most participants to this workshop made significant headway in finding solutions to the issues they were struggling with. All of the above mentioned strategies are intended to achieve personal and professional improvement through the attainment of a new insight. Once this new insight has nestled itself into one's system, the hold of irritation and dissatisfaction is ready to be lifted.

Turning inward can bring a number of critical insights to the surface, such as: (1) general awareness: the impermanence of everything; (2) specific awareness: the fickleness of positions; (3) holistic view: the ability to focus on the whole, and see past small irritations while recognizing the blessing of being where one is; (4) learning stance: the skill to understand that every seemingly negative occurrence serves a useful future purpose; (5) interconnectedness: the connection with others, even if they refuse to see it; (6) void: the awareness of one's non-self.

While there are other mental modes that could emerge, the six above qualities could be considered a good foundational package for anyone who wants to outgrow the agony of dissatisfaction at work. A brief elaboration of these six contemplation points is presented next.

1. *General awareness*: the impermanence of everything. This is usually a very strong beginning and ending point of every deep contemplation, in which one reviews his or her life and all the things that came and went through time: the losses and victories that were part of one's history, the friends, family members, positions, places, and experiences one encountered, which either changed over time, or disappeared from radar. The Dalai Lama (2005) suggests mindfulness meditation in which we become increasingly aware of the subtle but continuous changes that occur in our body and mind. Alternatively, the Dalai Lama suggests contemplation on "the complex web of circumstances that keep us alive, which leads to a deeper appreciation of the fragility of our continued existence" (p. 155). The awareness of impermanence spans over every area of our lives, and is usually the easiest one to communicate with those who struggle with senses of meaninglessness and isolation.

2. *Specific awareness*: the fickleness of positions. It is an easy transition to shift attention from the general scope to the workplace, and realize, as a result of the awareness generated in point (1) above, that the impermanence of matters does not exclude the workplace. Co-workers and their attitudes, problems, job losses, titles, influential positions, or powerlessness: they all arise and pass as everything else. Aside from the suggestions from the Dalai Lama in point (1) above, Thich (1998) recommends us to contemplate on the "Five Remembrances," which are embedded in Buddhist teaching, but make sense for every human being, regardless of his or her religious convictions:

1. We all grow old;
2. We all are prone to getting ill health;
3. We will all die;
4. Everything and everyone we cherish is prone to change; and
5. The only thing we own are our actions.

This quintet of realizations could be highly effective to us in understanding that it is not rewarding to become excessively upset about the things that don't seem right at work, because they, too, will once pass. Those who have adopted this understanding also know that releasing problems from their problem status by shifting one's paradigm is the quickest way to disarm them.

3. *Holistic view*: the ability to focus on the whole, and see past small irritations while recognizing the blessing of being where one is. Point (2) above is a good foundation for this contemplation point. Once there is solid understanding that everything passes, it also starts to become clear that those who obsess about their position, and engage in negative politics in the workplace are trapped in a superficial mindset, in which they cannot see beyond a single dimension. They got lost in details and became unable to enlarge their horizon. If, however, they decide to acquire a holistic perspective, a sense of gratitude can be obtained for all that is, without stressing too much on unpleasant but small details. According to Miller and Timothy (2010), the holistic view is on the rise and the narrow-minded, obsessively protective approach, is fortunately decreasing among workforce members.

> Many employees of all levels, in all industries, and in all parts of the country (and increasingly the world) wish to live a holistic life and bring their whole self to work, including their faith. This is often called the Faith at Work movement or Spirituality and Work movement.... The global economic crisis triggered in 2008 has, if anything, further strengthened this movement.
>
> *(Miller & Timothy, 2010, p. 53)*

4. *Learning stance*: the skill to understand that every seemingly negative occurrence serves a useful future purpose. With the previous thought of seeing the whole picture and refraining from becoming trapped in details, one can consider the expansiveness of life in all its facets and the magnitude of all there is to learn. In extension to that awareness, one can start appreciating all the lessons that are captured in those we meet: the pleasant and not-so pleasant teachers, who appear to provide us with what we need to know for our future. The realization that even the less pleasant occurrences of today will turn out to be useful tomorrow is a strong one that can make a world of difference in the way one deals with workplace circumstances. In addition, learning also entails the act of trying to understand others in order to help them and increase the sense of wellbeing for all. Thich (2003) particularly underscores the importance of right

understanding, which is one of the elements of the Noble Eightfold Path in Buddhist teaching. He asserts (p. 88):

> Deep listening and loving speech are wonderful instruments to help us arrive at the kind of understanding we all need as a basis for appropriate action. You listen deeply for only one purpose—to allow the other person to empty his or her heart. This is already an act of relieving suffering. To stop any suffering, no matter how small, is a great action of peace.

5. *Interconnectedness*: the connection with others, even if they refuse to see it. The thought expressed above that everything that happens today is a needed lesson for tomorrow is an important dimension of interconnectedness. Richmond (2000) suggests trying to keep track for a few days how many times we say "thank you" at work.

> And whenever you yourself say the words "thank you," see if you can step back from the habitual cadence of talking and say them with a little more depth and feeling. Yes, I automatically say thank you to you when you hand me the phone at work, but I can also be thankful for your presence, for all the people here, for this job, for the freedoms that I have, for my health, for this world, for everything.
>
> *(Richmond, 2000, p. 225)*

However, the notion of interconnectedness transcends mere occurrences. It manifests itself in things and in people. The notion can be further approached in numerous other ways, such as the thought that everyone appears to teach us something, and is therefore connected to us, but also, that everything we use (our food, clothes, cars, homes, etc.) was produced by millions of others in an immense web of interbeing, consisting of all humans, flora, and fauna, and that existence is only possible in relationship with those so-called "others."

6. *Void*: the awareness of one's non-self. As the contemplation point above sinks in, the realization starts dawning that we are part of something much greater than ourselves. Ashforth and Pratt (2003) refer to this awareness as, "a connection to something greater than oneself" (p. 93) and clarify that this "something" can be different things, such as other people, one or more causes, the environment, or believing in a higher power. This notion could also be described as being a dissolvable part of an evolving existential wheel, which keeps spinning through time, and which changes in substance from micro-moment to micro-moment. Kabat-Zinn (1994) points out the limiting context of the self, and the process of "selfing" that we engage in all day long by continuously referring to "I," "me," and "my." Kabat-Zinn (p. 237) notes:

> If you observe this process of selfing with sustained attention and inquiry, you will see that what we call "the self" is really a construct of our own mind, and hardly a permanent one, either. If you look deeply for a stable, indivisible self, for the core "you" that underlies "your" experience, you are not likely to find it other than in more thinking. You might say you are your name, but that is not quite accurate. Your name is just a label. The same is true of your age, your gender, your opinions, and so on. None are fundamental to who you are.

Our current notion of existence is a passing stage, and will be continued by another element of the whole that is the ultimate Self of which we are part.

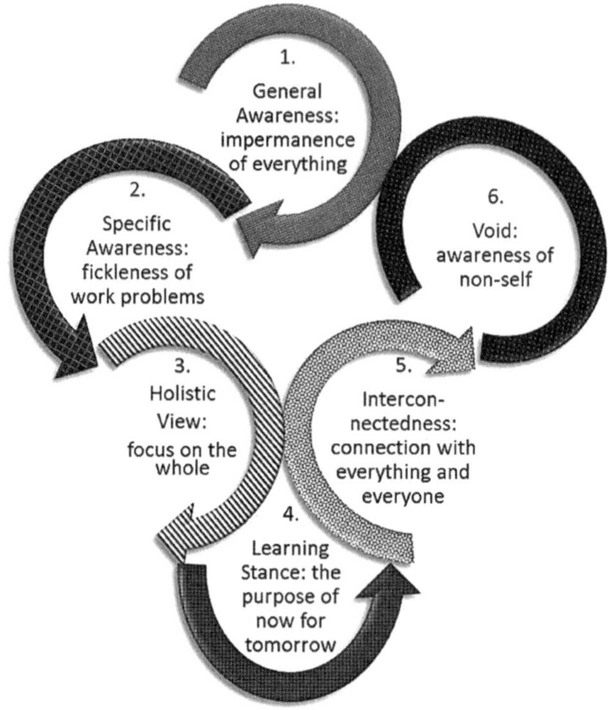

Figure 11.1 Turning Inward to Understand Interbeing at Work

Conclusion

The six contemplation points presented in this chapter form a synergistic mental approach toward personal and professional wellbeing in the workplace and any other environment. The points are closely interlinked, which makes them easy mental steps to follow on the path to less friction and greater tolerance, less ostracism and more togetherness, less antagonism and more peace. If these six contemplation points are nurtured, possibly one by one until they dissolve into one understandable whole, it becomes possible to elevate the mind beyond senses of meaninglessness or disengagement, as the understanding emerges that meaning and connection are part of an awareness that can only be gained by turning inward, and contemplating on essential existential points such as the six above.

References

Alexander, C. (1998). Creating new futures in turbulent times. *Empowerment in Organizations, 6*(8), 201.

Ashforth, B. E., & Pratt, M. G. (2003). *Institutionalized Spirituality: An Oxymoron?* in R. A. Giacalone & C. L. Jurkiewicz (Eds.), *Handbook of Workplace Spirituality and Organizational Performance*. New York: M. E. Sharpe, 93–107.

Baines, S., Bull, M., & Woolrych, R. (2010). A more entrepreneurial mindset? Engaging third sector suppliers to the NHS. *Social Enterprise Journal, 6*(1), 49–58.

Bennis, W., & Thomas, R. J. (2002, September). Crucibles of leadership. *Harvard Business Review*. Retrieved from https://hbr.org/2002/09/crucibles-of-leadership.

Camplin, J. (2011). A whole new mind: Why right-brainers will rule the future [review of *A Whole New Mind: Why Right-Brainers Will Rule the Future* from Daniel Pink, 2005, Riverhead]. *Professional Safety, 56*(5), 42–43.

Clem, A. H., & Mujtaba, B. (2010). Infusing value: Application of historical management concepts at a modern organization. *Journal of Management and Marketing Research, 4*(1), 135–149.
Dalai Lama. (2005). *The Universe in a Single Atom: The Convergence of Science and Spirituality*. New York: Broadway Books.
Fry, L. W. (2003). Towards a theory of spiritual leadership. *Leadership Quarterly, 14*, 693–727.
George, B., & Sims, P. (2007). *True North: Discover Your Authentic Leadership*. San Francisco: Jossey Bass.
Kabat-Zinn, J. (1994). *Wherever You Go There You Are: Mindfulness Meditation in Everyday Life*. New York: Hyperion Books.
Kinjerski, V., & Skrypnek, B. J. (2008). Four paths to spirit at work: Journeys of personal meaning, fulfillment, well-being, and transcendence through work. (Cover story). *Career Development Quarterly, 56*(4), 319–329.
Leonard, B., & Biberman, J. (2007). Utilizing multi-dimensionality in the workplace: A meta-study. *Managerial Finance, 33*(12), 935–946.
Lips-Wiersma, M., & Morris, L. (2009). Discriminating between "meaningful work" and the "management of meaning." *Journal of Business Ethics, 88*(3), 491–511.
McDonald, P. (2010). Teaching the concept of management: Perspectives from "six honest serving men." *Journal of Management and Organization, 16*(5), 626–640.
Marques, J., Biberman, J., & Dhiman, S. (2010). Asking the inner-consultant: The power of communicating, listening, trusting, and collaborating. *Journal of Global Business Issues, 4*(2), 21–28.
Miller, D., & Timothy, E. (2010). Rethinking the impact of religion on business values: Understanding its reemergence and measuring its manifestations. *Journal of International Business Ethics, 3*(2), 49–57.
Mitroff, I. I., & Denton, E. A. (1999). *A Spiritual Audit of Corporate America: A Hard Look at Spirituality, Religion, and Values in the Workplace*. San Francisco: Jossey-Bass.
Peters, T. (1999). *The Brand You 50: Or Fifty Ways to Transform Yourself from an "Employee" into a Brand That Shouts Distinction, Commitment, and Passion!* New York: Knopf.
Pfeffer, J. (2003). Business and the spirit: Management practices that sustain values. In R. Giacalone & C. Jurkiewicz (Eds.), *Handbook of Workplace Spirituality and Organizational Performance*. Armonk, NY: M. E. Sharpe, 29–45.
Pink, D. (2006). *A Whole New Mind: Why Right-Brainers Will Rule the Future*. New York: Riverhead Books.
Richmond, L. (2000). *Work as a Spiritual Practice: A Practical Buddhist Approach to Inner Growth and Satisfaction on the Job*. New York: Broadway Books.
Ross, L. (1997). The nurse's role on assessing and responding to patients' spiritual needs. *International Journal of Palliative Nursing, 3*(1).
Sachau, D. A. (2007). Resurrecting the motivation–hygiene theory: Herzberg and the positive psychology movement. *Human Resource Development Review, 6*(4), 377–393.
Schein, E. (1992). *Organizational Culture and Leadership*. San Francisco: Jossey Bass.
Sheep, M. L. (2006). Nurturing the whole person: The ethics of workplace spirituality in a society of organizations. *Journal of Business Ethics, 66*(4), 357–375.
Singer, J. (2011, March). Healing your workplace: Powerful prescriptions to prevent hardening of the attitudes among your employees. *Supervision, 72*(3), 11–13.
Tablan, F. (2015). Catholic social teachings: Toward a meaningful work. *Journal of Business Ethics, 128*(2), 291–303.
Thich, N. H. (1998). *The Heart of the Buddha's Teaching: Transforming Suffering into Peace, Joy, and Liberation*. New York: Broadway Books.
Thich, N. H. (2003). *Creating True Peace: Ending Violence in Yourself, Your Family, Your Community, and the World*. New York: Free Press.
Thich, N. H. (2007). *Two Treasures: Buddhist Teachings on Awakening and True Happiness*. Berkeley, CA: Parallax Press.
Udechukwu, I. I. (2009). Correctional officer turnover: Of Maslow's needs hierarchy and Herzberg's motivation theory. *Public Personnel Management, 38*(2), 69–82.
Vasconcelos, A. (2010). The effects of prayer on organizational life: A phenomenological study. *Journal of Management and Organization, 16*(3), 369–381.
Wärna, C., Lindholm, L., & Eriksson, K. (2007). Virtue and health: Finding meaning and joy in working life. *Scandinavian Journal of Caring Sciences, 21*(2), 191–198.
Williams, H. (2010, February). Employee engagement still a tough nut to crack for HR. *Personnel Today*, 8.

12

AWAKENING LEADERSHIP

The Outer Reaches of Inner Space

Cheryl De Ciantis and Ginger Grant

Introduction

The demand for innovation within organizations is a worldwide concern. The pre-conditions necessary for liberating creativity within the organizational context have been well described (Amabile, 1996), but the means for behaviorally engaging personal creativity "on the ground" within organizations are challenging to the managerial/administrative mindset and, paradoxically as this may seem, also to the visionary senior leadership perspective. Disengagement in the workplace is high (Mann & Harter, 2016). It is necessary to dig far deeper to find the sources of engagement in work and life, down to the wellsprings of emotion, empathy and imagination, and to the roots of both individual and collective sense of purpose.

One key issue which may be masked under all the measurement is that empowerment is seen as a neutral concept, a quantifiable factor that is necessarily disconnected from personal values, much the way we conceive of scientific method, regardless that our methods not infrequently have harmful consequences. Empathetic engagement is de-valued and the illusion of logical neutrality is too often disconnected from the real, ethical questions of who benefits from what and how, and why it matters.

Re-querying the wisdom of both myth and ancient philosophy is helpful in finding our way in a complex world. Technologies present both unprecedented opportunities and challenges, but we also still continually face the basic human conundrums and dilemmas that we have wrestled with for millennia, and perennial wisdom still raises fruitful questions about personal individuation and the dynamic nature of both personal and collective power within any given situation. There are no simple answers, there never have been. But there are countless questions that lead to wisdom. The concept of spirituality itself is very difficult to pin down. Recent research finds that, for example, the percentage of people in the US who describe themselves as "spiritual but not religious" is growing (Lipka & Gecewicz, 2017); interestingly 90% of US adults say they believe in some "higher power" though slightly fewer than half attribute daily involvement in their lives on the part of "God." How "God" is defined varies greatly (Fahmy, 2018).

In this chapter, we posit that we arrive at a spiritual aspect of leadership through two pathways:

1. Self-knowledge of values and unleashing of personal creativity through individuation, and
2. Participating in values-based phronetic dialogue that synergizes the creative instinct for the good of a community.

The ethical dimension of both individuation and phronesis takes account of both internal and external or shared loci of power, driving toward influencing outcomes that are beneficial. This chapter will present the preliminary aspects of a mythic model we have devised and use frequently to capture the tacit value system or what psychologist C. G. Jung called archetypes of transformation (1969b, para. 80) functioning both in individual psyches and in cultures. Much has been written about personified archetypes such as the hero or the outlaw that attempt an explanation as to their complex and multiple meanings (Campbell, 1968; Mark & Pearson, 2001). Archetypes of transformation are not personalities as such, but instead are ways and means, values, situations, or places that symbolize the transformation in question (Jung, 1969b, para. 80). Whether you are dealing with an organizational culture or a nation, finding the core archetypes of transformation that speak to the cultural identity is key. Jung emphasized that archetypes are symbols that cannot be reduced to a single meaning. They are symbols because they are ambiguous—promoting constant explorations as to both historical and current context. These both/and stages involve ongoing interpretation and reinterpretation through dialogue—at the intra-, interpersonal, and intercultural levels of engagement, ensuring participants are engaged in formulating the best possible course of collective action.

Methodology

Phenomenology involves the exploration of human experience though conscious, retrospective reflection. Phenomenological inquiry seeks to examine, understand, and interpret observable special events in our everyday life, with the benefit of sharing the meaning of these phenomena with others. Experiences are individual constructions which can illustrate the essence of an event, embedded into a particular context influencing or affecting experiences and psychological states. Phenomenology is an exploratory approach requiring an open attitude allowing unexpected meanings to emerge. This chapter also takes a Depth Psychology approach in raising questions about processes of individuation—most simply stated, cultivation of self-knowledge—in order to add to practical insights with regard to the meanings and consequences of the spiritual dimension of leadership.

Aristotle described three ways of knowing: episteme, techne, and phronesis. Episteme "concerns universals and the production of knowledge which is invariable in time and space, and which is achieved with the aid of analytical rationality" (Flyvbjerg, 2001, p. 55). Techne has as its objective the "application of technical knowledge and skills according to a pragmatic instrumental rationality" (p. 56). Phronesis is "a true state, reasoned and capable of action with regard to things that are good or bad for man" (p. 2). Our approach is phronetic and inherently dialogical. Aristotle saw phronesis, which he also referred to as prudence or practical wisdom, as the most important of intellectual virtues because its sphere comprises all human affairs, including the management of epistemé (universal truth) and techné (technical know-how) (p. 11). We also follow Bent Flyvbjerg in using the phenomenology of learning formulated by Hubert Dreyfus and Stuart Dreyfus, positing that the basic differences between competence and virtuosity in performance are in large part attributable to the performer's ability to transcend context-dependent rules and learn to trust and apply individual judgment according to the perceived demands of individual contexts, which in some cases requires that the "rules" be ignored, overridden by circumstantial requirements judged necessary in a given context by an expert practitioner (pp. 9–20).

We will use the heuristics that originated in the Stanford Creativity in Business program (Ray & Myers, 1989) to examine questions such as, how do people in organizational/institutional settings experience personal creativity, leadership, followership, or conflict? Using these heuristics as a starting point, the participant dictates the context of reflection and explores the belief system that motivates exploration of his or her creative force. This is a constructivist approach to workplace spirituality that seeks to transform the learning experience by having the participants deeply engage with their own story, discovering the foundation of their unique creative capacity.

Some Misconceptions about Creativity and Innovation

Education is under heavy criticism for failure to produce the workforce needed to meet the innovation challenge. We believe that the solution to this complex problem lies in the human imagination. Imagination and creativity are the seeds of innovation. Creativity is a matter of personal, qualitative "style" rather than the quantifiable notion of "level" that has typically characterized its conceptualization in creativity studies and in culture at large. It is the misconception of level that impels many people who say, "I'm not creative." Everyone is creative; it is a fundamental human capacity. *How* we are creative is a matter of individual difference and is generated from myriad possible factors in differing contexts (De Ciantis, 2017, p. 143). In a compounded misconception, creativity is generally confused with innovation. It is arguable that innovation is measurable, in novel products and process advances, whereas creativity is an immeasurable drive, which indeed Jung recognized as an "instinct" (Grant, 2005, 2012; Jung, 1969a, para. 245). Innovation is the introduction of visible change that impacts systems, and it relies on a generative combination of individual creativity and interaction within human systems, and as such can be best elucidated by the concept of phronesis.

Western habits of thinking since Plato and Aristotle tend to be categorical and excluding. The result is on one hand a great tradition of scientific advancement. On the other hand, misconceptions persist about the nature and possibilities of emotion, intuition, and the deep sense of spiritual interconnectedness with something larger than themselves that most people feel but are unable to directly access using categorical terms and methods of measurement. Though science can measure the chemistry of emotion, and even the psychological trait of "connectedness" that many of us think of as spirituality may be discerned through socio-psychological typologies such as the Gallup Strengths Finder (Buckingham & Clifton, 2001, p. 92), the deeper meanings of these phenomena remain ineffable. Even the ability to gather and systematize big data is limited by the lack of emotional value in artificial intelligence (AI) algorithmic conceptions (el Kaliouby, 2017)—we may generate and gather data mechanistically but nuanced interpretation, subtle judgment, often leading to deeper questions, is required to sufficiently understand what it means in order to make it actionable.

We have the advantage of Aristotelian episteme, the mode of knowledge that presumes that phenomena possess objective existence in a bounded form whose essential properties can be known through scientific method, and which we can also call "true." Likewise, we use and value techne, the mode of knowledge that is gained through interaction with material phenomena through the application of craft, by means of replicable procedures with reliable rules that can be taught and learned. Phronesis, or social/interactive knowing, Aristotle's third mode of human learning, has been historically less valued; indeed it has been viewed with suspicion as being subjective and therefore unreliable in the quest to find and productively exploit objective "truth" discoverable via episteme and validated through techne.

An additional way of knowing that is implicit in Greek thought and literature but evading categorization is metis. Metis is by nature spontaneous, opportunistic, and evasive, surpassing boundaries and capitalizing on capability based in experience in combination with readiness to seize the moment. The classicists Marcel Detienne and Jean-Pierre Vernant (1978) have shown

Table 12.1 Relationship of Episteme, Techne, Phronesis, and Metis to Objective "Truth"

	←					
What is True/ Verifiable: • Bounded • Absolute • Objective • Measurable by scientific method	*Episteme* (universal truth)	*Techne* (technical know-how based on experience)	*Limit of Subjectivity*	*Phronesis* (practical wisdom/ ethics)	*Metis* (wisdom, craft, cunning, opportunism)	*What is not True/ Unverifiable:* • Unbounded • Relative • Subjective • Describable through myth, metaphor and story

that, though it was not formally categorized by the Greeks as a way of knowing, it is nevertheless recognizable in story, for example in the exploits of "wily" Odysseus, a paradigmatic possessor of metis. Table 12.1 shows the relationship of the respective concepts of episteme, techne, phronesis, and metis to objective "truth" in the Aristotelian sense.

The placement of a "Limit of Subjectivity" between these concept sets suggests that phronetic and metic intelligence may encompass techne and indeed episteme, as each makes use of "proven" theorems and methodologies to suit contextual needs. However, this expansion is unidirectional, since what is objectively verifiable (episteme, techne) by definition does not surpass the limit of subjectivity. This seeming intractable one-sidedness is the fault of the artificial bifurcation of our concepts of knowledge, and our habit of defining rational thinking as a binary proposition that separates "judgment" from "intuition" and places them, mistakenly, in radical opposition (Flyvbjerg, 2001, p. 21). This bias is perpetuated in our psychological typologies (De Ciantis, 2017, pp. 143–44). The combination of techne and metis is often seen as unpredictable and ungovernable, and thereby threatening to the power of the ruling elite. In institutions and organizations the response to this perceived threat often takes the form of discrediting, marginalizing, and expulsion. And, unfortunately, it results in the loss of talent and, with it, competitive advantage (De Ciantis, 2005, p. 184).

Crossing the "Limit"

The ability to cross the "Limit of Subjectivity" is a matter of maturation. It is natural for people to have personality and cognitive preferences that make them feel relatively more at home with the realm we have labeled "true/verifiable" or "true/unverifiable." This is described in numerous psychological type indices. It tends to be a general assumption driven by binary thinking that those whose preferences tend toward the more bounded, absolute, and objective may not be able to "cross the line" to value what is unbounded, relative, and subjective. This categorical assumption is not accurate (Hyatt & De Ciantis, 2014). How one operates within and reaches outside of one's psychological "native" preference or comfort zone can be as varied as each individual's education, experience, and myriad other factors including the exigencies of context in a given situation. It can equally occur that people whose general preference is for the more unbounded, relative, and subjective may also simply fail to value the "opposite" perspective. What is far more important is to understand the processes by which one is able to find value in a complementary perspective when it differs from their native preference.

In order to build the capacity to understand multiple perspectives, the original "Creativity in Business" program was developed by Michael Ray and Rochelle Myers at the Stanford Graduate School of Business. Creativity in Business is a developmental process designed to leverage both personal and organizational performance. It is based on the premise that organizational success depends on an individual's ability to connect and sustain a link to that source from which they access what Jung called archetypes of transformation (1969b, para. 80). Core to this process is a set of heuristics ("Live-Withs") that aid in developing self- and other-awareness through practice, reflection, and dialogue that are each done for one week. The keystone set of live-withs are:

1. *Have no expectations.* Participants are asked to notice all of their expectations and ponder how such expectations might limit their perception not only of others but also of their own creative capacity.
2. *Silence the voice of judgment.* Participants are asked to become aware of how their self-judgment operates, the quantity and quality of their criticism of self and others, and question where such judgment originates.
3. *Pay attention.* Participants are challenged to become cultural anthropologists and to pay close attention to the world around them and how they experience it. They are also asked to do one thing differently each day and take note of their responses to change.
4. *Ask penetrating questions.* Participants are reminded of the creative child within that asked so many questions without fear. The ability to ask penetrating questions uncovers deeper conditions where creative possibilities may be hidden, particularly in groups. Phronetic dialogue starts here with the ability to ask "what if?" and then explore the results with the group. The foundations of trust are built here as participants re-learn to ask questions without fear of judgment.

In this process, the participant dictates the context of reflection and explores the belief system that motivates exploration of her or his creative force. Participants are asked to explore their attitude and experiences about judgment, fear of change, imagination, spontaneity, and links to individual passion and purpose; a spiritual quest of potential and possibility experienced through a 10-week reflective journey. The participants discover the foundation of their creative capacity and eventually expand their capacity for innovation.

The Call to Adventure—Individuation and Liberating Individual Creativity

C. G. Jung defined individuation as "the process by which individual beings are formed and differentiated [from other human beings]; in particular, it is the development of the psychological individual as a being distinct from the general, collective psychology" (1953, para. 757). Depth Psychology, following Jung, valorizes myths, dreams, and the stories we tell ourselves about ourselves as valid and relevant in process, throughout the course of a lifetime, of continually developing one's unique identity.

According to Joseph Campbell, one of myth's functions is to enforce a moral order within each successive coherent social group, within the context of its unique geographical and historical place. "The rise and fall of civilizations in the long, broad course of history can be seen to have been largely a function of the integrity and cogency of their supporting canons of myth" (Campbell, 1968, p. 5). A mythic canon persists as long as it has the power to inspire individual members of a group to experience a harmonious connection with the social order and their place in the universe. Myth is a cultural preserver, a kind of "glue" that adheres individuals to individuals and all to community identity (Grant, 2005).

The world, however, changes, and myth too changes under historical pressure. Campbell points out that when the canonical myth ceases to hold meaning for at least some members of the community or produces "deviant" effects, what arises is both a sense of dissociation and an urge toward a renewed quest for "meaning" (1968, p. 5). Campbell points toward historical times of dissolution as productive of new myths. In other words, one of the functions of myth is to generate new myths. Campbell uses the example of Christian Europe in the twelfth century, when "beliefs no longer universally held were universally enforced" (p. 5). Many people lost faith in Scripture, giving rise to what Campbell calls the "Waste Land" theme in the imagery of the Grail legend: a theme of spiritual death, of wandering, and "waiting, waiting." Campbell asserts that the work of Rousseau in the mid-18th century marks a further dissolution, this time a loss of faith in reason. Society came to be seen as a corrupting influence, and new myths appeared, of the "noble savage," the "natural man" (p. 5). These myths expressed a desire to return to an imagined state of nature, expressed in the creative impulse toward speculative fantasies like Mary Shelley's Frankenstein. According to Campbell, we still live in the larger epoch of dissolution, dissatisfaction, and yearning for meaning.

The status quo function of myth is embodied in the culture. The transforming function of myth originates with individuals. Campbell's "creative mythology" is not a product of the normative voice of the culture, but arises from the "insights, sentiments, thought, and vision of an adequate individual, loyal to his own experience of value" (p. 7). This individual voice provides a corrective to empty, left-over shells of forms that no longer inspire meaningful engagement. Unlike traditional forms of knowing, a myth remains alive not because it is completely fixed in meaning but because it is plastic and can be retold, rewritten, reinterpreted, remade, and told again (De Ciantis, 2005, p. 179). The Grail myth, more popularly known as The Hero/ine's Journey, can be read as a model for individuation (Grant, 2005, 2014, 2017).

Building on the work of Joseph Campbell, the Heroic Journey is a model or map that we find provides easy access by ordinary people to the world of mythological systems. Used as a life-stage model it resonates with any individual in an organizational setting, regardless of age or

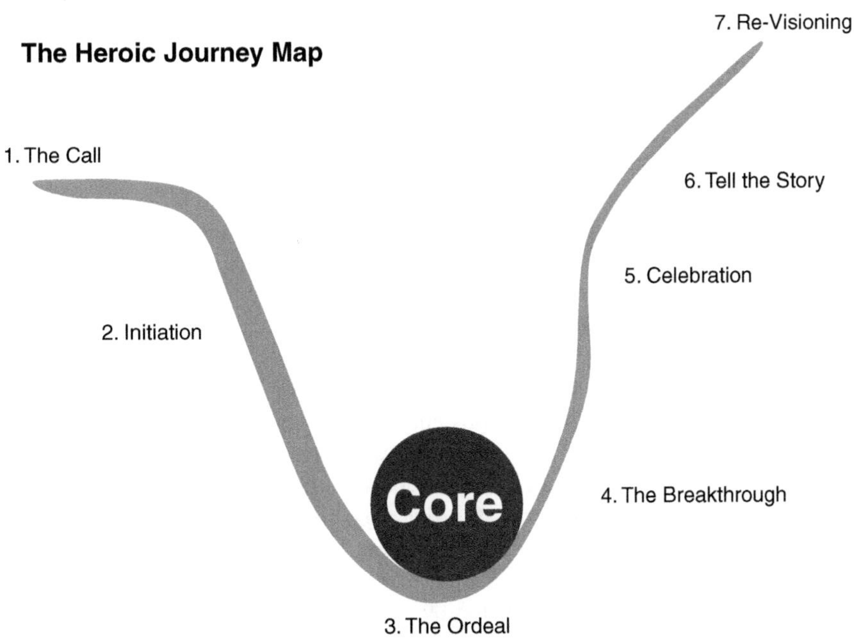

Figure 12.1 The Grail Myth

race (Grant, 2005). The map can be used to model the path of an individual, a team, a division, or of an organization. In the telling of the "journey," an archetype of transformation is introduced that permits a new myth to emerge from the fertile grounds of the old. Our ability to make new meaning—new myths—mythopoesis, is revealed and can now be used to enhance creative capacity in service of innovation.

Myths are not just told; they are felt, resonating through the body as well as the mind (Grant, 2005, p. 1). In our experience, traditional business teachings omit emotion from learning. Many have tried to "teach" creativity which results in a prescriptive focus on tools and processes but has limited, if any, emotional engagement. Capturing emotion is a necessary component as the creative drive is intrinsic, it originates from within. We concur with the view that "denial of feelings is denial of learning" (Boud, Keogh, & Walker, 1985, p. 15). How, then, to introduce emotion back into a business environment? Our answer is practice, practice, practice. There are many ways to break out of habits of thinking to arrive at transformative insights. Arts methodologies are very useful in circumventing habits of thought expressed in self-talk by immersion in image and gesture. The Creativity in Business heuristics are a particularly effective way to elicit reflection, particularly among groups such as business students, since they provide relatively simple, text-based instructions for practice which feels safe for the participant, who is not asked to express reflections in an unfamiliar medium.

What follows in Tables 12.2 and 12.3 are examples of some of the initial insights of business baccalaureate students participating in a 10-week course using these heuristics.

The 10-week course culminates in participants presenting an individual, creative project capturing their experiences, often taking the form of a video. The following are a sample of student responses to the question, "What did you learn about yourself?"

What these reflections show is that, in short, the "story" has changed for participants. A final comment summarizes a commonly expressed conclusion: "Now I know what to do."

The Greek concept of metis, often translated as "cunning intelligence," is named for the shape-shifting Okeanids of Greek mythology, such as the Old Man of the Sea who knows all, the sea-nymph Metis, with her daughter, Athena, the goddess of strategy who takes on differing guises to advise and direct mortals like her protégé Odysseus, famed for his cunning (De Ciantis, 2017, p. 136). In the learning stages described by Dreyfus and Dreyfus—(1) Novice, (2) Advanced Beginner, (3) Competent Performer, (4) Proficient Performer, and (5) Expert—possession of metis may be said to characterize experts, who "exhibit thinking and behavior that is rapid, intuitive, holistic, interpretive, and visual," having surpassed the "slow, analytical reasoning which characterizes rational problem-solving and the first three levels of the learning process" (cited in Flyvbjerg, 2001, p. 14). Techne—the ability to manipulate tools via replicable rules and techniques (De Ciantis, 2017, p. 137)—is assimilated into intuitive mastery: I know what to do *without thinking about it.* Instead of learning only from textbooks, the student now learns from life.

Though relatively little research has been done on the long-term impact programs that can be termed "non-traditional" in their approach, a research study combining qualitative and quantitative analysis on the impact of a leadership development program ("LeaderLab") conducted at the Center for Creative Leadership between 1992 and 2000 (Burnside & Guthrie, 1992) found that three to four months after the program, two program elements received a higher value-rating from participants than they had at the program conclusion. Elements that incorporated non-traditional modalities ("artistic activities") leading to personal storytelling in the context of a small peer-group facilitated by a "Process Advisor" (a professional executive coach) were shown to increase in value after the fact, compared with Action Planning, which was rated lower in perceived value 3 to 4 months later than it had been rated at the time of the

Table 12.2 Examples of Initial Insights of Business Baccalaureate Students

Week 1: Have No Expectations	*Week 2: Stamp Out the Voice of Judgment*	*Week 3: Pay Attention*	*Week 4: Ask Penetrating Questions*
"I found over the weekend a numerous amount of times where I would assume there was one right answer or one right outcome. After adopting an open mindset I noticed a change in the people around me as well as myself." "I like the idea of giving and not worrying about what you'll get back."	"I can see now that we form judgments based on a small percentage of the facts. We lack insight into the situation or person we are dealing with or we don't fully understand their story." "My main problem is being too harsh or critical of myself." "I have to remind myself that I am always learning and investigating new concepts, and that being open to different ideas only makes me a better person."	"It was comforting to reconnect with myself at a deeper lever and remind myself about how far I have come in my 23 years of life. This exercise brought me back down to earth and has helped me regain focus about where I want to go in life." "I learned the difference between 'spending time with someone' and 'being with someone.'"	"This live-with taught me the importance of understanding problems from differing points of view." "Sometimes what is obvious to one may not be obvious to another. Everyone is brought up differently with different experiences."

Table 12.3 Sample of Student Responses to the Question, "What Did You Learn About Yourself?"

Identity Formation	*Self-Confidence*	*Adaptability to Change*	*Owning One's Creative Capacity*
"I now know who I am. I'm a girl who wants love and respect in her life and relationships. I'm a girl who is going to take her life in her hands, and rock it." "I am writing my story of the life I want to live with my dreams, my knowledge, my courage, my love, my faith to make every page just as amazing as the last one written. No regrets." "I am thankful that I had the opportunity to do all these live-withs, because they all taught me something different. I realized that kind of person I am, what I need to improve, and how I want to approach things in the future."	"The weekly live-withs have helped me deal and cope with worrying, and I've found myself worrying less and less as the weeks went by." "All in all, this course has helped shape me into a better and more suited person for the fast-paced business world." "I am a different person now than I started out at the beginning of this semester and this is all because of a few simple activities I completed every week. I am excited to see what life holds just around the corner now that I feel more empowered than ever before."	"I found that the live-withs opened my mind, and let me explore different options and situations which I may, and probably would never have gone out of my way to do." "I believe that the live-withs really helped me. Each week, I either discovered something new about myself or I overcame something that I was struggling with." "Usually I learned everything straight from the textbooks, and lectures. I loved how during the course of these ten weeks, I learned by using life." "As I come full circle and reflect on all of the past live-withs, I discover how simple and impactful change can be."	"I assumed I knew the best ways to bring out my creativity, but with these exercises I learned some new techniques. I've learned a lot about myself in the past few months and I thank these exercises for that. I now have a better sense of who I am and who I want to be, and I feel more creative than ever." "I never thought I was creative. This changes everything!"

program conclusion (Young & Dixson, 1996). Significantly, these elements combined both individual creative exploration in a safe environment with dialogue within the facilitated peer-group. The dialogue was initiated by a simple, open-ended question: what happened for you?

The emphasis is on the "why" of the reflective process—questioning current beliefs about creativity and innovation, and, more fundamentally, about the search for personal meaning. Are spiritual beliefs and practices still valid under the current context? The answers are sometimes surprising. We may pause to note that the transformative moment in the Grail myth occurs when Gawain faces the shapeshifting hideous hag at the well and is able to answer her question of which shape he would prefer, with the statement "the choice must be yours my lady, for it is your body" (Grant, 2017, p. 7). The question and reply represents a shift in emphasis from command and control to the individual claiming personal power.

Making the Move to Phronesis

Reason and Hawkins (1988) believe that the primary key to using narrative in learning is allowing meaning to develop using reflective dialogue. Through dialogue, we increase our knowledge of self and enhance our relationship to others. We practice our power to choose.

The ancient practice of dialogue remains more than ever on the growing edge of cultural attainment. Increasingly we face problems that outdistance the individual power of any of us to solve. It can be said that the process of dialogue in fact begins internally. Hannah Arendt took special notice of the instance when Socrates recounts that when he goes home alone at the end of the day, he nevertheless finds himself in company (1971, p. 188). It is a voice within him which questions the assertions he made during his day in the Symposium. This "fellow" "asks me whether I am not ashamed of my audacity in talking about a beautiful way of life when questioning makes it evident that I do not even know the meaning of the word 'beauty.'" Thus Socrates questions even *himself*, in an internal dialogue. By contrast, his colleague Hippias enjoys peaceful quiet at night, content in the fact that no internal voice questions his daylight assertions. This internal process may be said to be a spiritual practice, whereby one comes to know oneself, and creates the conditions for being open to know others.

To know oneself requires circumambulation—the act of circling a referent—and defines boundaries of a space by relating to a center of value. Common in most religions, circumambulation is used to define a sacred space. Jung thought that the idea of the "circumambulatio" was to find your center and thus define a container for the Psyche (Grant, 2005, p. 25). A visual analogy would be something akin to peeling the skin from an onion in order to find the center. To find the tacit components of what is valued in an organization, a direct linear approach will not work. You must go "deeper," under the superficial skin in order to find out what is OK, not OK, and, more importantly, why. There is an emotional charge in what is valued and it must be approached indirectly and with an open mind that can "hear" the unconscious as well as conscious content. This dialogue between the core community identity and the aspects of identity that are changeable results in a field of common understanding—a place where participants can meet and continue the conversation. Psyche demands a system of both/and, not either/or. A phronetic dialogue creates this space that can hold the tension of the opposites, allowing the potential realization of both. It is through dialogue that we can create the conditions for crossing the Limit of Subjectivity—in either direction.

This phronetic process was learned by participants through the discussion of the live-withs. In the case of the business students, this was the first time that they had been encouraged to reveal and discuss what was most important to them as individuals. A variety of discussions were held in pairs, triads, small groups, and eventually the entire class. Each student worked with their own "story," their journey toward the future that they had yet to articulate. Through the discussions, archetypes of transformation—values—were revealed. If the values could not be clearly articulated, images were used to represent the attempt at expression. More discussions were the result, in an iterative process of circumambulation. As the individual value systems were explored and discussed, group values became articulated. As group values surfaced and were made clear, group norms were established and maintained. It is important to note that the role of the facilitator in this process is vitally important. Not to lead per se; rather, to support the emergent process. A safe space for these discussions needs to be created and then held in order for creativity to emerge and flourish. The processes are iterative: circumambulatio is in its nature a repetitive movement.

In his seminal work, *Making Social Science Matter* (2001), Bent Flyvbjerg states that the principle objective for social science in using a phronetic lens is to carry out analysis and interpretations of values and beliefs aimed at social commentary and social action. Our study draws on Flyvbjerg's elaboration of phronesis as the mode of inquiry "that opens up discussion of the 'good or bad for man' through exploration of the structures of power and rationality inherent in interactions between groups and individuals"; and allows for education of individual managers *not* as "morally neutral technician(s)" but rather as capable of engaging with complexities to make decisions according to the differing conditions presented in a given situation (Sliwa & Cairns, 2009, p. 229). Phronesis is the vehicle whereby our individual insights are made available; indeed often given voice and form for the first time within the vessel of phronetic dialogue. Once given voice, they are available for shared reflection, query, and evaluation grounded in real conditions. With regard to creating conditions for change that has the potential to serve the good of humankind in countless ways, phronetic dialogue puts the wheels on the bus.

Values, Contexts, and Power

Flyvbjerg (2001, p. 60) proposes the application of methodological guidelines for phronetic studies in which the following questions are addressed:

1. Where are we going?
2. Is this desirable?
3. What should be done?

However, these questions are not sufficient to the realities of context. Context here refers to the unique situation at hand with which a phronetic dialogue is concerned. What problem are we addressing? Who are the stakeholders? Where and in what relationships are they situated? What is the history of the problem? Generally, our Western, cultural definition of rationality assumes that we can apply consistent rules to problem situations to achieve solutions. But the realities "on the ground" render this assumption inadequate. Dialogues by nature do not have determined outcomes. The use of heuristics, especially "asking penetrating questions," tends to reveal not only previously unknown facts, but also surfaces information about attitudes, assumptions, and the values underlying them. For example, a dialogue about values may surface hitherto unrecognized differences in how participants define a value such as honesty. We may think we share the value; when asking the question "What does this mean to you?" may in fact surface entirely unexpected results. For example, a core value of honesty in one person's definition may be combined with an equally strong value of independence, while for another honesty combines with respect (Hyatt & De Ciantis, 2014, pp. 56–57). These differing values' definitions produce very different attitudes and behaviors that underlie each participant's ultimate objectives with regard to the outcome of the dialogue and desires as to the decisions that may result from it. According to Aristotle, the study of human activity "demands that one practice phronesis, that is, that one occupy oneself with values as a point of departure for praxis. And Aristotle considered that values and human behavior must be seen in relation to the particular" (Flyvbjerg, 2001, p. 70).

It is necessary too to distinguish between the intentions of participants in dialogue. If phronesis is directed by definition toward good for humankind, it becomes necessary to discern whether a participant intends *manipulation* (having hidden agenda, withholding information) or *coercion* (compulsion via threat or action). The Aristotelian definition indicates that *influence* is the correct intention with which to undertake phronetic dialogue: sharing information and allowing for possible alternative outcomes (an example of the "have no expectations" heuristic). Making these distinctions allows for influence to remain constructive and positive (K. Hyatt, private conversation). Holding an intention for positive influence returns personal power to the participants.

Flyvbjerg strongly argues that in real social settings, the realities of who holds power and what influences power relationships and structures may have on the outcomes must be examined and evaluated. This is the critical difference between social science as description and social science as uniquely effective in creating the conditions to achieve specific, desired changes in local contexts. Attitudes toward power can be seen at the core of phronesis. It thus becomes necessary to reappraise our societal assumptions toward power as being singular, centered, and static; often concentrated in individual roles and designated entities (for example, heads of state or officials), rather than dynamic and relational. In the West, we often view power as restrictive and negative, as in the view that "power corrupts and absolute power corrupts absolutely." Instead, awakened leaders must see power also as productive and positive; and, as distributed among heterogeneous individuals and groups of individuals with genuinely shared interests and values. Flyvbjerg (2001, p. 131) contributes additional caveats necessary to understanding the actual nature of power as follows:

- Power is viewed as a dense net of omnipresent relations and not only as localized in "centers" and institutions, or an entity one can "possess."
- The concept of power is seen as ultradynamic; power is not only something one appropriates, but also something one reappropriates and exercises in a constant back-and-forth movement in relations of strength, tactics, and strategies.
- Knowledge and power, truth and power, rationality and power are analytically inseparable from each other; power produces knowledge, and knowledge produces power.
- The central question is how power is exercised, and not only who has power, and why they have it; the focus is on process in addition to structure.
- Power is studied with a point of departure in small questions, "flat and empirical," not only, nor primarily, with a point of departure in "big questions."

It is only when participants see themselves as potentially, personally powerful and capable of influencing that they may become part of an actual, informal power node or a more formal power structure. This is how things change. Thus, the questions that necessarily must be added to phronetic dialogue aimed at real change become (Flyvbjerg, 2001, p. 131):

- Who gains, and who loses?
- Through what kinds of power relations?

- What possibilities are available to change existing power relations?
- And is it desirable to do so?
- Of what kinds of power relations are those asking questions themselves a part?

These are not easy questions to put forward. Convenors, facilitators, coaches, teachers, and group or team members need to create foundational conditions of safety in order for phronetic dialogue to occur. This involves confidentiality, as for example in structured values dialogues where the actual content of conversations is held as privileged and not to be repeated outside the dialogue setting without express permission. Phronetic dialogues must be conducted with the caveat of non-judgment, meaning that no question or statement may be considered a priori as more accurate or worthy than any other; rather, dialogue is conducted within the boundaries of well-understood, agreed-upon, and enforced norms (Hyatt & De Ciantis, 2014, pp. 14–16). These norms may range from refraining from profanity or ad hominem assertions to, for example as in the case of the South African Truth and Reconciliation Commission (1995) processes, access to application for amnesty in exchange for truth-telling by perpetrators of human rights abuses.

The Power of Story

To use the Heroic Journey Model provides this safe container to explore and document the path forward. The purpose of story has always been to act as a bridge between the past and the future. It is the stories of old that carry the cultural value system into the present and on into the future, recontextualized to suit the time at hand. Why is this important now? Our mode of production has shifted to organizational knowledge creation. In this new economic environment that is continuously unfolding, a traditional mode of production thinking is increasingly recognized as potentially counter-productive. A new paradigm is needed, one that recognizes that the future belongs to people who use their hearts as well as their heads. Awareness of this shift is the key to realizing a new paradigm. Using story transforms business and executive education and deepens the learning experience in a current context (McDrury & Alterio, 2002). White (1987, p. 1) suggests

> narrative might well be considered a solution to a problem of general human concern, namely the problem of how to translate *knowing* into *telling*, the problem of fashioning human experience into a form assimilable to structures of meaning that are generally human.

Narrative is an ancient method and a seminal form for sense making of experiences. Our research taps into the narratives of individuals as well as our own. Flyvbjerg reminds us that "good narratives typically approach the complexities and contradictions of real life" (2001, p. 84). Often such narratives may be difficult to summarize as they offer multiple interpretations that are diverse and sometimes conflicting. Therefore, this complexity leaves ample space for not only the researchers and the narrators but also the readers to make different interpretations and draw different conclusions. To use narrative as a tool for learning is to take seriously the need for students to make sense of their experiences and thus create meaning. By "story" we do not mean a whole-cloth beginning-middle-end structure; rather an iterative, evolving fabric of sense-making. Forming one's story or forming the story of a group is a lifelong process, which is aided by being spoken, and heard. This may be the essence of phronetic learning.

Implications

A number of precepts are emerging and therefore underpin and inform our ongoing practice (Grant, 2017):

1. Authenticity and integrity occur when individuals develop self-awareness together with an ability to pay attention to others and the current operating context. This attentiveness enables them to examine a situation from all angles, and communicate a clear vision of what needs to be done.
2. Potential change agents need tools to help them become more reflective and attentive. They need to journey into their own hearts, minds, and psyches to discover their core beliefs and perceptual filters to better understand and use the shared myths and stories that can align and inspire an organization to perform beyond the norm.
3. Those who wish to influence need to inspire, which is different from motivating. This ability to inspire is determined by integrity of character (who we are, what we stand for, and how we act), realizing an alignment of passion, purpose, and the presence of trust. People see who we are and make judgments about our message accordingly. In other words, "it's not what we say, it's what we do."
4. Organizations will not achieve results unless their practices, policies, and procedures reflect their espoused values and purpose and unless those values are aligned with those of their employees and other stakeholders. When actual values differ from espoused values, the actual values will be reflected in the stories stakeholders tell. The same occurs when espoused and actual values are aligned. One need only listen.

Conclusion

We have stated that spiritual wisdom resides in two critical factors, self-actualization (individuation) and the ability to ask a dialogic question: a question to which we do not already know the answer. Traditional business courses do not address these factors and, in most cases, avoid them. It has been our experience that the solution to this complex problem lies in the human imagination. We know that imagination and creativity are the seeds of innovation and it is time for educators to provide leadership based on hope and aspiration if we are to reach the untapped creative potential in our people. The participants in reflective practice programs such as "Creativity in Business" confirm our beliefs and ask for more. There is much work ahead of us—in academe and in industry.

We use the Stanford Creativity in Business program to examine questions such as, how do participants experience personal creativity, leadership, followership or conflict? In this instance creativity, leadership, followership, or conflict is the phenomenon of interest, but is a psychological abstraction. For example, what do you experience when you face conflict in teams? Here the meaning of conflict is being examined, the experience of facing conflict, as opposed to accepting the abstract word as conclusive. It is through such experiences that insights are obtained, spiritual sources reclaimed, and new practices defined. Social capital is built on these active connections among people that bind human networks and communities. Perhaps we need to reclaim something old in order to build something new. And what could be more practical than claiming the power inherent in your own story?

Performance storyteller and storytelling coach Doug Lipman, whose work is informed by Hasidic mystical tradition, retells the story of the Rabbi Zusia, who after a dream becomes fearful of what question the angels will ask him when he dies. His students gather around, seeking to comfort him by soothing the source of his trouble of mind, and in doing so they ask the same great question that in mystic Christian tradition, Parsifal, whose attainment of wisdom is long and arduous, at last asks of the spiritually wounded Grail King: "Master, what ails thee?" (Grant, 2017). Zusia's answer is that the angels who in his dream flank the gates of paradise do not ask him why he was not in life a Moses to his people, nor why he was not a Joshua. Instead, they ask him: "Why were you not Zusia?"

References

Amabile, T. (1996). *Creativity in Context: Update to the Social Psychology of Creativity*. Boulder, CO: Westview Press.

Arendt, H. (1971). *The Life of the Mind*. New York: Harcourt.

Boud, D., Keogh, R., and Walker, D. (1985). *Reflection: Turning Experience into Learning*. London: Kogan Page.

Buckingham, M., & Clifton, D. O. (2001). *Now, Discover Your Strengths*. Omaha, NE: Gallup Press.

Burnside, R. M. & Guthrie, V. A. (1992). *Training for Action: A New Approach to Executive Development*. Center for Creative Leadership, Greensboro, NC.

Campbell, J. (1968). *The Masks of God: Creative Mythology*. New York: Penguin Books.

De Ciantis, C. (2005). Gods and myths in the information age. *Agir 20–21: La societe de l'information*.

De Ciantis, C. (2017). The gait of Hephaistos: Crooked perceptions into consilience. *Icono 14, 15*(1), 128–148.

Detienne, M., & Vernant, J-P. (1978). *Cunning Intelligence in Greek Culture and Society* (Trans. Janet Lloyd). Atlantic Highlands: Humanities.

el Kaliouby, E. (2017, October 20). We need computers with empathy. *MIT Technology Review*. Retrieved from www.technologyreview.com/s/609071/we-need-computers-with-empathy/.

Fahmy, D. (2018). Key findings about Americans' belief in God. *Fact Tank*. Retrieved from www.pewresearch.org/fact-tank/2018/04/25/key-findings-about-americans-belief-in-god.

Flyvbjerg, B. (2001). *Making Social Science Matter: Why Social Inquiry Fails and How it Can Succeed Again*. Cambridge, UK: Cambridge University Press.

Grant, G. (2005). *ReVisioning the Way We Work*. Bloomington, IN: Trafford Press.

Grant, G. (2012). Jung's drive theory: Ideas to action. International C. G. Jung Conference proceedings, New Orleans, LA.

Grant, G. (2014, November). Re-visioning the heroes journey: Something old, something new. *Integral Leadership Review*.

Grant, G. (2017). The untapped power of imagination in the workplace. In J. Neal (Ed.), *Handbook of Personal and Organizational Transformation*. Berlin: Springer AG, 1–35.

Hyatt, K. and De Ciantis, C. (2014). *What's Important: Understanding and Working with Values Perspectives*. Tucson, AZ: Integral Press.

Jung, C. G. (1953). *Psychological Types* (Trans. R. F. C. Hull). *The Collected Works of C. G. Jung*. CW 6. Bollingen Series 20. Princeton, NJ: Princeton University Press, 1953, 2nd ed. 1968.

Jung, C. G. (1969a). *The Structure and Dynamics of the Psyche* (Trans. R. F. C. Hull). *The Collected Works of C. G. Jung*. CW 8. Bollingen Series 20. Princeton, NJ: Princeton University Press, 2nd ed. 1969.

Jung, C. G. (1969b). *Archetypes of the Collective Unconscious* (Trans. R. F. C. Hull). *The Collected Works of C. G. Jung*. CW 9. Bollingen Series 20. Princeton, NJ: Princeton University Press, 2nd ed. 1969.

Lipka, M., & Gecewicz, C. (2017). More Americans now say they're spiritual but not religious. *Fact Tank*. Retrieved from www.pewresearch.org/fact-tank/2017/09/06/more-americans-now-say-theyre-spiritual-but-not-religious.

Lipman, D. (n.d.). Why weren't you Zusia? Retrieved from www.hasidicstories.com/Stories/Other_Early_Rebbes/zusia.html.

McDrury, J., & Alterio, M. (2002). *Learning through Storytelling in Higher Education: Using Reflection and Experience to Improve Learning*. London: Kogan Page.

Mann, A., & Harter, J. (2016). The worldwide employee engagement crisis. *Gallup Business Journal*. Retrieved from http://news.gallup.com/businessjournal/188033/worldwide-employee-engagement-crisis.aspx.

Mark, M., & Pearson, C. S. (2001). *The Hero and the Outlaw: Building Extraordinary Brands Through the Power of Archetypes.* New York: McGraw Hill.
Ray, M. L., & Myers, R. (1989). *Creativity in Business.* New York: Doubleday.
Reason, P., & Hawkins, P. (1988). Storytelling as inquiry. In Peter Reason (Ed.), *Human Inquiry in Action: Development in New Paradigm Research.* Newbury Park, CA: Sage, 79–101.
Sliwa, M., & Cairns, G. (2009). Towards a critical pedagogy of international business: The application of phronesis. *Management Learning, 40*(3), 227–140.
South African Truth and Reconciliation Commission (TRC). (1995). Retrieved from www.justice.gov.za/trc/.
White, H. (1987). *The Content of the Form: Narrative Discourse and Historical Representation.* Baltimore: Johns Hopkins University Press.
Young, D. P., & Dixson, N. M. (1996). *Helping Leaders Take Effective Action: A Program Evaluation.* Center for Creative Leadership, Greensboro, NC.

13

WORKPLACE SPIRITUALITY AND WELLNESS

An Organizational Neuroscientific Perspective

Claude-Hélène Mayer and Dirk Geldenhuys

Introduction

Spirituality within the workplace has become a topic well addressed within the discourse of organizational management (Mayer, 2011) and leadership (Allison, Kocher, & Goethals, 2016). It has been pointed out that spirituality is closely linked to mental health, wellbeing, and wellness (Kamoche, 2000; Honiball, Geldenhuys, & Mayer, 2014; Mayer & Geldenhuys, 2014). However, at the same time, spirituality often in the past has been excluded from sciences because sciences and scholarly work have increasingly been influenced by materialistic worldviews, leading to a turn away from spirituality as a scientific research topic (Sheldrake, 2013). According to Mayer and Walach (2018), spirituality, therefore, has to (re-)gain legitimacy as a scientific research topic and should be addressed from various methodological and theoretical stances. The chapter focuses on spirituality as an important aspect in the workplace, from a neuroscientific perspective. Neurosciences have recently become favored within research contexts, exploring, for example, religious experiences (McNamara, 2009) or organizational and workplace contexts (Choi & Leroy, 2015). However, combined research on neuroscience and spirituality within workplaces and organizations seems still to be a void in research (Smith, 2008).

This theoretical chapter therefore aims at focusing on (workplace) spirituality with regard to wellness from neuroscientific perspectives. It further takes selected, related concepts to spirituality, such as mindfulness, into account to explore them within the workplace and organizational context. The discussion of these concepts from the described perspectives will lead toward new insights, conclusions, and recommendations regarding spirituality as an important research topic in the context of organizational and workplace studies and wellness.

In the following, spirituality and workplace spirituality will be defined and explored in the context of wellness during life and work. These concepts will furthermore be reflected from neuroscientific perspectives and explained with regard to leadership and managerial practices. The authors will present and describe more practical examples with regard to neuroscience and mindfulness as related concepts. Finally, conclusions are provided and recommendations for future research and practice given.

Defining Spirituality

Spirituality has been defined from various disciplinary perspectives (Salopek, 2004; Adams, 2017). Workplace spirituality has been referred to as a specific concept within the discourses on spirituality (Giacalone, 2004; Baldacchino, 2017). The discourses around the meaning of spirituality and workplace spirituality and the complexity of these concepts have led to in-depth discussions and challenges to define the concepts (Giacalone & Jurkiewicz, 2003; Mohamed, 2004; Jacobs, 2013) and scholars from theology (Klerk-Luttig, 2008) and other fields have been actively involved in the interdisciplinary discourses on spirituality (Mayer & Boness, 2011; Lean & Ganster, 2017). Spirituality has, however, also been discussed in the context of organizations and from management and industrial as well as organizational perspectives (Mayer & Geldenhuys, 2014; Mayer & Viviers, 2014a, 2014b).

Spirituality has been defined multifold; it is, however, often referred to as an inner concept which evolves from inner reflection and self-awareness (Han, 2006) and it usually develops throughout the course of life (Mayer, 2017) and represents a conscious attitude toward the self, the world, and beyond (Butts, 1999). To become aware of spirituality within daily life and activities, individuals need to become conscious of the interdependency and interconnectedness of things (Covey, 2005). Therefore, spirituality is always a subjective experience, which interrelates the self, the other, and the entire universe in a quest for meaning (Garcia-Zamor, 2003; Swinton, Bain, Ingram, & Heys, 2011), and connects to the purpose of life and meaningfulness which becomes part of the individual's identity (Krishnakumar & Neck, 2002).

Definitions of spirituality therefore range from concepts that place spirituality within the concept of meaning-making—the moving away from materialism toward transcendence and a certain value orientation (Jirásek, 2013). As described by Mayer and Walach (2018), definitions of spirituality often include that spirituality is based on a human experience in an embodied sense, relating to the self, others, and the world, and transcending in scope, reaching out for a consciousness beyond the materialistic world. Walach (2017) has therefore defined spirituality as the habit of being motivated by a reality beyond the immediate needs and wants of the ego and a holistic, comprising cognition, emotion, and motivation or behavior.

For several researchers, spirituality includes transcendence and a sense of calling, which is usually related to meaningfulness and leading a meaningful and purposeful life (Ashmos & Duchon, 2000). The growing interest in spirituality has been seen as an increase in the search for meaning (Honiball et al., 2014), as well as in a search for an increasing meaningfulness at work particularly (Mayer, Surtee, & May, 2015; Person, May, & Mayer, 2016). Meaningfulness becomes a motivational component and is created through work—particularly when it leads to personal growth and self-development (Sheep, 2004; Mayer, Surtee, & Barnard, 2015)—and increases productivity, as well as wellness in life and at work.

Besides meaningfulness, mindfulness is associated with spiritual traditions (Cashwell, Paige Bentley, & Bigbee, 2007) and defined as a multilayered construct that is connected to cognition, awareness, and emotion (Sauer, Walach & Kohls, 2011). Mindfulness keeps the person in the present moment, opens up multiple perspectives (Atkins, 2008), and is aligned with a non-judgmental, non-attached, gentle, and kind attitude through spiritual practice, which is further seen as being associated with psychological wellbeing and inversely associated with distress (Masuda, Price, & Latzman, 2012).

Mindfulness and meaningfulness are further discussed with regard to their neuropsychological angle and the pros and cons of the application. Practical examples are provided for the reader to gain a deeper understanding of the interconnectedness of the concepts.

Exploring Spirituality in the Context of the Workplace

Workplace spirituality has advanced to a specific concept, which refers to spirituality within the workplace and organizations and it has been pointed out that spirituality can shift the focus within the workplace from a culture of having to a culture of being (Labuschagne, 2013), which further increases effectiveness, creativity, freedom, and wellbeing within the workplace. However, although spirituality has been emphasized as being an important aspect of the *homo economicus* (Yamagishi, Li, Takasishi, Matsumoto, & Kiyonari, 2014), it still seems to be underestimated and neglected in management and organizational studies (Visser, 2009) and the understanding of spirituality within the workplace is still limited (Van Tonder & Ramdass, 2009).

Over the past years, however, workplace spirituality has gained interest in different cultural contexts (Mayer & Walach, 2018) and various definitions of workplace spirituality exist. These definitions range from passionate and energized employees who find their meaning in life in their work, to a spiritual workplace culture, which includes specific values such as autonomy, trust, support, recognition, fairness, and innovation (Kinjerski & Skrypnek, 2004, p. 27). It also includes a sense of transcendence and human and spiritual interconnection and feelings of completeness (Giacalone & Jurkiewicz, 2003, p. 13), including the foci on inner life or spiritual identity, meaning and purpose in work, and a sense of connection and community (Ashmos & Duchon, 2000).

With regard to the workplace, spirituality has been researched particularly in connection with leadership studies (Leigh-Taylor, 2000). Mayer and Boness (2011) have emphasized that spirituality is successfully applied in conflict, conflict management, and mediation in leadership and organizations and it has also been argued by other researchers that spirituality needs to be taken into account when leadership is discussed within the context of the workplace to address leadership and change (Barrett, 2006; Dadabhay, 2011). Full (2010) has described the growing movement among business leaders to turn to mindfulness and spiritual practices, which lead to reduced stress and changes in values and attitudes within workplaces.

Spirituality in the workplace is often connected to related concepts of mindfulness and meditation (Mayer, 2014). The concept of mindfulness in particular has been proven to increase quality of life, decrease symptoms of clinical conditions, and to contribute positively to psychological variables (Khoury, Sharma, Rush, & Fournier 2015; Kuyken et al., 2016). Mindfulness programs, as part of workplace spirituality programs, have increasingly been adopted in organizations and workplaces to reduce stress, but it should be noted that, in this regard too, there is no valid and reliable evaluation research (Ruprecht & Walach, 2016). An increased conscious application of spirituality, however, could support a more sustainable, wellness-oriented workplace culture and lead to an orientation beyond immediate ego-driven needs. It further leads to an increase in ethics and ethical behavior in the workplace (Lips-Wiersma & Mills, 2002), and, according to Glauner (2014), growing sociability and sustainability. Finally, Albertini and Smith (2009) have highlighted that workplace spirituality also leads to improved teamwork, trust, ethical and moral behavior, contentment, feelings of belonging, as well as meaningfulness in the workplace.

Spirituality and its Connection to Wellness in Life and in the Workplace

Spirituality has been described as generally improving human conditions with regard to mental, physical, and spiritual wellness. Wellness is often either defined as subjective wellbeing (SWB) or as psychological wellbeing (PWB) (Diener & Lucas, 2000); however, definitions of wellness, wellbeing, and mental health often overlap (Mayer, 2011). Wellness is defined as experiencing positive emotions (Goleman, 2000) and as a specific approach to personal health and wellbeing (Freidl, 2004). Wellness is viewed as a positive leadership task, which needs to be recognized as an integrative force of mind, body, and spirit (Mayer, 2011). Employees, when experiencing wellness, are described as being energetic, motivated, healthy, productive, and committed to the organization and its goals (Rothmann, Van der Colff, & Rothmann, 2006). The holistic approach of health and wellbeing includes emotional, intellectual, spiritual, occupational, social, and physical dimensions of the individual (Sapp, 2004). Wellness, as in this definition, includes spirituality as one dimension.

Researchers have described spirituality as an important aspect in medical sciences, psychiatry, and psychotherapy (Van Rensburg, 2014; Mayer & Walach, 2018). Others, such as Bojuwoye (2005), have highlighted its importance for therapies and healing interventions. According to Mayer (2011) and Honiball, Geldenhuys and Mayer (2014), workplaces need to expand their often rather rational and logical focus toward a more spiritual dimension to increase employees' health and wellbeing. Through spirituality, a balance between work and self is increased at work through improved interpersonal relationships, innovative practices, problem-solving, and creativity (Hankin, 2005). This leads to an increase in wellness (Mayer & Geldenhuys, 2014). However, spirituality also functions as a coping mechanism for challenges experienced at work, such as downsizing, risks, rapid changes, or threats of unemployment or increasing organizational diversity (Mayer, 2011). By functioning as a coping mechanism, spirituality increases wellness and enables organizations to flourish (Moore & Casper, 2006), thereby impacting positively on the organizational (wellness) culture.

The role of mindfulness as a spiritual activity in the work context has already become a popular topic in literature (Alberts & Hülsheger, 2015; Choi & Leroy, 2015; Reb & Atkins, 2015). Although the focus still seems to be on interventions, especially through training programs, attempts to scientifically study mindfulness in organizations have already started to gain attention (Ellen & Leroy, 2015). Theoretical studies have already been conducted on the role of mindfulness and wellbeing in the work context (Glomb, Duffy, Bono, & Yang, 2011), the relationship between mindfulness, performance, and turnover intention (Dane & Brummel, 2014), and the role of effective leadership (Boyatzis, 2015). Furthermore, Alberts and Hülsheger (2015) refer to empirical studies indicating initial evidence regarding the positive effect of mindfulness on aspects such as work–family balance, leadership, employee engagement, job satisfaction, stress reduction and quality of sleep, recovery during a short respite, emotion regulation at work, and job performance. Yet, there is still no consensus in conceptualizing mindfulness (with different frameworks and dimensions) (Choi & Leroy, 2015), as well as the practices and programs, ranging from differences of duration to mode of delivery (Alberts & Hülsheger, 2015).

Based on this overview, the authors argue that organizational neuroscience offers the possibility of synthesizing the constructs with specific implications for leadership and managerial practices.

Spirituality, Workplace Spirituality, and Wellness from a Neuroscientific Perspective

Organizational neuroscience as an emerging field of study investigates particular networks of brain systems responsible for attitudes and behavior in the workplace (Ghadiri, Habermacher, & Peters, 2012). Selective neuroscientific principles are applied in the study of intuition, emotions in organizations, ethical decision-making, organizational justice, and leadership (Becker, Cropozano, & Sanfey, 2011; Ghadiri, Habermacher, & Peters, 2012, Habermacher, Ghadiri, & Peters, 2014; Henson & Rossouw, 2013). It is a multidisciplinary field, translating neuroscientific principles, such as the functioning of the fear-based system, to topics related to the work context to further understand, enrich, validate, and offer a framework for management sciences.

Whereas wellness models in the organizational sciences traditionally rely on applied theories and models from psychology and psychotherapy, current organizational wellness models deriving from a neuroscientific perspective, are primarily based on neuroscientific principles and neuropsychotherapeutic models (Pillay, 2011), for example the work of Grawe (2007) and Grawe's model as refined by Rossouw (2014). These principles and this model serve as the foundation for this discussion. It differs from, but augments, the traditional analytical and humanistic schools of psychology, as the focus is on the neural processes underlying psychology.

Most of the research on organizational wellness interventions mainly studies the stress response with the purpose of determining the causal relationship between exposure to stressors in the workplace and health or organizational performance (Biron, Karanika-Murray, & Cooper, 2012); seemingly, without acknowledging the crucial role the brain plays in the stress response. The reason for this is probably the fact that the majority of the brain's responses occur before the organism is even aware of the stressful condition (Henson & Rossouw, 2013). It is the brain that determines if the environment poses a threat to the individual, and whether the course of action will be to approach or avoid the stressor, both physiological and psychological.

To understand the role of the brain in the stress response and the subsequent implications for spirituality, one first needs to consider the neuroscientific perspective on human development (Hanna, 2014). This theory is called the triune brain theory (three brains in one) developed by Paul MacLean (1990). According to MacLean, the human brain developed through evolution in a sequence, starting with the Reptilian Complex (the most primitive structure that we share with all animals), followed by the Paleomammilian Complex (that we share with mammals), and third the Neomammilian Complex as the most recent step in the evolution of the brain. This development, from the most primitive to the most advanced structures, can be recognized in human beings.

Although the specifics of the theory is today challenged by some neuroscientists (Brann, 2014), there is agreement that the human brain comprises three interconnected brain systems (Dahlitz & Rossouw, 2014) with the primitive brain comprising the brainstem, pons, and medulla, as the first system. This system is fully developed and fully functional at birth and is responsible for physical survival as it regulates breathing, heart rate, motor planning, and the physiological aspects of basic affect such as aggression and anxiety (Hanna, 2014; Henson & Rossouw, 2013; Rossouw, 2014). This is the most protected system of the brain and in need of constant blood flow.

The next is the limbic region (Hanna, 2014), also known as the emotional or impulsive brain and comprises the thalamus, hypothalamus, amygdala, hippocampus, basal ganglia, and nucleus accumbens. This system is fully developed at birth, but not fully functional. It interacts with the environment where it gets cues for learning and for protection. It enables emotions, social behavior, and the ability to refine basic affect (aggression and anxiety) that originates in the primitive brain (Henson & Rossouw, 2013). This is followed by the development of the cortical systems (especially the left and right pre-frontal systems) (Hanna, 2014), also known as the smart brain. This system is mostly underdeveloped at birth and develops until early adulthood. The cortical systems or frontal parts of the brain are responsible for executing control, namely the language, abstract cognition, sequential planning, and perception abilities. Another function of this system is that it serves to down-regulate the limbic system (Dahlitz & Rossouw, 2014). Other than in the case of the primitive systems (such as the brain stem region and the limbic system), damage in this part of the brain is in most instances not life threatening. As the primitive systems are better developed than the cortical systems, the primitive systems take precedence in activation in situations when danger or threat is perceived, leading to a stress response. The stress response is a psychological survival response of fight, flight, or freeze and is primarily initiated by the amygdala (Hanna, 2014). During the stress response, the hypothalamus–pituitary–adrenal axis (HPA axis) is activated, shutting down systems such as the immune system, digestion, and even the pre-frontal cortex (PFC). This explains why stress can lead to physical illness as well as psychological pathology.

The brain is thus primarily wired for survival (Hanna, 2014; Rossouw, 2014). It is only when survival is secured that the higher order systems, such as the smart brain, can function optimally.

The survival function of the brain is needed in times of danger. However, extensive or prolonged activation of these primitive systems leads to even stronger wiring in this area, the strengthening of neural connections due to the ongoing firing between neurons, the activation of stress chemicals such as corticotropin-releasing factor (CRF), adrenocorticotropic hormone (ACTH), adrenalin, and cortisol, and the inhibition of serotonin, which is associated with smart brain development (Dahlitz & Rossouw, 2014). This in turn leads to compromised neural proliferation in the frontal systems, resulting in the development of the "anxious brain." The stress response is thus not only a neurochemical reaction, but also changes the neural networks and even structures of the brain. It may lead to cell death and a decrease in brain volume (Henson & Rossouw, 2013).

Due to the principles of neuroplasticity and epigenetics, synapses are modified by experience (Dahlitz & Rossouw, 2014). The same gene can thus be expressed differently, depending on the experience of the influence of the environment. Experiencing a compromised environment constantly activates the protective patterns that surface in the stress response, leading to the development of motivational schemata of avoidance (Grawe, 2007). However, if the environment is experienced as physically and emotionally safe, the over-activation of these systems will be downregulated, leading to the development of approach motivational schemata (Dahlitz & Rossouw, 2014). According to Grawe (2007), motivational schemata of "approach" and "avoidance" are developed throughout life to satisfy consistently basic human needs and to protect human beings from the violation of these needs. These schemata form the basis of Grawe's consistency model (2007).

Grawe (2007) identified neural correlates for the basic human needs of Seymour Epstein's "cognitive-experiential self-theory" (Epstein, 1990, 1993) and postulates that the need for attachment (Ainsworth, Blehar, Waters, & Wall, 1978; Bolby, 1969, 1973) is one of the most fundamental needs for the infant's psychological wellbeing and development. This is the first survival need that needs to be fulfilled, as infants are not able to ensure their own survival (Hanna, 2014). As the infant's neocortex is still underdeveloped at this stage, the attachment processes entail more reactive responses than responses that are cognitively controlled. The development of secure or insecure attachment patterns therefore depends on the consistency of the caregiver's availability, proximity, and sensitivity (Bowlby, 1973; Hanna, 2014; Henson & Rossouw, 2013). If the basic need for attachment is met in a consistent manner, the infant feels safe to explore the environment further. This facilitates learning, resulting in optimal stimulation and neural growth (Grawe, 2007; Henson & Rossouw, 2013).

The interpersonal need for attachment is also linked to a sense of belonging (Hanna, 2014; Siegel, 2012). According to Hanna, Harper, and Nelson as cited in Hanna (2014), the interplay of belonging and individuality as elements of attachment, guide children as they gain a sense of identity in sibling roles.

Another crucial fundamental need for human functioning is the pervasive need for control and orientation (Epstein, 1990; Grawe, 2007). The need for control begins when an infant needs to respond to the environment in order to survive. As the mother is instrumental in satisfying the need for control, there is a clear relation between the need for control and the need for attachment. If the need for control is not met, the infant experiences incongruence between its goals and its perception of the extent to which the environment can satisfy these goals and hence a violation of this need. However, if the need is met, congruence is experienced and neural proliferations are enhanced.

Human beings need to experience that their environment, or their perceptions of their environment, is congruent with their activated goals (Dahlitz & Rossouw, 2014). They therefore need to experience a sense of control and orientation over their environment. For growth to happen, incongruence is hence needed, but to such an extent, that control is still experienced. Past life experiences, influence the perception of controllability and predictability, of the extent to which life makes sense in general, and about whether investing resources and approaching life is likely to be rewarding (Henson & Rossouw, 2013). The need for control does not only refer to control over the current situation but also to the maximum number of options available for the future. If there are options available for the future, a sense of control is thus experienced (Dahlitz & Rossouw, 2014; Grawe, 2007).

The need for orientation also forms part of the need for control (Grawe, 2007). Orientation refers to the ability to form an accurate appraisal of a situation and to make sense of what is happening (Dahlitz & Rossouw, 2014). If a situation is understood clearly, it will in most instances result in the experience of a greater sense of control.

According to Epstein (1998), another crucial need is the need for pleasure maximization (good, beautiful, etc.) or distress avoidance. Experiences are neurologically evaluated as either good or bad, with the motivation to maximize good experiences and minimize bad experiences. This even happens when people are prepared to suffer for the greater good, or to deny some short-term pleasure to obtain something better in the future (Dahlitz & Rossouw, 2014). Dopamine is released when a sense of pleasure is expected as well as when people are successful in avoiding pain or discomfort.

The evaluation of what is good or bad is subjective and influenced by the individual's activated goals and how the experience of the environment is consistent with satisfying the other basic needs (Rossouw, 2014). According to Grawe (2007, p. 244), we are in a maximal state of pleasure when our "current perceptions and goals are completely congruent with one another, and the transpiring mental activity is not disturbed by any competing intentions." This maximum state is similar to the concept of "flow" (Csikszentmihalyi, 1991), with its focus on intrinsic motivation and the alignment of perception of experience with intentions.

The fourth basic need, the need for self-esteem enhancement or protection, differs from the other needs in the sense that it is distinctly human (Grawe, 2007), probably because the neural circuits associated with this need seem to be more complex and perhaps more extensive than those associated with the other needs (Henson & Rossouw, 2013). Self-esteem is defined as an individual's subjective self-evaluation of his or her worth as a person. As a basic need, it is secure and congruent, as opposed to unstable, narcissistic, or discrepant (Grawe, 2007; Henson & Rossouw, 2013). Conscious self-awareness and the capacity for reflective thinking are required for the regulation of self-esteem and probably evolved as result of the survival value of social relationships. As these qualities are primarily facilitated by the cortical areas, they are still absent in young humans, and thus the last to mature. However, life experiences that occur before the development of these qualities already influence the self-image and self-esteem of the individual. According to Grawe (2007), the tendency to enhance self-esteem can be related to approach motivational schemata, whereas self-esteem protection can be related to avoidance schemata.

Grawe's consistency model (2007) was refined by Dahlitz and Rossouw (2014) who suggest that the need for self-esteem is an emerging property of the other basic needs and that the "*condition* of safety is essential for the satisfaction of those needs" (Dahlitz & Rossouw, 2014, p. 32). Furthermore, it is argued that the self-esteem concept does not seem to have an approach/avoidance reflex in relation to the environment. It should rather be seen as an emerging property of the other needs, "an *emergent* sense of *self*—shaped by basic need satisfaction and the motivational schemata that serve those needs—as a neural meta-structure that influences our approach/avoid violation" (Dahlitz & Rossouw, 2014, p. 32). Habermacher et al. (2014) also adapted Grawe's model by viewing control and orientation as two separate needs.

Organizational Neuroscience for Leadership and Managerial Practices

Although leadership theories and managerial practices are currently, in most instances, not developed from a neuroscientific perspective per se, using organizational neuroscience as a framework or as a benchmark for assessing these is becoming popular among scholars and practitioners. For example, coaching with compassion is an approach developed by Boyatzis, Smith, and Beveridge (2012), of which the aims can be regarded as congruent with basic neuroscience principles. According to the authors, compassion includes both increasing hedonic wellbeing in response to pain, but also eudemonic wellbeing in response to the need to grow. This correlates well with satisfying the basic human needs and providing stimulation for growth.

Henson and Rossouw (2013) applied Grawe's consistency theory to leadership development and Habermacher et al. (2014) and Brann (2014) to coaching as a leadership development intervention. Ghadiri, Habermacher, and Peters(2012) are of the opinion that leadership, from a neuroleadership perspective, means to lead one's own and others' brains and to satisfy the four basic neuroscientific needs. Hence, the goal of management is to strive for harmony with these basic needs, the brain, and the working environment. According to Henson and Rossouw (2013), optimal brain functioning in organizations is achieved when individuals are able to self-regulate the experiences of new stimulation. They can build resilience by including confidence and competence through exposure to, and adapting to increased levels of change. This implies an organizational culture that is characterized by safety and an optimal stimulation and cognitive load (Henson & Rossouw, 2013). Optimal stimulation refers to a "controlled disruption of inconsistency" (Henson & Rossouw, 2013, p. 80) and cognitive load refers to a thinking environment where the correct amount of time is dedicated to ensure deep thought, reflection, and analysis, while, at the same time maintaining a sense of urgency. Based on this discussion, we argue that organizational neuroscience can serve as a scientific validation for applying spiritual activities such as mindfulness in the workplace.

Spiritual Concept of Mindfulness from a Neuroscience Perspective

Studies about the relation between mindfulness as a spiritual practice and neuroscience are still in its infancy (Chiesa, Calati, & Serretti, 2011) and are regarded as a promising avenue for future research and practice (Brann, 2014; Choi & Leroy, 2015). However, preliminary studies have already indicated an association between the two major approaches in mindfulness training, namely focused attention and open monitoring, and portions of the cortical areas such as the prefrontal cortex, anterior cigulate cortex, and the parietal cortex (Tang & Posner, 2013).

Spirituality offers an advantage point for increasing wellbeing in organizations by lowering cortisol levels and enhancing the development of the neocortical systems (Henson & Rossouw, 2013). This in turn leads to the enhancement of wellbeing in organizations, improved leadership and managerial practices, and hence improved productivity. From the perspective of applied neuroscience, the capacity to reflect and the development of self-awareness are regarded as mainly as a smart brain function that develops throughout life. In essence, self-monitoring facilitates a shift from being a victim of external forces to taking control (Henson & Rossouw, 2013). The practice of spirituality with its emphasis on non-judgmental reflection and self-awareness can therefore assist in neural proliferation in these systems thereby enhancing well-being (Cloninger, 2007). Awareness of stress without judgment can decrease negative thoughts about the self and contribute to the enhancement of self-esteem. That is, according to Dahlitz and Rossouw (2014), an emerging property of the other basic needs.

Furthermore, another major component of spirituality, namely to become conscious about the interdependency and interconnectedness of things, probably also relates to approach motivational schemata whereby humans approach the environment instead of avoiding challenges that the environment may pose. Approach motivational schemata can be enhanced even further with the non-judgmental curiosity and kindness that is characteristic of practicing mindfulness as a spiritual activity.

It can also be argued that practicing mindfulness can assist in down-regulating fear-based avoidance motivation, as human beings cannot develop self-awareness when overly fearful, stressed, or angry (Hanna, 2014). More specifically, spirituality can probably address the basic human needs for attachment and control. As discussed earlier, making sense of life experiences can enhance the experience of being in control. Only when this need is satisfied on a basic level, are people able to strive for exercising control over their environment. According to Cloninger (2007), people find meaning in life by experiencing acts of kindness or compassion. In this sense, spirituality can assist in activating feelings of hope and life satisfaction. This corresponds with the relationship between the needs for attachment and control whereby the need for control can be satisfied by the proximity and sensitivity of a caregiver. The experience of belonging thus provides safety, allowing focus on approaching life and difficulties instead of avoidance behavior.

We also argue that the basic need for pleasure maximization relates to spirituality. As mentioned, the maximal state of pleasure is similar to the concept of flow. According to Seligman (2002) who built on the concept of flow, happiness in life entails three dimensions that can be developed, namely the pleasant life, the good life, and the meaningful life. The last dimension to be developed, the meaningful life, refers to a sense of fulfillment that is experienced when people use their personal strengths to serve a purpose greater than their own needs by contributing to the happiness of other human beings. As dopamine is released when a person experiences success in avoiding pain or discomfort as well as when pleasure is experienced, spirituality can assist in satisfying this need to such an extent that life is not only pleasurable but even experienced as meaningful.

Although links between mindfulness and neuroscience have already been made, there is still resistance to implementing mindfulness interventions in the workplace. According to Reb and Atkins (2015), the tension between spirituality and the workplace can, for instance, be ascribed to value conflicts between spiritual practices and workplaces, the growing secularization of society and the need for many to retain a separation between work life and personal life. According to Hall (2015), scholars and practitioners could frame mindfulness in a secular context in an attempt to address these concerns. This, however, could lead to concerns about losing the essence of mindfulness (Reb & Atkins, 2015). We argue that applied neuroscience can offer such a vantage point by not only providing a secular but, more importantly, a scientific lens for introducing mindfulness as a spiritual concept in the workplace.

An openness to the introduction of formal mindfulness programs in organizations can be facilitated by including a theoretical neuroscientific component as part of the program.

Furthermore, mindful leaders can imbed mindful practices in the organizational culture. This can be done by using self-awareness and self-regulation to create a safe, but stimulating, culture through instilling policies and processes that foster open communication. Simple but practical techniques could be, for instance, to learn to reflect on the motivational schemata that drive decisions; to make reflective rather than reactive decisions; to broaden thinking by asking how the opposite of your own assumptions might be true; to observe and name external and internal stimuli without judgment; to develop the habit for asking for alternatives before decision-making (Brann, 2014; Henson & Rossouw, 2013).

Conclusions and Implications for Theory and Practice

The aim of this chapter was to provide insights into spirituality and wellness from a neuroscientific perspective. The authors conclude that organizational neuroscience can assist in providing a scientific basis for applying mindfulness as spiritual practice in the work context.

Researchers and practitioners need to be mindful about organizational neuroscience becoming an applied field of study. In a world that is progressively characterized by interdisciplinary, multidisciplinary, and transdisciplinary studies, there does not seem to be a need for behavior specialists working in organizations to do clinical studies with functional magnetic resonance imaging (fMRI) and similar technology. Translating and researching the contribution of applied neuroscientific principles seem to be more appropriate and useful. In this sense, as organizational interventions to a large extent apply theories, models, and practices based on psychotherapeutic principles, it is reasoned that neuropsychotherapy can already serve this purpose and be adjusted to neuropsychological-based coaching in the workplace.

However, this being said, this field of study is still in its early stages. Empirical research to validate current hypotheses about the correlations between neuroscientific principles and mindfulness as spiritual activity in the workplace is still largely lacking. Multidisciplinary research and particularly neuroscience, for instance, can assist by identifying and offering insights into the neural correlates of mindfulness as spiritual activity in the workplace.

Regarding future practice, we argue that applied neuroscientific knowledge can form a theoretical component of skills training interventions and mindfulness. Equipping participants with the relevant knowledge of how the brain functions will assist in grounding the interventions and creating meaning and a deeper understanding of the workplace and workplace interactions for participants. Furthermore, applied mindfulness techniques can be practiced by employees, leaders, and workers alike to create a mindful and spiritual workplace culture in which all participants can strive for wellness and success.

References

Adams, K. (2017). Towards an interdisciplinary approach to understanding and nurturing spirituality and the whole child. *International Journal of Children's Spirituality, 22*(1), 1–3.

Ainsworth, M. D., Blehar, M. C., Waters, E., Wall, S. (1978). *Patterns of Attachment: A Psychological Study of the Strange Situation*. Hillsdale, NJ: Lawrence Erlbaum Associates Inc.

Albertini, S., & Smith, T. (2009). A spiritual audit of a retail branch of a South African bank. *South African Journal of Human Resource Management, 6*, 10–21.

Alberts, H. J. E. M., & Hülsheger, U. R. (2015). Applying mindfulness in the context of work. In J. Reb & P. W. B. Atkins (Eds.), *Mindfulness in Organisations: Foundations, Research, and Applications*. Cambridge, UK: Cambridge University Press, 100–132.

Allison, S. T., Kocher, C. T., & Goethals, G. R. (2016). *Frontiers in Spiritual Leadership: Discovering the Better Angels of Our Nature*. New York: Palgrave Macmillan.

Ashmos, D. P., & Duchon, D. (2000). Spirituality at work. *Journal of Management Inquiry, 9*, 134–145.

Atkins, P. (2008). Leadership as response not reaction: Wisdom and mindfulness in public sector leadership. In P. Hart & J. Uhr (Eds.), *Public Leadership: Perspectives and Practices*. Canberra, Australia: Anu Press, 73–82.

Baldacchino, D. (2017). Spirituality in the healthcare workplace. *Religions, 8*(12), 2060.

Barrett, A. M. (2006). Coherence, deference and difference: Primary school teacher identity in Tanzania. Paper presented at the British Association for International and Comparative Education Conference, Queen's University, Belfast, 8–10 September 2006. Retrieved from: www.edqual.org/edqual/educationquality/barrettbaice06.doc.

Becker, W. J., Cropozano, R., & Sanfey, G. (2011). Organizational neuroscience: Taking organizational theory inside the neural black box. *Journal of Management, 37*(4), 933–961.

Biron, C., Karanika-Murray, M., & Cooper, C. L. (2012). Organizational interventions for stress and well-being: An overview. In C. Biron, M. Karanika-Murray, & C. L. Cooper (Eds.), *Improving Organizational Interventions for Stress and Well-Being: Addressing Process and Context*. London: Routledge, 1–17.

Bojuwoye, O. (2005). Traditional healing practices in Southern Africa: Ancestral spirits, ritual ceremonies and holistic healing. In R. Moodley & W. West (Eds.), *Integrating Traditional Healing Practices into Counselling and Psychotherapy*. Thousand Oaks, CA: Sage, 61–73.

Bowlby, J. (1969). *Attachment and Loss. Vol 1: Attachment*. New York: Basic Books Inc.

Bowlby, J. (1973). *Attachment and Loss. Vol 2: Separation: Anxiety and Anger*. New York: Basic Books Inc.

Boyatzis, R. E. (2015). Building and maintaining better leadership relations through mindfulness. In J. Reb & P. W. B. Atkins (Eds.), *Mindfulness in Organisations: Foundations, Research, and Applications*. Cambridge, UK: Cambridge University Press, 239–255.

Boyatzis, R. E., Smith, M. L., & Beveridge, A. J. (2012). Aching with compassion: Inspiring health, well-being, and development in organisations. *Journal of Applied Behavioral Science, 49*(2), 153–178.

Brann, A. (2014). *Neuroscience for Coaches: How to Use the Latest Insights for the Benefit of Your Clients*. London: Kogan Page.

Butts, D. (1999). Spirituality at work: An overview. *Journal of Organizational Change Management, 12*, 328–333.

Cashwell, C. S., Paige Bentley, D., & Bigbee, A. (2007). Spirituality and counselor wellness. *Journal of Humanistic Counseling, Education and Development, 46*, 66–81.

Chiesa, A., Calati, R., & Serretti, A. (2011). Does mindfulness training improve cognitive abilities? A systematic view of neuropsychological findings. *Clinical Psychology Review, 31*, 449–464.

Choi, E., & Leroy, H. (2015). Methods of mindfulness: How mindfulness is studied in organisations. In J. Reb & P. W. B. Atkins (Eds.), *Mindfulness in Organisations: Foundations, Research, and Applications*. Cambridge, UK: Cambridge University Press, 67–99.

Cloninger, C. R. (2007). Spirituality and the science of feeling good. *Southern Medical Journal, 100*(7), 740–743.

Covey, S. R. (2005). The 8th habit. *Soundview Executive Book Summaries, 27*, 1–8.

Csikszentmihalyi, M. (1991). *Flow: The Psychology of Optimal Experience*. New York: Harper Perennial.

Dadabhay, M. (2011). The mediating role of workplace spirituality on perceptions of transformational leadership, organisational commitment and employee job satisfaction within a sample of South Africa Muslim school teachers. Master's thesis, Department of Industrial and Organisational Psychology, University of Witwatersrand, Johannesburg.

Dahlitz, M. J. & Rossouw, P. J. (2014). The consistency-theoretical model of mental functioning: Towards a refined perspective. In P. J. Rossouw (Ed.), *Neuropsychotherapy: Theoretical Underpinnings and Clinical Applications*. Brisbane, Australia: Mediros, 21–41.

Dane, E., & Brummel, B. J. (2014). Examining workplace mindfulness and its relations to job performance and turnover intention. *Human Relations, 67*, 105–128.

Diener, E., & Lucas, R. E. (2000). Subjective emotional well-being. In M. Levis & J. M. Haviland (Eds.), *Handbook of Emotions* (2nd ed.). New York: Guilford Press, 325–337.

Ellen, C., & Leroy, H. (2015). Methods of mindfulness: How mindfulness is studied in the workplace. In J. Reb & P. W. B. Atkins (Eds.), *Mindfulness in Organisations: Foundations, Research and Applications*. Cambridge, UK: Cambridge University Press, 67–99.

Epstein, S. (1990). Cognitive-experiential self-theory. In L. A. Pervin (Ed.), *Handbook of Personality: Theory and Research*. New York: Guilford Press, 165–192.

Epstein, S. (1993). Implications of cognitive-experiential self-theory for personality and developmental psychology. In D. C. Funder, R. D. Parke, C. Tomlinson-Keasey, & K. Widaman (Eds.), *Studying Lives through Time: Personality and Development*. Washington, DC: American Psychological Press, 399–438.

Epstein, S. (1998). Cognitive-experiential self-theory. In D. F. Barone, M. Hersen, & V. B. van Hasselt (Eds.), *Advance Personality*. New York: Springer Science & Business Media New York, 212–238.

Freidl, C. (2004). *Wellnessboom: Erholung oder zu viel des Guten?* Soziologische Studie. Saarbrücken: VDM Verlag.

Full, G. (2010). *Die Emanzipation des Geistes: Eine Betrachtung antiker Bildungswege für eine emanzipierende Bildung*. Kröning, Germany: Asanger Verlag.

Garcia-Zamor, J. (2003). Workplace spirituality and organizational performance. *Public Administration Review, 63*, 355–364.

Ghadiri, A., Habermacher, A., & Peters, T. (2012). *Neuroleadership: A Journey through the Brain for Business Leaders*. Berlin: Springer.

Giacalone, R. (2004). A transcendent business education for the 21st century. *Academy of Management Learning and Education, 3*, 415–420.

Giacalone, R. A., & Jurkiewicz, C. L. (2003). Right from wrong: The influence of spirituality on perceptions of unethical business activities. *Journal of Business Ethics Part 1, 46*, 396–405.

Glauner, F. (2014). Ethics, values and corporate cultures: A Wittgensteinian approach in understanding corporate action. Paper presented at the Proceedings of the CSR, Sustainability, Ethics and Governance Conference, Guildford, University of Surrey.

Glomb, T. M., Duffy, M. K., Bono, J. E., & Yang, T. (2011). Mindfulness at work. In J. Martocchio, H. Liao, & Joshi (Eds.), *Research in Personnel and Human Resource Management*. Bingley, UK: Emerald Group Publishing Limited, 115–157.

Goleman, D. (2000). *Emotional Intelligence*. New York: McGraw-Hill.

Grawe, K. (2007). *Neuropsychotherapy: How the Neurosciences Inform Effective Psychotherapy*. New York: Psychology Press.

Habermacher, A., Ghadiri, A., & Peters, T. (2014). The case for basic human needs in coaching: A neuroscientific perspective—The SCOAP Coach Theory. *Coaching Psychologist, 10*(1), 7–16.

Hall, L. (2015). Mindfulness in coaching. In J. Reb & P. W. B. Atkins (Eds.), *Mindfulness in Organisations: Foundations, Research and Applications*. Cambridge, UK: Cambridge University Press, 383–408.

Han, P. (2006). Nobodies to somebodies. *Soundview Executive Book Summaries, 28*, Part 2.

Hankin, H. (2005). *The New Workforce: Five Sweeping Trends that will Shape Your Company's Future*. New York: Amacom.

Hanna, S. M. (2014). *The Transparent Brain in Couple and Family Therapy: Mindful Integrations with Neuroscience*. New York: Routledge.

Henson, C., & Rossouw, P. (2013). *Brainwise Leadership: Practical Neuroscience to Survive and Thrive at Work*. Sydney, Australia: Learning Quest.

Honiball, G., Geldenhuys, D., & Mayer, C-H. (2014). Acknowledging others as whole beings: Managers' perceptions of spirituality and health in the South African workplace. In C-H. Mayer & D. Geldenhuys (Eds.), Spirituality, culture and health in management. Special Issue *International Review of Psychiatry, 26*(3), 289–301.

Jacobs, A. C. (2013). An evaluation of different kinds of spirituality. *Journal for Christian Scholarship, 49*(3), 143–180.

Jirásek, I. (2013). Verticality as non-religious spirituality. *Implicit Religion, 16*(2), 191–201.

Kamoche, K. (2000). From boom to bust: The challenge of managing people in Thailand. *International Journal of Human Resource Management, 11*, 452–468.

Khoury, B., Sharma, M., Rush, S. E., & Fournier, C. (2015). Mindfulness-based stress reduction for healthy individuals: A meta-analysis. *Journal of Psychosomatic Research, 78*, 519–528.

Kinjerski, V., & Skrypnek, B. J. (2004). Defining spirit at work: Finding common ground. *Journal of Organizational Change Management, 17*, 26–42.

Klerk-Luttig, J. de (2008). Spirituality in the workplace: A reality for South African teachers? *South African Journal of Education, 28*(4), 2076–3433.

Krishnakumar, S., & Neck, C. P. (2002). The "what", "why" and "how" of spirituality in the workplace. *Journal of Managerial Psychology, 17*, 153–164.

Kuyken, W., Warren, F. C., Taylor, R. S., Whalley, B., Crane, C., Bondolfi, G., et al. (2016). Efficacy of mindfulness-based cognitive therapy in prevention of depressive relapse: An individual patient data meta-analysis from randomized trials. *JAMA Psychiatry, 73*, 565–574.

Labuschagne, W. J. P. (2013). Towards developing a model for spirituality in the workplace. Doctoral thesis, Department of Industrial Psychology and Peoples Management, University of Johannesburg, Johannesburg.

Lean, E. R., & Ganster, D. C. (2017). Is there a common understanding of spiritual leader behaviors? *Journal of Management, Spirituality and Religion, 14*(4), 295–317.

Leigh-Taylor, C. (2000). Business leadership as a spiritual discipline. *Physician Executive, 26*, 20–28.

Lips-Wiersma, M., & Mills, C. (2002). Coming out of the closet: Negotiating spiritual expression in the workplace. *Journal of Managerial Psychology, 17*, 183–202.

MacLean, P. D. (1990). *The Triune Brain in Evolution: Role in Paleocerebral Functions*. New York: Plenum Press.

McNamara, P. (2009). *The Neuroscience of Religious Experience*. Cambridge, UK: Cambridge University Press.

Masuda, A., Price, M., & Latzman, R. D. (2012). Mindfulness moderates the relationship between disordered eating cognitions and disordered eating behaviors in a non-clinical college sample. *Journal of Psychopathology and Behavioral Assessment, 34*, 107–115.

Mayer, C-H. (2011). *The Meaning of Sense of Coherence in Transcultural Management*. Internationale Hochschulschriften Series. Münster: Waxmann.

Mayer, C-H. (2014). Spiritualität in Organisationen: Orientierung an Werten. *Wirtschaftspsychologie aktuell, 21*(4), 57–59.

Mayer, C-H. (2017). *The Life and Creative Works of Paulo Coelho: A Psychobiography from a Positive Psychology Perspective*. Cham, Switzerland: Springer International Publishing.

Mayer, C-H., & Boness, C. M. (2011). Spiritual insights in cross-cultural conflicts and mediation in ecclesiastical organizations in Tanzania. *Qualitative Research in Organizations and Management: An International Journal, 6*(2), 171–190.

Mayer, C-H., & Geldenhuys, D. (2014). Editorial: Spirituality, culture and health in management. *International Review of Psychiatry, 26*(3), 263–264.

Mayer, C-H., Surtee, S., & Barnard, A. (2015). Women leaders in higher education: A psycho-spiritual perspective. *South African Journal of Psychology, 45*(1), 102–115.

Mayer, C-H., Surtee, S., & May, M. (2015). The meaning of work for a diverse group of women working in higher education institutions. *South African Journal of Higher Education, 29*(6), 182–205.

Mayer, C-H., & Viviers, A. (2014a). "Following the word of God": Empirical insights into managerial perceptions on spirituality, culture and health. *International Review of Psychiatry, 26*(3), 302–314.

Mayer, C-H., & Viviers, A. (2014b) "I still believe..." Reconstructing spirituality, culture and mental health across cultural divides. *International Review of Psychiatry, 26*(3), 265–278.

Mayer, C-H., & Walach, H. (2018). Workplace spirituality in contemporary South Africa. In S. Dhiman, G. E. Roberts, & J. E. Crossman (Eds.), *The Palgrave Handbook of Workplace Spirituality and Fulfillment*. Palgrave Macmillan. In press.

Mohamed, A. A. (2004). Towards a theory of spirituality in the workplace. *Competitiveness Review, 14*, 102–107.

Moore, T. W., & Casper, W. J. (2006). An examination of proxy measures of workplace spirituality: A profile model of multidimensional constructs. *Journal of Leadership and Organisational Studies, 12*, 10–19.

Person, K., May, M. S., & Mayer, C-H. (2016). The meaning of work for South African women: A phenomenological study. *Journal of Psychology in Africa, 26*(2), 134–140.

Pillay, S. S. (2011). *Your Brain and Business: The Neuroscience of Great Leaders*. Upper Saddle, NJ: Person Education Inc.

Reb, J., & Atkins, P. W. B. (Eds.). (2015). *Mindfulness in Organisations: Foundations, Research, and Applications*. Cambridge, UK: Cambridge University Press.

Rossouw. P. J. (2014). Neuropsychotherapy: Towards a theory of brain-based therapy. In P. J. Rossouw (Ed.), *Neuropsychotherapy: Theoretical Underpinnings and Clinical Applications*. Brisbane, Australia: Mediros, 1–20.

Rothmann, S., Van der Colff, J. J., & Rothmann, J. C. (2006). Occupational stress of nurses in South Africa. *Curationis, 29*(2), 22–33.

Ruprecht, S., & Walach, H. (2016). Mindfulness at work: How mindfulness training may change the way we work. In M. Wiencke, M. Cacace, & S. Fischer (Eds.), *Healthy at Work: Interdisciplinary Perspectives*. Cham, Switzerland: Springer, 311–326.

Salopek, J. J. (2004). Engaging mind, body and spirit at work. *T+D, 58*, 17–19.

Sapp, A. (2004). Promoting wellness in employees [Online]. Retrieved from www.bsu/web/amsapp/employeewellness.htm.

Sauer, S., Walach, H., & Kohls, N. (2011). Gray's Behavioural Inhibition System as a mediator of mindfulness towards well-being. *Personality and Individual Differences, 50*(4), 506–511.

Seligman, E. P. (2002). *Authentic Happiness: Using the New Positive Psychology to Realize Your Potential for Lasting Fulfillment*. New York: Free Press.

Sheep, M. L. (2004). Nailing down gossamer: A valid measure of the person-organization fit of workplace spirituality. *Academy of Management Proceedings*, B1–B7.

Sheldrake, R. (2013). *The Science Delusion: Freeing the Spirit of Inquiry*. London: Hodder & Stoughton.

Siegel, D. J. (2012). *Pocket Guide to Interpersonal Neurobiology: An Integrative Handbook of the Mind*. New York: W. W. Norton.

Smith, A. C. T. (2008). The neuroscience of spiritual experience in organisations. *Journal of Management, Spirituality and Religion, 5*(1), 3–28.

Swinton, J., Bain, V., Ingram, S., & Heys, S. D. (2011). Moving inwards, moving outwards, moving upwards: The role of spirituality during the early stages of breast cancer. *European Journal of Cancer Care, 20*, 640–652.

Tang, Y., & Posner, M. I. (2013). Tools of the trade: Theory and method mindfulness neuroscience. *Social Cognitive and affective Neuroscience, 8*(1), 118–120.

Van Rensburg, A. B. R. J. (2014). South African Society of Psychiatrists: Guidelines for the integration of spirituality in the approach to psychiatric practice. *South African Journal of Psychiatry, 20*(4), 133.

Van Tonder, C. L., & Ramdass, P. (2009). A spirited workplace: Employee perspectives on the meaning of workplace spirituality. *South African Journal of Human Resource Management,* 7(1).

Visser, W. (2009). A new era for spirit at work. *Quality Life Journal*, September. Retrieved from www.qualitylife.co.za.sept2008.htm.

Walach, H. (2017). Secular spirituality—what it is. Why we need it. How to proceed. *Journal for the Study of Spirituality,* 7, 7–20.

Yamagishi, T., Li, Y., Takasishi, H., Matsumoto, Y., & Kiyonari, T. (2014). In search of homo economicus. *Psychological Science, 25*, 1699–1711.

14

ORGANIZATIONAL ONENESS

A Possible Vision or an Inescapable Reality?*

Duysal Aşkun

Organizational Oneness: A Possible Vision or an Inescapable Reality?

As the world is suffering today from myriad types of problems starting at individual, relational, cultural, societal, and national levels, the cultivation of the idea of oneness does not seem to be just a luxurious academic pursuit. The exploration, understanding, and later a possible application of the concept can be a very attractive ideal for those of us in the business of human development and evolution.

For the organizations, understanding and application of oneness even looks like a virgin field. Although oneness has been explored most prominently in physics, quantum physics, spirituality, philosophy, and recently as it applied to the self (Ivanhoe, 2017), organizational oneness has not been discussed extensively yet. There are many sources of oneness and its principles which all can be used for organizations though. It is the main aim of this chapter to promote oneness as it applies to organizations with support from whatever source is available in the current literature.

Oneness as a Concept

The idea and understanding of Oneness date back to ancient times since both Western and Eastern thinkers such as Aristotle, Plato, Confucius, Buddha, and many others had already said a good deal on the concept as it related to self, others, and the world around us. As a term, Oneness means healthy, whole, or holy (*Merriam-Webster's Collegiate Dictionary*, 2005), the original root exists in Anglo-Saxon language as "hal" (Thakadipuram, 2010) while its Sanskrit root is "sampoorna" that means totality, completeness, and wholeness (Apte, 2004; as cited in Thakadipuram, 2010).

Scientific and Philosophical Approaches to Oneness

As a pioneer thinker and academician on the concept of oneness which he defines as the worldview of the 21st century, Malcolm Hollick (2006), in his comprehensive book called *The Science of Oneness*, talks about two approaches to oneness: (1) the one from the many, and (2) the many from the one. The first he defines as the modern Western scientific approach and the latter as the mystic approach. According to Hollick, the science of oneness needs to synthesize the two approaches. Talking about the Western approach, Hollick refers to *classification* and *systems science* which he thinks are both necessary if we'd like to conceptualize oneness in terms of connections between independent phenomena. Here he refers to analyzing isolated parts which can be a sole scientific endeavor, on the other hand by exploring the connections between those parts thought of as belonging to a larger whole form, the systems scientific approach. Although systems science seems to make a lot of sense in terms of oneness inherent in all beings, Hollick strongly denotes that it is not usually the preferred scientific effort over the analytical one. The only philosopher who tried to reconcile both approaches was Johann Wolfgang von Goethe. Goethe's (Hollick, 2006) understanding of parts and wholes was something like this: each part is a unique expression of the whole, but they cannot be considered as independent units. Moreover, the interaction of those parts leads the whole to self-creation and this way whole provides the necessary context in which the parts acquire their meaning. Here Goethe purports the understanding of both "many are one" and "many from one."

As a philosopher who is approaching oneness from an albeit different but a related angle, Priest (2014) argued that parts exist even when a unity does not. He makes an analogy to the bricks of a house which exist even before a house exists or does not exist at all. Relying on the ideas of Aristotle, Priest argues that a unity is more than the sum of its parts. This leads to the discussion of parts and wholes are not the same thing. But because of that difference in nature, combining those parts together needs an additional binding function which he terms as *gluon*. The one thing which makes them unified as a single thing. This is more than the plurality of parts which do not necessarily form a unity. To further explain this gluon, Priest (2014) refers to *relationships* between those parts, while relationships also relate. However, this still doesn't explain how unity is formed as I might relate to a person but that does not necessarily create oneness between us. Coming back to the original argument, Priest (2014) adds by talking about the necessary dependence of the part on the whole which, to him, still remains inadequate in explaining the cooperation of the parts to form unity.

The Oneness Hypothesis

While how oneness comes to the fore and enables the whole functioning of the universe, all living organisms and systems still remains much of a scientific mystery, the Oneness hypothesis as suggested by Ivanhoe (2015; as cited in Ivanhoe, 2017) depicts a picture of oneness that reflects not a single theory but a family of views. Having roots in East Asian traditions such as Buddhism, Daoism, and Confucianism, it is defined as a view about the nature of the world, the nature of the relationship between self and others including not only people but also other creatures, plants, animals, and all sorts of beings. The main claim of the Oneness hypothesis is that we all are interrelated with other beings around us. The main argument is not more about how oneness comes about per se, but more of how its serves the deep need of all beings to belong to larger wholes, communities, and all (Baumeister & Leary, 1995; as cited in Ivanhoe, 2017).

A more expansive conception of self. The Oneness hypothesis entails a relational nature of the self as an alternative to individualistic versions. While it could be argued that this version of self means loss of independence, autonomy, and even self, Ivanhoe (2017) defends it by saying that this understanding of self implies an intimate connection with others which supposedly leads to an enhanced wellbeing and happiness of all concerned, hence the term "expansive" should be taken in this regard. How that translates into people and their relationships is as follows: as we understand our innate relatedness with all beings around us, this inherent interconnection is said to lead to a change in our personal views about ethics, social life, and spirituality. Ideally this understanding results in more compassion and greater care for all others around us. This obviously leads to a different world picture than it is now. In other words, Ivanhoe (2017, p. 11) beautifully puts it: "When we see other people, creatures, and things as part of ourselves, their welfare becomes parts of our happiness."

Oneness and Chinese philosophy. Starting with the idea that the universe actually began as an undifferentiated reservoir of *qi* which basically means a vital energy, the universe later on fractured into discrete layers which also differed in such dimensions as clarity, purity, density, and movement. Individual beings and things gradually were created out of this ongoing process of formation of layers and later different structures of energy with different qualities. The main understanding of this message that came from the early Chinese texts (Book of Changes as an example by Ivanhoe, 2017) was that the main essence of all these happenings and structures was *qi*.

Later, Daoists explained all of this as coming from an original state of nothing, not in an absolute sense but more of a description of a stage where there were no discrete and individual entities. At about the same time with Daoists, a related view emerged which purported a worldview as a unified system, interconnected, like living organisms and ecosystems. This idea suggested terms such as the "roots" and "branches" where each part holds a distinctive place and role and, further, some parts are more fundamental and more important than others (Ivanhoe, 2017).

Finally, mostly under the Buddhism influence, neo-Confucians turned more into the relationship between the self and the world. This meant that the world is not an interconnected system or web of patterns, but more of each entity containing a pattern of universe within (Cook, 1977; as cited in Ivanhoe, 2017). This type of self led the way to an understanding of humans' connection to others, coming with an expansive sense of responsibility with a natural tendency to care for others.

Consciousness in the Context of Oneness

However ideal and promising it may seem, unfortunately humans' connections with others and their sense of responsibility toward them does not reflect too much of a reality in our world today. In other words, we, as humans, do not seem to operate according to the oneness principle. Increased problems in our ecological, political, societal, and cultural systems have led to all sorts of problems ranging from intense violence such as terrorism, mass shootings, to diminishing sources of organic nutrients, unfavorable climate change, and many unresolved political disputes and economic downturns. As our technologies have evolved, we have enhanced ways of communication, however this did not lead to higher communication quality or collaboration in many different walks of life. Maybe even compared to the past, people are complaining more about "lack of voice," "problems in governmental policies," and even "feeling less safe" for their own selves and also their families and communities. This might be the right time to look at consciousness which might be the missing ingredient in trying to conceptualize and ideally apply oneness in our worlds and societies.

Unity Consciousness and How it Comes About

Hollick (2006) introduced a spiritual model that involved cosmic evolution based on consciousness. He wrote about Gnostic sources by Freke and Grandy (2001) which delineated the fundamental essence of reality as consciousness, not matter. This means that our bodies are not given life by their atomic particles, but by consciousness itself which is basically the awareness of the world around us and our own inner selves. If there was no conscious experience of our living, there would be no existence for an individual to know about. Again, according to Gnostics, the mystery from which existence comes is an undivided whole. This means mystery is not consciousness by itself, as consciousness requires an object to be conscious of. Therefore, consciousness is said to come into existence when the mystery was divided into the consciousness and its object.

According to Hollick (2006), unity consciousness is the awareness of all that is. It is described as beyond our experience, knowledge, or imagination. And the fundamental difference between unity consciousness and other types of consciousness mainly concerns the blurred boundaries of the self and not-self. In normal and transpersonal consciousness there is a boundary between the self and the non-self. In unity consciousness this boundary dissolves and distinct awareness of subject and object stops. But it would be misunderstanding, according to this view, to see self as a disappearing entity in all. But the sense of self here, similar to Ivanhoe's (2017) description, is expansive. The self expands to encompass all that is, separate and distinct, but actually as One. The self, before returning it its original individual position, feels that it is one with reality at least for a while. This, all by itself is an experiential state where the brain usually seems to be quiet and still, without active thought processes, but very much awake and alert.

Scientifically speaking, in spite of recent discoveries, the consciousness spot in the brain remains a mystery. And many practices of spirituality try to help people empty and still their minds till there is an ultimate awareness, desirably with no content/object. Accordingly, Hindu and Buddhist thinkers purport that human consciousness is what emerges from this state of emptiness and not from the brain itself (Hollick, 2006). This results in an understanding of the brain as a tool, not a creator of consciousness which exists outside the brain, that resides in all matter either as a parallel form of reality or as a fundamental one from which pretty much everything comes.

According to Priest (2014), it becomes less straightforward when we conceive of mind as not of a physical nature. He talks about Kant who acknowledges the existence of consciousness merely from an individual saying, "I think." This, according to Priest (2014), makes the thought as mine, as an individual, and that is what determines the unity of my consciousness. But Priest (2014) critically argues that even the thought is existent by the condition that one is conscious. Quoting Dennett (1993) who proposed that:

> There is no single stream of consciousness because there is no central Headquarters, no Cartesian theater where "it all comes together" for the perusal of a Central Meaner. Instead of such a single stream, there are multiple channels in which specialized circuits try, in parallel pandemoniums, to do their various things, creating Multiple Drafts as they go.
>
> *(Priest, 2014, p. 170)*

Following this understanding, Priest creates a reconciled view of self the quiddity of which is determined by its position in a network of relations. He further argues, because of all the relativity concerning self, consciousness, and how we approach ourselves in a sea of relations with all different beings, all of those relations combine to make us what we are. These relations include our parents' behaviors towards us and all our loved ones, albeit in some sort of a hierarchy of significance. This way our very own being is influenced by all those webs of relationships ranging from most to less essential.

Relational Consciousness as a Path to Oneness

As a possible glue that holds humans and related beings together, relational consciousness can be one possible factor to be entered into the equation of oneness. Originally appearing in the work of Hay and Nye in 1998 on children's spirituality, *relational consciousness* represented the ability of children to perceive their world in relational terms. As part of Nye's longitudinal studies with children, relational consciousness was defined as: "An unusual level of consciousness or perceptiveness, relative to other passages of conversation spoken by that child. Conversation was expressed in a context of how the child related to things, other people, him/herself, and God" (Hay & Nye, 1998, p. 113). The kind of consciousness that is being referred to here meant a specific relationship. The consciousness was mainly relational, existing in the intra- and interpersonal domain. More than a simple alertness and attentiveness, relational consciousness represents being aware of one's mental activity in a certain context. The sense of being objectively aware of oneself as "subject" was deemed as very important for the child to develop its ability to perceive its world in relational terms. Relational was applied in a very wide sense, encompassing I-Others, I-Self, I-World, and I-God.

Although the processes and the contexts in which relational consciousness appear relate to the developmental stage of each child, the consequences of this type of consciousness are of significant importance if we can also reflect on its meaning for the world of adults. Some of the positive consequences included feelings of calmness, peacefulness, holiness, and moral goodness. On the other hand, a sense of oneness, forgetting self, and feeling free were also consequences. Hay and Nye (1998) reported that those consequences were reactions to something outside, something with external reference. In her study, children reported a new desire to search for understanding or meaning and a greater sense of clarity. Nye (1998) concluded by saying that relational consciousness reflected a concept which served as a means to see the different dimensions of spirituality as members of any whole.

Oneness in Organizations

Earlier, we have talked about the parts and the whole in the context of oneness. Many explanations had been given by different philosophers and theoreticians. Among those, the one by Goethe (Hollick, 2006), seems to be a good one to apply for our organizations today. Goethe originally thought each part to be a unique expression of the whole, but which cannot be considered as independent units. And the interaction of those parts leads the whole to provide the necessary context in which the parts acquire their meaning.

Like an organization, a human is also a system, composed of parts, interrelationships between those parts, and something that goes beyond those interrelationships. An organization is another system, operating similarly, albeit on a larger scope. Therefore, humans are systems inside the organizational systems. And to make the picture clearer, the organizations are also part of their surrounding environmental systems (economy, ecology, politics, culture … etc.) which also operate with the same principles. So, the question would be, how do we locate humans as important and active agents in the organizational system? Can we make a distinction between the types of processes that take place in terms of oneness? How do we draw the line between different albeit interrelated entities: the individual and the organization?

The answer must lie in the distinction between understanding individual oneness and understanding oneness in terms of relationships between the individuals.

Intrapersonal Oneness

As a healthy system, when we talk about oneness within humans, we are talking about the alignment between the interrelated parts. And those parts need also to be healthy so that they can function properly within themselves and in relation to others. When we list those parts as mind, body, and soul, we need to consider the ways in which they remain healthy and functional. As no human is born and grows up the same in terms of their healthy make-up, we need to accept the fact that there is a variation in society in terms of individuals who we can name as "whole."

Individual Consciousness. In terms of the criteria to be used to understand the levels of healthiness inside the human as a system, consciousness has been one of the most prominent terms to use (Sadhguru, 2016). And to restrict our terminology to the workplace contexts, we can say that there are basically two approaches to consciousness at the workplace (Marques, 2012):

- Eastern conceptualizations that mainly stem from Buddhism,
- Western conceptualizations that involve approaches by various philosophers and thinkers coming from different orientations (Freud, Hegel, Sartre (Macann, 2015), later Hawkins (1995), Wilber (2002) … and others).

Focusing on the related definitions of those two different approaches, we can give the following for Marques (2012): "consciousness is an experience related to one's own experience rather than others'" (Bodhi, 1993; Narada, 1959). As an important aspect of spiritual growth, consciousness, being a continuous construct, enables us to make cognitive improvements while leading us to experience important realizations along the way (Dalai Lama, 1995).

One of the ways in which we can alleviate our consciousness at work was suggested as mindfulness practices. According to Brown, Ryan, and Creswell (2007), to reach desirable goals, people need to learn to be attentive to their inner states and behaviors, otherwise less conscious behaviors would be the result. In addition, Brown et al. (2007) suggest the cognitive element (Langer and Moldoveanu, 2000) to mindfulness related to how an individual makes sense of his/her environment in a mindful manner. In a similar vein, Purser and Milillo (2015) argued that mindfulness should be defined not as a passive individual position but as a more active approach which would happen through complex cognitive processes like memory, covering all time perspectives together (past, present, and future). The authors named it the "right mindfulness" where it defines knowing in all existence levels—the mind, body, and the soul. In other words, they followed Buddhist notions of "wholesome mind and body" which would be producing behaviors they called as wholesome. While the authors did not conduct an empirical study about what those types of behaviors might be, they gave examples of wholesome behaviors as ethical behavior and social responsibility and unwholesome behaviors such as destroying life, stealing, lying, harsh speech … etc.

The Holistic Self. Hollick (2006) defined us humans as both autonomous organisms and also as dependent and vital parts of the larger systems to which we all belong. In this way, we are parts and wholes at the same time. And he argues that for many of us this is very threatening for our independent conceptions of self. But from the system's perspective (Macy, 1990) there is an inescapable interaction with the whole system surrounding us which creates further wholes and patterns, leading to a diverse picture enabled through transpersonal consciousness (Hollick, 2006).

Interpersonal Oneness

How does oneness act out in relationships? Especially concerning organizations, what makes those gluons (Priest, 2014) reflect "feelings of unity, oneness or wholeness?" Is relational consciousness possible, especially by two conscious individuals, or does it suffice to have one individual to be more conscious than the other? Most of all, how do we draw the line between the more conscious and the less? Is mindfulness an adequate practice to demonstrate oneness in relationships?

If we think of persons as reflections of their feelings, thoughts, and behaviors, and something more than the sum of all three, behaviors might be the type of personal reflection that very much make sense in the context of relationships. It is the behavior which is clearly visible and observable, and sometimes much easier to measure compared to the others. When we talk about objective performance measures, for example, we are talking about "behavioral metrics" that were also very clearly identified by Brown (1982) in his book *Managing Behavior on the Job*, creating a guideline for managers to conduct objective performance appraisals based on clear, unbiased, and non-subjective methods of behavioral observation. In short, behaviors are the most visible of all parts and are more readily subject to objective analysis, and which, clearly is what is seen by both parties in the relationship dyad, no matter how much they are able to remain objective in their observations. This of course doesn't mean that "behaviors" form the only possible units of analysis of what happens between two individuals in terms of oneness. There are of course other psychological processes that happen between the two in terms of thoughts, feelings, mental reactions ... etc. But for the sake of rendering oneness as something more than a philosophy or just an idealized thought, to talk about it in terms of visible behaviors seems like an important scientific pursuit.

Introduction of Oneness Behaviors. As an important attempt to try to demonstrate the evidence of oneness in terms of human behaviors, Aşkun and Çetin (2017), as a result of their 4-year-long study, suggested a behavioral definition of oneness, calling it oneness behavior. They came up with a 27-item measure that represented oneness behaviors which take place in different social environments. The oneness behavior items fell into two categories: focus on one's self vs. consideration of the other. The individual behaved in one of those two ways which basically represented a self-centered vs. an interdependent state of being. In an attempt to define and understand oneness more from an interconnected state, Aşkun and Çetin (2017) aimed to demonstrate oneness as it applied to the day to day behavior of an individual. As an example, how does an individual react to an old person trying to cross the street? How does he or she behave when there is a line? What is the behavior during group projects/activities when there is more than one person involved? Does he/she adjust his/her style accordingly by considering the other person in that relationship context? Does he/she understand the mood the other is in, or does he/she even care? As a healthy and a whole individual would be composed of healthy cognition, emotion ,and behaviors, it seems necessary to highlight "oneness behaviors" as one of the possible indications of healthy cognition and emotion. In other words, thinking our behaviors as the most visible and evident parts of our individual systems, we are thinking that behaviors that reflect oneness would provide some significant clues to understand and hopefully cultivate oneness for every individual inside the organizational system.

As a consequence, to live in interconnectedness, the organizations need to stay healthy and be in a constant state of growth (Marques, 2012). Thinking about humans as whole systems, considering them as active agents playing critical roles inside the organizations, we can think of some competencies to be developed in addition to achieving the states of mindfulness. Competencies are the types of capacities that help the whole organization to perform in the short and the long run. Some organizations prefer to define their competencies according to their definite set of values, and some others prefer to define them based on their performance metrics. In any case, competencies as expressed by each individual (employee or a manager) are necessary building blocks of positive organizational outcomes that go beyond performance to also include sustainable growth, healthy culture, and happy workforce.

Competencies at the Intra-Individual Level

Consciousness. As extensively outlined above, consciousness is a necessity for a healthy organization (Marques, 2012) and it goes beyond thoughts, feelings, and behaviors and reaches far out to set the cultural tone of any type of organizational entity.

Mindfulness. In accordance with Buddhist ideology and literature, Western researchers studying mindfulness have theorized its strong relation with connectedness (Kabat-Zinn, 2003) while Brown and Ryan (2003) originally put forward its strong relation with relatedness.

Motivation. Self Determination theory (Deci & Ryan, 1980) sees human motivation a result of three interrelated human needs: autonomy, relatedness, and competence. The three interact to form a level of motivation for the individual which is a very fundamental area of exploration in today's business world to understand performance and related positive outcomes.

Autonomous-related self. In an attempt to reconcile Western and Eastern conceptions of self, Kagitcibaşi (1996) claimed that autonomy does not have to mean separateness from others. As the original psychological theories of self have promoted individual independence, autonomy, self-reliance, and many other related concepts, the development of the autonomous, independent self has been stressed more for its healthy and significant nature. However, Kagitcibaşi (1996) proposes that autonomy should be understood as what it is, mostly as an agency, not as separateness and there is a possibility that relatedness as another basic human need (Deci & Ryan, 1980) can coexist with it. If we can look closer, her depiction of the autonomous-related self is very similar to what Hollick (2006) described as holistic self.

Resilience. While originally it was defined as a positive adaptation to situations which carried a significant adversity or risk, resilience also means positive wellbeing (Masten & Reed, 2002). In terms of oneness, resilience by the individual reflects health and being wholesome.

Identification. This is the extent to which individuals perceive oneness with their organizations (Ashforth & Mael, 1989; Wieseke, Ahearne, Lam, & van Dick, 2009). In other words, Kim, Chang, and Ko (2010) describe it as the perception of belongingness to an organization and a sense of oneness with the organization.

Commitment. One of the possible outcomes of identification, commitment (Meyer & Allen, 1991) is a necessary competence for a healthy organization performance (Conway & Briner, 2012; Fu & Deshpande, 2014).

Competencies at the Inter-Individual Level

Relational Consciousness. Originally coined by Hay and Nye (1998) in an effort to understand children's spirituality, relational consciousness reflects a relationship process where the relationship enters time and space through the mediation of self-consciousness that leads to the objectification of the self and partner and influences mutual recognition by both parties (Wills, 2012).

Citizenship behaviors. Organizational citizenship behavior (OCB) coined as a term by Organ (1988) who originally followed Barnard's (1938) conception of an organization as a "cooperative system" which is composed of those willing individuals without whose efforts the organization cannot exist or evolve. In more specific terms, those persons needed to have a tendency to think with an interdependent consciousness that represented an interconnectedness which they truly believed to reflect the eventual benefit for the whole organization.

Emotional intelligence: In their article where they report a series of seven studies, Schutte et al. (2001) found significant high relationships between emotional intelligence and empathic perspective taking, self-monitoring in social situations, social skills, more cooperative responses, and higher scores for close and affectionate relationships. These are truly the building blocks of any kind of healthy interpersonal exchange between two or more individuals.

Empathic communication. Kameda (2014), while discussing Japanese business discourse on oneness, makes a very clear definition for communication as a competence to be developed. In his outline, there needs to be a you-consideration and you-attitude for at least two individuals to share perspectives and to identify with each other.

Respect. Respect especially as a behavior is the manifestation of belief that another person has value and people react accordingly when respected (Grover, 2013).

Authentic leadership. Leadership wholeness is implied in the definition of an authentic leader (George, 2007; as cited in Thakadipuram, 2010).

Whole-soul leadership. Originally proposed by Fairholm and Fairholm (2009) who mentioned the key elements of this type of leadership as: showing concern for and integration of the whole-soul of leader and the followers; liberating individuals to grow constantly; enabling individual wholeness in the community; developing an organization which is intelligent; setting moral standards; inspiring; freeing followers to build stewardship communities; modeling a service orientation.

Being-Centered Leadership. This is leadership based on oneness and constant reconciliation of apparent opposites (Fry & Kriger, 2009; as cited in Egel & Fry, 2017). Defined as the most inclusive, this is the level of being that only relies on the unity that is transcendent. At this level of being the leader exists in pure emptiness, fullness, and completeness. Here there remains no separation between the leader and the follower. In an idealized state of perception, the leader responds with an open system of knowing and being. There is pure self-actualization in all of the leader's pursuits.

Organizational Outcomes in Relation to the Oneness Principle

Organizational Change through the Wholeness Praxis

What happens when an organization is composed of conscious, wholesome beings? What is the mechanism that helps with the healthy transformation of an organization toward oneness? What is the outcome of oneness in relationships that include dyads, groups, and multi-functions? These are all useful questions that we can ask when we think of oneness either as an outcome or as a process.

In an extensive outline of a new paradigm of organizational transformation that needs to take place in the business world today, Li and Lin (2011) observed that the biggest hurdle on the road to organizational transformation was actually about how we collectively relate ourselves to our problems instead of how we framed those problems. Naming this new paradigm "wholeness praxis," the authors claim that learning organizations are no longer adequate in terms of handling complex problems while the wholeness praxis could serve as a functional integrator of the emerging global communities. In their attempt to formulate a new path to a sustainable organizational development, Li and Lin (2011) predict that learning organizations might transcend themselves toward being wholeness praxis organizations by envisioning possibilities. As a response to the questions about how different entities inside the organization work together for an envisioned world and how diverse perspectives can be reconciled toward a unified goal, they suggest forming horizontal network structures both inside and outside the organization, including the real world. Second, they suggest extending the vertical network from the real world to the envisioned ideal world by cultivating insights (consciousness as an individual competence). However, among the most important of those suggestions, the authors highlight building a bridge for diverse groups of people where they create a new language to communicate with one another between the worlds of the real and the ideal.

Similarly, Wilber (2002) made a distinction between the subjective world and the objective world of consciousness (Pandey & Gupta, 2007) as a transcendental view which encompasses the all level quadrant approach to consciousness. According to his model, it seems that consciousness at all levels have interrelationships with others. This means we can expect outcomes at the following levels:

- Individual (attitudes, behaviors, emotions),
- Subsystems (top management, departments, units, project groups, teams),
- Whole systems (organization, institution, society, culture),
- Interrelations between those systems.

In terms of how those outcomes come to play in each system, we would be dealing with many variables related to each entity. As an example, at the level of top management we might be talking about values and mission statements, whereas at the level of organization we might be talking about market share, performance, and profit margins. It mainly depends on our choice for the unit of analysis.

Organizational Culture and Practices. Whatever a personality is to an individual, culture is to an organization or groups of people. Following Schein's (1990) conceptualization, culture is composed of assumptions, values, and artifacts. How does a culture look like in an organization embodying oneness? How do people think at a conscious and unconscious level, what do they value, and how do they behave?

As consciousness is an important and an antecedent term for oneness, we believe that consciousness at all levels of cultural model would be significant to attain a oneness culture. And for some related culture types, we can just list the following:

- Compassionate culture (Barsade & O'Neill, 2014),
- Horizontal collectivistic culture (Triandis & Bhawuk, 1997).

Practices that help organizations express themselves in oneness with their surroundings can range from sustainability practices to several corporate social responsibility projects, while high performance and innovative products might be the natural outcome of healthy individual and team make up. In addition, how the organization treats its customers, suppliers, wholesalers, retailers, community, and both its immediate and extended social environment that exists in the network can all be the subject of oneness practice that transcends the organizational boundaries that expand far and beyond. In other words, if we think of organizations as whole entities themselves, their expanded version of self also would have enormously important outcomes.

Organizational Oneness: Just an Ideal or a Reality?

Priest (2014) makes a distinction between realism and idealism in the sense that realism represents more of our common-sense and scientific thinking. All things around us have come into existence somehow and there were some natural universal laws that might have helped with their existence, co-existence, and their relationships. On the other hand, idealism, according to Priest (2014) contends that we only perceive our world through our conceptual lens and even though there was a world before our conceptualization of it, it can only exist to our knowledge by our own understanding of it. In relation, argument of oneness changes if we come from a realist vs. an idealist standing. In more clear terms, if oneness is an inherent reality, all beings, groups of beings, and others, then it is something that we need to discover and possibly carve out of the current situation of the world, of the organizations, no matter how ugly, distorted, polluted, conflictual, and chaotic it may seem. This possibly requires all of us to dig into more self-awareness, mindfulness, consciousness training, and all else to find the true essence within all of us as individuals, groups, and organizations. In addition, healing all which contaminates our relationships as unhealthy, destructive, and even violent. Removing the barriers that prevent us from expanding to the other, by being open communicators, using perspective taking, listening, and empathizing, and considering the other at all times.

In her extensive discussion on the organizations she defines as Fractured Wholes, Hess (2018) defines individuals who are expected to behave "professionally, rational, goal-oriented" and who have to leave an important portion of themselves at home to be able to survive in an organizational context. The corporations (organizational bodies) are defined as usually large, organized collectives with hierarchies and with set goals that may or may not necessarily be welcomed by its individual members. And, more importantly, those large organizations operate according to rational point of view (RPV by Rovanne, 1998), their own norms of standard behavior, usually reinforced by the top. Here Hess (2018) sees the unity inside the organization not in pure essence of oneness but as a collective participation by the shared commitments of the members. Here that participation and commitment come with an exchange of self-interests and organizational goals through satisfaction of certain individual needs such as security, power, prestige, recognition, rewards … etc. Here this exchange happens at the expense of "leaving what is true about the whole self behind" as the members are not asked for their expression of their most true values, emotions, or personal choices about what is really important for the world and for them. This also includes their complex personal identities such as familial ties, religious orientations, and anything that belongs intimately to them. This way whatever makes them unique is left at the door. Bringing in only that part of the self which is accepted by the organization leads to fractured wholes which comprise fractured selves. Hess (2018) further argues that the way they are composed of the fractured selves, the resulting organizations would not be conscious entities, not feeling or experiencing anything real, but mostly driven by self-interests fueled by being oriented to their individual goals without a concern or compassion for other beings, groups of people, creatures, societies, and ecologies. This tendency is said to result in more harmful actions than good ones. Then what is the solution for the sake of oneness as a possibility in organizations?

Hess (2018) suggests that although it might seem to be the very practical way of approaching it, healing fractures may not be as an effective strategy as it may sound. She is arguing that actions and intentions of organizations go more beyond the sum total of the related actions of their members and that changing the members would not be the best way to reach positive outcomes as an organization. Rather, she suggests, making a change from the top by implementing related changes in the values, virtues, and the structural levels would be the most effective way to prevent external harms, which is actually more what counts. Here the "Being-centered leadership" by Fry and Kriger (2009) comes to mind as a leadership competency to develop. Through being-centered leadership, not only might the organizational practices and culture change, but also there would be a possibility for change at the level of the followers.

If oneness is just an ideal, not a reality-based principle, then what is the task for all of us and our organizations? In his exploration on the 21st century oneness, Flanagan (2018) talks about the concept starting with the United Nations' 17 Sustainable Development Goals signed by each country in Paris in 2015. According to the agenda, every nation should be working toward achieving the goals of ending war, corporate greed, poverty along with economic and political inequality, enabling access to health care and education for all, and work for the environmental sustainability for the future. Having outlined those goals and their rationale, Flanagan critically questions the power of the belief in oneness to motivate people and societies into related action. And he suggests additional motives for a real change to take place: moral commitment, states of faith and hope, including certain positive illusions of metaphysics which he defines in relation to five theses of oneness: cosmic oneness, sentient being oneness, historical oneness, shared fate oneness, and care oneness. The cosmic oneness entails interconnectedness with everything, historical oneness is about the causal dependency on others who were here before us, shared fate oneness involves dependencies with others existing near us, sentient being is about our common features that make all of us as humans, and care oneness is about our relation being fundamental to who we are, in other words, our core being. The main argument Flanagan (2018) makes here is that whatever the essence of our true nature is, be it oneness or separateness, it is worth believing in the idea of oneness and act accordingly.

In line with Flanagan's (2018) discussion, if oneness is conceptualized as an ideal state for organizations then it is our task to make necessary commitments and get involved in related actions that call for oneness. This understanding translates into transformative consciousness at both intra- and interpersonal levels, development of related competencies (outlined above) through further training, development and change programs, aligning goals of the organization with that of the employees through empowerment, whole-soul, and being-centered leadership, and, finally, enabling a culture of oneness through related value sets, norms, and practices. For the whole organization to become whole, there needs to be a promotion of change starting from both ends, bottom-up and top-down.

Conclusion

As oneness is a new concept for existence at all levels of being, from creatures, animals, humans, organizations to surrounding ecosystems, any attempt toward more understanding seems to be helpful for future prospects. From what is available so far, it seems pretty clear that oneness exists side by side with consciousness, health, expanded self, mindfulness, and relational consciousness. And it is quite imperative to accept the fact that many do not necessarily create oneness just by existing together. There needs to be a glue, a gluon, that connects each separate being together to form a unity. And it is also obvious that the unity is more than just the added sum of those existences.

As for the organizations which cannot be thought apart from its members, departments, management, culture, and practices, oneness offers a new way of being. A way of being that could be reinforced by the leadership but is only possible by the contributing members' evolved ways of existence through enhanced but a unique set of competencies. How competencies come about might be the art and science of hiring, training, and organizational development. Here the cultivation of consciousness at both intra- and interpersonal levels seems to be a priority for those who are responsible for the organization's change efforts.

References

Apte, V. (2004). *The Practical Sanskrit-English Dictionary* (4th rev. ed.). Delhi, India: Mothilal Banarsidas Publishers Private Ltd.

Ashforth, B. E., & Mael, F. (1989). Social identity theory and the organization. *Academy of Management Review, 14*(1), 20–39.

Aşkun, D., & Çetin, F. (2017). How do we demonstrate oneness as a behavior: Operationalizing oneness through scale measurement. *Journal of Spirituality in Mental Health, 19*(1), 34–60.

Barnard, C. I. (1938). *The Functions of the Executive*. Cambridge, MA: Harvard University Press.
Barsade, S. G., & O'Neill, O. A. (2014). What's love got to do with it? A longitudinal study of the culture of companionate love and employee and client outcomes in a long-term care setting. *Administrative Science Quarterly, 59*(4), 551–598.
Baumeister, R. F., & Leary, M. R. (1995). The need to belong: Desire for interpersonal attachments as a fundamental human motivation. *Psychological Bulletin, 117*(3), 497–529.
Bodhi, B. (1993). *Abhidhammattha Sangaha: A Comprehensive Manual of Abhidhamma—The Philosophical Psychology of Buddhism* (M. Narada, Trans.). Onalaska, WA: BPS Pariyatti Editions.
Brown, K. W., & Ryan, R. M. (2003). The benefits of being present: Mindfulness and its role in psychological well-being. *Journal of Personality and Social Psychology, 84*(4), 822–848.
Brown, K. W., Ryan, R. M., & Creswell, J. D. (2007). Mindfulness: Theoretical foundations and evidence for its salutary effects. *Psychological Inquiry, 18*(4), 211–237.
Brown, P. L. (1982). *Managing Behavior on the Job*. New York: John Wiley & Sons, Inc.
Conway, N., & Briner, R. B. (2012). Investigating the effect of collective organizational commitment on unit-level performance and absence. *Journal of Occupational and Organizational Psychology, 85*(3), 472–486.
Cook, F. H. (1977). *Hua-Yen Buddhism: The Jewel Net of Indra*. University Park: Pennsylvania State University Press.
Dalai Lama. (1995). *The World of Tibetan Buddhism*. Boston: Wisdom Publications.
Deci, E. L., & Ryan, R. M. (1980). Self-determination theory: When mind mediates behavior. *Journal of Mind and Behavior, 1*(1), 33–43.
Dennett, D. (1993). *Consciousness Explained*. London: Penguin Books.
Egel, E., & Fry, L. W. (2017). Cultivating a global mindset through "being-centered" leadership. In J. Neal (Ed.), *Handbook of Personal and Organizational Transformation*. Berlin: Springer International Publishing, 1–21.
Fairholm, M. R., & Fairholm, G. W. (2009). *Understanding Leadership Perspectives: Theoretical and Practical Applications*. New York: Springer.
Flanagan, O. (2018). Hallucinating oneness: Is oneness true or just a positive metaphysical illusion? In P. J. Ivanhoe, O. J. Flanagan, V. S. Harrison, H. Sarkissian, & E. Schwitzgebel (Eds.), *The Oneness Hypothesis: Beyond the Boundary of Self*. New York: Columbia University Press, 268–283.
Freke, T., & Grandy, P. (2001). *Jesus and the Goddess: The Secret Teachings of the Original Christians*. London: Thorsons.
Fry, L., & Kriger, M. (2009). Towards a theory of being-centered leadership: Multiple levels of being as context for effective leadership. *Human Relations, 62*(11), 667–696.
Fu, W., & Deshpande, S. P. (2014). The impact of caring climate, job satisfaction, and organizational commitment on job performance of employees in a China's insurance company. *Journal of Business Ethics, 124*(2), 339–349.
George, B. (2007). *True North*. San Francisco: Jossey-Bass.
Grover, S. L. (2013). Unraveling respect in organization studies. *Human Relations, 67*(1), 27–51.
Hawkins, D. R. (1995). *Power vs. Force: The Hidden Determinants of Human Behavior*. Carlsbad, CA: Hayhouse, Inc.
Hay, D., with Nye, R. (1998). *The Spirit of the Child*. London: HarperCollins.
Hess, K. (2018). Fractured wholes: Corporate agents and their members. In P. J. Ivanhoe, O. J. Flanagan, V. S. Harrison, H. Sarkissian, & E. Schwitzgebel (Eds.), *The Oneness Hypothesis: Beyond the Boundary of Self*. New York: Columbia University Press, 192–211.
Hollick, M. (2006). *The Science of Oneness: A Worldview for the Twenty-First Century*. Ropley, UK: John Hunt Publishing.
Ivanhoe, P. J. (2015). Senses and values of Oneness. In B. Bruya (Ed.), *The Philosophical Challenge from China*. Cambridge, MA: MIT Press, 231–251.
Ivanhoe, P. J. (2017). *Oneness: East Asian Conceptions of Virtue, Happiness, & How We Are All Connected*. New York: Oxford University Press.
Kabat-Zinn, J. (2003). Mindfulness-based interventions in context: Past, present, and future. *Clinical Psychology: Science and Practice, 10*(2), 144–156.
Kagitcibaşi, C. (1996). The autonomous-relational self: A new synthesis. *European Psychologist, 1*(3), 180–186.
Kameda, N. (2014). Japanese business discourse of oneness: A personal perspective. *International Journal of Business Communication, 51*(1), 93–113.
Kim, T., Chang, K., & Ko, J. Y. (2010). Determinants of organizational identification and supportive intentions. *Journal of Marketing Management, 26*(5–6), 413–427.

Langer, E. J., & Moldoveanu, M. (2000). Mindfulness research and the future. *Journal of Social Issues, 56*(1), 129–139.
Li, M., & Lin, K. (2011). A new paradigm of organizational transformation: Enacting wholeness praxis in the oneness of problem and possibility. *Systemic Practice and Action Research, 24*(2), 107–132.
Macann, C. (2015). Consciousness, self-consciousness, and the unconscious. *Existential Analysis, 26*(2), 328–339.
Macy, J. (1990). *The Greening of the Self.* Berkeley, CA: Parallax Press.
Marques, J. (2012). Consciousness at work: A review of some important values, discussed from a Buddhist perspective. *Journal of Business Ethics, 105*, 27–40.
Masten, A. S., & Reed, M. G. J. (2002). Resilience in development. In C. R. Snyder & S. J. Lopez (Eds.), *Handbook of Positive Psychology*. Oxford: Oxford University Press, 74–88.
Merriam-Webster's Collegiate Dictionary. (2005). Merriam-Webster, Incorporated, USA.
Meyer, J. P., & Allen, N. J. (1991). A three-component conceptualization of organizational commitment. *Human Resource Management Review, 1*(1), 61–89.
Narada, M. T. (1959). *A Manual of Abhidhamma*. Kuala Lumpur, Malaysia: Buddhist Missionary Society.
Organ, D. W. (1988). *Organizational Citizenship Behavior: The Good Soldier Syndrome*. Issues in Organization and Management Series. Lexington, MA: Lexington Books/D. C. Heath and Co.
Pandey, A., & Gupta, R. K. (2007). A perspective of collective consciousness of business organizations. *Journal of Business Ethics, 80*, 889–898.
Priest, G. (2014). *One*. Oxford: Oxford University Press.
Purser, R. E., & Milillo, J. (2015). Mindfulness revisited: A Buddhist-based conceptualization. *Journal of Management Inquiry, 24*(1), 3–24.
Rovanne, C. A. (1998). *The Bounds of Agency: An Essay in Revisionary Metaphysics*. Princeton, NJ: Princeton University Press.
Sadhguru. (2016). *Inner Engineering*. New York: Penguin Random House.
Schein, E. (1990). Organizational culture. *American Psychologist, 45*(2), 109–119.
Schutte, N. S., Malouff, J. M., Bobik, C., Coston, T. D., Greeson, C., Jedlicka, C., Rhodes, E., & Wendorff, G. (2001). Emotional intelligence and interpersonal relations. *Journal of Social Psychology, 141*(4), 523–536.
Thakadipuram, T. (2010). Leadership wholeness: A human resource development model. *Human Resource Development International, 13*(4), 463–475.
Triandis, H. C., & Bhawuk, D. P. (1997). Culture theory and the meaning of relatedness. In P. C. Earley & M. Erez (Eds.), *New Perspectives on International Industrial/Organizational Psychology*. San Francisco: New Lexington Press/Jossey-Bass Publishers, 13–52.
Wieseke, J., Ahearne, M., Lam, S. K., & van Dick, R. (2009). The role of leaders in internal marketing. *Journal of Marketing, 73*, 123–145.
Wilber, K. (2002). *Spectrum of Consciousness*. New Delhi, India: Motilal Bavarsidas.
Wills, R. (2012). Beyond relation: A critical exploration of "relational consciousness" for spiritual education. *International Journal of Children's Spirituality, 17*(1), 51–60.

15
EMOTIONAL INTELLIGENCE AND WORK

Isaac Wanasika

Emotional Intelligence

There are many definitions and applications of emotional intelligence (EI), some controversial and others even conflicting. This is, in part, due to widespread use of the concept without empirical support across multiple disciplines. It is widely acknowledged, however, that EI involves aspects of emotions and intelligence. Popular writers and practitioners have often been tempted to prescribe EI as a panacea to organizational ills such as interpersonal conflicts, organizational stress, and burnout. Some of these prescriptions can be supported empirically, while others are questionable. Regardless, the appeal of touting the positive effects of EI is quite high among practitioners and scholars.

The first step is to understand the interaction of emotions and intelligence. Interest in different attributes of EI has continued to evolve over the past 100 years. Early work on EI appears to have focused on social intelligence. Over time, however, EI has evolved to include four categories: perception, assimilation, understanding, and management. Emotional perception is the ability to be aware of your own emotions as well as the emotions of others. Ability seems to infer accurate perception of these emotions. The concept of intelligence is associated with the cognitive capacity to think in abstract terms, learn new knowledge, and adapt to new environments. Intelligence has many dimensions such as memory, critical thinking, abstraction, and judgment. General intelligence is often measured by the "G-factor" (Mayer, Salovey, & Caruso, 2004). Some studies have found support for intelligence as a genetic disposition. According to this line of thinking, intelligence is a trait you either have or do not have. This view has been completely debunked in recent studies (Nisbett et al., 2012). In the most recent findings, intelligence is determined by multiple factors. Many disciplines such as psychology, neuroscience, computer science, intelligence science, and others have made significant progress in understanding intelligence. This has created further complications in trying to understand how these factors are related. Perhaps the most important finding is how little we know about intelligence.

Emotions are intense feelings that are produced by, or related to, a specific cause or event. Emotions govern and signal a response to the specific event or situation. Emotions include intense feelings such as happiness, sadness, excitement, and anger. Emotions are often distinguished from moods. Moods tend to be long term in nature, often positive or negative, and are not necessarily elicited by a specific event or incident. A large body of work has explored emotions. Like intelligence, understanding emotions is work in progress with many unanswered questions. From an EI standpoint, the main interest is in understanding individual emotions and emotions of others, and identifying methods of selectively controlling these emotions. Emotions, however, are often not isolated. In some situations, emotions are intermingled such as in anger and sadness or jealousy and rage.

Mainstream research on EI acknowledges that EI involves a wide range of emotions and abilities that are relevant at the workplace. Generally, EI specifies how people recognize their own emotions, how they recognize the emotions of others, and how they regulate their own emotions in order to achieve desirable outcomes. From this description, there are many formulations of EI. The lack of agreement by scholars and practitioners regarding EI's attributes, measurement, and utility has not deterred assertions regarding its benefits. This may be, in part, because EI deals with a very active interaction between intelligence and the visible parts of human emotions that constantly pop up through personal and social interactions. EI can be defined as the ability to use emotions for the growth of the whole individual. This involves accurately perceiving one's own emotions, accurately perceiving emotions of others, and accurately understanding how individual behavior affects emotions of others (Mayer et al., 2004). This perspective of EI seems to conceive EI as a form of ability or competence. Such a formulation might have other important implications for understanding EI and the extent to which EI competence plans can be developed for workers.

Recent studies have formulated EI as a personality trait (Petrides, Pita, & Kokkinaki, 2007). In this model, EI is described as a set of behavioral dispositions and self-perceptions concerning one's ability to recognize, process, and utilize emotional-laden information (Petrides & Furnham, 2003, p. 278). This perspective of EI has identified four main dimensions. The first dimension is individual or worker wellbeing. Wellbeing encompasses happiness, self-confidence, and optimism. The second dimension is sociability. Sociability incorporates assertiveness, social competence, and emotional management of others. The third dimension is self-control. Self-control includes emotion regulation, stress management, and low impulsiveness. The last dimension is emotionality which includes empathy, emotion expression, and emotion perception of self and others (Santos, Mustafa & Gwi, 2015); Petrides et al., 2007). There are obvious differences and controversies between the trait and ability approaches. Some of these differences are theoretical, while others are related to how EI is measured. From a practical standpoint, it has been easier to scientifically measure traits than ability, since ability cannot be easily quantified unless an individual self-reports or is tested on a relevant task. Measuring traits, however, appears to diminish the importance of other determinants of EI that are not trait-determined. In addition, it creates a burden of creating EI developmental plans for workers if in the first instance the concept has indeed been cast as a trait.

A third group of EI paradigms seeks to combine the first two models of traits and ability. These mixed models are mainly practical-oriented with the intention of developing EI competences among individuals in business education and management consultancy areas. The Bar-On Model of Emotional-Social Intelligence (Bar-On, 2006), a popular EI model is a framework of interrelated emotional and social competencies, skills, and facilitators. This EI framework influences one's ability to recognize, understand, and manage emotions, relate with others, adapt to change, solve problems of a personal and interpersonal nature, and efficiently cope with daily demands, challenges, and pressures. The dimensions of this model are: intrapersonal (comprising self-regard, emotional self-awareness, assertiveness, independence, and self-actualization); interpersonal (comprising empathy, social responsibility, and interpersonal relationship); stress management (comprising stress tolerance and impulse control); adaptability (comprising reality testing, flexibility, and problem solving); and general mood (comprising optimism and happiness). These emotional-social intelligence competencies can be taught to individuals in a wide variety of contexts (Bar-On, 2006). A second popular example of mixed approaches is Goleman's Emotional Competence Inventory (Boyatzis & Sala, 2004; Boyatzis, Goleman, & Rhee, 2000; Goleman, 1998). In order to understand this perspective of EI, it should be noted that it was developed as a competence model. The competence inventory has certain key ingredients that relate to other models (Zeidner, Matthews, & Roberts, 2004). The first dimension is emotional self-awareness. This competence includes identification of emotion and understanding how emotions are related to one's goal, thoughts, behaviors, and accomplishments (Goleman, 1998). The second competence is the ability to regulate one's emotions. This competence involves intentionally eliciting and sustaining pleasant and unpleasant emotions when considered appropriate, effectively channeling negative affect, and restraining negative emotional outbursts and impulses (Goleman, 1998). One can only regulate one's own emotions, and the emotions of others, if one understands those emotions first. The third component is social awareness of emotions and empathy, which includes awareness of others' feelings, needs, and concerns, understanding and sympathizing with others' emotions, and responding to others' unspoken feelings (Goleman, 1998). Note the introduction of feelings in addition to emotions. Feelings implies other sensory tendencies such as feelings of suspicion or "funny feelings" that may extend to extra-sensory perceptions outside the realm of emotions. Next, is regulating emotions of others. This competence incorporates influencing others, effectively communicating with others, and managing conflicts (Weisinger, 1998). Motivational tendencies include such components as internal strivings, attributions, and need for achievement (Boyatzis et al., 2000; Goleman, 1998). The final dimension is character, which incorporates trust and integrity (Goleman, 1998; Weisinger, 1998). The Goleman's Emotional Competence Inventory is highly popular and widely used. Despite numerous criticisms among scholars, these mixed methods are alive and well among consultants and practitioners.

The Importance of EI at the Workplace

Our knowledge of EI is limited, yet we cannot ignore its importance at the workplace. In the past few decades, studies and anecdotal evidence have consistently demonstrated positive effects of leveraging EI at work. Empirical studies have shown that EI is beneficial in enhancing organizational performance, individual productivity, and wellbeing in the areas of customer satisfaction, goal alignment, motivation, leadership, organizational teams, interpersonal relationships, interpersonal communications, organizational citizenship behavior, corporate culture, dealing with toxic employees, managing a hostile environment, management of stress, and burnout. The extensive benefits have perhaps led others to inappropriately prescribe EI solutions and interventions even where there is no evidentiary proof of effectiveness or relatedness with the problem. While the academic war on EI rages on, the concept continues to flourish. The popularity of EI can be, in part, attributed to practitioner-interest in the mid-1990s following the publication of the runaway bestseller by Daniel Goleman (Goleman, 1995) and subsequent interest in mainstream media. The following year *TIME* magazine wrote extensively on the subject and even had a cover titled, "What's your IQ?" In the cover, it goes on to say, "It's not even a number. But emotional intelligence may be the best predictor of success in life, redefining what it means to be smart" (Gibbs, 1995). Even at this early stage, Gibbs, the *TIME* magazine author, was writing on potential misuse of the concept. A quick google search for EI yielded more than 196 million hits, while more than 1.6 million books related to the subject have been published. Clearly, despite the issues, EI continues to enjoy wide appeal.

EI and the Changing Workplace

Since the theory of EI was developed, the modern workplace, and the concept of work as perceived by employees and employers, has evolved. Due to technological advancements, work processes have become less mechanically digitized and spatial, resulting in a change in workflow processes and the way employees interact with each other. Workers are more likely to interact through some form of technology. Virtual organizations, flextime, and other work-related changes have reduced face time among workers in many industries. While these developments might diminish the role of EI at the workplace, they may also have potentially led to more isolation among some workers or even reduced emotional awareness.

The work environment itself has gone through a transformation. For a variety of reasons, many organizations can no longer guarantee lifetime or longtime employment. Temporary work, contingency work, and fixed term contractual employment have become the norm rather than the exception. The psychological contract between employers and workers has been diminished in many industries. Workers have to endure overwhelming gales of globalization and competitive pressure that is constantly looming over organizations. Workers can be forgiven for being conflicted about whether to invest emotional and social capital in a workplace that is temporary by many measures, or focus on personal wellbeing and employability.

Third, effects of globalization have led to increasingly diverse organizational populations. The ability to monitor and understand the emotions of co-workers is an important ingredient in job satisfaction and reduced conflicts at the workplace. However, a diverse workforce presents special EI and cultural intelligence challenges. Culture seems to have effects on most aspects of EI, and the ability to monitor and understand co-workers' emotions becomes increasingly challenging in a multicultural work environment. Workers realize they must effectively engage with other workers who may not share their worldview or may have different values and beliefs. In order to develop cultural competences that increase cultural intelligence, it is essential to first understand how culture affects EI.

EI and National Culture

Culture can be defined as the collective programming of the mind distinguishing one group or category of people from others (Hofstede, 2009). A nation develops a distinct culture that is unique and different. It has long been known that culture has considerable effects on emotions. Different cultures understand and interpret emotions differently. Different cultures have idiosyncratic emotional display rules that may, at times, be difficult to discern or even confusing to outsiders. Perceptions and judgments regarding emotions also vary on the basis of cultural orientation. Culture is central in determining our beliefs, values, and norms. These attributes have a major influence on the way individuals make sense of the world, life, and how they are likely to understand and control their own emotions. An individual with high EI in one culture may be considered to have a low EI in a different culture. Culture has a great effect on where people look, what they see, how they perceive what they see, and their interpretation and enactment of these perceptions through verbal and non-verbal language. Culture also determines emotional display rules. Individuals will display emotions that are culturally proper, in the most appropriate form. This implies that a person from a different culture with high EI is likely to display the wrong emotions, or none at all, even if they have a high degree of emotional understanding and control. This has led researchers to explore other forms of intelligence that are related to culture. Consequently, cultural intelligence is a different concept from EI. Cultural intelligence is concerned with a person's ability to adapt effectively to new cultures and contexts

(Earley & Ang, 2003). Some determinants of EI and cultural intelligence are related, since both perspectives deal with some form of inherited or acquired intelligence.

To understand how different cultural backgrounds might affect EI at the workplace, we need to first examine different national cultural dimensions. Geert Hofstede has conducted an extensive study spanning more than four decades of national cultural dimensions and how values at the workplace are influenced by culture (Hofstede, 1984). National cultural dimensions can be described as independent preferences for one state of affairs over another that distinguish countries (rather than individuals) from each other. Hofstede's study identified six distinct national cultural dimensions. These are power distance, individualism, masculinity, uncertainty avoidance, long-term orientation, and indulgence. Some of the dimensions have more relevance to EI than others.

In individualistic cultures, the needs, interests, and feelings of the individual are the focal point. In such cultures, individuals are focused on taking care of their individual interests and those of their immediate families. Individuals are more likely to recognize their own emotions and express those emotions more openly. Since individuals are focused on their own emotions, they may be less likely to pay attention to the emotions of others. In collectivist societies, individuals are more focused on the needs of the collective, a tight-knit group with shared interests. Individuals are more likely to put the needs of this in-group over and above their own interests. In collectivist societies, individuals are more likely to suppress their personal emotions, and focus more on collective feelings of the group.

Other cultural dimensions such as high context versus low context, and power distance relationships are likely to impact how emotions are managed and interpreted by others. For example, emotional cues used by people from one culture to ascertain another person's emotional state such as empathy may differ from those used in other cultures (Earley & Peterson, 2004). A "friendly" smile for a Canadian may seem straightforward until she encounters a Thai worker for whom over 20 separate smiles provide subtle cues for radically different frames of mind (Klausner, 1993).

EI and Emotional Labor

Emotional labor is the process of controlling and managing one's emotions and expressions to reflect the organization's desired emotional expressions. Emotional labor has been associated with dramaturgy theory (Goffman, 1949). According to this theory, human beings act out their lives by guiding and controlling the way others perceive and see them. Human beings act differently when they are in the presence of other people from when they are on their own. Goffman proposes human beings have a "front stage" where they act out or engage in impression management in order to portray a specific image to their "audience." On the other hand, the backstage is where the individual is alone and emotions on display are genuine. The paradigm is very similar to Shakespeare's "all the world's a stage" monolog. Going back to organizations and work, organizations often set rules and norms outlining how workers should interact with internal and external customers. For example, a hotel receptionist may be expected to demonstrate hospitality by smiling and making small talk with guests that are checking in. Physicians and nurses might be expected to show a bedside demeanor that reflects empathy and compassion to their patients. Organizations require workers to apply these emotional display rules even though they might have different off-stage emotions at the same time. For instance, the hotel receptionist that is required to smile and display warm feelings might be mourning the loss of his dog.

When employees' display rules are in conflict with their authentic emotions and feelings, they are compelled to suppress their authentic feeling, leading to self-censorial emotional dissonance (Santos et al., 2015). Emotional dissonance is a psychological state that can lead to deleterious effects of emotional labor. Emotional labor can be intense when surface acting is required. Surface acting involves displaying organizationally sanctioned emotions, while trying to suppress real emotions. Over time, surface acting may lead to unsustainable emotional dissonance and, ultimately, burnout. Burnout is a state of emotional exhaustion that creates a feeling of being emotionally drained, helpless, and fatigued from work. Emotional burnout has three main components, emotional exhaustion, depersonalization, and a reduced sense of personal accomplishment (Maslach & Jackson, 1981). Workers that burnout from emotional labor tend to lose the sense of caring about co-workers and customers, in the process acting in ways that are inconsistent with organizational display rules. Lack of intervention to relieve burnout can lead to more serious physical illness and even death.

A heightened sense of EI can alleviate or reduce the effects of emotional burnout at work. Deep acting implies that rather than engaging in surface acting, a worker endeavors to modify or transform internal feelings in order to align them with required display rules. It is expected that individuals with a high EI will be attuned to their own emotions in terms self-awareness, control, and empathy, as well as accurately communicating correct emotional cues. For such workers rather than faking their feelings, they will identify and portray positive aspects of the job. Since organizational rules tend to focus on suppressing negative emotions, individuals that are high in EI have the ability, and motivation, to focus on positive emotions, rather than negative emotions, as a means of sustaining their wellbeing. Given the significance of the service industry in the economy, increased incidences of mental illnesses at the workplace and an incentive to make work more meaningful and fun, this aspect of EI holds a lot of promise. More needs to be done, however, to fully understand physiological and psychological processes in play in order to effectively deploy such interventions.

EI Competence

Can EI competences be improved through training? There are many EI institutional and executive training programs. The exact psychological basis and processes for EI, however, have not been mapped. Consequently, most EI training content lacks theory and method justification. In addition, there is no agreement on the constitution of EI dimensions. While it may not be possible to overhaul individual EI competences, there are clear benefits in training for awareness of what is known, and evidence for incremental work-related benefits. In the most recent meta-analysis on the efficacy of EI training, most studies found that training involving ability EI models showed significantly higher efficacy than training involving trait and mixed EI models. Training effects of understanding emotions was more effective than training effects of facilitating thought (Hodzic, Scharfen, Ripoll, Holling, & Zenasni, 2018). It seems the verdict on training so far is clear; it is easier to enhance ability than traits. In addition, while EI has been associated with better organizational performance, most training modules seem to be focused on individual interventions such as mental health, interpersonal conflicts, and individual wellbeing. There is increased research on the efficacy of EI in resolving mental and other behavioral issues. While this is a welcome development, there is a potential danger of casting individuals with low emotional intelligence as diagnostic cases worthy of medical intervention. EI has been developed as part of cultural intelligence competence training. Cultural intelligence (CQ) captures this capability for adaptation across cultures and it reflects a person's capability to gather, interpret, and act upon these radically different cues to function effectively across cultural settings or in a multicultural situation (Earley & Ang, 2003). In a nutshell, cultural intelligence involves aspects of EI with a cultural context.

EI and the Changing Technology

Internal work environments continue to change, often in unpredictable ways. Technology and globalization have transformed how people communicate and with whom they communicate in organizations. Such developments call for a new way of perceiving co-workers' emotions, establishing meaningful relationships, working building teams, and communicating effectively. New forms of technology such as robotics and artificial intelligence are continuing to support, and even replace, workers rendering EI insignificant in such situations. Knowledge-mediate work processes in the modern organization appear to substitute, or even neutralize, the effects of EI.

The Dark Side of EI

Despite extensive interest, little has been done to understand the negative aspects of EI. Emotions and intelligence have no sense of morality per se. Whether EI is crafted as a trait or ability, there is potential for nefarious use. Individuals with EI can easily manipulate others as they pursue their own interests. History has shown that manipulative and Machiavellian leaders in the past had a deep understanding of their followers' emotions, fears, and weaknesses. Studies have attempted to link EI to positive and benign attributes such as empathy and good-natured behavior (Petrides, Vernon, Schermer, & Veselka, 2011). Since EI is not grounded in any value framework, it would be naïve to assume that all individuals with a heightened sense of EI are well intentioned. Manipulative individuals, narcissists, sociopaths, and con artists tend to pick their victims carefully after assessing their vulnerabilities. This skill or ability certainly entails the same elements of understanding other people's emotions, feelings, and weaknesses that EI defines.

Criticisms and Controversies of EI

Some controversies and issues related to EI have been discussed in different contexts. One pointed criticism by Locke (2005) is worth highlighting. Locke submits that EI is an invalid concept for a variety of reasons. First, the ability to monitor one's emotions does not require any special degree or type of intelligence. This is a factor of field of focus. People do learn to discriminate between emotions. A highly intelligent person is able to make subtle distinctions between similar emotions such as jealousy and envy, and use developed introspective skill to focus these distinctions inward. Locke suggests that whether one uses one's knowledge in everyday action is not an issue of intelligence per se. Other factors such as rationality, focus, and integrity are relevant. Redefining intelligence broadly to include multiple intelligences destroys the notion of true intelligence or the g-factor by making it seem that everyone has equal intellectual capacity. In addition, while some people are more intelligent, it may not be reflected in every skill that they choose to develop. Finally, Locke observes that EI proponents have developed a long list of characteristics that includes everything, but actual intelligence (Locke, 2005). Locke is one among many critics that have stepped forward, but their criticisms have not deterred proponents of EI to march on. The most pointed criticism appears to be in the way intelligence is described in the body of knowledge and demonstrating how this description is different from EI.

The Way Forward for EI

The emerging concept of work and the current organizational workplace are constantly changing in alignment with the fourth industrial revolution. EI is even more relevant and offers the promise of resolving many modern work-related issues such as job insecurity, misaligned psychological contracts, diverse workforce, and virtual organizations. The EI concept, however, must be nurtured in a number of ways. There is still lack of agreement on what constitutes EI, its dimensions, and measurement. A systematic empirical analysis of EI, its antecedents, and measurements is necessary. Such a body of knowledge will benefit those practitioners that are interested in enhancing EI awareness and training among their ranks.

EI is not a panacea for all work-related employee problems. The excitement and enthusiasm around EI has led some to perceive EI as a universal solution to many workplace social and psychological problems, without understanding its limitations. Perhaps more robust, empirical foundations will help to moderate this enthusiasm while making EI more effective. EI scholars and practitioners have a great opportunity to explore the impact of EI on modern work-related contexts such as digitization, multicultural work settings, globalization, and constant uncertainty affecting modern organizations.

Wong and Law (2002) have found that workers with high EI are capable of revising perceptions regarding their work environments. These workers regulate their emotions by intensifying, diminishing, prolonging, or curtailing certain emotions. Such employees are able to feel and behave appropriately in different work settings. For instance, a supervisor that works with a difficult boss will strive to curtail feelings of frustration while dealing with the boss by deliberately curtailing those emotions. On the other hand, the supervisor will portray upbeat feelings of energy and optimism while interacting with her subordinates. Workers with high EI are able to understand their own emotions, the emotions of others, and regulate their own emotions appropriately according to the situation. Workers with high EI are also able to achieve individual emotional growth and maturity over time since they have relevant emotional "tools" to cope and learn from different situations. They have a greater capacity to make adjustments in dynamic environments such as new leadership, new employees, and unpredictable performance outcomes in the organization.

There is a clear need to create a better understanding of what EI means, and separate the concept from other related concepts such as intelligence, introspection, and reflection. The romanticized view of EI as a solution to employee and organizational problems is unrealistic. Like many other psychological constructs, the effect of EI interventions on individual workers is modest though positive. However, the effect on organizational performance is indirect, through improved worker wellbeing and mental state of health. There are emerging organizational contexts and work situations that had not been contemplated when the concept was first developed. Clearly, there is more research to be done in all these areas.

References

Bar-On, R. (2006). The Bar-On model of emotional-social intelligence (ESI). *Psicothema, 18,* 13–25.

Boyatzis, R., & Sala, F. (2004). The Emotional Competency Inventory (ECI). In G. Geher (Ed.), *Measuring Emotional Intelligence: Common Ground and Controversy*. Hauppauge, NY: Nova Science Publishing, 147–180.

Boyatzis, R., Goleman, D., & Rhee, K. (2000). Clustering competence in emotional intelligence: Insights from the Emotional Competence Inventory (ECI). In R. Bar-On & J. D. A. Parker (Eds.), *The Handbook of Emotional Intelligence: Theory, Development, Assessment, and Application at Home, School, and in the Workplace*. San Francisco: Jossey-Bass, 343–362.

Earley, P., & Ang, S. (2003). *Cultural Intelligence: Individual Interactions Across Cultures*. Stanford, CA: Stanford University Press.

Earley, P., & Peterson, R. (2004). The elusive cultural chameleon: Cultural intelligence as a new approach to intercultural training for the global manager. *Academy of Management Learning and Education, 3*(1), 100–115.

Gibbs, N. (1995). What's your EQ. *Time*. October, 2.

Goffman, E. (1949). Presentation of self in everyday life. *American Journal of Sociology, 55*, 6–7.
Goleman, D. (1995). *Emotional Intelligence: Why It can Matter More Than IQ for Character, Health and Lifelong Achievement*. New York: Bantam Books.
Goleman, D. (1998). *Working with Emotional Intelligence*. New York, Bantam Books.
Hodzic, S., Scharfen, J., Ripoll, P., Holling, H., & Zenasni, F. (2018). How efficient are emotional intelligence trainings: A meta-analysis. *Emotion Review, 10*(2), 138–148.
Hofstede, G. (1984). *Culture's Consequences: International Differences in Work-Related Values* (Vol. 5). Newbury Park, CA: Sage.
Hofstede, G. (2009). Dimensionalizing cultures: The Hofstede Model in context. *Online Readings in Psychology and Culture, 2*(1). Retrieved from https://doi.org/10.9707/2307-0919.1014.
Klausner, W. (1993). *Reflections on Thai Culture*. Bangkok, Thailand: Siam Society.
Locke, E. A. (2005). Why emotional intelligence is an invalid concept. *Journal of Organizational Behavior, 26*(4), 425–431.
Maslach, C., & Jackson, S. (1981). The measurement of experienced burnout. *Journal of Occupational Behavior, 2*, 99–113.
Mayer, J., Salovey, P., & Caruso, D. (2004). Emotional intelligence: Theory, findings, and implications. *Psychological Inquiry, 15*(3), 197–215.
Nisbett, R. E., Aronson, J., Blair, C., Dickens, W., Flynn, J., Halpern, D. F., & Turkheimer, E. (2012). Intelligence: New findings and theoretical developments. *American Psychologist, 67*(2), 130.
Petrides, K., & Furnham, A. (2003). Trait emotional intelligence: Behavioural validation in two studies of emotion recognition and reactivity to mood induction. *European Journal of Personality, 17*, 39–57.
Petrides, K. V., Pita, R., & Kokkinaki, F. (2007). The location of trait emotional intelligence in personality factor space. *British Journal of Psychology, 98*(2), 273–289.
Petrides, K., Vernon, P., Schermer, J., & Veselka, L. (2011). Trait emotional intelligence and the dark triad traits of personality. *Twin Research and Human Genetics, 14*(1), 35–41.
Santos, A., Mustafa, M. J., & Gwi, T. C. (2015). Trait emotional intelligence, emotional labour, and burnout among Malaysian HR professionals. *Management Research Review, 38*(1), 67–88.
Weisinger, H. (1998). Emotional Intelligence at Work: The Untapped Edge for Success. San Francisco: Jossey-Bass.
Wong, C., & Law, K. (2002). The effects of leader and follower emotional intelligence on performance and attitude: An exploratory study. *Leadership Quarterly, 13*(3), 243–274.
Zeidner, M., Matthews, G., & Roberts, R. (2004). Emotional intelligence in the workplace: A critical review. *Applied Psychology, 53*(3), 371–399.

16

MANAGING SPIRITUALLY ADVERSE PEOPLE

Debra J. Dean

Introduction

When talking with employees in any organization Dean (2016, 2017) likes to explain that workplace spirituality is important because it is the right thing to do. The more she researched this topic, she realized that her efforts merely validated what God had already documented in the Sacred Text. She remembered setting off on her first organizational leadership adventure with a large, secular, global company to find that the answer to her quest was 1 Corinthians 13:13, "and now these three remain faith, hope, and love. But the greatest of these is love." Love was the single most significant predictor of employee engagement, job satisfaction, and organizational commitment; how could that be in a secular organization?

For far too many years, human beings have walked into their workplace with their body and mind, leaving their heart and soul at the door. Research shows that neglecting the whole person at work has caused increased amounts of stress as workers try to balance their personal needs along with the needs of their employer. Such stress may impact one's health or cause a lack of employee engagement, among other things. It may also cause absenteeism or high turnover. As a leader in the organization and a scholar, Dean (2016, 2017) found herself asking what can she do to help *nourish the soul at work* and how can she help each employee find meaning and purpose in the time spent earning a paycheck. Workplace spirituality was the answer for her to help co-workers and others move from their job to their vocation and research shows that spirituality in the workplace can increase job satisfaction, organizational commitment, and other workplace outcomes.

Workplace Spirituality—Businessmen on their Knees

This section of the chapter will introduce the concept of workplace spirituality. A 1953 article in *Fortune* magazine entitled, "Businessmen on their Knees" is possibly the first mention of the concept scholars now term "workplace spirituality." This article is referenced by many intellectuals who believe the concept of spirituality in the workplace dates back to the 1950s. Norton-Taylor (1953) penned the article explaining that "a considerable number of businessmen" (p. 140) around the country are talking about the application of religion to business. To understand the weight of this issue, many of the businessmen in 1953 did not even discuss religion in their own home as it was a personal issue and was not an issue they discussed even with their parents.

Norton-Taylor (1953) describes a phenomenon of increased church membership, increased tithing, and record sales of four religious books including the New Revised Standard Version of the Bible. Realizing that something different was happening in American businesses, Norton-Taylor (p. 140) questioned if businessmen were "promoting religion as a useful tool and God as a good partner to have in the firm?" Or if businessmen were "putting their religion to daily 'practical' uses" and "experiencing a spiritual awakening that is indeed genuine" (p. 140)?

Norton-Taylor (1953) called it a movement. He wrote about the movement that was changing the cocktail parties of the businessmen, noting that "to the bewilderment of outsiders, their cocktail parties are more apt than not to turn into religious discussions" (p. 253). He described the journey of Admiral Ben Moreell who questioned his existence in 1932 when the Navy assigned him to Paris, France. He explained that his search for answers about "man's existence and God's purpose for him became clearer ... with the practice of the two commandments: love God, and love your neighbor" (p. 141) Twenty years later, Moreell often found himself sitting at his desk in an "ultramodern" skyscraper talking about religion. Moreell said, "the subject is not only vital but respectable" (p. 141). Moreell also assembled a group of Pittsburg industrialists, including presidents, vice presidents, and executives of different organizations to "put Christianity to work" (p. 140). The group wrote the following statement and disbursed it to their employees:

> We attempt to work out too many of our human-relations problems without asking for divine guidance ... Actually, what we need is God's help ... We must be [Christ Bearers]. Our lives, our words, our inspired acts, our deeds of honesty and integrity and unselfishness, must be bridges across which He walks again into our world.
>
> *(p. 141)*

Many other businessmen were researched by Norton-Taylor (1953). The article references specific conversations of businessmen examining the Beatitudes in relation to routine business practices such as determining what leaders should do with aging workers who are becoming inefficient. Others compared the application of Christian principles to labor and human relations, quoting the president of Borg-Warner in saying religion "is the best solution we have found to the problem of getting along with each other" (p. 141). Norton-Taylor described a committee called Religion in Industry which started at the Russell Stover Candy Company and extended to a convention in Detroit, Michigan.

In another example, Norton-Taylor (1953) wrote that David Griffith, a worker at U.S. Steel's Homestead Works was fed up with a strike that lasted 8 weeks. He petitioned management to begin prayer meetings like they did at Stupakoff Ceramic and Manufacturing, which had been strike free for 11 years. Management at U.S. Steel was permissive of the prayer meetings if Griffith led them once a week in the corner of his department. With an average of 25 men in attendance, their meetings were amplified over the public address system for hundreds of employees to hear. Norton-Taylor wrote that "the singing of hymns out at Homestead is an unusual sound on that old and bloody ground." U.S. Steele also invested up to $150,000 to provide *Guideposts* magazines to their 125,000 employees monthly.

Additionally, religion was being discussed by businessmen at the golf club where Dr. Shoemaker conducted a 7-week series of lectures with an average attendance of 45–70 young married couples (Norton-Taylor, 1953). Putnam (Putty) McDowell was among those in attendance and acknowledged that he had not "needed" religion, which seemed to be the sentiment of many that described themselves as "happy, ethical pagans" that were not "broke or unhealthy"

(p. 248). Putty explained that praying was new to him, but he started to pray before situations arose at work and "things just worked out better" (p. 248). He was a graduate of Harvard, which he explained taught students to rely on "man's own endeavors" (p. 253). Post-graduation, Putty became a member of Pittsburgh's H-Y-P (Harvard, Yale, and Princeton) Club that studied the Bible and spiritual power of Christianity over lunch.

Workplace Spirituality—God in Business

Fast forward nearly five decades and a second article was written in *Fortune* magazine July 2001 entitled "God and Business." Gunther (2001) wrote that "bringing spirituality into the workplace ... is breaching the last taboo in corporate America" (p. 64). He stated that many still believe in "separation of church and boardroom" and explained that the business world had found ways to talk about "race, gender equality, sexuality, disability, and even mental illness" (p. 64), but not religion.

The 2001 article references the 1953 article by Norton-Taylor as the days where "women and non-Christians" (p. 64) were not welcome in the executive suite. Gunther (2001) cited an example of Warren Buffett and his planned franchise of the R. C. Wiley furniture store in Las Vegas, Nevada. The problem was that Buffett, who was a self-professed agnostic at the time, wanted the store to be open on Sundays, which was a direct violation of Bill Child's business model. Child, the chairman of R. C. Wiley Home Furnishings and devout Mormon who always observed the Sabbath, said that reputation was R. C. Wiley's biggest commodity and stemmed from being a family owned business that set aside Sunday for church, family, and rest. Honesty is also the best policy at R. C. Wiley, where Child tells his 2000 employees to be scrupulously honest. To convince Buffett that God would prevail, Child paid $9 million to set up a store in Boise, Idaho as a test. Buffett and Child agreed that if the store could make a profit while being closed on Sunday's then Buffett would move forward with the store in Las Vegas. Several months after the opening in 1999, Buffett recognized that the store was profitable and bought the store from Child who refused to accept any of the interest on the $9 million capital he had invested. The first Las Vegas store was approved in 1999 and there are now four R. C. Wiley furniture stores in Nevada, all are closed on Sundays.

Gunther's (2001) article reinforced the workplace spirituality verbiage from 1953 but added that more religions were in America than half a century ago. Gunther (2001) documented lunch meetings at LaSalle Bank in Chicago that included sandwiches and spiritual sustenance calling for employees to work less, slow down, and stop multi-tasking. Gunther also referred to the Business Leaders for Excellence, Ethics, and Justice (BEEJ) as an executive group that struggled with questions such as promoting family life, fair wages, justifying layoffs, and integrating faith in work. ServiceMaster was referenced in the article as being a "Fortune 500 company committed explicitly to serving God" (p. 64). Gunther also described the career of Jose Zeilstra, Vice President of J. P. Morgan Chase, who says she is "ultimately working for God" (p. 68).

David Miller, author of *God at Work* was quoted in Gunther's (2001) article as saying that "god is found in earth and rocks and buildings and institutions, and yes, in the business world" (p. 61). Gunther (2001) wrote about Thomas Crisman, a Jenkens and Gilchrist patent attorney and litigator that spends one-month per year in rural India for silence at a meditation retreat center. Additionally, the case study of Blistex was also noted in Gunther's article where President Dick Green explained that he tried for more than a decade to integrate his faith and his work before realizing that when seeking "harmony between God and business: sometimes the two collide, head-on" (p. 78). Blistex has a company policy to pay workers profit-sharing benefits worth about 15% of the employee's annual salary directly into their retirement accounts.

According to Gunther (2001), Laura Nash, a senior research fellow at Harvard Business School declared that "spirituality in the workplace is exploding" (p. 62). The author wrote about Julius Walls, Jr., chief executive at Greystone Bakery who lives his faith at work by hiring anyone because he believes everyone deserves a chance to succeed. Walls also begins meetings with a moment of silence and donates all of the bakery profits to the Greystone Foundation to help the needy. According to Walls, he "serves the poor by feeding the rich" and the bakery has been said to offer "sinful desserts that support saintly causes" (pp.72–73).

Gunther (2001) noted that the Baby Boomer generation was partially responsible for the workplace spirituality movement and recited that they brought the 1960s' youth culture, the 1980s' greedy culture, and now they want more than a paycheck as they anxiously want to know what really matters. Another area Gunther (2001, p. 64) notes as being responsible for the workplace spirituality movement is the fact that "post-World War II prosperity has created enough wealth that many Americans primary desires are not for material goods, but for spiritual and intellectual assets."

Introducing Workplace Spirituality

When introducing workplace spirituality to any audience, it is best to speak the words and identify the elephant in the room up front. Dean (2017) recommends probing the workplace with the spiritual terminology to get a feel for the temperature in the room. This section of the chapter will give some examples of how workplace spirituality has been introduced to a variety of audiences and the responses that were provided.

One of the first conversations about workplace spirituality was with a senior level executive in charge of modernization for a global, secular firm. The relationship was such that Dean referred to him as a mentor; whereas, she trusted him and his opinion on her career. When explaining workplace spirituality, his first reaction was that religion and spirituality in the workplace was an "oxymoron." He was quick to say that religion and spirituality do not belong in the workplace. Needless to say, the relationship changed at that point and he never asked about her research or education again. When managing spiritually adverse people from this perspective, the approach used by Dean (2017) was to show proof and lead by example. Although she did not have the support of this one leader in the organization, she did have support from others who championed the efforts; therefore, Dean continued her work and was eventually able to show proof that spirituality did belong in the workplace and resulted in positive work outcomes for the organization.

Shortly after the above deflating conversation, Dean went to a university about one hour from her home to present an article entitled "Employee Engagement and Servant Leadership" (Dean, 2016). While talking with the class, she was asked about her dissertation titled, "Religion and Spirituality in the Workplace: A Quantitative Evaluation of Job Satisfaction and Organizational Commitment" (Dean, 2017). The school is known for being a spiritual place and their response was positive. They discussed using different terminology so as to not scare off the audience or cause them to go on the defense. That conversation has been parked for a later date as there may be some value in using a different phrase instead of the word "spirituality." Overall, the day was full of positive remarks and excitement about the research. Meetings such as this are important when managing spiritually adverse people since being around like-minded people and those that support and encourage provides energy to keep going. So, it is important to recognize the support group(s) and acknowledge them as being a helpful part of the research process.

With much encouragement from a director of a secular organization, Dean (2017) mustered up the courage to introduce the topic of religion and spirituality to a small department of about

30 business professionals. In doing so, she hit the topic straight on and explained that religion and spirituality were not synonymous. She quoted from the Crazy Horse Memorial in South Dakota where she saw a sign that read, "We are not human beings having a spiritual experience; we are spiritual beings having a human experience." It is believed the quote came from Pierre Teilhard de Chardin (1976). Dean found only one employee that was offended and refused to attend the meeting. Unfortunately, he was not at the meeting to hear the opening where she stated that she was not trying to change anyone's religion and asked the crowd about what they thought was spiritual. She had answers to the question prepared from research including the following: connection, creator, energy, God, higher source, infinite, inner life, meaning, mysterious, one of a thousand names, one with nature, sources of all, that which remains unnamable, the universe, and wholeness. She then asked the audience what it felt like to be spiritual and words such as aware, balanced, caring, compassionate, content, creative, energized, joyful, mindful, peaceful, and receptive were spoken. This audience was usually a very quiet bunch and this 2-hour meeting was no exception; however, it was the aftereffect that was miraculous. After the meeting, several people emailed or talked to her verbally about their inner self. They asked good questions and she could tell they were searching for more meaning at work. They were tired and hungry for the nourishment of their soul. This one meeting has an insurmountable amount of significance. First, Dean was courageous in speaking about religion and spirituality in a secular workplace. Second, she was working with a senior leader that supported her research initiative. Third, she did have one employee that refused to participate, but that did not hold her back from continuing. Fourth, she had a quiet meeting, which some may see as failure, but she remained open after the meeting to communicating with the participants and found that the topic was sensitive enough that they were wanting private conversations as opposed to larger group discussions. With persistence and availability as two of her strengths, Dean met with many of the participants individually and found that they had a thirst for knowing more about the topic and finding a way to introduce the concept at work. And fifth, the one person that refused to participate sat back as an observer for more than a year and then became a vocal supporter of the research as he started seeing positive change in the workplace as a result of Dean's initiative.

After the meeting with about 30 business professionals, Dean found herself in another position of managing spiritually adverse people. She had one employee that was open to the idea but had a history of darkness. It was interesting to watch this relationship unfold as the employee was interested in helping with the research, but had not bought into the idea wholeheartedly. Dean simply persevered with the research and education at the workplace; she was consistent with her methodology and coached the participant along the way. Several conversations were held where the employee acknowledged the positive outcomes. With spiritually adverse people such as this, Dean recommends involving them in the process as well as coaching and mentoring. Eventually, the proof of the work should unfold.

In another meeting with a variety of professions, Dean (2017) asked similar questions as above. Additionally, she also asked how the audience members achieved feelings of joy, peace, and balance. They responded with walks in the park, yoga, attending a concert, and reading a book. The response in the room was amazing. She asked if anyone would like to work in this type of environment and their eyes were fixated on her as if she held a key to quenching their thirst. This meeting was inspiring for Dean, as well as those in the audience. It was a small meeting of 10–12 people, but it was a good group that did not seem to fear what others might think. The dynamic of this group was that there were not any direct reports in a hierarchy. They were simply business professionals meeting for another purpose and she was allowed to give a speech about workplace spirituality. Although this meeting did not have an immediate, direct impact on the research initiative, it did provide a way to sow some seeds. The 10–12 people in the meeting went back to their respective jobs and were able to communicate with others about this new information they had just heard. They were able to spread the word about workplace spirituality. And for those who may not have been vocal about it, they retained the information for later.

As president of her local speech guild, Dean (2017) gave many speeches to a secular audience about workplace spirituality as she prepared for conferences and other speaking engagements. She found that introducing workplace spirituality with questions such as "are you feeling nourished at work" and "are you happy with your workplace" opened the door to their undivided attention. She found that the audience was focused on every word and wanted more. In essence, they were hungry for this topic and wanted to know more about it. The practice at the speech guild provided Dean with several opportunities for success. First, she was able to deliver her speeches in a safe environment so she could communicate effectively to other audiences. Second, she was able to practice her speeches which continued to give her confidence and courage to speak to others. And the third benefit was that she educated another audience that could spread the information or retain it for their own use at a later date.

During a conference in 2017, Dean and other scholars spent several days talking about workplace spirituality and the growth the field has had in recent years. As mentioned above with the second example, she was surrounded by other like-minded professionals that shared her same passion for the topic. This was a week of encouragement and energy to continue the research. In addition to the academic reinforcement, she was surprised to find that many wanted to know more about how she applied spirituality in the workplace practically since she was able to do not only research but also the application of theory. This energized Dean to a new level and she has embarked on a new effort to write, educate, coach, and mentor as many as possible.

In this section of the chapter, Dean described her wins and failures as she introduced the topic of workplace spirituality to a variety of audiences. From a follower perspective, she has had two employees that were either adamantly against or lukewarm with regards to the topic. With both situations, she just continued her efforts without their participation and they eventually warmed to the idea. Dean also coached and mentored leaders, which is described more in the next section of this chapter.

Coaching and Mentoring Leaders and Followers

As a result of the meeting with about 30 business professionals, Dean began coaching and mentoring the leaders; after all their senior leader was one of her biggest supporters of the research. She embarked on a path where she educated the leaders via email, personal conversations, weekly meetings, and monthly workshops. She also surveyed their teams independently to see where each leader stood with their servant and spiritual leadership skills. There are many variables from the surveys that can be taught and/or coached. The variables are outlined in Table 16.1.

The Servant Leadership Assessment Instrument (SLAI) was developed by Dennis and Bocarnea (2005) to measure agapao love, altruism, empowering, humility, serving, trust, and vision. Dean used the Spiritual Leadership Scale developed by Fry, Vitucci, and Cedillo (2005) to measure Fry's three dimensions of spiritual leadership including altruistic love, hope/faith, and vision. Dean also used Ashmos and Duchon's (2000) Spirituality at Work Scale to focus on three aspects of workplace spirituality including inner life, meaningful work, and sense of community. Each of these variables were tested by Dean with the employees to see which variables correlated with the desired workplace outcome and which variables had predictive power. She

Table 16.1 List of Surveys and Variables

Servant Leadership Assessment Instrument (SLAI)	*Spiritual Leadership Scale*	*Spirituality at Work Scale*
• Agapao love • Altruism • Empowering • Humility • Serving • Trust • Vision	• Altruistic love • Hope/faith • Inner life • Meaning/calling • Membership • Organizational commitment • Productivity • Satisfaction with life • Vision	• Conditions for community • Inner life • Meaning at work • Positive work unit values • Work unit community

found that all of the variables on the SLAI correlated significantly with employee engagement. Her research also indicated that altruistic love was the most significant predictor of job satisfaction and organizational commitment. In addition to altruistic love, a sense of community and meaningful work were significantly predictive of job satisfaction. With this information available, she was able to work with the leaders and followers of the department to educate them on the topics of workplace spirituality, servant leadership, spiritual leadership, employee engagement, job satisfaction, and organizational commitment. She was then able to work with the team from the leader and follower perspective. The outcome was a sub-culture within the larger secular company that had some of the highest employee engagement scores in the company. They also had concerted efforts put into place with investigation and training on meaningful work. And, they built a community that supports one another on a daily basis in addition to life events such as births, marriages, retirements, new jobs and/or promotions, deaths, and other exciting and/or difficult times.

Spiritual Companies

This chapter follows Dean (2017) as she managed spiritually adverse people by educating, coaching, and mentoring participants. She is not the first person to apply the concept of workplace spirituality practically. Throughout her research, many companies were listed as being spiritual. The list in Table 16.2 is a compilation of those company names. Keep in mind, that the companies listed in Table 16.2 may have been considered spiritual years ago and something may have changed since then, so this list is not up-to-date by any means. In fact, some of these companies are no longer in business or have been bought out and the name has changed. It is, however, a list Dean (2017) found intriguing and inspiring as so many secular companies had once been deemed spiritual.

Additionally, once upon a time, there was an International Spirit at Work Award. Judi Neal (President and CEO of the International Center for Spirit at Work) and other scholars would receive applications for the annual award and then chose a company that met their spirituality requirements. Unfortunately, that award was disbanded due to the lack of applications. Perhaps the issue is that few companies understand the importance of being spiritual.

Dean (2017) hopes that one day, the Spirit at Work Award will be resurrected and companies, as well as their customers and employees, will find value in working with a spiritual business.

Table 16.2 List of Spiritual Companies

• Alcoa	• IBM	• Pittsburg Plate Glass
• Alcoholics Anonymous	• Interstate Battery J. Rene Ouimet Holding	• Price Waterhouse Cooper
• American Express	• Jenkins and Gilchrist	• Procter and Gamble
• Amoco	• Jones and Laughlin	• R.C. Wiley Furniture Stores
• Australia and New Zealand Banking (ANZ)	• JP Morgan Chase	• Russell Stover
• Ben and Jerry's	• LaSalle Bank	• SAS Institute
• Berkshire Hathaway	• Legatos	• Scaife Company
• Big Horne Department Store	• Maxwell, Locke, and Ritter	• Service Master
• Blaw-Knox	• Medtronic	• Shell Oil Company
• Blistex	• Memorial Herman Healthcare	• Sherwin Williams
• Body Shop	• Missouri Ascension Health	• Southwest Airlines Starbucks
• Borg-Warner	• NEC Corporation	• Stupakoff Ceramic and Manufacturing
• Catalytica	• New Balance	• Timberland
• Chick-Fil-A	• Nike	• Tom's of Maine
• Cordon Bleu Tomasso	• Outdoor Recreation	• Tyson
• Disney		• U.S. Steel
• Dow Chemical		• UniLever
• Exxon		• Weleda
• Ford		• Whole Foods
• General Electric		• YMCA
• Google		
• Greystone Bakery		
• Herman Miller		

Culture and Climate

This section of the chapter examines organizational culture and climate, the process of transformation, and presents empirical evidence to suggest that transformation is a journey requiring involvement and commitment from all areas of the company, including leaders and followers. Evidence from this research supports the need to align the culture and climate with corporate values, strategies, and driving forces of the company. The theoretical foundation for Dean's (2016, 2017) efforts revolved around servant leadership, spiritual leadership, and workplace spirituality. Ultimately, her goal was to change the culture to become spiritual.

Although efforts began to transform the culture of the large, global, secular company in 2012, it was not fully understood how long it would take to see results. In the beginning, the company recruited volunteers to help, but there was not enough investment throughout the entire organization to see a real change of heart. To get a pulse on the status of the environment, a simple survey in 2014 asked employees to describe the culture of the organization in just one word. The results were shocking as words such as achievers, awesome, cliquey, cold, distracted, evolving, flux, inconsistent, joke, nightmare, petty, progressive, sterile, and worldly showed up. This proved that the work was far from over. It was about this time that Dean stepped in to focus on just one department. Her efforts were supported by one senior director, but not all in the organization saw the value of her efforts at the time. This work shows the power of one person and the influence one can have on a large organization.

Changing the culture of a century-old company is not an easy task. Many factors come into play when trying to transform a culture; however, great benefits can result from persevering. To begin, it is important to understand the difference between culture and climate. Culture is the personality of the organization. The culture is the sum of multiple characteristics within the workgroup. Managerial values and beliefs are embedded in the corporate culture. Culture is rooted in the organization's people and routine (Wei, O'Neill, Lee, & Zhou, 2013). The culture of an organization includes artifacts, assumptions, beliefs, collective behaviors, collective programming, common sets of values, consensus, control systems, environment, norms, organizational structures, power structures, rituals and ceremonies, stories, symbols, underlying shared assumptions, and values (Simoneaux & Stroud, 2014). Artifacts are what you see, smell, and hear. They are often the only tangible part of an organizational culture. When considering one's culture it is important to reflect on each one of these items to question what is this and why is it important to the company. One may find that an artifact, as an example, is outdated and conflicting with the direction the company is trying to move toward.

Culture can take a long time to change. The culture of the organization is reflected in the business hours, client satisfaction, dress code, employee benefits, hiring decisions, office setup, treatment of clients, turnover, and every other aspect of the operation (Simoneaux & Stroud, 2014). The culture is to be clearly expressed and understood by most personnel within an organization in order to enable members to behave in meaningful ways toward one another and interpret the meaning of other member behaviors (Simoneaux & Stroud, 2014). Take for example a dress code where males are expected to dress in suits with ties and females are expected to wear stockings with their dresses. If the desired culture is one of professionalism and strict adherence to rules then this dress code may be appropriate. On the other hand, if the desired culture is one of flexibility and empowerment, the dress code may cause employees frustration or uncertainty.

Kurt Lewin was the first to talk about organization climate. The climate of a company is the attitude of the organization. It is how the company feels, like a temperature. The climate is what the company rewards their employees for or what they pay attention to. Examples may include safety and service if the organization rewards employees for having positive feedback (service) or zero accidents (safety). Climate is easier to change than culture; however, it is important to note that culture and climate work hand-in-hand. Dean (2017) found that the culture of her department was initially cold and abrasive. Her intention was to transform the department into a spiritual workplace; that is a workplace where people care for one another and feel connected.

Spiritual Leadership Theory

To analyze the importance of workplace spirituality and the predictive power with common workplace outcomes, Dean (2017) chose job satisfaction and organizational commitment as two dependent variables. She used two popular workplace spirituality scales. The independent variables included the likes of altruistic love, hope/faith, and vision based on the Fry et al. (2005) Spiritual Leadership Scale and the variables of inner life, meaningful work, and sense of community-based on Ashmos and Duchon's (2000) Spirituality at Work Scale. Additionally, she controlled for age, education, gender, income, meditation experience, religion, and tenure. Her research included 147 participants from 21 different industries and three different countries. She found that altruistic love was the one variable that significantly predicted both job satisfaction and organizational commitment. The sense of community and meaningful work also significantly predicted job satisfaction.

Although workplace spirituality has been a movement since the 1950s there is not an agreed upon definition. Giacalone and Jurkiewicz (2003, p. 13) define it as "a framework of organizational values evidenced in the culture that promotes employees' experience of transcendence through the work process, facilitating their sense of being connected to others in a way that provided feelings of completeness and joy." Ashmos and Duchon (2000, p. 137) define workplace spirituality as "recognition of an inner life that nourishes and is nourished by meaningful work that takes place in the context of community."

The workplace spirituality movement is about "employees who understand themselves as spiritual beings whose souls need nourishment at work" (Ashmos & Duchon, 2000, p. 134). It is about employees having more meaningful work and a connection between one's soul and their work (Ashmos & Duchon, 2000). Human beings have both mind and spirit, and spiritual workplaces realize that developing the spirit is just as important as developing the mind (Ashmos & Duchon, 2000). Spirituality in the workplace, according to Ashmos and Duchon involves the community, inner life, and meaningful work.

A spiritual workplace is quite possibly the answer to many organizations that are seeking to provide an environment for their employees to feel fulfilled and realize they are coming to work to do a meaningful job. While a spiritual workplace is a phrase many may not be familiar with, it is a movement that has been underway in corporations since the 1950s. Giacalone, Jurkiewicz, and Fry (2005) stated: "workplace spirituality is one of the fastest growing areas of new research and inquiry by scholars and practitioners alike" (p. 515). In what is considered the first empirical study on workplace spirituality, Mitroff and Denton (1999) explained that the word interconnectedness is a single word that describes the meaning of spirituality (p. 83). Their groundbreaking research found that spiritual employees were hungry to "bring more of their 'complete selves' to work" (p. 83). The scholars explained, "unless organizations learn how to harness the whole person and the immense spiritual energy that is at the core of everyone, they will not be able to produce world-class products and services" (p. 84).

Servant Leadership Theory

In addition to spiritual leadership theory, the scholar investigated servant leadership theory within her department and found that agapao love, altruism, empowering, humility, serving, trust, and visionary all correlated with employee engagement. Dean (2016) used the Dennis and Bocarnea (2005) SLAI to survey 126 participants in seven different states. Servant leadership was a term first coined by Robert Greenleaf in 1970. Berger (2014) wrote that servant leadership is a leadership style that re-engages employees by focusing on people. Servant leadership, therefore, is emerging as a theory with the potential to create a positive organizational culture, produce socially responsible organizations, and cultivate engaged employees (Berger, 2014).

Robert Greenleaf (quoted in Berger, 2014) argued that the purpose of servant leadership is to serve first instead of lead. Greenleaf believed that followers of servant leaders would grow as a person and become more autonomous, freer, healthier, and wiser as a result of being served. Servant leaders listen receptively, display empathy, heal the self and others, and are aware of their self, their strengths, and their surroundings. Servant leaders are persuasive. They can conceptualize by looking beyond the day-to-day issues. Servant leaders have the foresight to learn from the past, understand the present, and forecast the future. Servant leaders are also stewards that play a role in holding their organization to a high standard of ethics. Servant leaders grow people and are personally committed to developing others. Servant leaders also build community and look for ways to improve the areas in which they work (Berger, 2014).

Conclusion

Practically applying academic concepts and theories in the workplace is a highly desired skill in today's marketplace. This chapter has followed a multi-year journey as Dean (2016, 2017) worked with a large, global, secular organization to transform the culture and climate. The company employed more than 12,000 people and boasted a history of more than 100 years. As a lone person pursuing her research initiative, she was faced with a variety of challenges and obstacles including spiritually adverse people, but her efforts resulted in a subculture that earned accolades for some of the highest employee engagement scores in the company. Despite the adversity along the way, she experienced many successes and gained valuable support that ultimately earned her a reputation of being a leader that cares and a scholar that practically applies theory. Her work may give a glimpse into the strategy used to make a difference in a large organization by starting with a smaller population and persevering.

References

Ashmos, D., & Duchon, D. (2000). Spirituality at work. *Journal of Management Inquiry, 9*(2), 134.

Berger, T. A. (2014). Servant leadership 2.0: A call for strong theory. *Sociological Viewpoints, 30*(1), 146–167.

Dean, D. (2016). A correlation study of employee engagement and servant leadership. *Journal of Strategic and International Studies, XI*(2), 32–43.

Dean, D. (2017). Religion and spirituality in the workplace: A quantitative evaluation of job satisfaction and organizational commitment (Order No. 10260968). Available from ProQuest Dissertations & Theses Global (1881834070).

Dennis, R., & Bocarnea, M. (2005). Development of the servant leadership assessment instrument. *Leadership and Organization Development Journal, 25(8)*, 600–615.

Fry, L. W., Vitucci, S., & Cedillo, M. (2005). Spiritual leadership and army transformation: Theory, measurement, and establishing a baseline. *Leadership Quarterly, 5*, 835.

Giacalone, R., & Jurkiewicz, C. (2003). Toward a science of workplace spirituality. In R. A. Giacalone & C. L. Jurkiewicz (Eds.), *The Handbook of Workplace Spirituality and Organizational Performance*. Armonk, NY: M. E. Sharpe,13.

Giacalone, R., Jurkiewicz, C., & Fry, L. (2005). From advocacy to science: The next steps in workplace spirituality research. In R. Paloutzian (Ed.), *Handbook of the Psychology of Religion and Spirituality*. Newbury Park, CA: Sage, 515–528.

Gunther, M. (2001). God and business. *Fortune*.

Mitroff, I., & Denton, E. (1999). A study of spirituality in the workplace. *Sloan Management Review, 40*(4), 83–92.

Norton-Taylor, D. (1953). Businessmen on their knees. *Fortune*.

Simoneaux, S. L., & Stroud, C. L. (2014). A strong corporate culture is key to success. *Journal of Pension Benefits: Issues in Administration, 22*(1), 51–53.

Teilhard de Chardin, P. (1976). *The Phenomenon of Man*. New York: Harper Perennial.

Wei, Y., O'Neill, H., Lee, R. P., & Zhou, N. (2013). The impact of innovative culture on individual employees: The moderating role of market information sharing. *Journal of Product Innovation Management, 30*(5), 1027–1041.

PART IV

Leadership and Spirituality

17

LEADING WITH A MORAL COMPASS

Eugene Ohu and Princess Anifowose

Introduction

The burgeoning literature on leadership is either a testament to the rapid evolution of the times and the effort of education, research, and learning to catch up, or it may be proof that we need to improve our understanding of an old term. There is as yet little consensus in management literature on the meaning of leadership and how it works, even though no topic has been studied and written about the most in the behavioral sciences.

The advancement and development of society and of the small and large units that make it up, the family and organizations, are to a large extent products of leadership and the exercise of power and of authority (Ciulla, 1995; Kort, 2008). In private and public organizations, small and big businesses and in all enterprises requiring team effort, there are individuals at the forefront taking the lead and providing direction toward the accomplishment of mutually agreed objectives (Braun & Nieberle, 2017; Williamson, 2008). Leaders influence a set of followers to feel, think, and act in particular ways (Zhu, Treviño, & Zheng, 2016).

Several attributes have been used in literature to qualify leadership, each of which is intended to highlight a higher and exemplary standard which people who occupy such positions ought to possess and by which they should be judged. Some of these traits include "responsible" as in "responsible leadership," "servant" as in "servant leader," this latter being a double entendre intended to unravel some hitherto ignored meanings of "servant" (Cameron, 2011; Ciulla, 1995; Graham, 1991; Pless, 2007). Cameron (2011) identifies responsible leadership with virtuousness. She equates "responsibility" first with accountability and dependability, second with discretion (or volition), third with the task of caring for "others" (tasks, objectives, people, etc.); and finally the author (citing Walsh, Weber, & Margolis, 2003) proposes a fourth conception of responsible leadership as the ability to

> act in an appropriate fashion (as when an individual acts responsibly). The concept of appropriateness is key to this connotation in that it associates responsible action with what is right, correct, or best. Behaving responsibly in this sense means being good or doing good.
>
> *(Cameron, 2011)*

The rest of the chapter is arranged as follows. First is an attempt to provide some clarity to the definition of leadership, which provides the opportunity to explain some key concepts.

There is a brief treatment of the two parties involved in the leadership relationship followed by some comments on a few selected leaders. The concept of a moral compass is then considered which leads to the introduction of the virtues. The chapter then proceeds to address the topic of freedom, particularly in the context of the role of the followers, ending with the suggestive term, virtuous followership. Persuasion is then introduced as the tool leaders use to influence the followers. The chapter ends with a focus on some key virtues required of the leadership function.

Toward Definitional Clarity

Despite hundreds of books and articles written on leadership, there is as yet neither clarity nor agreement on the meaning of the terms of "leadership" and "leader", and sometimes one is confused for the other. Citing Rost (1993), Gini offers the following which is here adopted as a working definition and a guide to the framework adopted in this chapter: "Leadership is a power and value laden relationship between leaders and followers/constituents who intend real change(s) that reflect their mutual, purpose(s) and goal(s)" (1997, p. 324). This definition highlights certain key ideas, one of which is power. This capability of exerting control and effecting change is often attributed to leadership, even though not all with power can be considered leaders. Gini (1997) suggests that power is universal and that it always fills a vacuum in any organization. One assumption that comes up from this treatment is that power is a deliberate process (Gini, 1997). A point that may not be so obvious is the possibility of a leader unconsciously exercising influence (control and change) without intending to, merely by the force of moral persuasion or good example that is visible to others for whom this person is a model. The exercise of leadership may thus not always be a deliberate process, either for the leader or for the followers.

The definition also draws attention to the importance of values. Arguing that managing the values of any undertaking constitutes the main task of leadership, Gini (1997) says that "all leadership is value laden" (p. 325), a direct allusion to the moral nature of the leadership function.

Managing values implies taking a position in some particular direction whether good or bad, so long as the leader's point of view (and at that point, those of the followers that choose to emulate them) suggests that as the correct view to adopt (Padilla, Hogan, & Kaiser, 2007; Zhu et al., 2016). It is perhaps in this light one understands the power to influence that some like Hitler and Stalin were able to exert (Cooper, Scandura, & Schriesheim, 2005; Potts, 2009; Sy, Horton, & Riggio, 2018). Could Hitler and Stalin be described as leaders even if later history would consider them despicable (Braun, Sloan, Aldor, & Trenker, 2014; Kershaw, 2014; Ciulla, 1995)?

A Tale of Two Parties: The Leader and the Follower

Since leadership involves a relationship between two parties, Gini (1997) suggests that a clear distinction be made between the process (involved in the relationship), the person, and the job, while stating the importance and co-existence of all three in a delicate balance. If as Zaleznik (1990, p. 12) states that "Leadership is based on a compact that binds those that lead with those who follow into the same moral, intellectual and emotional commitment," we ought to acknowledge a relationship between thinking beings who have come together to achieve a common goal and who freely choose the means to attain these goals, including how they relate with others in that environment (Rego, Vitória, Magalhães, Ribeiro, & e Cunha, 2013).

The leader, a specific individual is singled out to lead the others, either by the free choice of those led or by some other circumstance (Hollander, 1995; Rego et al., 2013; Williamson, 2008). This individual has certain characteristics that others do not seem to possess and which therefore are worth a closer look. Gini (1997) further suggests that the circumstances of some particular task or job can differentiate manifestations of the leadership relationship and the traits of the individual leader. To this end, he suggests that qualities of leadership can only be measured in a "particular instantiation of a leader doing a job" (p. 324).

Leader Exemplars

Mahatma Gandhi, who led the Indian independence movement against British colonial rule was described as a shy person and was not particularly an impressive speech maker (Bligh & Robinson, 2010). He however remains known as one of history's greatest human rights activists whose leadership style endeared him to millions, then as now (Parekh, 2001). He referred to his followers as co-workers, with whom he shared his visions of a hope for a better future for his native land India (Shamir, Dayan-Horesh, & Adler, 2005). Heavily influenced by his Hindu religion, Gandhi's philosophy was that of non-violent protest against oppressive rule. This approach was an inspiration to a later leader in another clime and environment, Martin Luther King Jr. and remains an influence to many to this day (Jacobs & Longbotham, 2011).

Adolf Hitler of Nazi Germany (1889–1945) (Kershaw, 2014) was by many accounts a charismatic influencer for the "full-blooded German" and Aryan race superiority campaign (Rosenbloom & Althaus, 2010). He led a revolution whose outcome (World War II) still defines history to date. Hitler's followers accorded him godlike reverence and many considered him superhuman (Potts, 2009; Graham, 1991).

Joseph Stalin of Russia championed Stalinism, a political system which involves ideologies of communism, and which influenced the Russian and Soviet Union citizenry in the 1930s (Fitzpatrick, 2000). Joseph Stalin's government was accused of incompetence, corruption, and mismanagement of the country's resources. The people could only "grumble" about it but were largely helpless (Fitzpatrick, 2000). Stalin was himself influenced by a previous leader from another environment, Russia's Vladimir Lenin (Potts, 2009; Fitzpatrick, 2000).

The Albanian Catholic nun and missionary, Mother Teresa whose service to the poor in Calcutta, India and other parts of the world was a great influencer in life and in death. She found purpose in her numerous charitable works for destitutes and people confined to slums (Jacobs & Longbotham, 2011). Her life and works endeared her to many across the globe, from the highly placed socially to the lowest. She received many notable awards throughout the world, including the Nobel Peace Prize (Cooper et al., 2005). Mother Teresa founded a religious congregation, the Daughters of Charity that has continued her work, and the Catholic Church by *canonizing* her a saint, has held her up as a universal model.

Influence is important to the leadership process and Burns, in Gini (1997), says that the leadership process: "must be defined as carrying through from decision-making stages to the point of concrete changes in people's lives, attitudes, behaviours and institutions." Influence has been defined as, "the capacity to have an effect on the character, development or behaviour of someone or something, or the effect itself" (English Oxford Living Dictionary, 2018). Hitler and Stalin were examples of leaders because they adopted and had others follow some shared vision, and they had powerful influence on their followers (Gini, 1997).

To the extent that Hitler and Stalin were as much influencers as the likes of Pope John Paul II, Mahatma Gandhi, Mother Teresa, Martin Luther King Jr. or Winston Churchill, they could all be considered leaders (Ciulla, 1995; Kort, 2008; Padilla et al., 2007).

They were in positions of authority and they influenced the followers with whom they shared a common goal. The difference is in the different values, or moral stance, they both lived and upheld. In this light, moral leadership is therefore not a moot point and must be taken into account in the leadership question (Ciulla, 1995).

Leaders, such as the examples given here, had charisma (Bligh & Robinson, 2010; Potts, 2009). Whether or not the position they occupied in the minds of their followers was established by law or not, each had an emotional relationship with those who followed their lead (Sy et al., 2018). The authority and power a leader wields has a great impact on the followers, the perceptions of the followers on the leadership, and also some behavioral patterns (Hollander, 1995). Leaders possess some force of conviction and power that wins their followers over, sometimes in spite of the former's intentions. This has led to such extreme cases as that of Eva Braun, Hitler's lover who committed suicide for his sake (Braun et al., 2014). Thus the outcome of the leadership function on the followers varies from beneficial to harmful (Padilla et al., 2007).

Ciulla (1995) suggest that leadership cannot be devoid of ethics and morality and that these are at the core of what a leader and leadership is, adding that for someone to be properly described as a leader, the process must be a force destined for good. This is why several studies disagree that Adolf Hitler could properly be described as a leader because his leadership caused more harm than greater good (Padilla et al., 2007; Sy et al., 2018). If however the focus is on influencing per se, irrespective of whether the outcome was good or bad, Ciulla (1995) agrees that Hitler could indeed be described as a leader.

The extent to which one person's actions can be held up to an agreed standard, such actions may therefore be considered as upright or appropriate. If the person is a leader, such "appropriate" behaviors may be taken or offered as an imitable model or compass for others to follow (Rego, Cunha, & Clegg, 2012).

A Moral Compass

Like a navigator relies on a compass for direction, people need a guide to lead them to a desired destination for their good. This person, the leader, is the compass, pointing to the objective.

A magnetic compass is an instrument used for navigation on land and at sea. In order to show the way, the "north" on a compass is not aligned unto itself, but to the Earth's geographic north which is why it is able to guide people irrespective of weather, time, or place. A compass in good condition ought to maintain the Earth's geographic (or true) north as its reference point. The Earth is a magnet and, like all magnets, the poles (negative or positive) attract or deflect the poles on other magnets depending on whether the charge is negative or positive, with opposing poles attracting and like poles deflecting. A compass has a loosely held magnetic pin which rotates as it is alternately attracted and deflected by the different poles of the Earth's magnetic field. Technically, it is the Earth's south pole (which is different though near, to its geographic—or true—north pole) that is attracted to the compass' magnetic north pole. The aim of a navigator is to always align the compass' magnetic north pole to the Earth's "true north." He therefore has to take into account and compensate for this difference (or declination) between the magnet's north and the Earth's true north. This they do by means of "charts of declination" or by "local calibration" (Sheppard, 1970).

Who Leads the Compass

What the compass is to the navigator, the virtues are to the leader and the followers. Like the followers, the leader needs an objective guide which we propose to be the moral virtues (Rego et al., 2012; Thompson, 2010); but he also relies on the free choice of followers who deliberately give themselves up to be led by a particular person (Oc & Bashshur, 2013).

As a human being with often fluctuating needs, desires, emotions, and abilities (Govind, Singh, Garg, & D'Silva, 2017; Rego et al., 2012), a leader may not always be a perfect model or compass, hence the need for a constant unchanging reference point for himself and those he leads (Thompson, 2010).

Brown, Trevino, and Harrison (2005, p. 120) equate moral leadership with ethical leadership defining the latter as "the demonstration of normatively appropriate conduct through personal actions and interpersonal relationships, and the promotion of such conduct to followers through communication, reinforcement, and decision-making." Virtues make up the "north" of the "compass" that guides the direction to which the leader heads himself and leads his followers.

What is Good? Toward a "True North"

The conversation about whether there are objective standards of "good" and "bad," "right" and "wrong" that are valid for everyone and at every time, is as old as life, and remains controversial (Chonko, Wotruba, & Loe, 2003). Cameron's (2011) analysis of the leadership literature finds some equating ethics with the avoidance of harm or the fulfillment of some prescribed duties. One ethical theory suggests that the standard should be to aim to attain the greatest happiness for the majority; another simply invites people to do the right thing; yet another enjoins people to practice a duty of care toward others; yet another is the so-called "virtue ethics" which says that the right thing is for everyone to strive to be ethical through practicing the virtues (Bray, Johns, & Kilburn, 2011; Song & Kim, 2016). Although the different approaches do not necessarily all contradict themselves, the virtue-ethics approach seems more appropriate for the present study, particularly because of its focus on good habits.

Virtues as Compass

There seem to be some confusion, or disagreement, among authors about the meaning of virtues. This confusion ironically offers light and an opportunity to understand virtues and how they work particularly when viewed through the Aristotelian lens. Aristotle identifies virtue (Greek *arete*) with "excellence in the human soul" (Hardie, 1978, p. 63). This conceptualization places virtue as a characteristic or attribute of the individual person. It is a person who is virtuous or has virtues, and therefore it is within a person that we must seek to discover virtues. If it is by observing a person that virtue can be understood, this should therefore become apparent through what the person thinks, says, or does. As thoughts can be inferred only through speech and action, the latter two remain the only way of judging the individual as either possessing virtues or not.

Cameron (2011) argues that some authors equate virtue with character strengths and disagrees that they are synonymous. One example the author gives to buttress this position is that one can have too little or too much character strength with possibly negative consequences, and since virtue (or the consequence in man, virtuousness), ought to refer to a desirable or favorable outcome, these defects or excesses cannot therefore be "virtuous" because "Virtuousness, on the other hand cannot be exceeded" (p. 27).

We agree with Cameron (2011) that character strength is not another name for "virtue" (in general), but we suggest that it is indeed an example of a virtue. We also agree that an excess or a defect in something can result in negative consequences, but do not agree that virtuousness (the attribute of virtue in a person) cannot be exceeded. Virtues can be exceeded when it is done with the wrong measures or with a wrong object or end. The reason for the issue of the possibility of a defect or excess does not lie in the inequivalence of character strength with virtues, but rather that as character strength is itself a virtue, like other virtues, it requires another virtue (anchor, moderator, measure) in order for it not to "exceed" or "fall short" and hence remain desirable and good.

Grant and Schwartz (2011) cite Aristotle to suggest that the best exercise of the virtues is to be found when there is proportion or an adequate mean.

> Both excessive and defective exercise destroys the strength, and similarly drink or food which is above or below a certain amount destroys the health, while that which is proportionate both produces and increases and preserves it. So too is it, then in the case of temperance and courage and the other virtues.
>
> *(Aristotle, trans. 1999, p. 22, cited in Grant & Schwartz, 2011, p. 1)*

The remainder of the Aristotelian quote cited above gives examples illustrating respectively the four cardinal virtues of fortitude, prudence, temperance, and justice:

> For the man who flies from and fears everything and does not stand his ground against anything becomes a coward (*fortitude*), and the man who fears nothing at all but goes to meet every danger becomes rash (lack of *prudence*); and similarly the man who indulges in every pleasure and abstains from none becomes self-indulgent (lack of *temperance*), while the man who shuns every pleasure, as boors do, becomes in a way insensible (lack of *justice*, as such a pleasure may be a need due to one).
>
> *(Aristotle, trans. 1999, p. 22 cited in Grant & Schwartz, 2011, p. 1)*

Thus we see that for an act to be considered virtuous, the four cardinal virtues have to intervene and they hardly act in isolation and so are the measure to be taken into account for every act to be considered virtuous. Fortitude is the strength needed to overcome obstacles in the way of doing that which is considered appropriate; prudence provides the wisdom to determine the appropriateness and object; justice considers the benefitting stakeholders of that action and apportions it to whom it is rightly due, while temperance exercises control, introducing a mean or due proportion.

Virtues as the Fruit of Exercise

In the pursuit of what is beneficial to themselves and others, people have to freely make choices between alternatives with possibly different end points. Frequent exercise of good deeds make virtues possible and easier. This is like what happens in the physical fitness and health domain.

Frequent bodily exercises make the muscles more flexible and pliable and thus increasingly capable of both more complex and arduous actions. The body becomes habituated to these movements and demands and thus repetition makes successive actions easier, as the person gets used to them. The first efforts at bodily exertions demanded by physical exercise are usually harder and require effort. There are obviously easier alternatives to these efforts, which the actor is free to choose, such as doing nothing. Will power, helped by rationalizations about the benefit of exercise, is needed to choose that which is more difficult. This analogy applies to all actions from which benefits accrue either to oneself or to others such as an act of kindness or duty, when ignoring a person in need may be less tasking or arduous. Good repeated actions (habits) are virtues, while the bad repeated actions (habits) are vices. Virtuous behaviors or those acts that can be called virtues may therefore be equated with ethical behaviors. Aristotle describes virtues as a range of passions and actions, and that is a mean between extremes (Hardie, 1978). If ethical choices redound to the benefit of people, planet, and society (Bond, 2005;

Lopez-Rodriguez, 2017; Sheth, Sethia, & Srinivas, 2011), and if the cardinal virtues help determine the correct judgment call and actions for particular circumstances (Bauman, 2018; Harris, 2001; Morales-Sánchez & Cabello-Medina, 2013), we can in the context of this chapter conclude that a virtuous person is an ethical person.

Freedom to Choose a Leader

War and conflict provide good illustrations of leadership and many great leaders in history have been linked to such occurrences of conflict, either physical or moral, from Alexander the Great, generals from the World Wars, Martin Luther King Jr. in the USA civil rights movement, Lech Wałęsa of Poland, and more recently Nelson Mandela in the Apartheid struggle of South Africa. Of the several patterns that emerge from the leader–follower relationship (even in the so-called dictatorial or tyrannical leadership contexts), one thing common to all is the role the followers play in determining who becomes their leader.

Everyone has a right to pursue that which will result in the greater good, beginning with what is good for oneself. The leadership relationship is directed toward the common good of the parties involved. It is therefore important to respect people's freedom to choose the means to achieve these goods (see Clark, 1978). Since the attainment of individual objectives is not exclusive of the objectives sought by or due to others, neither should the means or ends be indifferent. They should instead be subjected to a judgment of the moral rectitude or lack thereof. Moral responsibility can thus be imputed depending on whether the outcome is considered good or bad. It is generally recognized in law that total guilt cannot be imputed to a person temporarily or permanently bereft of reason such as a person acting under the influence of a mental illness. Thus, a mental illness or a drunken state can reduce the freedom attributable to the actor. Moral responsibility for the consequences of an action can only be rightly imputed on a person acting with full freedom. Merit can likewise only be imputed to acts that are performed freely. Freedom, and the consequent responsibility, is essential to and required of the dignity of the human person.

A quote from Thomas Aquinas' *Summa Theologiae* can further illustrate the concept of "free will," why it is a proper and necessary attribute of rational beings and why it is an important determinant of the morality of an act:

> Man has free-will: otherwise counsels, exhortations, commands, prohibitions, rewards, and punishments would be in vain. In order to make this evident, we must observe that some things act without judgment; as a stone moves downwards; and in like manner all things which lack knowledge. And some act from judgment, but not a free judgment; as brute animals. For the sheep, seeing the wolf, judges it a thing to be shunned, from a natural and not a free judgment, because it judges, not from reason, but from natural instinct. And the same thing is to be said of any judgment of brute animals. But man acts from judgment, because by his apprehensive power he judges that something should be avoided or sought. But because this judgment, in the case of some particular act, is not from a natural instinct, but from some act of comparison in the reason, therefore he acts from free judgment and retains the power of being inclined to various things. For reason in contingent matters may follow opposite courses, as we see in dialectic syllogisms and rhetorical arguments. Now particular operations are contingent, and therefore in such matters the judgment of reason may follow opposite courses, and is not determinate to one. And forasmuch as man is rational is it necessary that man have a free-will.
>
> *(Aquinas, 1485)*

During World War II, there were instances when soldiers decided that a commanding officer no longer deserved their respect, and subsequently decided to stop obeying him. Such was the case when some non-commissioned officers (NCOs) from the US side of the allied forces gave an ultimatum requesting the regimental commander to replace their commanding officer, else they resigned their commission. Although the soldiers in question were punished for the apparent mutiny, the regimental commander made the requested change. Whether or not the mutinous soldiers were right, it was clear that having put into question the credibility of their leader to lead them, their will to obey had been compromised. Freedom of the followers is therefore necessary for the leadership relationship, and it is through persuasion of the moral kind that leaders convince the followers that they have the qualities needed to lead them toward a common goal.

Followers do not always have a chance to choose their leaders. We are not therefore arguing that this would imply that either the leadership relationship or the outcome be considered bad. Consider a government led by the so-called "benevolent dictator," who although not elected to government by the people (such as military dictatorships), work only for the attainment of the good of the people.

Virtuous Followership

The exercise of freedom is not by itself a guarantee of a correct choice. The fact also that followers are able to choose their leaders freely (as in a democratic government) does not imply that the person of the leader or the outcome of leadership will redound to the common good. Man can freely choose that which is bad, which in this context can be a vicious leader (prone to vice) or an end that does not benefit the common good.

Chaos would result were followers to make their choices without a stable moral standard. Freedom cannot be a guide unto itself, otherwise we would not have the emergence of leaders like Adolf Hitler whom many followed in his anti-Semitic campaign. Freedom in choosing a leader needs a moral compass to ensure that the followers are right. Similar to how virtues serve the function of a compass for the virtue-inclined leader, they aid the followers in choosing who to lead them. We therefore define virtuous followership as the recourse that followers have to the virtues as the standard against which they measure those they select to lead them, and the criteria guiding their relationship with these persons.

Influence, Power, and Persuasion

Recall the Oxford Dictionary's definition of "influence" above as "the capacity to have an effect on the character, development or behaviour of someone or something, or the effect itself." One definition of "power" that is similar to this describes it as the extent to which one person can influence another. Power, in an organization, results from the interaction or relationship between supervisors and subordinates. Were the focus to be on the ability to influence others, it becomes clear that different types of power (influencing ability) proceed from different sources. *Expert* power, for example, depends on the superior knowledge or expertise subordinates perceive their superiors to have; *referent* power is based on how likeable and popular a superior is; *legitimate* power derives its force from the official position, post, or job title that a superior holds; and, finally, *reward and coercive* power derives from one's ability to reward or punish subordinates according to their actions.

The aforementioned categorization of power into four types may cause some confusion, because it would seem to suggest that "power" is inherent in all kinds of relationships where influence and control is exerted. Gini (1997) on the one hand warns against equating leadership with power, and on the other hand describes leadership as a power laden relationship.

To make it clearer, we clarify our understanding of power and how we use it here. In the first place, when considering the source of the legitimacy that a leader has over those led, power can be categorized as expert, referent, legitimate, and reward/punish types. When considered however in terms of the instrument of influence, we lean toward Aristotle's differentiation between *autoritas* (authority) and *potestas* (power). According to the Greek philosopher, the first refers to the moral uprightness of the subject as the instrument of influence, while the second refers properly to the official, legal position, rank, or title as the instrument those people use to lead. Thus we differentiate between authority and power, and if we suggest leadership to be a value laden relationship where the compass is provided by virtues, we will equate authority with leadership and power with management or other kinds of superiority exercise whose force of influence arises, not from the moral standing of the person at the top, but from an appointed official position. Put it another way, authority achieves the goals of the group through moral persuasion (which relies on the free choice of the followers to be persuaded), while the second relies on coercion, force, threat, or reward.

In a true leader–follower relationship, the followers freely allow themselves to be influenced by the leader, because they want to and because they are convinced that she/he deserves the respect. Thus authority is awarded to and earned by the leader through passing a moral test with the followers as arbiters. Followers hold leaders to a moral standard and when they pass it, the former freely surrender their obeisance to the one who has thus earned their trust and confidence. Authority is independent, and indeed can exist without the official position occupied by the leader. Thus an army captain commander of a platoon may have the official position of commanding officer, but may not enjoy the confidence and trust of the soldiers under his command. He would be able to make them obey orders by the use of the power of reward or threats, but not through the force of his character. The real authority (and hence true leadership position) in that platoon may be a peer member that the other soldiers deeply respect. Aristotle's art of persuasion may help to explain the process by which leaders persuade followers.

Leadership as Persuasion

"The supreme quality for leadership is unquestionably integrity. Without it, no real success is possible, no matter whether it is on a section gang, a football field, in an army, or in an office" (Dwight D. Eisenhower, cited in Krylova, Jolly, & Phillips, 2017).

The process of influencing others is not always intentional and deliberate. Some may be leaders without being aware they exert such moral force on others, yet there may be people who emulate them and consider them exemplars and guides. In other cases, however, the intending leader needs to both express the intention as well as provide proof through displays of some character and competency traits. Irrespective of whether the process is intentional or unintentional, the follower needs to be persuaded to freely surrender his or her "allegiance" to a particular leader.

According to Aristotle, persuading or convincing others to adopt a different point of view rests on the tripod of *Ethos*, *Pathos*, and *Logos*, Greek words that respectively refer to the speaker/writer, the listeners/readers, and the content.

Ethos is Greek for character (Bauman, 2018), and in the context of persuasion refers to the integrity (moral uprightness) *and* competence (professional preparation and standing) of the speaker or writer, both of which confer prestige or "authority." According to Bauman ethos is an *in-actu* concept, as its focus is on how one becomes a virtuous person, rather than on being guided by principles or norms. For this reason, Bauman differentiates a so-called "virtue ethic" from "principle ethic." These need not be mutually exclusive. Virtues for a leader can mean both the set of good habits that one practices and a list of guidelines by which one leads others. The guide for the followers would thus be the very life of the leader, which reflects the virtues, as well as virtues which the leader espouses to them as guidelines. A leader who is both trustworthy and learned in her subject area has a strong ethos and is likely to be believable even when she tells the followers to come along a particularly difficult path. They would obey because they trust the leader, not because they have proof in support of the suggested position. Leadership coherence would be when the habits a leader portrays align perfectly with the good habits (virtues) he or she proposes to the followers.

Pathos is Greek for "suffering," which by extension implies "to suffer with," "experience with," "feel with." It is the root for the English words "empathy" and "pathetic." It is an appeal to the emotions or feelings of the audience of the persuasion. Communication as an appeal to the emotions can be verbal or non-verbal, intentional or unintentional and can use conventional or non-conventional means. Examples of emotions could be love, hate, fear, anger, pity, remorse, or shame. As it is, the leader may not need to do anything in order to "cause" the audience to experience any one of these emotions. The strong emotions the audience feel (fear, envy, hope, etc.) can affect how they respond to cues from the leader. The leader may be able to take advantage of the emotions of the followers to convince them that he is a "virtuous" leader (Sy et al., 2018).

Logos is Greek for "word" and, more precisely, a word that expresses some inner thought. Since words are projected outside the person, *logos* refers to the information, data, facts, or logic in support of a point of view. It is what is said or written to back a claim in persuasive communication. That which is said must also make sense and being logical contributes to this sense.

Whatever will make a leader more credible will be the most important of these three. While Ethos refer directly to the integrity and competence of the person who leads, pathos is how the audience reacts emotionally to the person of the leader as well as to what he or she espouses. Therefore all three are simultaneously important and will be deployed in varying proportions depending on the context and the stage of the persuasive encounter.

Leadership Virtues

A leader should be like the people he leads. That is the only way to show that the virtues he proposes are imitable. Possession of the virtues is demonstrated through the activities that flow from the person who has them (Hardie, 1978). All the virtues are important for everyone, but for a leader they are lived with particular nuances as of one who is responsible for more than himself.

Aristotle exalts the virtue of magnanimity in a special way. It means "greatness of soul" or "large hearted," and Aristotle describes it variously as "what is great in every virtue" and a "sort of ornament" of the virtues (Hardie, 1978, pp. 63, 71). A magnanimous person is portrayed as "large" in many senses: in the great way in which he practices all the virtues, and the greatness and worth that such practice brings about. The magnanimous person is detached from everything, primarily from self and from honor, and although is a citizen like all others, is more focused on trying to promote the common good.

It is easy to see how magnanimity is an important virtue for a leader. Such a person, through a heroic struggle to practice all the virtues well becomes a good model of a good life to the followers. Large heartedness also means being open and understanding with everyone in spite of differences and the shortcomings of those being led. This attitude will manifest other related virtues, such as patience, which will be essential to allow the followers to safely be themselves, make mistakes, express their quirks and idiosyncrasies, have time to learn and improve in their life and tasks. A magnanimous person does not apply a "one size fits all" approach to judging and dealing with people, but recognizes each individual as unique, thus "customizing" the approach required by their need.

A magnanimous person is also less conflicted because, thanks to being more concerned about the common good, the cardinal virtues find it easy to play their moderating role in the decision-making of the leader. He or she practices justice as it is easy to see to whom a particular good is due. The magnanimous person is prudent as Aristotle notes that all "ethical virtues are all inseparable from each other and from practical wisdom" (Hardie, 1978, p. 63).

The magnanimous person is temperate and most of all courageous. Experienced soldiers know it is normal to be afraid in war. They force themselves to be courageous in spite of their fear in order to function according to their training. A leader has an obligation to be particularly brave for the sake of those he leads. When asked to summarize what he regarded as the top three leadership skills, Lt. General (retired) James Ronald Helmly, a US OCS Hall of Fame member would indeed list the three skills of critical thinking and communication but quickly add that he considered the virtue of physical and ethical courage as exceptionally important (Ariail, Hiatt, & Quinet, 2013).

Conclusion

This chapter sought to present a relationship model of leadership that has the leader and followers as two important parties with mutual responsibilities for its success. Of the many ethical theories in literature, preference is given to virtue ethics with its focus on acting ethically, that which is directed toward attaining the common good. This approach suggests a stable reference point for moral choices. Like the magnetic compass which retains its orientation to the Earth's geographic north pole and helps navigators keep the course, the virtues are proposed as the reference point for leadership. Virtues are good habits, which Aristotle describes as a range of passions and actions, and which are a mean between extremes. They are the model and currency of transaction for the leadership relationship. The cardinal virtues of justice, prudence, temperance, and fortitude are introduced as those responsible for establishing the required mean. The chapter also makes a strong case for freedom, since merit can only be imputed to an actor when the will freely decides a course for itself. This approach is in agreement with the dignity of the human person who is a rational being with freedom and will. Furthermore, it is when virtue is freely chosen that one has a motivation to keep doing what is good, thus making the practice thereof subsequently easier. Finally, although all the virtues are important to leaders and followers, magnanimity (largeness of heart) is highlighted as particularly essential to the leader.

References

Aquinas, T. (1485). *Summa Theologiae*.

Ariail, D. L., Hiatt, M. S., & Quinet, G. (2013). Leadership lessons from an OCS infantry hall of fame member: A conversation with Lt. General (retired) James Ronald Helmly. *Journal of Applied Management and Entrepreneurship, 18*(4), 94.

Bauman, D. C. (2018). Plato on virtuous leadership: An ancient model for modern business. *Business Ethics Quarterly*, 1–24.

Bligh, M. C., & Robinson, J. L. (2010). Was Gandhi "charismatic"? Exploring the rhetorical leadership of Mahatma Gandhi. *Leadership Quarterly, 21*(5), 844–855.

Bond, S. (2005). The global challenge of sustainable consumption. *Consumer Policy Review, 15*(2), 38–44.

Braun, S., & Nieberle, K. W. A. M. (2017). Authentic leadership extends beyond work: A multilevel model of work-family conflict and enrichment. *Leadership Quarterly, 28*(6), 780–797.

Braun, E., Sloan, S., Aldor, F., & Trenker, L. (2014). *The Private Life of Adolf Hitler: The Intimate Notes and Diary of Eva Braun* (Ed. P. Tabori). New York and Tokyo: Ishi Press.

Bray, J., Johns, N., & Kilburn, D. (2011). An exploratory study into the factors impeding ethical consumption. *Journal of Business Ethics, 98*(4), 597–608.

Brown, M. E., Trevino, L. K., & Harrison, D. A. (2005). Ethical leadership: A social learning perspective for construct development and testing. *Organizational Behavior and Human Decision Processes, 97*(2), 117–134.

Cameron, K. (2011). Responsible leadership as virtuous leadership. In B. N. Pless & T. Maak (Eds.), *Responsible Leadership*. Dordrecht, Germany: Springer, 25–35.

Chonko, L. B., Wotruba, T. R., & Loe, T. W. (2003). Ethics code familiarity and usefulness: Views on idealist and relativist managers under varying conditions of turbulence. *Journal of Business Ethics, 42*(3), 237–252.

Ciulla, J. B. (1995). Leadership ethics: Mapping the territory. *Business Ethics Quarterly, 5*(1), 5–28.

Clark, M. (1978, January). The meritorious and the mandatory. *Proceedings of the Aristotelian Society, 79*(1), 23–33.

Cooper, C. D., Scandura, T. A., & Schriesheim, C. A. (2005). Looking forward but learning from our past: Potential challenges to developing authentic leadership theory and authentic leaders. *Leadership Quarterly, 16*(3), 475–493.

English Oxford Living Dictionaries. (2018). influence | Definition of influence in English by Oxford Dictionaries. Retrieved from https://en.oxforddictionaries.com/definition/influence.

Fitzpatrick, S. (2000). *Everyday Stalinism: Ordinary Life in Extraordinary Times: Soviet Russia in the 1930s* (New ed.). Oxford, UK: Oxford University Press.

Gini, A. (1997). Moral leadership: An overview. *Journal of Business Ethics, 16*(3), 323–330.

Govind, R., Singh, J. J., Garg, N., & D'Silva, S. (2017). Not walking the walk: How dual attitudes influence behavioral outcomes in ethical consumption. *Journal of Business Ethics*, 1–20.

Graham, J. W. (1991). Servant-leadership in organizations: Inspirational and moral. *Leadership Quarterly, 2*(2), 105–119.

Grant, A. M., & Schwartz, B. (2011). Too much of a good thing: The challenge and opportunity of the inverted U. *Perspectives on Psychological Science, 6*(1), 61–76.

Hardie, W. F. R. (1978). "Magnanimity" in Aristotle's "Ethics." *Phronesis, 23*(1), 63–79.

Harris, H. (2001). Content analysis of secondary data: A study of courage in managerial decision making. *Journal of Business Ethics, 34*(3–4), 191–208.

Hollander, E. P. (1995). Ethical challenges in the leader–follower relationship. *Business Ethics Quarterly, 5*(1), 55–65.

Jacobs, G. A., & Longbotham, G. J. (2011). The impact of spirituality on the formation of a leader's purpose. *Journal of Management, Spirituality and Religion, 8*(1), 69–91.

Kort, E. D. (2008). What, after all, is leadership? "Leadership" and plural action. *Leadership Quarterly, 19*(4), 409–425.

Krylova, K. O., Jolly, P. M., & Phillips, J. S. (2017). Followers' moral judgments and leaders' integrity-based transgressions: A synthesis of literatures. *Leadership Quarterly, 28*(1), 195–209.

Lopez-Rodriguez, S. (2017). Ethics and morality in consumption: Interdisciplinary perspectives. Edited by Deidre Shaw, Andreas Chatzidakis, & Michal Carrington. *Business Ethics Quarterly, 27*(4), 637–640.

Morales-Sánchez, R., & Cabello-Medina, C. (2013). The role of four universal moral competencies in ethical decision-making. *Journal of Business Ethics, 116*(4), 717–734.

Oc, B., & Bashshur, M. R. (2013). Followership, leadership and social influence. *Leadership Quarterly, 24*(6), 919–934.

Padilla, A., Hogan, R., & Kaiser, R. B. (2007). The toxic triangle: Destructive leaders, susceptible followers, and conducive environments. *Leadership Quarterly, 18*(3), 176–194.

Parekh, B. (2001). *Gandhi: A Very Short Introduction* (1st ed.). Oxford, UK and New York: Oxford University Press.

Pless, N. M. (2007). Understanding responsible leadership: Role identity and motivational drivers. *Journal of Business Ethics, 74*(4), 437–456.

Potts, J. (2009). *A History of Charisma*. Houndmills, UK and New York: Palgrave Macmillan.

Rego, A., e Cunha, M. P., & Clegg, S. R. (2012). *The Virtues of Leadership: Contemporary Challenges for Global Managers* (1st ed.). Oxford, UK: Oxford University Press.

Rego, A., Vitória, A., Magalhães, A., Ribeiro, N., & e Cunha, M. P. (2013). Are authentic leaders associated with more virtuous, committed and potent teams? *Leadership Quarterly, 24*(1), 61–79.
Rosenbloom, A., & Althaus, R. (2010). Degussa AG and its holocaust legacy. *Journal of Business Ethics, 92*(2), 183–194.
Rost, J. C. (1993). *Leadership for the Twenty-First Century*. Westport, CT: Greenwood Publishing Group.
Shamir, B., Dayan-Horesh, H., & Adler, D. (2005). Leading by biography: Towards a life-story approach to the study of leadership. *Leadership, 1*(1), 13–29.
Sheppard, T. H. (1970). Desert navigation. *Geographical Journal, 136*(2), 235–239.
Sheth, J. N., Sethia, N. K., & Srinivas, S. (2011). Mindful consumption: A customer-centric approach to sustainability. *Journal of the Academy of Marketing Science, 39*(1), 21–39.
Song, S. Y., & Kim, Y. K. (2016). Theory of virtue ethics: Do consumers' good traits predict socially responsible consumption? *Journal of Business Ethics, 152*(4), 1159–1175.
Sy, T., Horton, C., & Riggio, R. (2018). Charismatic leadership: Eliciting and channeling follower emotions. *Leadership Quarterly,* 29(1), 58–69.
Thompson, L. J. (2010). The global moral compass for business leaders. *Journal of Business Ethics, 93*(1), 15–32.
Walsh, J. P., Weber, K., & Margolis, J. D. (2003). Social issues and management: Our lost cause found. *Journal of Management, 29*, 859–881.
Williamson, T. (2008). The good society and the good soul: Plato's republic on leadership. *Leadership Quarterly, 19*(4), 397–408.
Zaleznik, A. (1990). The leadership gap. *Academy of Management Perspectives, 4*(1), 7–22.
Zhu, W., Treviño, L. K., & Zheng, X. (2016). Ethical leaders and their followers: The transmission of moral identity and moral attentiveness. *Business Ethics Quarterly, 26*(1), 95–115.

18

MANA AND THE EXISTENCE OF LEADERSHIP

Chellie Spiller, Matthew Mudford, and Rachel Wolfgramm

Mana and the Existence of Leadership

> The same stream of life that runs through my veins night and day runs through the world and dances in rhythmic measures. It is the same life that shoots in joy through the dust of the earth in numberless blades of grass and breaks into tumultuous waves of leaves and flowers. It is the same life that is rocked in the ocean-cradle of birth and of death, in ebb and in flow. I feel my limbs are made glorious by the touch of this world of life. And my pride is from the life-throb of ages dancing in my blood this moment.
>
> *(Tagore, 2002)*

Tagore's poem illuminates a wisdom of the ages, an eternal now-ness, where we are a movement through time, and inseparable from the world around us; a refraction of existence where the universe expresses itself through us. Cajete's (2015, p. 259) description of Indigenous spirituality resonates with Tagore's as Cajete explains that

> spirituality comes from the process of exploring and coming to know the nature of the living energy that moves in each of us, through us, and around us. Coming to know this knowledge is considered completeness in its most profound form.

Māori recognize many forms of *mana* in the world, which flow through us; we are born with divinely endowed *mana* that comes, for example, from our kinship relationships, our ancestral lines, and our sacred lands and bodies of water (Porter, 2009). Tagore's rendering of pride as a "life throb of ages dancing in my blood this moment" captures the essence of what we are exploring in this chapter: *mana*. Pride as dignity, as *mana* drawn from the wellspring of our ancestors, sacred places, and communities, as our spiritual agency to take up respectful, right, and loving action. Contemporary explanations of *mana* reverberate with ancient meaning. *Mana* flows to us and from us. The following words from Māori leader, Tame Iti, point to this sense of connection: "Mana, everyone has it. It's about knowing who you are, where you come from, and connects you to your land. Mana grounds you. In the past, present and future" (Iti, 2015).

In early Hawaiian and Tahitian cultures *mana* referred to a spiritual energy and healing power that was possessed by people, places, and objects. Early anthropological accounts of Samoan culture defined *mana* as supernatural power (Pratt, 1862). Various anthropological accounts of religion and spirituality throughout the Pacific in the 1800s, including Melanesia and Polynesia, struggled to accurately define *mana* and explain the nuances between each group of peoples (Tomlinson & Kāwika Tenga, 2016). Some anthropologists also drew parallels between *mana* and a range of elementary principles contained within cultures of the diaspora of Indigenous peoples across the continent of Australia. In a Māori worldview, according to Marsden (2003), *mana* is spiritual authority and power derived from the gods and accompanied by the endowment of spiritual power to act in accordance with divine will. *Mana* can also refer to the enduring, indestructible power of the gods that is a sacred fire without beginning or end. Tāne (the first human) ascended by the sacred vine in order that he might retrieve *mana*, or the sacred power of the gods, which was known to ancestors as the *ahi komau* (Barlow, 1991). *Mana* has several sources, including that which rests on the prestige of ancestors and is ascribed by birth (*mana tūpuna*) and came to the ancestors from pre-human deities, from whom authority and power flowed (*mana atua*). *Mana atua* is acknowledged as sacred power that comes from spiritual forces. Humankind as part of a larger creative order can be agent, channel, and conduit, but not the *source* of *mana*. *Mana* has a part to play in almost every ceremony, ritual, and daily activity and is central for the group and the individual to maintain their integrity (Marsden, 2003, p. 288).

Mana tūpuna is a source of power and authority that comes from ancestors. It is held in our collective consciousness and valued as a source of ancestral efficacy (Henare, 2003; Marsden, 2003; Metge, 1976). *Mana tūpuna* is expressed through *whakapapa* (genealogical recital) and is considered one of the most prized forms of knowledge and an essential medium by which kinship, political, economic, and social ties are cemented and maintained. Therefore significant effort is associated with the retention and transmission of *whakapapa*, as evidenced in rituals such as *pōwhiri*, ritual greeting and welcome (Barlow, 1991; Metge, 1976; Royal, 2002; Salmond, 1991, 1998). Salmond noted in a Waitangi Tribunal Hearing (1998, p. 23, cited in Henare, 2003) that in 1840 in Northland, Māori were operating in a world governed by *whakapapa*. Ancestors intervened in everyday affairs, *mana* was understood as proceeding from the ancestor gods, and *tapu* (sanctity) was the sign of the gods' presence in the human world. Life was kept in balance by the principle of *utu* (reciprocal exchange), which operated in relationships between individuals, groups, and ancestors.

Connections to the natural world and the deities that comprised the polytheistic spiritual realm of Oceanic cultures were key in the expression of *mana* that tied into every aspect of daily life and brought about a close relationship with the natural world (Codrington & Murray, 1892). In the Māori world, *mana whenua* is a source of power associated with land and the environment. Metge (1995) and Tate (in Wolfgramm, 2007) note how, for Māori, *whenua* has more than one meaning: land in the sense of earth, as distinct from but associated with water; land in contrast to sea, in which case it includes the waters of the land (streams, rivers, lakes, springs, and the water table); and land meaning country or territory as a whole, comprising earth and oceans. This binding of humanity to the natural world is also shown in the word for a human placenta and for land being the same in Māori: *whenua*. In addition, *mana wahine* (*mana* of women) is often linked to *Papatūānuku* (earth mother) and is associated with the generative and nurturing forces demonstrated in a variety of areas related to women's leadership (Henry, 2015).

Whakapapa—*Divine Genealogical Order*

Every aspect of creation has a *whakapapa*, a divine genealogical order that takes us back through layers to a shared point of coalescence that is Io, creator of the cosmos (Marsden, 2003). In this world of relatedness, manifestations of life are unified through a common source in Io and are bound by life energies. Also, importantly, this is not a static account but rather a living unfolding, a process of transformation, as illuminated by Māori Marsden who says that to understand a rock one must look to the "crystal into which it is becoming" (2003, p. 45). In his view there is deep appreciation that all things are in a process of "becoming."

When introducing themselves Māori will stand to share their genealogical connections, which trace relationships to land, waterways, and sacred places, to peoples and ancestors, to origins. These relationships evoke the manifold *mana* that flows to and from that person. In expressing *whakapapa*, a person is expressing oneness with the land and people. In this state of oneness, humans "become one with the *atua*, the spiritual powers" (Shirres, 1997, p. 57; see also Durie, 2003, p. 84). *Whakapapa* is not just a rote recital; it is a narration of belongingness, beingness, of respect and inseparable recognition of who we are. Through the evoking of *whakapapa* there is a deep appreciation and understanding that self-actualization involves spiritual unification with all creation (Shirres, 1997). Cycling back to Tagore's poem that opened this chapter, the "life-throb of ages dancing in my blood this moment" is how *whakapapa* can feel, as we recognize we are part of a movement through time.

Te Rito (2007) observes that *whakapapa* represents an ongoing, continuing narrative stretching back hundreds of years, and notes the critical role this chronicled process plays in grounding individuals firmly in place and time, past and present, and in confirming one's identity and overall sense of being. The notion of *whakapapa* is of integral importance to a Māori worldview upon which an identity narrative is constructed; an ordering of the universe which recognizes spiritual kinship with all creation. Wolfgramm (2007, p. 80) says: "Māori continue to see themselves as agents in an evolving cosmological community, and use *whakapapa* [genealogies] to actively interpret relationships in order to bring the sacred to the centre of being."

Many Indigenous spiritualities are based on an appreciation that humans share kinship with all of life (Spiller & Wolfgramm, 2015) wherein "relatedness is a physical and metaphysical connection to everything temporal, spatial and material" (Deloria, Deloria, Foehner, & Scinta, 1999, in Gladstone, 2015, p. 23). Māori aspire to unify the spiritual and material worlds whereby the "cultural milieu is rooted both in the temporal and the transcendent world, this brings a person into intimate relationship with the gods and his universe" (Marsden, 2003, p. 23). In Royal (2011, p. 7) Marsden states:

> We dwell within "the woven universe", within the web of existence and no part of the whole is comprehensively autonomous. The purpose of life is to live within this intricate web of relationships and to become a conduit for the energies of life, to enable these energies to rise and fall within us.

Flourishing in Organizations

Royal (2006, p. 4) describes *mana* as a "special and non-ordinary presence or essence that can flow in the world." He makes the point that *mana* lies at the heart of people's health and well-being and involves feeling empowered, illuminated, and warm about ourselves and our life. He also notes the importance of restoring *mana* for those who have lost it and argues that community involvement, connection to *iwi* tribal background, and connection with their personal history, identity, and background could be important pathways for the restoration of *mana*. The key tenet of this pursuit is essentially the empowerment of others. In organizations, people, especially those in leadership and management roles, are encouraged to reciprocally uplift the collective (Spiller & Stockdale, 2013).

Mana enables flourishing, a spiritual encounter with a complex of interwoven energies that bind humans together, in kinship with all of creation, and is itself a creative force (Henry, 2015; Spiller, Erakovic, Henare, & Pio (2011). Flourishing unfolds through the co-creative narratives of people in an organization in which people produce and aspire to make sense of the organization's highest ideals and possibilities (Cooperrider, Whitney, & Stavros, 2008; Fredrickson & Dutton, 2008). When organizations are flourishing they have healthy relationships across many dimensions, including with ecologies, the *atua* (divine, gods), and the ancestors as well as human groupings—which, in organizational vernacular, includes employees, suppliers, and communities. Spiller and Stockdale (2013, p. 149) argue that "attending to the life-energy of an organization is an important, yet often overlooked aspect of management and leadership" and to ignore life energies leads to workplaces that do not flourish.

Spiritual life energies include (but are not limited to): *mauri* (life-force); *mana* (inherited and endowed authority); *wairua* (spirituality); and *hau* (reciprocity). *Mauri* is an immanent energy that weaves, binds, and unifies all things. It is a life-force that brings unity to the diversity in creation (Marsden, 2003). Even aspects of life such as our intentions, plans, relationships, words, and creations have a *mauri* (Kereopa, in Moon, 2003) and, thus, in the context of organizations, people are encouraged to support and strengthen *mauri*, as explained by Spiller and Stockdale (2013, p. 163):

> Strong interconnected life-forces create and facilitate the conditions for thriving and realisation of individual and collective potential. The emergent whole is more than the sum of the parts—it is the coalescence of each person's *mauri*, along with other aspects such as processes, protocols, behaviors, attitudes, and intentions within an organisation, that give it an overall *mauri*...
>
> *Mauri* can become contaminated. The vitality of an organisation can be greatly diminished, and can even become toxic, if the *mauri* of the organisation is allowed to become unhealthy.

Mana is transformed by *manaakitanga*, that is, through acts of generosity that enhance the wellbeing of all (Durie, 2001). Marsden (2003) claims that Māori social interactions require structures that enhance *mana Māori*, as *mana* involves the wholeness of social relationships, wellbeing, integrity, and continuity through time and space. In this sense, *mana* is derived from the support of one's people, requiring their active cooperation (*mana tangata*). Hence *mana tangata* acts to enhance the promotion of the common good and unity within plurality. The dynamic relationship between leaders and followers in Māori society involves an exchange of *mana* (Barlow, 1991; Durie, 1998; Henare, 2003; Henry & Pene, 2001; Marsden, 1975). Thus *mana* is associated with leadership and signifies social status, influence, and respect (Barlow, 1991; Durie, 1998; Henare, 2003; Marsden, 2003; Moko-Mead, 2003).

Spiller and Stockdale (2013, pp. 162–163) offer a contemporary model with seven key considerations for the expression of *mana* by managers as part of the wellbeing of an organization:

- Recognize that managers and leaders stand in the power of the authority of the ancestral, tribal and family connections of the people who work for the organisation.

- In conflict situations consider the innate authority of the person, whilst honouring one's own, and search for win-win outcomes.
- Accept and respect that all people have their own innate authority—create the conditions so this can flourish in others, in a spirit of generosity.
- Encourage the release of a person's potential through training, supervision and personal growth.
- Always seek to enhance the collective.
- Be in integrity, about making and keeping promises.
- Seek the guidance and wisdom of a mentor or elder in the tribal/local community.

A *mana*-based approach suggests that *mana* is gained by growing it in others and thus represents a reciprocal relationship. Leaders who acknowledge a *mana*-based approach seek to build mutual relationships of respect and reciprocity (Roche, Haar, & Brougham, 2015; Spiller, 2010). Acts of kindness, humility, and respect offer opportunities for individuals to obtain *mana* through a style of leadership that is more distributed and shared than it is hierarchical.

Narrating Existence and Identity

Heil and Whittaker (2007) argue that narratives "are a powerful means to shaping peoples [*sic*] thinking and actions" (p. 369) and "have the capacity to alter the world we find ourselves in, in the most fundamental ways" (p. 382). Hammack (2008) and McAdams (2001) have described how the narratives can transform the ideals individuals live by and adhere to, which in turn transforms and sustains the culture itself. Stories serve as a particular form of narrative that have powerful sense-making potential yet are too often ignored in the deluge of organizational rationalistic, logical, and efficient noise that claims attention in organizations (Gabriel, 2004, p. 63). Yet, stories provide ample fertile ground for the reaffirmation and adaptation of one's identity within the cultural and organizational milieu.

Rukeyeser (cited in McLean, Pasupathi, & Pals, 2007) holds up identity stories as crucial to a sense of self—stories support the individual to build an identity narrative over time, situating their unique experiences and personhood in an equivalently transformative cultural milieu. In this process, sustained through repeated interactions with others, the identity narrative is "processed, edited, reinterpreted, retold, and subjected to a range of social and discursive influences" (McAdams & McLean, 2013, p. 235) as the individual narrator gradually begins to broaden and integrate the various complementary threads of their personal narrative.

Many Māori narratives reflect a cultural attribution to, and emotional relationship with, not just people but a sacred place, *atua* (gods), and ancestors. The wider environment self-concept and a sense of communal belonging are fused. Every action is an imprint on our world; it creates our reality. Cajete (2015, p. 261) notes that "language used in a spiritual, evocative, or affective context is 'sacred' and has to be used responsibly." This is consistent with the notion of *mana reo*, for Māori, *te reo*, the language, is the food of leadership "*te reo i te kai o te rangatira.*"

According to Rappaport (1995, p. 803), a community narrative is not only something a group of people have in common, shared narratives may be what creates a community. Narratives may represent historical or mythological accounts (or an amalgamation) through which members of the community come to understand themselves and the community. Community narratives create distinctness in a community, which shows its members as uniquely identifiable from the wider society in which they are embedded. Further, narratives create a rallying point for communities: a focus for belief, aspiration, and meaning, as well as a means for promoting

Table 18.1 Exploring Some Core Dimensions of Mana

Mana in Worldviews	*Mana Dimensions*	*Mana in Leadership*
Mana o te wa—I nga wa o mua Multidimensional view of time and space—plurality	Honoring the *mana* and *tapu* of the past, present, and future	Leaders commit to 500-plus years in strategic planning Long-term intergenerational succession planning in leadership and governance Panoramic view of trends in the wider environment and a well-considered understanding of followership
Mana atua The spiritual sources of *mana* linked to a pantheon of spiritual beings	Honoring the intelligence of nature through according it divine status, for example, in divine beings such as *Tangaroa* (guardian of oceans), *Papatūānuku* (earth mother)	Rituals and ceremonies including *karanga*, *pōwhiri* highlight an enduring relationship with a cosmological community Highly evident in *tangi* (funerals of leaders) and in succession rituals
Mana whenua Terrestrial relationships to lands, seas, oceans, rivers, springs, and so forth	We are of the land, with the land, and for the land—connecting and respecting the lands and environs	Identities are affirmed and lived through these relationships—in leadership, the focus is on growth and guardianship *Papatūānuku* (earth mother) gives generously—therefore how do we as leaders in our strategic focus emulate this generosity in our decisions
Mana Rangi *Ranginui* (sky father) holds the *mana* of the heavens—see proverb at the conclusion	The ancestral partner of *Papatūānuku*; *mana* derives from heavenly sources held in care by *Ranginui*	Utilizing technologies—alternatives to land-based economies
Mana motuhake Self/collective determination	Māori aspiration for greater control over their own destinies and resources Ongoing search for sovereignty, autonomy, independence, self-governance, self-determination, *tino rangatiratanga*, and *mana motuhake* (Durie, 1998, p. 218)	Māori economic self-sufficiency, social equity, cultural affirmation, and political strength (Durie, 1998) *Ka whawhai tonu mātou*: struggle without end and the long tail of colonization (Walker, 1990/2004)

continued

Table 18.1 Continued

Mana in Worldviews	*Mana Dimensions*	*Mana in Leadership*
Mana reo The language and the voice must empower lives in positive transformation	Expressing self/identity and collective through voice and language	Empowering to be able to fully express oneself in one's own language; important identity milestone now for many
Mana tūpuna Living faces of those who came before us and those who will come after us	We are our ancestors and our ancestors are us	Moving beyond anthropocentric worldview to connectivity to lands, rivers, mountains, oceans: these are our ancestors
Mana wai Water is spiritual source of *mana* and *wai* is the essence of *wairuatanga*, spirituality	*Te wai e whakaora ia tātou*: water heals and sustains us *Te wai i te ora*: water is life	Leadership with regard to our relationship with water Particular focus on what we are basing our decisions on with regard to water, *wai*, which has symbolic, spiritual, and physical meaning
Whakapapa (expressing mana through connecting) Genealogical recital explicitly making connections to lands, seas, ancestors, mountains	Layering of relationships across time and space	Practiced prolifically in Māori leadership As ritual heuristic practice, it is used to articulate relationships of self with others in terrestrial, ancestral, spiritual, and social spheres (tribes) In practice, layering of relationships (*whakapapa*) is a transformative process that shifts the focus of embodied leadership to enacted decision making (Henry & Wolfgramm, 2015) Highly evident in symbolism and ritual
Tūrangawaewae (a place to stand)	Belonging	Affirmations of identity to place; for example the significance of a *marae* complex, the sense of belonging in an *iwi*, *hapū*, and *whānau* context and beyond
Hau	Relational reciprocity	Expressing *manaakitanga*, generosity, remembering such things from the past; consideration of this into the future as legacies
Tiakitanga	Role as guardians	Long-term strategic planning and decision -making that aligns both growth and guardianship

Source: Whai Rawa research project, see Acknowledgements at end.

civic engagement and discourse in the community. Humphreys (2000) observes that community narratives affirm traditions and promote a sense of wonder and awe as regards the positive and generative qualities of the community.

Fishbane (2001) observes that people are in a constant, fluctuating state of connection and disconnection, oscillating between the intimacy of relationships and the disembodied nature of isolation, with the former facilitating healthy personal development and the latter creating personal distress, inauthenticity, and depression. Lefebvre (1991) states that socio-relational narratives embolden and fortify the opportunity one has for connection and subsequent self-development, specifically by way of providing the communicative means by which one can make sense of one's experience of relational complexity and belonging. In addition, Somers (1994) notes that relational narratives allow for a fruitful transformation of the prevailing self/other dichotomy into social patterns, practices, and institutions that exist, not as mere abstractions, but as the mechanisms by which personal agency can be realized in the context of the highly social sphere that humans inhabit. Conceptualizations of self are, by these lights, predicated on an intricate interweaving of narratives concerning historical and social knowledge, and of institutional and cultural practices. Somers (1994) argues that relational narratives provide a means by which the coupling of social identity and personal agency can be better realized. Echoing these sentiments, Tamboukou (2010) and Rockquemore and Laszloffy (2003) concur that relational narratives are a means through which individual personhood is conceived and identity developed in mutually constitutive relationships with others.

Mana *in Leadership*

As the essence of *mana* is actualized in relationships, *mana* underpins an integrative Māori leadership ontology (Henry & Wolfgramm, 2015). *Mana* in leadership is steeped in a "cosmological community of archetypal leaders" and, albeit there are tribal variations, this community includes Io (a multifaceted numinous Being), *Papatuānuku* (earth mother), and *Ranginui* (sky father). In the lived wisdom traditions of Indigenous peoples (Cajete, 2000; Spiller et al., 2011) perspectives of relational wellbeing inquire into how *mana* is expressed in contemporary leadership practice, highlighting an ethic of care approach based on reciprocity and respect, along with a multidimensional, integrative view of purpose that includes spiritual wellbeing (Spiller et al., 2011; Spiller & Wolfgramm, 2015).

Table 18.1 summarizes core dimensions of *mana* as developed throughout this chapter and shows how *mana* can be expressed and enacted in leadership.

Conclusion

We can learn much about the role *mana* plays in leadership, but it is merely part of a greater wisdom that views the world, not as a collection of disparate coincidences, but as connected by interlacing principles such as respect, reciprocity, care, family, and guardianship. *Mana* today is thus very important in a world of escalating environmental degradation and growing economic disparities. The role *mana* can play is a part of a greater wisdom about how the world is interconnected through people and nature.

In Te Ao Māori, a Māori worldview, there are a number of energies that were not explored in this chapter, such as *tapu* (sacredness, restriction) and *noa* (ordinariness, unrestricted) which are deeply connected to *mana*. It is important to set appropriate boundaries on knowledge, and we acknowledge that *mana* is not a stand-alone energy. However, given the constraints of space, and awareness of the context, we have set a boundary around our work taking up Spiller, Kerr, and Panoho's (2015, p. 151) explanation:

> In a Māori world, knowledge is living and full of energy. Words are not lifeless and static, but have power. For example, the use of karakia [prayer/invocation] to invoke intention is not a recital of words but a powerful calling for spiritual guidance and manifestation of reality. Not all knowledge is for immediate consumption. Some of it must be guarded, and as such, it is kept tapu—set apart and restricted. This is not so that cultural elites can use it to wield power over others: rather, it has a very practical purpose. In wayfinding, there is knowledge that needs to be guarded until such time as a person is ready. It is about safety, as some knowledge can have powerful, even harmful consequences.

The task of leaders and managers is to recognize the various elements of a situation, to pay attention to the unfolding dynamics, cultivate reciprocal relationships of respect, and ultimately to perceive flourishing as a complex of spiritual energies, a revealed state, and a process of being. Recognition narratives are reflections of a cosmological order that calls humans to self-actualize in relationship with each other and in kinship with all of creation. These narratives are deeply scripted imprints in dialectical individual and collective worldviews, formed within an understanding of an "eternal present" which, as it relates to the Māori worldview, acknowledges the ancestors, the *atua* (gods), and a divine genealogical order that reminds humans they are *kaitiaki*, custodians, and guardians of the planet, with responsibilities to ensure flourishing.

> Mai i te rangi, ki te nuku o te whenua,
> ka puta te ira tangata i te pō, i te whaiao, i te ao mārama.
>
> From the sky and the land came people,
> from the night, to the old world, to the world of light.

Acknowledgments

This chapter is part of a series of articles, chapters, and papers examining effective Māori leadership and integrated decision-making, and how these processes deliver pluralistic outcomes that advance transformative and prosperous Māori economies of wellbeing. Professor Spiller and Dr. Wolfgramm are principal investigators within Ngā Pae o te Māramatanga's Whai Rawa Māori economy group.

References

Barlow, C. (1991). *Tikanga Whakaaro: Key Concepts in Māori Culture*. Auckland, New Zealand: Oxford University Press.

Cajete, G. (2000). *Native Science: Natural Laws of Interdependence* (1st ed.). Santa Fe, NM: Clear Light.

Cajete, C. (2015). That place that Indians talk about. In C. Spiller & R. Wolfgramm (Eds.), *Indigenous Spiritualties at Work: Transforming the Spirit of Business Enterprise*. Charlotte, NC: Information Age, 259–272.

Codrington, R. H., & Murray, C. (1892). The Melanesians: Studies in their anthropology and folk-lore. *Journal of the Polynesian Society, 1*(3), 137–142.

Cooperrider, D. L., Whitney, D. K., & Stavros, J. M. (2008). *Appreciative Inquiry Handbook: For Leaders of Change*. San Francisco: Crown Custom.

Durie, M. (1998). *Te Mana, Te Kawanatanga: The Politics of Māori Self-determination*. Auckland, New Zealand: Oxford University Press.
Durie, M. (2001). *Mauri Ora: The Dynamics of Maori Health*. London: Oxford University Press.
Durie, M. (2003). *Ngā Kāhui Pou: Launching Māori Futures*. Wellington, New Zealand: Huia.
Fishbane, M. D. (2001). Relational narratives of the self. *Family Process, 40*(3), 273–291.
Fredrickson, B. L., & Dutton, J. E. (2008). Unpacking positive organizing: Organizations as sites of individual and group flourishing. *Journal of Positive Psychology, 3*(1), 1–3.
Gabriel, Y. (2004). Narratives, stories and texts. In D. Grant, C. Hardy, C. Oswick, & L. Putnam (Eds.), *The SAGE Handbook of Organizational Discourse*. London: Sage, 61–77.
Gladstone, J. (2015). Native American transplanar wisdom. In C. Spiller & R. Wolfgramm (Eds.), *Indigenous Spiritualties at Work: Transforming the Spirit of Business Enterprise*. Charlotte, NC: Information Age, 21–32.
Hammack, P. L. (2008). Narrative and the cultural psychology of identity. *Personality and Social Psychology Review, 38*(7), 867–883.
Heil, D., & Whittaker, L. (2007). An ontological foundation for strategic management research: The role of narrative. *Research Methodology in Strategy and Management, 4*, 369–397.
Henare, M. A. (2003). *The changing images of nineteenth century Māori society, from tribes to nations*. (Unpublished doctoral dissertation), Victoria University of Wellington, Wellington, New Zealand.
Henry, E. (2015). Te whare ako: Architecture speaks to heart, mind, and spirit. In C. Spiller & R. Wolfgramm (Eds.), *Indigenous Spiritualties at Work: Transforming the Spirit of Business Enterprise*. Charlotte, NC: Information Age, 51–67.
Henry, E. & Pene, H. (2001). Kaupapa Māori: Locating Indigenous ontology, epistemology and methodology in the academy. *Organization, 8*(2), 234–242.
Henry, E., & Wolfgramm, R. (2015). Relational leadership: An indigenous Māori perspective. *Leadership, 0*(0), 1–17.
Humphreys, K. (2000). Community narratives and personal stories in Alcoholics Anonymous. *Journal of Community Psychology, 28*(5), 495–506.
Iti, T. (2015, June 17). Mana: The power in knowing who you are | Tame Iti | TEDx Auckland. Retrieved from www.youtube.com/watch?v=qeK3SkxrZRI.
Lefebvre, H. (1991). *The Production of Space*. Oxford: Blackwell.
McAdams, D. P. (2001). The psychology of life stories. *Review of General Psychology, 5*, 100–122.
McAdams, D. P., & McLean, K. C. (2013). Narrative identity. *Current Directions in Psychological Science, 22*(3), 233–238.
McLean, K. C., Pasupathi, M., & Pals, J. L. (2007). Selves creating stories creating selves: A process model of self-development. *Personality and Social Psychology Review, 11*(3), 262–278.
Marsden, M. (1975). Man, God and universe: A Māori view. In M. King (Ed.), *Te Ao Hurihuri, Aspects of Māoritanga*. Wellington, New Zealand: Hicks Smith, 191–220.
Marsden, M. (2003). *The Woven Universe: Selected Writings of Rev. Māori Marsden*. Otaki, New Zealand: Estate of Rev. Māori Marsden.
Metge, J. (1976). *The Māoris of New Zealand: Rautahi*. London: Routledge & Keegan Paul.
Metge, J. (1995). *New Growth from Old: The Whanau in the Modern World*. Wellington, New Zealand: Victoria University Press.
Moko-Mead, H. (2003). *Tikanga Māori: Living by Māori Values*. Wellington, New Zealand: Huia Publishers.
Moon, P. (2003). *Tohunga: Hohepa Kereopa*. Auckland, New Zealand: David Ling.
Porter, P. (2009). *Four Themes of Māori Leadership, Te whakaarotanga o ngā whakatōranga o ngā mātua, ngā tūpuna: Capturing the Thoughts of the Elders*. Auckland, New Zealand: Te Ringa Whero, Mira Szászy Research Centre, University of Auckland.
Pratt, G. (1862). *A Samoan Dictionary: English and Samoan, and Samoan and English; With a Short Grammar of the Samoan Dialect*. Malua, Samoa: London Missionary Society Press.
Rappaport, J. (1995). Empowerment meets narrative: Listening to stories and creating settings. *American Journal of Community Psychology, 23*(5), 795–807.
Roche, M. A., Haar, J. M., & Brougham, D. (2015). Māori leaders' well-being: A self-determination perspective. *Leadership, 0*(0), 1–15.
Rockquemore, K. A., & Laszloffy, T. A. (2003). Multiple realities: A relational narrative approach in therapy with black-white mixed-race clients. *Family Relations, 52*(2), 119–128.
Royal, T. A. C. (2002). *Indigenous Worldviews: A Comparative Study*. Wellington, New Zealand: Te Wananga-o-Raukawa, Te Puni Kokiri for Māori Development.

Royal, T. A. C. (2006). A modern view of mana. Paper presented at the Joint Conference of the Australian Psychological Society and the New Zealand Psychological Society, SkyCity Auckland Convention Centre, September 26–30.

Royal, T. A. C. (2011). New expressions of indigeneity through *whare tapere*. Paper presented at the Building Reconciliation and Social Cohesion through Indigenous Festival Performance, Centre for International Theatre and Performance Research, Department of Theatre and Drama, Royal Holloway, University of London, Paris, France, November 17–18.

Salmond, A. (1991). *Two Worlds, First Meetings between Māori and Europeans 1642–1772*. Auckland, New Zealand: Viking Press.

Salmond, A. (1998). *Between Worlds: Early Exchanges Between Māori and Europeans 1773–1815*. Auckland, New Zealand: Viking Press.

Shirres, M. P. (1997). *Te tangata: The Human Person*. Auckland, New Zealand: Accent Publications.

Somers, M. R. (1994). The narrative constitution of identity: A relational and network approach. *Theory and Society, 23*(5), 605–649.

Spiller, C. (2010). *How Māori cultural tourism businesses create authentic and sustainable well-being*. (Unpublished PhD Thesis). University of Auckland, Auckland, New Zealand.

Spiller, C., Erakovic, L., Henare, M., & Pio, E. (2011). Relational well-being and wealth: Māori businesses and an ethic of care. *Journal of Business Ethics, 98*(1), 153–169.

Spiller, C., Kerr, H., & Panoho, J. (2015). *Wayfinding and Leadership*. Wellington, New Zealand: Huia Publications.

Spiller, C., & Stockdale, M. (2013). Managing and leading from a Māori perspective: Bringing new life and energy to organizations. In J. Neale (Ed.), *Handbook for Faith and Spirituality in the Workplace*. New York: Springer, 149–173.

Spiller, C., & Wolfgramm, R. (Eds.). (2015). *Indigenous Spiritualities at Work: Transforming the Spirit of Business Enterprise*. Charlotte, NC: Information Age.

Tagore, R. (2002). *Gitanjali*. New Delhi, India: Rupa Publications.

Tamboukou, M. (2010). Relational narratives: Auto/biography and the portrait. *Women's Studies International Forum, 33*(3), 170–179.

Te Rito, J. S. (2007). Whakapapa: A framework for understanding identity. *Mai Review, 2*, 1–10.

Tomlinson, M., & Kāwika Tenga, T. P. (2016). *New Mana: Transformations of a Classic Concept in Pacific Languages and Cultures*. Acton, Australia: ANU Press.

Walker, R. (1990/2004). *Ka whawhai tonu mātou: Struggle without End* (Rev. ed.). Auckland, New Zealand: Penguin.

Wolfgramm, R. M. (2007). Continuity and vitality of worldview(s) in organisational culture: Towards a Māori perspective. (Unpublished PhD Thesis). University of Auckland, Auckland, New Zealand.

19

SPIRITUAL LEADERSHIP AND ITS EMOTIONAL AND PROSOCIAL CONSEQUENCES

A Review and Synthesis

Sukumarakurup Krishnakumar

Introduction

The core concept of spirituality has been defined in a multitude of ways and in multiple domains including leadership (Correa & Sandage, 2018; Culatto & Summerton, 2015; Giske, 2012; Norenzayan, 2016). Inherent in the diversity of these conceptualizations of spirituality is its dimensionality, purpose, and the process—the "what," "why," and the "how" respectively (Hill, Jurkiewicz, Giacalone, & Fry, 2013; Houghton, Neck, & Krishnakumar, 2016; Krishnakumar & Neck, 2002; Oman, 2013). Even with such diverse opinions, conceptualizations, and empirical investigations, interest in studying the role of spirituality at work has been steadily increasing especially in the past few years (Anselmo Ferreira, 2018; Moon, Youn, Hur, & Kim, 2018). Using the three dimensional model proposed and empirically tested by Liu and Robertson (2011), spirituality was defined by Moon et al. (2018, pp. 1) as "the basic feeling amongst employees of being connected with a higher power, feeling interconnected with other human beings, and experiencing an interconnection with nature and all living things." A part of this definition is the notion that an individual is interconnected with others and/or to a sacred entity. The topic of spirituality has been extended into the study and understanding of leadership by researchers and practitioners beginning in the early 20th century (Tarbell, 1933). Just as there are diverse characterizations of workplace spirituality, there are also a broad array of theories and conceptualizations of spiritual leadership (Fry, 2005).

Spiritual Leadership

Leadership is undoubtedly a complex process that involves a leader (or more) influencing a group of people to achieve a certain goal or outcomes. In fact, after examining several definitions, Hughes, Ginnett, and Curphy (2012, p. 5) defined leadership as "the process of influencing an organized group toward accomplishing their goals." Spiritual leadership is a specialized form of leadership that has been defined as

> the values, attitudes, and behaviors that one must adopt in intrinsically motivating one's self and others so that both have a positive increase in the sense of spiritual

> well-being through calling and membership, that is, they experience meaning in their lives, have a sense of making a difference, and feel understood and appreciated.
>
> *(Fry, Vitucci, & Cedillo, 2005, p. 836)*

Inherent in this definition, and many others, is the role of experience and emotion, that of purpose and calling, and the need to engage in prosocial behaviors—activities that benefit the society as a whole. Just as spirituality has different definitions and viewpoints, spiritual leadership has been conceptualized in different ways. For example, Reave (2005) has incorporated the notions of leader integrity and character including constructs relating to the spiritual leader's character including his/her humility and concern for others. Another approach to spiritual leadership describes a multi-stage framework in which individuals progress from an initial stage of awakening and then through several intermediate stages of uncertainty and doubt, and finally ending at the "dawn" stage in which there is a sense of interconnectedness and transcendence (Benefiel, 2005). Other discussions of spiritual leadership relate to conditions and factors that affect the process itself. Krishnakumar, Houghton, Neck, & Ellison (2015) suggested the role of leader characteristics such as charisma, interconnectedness, and religious or existential faith, and boundary conditions such as narcissism, pro-social motivation to lead, follower perceptions of leader integrity (ethics), and perceived organizational support. The substantial role of leader integrity in Krishnakumar et al.'s (2015) model was empirically tested and confirmed by Yang, Liu, Wang, and Zhang (2017). Yang et al. (2017) also found that spiritual leaders exert their influence on their followers by making them feel more energized and enthusiastic to achieve task outcomes. The phenomenon of feeling energized when being with the spiritual leader was more effective when there was high levels of leader integrity. Yet another approach to studying spiritual leadership was suggested by Parameshwar (2005), who proposed a multistage model in which transcendental processes help spiritual leaders accomplish a higher purpose and empathy, consideration, and vision, which then helps them to steer a group of followers to extraordinary actions based on an ego-transcendent state.

In each of these approaches to studying spiritual leadership, there are a few common themes. First, most models suggest the role of spiritual flourishment and getting to a stage of ego transcendence in leaders and followers. Transcending one's ego would enable a leader to think about a larger purpose—purpose that is oriented communally rather than about the self. Second, although not necessarily clearly delineated, most models have active and engaging emotional contents in them. For example, in Fry's (2003) model, hope, faith, and altruistic love form the affective dimensions whereas in Benefiel's (2005) model, frustration and joy are interspersed in the leadership process as it unfolds. Third, most models include a sense of interconnectedness—a phenomenon where both the leader and the followers feel a sense of sameness with other individuals either within the leadership unit (e.g., a team which is led by a spiritual leader) or outside (e.g., customers of a company). Fourth, and finally, most spiritual leadership models include accomplishing extraordinary goals as the final outcome. Again, in Benefiel's (2005) spiritual transformation model, emphasis is on the greater good and finding meaning for a higher purpose. Similarly, in Fry's (2003) model, the final outcomes that are expected include organizational commitment, increased productivity, and life satisfaction (Fry et al., 2005). These four common themes point to the importance of spirituality, emotions, and the influence process that the spiritual leader has to ultimately employ to elicit outcomes.

In this chapter, I argue that spiritual leadership, just as leadership in general, manifests through and in the context of affect/emotions and social interactions. Thus, emotional intelligence, the ability to process and manage emotions appropriately, will be an important part of this leadership process and will make it effective through the facilitation of prosocial influence processes.

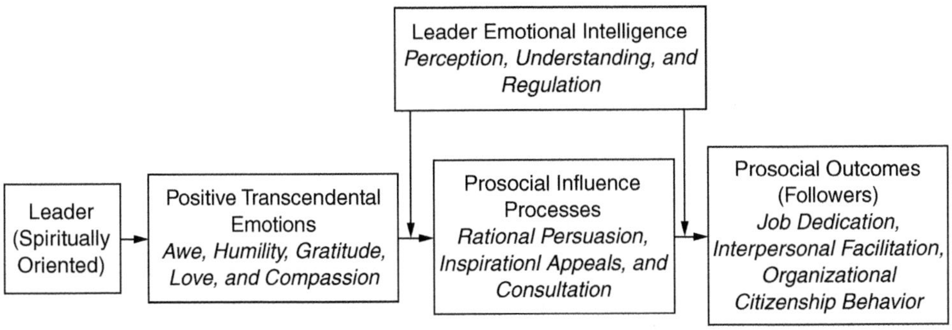

Figure 19.1 An Emotion-Influence Model of Spiritual Leadership and Prosocial Outcomes

Prosocial influence processes will involve those processes that steer a group of followers toward communal and socially relevant outcomes rather than agentic (or task-based) outcomes. In essence, I propose an Emotion-Influence model of spiritual leadership. This conceptual model is presented in Figure 19.1.

To begin discussing the model, first, I briefly review the role of emotions in leadership, particularly as it relates to spiritual leadership, before discussing the role of emotional intelligence.

The Role of Emotions in Leadership

The process of leadership and emotions are inseparable concepts. The role of affect/emotions in leadership in general has been recognized by scholars and practitioners alike. For example, recently, *Leadership Quarterly*, one of the premier journals in leadership, published a special issue specifically dedicated to affect/emotions in leadership (Connelly & Gooty, 2015). Leaders who feel, display, and appropriately regulate emotions are better at influencing their followers and accomplishing goals (Ashkanasy & Humphrey, 2014; Riggio, 2010). In one of the most commonly used theories of leadership, transformational leadership, leader charisma and individualized consideration have been shown to help followers express positive and action-oriented emotions without inhibition (Menges, Kilduff, Kern, & Bruch, 2015). Charismatic leadership is said to be effective when the leader is able to channel emotions through followers and inspire action from them using those emotions (Sy, Horton, & Riggio, 2018).

In many instances, the feeling or experience of an emotion correlates with the display of emotions. In a leadership context, however, the leader's *felt* emotions need not necessarily be the most appropriate or effective emotions that are *displayed* to his or her followers. For example, a leader that faces a strenuous situation is highly likely to feel such negative emotions as fear, anxiety, anger, frustration depending on the situation that arises. If this leader expresses the same negative emotions to his/her followers, then, they can potentially induce such negative emotions in the followers (Lindebaum, Jordan, & Morris, 2016). Negative emotions encourage deviant behaviors in people such as withdrawal, lack of motivation, abusive and rude behaviors, and sabotaging other people's performances (Rupprecht, Kueny, Shoss, & Metzger, 2016) and not the positive and extraordinary prosocial behaviors that an organization needs or wants. Thus, for leadership to be effective, a leader should be able to intelligently regulate *felt* emotions and subsequently be able to *display* emotions and behaviors that will positively facilitate proactive and prosocial behaviors in their followers (Edelman & van Knippenberg, 2017; Jordan & Lindebaum, 2015). Research supports this idea. For example, Edelman and van Knippenberg

(2017) found that training leaders in expressing and displaying *felt* emotions, a strategy known as deep acting, and the positive emotions that emanate from it, had positive effects on leader effectiveness. In sum, the process in which leaders feel and display emotions can have a significant impact on proximal (e.g., influence tactics, style) and distal outcomes (e.g., job performance, organizational outcomes).

Leader Emotional Intelligence

Leaders are not just passive conduits for emotions to flow—they actively process and regulate emotions using their emotional abilities (Riggio, 2010). The leader's emotional abilities, especially their emotional intelligence (EI), can play a major role in the spiritual leadership process. EI is defined as the ability to perceive, assimilate, understand, and manage emotions for productive purposes (Mayer & Salovey, 1997). In this regard, leader-EI has significant impacts on leadership outcomes (Kim & Kim, 2017; McCleskey, 2014; Walter, Cole, & Humphrey, 2011; Walter, Humphrey, & Cole, 2012). Leaders that can effectively perceive, understand, and manage emotions can prioritize tasks, organize action, and consider the needs and wants of followers and concurrently strive with them to attain goals and objectives (Walter et al., 2011). This speaks to the importance of abilities relating to emotions or emotional competence. Competences or abilities associated with the processing and regulation of emotions helps leaders not only to be "nice," but also to motivate his/her followers to accomplish tasks (Riggio, 2010; Rong, Sui, & Yang, 2015). A leader with higher levels of such competences will have the ability to discern the different verbal and nonverbal cues and mannerisms of his/her followers and attend to those followers appropriately (Vidyarthi, Anand, & Liden, 2014). A highly emotionally competent leader can assuage fears, reduce anxiety, and increase inspiration and other positive emotions (Neil, Wagstaff, Weller, & Lewis, 2016). Taken together, findings on *felt* emotions, *displayed* emotions, and the competences that may integrate them, i.e., EI, coalesces well with the findings on the effects of spirituality on felt emotions and emotional displays of the leader (Edelman & van Knippenberg, 2017; Van Cappellen, Toth-Gauthier, Saroglou, & Fredrickson, 2016).

Spirituality, Emotions, and EI

For ages, spiritual traditions, driven mostly from a religious-philosophical perspective, have highlighted the importance of taming or controlling negative emotions and enhancing positive emotions (Macavei & Miclea, 2008). In most of the religious traditions, emotions are never shunned or supposed to be eliminated—their presence is often acknowledged and accommodated in such a manner as to guide or facilitate social functioning (Correa & Sandage, 2018). Spirituality has been shown to facilitate positive and prosocial feelings at work because spirituality imparts a sense of "greater good" and the need for communal actions (Day, 2017). The effects of spirituality can be specifically related to the experience and expression of positive transcendental emotions—emotions that concern others and transcends self-interests of the individual that experiences those emotions (Tong, 2017). Although an exhaustive list and a detailed review of such transcendental emotions is outside the purview of this chapter, many researchers include such emotions as compassion, love, awe, humility, and gratitude (Tong, 2017; Van Cappellen, 2017). Research clearly shows that such emotions, by their very nature and purpose tend to facilitate concern for the other, and hence are prosocial in nature (DeSteno, Bartlett, Baumann, Williams, & Dickens, 2010). This is particularly pertinent to the emotion-influence spiritual leadership model (Figure 19.1), as a sense of the other or a sense of a community can help spiritual leaders better influence his or her followers.

Let us examine each of the major transcendental emotions. Compassion and love have been shown to be associated with higher levels of spirituality and have been implicated in spiritual leadership (Chen, Yang, & Li, 2012; Fry, 2003). Compassion significantly mediates the effects of spirituality on altruistic behavior (Saslow et al., 2013). An emotion that is closely related to compassion, love, has been shown to be effective in the leadership process (Dennis & Bocarnea, 2005; Fry, 2003; Van Cappellen, 2017). From a religious perspective, most world religions advocate showing compassion and subsequently engaging in compassionate acts and research supports this idea (Saslow et al., 2013). Awe, defined as "a positive emotion of wonder in response to something vast and beyond comprehension" is closely associated with spirituality (Preston & Shin, 2017) and leadership (McCann, Langford, & Rawlings, 2006). Followers are particularly influenced by feelings of awe toward the leader which then affects their affective commitment. Humility, next on the list of transcendental emotions, is defined as "an interpersonal characteristic grounded in a perspective of self-transcendence that is manifested by a willingness to view oneself accurately, an appreciation of others' strengths and contributions, and teachability" (Wang, Owens, Li, & Shi, 2018). Leader humility, overall, has been shown in prior research studies to help facilitate such positive employee outcomes as increased voice (Hu, Erdogan, Jiang, Bauer, & Liu, 2018), reduced turnover (Ou, Seo, Choi, & Hom, 2017), increased task performance and creativity (Hu et al., 2018; Wang et al., 2018). The final transcendent emotion is gratitude. Gratitude is defined as "a feeling of thankfulness directed toward others that emerges through social exchanges between helpers and beneficiaries" (Grant & Gino, 2010, p. 946). Gratitude has been shown to be an extremely important emotion in the workplace (Mills, Fleck, & Kozikowski, 2013). Followers' perception of a leader's gratitude can facilitate the emulation of ethical behaviors (Badrinarayanan, Ramachandran, & Madhavaram, 2018). Leaders who express gratitude can influence others to achieve prosocial outcomes (Grant & Gino, 2010).

In addition to its effect on positive transcendental emotions, spirituality buffers individuals from the stressors and blocks affective responses that signal strain (Byrne, Morton, & Dahling, 2011). In a large study of patients with coronary heart disease, researchers found that higher levels of spirituality were associated with lower levels of depression, anxiety, and anger (Ginting, Näring, Kwakkenbos, & Becker, 2015). Using the event sampling method in a group of 390 managers, a researcher found that managers that had higher levels of daily spiritual experiences showed a greater switch from negative to positive emotions when compared to those managers who had less daily spiritual experiences (Tong, 2017). In effect, spirituality helps block negative thoughts and emotions and facilitates positive transcendental emotions.

From a spiritual leadership perspective then, the spiritual leader should be able to better understand and process emotions such that they are processed, felt, and displayed in a productive way (Yadav & Yadav, 2018). This will involve the reduction of negative emotions and stress, and the amplification of positive transcendental emotions, both in the followers and in the leader. To enable a leader to use such emotions and emotional competences, the leader has to exert influence over his or her followers. Next, we discuss how spirituality will help leaders exert self-transcendental and prosocial influence processes.

Influence Processes in Leadership

Influence processes are central to any leadership. In fact, by definition, the core of every leadership situation involves some kind of influence process (Falbe & Yukl, 1992). Leaders choose many influence processes in their leadership activities. While a comprehensive review is outside the purview of this chapter, I will review the most important and pertinent influence tactics before explaining their roles and mechanisms in spiritual leadership.

Overall, research shows that the influence tactics that any leader uses fall into three categories: hard tactics, soft tactics, and rational persuasion (Clarke & Ward, 2006; Kipnis & Schmidt, 1985). Hard tactics involve the use of one's position as a power base, instilling pressure in one's followers, and forcing followers to engage in certain behaviors that the leader demands. Soft tactics involve the use of supportive and developmental influences and relies on the leader's personal rather than position power. One example of a soft influence tactic is inspirational appeal which is defined as a process where the "agent appeals to the target's values and ideals or seeks to arouse the target person's emotions to gain commitment for a request or proposal" (Yukl, Seifert, & Chavez, 2008, p. 610). Finally, rational persuasion involves the use of facts and logic to persuade or influence the follower. Research suggests that different types of leaders tend to use more (or less) of these influence tactics. For example, charismatic leaders, due to their focus on a future vision that is typically hopeful and positive, tend to use soft tactics as they have to appeal to the followers' positive emotions to be successful (Griffith, Connelly, Thiel, & Johnson, 2015). In a study that involved safety performance and climate, researchers showed that transformational leaders use such tactics as consultation and inspirational appeals and transactional leaders have been shown to use rational persuasion and coalition building (Clarke & Ward, 2006). In an open task setting where a leader manages individuals that engage in highly creative and innovative tasks, the leader should use appropriate influence tactics such as collaboration and participation to stimulate creative thinking in followers (Mumford, Scott, Gaddis, & Strange, 2002). Other studies also show that rational persuasion and inspirational appeals are used by transformational leaders (Charbonneau, 2004). Overall, soft and rational influence tactics are used more frequently by leaders than other tactics (Yukl & Tracey, 1992).

Spirituality, Emotions, and Influence Tactics

While there is ample research relating to the role of influence tactics in leadership in general, there is virtually no research on the role of spirituality and spiritual leadership on influence tactics. In my model of spiritual leadership, I suggest that leader spirituality, emotions, and EI together facilitate the appropriate choice of influence tactics employed by the leader. Research indicates that there is no one influence tactic that is better than others for all leadership situations. Even so, it has been shown that soft influence tactics and rational persuasion used singly or in combination, generally works better than most other ones (Charbonneau, 2004; Roth & Schwarzwald, 2016). I discussed earlier that a spiritual leader will be likely to experience and express positive transcendent emotions more often than negative emotions. The prevalence of such positive emotions facilitates two processes in the leadership situation. First, positive emotions generally have been shown to increase or broaden the scope of cognitive processing both in leaders and followers (Vacharkulksemsuk & Fredrickson, 2013). This will result in more creativity and subsequently more problem solving behavior. I propose that the opening up of possibilities by positive emotions further facilitates flexibility in the employment of the various influence tactics by the leader. A leader could switch from an inspirational influence tactic to rational persuasion based on the situation at hand. For example, inspirational appeals may work once a group of followers are influenced using data, figures, and logic (Yukl, Falbe, & Joo, 1993). Second, research evidence from multiple domains suggests that positive emotions tend to increase prosocial attitudes and cognitions in individuals facilitating such behaviors as cooperation, relationship building, and increased commitments (Berry & Hansen, 1996; Yee, Gonzaga, & Gable, 2014). Emotions can act as signals that inform others about the intentions of an individual (Barasch, Levine, Berman, & Small, 2014). In this context, a spiritual leader, by the elicitation of transcendent emotions can signal to his or her followers that he or she is prosocially motivated, which includes intentions for facilitating the long-term benefit of the followers.

The same transcendent positive emotions such as awe, humility, gratitude, love, and compassion discussed above can play a major role in facilitating the appropriate use of influence tactics by a spiritual leader. Experiencing and displaying awe can impart a sense of humility in an individual (Prade & Saroglou, 2016). By experiencing and displaying awe, a leader can, in fact, be perceived as being more humble by his/her followers, which then helps his or her followers to be more productive, more open in communication, and foster a more creative and innovative work environment (Stellar et al., 2018; Wang, Zhang, & Jia, 2017). Additionally, humility can counteract Machiavellian and Narcissistic tendencies, which can be deleterious for leaders (Owens, Wallace, & Waldman, 2015). Gratitude has also been shown to influence individuals in a positive manner (Armenta, Fritz, & Lyubomirsky, 2017). For example, studies have shown that gratitude helps people feel more connected to one another, which, again, relates back to the prosocial tendencies mentioned earlier (Algoe, 2012; Wood, Maltby, Stewart, Linley, & Joseph, 2008). Gratitude exerts strong effects on interpersonal relationships as well (Algoe & Haidt, 2009). The nature of gratitude being closely connected with spirituality is also well documented (Tudder, Buettner, & Brelsford, 2017; Uhder, McMinn, Bufford, & Gathercoal, 2017). If gratitude is expressed/displayed, then, the leader can influence followers to engage in prosocial behavior toward organizational stakeholders, but also to each other increasing both performance as well as group cohesion and unity (Froh, Bono, & Emmons, 2010; Layous, Nelson, Kurtz, & Lyubomirsky, 2017). Specifically, by showing gratitude, a leader not only implies humility, but also signals to his or her followers that he or she is open to consultation and is willing to listen to their suggestions and feedback.

Inspiration, which is an important emotional state closely associated with transcendental emotions, is elicited by leaders (through inspirational communication and leader behaviors). Inspiration occurs when an extremely successful individual (leader) or being actively encourages and motivates extraordinary action in individuals. The inspired individuals then strive to achieve the same success and qualities as that of the inspiring leader (Klein, Case, & Fitness, 2018; Thrash & Elliot, 2004). Positive transcendent emotions experienced and displayed by leaders (and followers) encourage the elicitation of inspiration among followers. As is prevalent in the leadership literature, inspiration can be a powerful tool for leaders. Spirituality, through its effects on transcendental positive emotions, further enhances the elicitation of an inspired state, which subsequently motivates followers to engage in extraordinary prosocial behaviors. While inspirational appeals can be an effective influence tactic, consultation can also be chosen depending on the situation. Consultation can only occur if the leader believes that he or she can benefit from the thoughts and knowledge that followers possess—this is often seen when leaders are humble and generally prosocial in their motivations.

The Effects of Spirituality, Emotions, and Influence Tactics

When an individual, particularly a leader, uses influence tactics, various outcomes can be elicited from his/her followers. Falbe and Yukl (1992) suggest outcomes from influencing a target consist of *commitment, compliance,* and *resistance*. Commitment is when the target (of the influence tactic) is intrinsically motivated to exert effort. As a result of commitment, the follower exerts extraordinary effort and goes over and above what is expected of him/her. Compliance is a response from the target of the influence (or the follower) where they will exert average effort to follow orders or respond to the specific actions requested by the leader, but will not exert extra effort. Finally, resistance is the response to an influence tactic where the target tries to not follow through on the requests by the leader by recusing himself/herself or counter arguing with the leader. Subsequent research has suggested that such soft influence tactics as inspirational appeals and consultation tend to generally favor commitment and so does rational persuasion. Hard tactics generally achieved compliance and/or resistance. Research further suggests that using combinations of influence tactics may be much more effective than using just one type of tactic. Soft tactics such as inspirational appeals and consultation were considered to be generally more effective than other influence tactics. Rational persuasion is typically effective if used with other soft tactics.

Integrating Spirituality, Emotions, and Influence Tactics

As seen from the model (Figure 19.1), I propose that the spiritually oriented leader will be able to effectively lead a group of followers to accomplish extraordinary outcomes such as prosocial behaviors. This process is accomplished by a three-step process. In the first step, the spiritual leader will engage with his or her spiritual beliefs or cognitions by recalling spiritual experiences, synchronizing his or her thoughts, values, and intentions, and the expression of positive transcendental emotions. In the second step, the leader will select the appropriate influence tactics by analyzing and processing the positive transcendental emotions that were elicited in step 1. At this stage, leader-EI will play an important moderating role where higher levels of EI will facilitate better selection of influence tactics. Step 3 will involve the use of influence tactics to achieve outcomes such as prosocial behaviors. Prosocial behaviors are defined as "helping behaviors performed to benefit or help an individual, group, or an organization with whom an individual interacts while carrying out his or her organizational role" (Lee, 1995, p. 197). Here, I define prosocial behaviors more broadly as a group of behaviors, that enhances outcomes for others—the organization as well as the society as a whole.

These include increased dedication to one's task, interpersonal facilitation (helping), and organizational citizenship behaviors (Borman & Motowidlo, 1997). Note that prosocial behaviors can be both in-role (prescribed job-related responsibilities) and extra-role (behaviors that fall outside the prescribed duties). In this step, leader-EI will again play an important role in facilitating the use of influence tactics such that prosocial behaviors are elicited from followers. Specifically, leader-EI will moderate the relationship between the selection and use of influence tactics and the elicitation of prosocial behaviors such that higher leader-EI will lead to a stronger relationship between influence tactics employed and the amount of prosocial behaviors. This happens because a leader with high-EI will be able to better read, analyze, and understand follower emotions and respond to those emotions in a more accurate and appropriate manner, thereby enabling the appropriate use of influence tactics. For example, in a team that has been already convinced by logic and facts, but is feeling less positive and less energetic, a leader with high EI can use inspirational appeals as an influence tactic.

Implications and Future Directions

In this chapter, I proposed a spiritual leadership model in which a leader influences his/her followers through the elicitation of positive transcendental emotions thereby, with the help of leader-EI, chooses appropriate influence processes, and ultimately enhances prosocial behaviors in his or her followers. With this model, I suggest that the spiritual leadership process is most effective when accomplished through the elicitation and management of positive emotions. This is not to posit that negative emotions are not important—on the contrary, it is important to make sure that the leadership process is unaffected by negative emotions. Positive transcendental emotions further help the spiritual leader to be open with his or her influence processes, to be humble, and to invite feedback and suggestions from his or her followers, to motivate them by inducing action-oriented positive emotions such as inspiration, and, ultimately to achieve extraordinary outcomes in the form of prosocial behaviors. Whether one is religious or not, the spiritual aspects of one's life, when incorporated into leadership processes and in the ways of influencing people, will be extremely effective in eliciting prosocial and proactive outcomes that are useful for the organization and the society as a whole. A major implication of this line of thought is that leadership outcomes, then, will subsequently increase the overall accomplishment of goals. Additionally, the prosocial and communal nature of the tasks and the leadership style will help make sure that the employees achieve outcomes in an ethical fashion rather than through shortcuts. In this model, I have suggested that the experience and display of positive transcendental emotions are an important part of the spiritual leadership process. Thus, an organization that is engaged in the development of spiritual leadership should train and develop leaders to authentically experience and express such positive transcendental emotions as awe, humility, love, compassion, and gratitude. Organizations should also encourage potential leaders to develop their EI skills, particularly their perceptive skills which can help such leaders to be continuously aware of their followers' needs, wants, challenges, and accomplishments. Future research should examine the role of spirituality and EI in the perception, understanding, management, and display of positive transcendental emotions. This is especially important in a leadership context. Research should also examine the role of emotions and EI in the selection and employment of appropriate and effective influence processes.

Conclusion

To conclude, leadership in organizations can often predispose leaders and their followers to set highly difficult goals, engage in hard influence tactics, and attempt to achieve goals by any means necessary. While this may be productive in the short run, this may prove to be costly and deleterious for organizations in the long run. Thus, organizations may be able to sustain longer-term performance by encouraging leaders to lead spiritually by feeling and expressing positive transcendental emotions and ultimately facilitating prosocial performance behaviors in their employees.

References

Algoe, S. B. (2012). Find, remind, and bind: The functions of gratitude in everyday relationships. *Social and Personality Psychology Compass, 6*(6), 455–469.

Algoe, S. B., & Haidt, J. (2009). Witnessing excellence in action: The "other-praising" emotions of elevation, gratitude, and admiration. *Journal of Positive Psychology, 4*(2), 105–127.

Anselmo Ferreira, V. (2018). Workplace spirituality: Empirical evidence revisited. *Management Research Review, 41*(7), 789–821.

Armenta, C. N., Fritz, M. M., & Lyubomirsky, S. (2017). Functions of positive emotions: Gratitude as a motivator of self-improvement and positive change. *Emotion Review, 9*(3), 183–190.

Ashkanasy, N. M., & Humphrey, R. H. (2014). Leadership and emotion: A multilevel perspective. In D. V. Day (Ed.), *The Oxford Handbook of Leadership and Organizations*. New York: Oxford University Press, 783–804.

Badrinarayanan, V., Ramachandran, I., & Madhavaram, S. (2018). Mirroring the boss: Ethical leadership, emulation intentions, and salesperson performance. *Journal of Business Ethics*. doi:10.1007/s10551-018-3842-1.

Barasch, A., Levine, E. E., Berman, J. Z., & Small, D. A. (2014). Selfish or selfless? On the signal value of emotion in altruistic behavior. *Journal of Personality and Social Psychology, 107*(3), 393–413.

Benefiel, M. (2005). The second half of the journey: Spiritual leadership for organizational transformation. *Leadership Quarterly, 16*(5), 723–747.
Berry, D. S., & Hansen, J. S. (1996). Positive affect, negative affect, and social interaction. *Journal of Personality and Social Psychology, 71*(4), 796–809.
Borman, W. C., & Motowidlo, S. J. (1997). Task performance and contextual performance: The meaning for personnel selection research. *Human Performance, 10*, 99–109.
Byrne, C. J., Morton, D. M., & Dahling, J. J. (2011). Spirituality, religion, and emotional labor in the workplace. *Journal of Management, Spirituality and Religion, 8*(4), 299–315.
Charbonneau, D. (2004). Influence tactics and perceptions of transformational leadership. *Leadership and Organization Development Journal, 25*(7), 565–576.
Chen, C. Y., Yang, C. Y., & Li, C. I. (2012). Spiritual leadership, follower mediators, and organizational outcomes: Evidence from three industries across two major Chinese societies. *Journal of Applied Social Psychology, 42*(4), 890–938.
Clarke, S., & Ward, K. (2006). The role of leader influence tactics and safety climate in engaging employees' safety participation. *Risk Analysis, 26*(5), 1175–1185.
Connelly, S., & Gooty, J. (2015). Leading with emotion: An overview of the special issue on leadership and emotions. *Leadership Quarterly, 26*(4), 485–488.
Correa, J. K., & Sandage, S. J. (2018). Relational spirituality as scaffolding for cognitive-behavioral therapy. *Spirituality in Clinical Practice, 5*(1), 54–63.
Culatto, A., & Summerton, C. B. (2015). Spirituality and health education: A national survey of academic leaders UK. *Journal of Religion and Health, 54*(6), 2269–2275.
Day, J. M. (2017). Religion and human development in adulthood: Well-being, prosocial behavior, and religious and spiritual development. *Behavioral Development Bulletin, 22*(2), 298–313.
Dennis, R. S., & Bocarnea, M. (2005). Development of the servant leadership assessment instrument. *Leadership and Organization Development Journal, 26*(8), 600–615.
DeSteno, D., Bartlett, M. Y., Baumann, J., Williams, L. A., & Dickens, L. (2010). Gratitude as moral sentiment: Emotion-guided cooperation in economic exchange. *Emotion, 10*(2), 289–293.
Edelman, P. J., & van Knippenberg, D. (2017). Training leader emotion regulation and leadership effectiveness. *Journal of Business and Psychology, 32*(6), 747–757.
Falbe, C. M., & Yukl, G. (1992). Consequences for managers of using single influence tactics and combinations of tactics. *Academy of Management Journal, 35*(3), 638–652.
Froh, J. J., Bono, G., & Emmons, R. (2010). Being grateful is beyond good manners: Gratitude and motivation to contribute to society among early adolescents. *Motivation and Emotion, 34*(2), 144–157.
Fry, L. W. (2003). Toward a theory of spiritual leadership. *Leadership Quarterly, 14*(6), 693–727.
Fry, L. W. (2005). Introduction to the Leadership Quarterly special issue: Toward a paradigm of spiritual leadership, Editorial. *Leadership Quarterly*, 619–622.
Fry, L. W., Vitucci, S., & Cedillo, M. (2005). Spiritual leadership and army transformation: Theory, measurement, and establishing a baseline. *Leadership Quarterly, 16*(5), 835–862.
Ginting, H., Näring, G., Kwakkenbos, L., & Becker, E. S. (2015). Spirituality and negative emotions in individuals with coronary heart disease. *Journal of Cardiovascular Nursing, 30*(6), 537–545.
Giske, T. (2012). How undergraduate nursing students learn to care for patients spiritually in clinical studies: A review of literature. *Journal of Nursing Management, 20*(8), 1049–1057.
Grant, A. M., & Gino, F. (2010). A little thanks goes a long way: Explaining why gratitude expressions motivate prosocial behavior. *Journal of Personality and Social Psychology, 98*(6), 946–955.
Griffith, J., Connelly, S., Thiel, C., & Johnson, G. (2015). How outstanding leaders lead with affect: An examination of charismatic, ideological, and pragmatic leaders. *Leadership Quarterly, 26*(4), 502–517.
Hill, P. C., Jurkiewicz, C. L., Giacalone, R. A., & Fry, L. W. (2013). From concept to science: Continuing steps in workplace spirituality research. In R. F. Paloutzian & C. L. Park (Eds.), *Handbook of the Psychology of Religion and Spirituality*. New York: Guilford Press, 617–631.
Houghton, J. D., Neck, C. P., & Krishnakumar, S. (2016). The what, why, and how of spirituality in the workplace revisited: A 14-year update and extension. *Journal of Management, Spirituality and Religion, 13*(3), 177–205.
Hu, J., Erdogan, B., Jiang, K., Bauer, T. N., & Liu, S. (2018). Leader humility and team creativity: The role of team information sharing, psychological safety, and power distance. *Journal of Applied Psychology, 103*(3), 313–323.
Hughes, R. I., Ginnett, R. C., & Curphy, G. J. (2012). What do we mean by leadership? In R. I. Hughes, R. C. Ginnett, & G. J. Curphy (Eds.), *Leadership: Enhancing the Lessons of Experience*. New York: McGraw-Hill Irwin, 2–42.

Jordan, P. J., & Lindebaum, D. (2015). A model of within person variation in leadership: Emotion regulation and scripts as predictors of situationally appropriate leadership. *Leadership Quarterly, 26*(4), 594–605.
Kim, H., & Kim, T. (2017). Emotional intelligence and transformational leadership: A review of empirical studies. *Human Resource Development Review, 16*(4), 377–393.
Kipnis, D., & Schmidt, S. M. (1985). The language of persuasion. *Psychology Today, 4*(1), 40–46.
Klein, J. W., Case, T. I., & Fitness, J. (2018). Can the positive effects of inspiration be extended to different domains? *Journal of Applied Social Psychology, 48*(1), 28–34.
Krishnakumar, S., Houghton, J. D., Neck, C. P., & Ellison, C. N. (2015). The "good" and the "bad" of spiritual leadership. *Journal of Management Spirituality and Religion, 12*(1), 17–37.
Krishnakumar, S., & Neck, C. P. (2002). The "what", "why" and "how" of spirituality in the workplace. *Journal of Managerial Psychology, 17*(3), 153–164.
Layous, K., Nelson, S. K., Kurtz, J. L., & Lyubomirsky, S. (2017). What triggers prosocial effort? A positive feedback loop between positive activities, kindness, and well-being. *Journal of Positive Psychology, 12*(4), 385–398.
Lee, C. (1995). Prosocial organizational behaviors: The roles of workplace justice, achievement striving, and pay satisfaction. *Journal of Business and Psychology, 10*(2), 197–206.
Lindebaum, D., Jordan, P. J., & Morris, L. (2016). Symmetrical and asymmetrical outcomes of leader anger expression: A qualitative study of army personnel. *Human Relations, 69*(2), 277–300.
Liu, C. H., & Robertson, P. J. (2011). Spirituality in the workplace: Theory and measurement. *Journal of Management Inquiry, 20*(1), 35–50.
Macavei, B., & Miclea, M. (2008). An empirical investigation of the relationship between religious beliefs, irrational beliefs, and negative emotions. *Journal of Cognitive and Behavioral Psychotherapies, 8*(1), 1–16.
McCann, J. A. J., Langford, P. H., & Rawlings, R. M. (2006). Testing Behling and McFillen's syncretical model of charismatic transformational leadership. *Group and Organization Management, 31*(2), 237–263.
McCleskey, J. (2014). Emotional intelligence and leadership: A review of the progress, controversy, and criticism. *International Journal of Organizational Analysis, 22*(1), 76–93.
Mayer, J. D., & Salovey, P. (1997). What is emotional intelligence? In P. Salovey & D. J. Sluyter (Eds.), *Emotional Development and Emotional Intelligence: Educational Implications*. New York: Basic Books, 3–34.
Menges, J. I., Kilduff, M., Kern, S., & Bruch, H. (2015). The awestruck effect: Followers suppress emotion expression in response to charismatic but not individually considerate leadership. *Leadership Quarterly, 26*(4), 626–640.
Mills, M. J., Fleck, C. R., & Kozikowski, A. (2013). Positive psychology at work: A conceptual review, state-of-practice assessment, and a look ahead. *Journal of Positive Psychology, 8*(2), 153–164.
Moon, T.-W., Youn, N., Hur, W.-M., & Kim, K.-M. (2018). Does employees' spirituality enhance job performance? The mediating roles of intrinsic motivation and job crafting. *Current Psychology*. doi:10.1007/s12144-018-9864-0.
Mumford, M. D., Scott, G. M., Gaddis, B., & Strange, J. M. (2002). Leading creative people: Orchestrating expertise and relationships. *Leadership Quarterly, 13*(6), 705–750.
Neil, R., Wagstaff, C. R. D., Weller, E., & Lewis, R. (2016). Leader behaviour, emotional intelligence, and team performance at a UK government executive agency during organizational change. *Journal of Change Management, 16*(2), 97–122.
Norenzayan, A. (2016). Theodiversity. *Annual Review of Psychology, 67*(1), 465–488.
Oman, D. (2013). Defining religion and spirituality. In R. F. Paloutzian & C. L. Park (Eds.), *Handbook of the Psychology of Religion and Spirituality*. New York: Guilford Press, 23–47.
Ou, A. Y., Seo, J., Choi, D., & Hom, P. W. (2017). When can humble top executives retain middle managers? The moderating role of top management team faultlines. *Academy of Management Journal, 60*(5), 1915–1931.
Owens, B. P., Wallace, A. S., & Waldman, D. A. (2015). Leader narcissism and follower outcomes: The counterbalancing effect of leader humility. *Journal of Applied Psychology, 100*(4), 1203–1213.
Parameshwar, S. (2005). Spiritual leadership through ego-transcendence: Exceptional responses to challenging circumstances. *Leadership Quarterly, 16*(5), 689–722.
Prade, C., & Saroglou, V. (2016). Awe's effects on generosity and helping. *Journal of Positive Psychology, 11*(5), 522–530.
Preston, J. L., & Shin, F. (2017). Spiritual experiences evoke awe through the small self in both religious and non-religious individuals. *Journal of Experimental Social Psychology, 70*, 212–221.
Reave, L. (2005). Spiritual values and practices related to leadership effectiveness. *Leadership Quarterly, 16*(5), 655–687.

Riggio, R. E. (2010). Emotional intelligence and interpersonal competencies. In M. G. Rothstein & R. J. Burke (Eds.), *Self-management and Leadership Development*. Northampton, MA: Edward Elgar Publishing, 160–182.

Rong, Y., Sui, Y., & Yang, B. (2015). The effect of leader emotional intelligence on group performance and employee attitude: Mediating effect of justice climate and moderating effect of group power distance. *Acta Psychologica Sinica, 47*(9), 1152–1161.

Roth, R. L., & Schwarzwald, J. (2016). Rationale and emotion in the selection of influence tactics by managers in conflict with subordinates. *Leadership and Organization Development Journal, 37*(1), 42–70.

Rupprecht, E. A., Kueny, C. R., Shoss, M. K., & Metzger, A. J. (2016). Getting what you want: How fit between desired and received leader sensitivity influences emotion and counterproductive work behavior. *Journal of Occupational Health Psychology, 21*(4), 443–454.

Saslow, L. R., John, O. P., Piff, P. K., Willer, R., Wong, E., Impett, E. A., Kogan, A., Antonenko, O., Clark, K., Feinberg, M., Keltner, D., & Saturn, S. R. (2013). The social significance of spirituality: New perspectives on the compassion–altruism relationship. *Psychology of Religion and Spirituality, 5*(3), 201–218.

Stellar, J. E., Gordon, A., Anderson, C. L., Piff, P. K., McNeil, G. D., & Keltner, D. (2018). Awe and humility. *Journal of Personality and Social Psychology, 114*(2), 258–269.

Sy, T., Horton, C., & Riggio, R. (2018). Charismatic leadership: Eliciting and channeling follower emotions. *Leadership Quarterly*. doi:10.1016/j.leaqua.2017.12.008.

Tarbell, I. M. (1933). Lincoln's spiritual leadership. *Homilectic Review, 105*, 142–142.

Thrash, T. M., & Elliot, A. J. (2004). Inspiration: Core characteristics, component processes, antecedents, and function. *Journal of Personality and Social Psychology, 87*(6), 957–973.

Tong, E. M. W. (2017). Spirituality and the temporal dynamics of transcendental positive emotions. *Psychology of Religion and Spirituality, 9*(1), 70–81.

Tudder, A., Buettner, K., & Brelsford, G. M. (2017). Spiritual well-being and gratitude: The role of positive affect and affect intensity. *Journal of Psychology and Christianity, 36*(2), 121–130.

Uhder, J., McMinn, M. R., Bufford, R. K., & Gathercoal, K. (2017). A gratitude intervention in a Christian church community. *Journal of Psychology and Theology, 45*(1), 46–57.

Vacharkulksemsuk, T., & Fredrickson, B. L. (2013). Looking back and glimpsing forward: The broaden-and-build theory of positive emotions as applied to organizations. In A. B. Bakker (Ed.), *Advances in Positive Organizational Psychology* (Vol. 1). Bingley, UK: Emerald Group Publishing, 45–60.

Van Cappellen, P. (2017). Rethinking self-transcendent positive emotions and religion: Insights from psychological and biblical research. *Psychology of Religion and Spirituality, 9*(3), 254–263.

Van Cappellen, P., Toth-Gauthier, M., Saroglou, V., & Fredrickson, B. L. (2016). Religion and well-being: The mediating role of positive emotions. *Journal of Happiness Studies, 17*(2), 485–505.

Vidyarthi, P. R., Anand, S., & Liden, R. C. (2014). Do emotionally perceptive leaders motivate higher employee performance? The moderating role of task interdependence and power distance. *Leadership Quarterly, 25*(2), 232–244.

Walter, F., Cole, M. S., & Humphrey, R. H. (2011). Emotional intelligence: Sine qua non of leadership or folderol. *Academy of Management Perspectives, 25*(1), 45–59.

Walter, F., Humphrey, R. H., & Cole, M. S. (2012). Unleashing leadership potential: Toward an evidence-based management of emotional intelligence. *Organizational Dynamics, 41*(3), 212–219.

Wang, J., Zhang, Z., & Jia, M. (2017). Understanding how leader humility enhances employee creativity: The roles of perspective taking and cognitive reappraisal. *Journal of Applied Behavioral Science, 53*(1), 5–31.

Wang, L., Owens, B. P., Li, J., & Shi, L. (2018). Exploring the affective impact, boundary conditions, and antecedents of leader humility. *Journal of Applied Psychology*. doi:10.1037/apl0000314.

Wood, A. M., Maltby, J., Stewart, N., Linley, P. A., & Joseph, S. (2008). A social-cognitive model of trait and state levels of gratitude. *Emotion, 8*(2), 281–290.

Yadav, M., & Yadav, R. (2018). Impact of spirituality/religiousness on cyber bullying and victimization in university students: Mediating effect of emotional intelligence. *Journal of Religion and Health*. doi:10.1007/s10943-018-0637-8.

Yang, F., Liu, J., Wang, Z., & Zhang, Y. (2017). Feeling energized: A multilevel model of spiritual leadership, leader integrity, relational energy, and job performance. *Journal of Business Ethics*. doi:10.1007/s10551-017-3713-1.

Yee, C. I., Gonzaga, G. C., & Gable, S. L. (2014). Positive emotions in close relationships. In M. M. Tugade, M. N. Shiota, & L. D. Kirby (Eds.), *Handbook of Positive Emotions*. New York: Guilford Press, 215–228.

Yukl, G., Falbe, C. M., & Joo, Y. Y. (1993). Patterns of influence behavior for managers. *Group and Organization Management, 18*(1), 5–28.
Yukl, G., Seifert, C. F., & Chavez, C. (2008). Validation of the extended Influence Behavior Questionnaire. *Leadership Quarterly, 19*(5), 609–621.
Yukl, G., & Tracey, J. B. (1992). Consequences of influence tactics used with subordinates, peers, and the boss. *Journal of Applied Psychology, 77*(4), 525–535.

20

SOFT SKILLS AND SPIRITUAL LEADERSHIP

Debra J. Dean

God and Business

Workplace spirituality is still an emerging field of study, and one of the original debates revolves around the separation of religion and spirituality. Giacalone, Jurkiewicz, and Fry (2005) wrestled with the concept of religion and spirituality and noted, "Spirituality is necessary for religion, but religion is not necessary for spirituality" (p. 517). It is important to discuss this right up front as many business professionals prefer to keep their church or religious life and their business life separate. In fact, some even become uncomfortable when the subject of workplace spirituality is broached. When introducing this topic, Dean (2017) asked questions such as (a) what activities have you been involved with that have caused a spiritual experience and (b) what does it feel like to be spiritual? In answering the first question, responses such as attending a concert, meditating, reading a book, or walking in nature were spoken. The second question had replies of feeling balanced, energized, a feeling like one is aware, or peaceful. In short, one does not need to be religious to be spiritual.

The Dalai Lama said,

> Religion, I take to be concerned with faith in the claims of one faith tradition or another, an aspect of which is the acceptance of some form of heaven or nirvana. Connected with this are religious teachings or dogma, ritual prayer, and so on. Spirituality I take to be concerned with those qualities of the human spirit—such as love and compassion, patience, tolerance, forgiveness, contentment, a sense of responsibility, a sense of harmony—which brings happiness to both self and others.
>
> *(Craig, 2002)*

According to Fry (2003)

> the Dalai Lama notes that while ritual and prayer, along with the questions of heaven and salvation, are directly connected to religion, the inner qualities of spirituality, spiritual survival, and the quest for God and, ultimately, joy, peace, and serenity and commitment to organizations that include and reinforce those qualities need not be.

So, if God or religion is part of your spiritual practice, then workplace spirituality may relate to your relationship with a higher being. If God or religion is not part of your spiritual practice, then workplace spirituality may relate to something such as meditation, music, walking, or yoga. In short, "we are not human beings having a spiritual experience, we are spiritual beings having a human experience" (Teilhard de Chardin, 1976). This chapter is not about a religious conversion, but rather about an inner life experience of spirituality related to the workplace.

Spirituality at Work Instruments

The purpose of this research was to answer the call of exploring two main instruments used to empirically test spirituality at work and contribute to the three most promising theoretical approaches to date, according to Benefiel, Fry, and Geigle (2014). The two main instruments used to test workplace spirituality include the Spiritual Leadership Scale and the Spirituality at Work Scale. Additionally, the Minnesota Satisfaction Questionnaire short-form and Organizational Commitment Questionnaire evaluated work outcomes of job satisfaction and organizational commitment. Furthermore, the Religious Commitment Index and demographic questions examined control variables of age, education, gender, income, meditation experience, religion, and years of work experience. To date, the two main instruments used to empirically test spirituality at work were developed by Ashmos and Duchon (2000) and Fry, Vitucci, and Cedillo (2005). For the purpose of this research Altruistic Love, Hope/Faith, Vision, Inner Life, Meaningful Work, and Sense of Community were the variables examined with the two Spirituality at Work instruments.

The Spiritual Leadership Scale

The Spiritual Leadership Scale was developed by Fry et al. (2005) and revised in 2016. This 42-item scale measures Altruistic Love, Hope/Faith, Inner Life, Meaning/Calling, Membership, Organizational Commitment, Productivity, Satisfaction with Life, and Vision. For the purpose of this research, Altruistic Love, Hope/Faith, and Vision were evaluated from this scale.

The Spirituality at Work Scale

The Spirituality at Work Scale was developed by Ashmos and Duchon (2000). This 66-item scale measures Conditions for Community, Inner Life, Meaning at Work, Positive Work Unit Values (also called Work Unit and Meaningful Work), and Work Unit Community. For the purpose of this research, Inner Life, Meaningful Work, and Sense of Community were evaluated from this scale. Figure 20.1 provides a visual of the six independent variables and two dependent variables.

The theories and concepts that applied to this research include (a) Fry's (2003) model of spiritual leadership, (b) Heaton and Schmidt-Wilk's (2011) meditation integration approach (also known as the Consciousness-Based Theory of Management, (c) Hicks' (2003) respectful pluralism, and (d) workplace spirituality.

Spiritual Leadership Theory

Spiritual Leadership Theory is the most effective theory to promote workplace outcomes and to stimulate human beings to behave in positive ways. In thinking about leadership theories of the past, names such as Lewin's autocratic, democratic, or laissez-faire leadership styles, Weber's

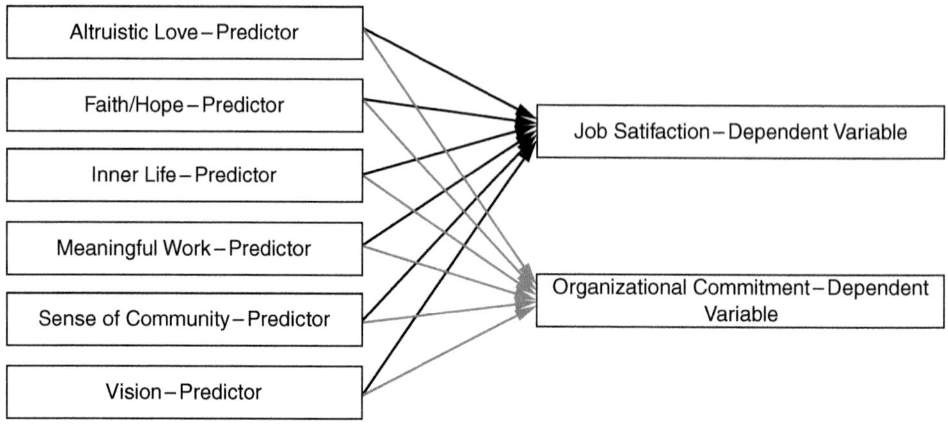

Figure 20.1 Independent Variables and Dependent Variables

charismatic leadership style, Bass' transactional leadership theory, Burn's and Bass' transformational leadership theory, Avolio's authentic leadership theory, and Greenleaf's servant leadership theory, show varying characteristics of leaders using persuasion or power to get work done. As decades progress, so do leadership styles. Leadership styles such as autocratic or transactional focus on managing the employee's body (hands and feet) or their head (mind). There are still plenty of situations where such leadership styles are necessary; such as an emergency situation or short-term urgent project. Theories such as transformational and authentic begin to shape the leader and follower in the relationship. They begin to hold one another up to higher standards. Servant leadership and spiritual leadership theories take it a step further and bring in the whole person; including the body, heart, mind, and spirit. Servant leaders focus on how they can serve the needs of their followers above all else and spiritual leaders spend time reflecting on their inner life so they too can serve others in a holistic approach. It is with these latter theories that leaders recognize their followers are not compartmentalizing their work as separate from the rest of their body. In other words, employees bring their whole self into the workplace.

Fry (2003) introduced the causal theory of spiritual leadership to include intrinsic motivation of Altruistic Love, Hope/Faith, and Vision as a holistic leadership theory to address the four areas that define the essence of human existence, which include the body, heart, mind, and spirit. Fry first examined leadership theories and the basic concept of leadership being the motivation to change. Second, Fry qualified the growing need for spirituality in the workplace by describing the "human need for spiritual survival through calling and membership" (p. 693). He then explained the difference between religion and spirituality, which included a generic definition of God as a "higher power with a continuum upon which humanistic, theistic, and pantheistic definitions of God can be placed" (p. 693). Fry also reviewed ethics, religious, and values-based leadership theories to explain that motivating followers requires leaders to be in touch with their core values and an ability to communicate those values to followers through vision and actions, creating a "sense of spiritual survival through calling and membership" (p. 693). Spiritual leadership is inclusive of other major leadership theories; however, it "is more conceptually distinct, parsimonious, and less conceptually confounded" (p. 693). Fry and Nisiewicz (2013) explained that the source of spiritual leadership is tapping into the inner life, which requires mindful practice to draw strength from something spiritual. This requires a commitment to embark on a spiritual journey or pilgrimage. The journey becomes one of transforming from an ego-centric self to other-centric self. The causal Model of Spiritual Leadership demonstrated how Hope/Faith and a Vision of love and service to others through the values of Altruistic Love fulfill the fundamental human needs of calling and membership, which are also referred to as purpose and belonging. Organizational outcomes of spiritual leadership include (but are not limited to) commitment and productivity.

Fry (2003) documented qualities of spiritual leadership with categories of (a) Vision, (b) Altruistic Love, and (c) Hope/Faith. A couple of vision qualities include a broad appeal to key stakeholders as well as defining the destination and journey. Some of the Altruistic Love qualities include attributes such as courage, empathy, patience, and trust. And, Hope/Faith characteristics include stretch goals, perseverance, and endurance. Fry defined spiritual leadership as "comprising the values, attitudes, and behaviors, that are necessary to intrinsically motivate one's self and others so that they have a sense of spiritual survival through calling and membership" (pp. 694–695).

Meditation Integration Approach, Also Known as Consciousness-Based Theory of Management

During this research effort to explore two main instruments used to empirically test spirituality at work and contribute to the three most promising theoretical approaches to date, according to Benefiel, Fry, and Geigle (2014), a concerted effort went into exploring and understanding Heaton and Schmidt-Wilk's (2011) Meditation Integration Approach, also known as the Consciousness-Based Theory of Management. The essence of this approach, through meditation, was to take time daily to calm the inner being, clear the mind, and discover bliss. This meditation becomes a way of life and research shows a plethora of positive outcomes for the practitioner.

Heaton and Schmidt-Wilk's (2011) Meditation Integration Approach, also known as the Consciousness-Based Theory of Management, is centered on the Maharishi Mahesh Yogi Transcendental Meditation (TM) program. The program is designed to develop the total brain, increase intelligence, improve creativity, reduce stress and anxiety, promote health and longevity, enhance relationships, and promote peace (Maharishi, 2012). There are more than 600 studies from 250 independent universities evaluating the benefits of TM (Maharishi, 2012). Schmidt-Wilk, Alexander, and Swanson (1996) found that TM "appears to improve employee health, well-being, job satisfaction, efficiency, and productivity, in turn influencing organizational climate, absenteeism, and financial performance" (p. 429). Frew (1974) documented that "meditators report they experience more job satisfaction, improved performance, less desire to change jobs (turnover), better interpersonal relationships, and decreased climbing orientation" or the motivation to climb the hierarchy (p. 366). Elder, Nidich, Moriarty, and Nidich (2014) stated that TM was "among the most widely studied meditation and relaxation programs" and found a significant reduction of perceived stress, depression, and burnout (p. 19).

Respectful Pluralism

Respectful Pluralism is another one of the "most promising theoretical approaches to workplace spirituality" according to Benefiel, Fry, and Geigle (2014). Respectful Pluralism is a constructive approach proposed as an alternative to the "generic-spirituality approach or a Christian establishment approach" (Hicks, 2003, p. 25). Hicks acknowledged that the workplace comprises human beings with a variety of religious interests including Buddhist, Christian, Hindu, Jewish, and Muslim (pp. 26–27). His approach involved a discussion of religious symbols, clothing, and holiday time, which was primarily Christian based in the United States of America until the 1965 Immigration and Naturalization Act (Hicks, 2003).

In recent history, the buzz phrase of "political correctness" has caused various responses. Regardless of one's feelings about being politically correct, the result has been an emergence of realizing that each person on this Earth is unique. In the past, discrimination referred to one's disability, gender, or skin color. The reality that has emerged to date is that each character quality or trait of a person is unique, and thereby different from another person. When explaining Respectful Pluralism to students in a classroom or employees in an organization, this concept is basically having respect for each other as all are unique. The concept of Respectful Pluralism is then boiled down to respecting the person because they are a human being.

Hicks (2003) compared religious diversity in the United States to that of India and Singapore. Using India as an example, they recognize 14 national holidays, 11 of which are religious: one Buddhist, two Christian, two Hindu, four Islam, one Jainism, and one Sikhism (p. 144). Hicks wrote that "Indian secularism does not generally mean the absence of religion from public life; on the contrary, secularism-as-pluralism calls for a kind of religious tolerance in public life or, at a minimum, the absence of violence motivated by religion" (p. 143). In Singapore, several religions are outlawed as they present a threat to the order of harmony or represent a threat to public order and political stability (p. 148). Singapore recognizes 10 national holidays, seven of which are religious: one Buddhist, two Christian, one Hindu, two Muslim, and one related to Chinese religion (p. 152).

Hicks argues that "like it or not, employees bring their own identity, problems, and beliefs to work" (p. 160). Further, he states that "for many employees, religious or spiritual beliefs and practices are an essential and inseparable part of their life" (pp. 160–161). Hicks wrote that "persons simply have dignity and deserve to be accorded respect because they are human" (p. 167). And confirms that to "achieve morally acceptable working conditions and employee health, it is necessary to discuss the proper role of religious, spiritual, political, and cultural expression by individuals while at work" (p. 171).

Research Findings

Dean (2017) conducted her research and found that altruistic love was worthy of attention with regard to job satisfaction and organizational commitment. In addition to Altruistic Love, Sense of Community and Meaningful Work were significantly predictive of job satisfaction; however, Altruistic Love clearly stood out as the most important variable. This finding caused her to coach leaders to develop and use their soft skills. She encouraged them on a frequent basis to display acts of love to their followers. Those acts included talking with them, asking about their family, and cultivating a relationship that went beyond getting the job done. The soft skills were extremely important to unite the group and resulted in a plethora of favorable work outcomes. The next few sections will delve a little deeper into the three variables Dean found to be most important based on her research. Those three variables included Altruistic Love, Sense of Community, and Meaningful Work.

Altruistic Love

The most significant variable found in Dean's (2017) research was Altruistic Love. According to Fry (2003), the spiritual leadership characteristic of Altruistic Love includes courage, empathy/compassion, forgiveness, honesty, humility, integrity, kindness, patience, and trust/loyalty. And Fry defined Altruistic Love as a "sense of wholeness, harmony, and well-being produced through care, concern, and appreciation for self and others" (p. 712). Fry and Matherly (2006, p. 6) also explained that Altruistic Love is

> given unconditionally from the organization and is received in turn from followers in pursuit of a common vision that drives out and removes fear associated with worry, anger, jealousy, selfishness, failure, and guilt and gives one a sense of membership.

Dean (2017) believes Altruistic Love refers to the core values found in 1 Corinthians 13: 4–8, 13: love is kind and patient; love rejoices in the truth; love always hopes, perseveres, protects, and trusts; love never fails; love does not boast, delight in evil, dishonor, envy, or keep a record of wrongs; and love is not easily angered, proud, or self-seeking. Using this scripture as a guide, one can assess one's own personal inner life and determine if one are offering Altruistic Love to others or not.

How does one demonstrate Altruistic Love in the workplace? Loving others is not always easy and many people overlook the importance of loving neighbors or co-workers. Demonstrating Altruistic Love in the workplace involves being patient. This can be demonstrated by listening patiently or taking time to ask questions such as how their day is, how was their weekend, and how members of their family are doing. Showing Altruistic Love can also involve protecting co-workers by offering to work overtime so they can recover from an illness or stand up for a colleague if they are being harassed or bullied. Displaying Altruistic Love may also involve forgiveness of past wrongs or failures in the workplace and optimistically hoping for a better outcome in the future. Altruistic Love played out in the workplace could also include acknowledging virtuous behavior of others such as honesty. There are many ways to display Altruistic Love in the workplace and this paragraph provides a small glimpse into what it may look like. Dean (2017) encourages others to get creative and spend some time thinking about how to love neighbors or co-workers well and how to do it on a consistent and frequent basis.

Meaningful Work

The second of three variables found to have significance in Dean's (2017) research was Meaningful Work. How does one find Meaningful Work in one's job? Finding meaning in one's work is not always easy. One is given a task to do and it is not always obvious as to how a mundane task relates to the bigger picture. Finding meaning in work may take time and effort. Employees or direct reports can also ask their manager how their work ties into the mission of the organization. If the manager cannot answer that question, and in many cases they cannot, this can be an opportunity to track down the answer and share it with colleagues. During this discovery period, employees or direct reports may find that what they are doing is very important and will give them a new perspective on coming into the workplace each day. If one cannot decipher meaning in their work based on the corporate mission, vision, and value statements then it may be necessary to create meaning in work for one's self. Below are a few examples that may help one find meaning in work on a personal level.

Dean (2017) used the following story to describe this concept of Meaningful Work to a large group of corporate professionals. As an example, let's say a high school girl or boy applies for a job as a lifeguard. Their purpose for getting the job is to spend their summer outside and get a tan. After the first week on the job, the lifeguard witnessed a small child fall into the pool and struggle to swim. The lifeguard jumped from their chair, dove into the pool, and pulled the lifeless child to the side. They proceeded to resuscitate the child successfully. After that day, the lifeguard discovered that their work had much more meaning than simply spending the summer outside and getting a tan. With their new perspective on their job, they were eager to get work and maintain vigilance. They had found meaning in their work.

As another example, Marques, Dhiman, and King (2009) wrote in their book about Johnny the Bagger (pp. 102–103). Johnny the Bagger was working at a grocery store. Johnny had Down syndrome and wanted to provide a positive message each day at work. In the evenings, Johnny would find a thought of the day, make copies, cut out each slip of paper, and sign his name. He would then put a slip of paper in a grocery bag for each customer. As a result, Johnny's line got longer as more customers preferred to wait for him. Johnny had found his purpose at work. He was not only bagging groceries but providing each customer with a positive message.

Also in the Marques, Dhiman, and King book was the story of Sue the Bus Driver (Ferguson, 2009, pp. 29–30). Sue had a job where she was responsible for driving a bus. Her job could have been mundane as she drove the same route each day but, for Sue, she found meaning in her work by using her skills as an outgoing and friendly person to talk to everyone as they got on the bus. Sue showed interest in her passengers and genuinely cared about her customers. Over time, riders would time their day so they could ride Sue's bus instead of taking a more convenient bus because they liked how they felt when they were greeted by Sue and how she cared for them. In the story, Sue explained that she felt connected to her passengers and driving a bus was her way of doing church; it was her ministry. She could care for others while she drove them from one place to another.

Regardless of how Meaningful Work is defined, it is important to know why one is waking up each day and going to work. It is important to know why a major portion of one's day is spent doing work. If the meaning of work is not evident, Dean (2017) encourages each person to discover the meaning of their work on their own as there are benefits from a personal and professional standpoint for having such meaning.

Sense of Community

The third of three variables found to have significance in Dean's (2017) research was Sense of Community. How does one have a Sense of Community in their business? Relationships matter and this is another area of work that is often overlooked. Planning lunch outings, celebrations for birthdays and anniversaries, recognition for achievements, cards and flowers for funerals of employee loved ones, and get-togethers after work are all ideas for building a Sense of Community with the team. It is perfectly acceptable to start small and start asking one or two co-workers to lunch every now and then, but make a conscious effort to build the community. This too will take time, but it is well worth the effort.

Workplace Spirituality

Workplace spirituality, as defined by Ashmos and Duchon (2000), is the "recognition of an inner life that nourishes and is nourished by Meaningful Work that takes place in the context of community" (p. 139). During this research, several presentations were given to college students and corporate professionals. Although the phrase workplace spirituality was new to them, they were eager to learn more about it. Dean (2017) found it encouraging to see the audience members' enthusiasm and attention during and after the presentations. It appeared that workplace spirituality was relevant to each person and they were hungry to learn more about how to nourish their soul and have a more holistic experience in the workplace.

When Dean (2017) introduced the topic to senior leaders of an organization, the leaders were supportive and followed up many times to confirm that the presentation would take place and their staff could hear about workplace spirituality. It is important to note that the term spirituality was defined early on in conversations with senior leaders and the audience. It was made clear that spirituality at work was about connecting with something other than one's self and not necessarily about religion; although for some they may be synonymous. The overarching theme of workplace spirituality was communicated as interconnectedness; whereas, Mitroff and Denton (1999) explained that the word "interconnectedness" is a single word that describes the meaning of spirituality and their groundbreaking research found that spiritual employees were hungry to "bring more of their 'complete selves' to work" (p. 83). There was a concerted effort early in the presentation to question the audience about what nourished their soul and examples such as reading, walking through nature, and yoga were given in addition to examples such as prayer and quiet time. This differentiation between religion and spirituality early in the presentation seemed to help the audience of the secular corporate workplace open their minds to the concept of workplace spirituality without the fear of being converted to any particular religion.

Application of Spiritual Leadership Theory

To answer the question in the 1984 song by Tina Turner entitled, "What's love got to do with it," Dean (2017) believes love has everything to do with it. However, explaining Altruistic Love as an important character trait to a room of executives can be a challenging concept to (a) have anyone show up and (b) keep their attention. Altruistic Love was the most important predictor variable of job satisfaction and organizational commitment; therefore, it deserves attention from the scholar and practitioner viewpoint.

For many, the concept of leaders loving followers is foreign and not applicable in the workplace. Dean (2017) recalls one student in the classroom chuckling and saying "everyone needs to man up and just do their job; after all that is what they are getting paid to do." Another conversation with a senior level executive at a large company included the word "oxymoron" as he explained that leaders cannot love their followers; that is just not how the real business world works.

One way to defend the importance of Altruistic Love in the workplace is with the use of Maslow's Hierarchy of Needs. Many college graduates are familiar with this hierarchy that explains how a human being has basic needs that must be met first in order to progress up to the next level of the hierarchy. In essence, if a person's basic needs of food, water, safety, and shelter are not met then they are not going to be very concerned with relationships or feelings of prestige. However, as many people are having their basic needs met in the 21st century, they are progressing up to the next level of the hierarchy. This means that relationships are becoming more important. Additionally, feelings of prestige, accomplishments, and achieving one's full potential are showing up in the workplace. This also means that leadership theories that once worked may need to shift to become more attentive to nurturing the soul of the follower at work.

Figure 20.2 displays each layer of Maslow's hierarchy. It is important to note that Maslow's Hierarchy of Needs was presented in a 1934 paper on the theory of human motivation. Over the past eight decades, many scholars have expanded the hierarchy to include more needs. Dean (2017) expanded the list of needs into Figure 20.2.

According to Buckingham and Coffman (1999), pay and benefits are "like tickets to the ballpark—they can get you into the game, but they cannot help you win" (p. 29). Monetary compensation and benefits may satisfy the basic human need for food, water, and shelter. But, if the human being has progressed into the higher levels of the hierarchy, pay and benefits are not going to satisfy them entirely. Madden (2015) reinforced the idea of "finding meaning through work that is deeper than material success" and noted that "the journey toward such purposeful work is one in which many people find themselves engaged" (p. 70). Giacalone, Jurkiewicz, and Fry (2005) stated, "Workplace spirituality is one of the fastest growing areas of new research and inquiry by scholars and practitioners alike" (p. 515).

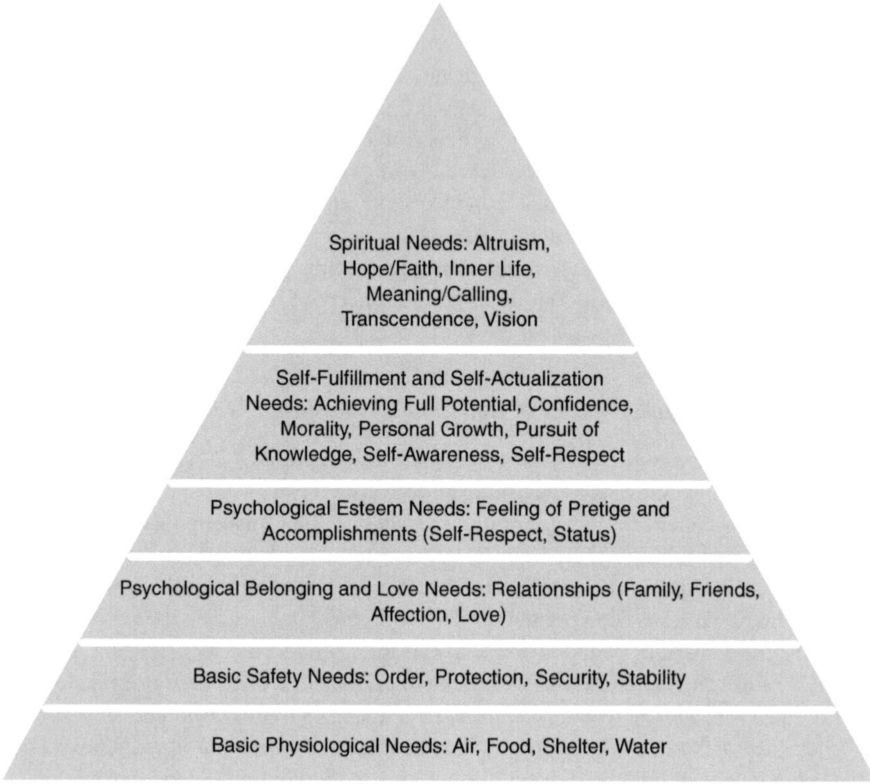

Figure 20.2 Maslow's Hierarchy of Needs

In what is considered the first empirical study on workplace spirituality, Mitroff and Denton (1999) explained that the word *interconnectedness* is a single word that describes the meaning of spirituality (p. 83). Their groundbreaking research found that spiritual employees were hungry to "bring more of their 'complete selves' to work" (p. 83). Since the pioneering efforts of Mitroff and Denton, numerous studies have assessed the relationship of workplace spirituality on organizational outcomes such as employee health and stress (Daniel, 2015; Kumar & Kumar, 2014), job involvement (Van der Walt & Swanepoel, 2015; Kolodinsky, Giacalone, & Jurkiewicz, 2008), job satisfaction (Milliman, Czaplewski, & Ferguson, 2003; Ghazzawi, Smith, & Cao, 2016), organizational commitment (Milliman et al., 2003; Rego & Pina e Cunha, 2008), organizational frustration (Kolodinsky et al., 2008), organizational identification (Kolodinsky et al., 2008), work rewards satisfaction (Kolodinsky et al., 2008), and work unit performance (Duchon & Ashmos-Plowman, 2005).

Applying workplace spirituality to the workplace is not difficult. Some will find they have the support from senior leaders and others may not have support. Some may find they are in a position as a leader to make change and others may think they are just a follower and cannot do anything to make their workplace better. Dean (2017) believes every human being can make their workplace better; regardless if they are the leader or the follower and regardless if they have support from senior leaders or not.

In summary, this journey progresses through Maslow's hierarchy; the challenge of finding psychological belonging and love needs, psychological esteem needs, self-fulfillment and self-actualization, and spiritual needs is attainable. In this experience, Altruistic Love, Meaningful Work, and Sense of Community are keys to starting a culture of workplace spirituality. The main idea of Altruistic Love is an aspect of caring for colleagues that transcends the workplace into a better place and moves the human being into the higher levels of the hierarchy. Simply speaking, when leaders take care of their followers, positive workplace outcomes happen because the people are vested in the corporate culture where their spiritual needs are met.

Lessons Learned and Recommendations for Next Steps

As with any journey of discovery, there are moments that are more challenging than others. In this research experience, Dean (2017) found herself to be the biggest obstacle as she worried about what others would think. She worried about discussing the taboo topic of religion in the workplace and worried about the connotation of the word spirituality. Dean was surprised to see a thirst and hunger from the audience members about how their soul could be nourished. Her first step with the research was to have the courage to speak up.

Dean (2017) had the "excuse" of her school assignment to survey her colleagues and find out what variable was more important. Once she found the variables that stood out as important to workplace spirituality she began coaching and mentoring others on the team. Some may think that Altruistic Love, Meaningful Work, or Sense of Community are silly. But, she found that the more she showed she cared for her colleagues, the more the department transcended into a spiritual community.

The main thing is to not get discouraged by the one or two employees that think the exercise is worthless. During one meeting, she invited the entire department to a meeting where she was going to discuss workplace spirituality. One person refused to attend the meeting. They also refused to take the survey. That is okay. Although they did not want to participate, they reaped the benefits of a spiritual workplace and just about 1 year later commented about the positive difference made in the department.

For those not in a position of leadership, but wanting to make a change in the workplace, the academic review of followership may help one to understand the different options for the follower position. Followership is the study of followers and their impact on the leadership relationship. There are several scholars pioneering the way with research on followership including Barbara Kellerman, Ira Chaleff, and Robert Kelley. Each scholar has identified typologies. Kelley identified alienated, conformist, exemplary, passive, and pragmatic. Chaleff identified implementer, individualist, partner, and resource. And, Kellerman identified activist, bystander, diehard, isolate, and participant. By understanding followership types, one may be able to understand more about how they can support the change they want to see in their workplace.

Overall, using Altruistic Love, Sense of Community, and Meaningful Work as a guide will help move the culture of the workplace toward a more spiritual culture that nourishes the soul of employees at work. To get started, simply pay attention to the little things. Schedule time to walk around and talk with others for the purpose of building community. Take time to care for others. And, take the time to find the company's mission, vision, and value statements. Then inquire with persistence to find out how the daily work of each person on the team makes a difference; knowing why one wakes up and goes to work each day is a first step to having Meaningful Work.

References

Ashmos, D., & Duchon, D. (2000). Spirituality at work. *Journal of Management Inquiry, 9*(2), 134.

Benefiel, M., Fry, L., & Geigle, D. (2014). Spirituality and religion in the workplace: History, theory, and research. *Psychology of Religion and Spirituality, 6*(3), 175–187.

Buckingham, M., & Coffman, C. (1999). *First, Break All the Rules: What the World's Greatest Managers Do Differently*. London: Simon & Schuster.

Craig, M. (2002). *The Pocket Dalai Lama*. Boulder, CO: Shambhala.

Daniel, J. (2015). Workplace spirituality and stress: Evidence from Mexico and US. *Management Research Review, 38*(1), 29.

Dean, D. (2017). Religion and spirituality in the workplace: A quantitative evaluation of job satisfaction and organizational commitment (Order No. 10260968). Available from ProQuest Dissertations & Theses Global (1881834070).

Duchon, D., & Ashmos-Plowman, D. (2005). Nurturing the spirit at work: Impact on work unit performance. *Leadership Quarterly, 16*(5), 807–833.

Elder, C., Nidich, S., Moriarty, F., & Nidich, R. (2014). Effect of transcendental meditation on employee stress, depression, and burnout: A randomized controlled study. *Permanente Journal, 18*(1), 19–23.

Ferguson, L. (2009). Working spiritually: Aligning gifts, purpose and passion. In J. Marques, S. Dhiman, & R. King (Eds.), *The Workplace and Spirituality: New Perspectives on Research and Practice*. Woodstock, VT: SkyLight Paths, 23–34.

Frew, D. (1974). Transcendental meditation and productivity. *Academy of Management Journal, 17*(2), 362–368.

Fry, L. W. (2003). Toward a theory of spiritual leadership. *Leadership Quarterly, 14*(6), 693.

Fry, L. W., & Matherly, L. (2006). *Spiritual Leadership and Organizational Performance: An Exploratory Study*. Atlanta, GA: Academy of Management Conference.

Fry, L. W., & Nisiewicz, M. (2013). *Maximizing the Triple Bottom Line through Spiritual Leadership*. Stanford, CA: Stanford Business Books.

Fry, L. W., Vitucci, S., & Cedillo, M. (2005). Spiritual leadership and army transformation: Theory, measurement, and establishing a baseline. *Leadership Quarterly, 16*(5), 835.

Ghazzawi, I., Smith, Y., & Cao, Y. (2016). Faith and job satisfaction: Is religion a missing link? *Journal of Organizational Culture, Communications and Conflict, 20*(1), 1–29.

Giacalone, R., Jurkiewicz, C., & Fry, L. (2005). From advocacy to science: The next steps in workplace spirituality research. In R. Paloutzian (Ed.), *Handbook of the Psychology of Religion and Spirituality*. Newbury Park, CA: Sage, 515–528.

Heaton, D., & Schmidt-Wilk, J. (2011). Consciousness-based management education and development. In D. Llewellyn & C. Pearson (Eds.), *Consciousness-based Education: A Foundation for Teaching and Learning in the Academic Disciplines*. Fairfield, IA: Consciousness-Based Books, 1–424.

Hicks, D. (2003). *Religion and the Workplace: Pluralism, Spirituality, Leadership*. Cambridge, UK: Cambridge University Press.

Kolodinsky, R., Giacalone, R., & Jurkiewicz, C. (2008). Workplace values and outcomes: Exploring personal, organizational, and interactive workplace spirituality. *Journal of Business Ethics, 81*(2), 465–480.

Kumar, V., & Kumar, S. (2014). Workplace spirituality as a moderator in relation between stress and health: An exploratory empirical assessment. *International Review of Psychiatry, 26*(3), 344–351.

Madden, T. (2015). Journeys of purpose: A review of literature about work and spirituality. *International Journal of Religion and Spirituality in Society, 5*(4), 69–76.

Maharishi (2012). The Transcendental Meditation Program [Brochure].

Marques, J., Dhiman, S., & King, R. (2009). The S-word revisited: New horizons in workplace spirituality. In J. Marques, S. Dhiman, & R. King (Eds.), *The Workplace and Spirituality: New Perspectives on Research and Practice*. Woodstock, VT: SkyLight Paths, 99–110.

Milliman, J., Czaplewski, A., & Ferguson, J. (2003). Workplace spirituality and employee work attitudes: An exploratory empirical assessment. *Journal of Organizational Change Management, 16*(4), 426–447.

Mitroff, I., & Denton, E. (1999). A study of spirituality in the workplace [cover story]. *Sloan Management Review, 40*(4), 83–92.

Rego, A., & Pina e Cunha, M. (2008). Workplace spirituality and organizational commitment: An empirical study. *Journal of Organizational Change Management, 21*(1), 53–75.

Schmidt-Wilk, J., Alexander, C., & Swanson, G. (1996). Developing consciousness in organizations: The transcendental meditation program in business. *Journal of Business and Psychology, 10*(4), 429–444.

Teilhard de Chardin, P. (1976). *The Phenomenon of Man*. New York: Harper Perennial.

Van der Walt, F., & Swanepoel, H. (2015). The relationship between workplace spirituality and job involvement: A South African study. *African Journal of Business and Economic Research, 10*(1), 95–116.

21

THE ROLE OF EMPATHY IN THE PROFESSIONAL WORKPLACE

Jody A. Worley

Why Empathy, and Why Now?

The modern workplace environment is likely one of the most dynamic and pervasive social relational processes in which humans interact. There are hundreds of thousands of books and research articles on organizational behavior, business management, and leadership in organizations. Empathy, although not a concept that frequently appears in the organizational research literature, has important implications for understanding performance, leadership, communication, and collaboration, among other valued processes in the professional workplace. Organizational outcomes that do receive a great deal of attention are likely influenced by the underlying role of empathy, its absence or presence, and which therefore warrants more attention than it receives.

This chapter aims to highlight the role of empathy in the professional workplace by presenting evidence for internal and external benefits to a company when the notion of empathy is embraced and practiced as an integral part of the organizational climate. First, two components of empathy, cognitive (perspective-taking) and emotional concern, are briefly described. Then, ways that empathy contributes to the professional workplace are discussed by focusing on internal and external benefits for companies. Although the range of possible benefits is broad, this chapter will focus on internal contributions of empathy for workplace communication, collaboration, performance, and leadership. The role of empathy in the workplace also has implications for relationships in the external social context in which the organization operates. Potential benefits outside the organization might include global market collaborations, philanthropy and social impact.

Empathy in the Workplace

The role of empathy in the workplace is relevant precisely due to a crossover or transmission process in human relations (Jones & Fletcher, 1993; Westman, 2001). Employees relate with each other, and with their respective supervisors, managers, leaders, other stakeholders, and so on, in order to communicate, collaborate, and work effectively to produce results. Although trust formation is important for relationship building, the empathic role in establishing trust requires the ability to interact and communicate effectively (empathically). The relational process is a crossover process. There is an empathic reaction at work.

Table 21.1 The Role of Empathy in the Workplace: Internal and External Benefits to the Company

Internal	*External*
Communication and collaboration	Global market collaboration
Performance and profitability	Philanthropy and social impact
Leadership	

The literal root meaning of empathy (*em pathos*; "feeling into") implies a clear emotional component. However, empathy may best be considered as a set of related constructs including emotional and non-emotional components (Davis, 1983). *Perspective-taking* is the cognitive component where individuals imagine how they would feel in the position of another (Salovey & Mayer, 1990). This is the non-emotional component of empathy. Social learning theorists (e.g., Bandura, 2001; Stotland, 1969) support this view, and have explained the transmission of emotions as a conscious processing of information. Whereas *empathic concern* is an emotional responsiveness in which individuals experience and share others' feelings and actively respond (Davis, 1983). The core relational theme for empathy would involve the sharing of another person's emotional state, distressed or otherwise. Starcevic and Piontek (1997) define empathy as interpersonal communication that is predominantly emotional in nature and involves the ability to be affected by other's affective state, as well as to be able to read in oneself what that affect has been. Likewise, Lazarus (1991) defined empathy as "sharing another's feelings by placing oneself psychologically in that person's circumstances" (p. 287). So, empathy is the ability to understand and communicate one's understanding of another person's emotion (Vignemont & Singer, 2006). Consider that empathy is an ability-based, interactional relationship building process, rather than strictly as a subjective, affective-based emotional concept. Therefore, empathy is not simply a feeling that we have for others, but also a responsive action that we share with others in work relations with them.

The role of empathy in the workplace has implications for relationships within organizations. Organizations benefit internally when empathy is present and shared in the workplace through enhanced communication and improved relations between leaders and followers. Communication effectiveness and healthy leader–member exchanges, then, contribute to organizational performance and profitability. Likewise, empathy contributes to external business development through stronger market collaborations, as well as through philanthropic initiatives and social impact. A summary of these proposed benefits is presented in Table 21.1.

Internal Benefits for the Role of Empathy in the Workplace

Communication and Collaboration

Conrad and Newberry (2012) recognized the importance of communication skills to drive effective leadership including the ability to communicate openly and honestly. Communication without this people-focused element may be constructed as command and control orders. Effective business leadership, however, is dependent upon communicating in optimistic yet realistic terms, and empowering people to help build the future. Workers prefer a sense of security and optimism about the future of their work. When empathic communication is encouraged at work, employees feel more comfortable speaking openly and that their perspectives matter. Culture building is a business necessity and that is achieved through communication that inspires and encourages the value of commitment, collaboration, cohesiveness, and collective identity.

Empathy is related to personality traits of openness and agreeableness (Davies, Stankov, & Roberts, 1998). In their review of interpersonal communication skills in organizational scholarship literature, Conrad and Newberry (2012) found consistent emphasis on the need to manage emotions and concentrate on controlling reactions to stressful situational factors. They found that by learning to manage emotions and control reactions to work-related stress, managers and supervisors were more effective at communicating stability and encouraging harmony among organizational staff. This type of emotional and social intelligence is commonly understood as a contributing factor in the ability to build relationships, inspire trust, control emotions, and express empathy through the art of listening. In fact, theorists propose that human bonding is achievable through developing awareness for communication needs, along with initiating communication that reduces barriers and conflict, while sustaining trust in a climate that invites dialogue. The ability to build and foster trust in workplace relationships requires interpersonal skills, or "soft skills," such as empathy.

Soft skills include techniques and methods of developing written communication, oral communication, leadership communication, team skills, listening skills, presentation skills, global/cultural awareness, and interpersonal communication. Evidence from the World Economic Forum (2016, p. 3) suggests that employers in all occupational fields place greater value on employees' communication skills than they do on their technical skills:

> Overall, social skills— such as persuasion, emotional intelligence and teaching others— will be in higher demand across industries than narrow technical skills, such as programming or equipment operation and control. In essence, technical skills will need to be supplemented with strong social and collaboration skills.

The reality is that organizational members may have brilliant ideas for product development, innovation, growth, and expansion of the company, but to succeed they must be able to communicate those ideas. In short, empathy, the ability to express one's emotions, and the ability to identify others' emotions, represents a complex set of skills that vary among individuals (Ickes, Stinson, Bissonnette, & Garcia, 1990) and may assist in the development of positive relationships, problem-solving, decision-making, and accomplishment of personal goals. Therefore, a few suggestions for enhancing your ability to engage in empathic conversation are presented in Table 21.2.

Leadership Development

A key point in the discussion of the role of empathy in workplace communication is the notion that expressing one's own emotions involves the ability to communicate feelings accurately and to express related needs. George (2000, p. 1034) states, "the accurate expression of emotion ensures that people are able to effectively communicate with others to meet their needs and accomplish their goals or objectives" and notes "ambivalence over expression of emotions can

Table 21.2 Recommendations for Enhancing Empathic Conversation

- Be present, physically and mentally, to what is happening in the exchange.
- Listen carefully and pay attention to the use of words and phrases.
- Respond to the central message.
- Adapt and be flexible in responding as the other person's thoughts and feelings change.
- Look for behaviors and listen for verbal cues to confirm that you understand correctly.

hamper an individual from developing beneficial interpersonal relationships in life." Likewise, the ability of leaders to display and communicate emotions may influence how followers perceive them in the workplace, and thus their ability to develop effective relationships with employees (Dasborough & Ashkanasy, 2002; Newcombe & Ashkanasy, 2002). This may explain why people who rate highly on empathy are more likely viewed by their peers as having leadership qualities (Kellett, Humphrey, & Sleeth, 2006).

By now, it is generally accepted that results in the workplace are associated with emotional intelligence. Emotional intelligence has been defined as the ability to perceive emotion in oneself and others, use emotions to facilitate thinking, understand emotions and emotion processes, and manage the experience and expression of emotions in oneself and others (Mayer, Salovey, Caruso, & Sitarenios, 2001). This has been demonstrated by an order of magnitude across industries and organizational contexts (Coté & Morgan, 2002; Wong & Law, 2002). More recent research also shows that the mood of leaders plays a role in that dynamic (Gooty, Connelly, Griffeth, & Gupta, 2010; Kellett et al., 2006; Wolff, Pescosolido, & Druskat, 2002). A leader's positive or negative mood and emotions sets the tone for everyone else; it is contagious. A grumpy and detached boss, for example, creates a toxic workplace climate filled with negative attitudes that gets in the way of recognizing opportunities for improvement or increased performance. An engaged and optimistic supervisor inspires followers to take initiative and overcome obstacles rather than getting distracted by what or whom might be considered the source of "the problem" when challenges arise.

Although research on the role of emotion and the contagious effects it has on others is often received with responses from business professionals as, "of course, we have known that all along," the reality is that if the process is recognized at all, it is still not often discussed. The conversation about a leader or co-worker's emotional style and its impact on the work climate is largely ignored or avoided. For many people, the topic is viewed as "soft" and perhaps trivial. Indeed, the physiological processes responsible for shared emotional experiences is a naturally occurring product of the human limbic system—the brain's central processor of emotion. This is relevant for understanding the role of empathy in the professional workplace because although it may sound like "common sense" when we read or hear about it, we usually do not notice the process or consider its impact on interpersonal relationships at work. There is an increasing interest in research evidence on emotional intelligence among leaders because a leader with emotional intelligence can monitor his or her moods through self-awareness and then change or improve upon them through self-management. More specifically, someone in a leadership position can better understand moods with empathy, and act in ways that influence the positive moods of others through relationship management.

Research evidence has shown a relationship between empathy and the cognitive skills that underlie effective leadership behaviors (Wolff et al., 2002). According to their model, Wolff et al. (2002) suggest that because task leaders organize and plan group work, a leader must develop a vision that encompasses a wide variety of often confusing information about environment, task characteristics, and group members' abilities and personalities. To do so requires a pattern recognition and perspective taking. Because empathy consists of the ability and desire to understand others' feeling, Wolff et al. argue that empathy should correlate with pattern recognition and perspective taking. Their findings supported their model of an indirect relationship between empathy and task leadership as a function of cognitive abilities.

Kellett et al. (2006) makes an important distinction between interactive empathy and passive empathy. Interactive empathy is a more engaged process such that followers recognize the leader's concern through his or her role in creating a shared emotional experience. Examples of interactive empathy include words of encouragement or inspiration, or the optimistic expression of a vision for positive change. Passive empathy is demonstrated when a person feels sympathy for others but does not influence the shared emotional tone of the group. With regards to the role of empathy in workplace leadership, there is perhaps less concern with the individual's internal emotional state than whether or not the individual has exerted leadership by creating an emotional tie with others.

While visible leader behavior and action might reflect the competencies and traits of a leader, there is general agreement that supportive communication and relationship building that empowers others also characterize effective leadership. Empathic communication includes listening, encouraging, facilitating, clarifying, and providing emotional support. Specific behaviors aimed at establishing norms for collaboration through communication and encouraging followers to voice ideas helps facilitate the emergence of shared leadership (Kramer & Crespy, 2011). The emergence of an exchange relationship can flourish when there is supportive communication. It is reasonable to assume that this relationship building process contributes to performance and profitability in the professional workplace.

Performance and Profitability

The crossover of emotion that occurs between leaders and followers can substantially influence job attitudes and performance. Pescosolido (2002) argued, and his case examples illustrated, that emergent leadership in self-managed work teams involves a process of managing group members' emotions in order to improve group performance. Furthermore, emergent leaders in the context of self-managed teams are empathic and responsive to the needs of followers. Specifically, empathy ability is positively related to perspective-taking skill and pattern recognition ($r=0.20$, and $r=0.25$, $p<0.05$, respectively; Wolff et al., 2002). This evidence provides a reasonable foundation for better understanding the role of empathy in workplace performance and profitability.

An empathic supervisor or manager is more likely to provide the type of support that facilitates recovery from a workplace incident that might otherwise thwart employee performance. Research evidence shows that emotion-focused coping (EFC) in the workplace is positively related to task performance (Gooty, Gavin, Ashkanasy, & Thomas, 2014; Miner & Glomb, 2010). EFC refers to an individual's attempts to let go or detach from the actual occurrence of work events as a way to deal with the emotional experience that may be associated with those events (Weiss & Cropanzano, 1996). It is important to note that EFC is not the suppression of emotions from a critical incident. Rather, EFC is an acknowledgment of the event and the conscious effort by an individual to choose how they will emotionally respond. The management of emotions in this way through EFC fosters workplace relationships such that workers can effectively perform their assigned duties and meet the requirements of the job. There is evidence to support this on an individual level within-person (Miner & Glomb, 2010; Weiss & Cropanzano, 1996), but also in between-person relationships in the workplace as with the supervisor–employee exchange or in the context of teams and team performance (Akgün, Keskin, Cebecioglu, & Dogan, 2015; Gooty et al., 2014).

Team member trust, for example, is reinforced when expectations and project-related outcomes align. This contributes to the formation of collective empathy, sometimes referred to as affective-based trust, where team members learn to understand each other's feelings. As it forms, collective empathy functions to reduce any sense of emotional vulnerability and allows for openness and transparent communication. So, what is that process? How does it work? There is evidence that it begins with familiarity with team members (Akgün et al., 2015). Specifically, Akgün et al. were able to show that when people know each other, perhaps from prior work projects, that they are more present with each other, open to change, empathically attuned, and emotionally responsive to each other. The consequence of this collective empathy, then, is that it influences the learning behaviors, in this case among software development teams. They observed that when team members understood and shared each other's feelings they were more effective at discovering and correcting software product-related issues and problems in the workplace.

In addition to the influence that collective empathy had on learning behaviors, it also influenced the ability of the project team to develop and implement products much faster in terms of speed-to-market. The management of emotions and collective empathy within the project team contributed to faster implementation and production over and above the use of advanced technology for information processing and dissemination. But there is more.

In addition to the influence that collective empathy had on learning behaviors and speed-to market production, it also contributed to a reduction in development costs. As the ability to adapt and take advantage of shared feelings developed among team members, there was an observed reduction in quality control problems, redundancies, and the need to rework elements of the product, which ultimately reduced the implementation and software development costs. In summary, then, Akgün et al. observed that collective empathy accounted for 28% of the variability in team learning, 15% of the variability in speed-to-market production, and 7% of the variance in reduced development costs.

There are other examples of research evidence demonstrating that leaders strongly influenced their subordinates' feelings of frustration and feelings of optimism, which in turn influenced objective sales performance (McColl-Kennedy & Anderson, 2002). Pirola-Merlo, Haertel, Mann, and Hirst (2002) also found that leaders had a strong impact on affective team climate, which in turn influenced team performance.

External Benefits for the Role of Empathy in the Workplace

Global Collaboration

Empathy must be at the core of any collaborative effort involving cross-cultural teams. Empathy extends well beyond feeling to understanding, and it extends beyond individuals to groups, and communities of people. Empathy is a key feature of clear judgment and rational decision-making in the context of effective global collaboration because empathy is a core component of individual and collective values that are the foundation of shared sense of justice.

Collaboration from a cross-cultural perspective can be defined as the study of similarities and differences in the processes and behavior at work across different cultures (cf. Gelfand, Erez, & Aycan, 2007). Unfortunately, despite rapid global commercialization of products in a dynamic and evolving global business environment, there is still limited attention to the process of addressing cultural differences. There is strong emphasis on understanding cultural differences with the intent to recognize and manage those differences. However, there is still little that is actually known about the process for optimizing the similarities and differences across cultures (Hinds, Liu, & Lyon, 2011).

When considering global innovation systems as social systems, there is a process of "social making" of innovations that can define a socially accepted space determined by cultural interactions including affective frames of identity and difference, cognitive frames of knowledge, and normative sets of values (Pohlmann, Gebhardt, & Etzkowitz, 2005). The development of a shared mental model and shared organizational climate that supports cross-cultural collaboration serve as important factors in sustaining global innovation. In order to fully understand cross-cultural team interactions, it is necessary to examine how disagreements, miscommunications, and critical incidents emerge. Cultural standards generally provide more insight on how critical incidents emerge because they show how critical incidents occur in the first place when choosing actions based on particular cultural standards and values and disregarding the values and standards of the other party. This is where empathic concern plays a valuable role in cross-cultural collaboration.

A project leader on cross-cultural collaborations will benefit greatly from skills that facilitate cultural empathy. For example, in global product innovation projects that involve cross-cultural collaborations, there is an inherent interdependence between global and local perspectives. If information and knowledge-sharing is directed from the global perspective to the local market, the local teams are in an implementation role and the collaboration process may collapse if the global perspective-taking does not include necessary elements of the culture for local execution.

Perspective-taking and empathy can be encouraged by promoting conversations that reveal people's experiences as they work through the challenges of working across cultures or languages. For example, in a study of cross-national teams that included members whose native language was German or English, few of the native English speakers recognized the struggle to communicate in English among some of their German colleagues (Neeley, Hinds, & Cramton, 2012). Likewise, the native German speakers were unaware of the feelings of exclusion and ostracism experienced by the non-German speaking colleagues when the Germans spoke their native language. Members from both cultures were open to changing their own behavior to be more accommodating once the issue was raised and discussed. Promoting transparency and candid sharing of experiences and emotions allows team members to empathize with each other. This reduces the emotional burden for everyone.

Jensen (2015) provides a case study illustration of the role that cultural empathy plays following a failed collaboration in which the local team did not feel the global project leader and management team were open or responsive to local customer needs. In that case, the global team developed an innovation strategy composed ofjoint planning with local teams to emphasize responsiveness in the local target market, but also as a way to build trust and values for transparent communication. Because the project leader from the global team invited local teams to participate in planning, local team members could actively collaborate and shape ideas for the global concept. This helped create a more collaborative approach for the project leader and resulted in a faster time to market, a localized product, increased customer demand, and motivation to launch and sell the new concept. Efforts to achieve these outcomes had failed until members of the global team exercised skills to facilitate cultural empathy. The us–them perspective that can sometimes be a barrier on cross-cultural teams, but empathy can buffer this attitude and enhance productivity.

Philanthropy and Social Impact

Corporate philanthropy in the professional workplace has been described as a marketing instrument that highlights the reputation of the company as a good corporate citizen (Brammer & Millington, 2005; Sen, Bhattacharya, & Korschun, 2006), or as a tool to manage financial benefits (Lev, Petrovits & Radhakrishnan, 2010). In contrast to this primarily top-down rational interpretation, researchers have increasingly recognized that, along with executive decision-makers, other employees are also important actors in corporate philanthropy (Kim, Lee, Lee, & Kim, 2010). Specifically, employees are important drivers of and participants in corporate philanthropy initiatives (Aguilera, Rupp, Williams, & Ganapathi, 2007). Employee involvement appears to be guided more by emotional mechanisms, such as collectively shared desire to help others in need, than by individual rational or cognitive considerations, such as job skills enhancement, or organizational rewards.

The notion of collective empathy has only recently been introduced and explicitly considered in relation to corporate philanthropy (Muller, Pfarrer, & Little, 2014) as a more participative approach that involves the influence that employees have on executive leadership decisions about philanthropic initiatives. Traditionally, corporate philanthropy decisions have often been limited by the same strategic and rational process that is used to make business decisions, rather than a broader perspective held by all stakeholders including employees and clients. In other words, corporate philanthropy decisions are largely purposeful decisions that align with the company's strategy. This is not necessarily a bad thing, but the reality in practice is that there remains a great deal of uncertainty in corporate philanthropy decisions. The connection between corporate philanthropy and organizational strategy and business objectives is not always clear. Moreover, there are few rules on when to engage in corporate giving, at what scale, or in what form. This ambiguity allows for the role of emotion in general, and empathy in particular, to influence corporate philanthropy decisions.

Consider that corporate social responsibility arises from a sense of altruism or prosocial behavior. As these acts of altruism are often based on feelings of empathy (Bar-Tal, 1976; Batson, 1987), the motivation to give is likely to be influenced by how the cause is perceived by the manager or executive decision-maker. Therefore, it is reasonable that managers rely on their own attitudes and feelings of social consciousness when making corporate philanthropic decisions. As stated by Brown and Ferris (2007), "Selfless or not, those acts involve a degree of compassion and commitment to others" (p. 85). Likewise, there is research evidence showing that when employees receive more positive attention from managers and supervisors in the professional workplace, management is viewed as more fair, just, and empathic (Cropanzano, Bowen, & Gilliland, 2007; Kellett et al., 2006). Further, this modeling of positive supervisory support can also prompt employees to advocate for prosocial helping behaviors beyond the workplace setting, including corporate philanthropy (Aguilera et al., 2007; Frey & Meier, 2004).

A model of collective empathy in corporate philanthropy decisions developed by Muller et al. (2014) is consistent with evidence showing the importance of empathy for helping behaviors outside organizational contexts (Batson, 1987; Frey & Meier, 2004). Psychologists and social scientists understand emotions as perceptual and motivational systems of feelings. We assign meaning to feelings as a result of an internal appraisal process that is followed by action tendencies that influence decision-making. The appraisal process and the action tendencies interrupt the cognitive thinking process and redirect our attention and judgment. By strengthening the bonds of group membership, shared emotions carry more powerful action tendencies than individual emotions (Barsade & Gibson, 2012). Given that leadership decisions can be influenced by shared mental models through rational and cognitive processes, but likely also by collective emotions (cf. Parkinson & Simons, 2009), collective empathy can influence leaders to make decisions that reflect empathic action tendencies of workers in the organization (Smith, Seger, & Mackie, 2007). Therefore, corporate philanthropy decisions are not exclusively purposeful, calculated, rational decisions made in isolation by strictly business minded corporate leaders (Grant, 2012; Marquis and Lee, 2013). Rather, corporate philanthropy decisions can be linked to shared empathic concerns of employees in the professional workplace with regards to their action tendencies to respond to the needs of individuals and groups external to the organization.

Conclusion

The role of empathy in the professional workplace has implications for organizational outcomes that are internal and external to the company. Empathy is generally defined as an ability or capacity to understand and experience the feelings, thoughts, and perspectives of another person. Empathy is a process of relating with others on a cognitive level of perspective-taking, and on an emotional level. Rational perspective-taking and emotional empathy, where one is attuned to the feelings and emotions of others, may be beneficial in a variety of professional workplace settings from local or global sales teams, to health professions, and in most management or leadership position.

The role of empathy in the professional workplace contributes to relationship building and the development of trust through more effective communication and collaboration. Therefore, empathy plays a role in service orientation when working with others as part of a team within an organization, or with individuals or project teams across organizational boundaries. This was discussed in the context of international or cross-cultural workplace environments. However, the role of empathy is also vital to other aspects of those professional work relationships that were not presented in this chapter due to space limitations. For example, empathy has a role in implementing initiatives for inclusion and diversity. Likewise, empathy plays a role in political awareness in the workplace when sensing and responding to power relationships in decision-making processes. Empathy as perspective-taking and emotional awareness is critical for negotiation strategies and conflict resolution as well. While there are many other possible implications, this chapter has underscored the role of empathy when it is embraced and practiced as an integral part of the professional workplace.

References

Aguilera, R. V., Rupp, D. E., Williams, C. A., & Ganapathi, J. (2007). Putting the S back in corporate social responsibility: A multilevel theory of social change in organizations. *Academy of Management Review, 32*, 836–863.

Akgün, A. E., Keskin, H., Cebecioglu, A. Y., & Dogan, D. (2015). Antecedents and consequences of collective empathy in software development project teams. *Information and Management, 52*, 247–259.

Bandura, A. (2001). Social cognitive theory: An agentic perspective. *Annual Review of Psychology, 52*, 1–26.

Barsade, S. G., & Gibson, D. E. (2012). Group affect: Its influence on individual and group outcomes. *Current Directions in Psychological Science, 21*(2), 119–123.

Bar-Tal, D. (1976). *Prosocial Behavior: Theory and Research*. Washington, DC: Hemisphere.

Batson, C. D. (1987). Prosocial motivation: Is it ever truly altruistic? *Advances in Experimental Social Psychology, 20*, 65–122.

Brammer, S., & Millington, A. (2005). Corporate reputation and philanthropy: An empirical analysis. *Journal of Business Ethics, 61*(1), 29–44.

Brown, E., & Ferris, J. M. (2007). Social capital and philanthropy: An analysis of the impact of social capital on individual giving and volunteering. *Nonprofit and Voluntary Sector Quarterly, 36*, 85–99.

Conrad, D., & Newberry, R. (2012). Identification and instruction of important business communication skills for graduate business education. *Journal of Education for Business, 87*, 112–120.

Coté, S., & Morgan, L. M. (2002). A longitudinal analysis of the association between emotion regulation, job satisfaction, and intentions to quit. *Journal of Organizational Behavior, 23*, 947–962.

Cropanzano, R., Bowen, D. E., & Gilliland, S. W. (2007). The management of organizational justice. *Academy of Management Perspectives, 21*, 34–48.

Dasborough, M. T., & Ashkanasy, N. M. (2002). Emotion and attribution of intentionality in leader–member relationships. *Leadership Quarterly, 13*, 615–634.

Davies, M., Stankov, L., & Roberts, R. D. (1998). Emotional intelligence: In search of an elusive construct. *Journal of Personality and Social Psychology, 75*, 989–1015.

Davis, M. H. (1983). Measuring individual differences in empathy: Evidence for a multidimensional approach. *Journal of Personality and Social Psychology, 44*, 113–126.

Frey, B. S., & Meier, S. (2004). Pro-social behavior in a natural setting. *Journal of Economic Behavior and Organization, 54*, 65–88.
Gelfand, M. J., Erez, M., & Aycan, Z. (2007). Cross-cultural organizational behavior. *Annual Review of Psychology, 58*, 479–514.
George, J. M. (2000). Emotions and leadership: The role of emotional intelligence. *Human Relations, 53*, 1027–1055.
Gooty, J., Connelly, S., Griffeth, J., & Gupta, A. (2010). Leadership, affect and emotions: A state of the science review. *Leadership Quarterly, 21*, 979–1004.
Gooty, J., Gavin, M. B., Ashkanasy, N. M., & Thomas, J. S. (2014). The wisdom of letting go and performance: The moderating role of emotional intelligence and discrete emotions. *Journal of Occupational and Organizational Psychology, 87*, 392–413.
Grant, A. M. (2012). Giving time, time after time: Work design and sustained employee participation in corporate volunteering. *Academy of Management Review, 37*, 589–615.
Hinds, P., Liu, L., & Lyon, J. (2011). Putting the global in global work: An intercultural lens on the practice of cross-national collaboration. *Academy of Management annals, 5*(1), 135–188.
Ickes, W., Stinson, L., Bissonnette, V., & Garcia, S. (1990). Naturalistic social cognition: Empathic accuracy in mixed-sex dyads. *Journal of Personality and Social Psychology, 59*, 730–742.
Jensen, K. R. (2015). Global innovation and cross-cultural collaboration: The influence of organizational mechanisms. *Management International/International Management, 19*, 101–116.
Jones, F., & Fletcher, B. (1993). An empirical study of occupational stress transmission in working couples. *Human Relations, 46*, 881–902.
Kellett, J. B., Humphrey, R. H., & Sleeth, R. G. (2006). Empathy and the emergence of task and relations leaders. *Leadership Quarterly, 17*, 146–162.
Kim, H. R., Lee, M., Lee, H. T., & Kim, N. M. (2010). Corporate social responsibility and employee–company identification. *Journal of Business Ethics, 95*, 557–569.
Kramer, M. W., & Crespy, D. A. (2011). Communicating collaborative leadership. *Leadership Quarterly, 22*, 1024–1037.
Lazarus, R. S. (1991). *Emotion and Adaptation*. New York: Oxford University Press.
Lev, B., Petrovits, C., & Radhakrishnan, S. (2010). Is doing good good for you? How corporate charitable contributions enhance revenue growth. *Strategic Management Journal, 31*(2), 182–200.
McColl-Kennedy, J. R., & Anderson, R. D. (2002). Impact of leadership style and emotions on subordinate performance. *Leadership Quarterly, 13*, 545–559.
Marquis, C., & Lee, M. (2013). Who is governing whom? Executives, governance, and the structure of generosity in large US firms. *Strategic Management Journal, 34*, 483–497.
Mayer, J. D., Salovey, P., Caruso, D. R., & Sitarenios, G. (2001). Emotional intelligence as standard intelligence. *Emotion, 1*, 232–242.
Miner, A. G., & Glomb, T. M. (2010). State mood, task performance, and behavior at work: A within-persons approach. *Organizational Behavior and Human Decision Processes, 112*(1), 43–57.
Muller, A. R., Pfarrer, M. D., & Little, L. M. (2014). A theory of collective empathy in corporate philanthropy decisions. *Academy of Management Review, 39*, 1–21.
Neeley, T. B., Hinds, P. J., & Cramton, C. D. (2012). The (un)hidden turmoil of language in global collaboration. *Organizational Dynamics, 41*, 236–244.
Newcombe, M. J., & Ashkanasy, N. M. (2002). The role of affect and affective congruence in perceptions of leaders. *Leadership Quarterly, 13*, 601–614.
Parkinson, B., & Simons, G. (2009). Affecting others: Social appraisal and emotion contagion in everyday decision making. *Personality and Social Psychology Bulletin, 35*(8), 1071–1084.
Pescosolido, A. T. (2002). Emergent leaders as managers of group emotion. *Leadership Quarterly, 13*, 583–599.
Pirola-Merlo, A., Haertel, C., Mann, L., & Hirst, G. (2002). How leaders influence the impact of affective events on team climate and performance in R&D teams. *Leadership Quarterly, 13*, 561–581.
Pohlmann, M., Gebhardt, C., & Etzkowitz, H. (2005). The development of innovation systems and the art of innovation management: Strategy, control and the culture of innovation. *Technology Analysis and Strategic Management, 17*(1), 1–7.
Salovey, P., & Mayer, J. (1990). Emotional intelligence. *Imagination, Cognition, and Personality, 9*, 185–211.
Sen, S., Bhattacharya, C. B., & Korschun, D. (2006). The role of corporate social responsibility in strengthening multiple stakeholder relationships: A field experiment. *Journal of the Academy of Marketing science, 34*(2), 158–166.

Smith, E. R., Seger, C. R., & Mackie, D. M. (2007). Can emotions be truly group level? Evidence regarding four conceptual criteria. *Journal of Personality and Social Psychology, 93*(3), 431–446.

Starcevic, V., & Piontek, C. M. (1997). Empathic understanding revisited: Conceptualization, controversies, and limitations. *American Journal of Psychotherapy, 51*, 317–328.

Stotland, E. (1969). Exploratory investigations of empathy. In L. Berkowitz (Ed.), *Advances in Experimental Social Psychology* (Vol. 4). New York: Academic Press, 271–314.

Vignemont, F., & Singer, T. (2006). The empathic brain: How, when and why? *Trends in Cognitive Sciences, 10*, 435–441.

Weiss, H. M., & Cropanzano, R. (1996). Affective events theory: A theoretical discussion of the structure, causes and consequences of affective experiences at work. In B. M. Staw & L. L. Cummings (Eds.), *Research in Organizational Behavior: An Annual Series of Analytical Essays and Critical Reviews* (Vol. 18). Greenwich, CT: JAI Press, 1–74.

Westman, M. (2001). Stress and strain crossover. *Human Relations, 54*, 717–751.

Wolff, S. B., Pescosolido, A. T., & Druskat, V. U. (2002). Emotional intelligence as the basis of leadership emergence in self-managing teams. *Leadership Quarterly, 13*, 505–522.

Wong, C., & Law, K. S. (2002). The effects of leader and follower emotional intelligence on performance and attitude. *Leadership Quarterly, 13*, 243–274.

World Economic Forum. (2016). *The Future of Jobs: Employment, Skills and Workforce Strategy for the Fourth Industrial Revolution*. Geneva, Switzerland. Retrieved from www3.weforum.org/docs/WEF_FOJ_Executive_Summary_Jobs.pdf.

22

LEADING IN TIMES OF CULTURAL DIVERSITY

Achieving Wellbeing, Inclusivity, and Organizational Performance

Wanda Krause

Introduction

At its basic level, wellbeing is about personal happiness—feeling good, healthy, working safely, and achieving productivity. Recognizing and embracing diversity means to be inclusive. An inclusive environment has everything to do with wellbeing. Yet, it is still little understood that if a company or an organization wants to thrive in the long term, keep a competitive edge, and make a difference in some key way, wellbeing must be an immediate organizational imperative. Indeed,

> [hu]manity needs to cultivate sustainability practitioners with the skills and capacities to engage and work effectively with complexity; to be adaptive, creative, and generative; to collaborate with diverse stakeholders; and to communicate effectively with a diversity of worldviews and value systems.
>
> *(Lynam, 2014, p. 3)*

Gallup has illustrated the link between wellbeing and workplace performance. Yet, according to a 2013 Gallup poll, in the US more than two in three workers are unhappy in their jobs with 52% of US workers "not engaged," meaning that even if they don't actively hate their jobs, they're unhappy and don't invest themselves in their job. Another 18% are "actively disengaged," meaning they can't stand their jobs and sometimes even sabotage co-workers or their companies. As our workplaces become more diverse, organizational leaders and management will have to grapple with how to lead with the values and qualities it will take when it comes to ensuring wellbeing for a diverse group of people with differing cultures, backgrounds, or religion, among so many more attributes that make us all different.

As such, leaders are recognizing that it is critical to create an environment where individuals can enjoy equal opportunity, dignity, and wellbeing. Thus, how might leaders and managers bridge this knowledge with capability to create the culturally safe and inclusive environment where individuals thrive? Research also shows that diversity in the workplace can contribute to better performance. How might organizational leaders and managers grappling with conflicts in the workplace around cultural differences in teamwork and perspectives harness this knowledge to move past differences and potential sites of conflict to greater performance? The real question then becomes: what values and qualities do we need to possess as organizational leaders and managers to achieve cultural diversity, individual wellbeing, and better performance? Bias and preference related to sameness as part of our human prejudices might be limiting our ability to answer this question and put into practice what it takes to ensure wellbeing and inclusion in our organizations. I propose that by overcoming misunderstandings and biases to learn how to lead in times of intensifying cultural diversity, we can be well positioned to create wellbeing for all. We know how to harness diversity in the workplace which then leads to greater ability to problem solve, be creative, build strong teams, achieve organizational performance, and sustainability.

Why Achieving a Culture of Wellbeing and Inclusion is Critical for Performance

Embracing diversity is the first and critical step to team building and creating sustainability within organizations. Wellbeing in the workplace includes physical, mental, emotional, psychological, and community wellbeing and, therefore, to be *well* is largely about being inclusive. It's about individual wellbeing and collective wellbeing. It relates to feeling safe and expressing oneself creatively and purposefully without fear of repression, prejudice, and exclusion. Economic growth as the ultimate goal has dominated company strategy but cannot remain the end goal if companies hope to survive into the coming decades. Yet, people tend to have a bias toward sameness both in their personal and professional lives. It would seem that when people can all agree on issues that teamwork is simpler and smoother but when people from diverse cultures, backgrounds, and experiences come together they offer more varied perspectives and experiences that are essential for continued growth and creativity of the collective. There are several further reasons why it is essential to consider why achieving a culture of wellbeing and inclusion is critical for the health of an organization, its sustainability, and its impact in the economy or wider world, as described in this section.

We begin with individual wellbeing and performance. High performers cannot sustain their output in a company culture where they are driven to keep producing under pressure and stress. Human beings are not machines; they will become ill, costing the economy in medical care and the organization in low performance and sick leave. If conditions do not enable wellbeing, the organization will be used as a stepping stone for something better. People are increasingly fed up with putting nose to grind with no joy or purpose, as illustrated through people increasingly leaving paid employment to start up their own businesses. Clients of mine and of colleagues are increasingly seeking out support not just around life coaching but more so on two levels—purposefully to brainstorm, plan out, and strategize how they can leave their stressful jobs to becoming their own bosses making a bigger impact around issues they can finally give voice to and to discover and learn how to create stronger relationships for which they have long not exercised skills or created capacities. They are seeking ways to live more purposefully and impactfully from an experience of exclusion, overwork, and lack of a sense of being valued. They will leave the organization, also forcing the organization to rehire and retrain, and the organization will not attract and retain talent. A lack of wellbeing can be costly to the organization.

Emerging leaders require nurturing. Indeed, in every individual is a leader, regardless of a defined role, although not all individuals experience being seen and valued as contributors to their organization and the world. Evidence has shown that leaders rarely emerge on their own but through an environment and culture that value and nurture their potentials. Employers are wasting opportunities for nurturing talent within their organization, and likely contributing to individuals "not engaged" if not "actively disengaged" if they're not actively creating a culture of wellbeing, engagement, and inclusion. Overworking is correlated with lower performance.

Putting off addressing underlying causes for burnout, the related retention issues, and lack of engagement is costing, and costing not just money but individual willingness to go the extra mile for the team or organization when needed.

There are numerous studies that show the impact of adequate sleep over a period of time on physical performance. In a study appearing in *SLEEP*, Cheri Mah, a researcher in the Stanford Sleep Disorders Clinic and Research Laboratory, showed that basketball players at the elite college level were able to improve their on-the-court performance by increasing their amount of total sleep time. Those players who got more sleep saw their free-throw shooting go up by 9% and their three-point shooting go up by 9.2%. Results are similar regarding mental performance. Amazon CEO Jeff Bezos (2017) explains:

> Making a small number of key decisions well is more important than making a large number of decisions. If you shortchange your sleep, you might get a couple of extra "productive" hours, but that productivity might be an illusion. When you're talking about decisions and interactions, quality is usually more important than quantity.

Good cognitive functioning, including decision-making under conditions of uncertainty, are directly correlated to sleep (Killgore, Balkin, & Wesensten, 2006). Good cognitive function is critical for good leadership and performance.

As a result, leaders, such as Arianna Huffington, are teaching organizations to embrace such key aspects to individual wellbeing and performance in the workplace as sleep. Huffington (2017) reasons, "If performance at your job or in your life involves focus, attention, decision-making, productivity, creativity, resilience or learning, sleep can be just as effective as a performance enhancer in your life." But sleep is one part to wellbeing. In the *Training Journal*, Derek Mowbray (2013) says,

> The ingredients for feeling well are clustered around having a purpose in life, feeling personal success and happiness in relation to a number of key elements—relationships, resources, the environment, personal growth, personal control and other items that individuals feel are important to them.

He adds, "if [people] cannot focus and concentrate on completing a task, they are not performing effectively."

In addition to her own research, Caroline Mbaabu cites several studies conducted in workplaces to track the performance of individuals who engaged in workplace wellness activities and found that "that majority of employees who participated in physical fitness programmes had above average performance, lower rates of absenteeism, higher commitment to work, and lower employee turnover" (2013, p. 15). Some of her research showed enormous increases in performance. According to Mowbray (2013), the link between wellbeing and performance is that people who feel well usually feel in control of themselves and so it's the attitude that determines the level of performance. Strategy is also of importance. Results-oriented people, instead of simply being "busy," have the greatest results. According to Benjamin Hardy (2016), it is important to have "intensive activity followed by high quality rest and recovery." That means that one focuses on the goal and does what is needed in order to reach that goal in intensive spurts.

Similarly, creativity doesn't happen by working long hours to get through tasks and figure things out, but instead requires those spaces in between for the brain to wander and the person to reflect. Hardy adds, "when you're working, be at work. When you're not working, stop working. By taking your mind off work and actually recovering, you'll get creative breakthroughs related to your work." But such practice requires that leaders trust that individuals can have the capacity to self-manage their own energy and time and invest in capacity development to support such practice. In the *Harvard Business Review*, Ron Friedman (2015) says we need to reframe why we are disengaging at the end of the day. He explains, it's much like exercise where we are doing something that is not just for your own personal, selfish benefit, but rather something that can help us be more effective at work. He emphasizes that the people who don't disengage, the people who are constantly checking their emails on evenings and on weekends, are the ones who tend to be less engaged a year later—because they're burnt out. Thus, how do we create individual and organizational wellbeing as well as the inclusion of diverse people?

One key is creating a shared understanding of the benefits of wellbeing not only to one's own life but to the enhancement of those one shares one's life with, one's team, and the good of one's whole organization. Hence, another key includes the supports that an organization can create for everyone to practice wellbeing, and the supports that must necessarily be put in place, such as through a buddy system where individuals take on responsibility to support each other. Further, while leaders can build supports within the workplace, they can also work toward building the right mindset and culture supportive of wellbeing that the individual takes outside work, too. Such is a leap in reframing. But as Hardy (2016) also points out, "what you do outside work is just as significant for your work-productivity as what you do while you're working." In his TED talk, Stuart Brown (2008) refers to a large body of literature on the role play has on the brain and performance. But for wellbeing to really become a value, organizational leaders would need to embrace this value as something that is a life skill and capacity, exercised in and outside the work environment.

Changing organizational culture is one of the hardest tasks for any leader. But when we have a shared understanding of what wellbeing means to us as individuals and as a collective in an organization, and have critical social supports in place, we can be well placed to keep disciplined in reaching and maintaining wellbeing and inclusion as values. All cultures are based on value systems and to create change in any value system takes a common framework, support, and discipline until wellbeing and inclusion of diverse ways of being is an intrinsic value. There will be times ahead in an increasingly turbulent world when the market share sees even greater competition but that is when we will need to rely on individual wellbeing and engaged individuals to make it through. Individual wellbeing and diversity is the new model for economic growth that leading organizations are now embracing.

The Values Required for Wellbeing and Inclusivity in Leading through Greater Diversity

As our organizations become increasingly diverse, workplace culture around wellbeing and inclusivity is a key determinant of how valued and supported people feel in their roles and how productive the organization becomes. Hence, we need to ask what values we need to embody or, essentially, who we need to become in order to enhance how well and included people feel in their organizations. Employee and team relationships are much like any personal relationship. From this basis, we can grasp how important it is to create conditions and opportunities that enable wellbeing to occur and inclusivity to be felt that are embedded in values that we share similarly in our personal relationships. These include foremost trust, belonging, and reciprocity.

The values of trust, belonging, and reciprocity support one another. When there is a sense that the leadership and staff at all levels invest in building trust and belonging, employees are inspired to reciprocate with greater investment in the organization. Practices that support belonging, trust, and reciprocity, in turn boost productivity. When employees feel they have contributed shared perspectives on how well they feel in their workplace, leaders will have greater success at creating a culture of wellbeing and sustained productivity. Such is achieved by including everyone's ideas, input, experiences, and wishes for how they feel they can get on board with their own wellness, and also how to support each other to achieve wellness and a sense of safety.

Even if well meaning, when ideas of wellbeing and inclusion are imposed, leaders may discover few are on board. In one workplace, the owner generously bought every individual a year's pass to the gym in the same building as a Christmas present. But nearly no one went to the gym. Some employees felt guilty that money was wasted on something they didn't want and the company owner was mad at everyone that she wasted the money. Resentment grew on both sides. Had she solicited feedback on what wellness looked like and what would support different notions of wellness, she would have had different results. Getting everyone on board by gathering a shared understanding of what wellbeing looks like is step one. Had she explored further she might have discovered that some individuals would prefer to exercise in nature, rather than a gym, or at times that were not connected to work. She might have discovered, too, that some people might feel exercising in public, not least at the workplace with co-workers, might be uncomfortable, if not even a cultural oddity, or even taboo. When our ideas around the experiences we want for our own happiness are heard, we feel valued.

Having conversations with people about what people want has everything to do with trusting that they know. When people feel trusted, their motivation to achieve things in the workplace tends to come from the inside, rather than the outside. As a leader, the best approach to ensuring performance is to inspire and motivate. The inducements and punishments approach is still evident in most organizations and awareness around how those methods miss the objective of facilitating belonging and trust is key. Trust must be an objective if leaders want to facilitate wellbeing, sense of inclusion, and one's voice being heard. While few leaders would argue against trust being necessary for performance, many still view trust-building as a "soft" or "secondary" competency (Covey & Covant, 2016). Covey and Covant remind us "It's not a nice-to-have; it's a must-have. Without it, every part of your organization can fall, literally, into disrepair. With trust, all things are possible—most importantly: continuous improvement and sustainable, measurable, tangible results in the marketplace." In one study published in the *Journal of Happiness Studies* (Helliwell & Huang, 2011), an increase of trust in management at one-tenth of the scale was equivalent to more than 30% increase in monetary income.

The Great Place to Work Institute partnered with *Fortune* to produce the "100 Best Companies to Work For" in which trust comprised two-thirds of the criteria. They similarly found that those companies beat "the average annualized returns of the S&P 500 by a factor of three" (Fortune 100, 2017). Covey and Covant (2016) explain how trust affects two measurable outcomes, speed and cost: "When trust goes down (in a relationship, on a team, in an organization, or with a partner or customer), speed goes down and cost goes up." All leaders need to consider trust-building as a key component to employees' positive experience and sense of wellbeing.

Reciprocity is enhanced when one is feeling valued and supported which correlates to better performance. Social reciprocity goes far beyond "you scratch my back and I'll scratch yours." It's a means to effective collaboration. Effective collaboration is where each person brings their strengths, capacities, experience, assets, and value to the table that another does not have and can benefit from. In this sense, each person adds to effectiveness by sharing what he or she uniquely can bring and receiving what others uniquely can bring in a relationship of any form. But reciprocity is almost a natural response to feeling included, trusted, their ideas heard, their presence embraced. This aspect to collaboration and performance is often overlooked but has comprised one of my biggest research findings among the organizations I have studied where people facilitate the changes they want to see, especially in challenging situations and environments.

Studies illustrate the connection between reciprocity and performance that organizational leaders will need to consider. Economists show that employers who are perceived as distributionally fair by their employees generate comparatively more value due to the positively reciprocal behavior of those employees (Bosse, Phillips, & Harrison, 2009). But it's not just fairness that is critical to higher performance but rather the mentality of giving in a relationship, whether a personal one or within an organization, where service entails that you bring your best to the table for the betterment of others and the benefit of the whole. As Englmaier, Kolaska, and Leider (2015) conclude through their research, by practicing reciprocity as a value employees develop more team-working and are generally more successful. Hence, performance in the organization is directly related to the values of reciprocity, trust, giving, collaboration, being included, and being valued.

Creating and Embracing a Culture of Wellbeing and Diversity

There are steps leaders can take to enable the development of a culture of wellbeing, engagement, and inclusivity among diverse groups in the organization supportive of productivity, impact, and/or profit.

Define Wellbeing, Inclusivity, and Diversity

For leaders to create awareness and demonstrate wellbeing and inclusivity, it is important to be clear on what the workplace needs in order to be inclusive in practice and not just in theory. It helps if leaders define what wellbeing, inclusivity, and the embracing of diversity means to them and all individuals in the organization by holding conversations around these topics. Leaders often focus on best practices and strategies to the neglect of engagement with the very people in the organization that any changes or adoption of new practices and strategies impact. Defining wellbeing and what it means to be inclusive involves a process of inquiry and engagement with individuals. Inquire into what wellness, happiness, safety, and health means to individuals within the organization. Surveys also comprise a favorite tool among employers and those they consult to collect data for change management. They are usually cheap to administer, quick to answer, and quick to tabulate, given their quantitative nature. While surveys further offer the safety of anonymity, they do not allow leaders to truly engage. The crux of engagement is the conversations that can emerge through the lengthier process of inquiry and circular discussions that can go in unexpected and new directions. Leaders cannot design steps toward and get buy-in for wellbeing and inclusivity if they do not know how everyone defines wellbeing and inclusivity in the complexity and breadth of developing the capacities and practices for enhancing these values.

Diversity is not simply about color, race, ethnicity, gender, sexual orientation, religion, age, or educational level. Lynam explains there is a "hidden form of diversity," which Drago-Severson calls "the new pluralism", that functions like an internal operating system in the individual (cited in Lynam, 2014, p. 51). Diversity must be recognized in a much broader spectrum. It includes disabilities and various challenges. It includes approaches and ways of learning information—it's not just about speed of learning. Diversity critically encompasses the logic a person holds to make sense of the world and process information, which differs from person to person. Lynam also points out that "[ho]w adults make meaning, how they respond to different educational experiences, and their capacities for and styles of self-reflection, self-direction, and collaborative learning are all significantly influenced by a … developmental stage" (2014, p. 54). Some people are introverts and others extroverts, and while this is one aspect to the way people show up in teamwork and life, it is also essential to understand therefore the different areas for growth and development that individuals want and need. Some individuals exhibit a need for control of their environment and even people. Others are contemplative or thinkers, while others are doers, or tend to delegate, collaborate better, or are highly trusting of their colleagues, etc. People show up differently depending on training, experience, personality, character, psychological make up, and a variety of other reasons. It is important to have conversations about and explore what these differences are from a place of understanding. It is essential to explore how to embrace and support people with their differences so that they feel safe, well, honored, respected, and can perform to their greatest capacities. In sum, the work environment should be one in which people can become their greater versions of themselves continuously.

Create Awareness

Leaders can help their organization understand the utility of wellbeing and inclusivity by linking these to values which staff, or influencers within and related to the organization, hold. There is a readiness to get on board that starts with awareness. For example, if a "why" for the administration, stakeholders, or shareholders is "profit" it helps to make the connection to wellbeing explicit by pointing to the outcome of greater individual productivity and capacity modeled in other organizations or among teams in the same organization when a culture embracing of wellbeing and diversity is supported. If a "why" is increasing performance, leaders can point to the value of diversity or the value of wellbeing within the organization to it doing better in growing its market share or doing better at achieving the impacts it envisions, among which includes statistics. There are different levels of awareness that people can hold depending on the logics they hold about the world and their place in it. Ultimately, leaders should strive to work with the higher levels of logic around wellbeing and diversity, such as embracing these as a moral imperative or as human values for dignity. However, creating awareness might also require coming from a utilitarian perspective if biases toward sameness to the exclusion of others who are different has been a strong aspect of the company culture.

Model Wellbeing and Inclusion

All cultures are based on value systems and to create change in any value system takes a common framework, institutional and social support, and, above all, discipline in modeling the value until it is an intrinsic value. Leaders will need to be bold in demonstrating that wellbeing is important by carving wellbeing into their day as daily practice. In other words, leading in times of cultural diversity entails modeling wellbeing and inclusion. Modeling wellbeing comes in the forms of ensuring physical wellbeing to how we interact with one another and make choices that affect others. Considering how physical wellbeing affects productivity, the countries performing the highest have the shortest workdays. Seven countries among those with the highest GDP rank have the fewest working hours. They include Luxembourg, then Norway, Switzerland, Netherlands, Germany, Denmark, and Sweden. However, we still live in a culture of bragging about how hard we work and how little we sleep to work. But bragging is actually a sign that one is not performing. In a 2015 interview, LinkedIn's Chief Human Resource Officer, Pat Wadors tells us:

> Trust me, it's not a badge of honor to brag that you can get by on 4 hours or 5 each night … You intimate that with fewer hours "wasted on sleep" you are more

> productive. Nope. Can't buy that. When you brag about that, you are telling me that it's ok for you to harm your health and not perform your best at work or at home. Is that something to brag about?
>
> *(Cited in Huffington, 2017)*

Modeling physical wellbeing might require taking major steps outside company culture and the country context in which we live to embrace wellbeing. This could be from initiating structural changes within the organization to providing example on how one lives one's work–life balance. Modeling wellbeing includes leading through a stressful company culture with examples of how one creates work–life balance and leading others on how to do the same by providing opportunity. Leading means modeling not only how one lives the values of wellbeing and inclusivity but by actually creating opportunities and means for all to be included, taking steps to provide different ways to learn, personal development time to learn and be creative, and making the embracing of diversity an imperative through advocating for organizational policy and in personal action.

To lead in embracing a culture of diversity, leaders will need to design where and how they will nurture seeds and take bold steps for wellbeing and inclusivity. Leading in this era means being a transformational leader because organizations are just beginning to recognize the need to embrace diversity as a value. Such, then, requires planning on how one can position him/herself within the organization, model the way, and introduce these concepts within the organization's culture, policies, and structure. A strategic plan in consultation with individuals will be important so that one can set a vision, mission, expectations, actionable steps, and therefore garner buy-in. Within such planning at such times, leading effectively can best occur through indices for monitoring success in changing organizational culture to the embracing of wellbeing and diversity. Monitoring starts with evaluating how one is leading and the milestones one is achieving. Because leading these changes is about transforming old systems of making profit and this as central focus requires control as method of leading versus embracing a new system of balance, wellbeing, and inclusion, leaders will have to take care to not get burned out in the process, by practicing wellbeing and balance. There will be times creating awareness and getting buy-in might feel like one is pushing upstream. But the process must be sustainable and as a result monitoring and evaluation must begin with oneself.

Conclusions

Organizations need greater diversity in order to grow and keep their competitive edge in the marketplace and in the world. This is at a time when the world is fast changing and, as a result, solutions to emerging challenges require a greater breadth of perspectives, experiences, and individual propensities. However, as our workplaces become more diverse, leaders are challenged to create the culturally safe and inclusive environments where diversity may be embraced so that all individuals experience dignity, respect, and can thrive and truly contribute. Leading in times of increasing diversity requires learning and embodying the qualities to lead during these challenging times for the success of individuals within their organizations and the sustainability and impact of their organizations in the world. The qualities and values important for leading through such times include, critically, awareness, trust, reciprocity, and giving as corner stones to wellbeing and inclusivity, and modeling the way to wellbeing and inclusivity. To lead in embracing a culture of diversity, further, requires a transformational role where leaders imbue the critical values and introduce concepts of wellbeing and diversity within the organization's culture, policies, and structure.

Leading into the future with these qualities, values, and planning processes is a moral imperative as much as it is the only real means for continued and sustained organizational performance. In other words, embracing wellbeing and diversity is the right thing to do. Working toward progress will indeed be challenging as leaders are transforming old approaches, systems, and paradigms around impacts and profit to new ways of thinking, acting, and being in their organizations around wellbeing, balance, and inclusion, and even profit itself. Such will require sticking to values of wellbeing and inclusion from a developmental perspective that will often be slow, challenged by those who fear change, fear cultural diversity, and fear the new perspectives that cultural diversity will force to emerge. The process will require that they challenge their own perspectives and biases. Such encompasses changing attitudes toward others and around other perspectives that are often rooted deeply in culture. Yet, changing attitudes and developing broader perspectives will need to come first before decision-makers can grasp the utility of changing organizational policies and structure.

Leading in times of cultural diversity is truly a purposeful and noble endeavor. One is not only taking on the task of ensuring success of his or her organization and creating safe environments where individuals can exercise the human right to live in dignity in diversity. Such a leader is facilitating the development of individual awareness and growth into greater humanity when individuals are growing into greater versions of themselves by breaking past bias and limitation into acquiring greater development, perspective and awareness. Steps to achieve these transformations include, at the basic level: engagement in defining wellbeing inclusivity and diversity; encouragement of expression; creating awareness around these concepts and the utility of wellbeing and inclusion; and at the very least, though most critically, modeling the way for wellbeing and inclusion.

References

Bezos, J. (2017, November). Why getting 8 hours of sleep is good for Amazon shareholders. Retrieved from https://journal.thriveglobal.com/jeff-bezos-sleep-amazon-19c617c59daa.

Bosse, D. A., Phillips, R. A., & Harrison, J. S. (2009). Stakeholders, reciprocity, and firm performance. *Strategic Management Journal, 30*(4), 447–456.

Brown, S. (2008, May). Play is more than just fun. TED talk. Retrieved from www.ted.com/talks/stuart_brown_says_play_is_more_than_fun_it_s_vital?language=en.

Covey, S., & Covant, D. (2016, July). The connection between employee trust and financial performance. Retrieved from https://hbr.org/2016/07/the-connection-between-employee-trust-and-financial-performance.

Englmaier, F., Kolaska, T., & Leider, S. (2015, January). Reciprocity in organisations: Evidence from the WERS. CESifo Working Paper Series No. 5168.

Fortune 100. (2017). Fortune 100 best companies to work for. Retrieved from www.greatplacetowork.com/best-workplaces/100-best/2017.

Friedman, R. (2015, March). Your brain's ideal schedule. *Harvard Business Review*. Retrieved from https://hbr.org/ideacast/2015/03/your-brains-ideal-schedule.html.

Gallup. (2013, October). Worldwide, 13% of employees are engaged at work. Retrieved from www.gallup.com/poll/165269/worldwide-employees-engaged-work.aspx.

Hardy, B. (2016, August). This morning routine will save you 20+ hours per week. *Mission*. Retrieved from https://medium.com/the-mission/how-to-structure-your-day-for-optimal-performance-and-productivity-dcbf0665e3f3#.cmq1lmhw7.

Helliwell, J., & Huang, H. (2011). Well-being and trust in the workplace. *Journal of Happiness Studies, 12*(5), 747–767.

Huffington, A. (2017). 10 years ago I collapsed from burnout and exhaustion, and it's the best thing that could have happened to me. Retrieved from https://journal.thriveglobal.com/10-years-ago-i-collapsed-from-burnout-and-exhaustion-and-its-the-best-thing-that-could-have-b1409f16585d.

Killgore, W., Balkin, D., & Wesensten, T. J. (2006, March 15). Impaired decision making following 49 hours of sleep deprivation. *Journal of Sleep Deprivation*, 7–13.

Lynam, A. (2014). *Embracing developmental diversity: Developmentally aware teaching, mentoring, and sustainability education*. (Doctor of Philosophy dissertation), Prescott College in Sustainability Education.

Mah, C. D., Mah, K. E., Kezirian, E. J., & Dement, W. C. (2011). The effects of sleep extension on the athletic performance of collegiate basketball players. *SLEEP, 34*(7), 943–950.

Mbaabu, C. (2013). Effect of workplace recreation on employee wellbeing and performance: A case of the commission or University Education (CUE). Research Project report submitted to School of Business Kenyatta University. Retrieved from http://irlibrary.ku.ac.ke/bitstream/handle/123456789/10165/Effect%20of%20workplace%20recreation%20on....pdf?sequence=1.

Mowbray, D. (2013). Performance is all about wellbeing. *Training Journal*. Retrieved from www.trainingjournal.com/articles/feature/performance-about-wellbeing.

PART V

Treading a Spiritual Path Toward Stakeholders

23

WHERE ETHICS, SUSTAINABILITY, AND SPIRITUALITY MEET

The Holy Trinity or Dystopia of the Three Stooges?

Timothy Ewest

Introduction

The ethical landscape in America is currently marked by failure, primarily because most people live a solitary insular life resulting in a complacency which ignores justice toward the communities that surround (Allen, 2004). According to Putnam (1995) the collective common good which has acted as a foundation for personal and ethical community behavior is now waning. Ewest and Kliegl (2012) suggest the lack of concern for the common good is clearly evidenced by many businesses and those who lead them, through ongoing corruption (e.g., Wells Fargo account sandal), scandals concerning harassment (e.g., #metoo), and environmental apathy (e.g., Volkswagen cheating on emission standards). For more than a decade, public opinion of businesses suggests a trust-starved environment, and the belief that many businesses are detached from societal interests (Schwab, 2003).

Research suggests one solution would be to focus on leadership development which is essential for the implementation of corporate social responsibly (CSR) within firms (Lawrence & Beamish, 2012; Wirtenberg, Wirtenberg et al., 2008; Strand, 2011). But, if leaders are under no ethical obligation to act, they cannot be held accountable for taking responsibility for the environment or social issues. Moreover, leadership theories have done little to establish a theoretical connection between ethics and leadership (Ciulla, 2005; Ewest, 2018), thus offering no grounds for leadership accountability and ultimately no requirements for leaders to engage in CSR strategic initiatives. However, if leaders can be held accountable to essential elements of their own human nature, which alternatively for some is considered spirituality, such a connection would be both catalytic and synergistic. Yet, if these connections are simply positive projections, factious, and intended to foster and create buoyant expectations, then their connection may be comical.

This chapter explores the connections between sustainability, ethics, and spirituality. The chapter argues that if there are innate universal characteristics to human nature, they may provide a constraint to unethical behavior as well as a means to guide human behavior. The chapter then illustrates the polarities of the understandings and theories of human nature by delineating the classic debate between Foucault, representing an anti-essentialist perspective, and Chomsky, representing an essentialist perspective. The chapter resolves by considering how prosocial research, which posits human values as an essential innate and universal quality of human nature, may act as a means to build a case for the connection between spirituality, sustainability, and ethics.

Constrained to Our Human Nature

"Ethics" typically refers to innate knowledge of right/wrong, transcending culture, religion, and time. "Morals" typically draws from culture, religion, or rationality to create distinctions of right/wrong (Gill, 2014; Stackhouse, 1995). Ethics are thus a standard by which we tell humans who they "ought" to be, think, believe or do (Gill, 2014). In the case of using human nature, ethical or moral moorings within human nature suggest that whatever is endemic to our human nature is indicative and predicative of what humans should be thinking acting and behaving (Horodecka, 2014; Southwood, 2015). Scholars have argued that specific features of human nature, if consistent and universal, act as an ethical constraint for human behavior (Southwood, 2015).

But the theories regarding what human nature is, and the analogous ethical expectations, are wide ranging (Horodecka, 2014). Loptson (2006) in his book, *Theories of Human Nature*, accounts for numerous theories or perspectives on human nature coming from a variety of academic sources. For example, Loptson cites one Christian perspective on human nature would suggest man as inherently sinful, but as made in the image of a holy God. Other views include Aristotle, who believed that human nature should be defined by the ability to reason. Or, John Locke believes that humans are born as blank slates, and what or who they become is determined by outside forces (Loptson, 2006). Turek (2010) ossifies the various perspectives or concepts regarding human nature, suggesting man is either economic and rational, humanistic and altruistic, imperfect and egotistical, or emotional and social. Each concept for human nature corresponds with various assumptions about human nature. See Table 23.1.

But, regardless of the theory of human nature one posits, Horodecka (2014) argues that humans use these theories as a means to reduce complexity and provide an interpretative frame for their individual (self-concept) and in turn connect their personal ethics and expectations to this image. However, these various perspectives regarding human nature can be further reduced and possibly find the best codification in the philosophical positions of Foucault and Chomsky (Chomsky & Foucault, 2006).

Foucault and Chomsky, Essentialist and Non-Essentialist

The debate between Chomsky and Foucault considered what qualities are essential to being a human. Specifically, which human qualities if removed would mean humans would cease to be humans; and, therefore, these qualities would be essential to being human (Chomsky & Foucault,

Table 23.1 Concepts of Human Nature

Concepts of Human Nature				
Perspective	*Economic Man*	*Humanistic Man*	*Imperfect Man*	*Social Man*
Concept	Rationality is based on goals	Altruism, others directed, values driven behavior	Egoism, values the self and personal aspirations above others	Emotionality, not values or rationality driven instinctual responses

2006). However, if a quality can be removed, be changed, or have variance (e.g., height, weight, or ethnicity) then these human qualities are referred to as nonessential traits. Therefore, if the essence of the human can be determined, there can be corresponding ethical expectations regarding human actions, thoughts, feelings, or social interaction which make them "essentially" human. And, if the essence of humanity can be determined and agreed upon, then it acts as a constraint to human behavior (Ellis, 2014; Wilkin, 1999).

As mentioned earlier, the theories regarding human nature are wide ranging and nuanced, extending far back into the history of thought, yet two fundamental positions can ossify the plethora of other theories regarding our human nature; the essentialist perspective and anti-essentialist perspective. The essentialist believes that human nature is derived from external factors from our environment and has no fixed modality, and the second alternative suggests that our human nature is innate (e.g., reason, language) and thus common to us all as humans (Ellis, 2014; Wilkin, 1999).

Chomsky and Foucault held a televised debate in 1971, and both addressed the question "is there such a thing as innate human nature which is independent of experience and external influence?" (Chomsky & Foucault, 2006, p. 31) Each argued for two contrasting concepts of human nature; these two perspectives create a soliloquy for humans seeking their own interpretative frame (self-concept) for what human nature is, and also provides a foundation for ensuing personal ethics. Foucault and Chomsky understood the essence of human nature differently, Chomsky believing human nature was consistent and had elements that were fixed, while Foucault believed human nature was evolving; these two perspectives, essentialism and anti-essentialism, represent two modern distinctive polarities (Loptson, 2006; Wilkin, 1999).

Foucault argued from an anti-essentialist perspective, suggesting that human nature has no essential essence. As an anti-essentialist, Foucault believed that essentialists are too quick to reduce human phenomena, including people and institutions, to a single transcendent principle and then they used this single principle as an interpretative frame for various cultures, historical epochs, and societies. Essentialists argue that there are universal identifiers or characteristics which do not change over time, being part of our biology (neurology) or transcendent element (e.g., soul). The result of essentialist thinking, Foucault believed, was if one could ascribe universal characteristics or norms which applied to the human, then one could reduce individuals, states, institutions, and societies to these principles or norms and thus study them like any other scientific object. Alternatively, Foucault believed human nature to be formed by societal forces and nothing innate to the human (Chomsky & Foucault, 2006; Ellis, 2014; Wilkin, 1999).

Foucault believed that humans were at times controlled by repressive power, that is, some entity who has the power to force the individual to do as they demand. But, this power is secondary to normalizing power, since repressive power is dependent on coercion. However, normalizing power makes the individual want to do what we are required to do anyway without coercion. Normalizing power occurs when individuals accept the characteristics or norms of what the human is to be. Specifically, normalizing power has the ability to determine what is "normal," that is, how life should be lived. The sources of normalizing power come from multiple places such as family, institutions, and society. Thus, any attempt by the social sciences to define an essential human essence, or human nature, acts as a normalizing power, and marginalizes alternatives, which may be a more complex understanding, but possibly more accurate (Ellis, 2014; Wilkin, 1999).

But, for Foucault, the outcome of essentialist thinking has been to restrain human development, which he proposed is open-ended and limitless—echoing the thoughts of Nietzsche (Milchman & Rosenberg, 2018). Foucault understood human practices as contingent on a person's belief in restraints, arguing that humans' potential should not be understood as being limited or constrained by belief in normalized or innate human nature. In reality, the definition of human nature was a compilation of present external social forces and not of anything transcendent, inherent, or innate in the human condition—diversity and potential is the real nature of the human. Foucault argued if there are no innate human constraints, no transcendent principles, no common goal for humans, then human potential is a matter of human imagination and will power, and those who wish to change society must simply take power, ignoring justice, and endeavor to win. Justice, as a transcendent ideal did not exist, but was only an idea (Chomsky & Foucault, 2006; Ellis, 2014; Wilkin, 1999).

Chomsky understood the accusation of language was an innate component of human nature. Chomsky echoed *Plato's Problem*, which considered how people acquire language at an early age even with fragmented information (Goldstein, 2011). Children acquire language with relative ease, even though they have had no instruction regarding grammar. Thus Chomsky believed it was not possible to explain language acquisition from an anti-essentialist perspective, wherein the language acquisition would be derived by societal forces. Instead from a small set of existing structures in the brain, humans are able to generate an infinite number of sentences (Chomsky & Foucault, 2006; Ellis, 2014; Wilkin, 1999). Chomsky believed this evidence suggested the mind is composed of neural modes which have distinct functions or structures enabling concept recognition (Pylyshyn, 1991).

For Chomsky, the formation of language involved interchanges with society and objects that are real and independent of humans, but these interchanges were confined or constrained by innate modes within the mind. The existing exchange between the person and society, while free to be developed in diverse ways, was also constrained by the existing model neurological categories. A good society for Chomsky, unlike Foucault, was not one in which the person was untethered and free to personally develop, instead societies should equitably enable the development of individuals whose interchange with the world fosters personal development which had similitude among humans (Chomsky & Foucault, 2006; Ellis, 2014; Steele, 2012; Wilkin, 1999).

Chomsky's essentialist position was also representative of a realist position, wherein realists believe that ethical truths are reliant on and linked to the human state. Here ethics are universal, but not necessarily found in theistic or platonic ideals, but tied to the nature of human essence or existence, regarded as the naturalistic tradition (Ewest, 2017). The naturalist tradition of realism, constrains human behavior to agree upon universal features of characteristics (Lillehammer, 2002; Little, 1994; McNaughton, 1988). One such example comes from prosocial psychologist consideration of human value, wherein human values are regarded as innate and motivational, constraining and directing human behavior thus providing a means to ethically constrain human behavior (Schwartz & Bilsky, 1987).

Human Values Essential to Human Essence

Rokeach (1973) describes human values as being "desirable, trans-situational goals, varying in importance that serves as guiding principles in people's lives" (p. 21). Human values can be employed by humans as a motivator, being used instrumentally or alternatively, they can be used as desired end or ultimate goals, thus being terminal or an end goal. Rokeach identified 18 terminal values and 18 instrumental values. See Table 23.2.

Schwartz (1999), building off the work of Rokeach (1973), was also known for identifying human values, and argued there were 10 motivational or instrumental values and four terminal values, or values which act as objectives or goals. Each of the terminal values has specific motivational goals associated with it. Moreover, the four terminal goals stand in opposition to each other. For example, if someone is motivated by the value of Self-Direction and Stimulation,

Table 23.2 Rokeach Human Values

Terminal Values	*Instrumental Values*
True	Cheerfulness
Mature love	Ambition
Self-respect	Love
Happiness	Cleanliness
Inner harmony	Self-control
Equality	Capability
Freedom	Courage
Pleasure	Politeness
Social recognition	Honesty
Wisdom	Imagination
Salvation	Independence
Family security	Intellect
National security	Broad-mindedness
A sense of accomplishment	Logic
World of beauty	Obedience
A world at peace	Helpfulness
A comfortable life	Responsibility
An exciting life	Forgiveness

they have as an end goal, Openness to Change, but their values oppose Conservationism, which is motivated by antithetical values of Security, Conformity, and Tradition. See Table 23.3. Again, Schwartz believed that these values were in keeping with the naturalist tradition of realism, were universal, and apply to all humans.

The research of Rokeach (1973) and Schwartz (1999) demonstrate the full range of innate motivational human values, which predict, describe, confine, and direct human behavior, including ethical behavior. In Rokeach' s model, two end goals, a World of Beauty and World at Peace represent values which have direct and positive impacts on others. Alternatively, Schwartz understood benevolence and universalism as the two values which motivate ethical behavior in others. These ethical innate human values, Batson (2010) argues, are the result of an empathic response, that is, a human being able to understand the needs, suffering of another in distress.

Batson (2010) suggests that all other directed ethical or prosocial behavior is the result of an empathic response. Batson uses the terms empathy and altruism to identify what Schwartz (1999) labeled as the terminal value of Self-Transcendence and Rokeach (1973) labeled Beauty

Table 23.3 Schwartz Human Values

Motivational Value	*Terminal Values*
Self-direction, stimulation	Openness to change (opposes conservatism)
Hedonism, achievement, power	Self-enhancement (opposes self-transcendence)
Security, conformity, tradition	Conservatism (opposes openness to change)
Benevolence, universalism	Self-transcendence (opposes self-enhancement)

and World at Peace. Batson posits empathy as being instrumental, whereby a person feels sympathy, compassion, or tenderness toward a person in need, and altruism as the terminal goal which seeks the welfare of the other person.

These three researchers, among others, suggest innate human values are motivational and essential qualities of human nature, thus supporting a naturalist tradition of realism, and a correspondingly and essentialist perspective regarding human nature. Specifically, the research of Batson (2010), who suggested the motivational state of empathy and suggested empathic response, has been evidenced in neuroscience research on mirror neurons (Decety, Jackson, Sommerville, Chaminade, & Meltzoff, 2004; Lieberman, Gaunt, Gilbert, & Trope, 2002). Consequently, the implication for human nature, is that empathetic response is an essential, biological aspect of the human being; thus, representative of the essentialist position, and does allow for the possibility of ethical guidance if not constraint of unethical human behavior. But, how this relates to sustainability and spirituality needs to be addressed.

Prosocial Ethical Values, Sustainability, and Spirituality

Research has indicated that executives and key organizational leaders with the core values of altruism are instrumental in implementing and maintaining sustainable practices (Ewest, 2017; Wirtenberg et al., 2008; Lawrence & Beamish, 2012). Numerous initiatives such as Conscious Capitalism (Mackey & Sisodia, 2014), the United Nations Global Compact (UN Global Compact, 2007), and its corresponding venture Principles of Responsible Management Education (Waddock, Rasche, Werhane, & Unruh, 2010), anecdotally suggest the importance of leadership in organizations and initiatives which are committed to address environmental and social concerns. But, these values, while substantive and important as a catalyst for organizations to become environmentally and socially responsible, in no way suggest that leaders need to constrain their actions to ensure their organizations act in a responsible way.

However, if one can accept that one aspect of essential human nature is innate human values (Schwartz, 1999), and among these values which are genetically and/or neurologically wired into the human person is empathetic response (Decety et al., 2004; Lieberman et al., 2002), which is one if not the primary causation of leaders to pursue altruistic action (Ewest, 2017; Wirtenberg et al., 2008; Lawrence & Beamish, 2012); the possibility of leaders to be held to account for their non-altruistic actions exists. And, research considering spirituality provides one means to foster and identify altruism in lives of leaders and organizations.

However, the nature of the relationship of spirituality to altruism is nuanced, so while there is an empirically validated connection between spirituality and altruism, it is multivariate and indicates that spirituality is not the sole property or causation of altruism (Saroglou, 2013). Yet, Greenwald and Harder (2003) explored dimensions of spirituality, and one of the factors that emerged from their research participants was self-effacing altruism. Alternately, their research had one factor garner low ratings with little shared variance, selfishness. Collectively, their research indicates altruism, or selflessness, is an important dimension to spirituality. This connection is also clearly seen as a component within spiritual leadership (SL) (Fry, 2003) and prosocial leadership (PL) (Ewest, 2017).

SL (Fry, 2003) is demonstrated by leaders who are motivated by altruistic love, and their others directed behavior inspires followers to have hope and faith in a collective vision to stakeholders. SL also is concerned about the needs of their followers and addresses the needs of followers to make a difference in their life and find personal meaning. Arguably the leaders who guide their organizations to sustainable change, as posited by Wirtenberg et al. (2008) and Lawrence and Beamish (2012), may fit within the characterization of SL.

In their book, *Maximizing the Triple Bottom Line*, Fry and Nisiewicz (2013) identify spiritual leaders and their ethical, others directed behavior, as being motivated by the essential universal human value of altruism. And, SL is instrumental in leading organizations to sustained profits, as well as socially and environmentally sustainable practices, capturing the harmony of ethics, sustainability, and spirituality.

PL (Ewest, 2017) does not propose itself as a new leadership theory, but as a means to use prosocial behavior theory (e.g., Batson, 2010; Schwartz, 1999) to identify leaders who are prosocial and outlines the development process these leaders go through as they choose altruistic personal development and leadership action.

Ewest (2017) in his book, *Prosocial Leadership: Understanding the Development of Prosocial Behavior within Leaders and their Organizational Settings*, considered the question, "How does the prosocial leadership development process apply to existing leaders within the context of the organizational life?" (p. 147). The research considered 22 organizational founders of small to medium enterprises (SMEs) who had a social or environmental mission built into the cause. Quantitative and qualitative research methods were used to determine how active prosocial leadership values were within the management and oversight of the SME ventures. Ewest (2017) found that PLs were motivated by the prosocial value of altruism, and found that, as with SL, PL also was concerned about the needs of their followers and addressed their needs to make a difference and help them find personal meaning, and that this action is what developed others' performance and sustained the organization. PL and SL join other leadership theories which can be identified as positivist leadership theories as codified by MacKie (2017) and Ewest (2018).

Conclusion

This chapter explored the connections between sustainability, ethics, and spirituality. The chapter argued that if there are innate universal characteristics to human nature, they may provide a constraint to unethical behavior as well as a means to guide human behavior. The chapter then illustrated the polarities of the understandings and theories of human nature by delineating the classic debate between Foucault, representing an anti-essentialist perspective, and Chomsky, representing an essentialist perspective. The chapter resolved by considering how prosocial research, which posits human values as an essential innate and universal quality of human nature, may act as a means to build a case for the connection between spirituality, sustainability, and ethics.

In the book, *The Three Stooges: An Illustrated History, from Amalgamated Morons to American Icons*, Michael Fleming (2013) traces the history of the three stooges, as they moved through media. The book describes how the three stooges, with their slapstick humor, stuck around for over 24 years, because they were highly disparate "where each stooge created his own reality in an unreal situation and never wavered from it" (p. 128). The stooges were comical and refreshing because they were placed together in a situation, but were never really "together." Metaphorically, at one time, this was the perception of suggesting leaders should take an ethical values centered approach to running their companies for the good of the environment and the good of society. The very suggestion ran as a counter narrative to neoclassical economics, where the responsibility of managers was to look out for themselves and the profitability of their shareholders.

Today, we understand the importance of leading socially and environmentally sustainable organizations as a way to increase shareholder wealth, and expand their stakeholder network. For some, this is best exemplified by the human value of empathy or spirituality and thus its inclusion becomes vital for effective organizational performance (Fry & Nisiewicz, 2013;

Wirtenberg et al., 2008). And, in reality, this is the trend happening today within the executive office, leaders are moving toward the synergies of the three (ethics, sustainability, and spirituality) that act as one, and not away (Bonini & Bové, 2014).

References

Allen, A. L. (2004). *The New Ethics: A Guided Tour of the Twenty-First Century Moral Landscape.* New York: Miramax.

Batson, C. D. (2010). Empathy-induced altruistic motivation. In M. Mikulincer & P. R. Shaver (Eds.), *Prosocial Motives, Emotions, and Behavior: The Better Angels of our Nature.* Washington, DC: American Psychological Association Press, 15–34.

Bonini, S., & Bové, A. T. (2014). Sustainability's strategic worth. McKinsey Global Survey results.

Chomsky, N., & Foucault, M. (2006). *The Chomsky-Foucault Debate: On Human Nature.* New York: The New Press.

Ciulla, J. B. (2005). The state of leadership ethics and the work that lies before us. *Business Ethics: A European Review, 14*(4), 323–335.

Decety, J., Jackson, P. L., Sommerville, J. A., Chaminade, T., & Meltzoff, A. N. (2004). The neural bases of cooperation and competition: An fMRI investigation. *Neuroimage, 23*(2), 744–751.

Ellis, B. (2014). *The Philosophy of Nature: A Guide to the New Essentialism.* London: Routledge.

Ewest, T. (2017). *Prosocial Leadership: Understanding the Development of Prosocial Behavior within Leaders and their Organizational Settings.* New York: Springer.

Ewest, T. (2018). Emerging forms of leadership and their ethical and prosocial moorings. In S. Dhiman, G. Roberts, & J. Crossman (Eds.), *The Palgrave Handbook of Workplace Spirituality and Fulfillment.* New York: Palgrave Macmillan, 795–810.

Ewest, T., & Kliegl, J. (2012). The case for change in business education: How liberal arts principles and practices can foster needed change. *Journal of Higher Education Theory and Practice, 12*(3), 75–86.

Fleming, M. (2013). *The Three Stooges: An Illustrated History, from Amalgamated Morons to American Icons.* New York: Broadway Books.

Fry, L. W. (2003). Toward a theory of spiritual leadership. *Leadership Quarterly, 14*(6), 693–727.

Fry, L. W., & Nisiewicz, M. S. (2013). *Maximizing the Triple Bottom Line through Spiritual Leadership.* Stanford, CA: Stanford University Press.

Gill, R. (2014). *A Textbook of Christian Ethics.* London: Bloomsbury Publishing.

Goldstein, J. (2011). Probing the nature of complex systems: Parameters, modeling, interventions—Part 1. *Emergence: Complexity and Organization, 13*(3).

Greenwald, D. F., & Harder, D. W. (2003). The dimensions of spirituality. *Psychological Reports, 92*(3), 975–980.

Horodecka, A. (2014). The meaning of concepts of human nature in organizational life in business ethics context. *Annales: etyka w życiu gospodarczym, 17*(4), 53–64.

Lawrence, J. T., & Beamish, P. W. (Eds.). (2012). *Globally Responsible Leadership: Managing According to the UN Global Compact.* Thousand Oaks, CA: Sage.

Lieberman, M. D., Gaunt, R., Gilbert, D. T., & Trope, Y. (2002). Reflection and reflexion: A social cognitive neuroscience approach to attributional inference. *Advances in Experimental Social Psychology, 34,* 199–249.

Lillehammer, H. (2002). Moral realism, normative reasons, and rational intelligibility. *Erkenntnis, 57*(1), 47–69.

Little, M. (1994). Moral realism II: Non-naturalism. *Philosophical Books, 35*(4), 225–233.

Loptson, P. (2006). *Theories of Human Nature.* Peterborough, Canada: Broadview Press.

Mackey, J., & Sisodia, R. (2014). *Conscious Capitalism, with a New Preface by the Authors: Liberating the Heroic Spirit of Business.* Boston: Harvard Business Review Press.

MacKie, D. (2017). Positive approaches to leadership development. In L. G. Oades, M. F. Steger, A. Delle Fave, & J. Passmore (Eds.), *The Wiley Blackwell Handbook of the Psychology of Positivity and Strengths–Based Approaches at Work.* Oxford, UK: John Wiley & Sons, Ltd, 297–316.

McNaughton, D. (1988). *Moral Vision: An Introduction to Ethics.* Hoboken, NJ: Wiley-Blackwell.

Milchman, A., & Rosenberg, A. (2018). Nietzsche and Foucault. In J. Westfall & A. Rosenberg (Eds.), *Foucault and Nietzsche: A Critical Encounter.* New York: Bloomsbury Academic, 99.

Putnam, R. D. (1995). Bowling alone: America's declining social capital. *Journal of Democracy, 6*(1), 65–78.

Pylyshyn, Z. (1991). *Rules and Representations: Chomsky and Representational Realism. The Chomskian Turn*. Oxford, UK: Basil Blackwell Limited.

Rokeach, M. (1973). *The Nature of Human Values*. New York: Free Press.

Saroglou, V. (2013) Religion, spirituality, and altruism. In K. I. Pargament (Ed.), *APA Handbook of Psychology, Religion and Spirituality* (Vol. 1). Washington, DC: American Psychological Association Publishing, 439–457.

Schwab, K. (2003, February 24). Capitalism must develop more of a conscience. *Newsweek*,41–42.

Schwartz, S. H. (1999). A theory of cultural values and some implications for work. *Applied psychology, 48*(1), 23–47.

Schwartz, S. H., & Bilsky, W. (1987). Toward a universal psychological structure of human values. *Journal of Personality and Social Psychology, 53*(3), 550.

Southwood, N. (2015). The relevance of human nature. *Journal of Ethics and Social Philosophy, 9*(3), 1–9.

Stackhouse, M. (1995). Introduction: Foundations and purpose. In M. L. Stackhouse, D. P. McCann, S. J. Roels, & P. N. Williams (Eds.), *On Moral Business: Classical and Contemporary Resources for Ethics in Economic Life*. Grand Rapids, MI: William B. Eerdmans Publishing Company, 10–36.

Strand, R. (2011). Exploring the role of leadership in corporate social responsibility: A review. *Journal of Leadership, Accountability, and Ethics, 8*(4), 84–96.

Steele, C. (2012). Conversation with Noam Chomsky about social justice and the future. *Jesuit Higher Education, 1*(2), 32–42.

Turek, (2010). "Koncepcje człowieka" a modele pracownika. Inspiracjedla ZZL, *"Edukacja Ekonomistów i Menedżerów"* 16, pp. 11–25.

UN Global Compact, N. (2007). *The Principles for Responsible Management Education*. New York: United Nations.

Waddock, S., Rasche, A., Werhane, P. H., & Unruh, G. (2010). The principles for responsible management education. In D. L. Swanson & D. G. Fisher (Eds.), *Got Ethics? Towards Assessing Business Ethics Education*. Charlotte, NC: Information Age Publishing, 13–28.

Wilkin, P. (1999). Chomsky and Foucault on human nature and politics: An essential difference? *Social Theory and Practice, 25*(2), 177–210.

Wirtenberg, J., Russell, W. G., & Lipsky, D. (Eds.). (2008). *The Sustainable Enterprise Fieldbook: When it All Comes Together*. Austin, TX: Greenleaf Press.

24

A THEORETICAL APPROACH TO SPIRITUAL LEADERSHIP IN PUBLIC ORGANIZATIONS

Is Spiritual Leadership a Good Fit for Public Managers?

Kira Haensel and Jean-Claude Garcia-Zamor

Defining Spiritual Leadership

While a consensual definition of spirituality in the management literature doesn't exist, one common definition that combines a number of preexisting definitions and was suggested by Ashar and Lane-Maher reads as follows:

> Spirituality is an innate and universal search for transcendent meaning in one's life. In addition, although it can be expressed in various ways, we submit that spirituality at work involves some common behavioral components. Above all, it involves a desire to do purposeful work that serves others and to be part of a principled community. It involves a yearning for connectedness and wholeness that can only be manifested when one is allowed to integrate his or her inner life with one's professional role in the service of a greater good.
>
> *(Ashar & Lane-Maher, 2005, p. 252)*

In line with this definition, it can be said that spirituality in general concerns the feeling of interconnectedness (Mitroff & Denton, 1999). With reference to the workplace, spirituality thus addresses the level of interconnectedness between an organization and its employees, including the level of interconnectedness among the employees and with their leader.

Spirituality in the workplace has received increasing attention over the last two decades. According to Giacalone and Jurkiewicz (2003), the emergence of workplace spirituality can be connected to three thematic sections. The first addresses changes in the social and business environment, which require employees to deal with the consequential tensions. In times of instability, budget cuts, downsizing, and the increased replacement of employees through technology, people begin to distrust the organizations they work for (Cash & Gray, 2000; Giacalone & Jurkiewicz, 2003). "This diminishing view of self and work exacerbates feelings of social alienation and fear, compelling the employee to search for deeper meaning in life (Ali and Falcone [& Azim], 1995) and thus integrating a spiritual-work identity" (Giacalone & Jurkiewicz,

2003, p. 3). That is, employees experience the need for satisfaction in the workplace, which goes beyond factors such as pay satisfaction (Izzo & Klein, 1998; Giacalone & Jurkiewicz, 2003). The second thematic section emphasizes the global change in values. Accordingly, self-actualization has become an important component of the workplace. Employees do not just want to go to work for financial and material reasons, but actually identify themselves with their job. People feel the need for meaning in their work and the impression to have a positive impact on society. Furthermore, increasing social consciousness has led to the development of the idea of corporate social responsibility. Corporate social responsibility can be roughly defined as "actions that appear to further some social good, beyond the interests of the firm and that which is required by law" (McWilliams & Siegel, 2001, p. 513). A third thematic section addresses the influence of Eastern philosophy on Northern American popular culture. Over the last two decades, the Eastern influence on aspects such as lifestyle choices, fitness, cuisine, and fashion has increased, which can be attributed to "societal shifts towards diversity and increasing interest in other cultures" accordingly (Giacalone & Jurkiewicz, 2003, p. 4).

Reconsidering the definition of spirituality mentioned earlier, "Spiritual leadership involves motivating and inspiring workers through a transcendent vision and a culture based in altruistic values to produce a more motivated, committed and productive workforce" (Fry & Matherly, 2006, p. 4). Accordingly, it is the leader's task to create an environment in which on the one hand the leader herself/himself is able to intrinsically motivate her/him through attitudes, behaviors values, and behaviors that facilitate this motivation. On the other hand, the leader has the job to generate a climate within which the followers "experience a sense of calling in that life [or work] has meaning and makes a difference" (Fry & Matherly, 2006, p. 4) based on values such as appreciation, concern for others, and genuine care. Spiritual leadership theory builds on the idea that a spiritual leader is able to motivate her/his followers through the emphasis on "meaning and purpose rather than rewards and security, thus encouraging employees to transcend their self-interest" (Rego, Cunha, & Oliveira, 2008, pp. 169–170). Leaders consequently have an impact on followers through their influence on workplace spirituality. Thus, according to Strack, Fottler, Wheatley, and Sodomka, "the management of individual spirituality as well as the leadership of others from a spiritual perspective are among the most fundamental of all management tasks" (2002, p. 16).

Finally, Fry (2003) states that spiritual leadership theory includes several different major motivation-based leadership theories but that it is less conceptually confounded. For the purpose of the conceptualization of spiritual leadership, Fry argues that in order to respond to the global societal demands of organizational change, a paradigm shift toward a learning organizational paradigm which focuses on intrinsic motivation, team empowerment, flexibility, diversity, and innovation is necessary. This implies a radical shift away from the traditional, hierarchical, bureaucratic, centralized, and formal organizational structure. "For the learning organization, developing, leading, motivating, organizing, and retaining people to be committed to the organization's vision, goals, culture, and values are the major challenge" (Fry, 2003, p. 694). In order to successfully transition to a learning organization, spiritual leadership is necessary. Accordingly, a spiritual leader is concerned about her/his and the followers' needs of any kind in order to trigger greater organizational commitment and therewith productivity. Fry defines spiritual leadership "as comprising the values, attitudes, and behaviors that are necessary to intrinsically motivate one's self and others so that they have a sense of spiritual survival through calling and membership" (2003, pp. 194–195).

Fry's model of spiritual leadership consists of the idea that a spiritual leader creates a vision, which then leads to a sense of calling in the leader and her/his followers, which in turn leads to spiritual well-being, since people feel that their work is meaningful. The second notion refers to the leader as creator of an organizational culture that incorporates the values of altruistic love through which a sense of membership is created (Fry, 2003). In more recent work, Fry revised the model and added inner life and life satisfaction as additional factors of spiritual leadership. Accordingly, inner life refers to people's perception of who they are and how and what they are contributing. Life satisfaction addresses an individual's perception of her/his life in terms of wellbeing. Higher levels of life satisfaction can function as a motivator (Fry, 2005). The theory behind the model is that through the sense of calling and membership, people feel attached to the organization and develop loyalty toward it. Furthermore, through the sense of calling and membership, people will be motivated to be productive and therewith support the organization's success. Finally, people with a sense of calling and membership will reach higher levels of life satisfaction due to the creation of a sense of purpose and belonging (Fry, Latham, Clinebell, & Krahnke, 2017). Other scholars have tested both, the original and the revised model (e.g., Jeon, Passmore, Lee, & Hunsaker, 2013; Bodla & Ali, 2012). The results show that the original model is able to predict a number of organizational as well as individual level aspects within different cultures and countries (Fry et al., 2017). The revised model was tested by Jeon et al. (2013) who found "initial support that inner life is an essential source of inspiration and insight that positively influences spiritual leadership, which then positively predicted calling and membership. In turn, calling and membership positively predicted organizational commitment, productivity, and life satisfaction" (Fry et al., 2017, p. 5).

Differences between Administrative Leadership and Leadership in the Private Sector

Most research on workplace spirituality related aspects such as value congruence between leaders and followers has been conducted in the private sector setting. The distinct compositions of the public and private sector however lead to doubts whether results from research conducted in the private sector setting are transferable to the public sector. Differences in the degree of political pressure (Wamsley & Zald, 1973), in the type of goods and services manufactured and or provided (Alford, 2002; Rainey, 2014), and the level of liability toward the public (Moore, 1995) form environments which require distinct management strategies (Rainey, 2014). Accordingly, leadership in public sector organizations is different and can be more complex than in private sector organizations, since political and ideological aspects, as well as concerns for values, are distinct. However, while there are some important similarities between cultures of private sector and public sector organizations, the differences at the structural and operational level in public sector organizations compared to private sector organizations cultures create unique challenges for public sector managers trying to evoke change (Schraeder, Tears, & Jordan, 2005).

Besides from the above-mentioned aspects, public sector leaders are also dealing with distinct types of employees, especially in terms of their motivation. Research on public and private sector work motivation revealed that public sector employees are less extrinsically motivated than private sector employees (e.g., Buelens & Van den Broeck, 2007). Extrinsic motivation refers to motivation that is driven by goals such as financial benefits or awards earned through the performance of an activity. Intrinsic motivation on the other hand concerns the engagement in an activity out of interest or the pleasure that might be gained through it (Lin, 2007). As one vital task of a leader is to ensure that employees are motivated (since motivation is also related to performance) the type of motivation that drives employees thus requires distinct leadership approaches.

Andersen (2010) empirically tested this assumption and found significant differences between managerial styles in the private and public sector. The scholar analyzed data from 495 Swedish managers on leadership style, decision-making style, and type of motivation. The results reveal that public and private managers apply different types of leadership styles, and have similar approaches to decision-making. Leaders in the public sector were found to have change-oriented leadership styles, which are defined through openness to new ideas and change, future planning, and experimentation with new approaches (Arvonen & Ekvall, 1999; Andersen, 2010). Private sector leaders in contrast show a leadership style that is focused on relationships. Accordingly, private managers tend to have a stronger bond with their subordinates through a relationship based on trust and are also more likely to delegate authority to subordinates (Anderson, 2010). Other findings show that private and public managers have similar decision-making styles which are based on intuition. Thus, both types of managers are open to new possibilities, are future oriented, and use their imagination in the decision-making process (Andersen, 2010). Regarding motivation, the results show that public sector managers are driven by the "desire to outperform someone else, meet or surpass some self-imposed standard of excellence, do something unique, be involved over long term in doing something" (Andersen, 2010, p. 137). Private sector managers in contrast feel motivated through power, meaning the desire to have an impact, to impress others, and to maintain a good reputation and position. Accordingly, Andersen's findings regarding public and private managers' leadership styles reveal that there are significant differences regarding their motivation and orientation. Possible explanations for that include organizational differences in terms of structure which lead to behavioral differences, the type of profession, and the criteria used for promotion decisions (Andersen, 2010).

Does Leadership in the Public Sector Matter?

The traditional bureaucratic paradigm, typified by "internal productive efficiency, functional rationality, departmentalization, hierarchical control and rule-based management" (Kaufman, 1977; Ndou, 2004), has continuously been challenged over the last years. While hierarchical control and rule-based management were established and accepted structures within the public sector for a long time, its efficiency has been questioned, not only in the private but also in the public sector. A look at the evolution of management theory and the way organizational behavior has been addressed in theory and research reveals that the perception of employees, their role in the organization as well as their needs underwent significant changes over the timespan of roughly the last 100 years. With the emergence of human relations theory in the earlier 20th century at the latest, we came to realize that an exclusively technical approach is not sufficient to explain organizational behavior. Human relations theory shifted the focus from efficiency, the principle of the scientific approach, to the human element in organization. The movement can be interpreted as reaction to the deficiencies of theories of scientific management, offering "solutions" for the very same (Bruce, 2006). Thus, the main focus of human relations theory lies on the social context of organizations and the "relationships among changes in the organization, worker satisfaction, and productivity" (Fry & Raadschelders, 2013, p. 189). The main concern is the

> "human factor" in industry and the unit of analysis is the social person and its central role in organizations: [...] humans are not merely the egoistic, utilitarian animal of neoclassical economics and Scientific Management, but they have other (high-level) psychosocial needs, and their social relationships at work play an important role in their productivity.
>
> *(Bruce, 2006, p. 177; Dingley, 1997; Wren & Greenwood, 1998; Duncan, 1999)*

Human relation theorists emphasize that besides from organizational level aspects, we must also consider personal as well as inter-personal factors and their impact on organizational behavior. That is, while organizational level aspects are important, we must not forget individual level factors that impact organizational behavior. The latter includes the role of the leader. Box's argument in 1999 that we are in the midst of an "apparent fragmentation of meaning, [which entails that] the daily mechanics and values of the market permeate social, political, and economic life" (Box, 1999, p. 25) is still relevant today, and therewith human relations theory. Box's (1990) statement indicates that there is a need to refocus on the identification of grand themes of common belief or interest in order to build productive organizational culture, which, as a body of literature and research reveals, is essential to organizational performance (Garnett, Marlowe, & Pandey, 2008; Moynihan & Pandey, 2005; Popoli, 2016). The role the leader takes in this process is closer defined by Fry (2003), who argues that organizational change toward a learning organization is led by a spiritual leader. This is substantiated through the notion that, "from an ethics and values perspective, leaders have an impact on establishing and reinforcing personal, team, and organizational values" (Northouse, 2001; Fry, 2003, p. 708).

As the comparison of administrative leadership and leadership in the private sector has shown, the role of a leader in the public sector compared to a private sector leader is distinct. This is attributable on the one hand to the different organizational environment of public sector agencies (e.g., regarding funding and promotion) and the associated liabilities and on the other hand to the distinct bodies of employees, their motifs, and motivations. Thus, public sector leaders' work is complicated through high levels of bureaucracy, which at the same time makes it more difficult for them to reach their subordinates on an interpersonal level and accommodate according changes. Considering the purpose of public organizations and the way they are expected to operate in terms of liability and ethical behavior, it is clear that public sector leaders play an important and influential role. Relating to this aspect, Downe, Cowell, and Morgan (2016) asked the question whether rules or leadership determine ethical behavior in public organizations. The research which was conducted within the local government setting revealed that constantly ethically behaving organizations mainly have multiple leaders who lead by good example and further informally react to problems in order to prevent the necessity of use of formal regulation. According to this finding, public sector managers play a vital role in terms of the determination of ethical behavior (Downe et al., 2016).

Yet, again, since public sector organizations in general and especially compared to their private counterparts have the reputation of high levels of red tape and therewith limited leeway for leaders to have a personal and distinct impact on the work environment and culture as well as on organizational change, it is more difficult for leaders who operate within a highly bureaucratic environment to impact organizational commitment, performance, and employee well-being than for leaders who work for organizations with less rule-oriented organizational cultures. Within the frame of research on the impact of succession, Lynn (2001) reviewed the development of succession management strategies in public service organizations. The researcher found a direct link between organizational culture and leadership and identified "the need for new human resource management initiatives to foster the systematic identification, recruitment, development, and selection of high-potential candidates to improve leadership growth in the public sector" (Lynn, 2001, p. 114). Hence, the pointed out differences between public sector and private sector employees and leaders emphasize the necessity of public sector leadership as a separate branch from private sector leadership in research, theory, and in practice.

Why is Spiritual Leadership a Good Fit for Public Sector Leadership?

As outlined beforehand, one of the objectives of spiritual leadership is to create self-awareness and enhance spiritual engagement, which are powerful tools in terms of identity-shaping and resilience-strengthening. Self-awareness and a resilient identity are crucial characteristics for public sector leaders, since the sector's nature requires leaders to respond to the demands of different stakeholders, while keeping the focus on the public interest and ensuring ethical behavior. Hence, building a resilient identity is crucial for public sector leaders who need to stand "against the pressures of culture and complexity" (Roof, Bocarnea, & Winston, 2018).

Another important factor regarding identity is the identification of an individual with the organization. In order to identify with an organization, one must stand behind the organization's work and values. Depending on the level of authority, leaders have the unique opportunity to impact organizational structures and functions and therewith also the work and values. A study conducted by Feeney and Boarman (2010) investigated which individual and organizational factors lead to high organizational confidence. Related to spirituality, the scholars define organizational confident workers as "workers reporting high levels of pride in the organization for which they work, and who believe that the organization provides high-quality public services and operates by highly ethical standards" (Feeney & Boardman, 2010, pp. 673–674). The research was conducted with a sample of public sector employees. According to the findings, factors that are related to highly positive attitudes toward public organizations and highly motivated public employees are low organizational red tape, an increased desire to serve the public, high levels or perceived client satisfaction, as well as work motivation that stems from security factors such as a steady income and career advancement factors such as the opportunity for promotion. All of these factors are related to spirituality insofar as they are related to aspects that create a meaning in work, e.g., employees being able to deploy creativity, emotions, and intelligence, the ability to realize one's full potential, having an income, and serving the public (Feeney & Boardman, 2010; Mitroff & Denton 1999). Furthermore, according to a study by Mitroff and Denton (1999), employees who rated their organization as "more spiritual" were more likely to rate their organization as "more profitable" as well. The results of these studies show the importance of spirituality in public sector leadership not only in terms of the leader herself/himself, but also in terms of followers' satisfaction and therewith performance; not only on the individual but also on the organizational level.

Another argument for why spiritual leadership is a good fit for public sector leadership refers to public sector motivation. Motivational factors provide valuable insight into the way employees work and how their needs can be met. As outlined beforehand, public sector respondents attribute greater value to work that is beneficial to others and to society, to involvement in important public policies, and to self-sacrifice, responsibility, and integrity (Kakabadse, Kakabadse, & Kouzmin, 2003; Khuntia & Suar, 2004). At higher management and professional levels, in particular, public sector respondents place less emphasis on money and high income as ultimate ends in work and life (Fernandez, 2005; Bjugstad, Thach, Thompson, & Morris, 2006). The mentioned aspects as well as esteem needs and self-actualization are closely related to intrinsic motivation, a type of motivation frequently found in the public sector (Buelens & Van den Broeck, 2007). Within that context, spiritual leadership focuses on the development of values that lead to intrinsic motivation and therewith to "spiritual survival through calling and membership" (Fry, 2003, pp. 194–195).

The fact that many public sector employees show commitment toward altruistic values calls for the adjustment of leadership strategies. Leaders need to be aware of the type of reward system their employees respond to and which organizational culture they feel comfortable working in. The idea behind spiritual leadership is to intrinsically motivate followers in order for them to develop a personal bond with their work which in turn leads to higher levels of commitment. As the referenced research shows, public sector employees already show intrinsic motivation, which is why leaders need to focus on the advancement of this value in order to fully unlock workers' potential with respect to their own wellbeing as well as the organization's performance.

Finally, one further thought on spiritual leadership and the public sector concerns the role of ethics. Ethics play a decisive role in public sector work, since public sector organizations are highly liable toward the public mainly due to their nature of funding, i.e., publicly funded organizations have the obligation to act for the purpose of the society. The leader is the one who sets ethical standards by example. Ethical leadership entails honesty, empathy, altruism, and humility, values that are part of the concept of spiritual leadership. Due to the nature of public sector organizations, leaders of such organizations are dealing with ethical dilemmas such as competing values of different stakeholders. It therefore is crucial for public sector leaders to develop a clear vision to be followed and resilience to unethical behavior and outside pressure. As outlined earlier, empirical research revealed the importance of leadership in terms of ethical organizational behavior. Spiritual leaders focus on the creation of a shared vision and the mediation of ethical behavioral values. Thus, spiritual leadership emphasizes and facilitates the vital factor of ethical behavior in public organizations.

References

Alford, J. (2002). Defining the client in the public sector: A social–exchange perspective. *Public Administration Review, 62*, 337–346.

Ali, A. J., Falcone, T., & Azim, A. A. (1995). Work ethic in the USA and Canada. *Journal of Management Development, 14*(6), 26–34.

Andersen, J. A. (2010). Public versus private managers: How public and private managers differ in leadership behavior. *Public Administration Review, 70*(1), 131–141.

Arvonen, J., & Ekvall, G. (1999). Effective leadership style: Both universal and contingent? *Creativity and Innovation Management, 8*(4), 242–250.

Ashar, H., & Lane-Maher, M. (2004). Success and spirituality in the new business paradigm. *Journal of Management Inquiry, 13*(3), 249–260.

Bjugstad, K., Thach, E. C., Thompson, K. J., & Morris, A. (2006). A fresh look at followership: A model for matching followership and leadership styles. *Journal of Behavioral and Applied Management, 7*, 304–319.

Bodla, M. A., & Ali, H. (2012). Workplace spirituality: A spiritual audit of banking executives in Pakistan. *African Journal of Business Management, 6*(11), 3888.

Box, R. C. (1999). Running government like a business. *American Review of Public Administration, 29*(1), 19–43.

Bruce, K. (2006). Henry S. Dennison, Elton Mayo, and human relations historiography. *Management and Organizational History, 1*(2), 177–199.

Buelens, M., & Van den Broeck, H. (2007). An analysis of differences in work motivation between public and private sector organizations. *Public Administration Review, 67*(1), 65–74.

Cash, K. C., & Gray, G. R. (2000). A framework for accommodating religion and spirituality in the workplace. *Academy of Management Executive, 14*(3), 124–133.

Dingley, J. C. (1997). Durkheim, Mayo, morality and management. *Journal of Business Ethics, 16*, 1118.

Downe, J., Cowell, R., & Morgan, K. (2016). What determines ethical behavior in public organizations: Is it rules or leadership? *Public Administration Review, 76*(6, 898–909.

Duncan, W. J. (1999). *Management: Ideas and Action*. New York: Oxford University Press, 162–167.

Feeney, M. K., & Boardman, C. (2010). Organizational confidence: An empirical assessment of highly positive public managers. *Journal of Public Administration Research and Theory, 21*(4), 673–697.

Fernandez, S. (2005). Developing and testing an integrative framework of public sector leadership: Evidence from the public education arena. *Journal of Public Administration Research and Theory, 15*, 197–217.

Fry, L. W. (2003). Toward a theory of spiritual leadership. *Leadership Quarterly, 14*(6), 693–727.

Fry, L. W. (2005). Toward a theory of ethical and spiritual well-being, and corporate social responsibility through spiritual leadership. In R. A. Giacalone, C. L. Jurkiewicz, & C. Dunn (Eds.), *Positive Psychology in Business Ethics and Corporate Responsibility*. Greenwich, CT: Information Age, 47–83.

Fry, L. W., Latham, J. R., Clinebell, S. K., & Krahnke, K. (2017). Spiritual leadership as a model for performance excellence: A study of Baldrige award recipients. *Journal of Management, Spirituality and Religion, 14*(1), 22–47.

Fry, L. W., & Matherly, L. L. (2006). Spiritual leadership and organizational performance. Paper presented at the Academy of Management, Atlanta, GA.

Fry, B. R., & Raadschelders, J. C. (2013). *Mastering Public Administration: From Max Weber to Dwight Waldo.* Thousand Oaks, CA: CQ Press.

Garnett, J. L., Marlowe, J., & Pandey, S. K. (2008). Penetrating the performance predicament: Communication as a mediator or moderator of organizational culture's impact on public organizational performance. *Public Administration Review, 68*(2), 266–281.

Giacalone, R. A., & Jurkiewicz, C. L. (Eds.). (2003). *Handbook of Workplace Spirituality and Organizational Performance.* New York: M. E. Sharpe.

Izzo, J., & Klein, E. (1998). The changing values of workers: Organizations must respond with soul. *Healthcare Forum Journal, 41*(3), 62.

Jeon, K. S., Passmore, D. L., Lee, C., & Hunsaker, W. (2013). Spiritual leadership: A validation study in a Korean context. *Journal of Management, Spirituality and Religion, 10*(4), 342–357.

Kakabadse, N. K., Kakabadse, A., & Kouzmin, A. (2003). Reviewing the knowledge management literature: Towards a taxonomy. *Journal of Knowledge Management,* 7, 75–91.

Kaufman, H. (1977). *Red Tape: Its Origins, Uses and Abuses.* Washington, DC: Brookings Institution.

Khuntia, R., & Suar, D. (2004). A scale to assess ethical leadership of Indian private and public sector managers. *Journal of Business Ethics, 49*(1), 13–26.

Lin, H. F. (2007). Effects of extrinsic and intrinsic motivation on employee knowledge sharing intentions. *Journal of Information Science, 33*(2), 135–149.

Lynn, D. B. (2001). Succession management strategies in public sector organizations: Building leadership capital. *Review of Public Personnel Administration, 21*(2), 114–132.

McWilliams, A., & Siegel, D. (2001). Corporate social responsibility: A theory of the firm perspective. *Academy of Management Review, 26*(1), 117–127.

Mitroff, I. I., & Denton, E. A. (1999). A study of spirituality in the workplace. *MIT Sloan Management Review, 40*(4), 83.

Moore, M. H. (1995). *Creating Public Value: Strategic Management in Government.* Cambridge, MA: Harvard University Press.

Moynihan, D. P., & Pandey, S. K. (2005). Testing how management matters in an era of government by performance management. *Journal of Public Administration Research and Theory, 15*(3), 421–439.

Ndou, V. (2004). E-Government for developing countries: Opportunities and challenges. *Electronic Journal of Information Systems in Developing Countries, 18*(1), 1–24.

Northouse, P. G. (2001). *Leadership Theory and Practice* (2nd ed.). Thousand Oaks, CA: Sage Publications, Inc.

Popoli, P. (2016). The impact of organizational culture on corporate performance. *Walden University, 16*(September), 210–216.

Rainey, H. G. (2014). *Understanding and Managing Public Organizations* (5th ed.). San Francisco: Jossey-Bass.

Rego, A., Pina E Cunha, M., & Oliveira, M. (2008). Eupsychia revisited: The role of spiritual leaders. *Journal of Humanistic Psychology, 48*(2), 165–195.

Roof, R., Bocarnea, M. C., & Winston, B. E. (2018). Spiritual engagement and positive leadership: The promise of identity-focused leader development. In S. Dhiman, G. Roberts, & J. Crossman (Eds.), *The Palgrave Handbook of Workplace Spirituality and Fulfillment.* Cham, Switzerland: Palgrave Macmillan, 719–731.

Schraeder, M., Tears, R. S., & Jordan, M. H. (2005). Organizational culture in public sector organizations: Promoting change through training and leading by example. *Leadership and Organization Development Journal, 26*(6), 492–502.

Strack, G., Fottler, M. D., Wheatley, M. J., & Sodomka, P. (2002). Spirituality and effective leadership in healthcare: Is there a connection?/commentaries/replies. *Frontiers of Health Services Management, 18*(4), 3.

Wamsley, G. L., & Zald, M. N. (1973). The political economy of public organizations: A critique and approach to the study of public administration. *Public Administration Review, 33*, 62–73.

Wren, D., & Greenwood, R. G., (1998). *Management Innovators: The People Who Have Shaped Modern Business.* New York: Oxford University Press, 173–176.

25

APPLIED VEDANTA PHILOSOPHY

Improving Stakeholder Relations Through Inner Transformation

Anke Turner, Subhasis Chakrabarti, Joanna Rowe, and Nikhil Somaru

Introduction

Today, individuals and societies face massive disruptive change, an uncertain future, and unprecedented levels of complexity. The world seems to be heading toward ecological disaster. Despite intervention, poverty persists and inequality is steadily growing. Individuals and societies are responding with fear and protectionism. The next disruptive technological transformation is yet another potential threat to global social peace. Business as usual is not an option. Greater care toward all living beings, future generations, and nature is needed. How can the ancient Vedanta philosophy from India guide managers to act in a more responsible and caring manner in the face of these challenges?

The Stakeholder Theory canvas is proposed here as a useful framework to bring spirituality or religion into the business ethics discussion (Wicks, 2014). Stakeholder Theory has broadened the field of vision with regard to recognition of stakeholder groups, from exclusive focus on profit for shareholders to questions such as "Why does a firm exist?" and "For whom is the firm creating value?" Stakeholder Theory considers all groups and individuals who influence business decisions or who are influenced by them, including investors (Freeman, Wicks, & Parmar, 2011). All stakeholders are interconnected and reinforce each other in fundamental ways. Recent debate has elucidated the reality that value creation for stakeholders is not just about products, services, and financial returns. Fairness, sense of meaning, and opportunity costs can be valuable to stakeholders as well (Harrison & Wicks, 2013).

Stakeholder Theory assumes that, more often than not, most actors "want to and do accept responsibility for the effects of their actions on others" (Freeman et al., 2011, p. 54). So, in theory, if all managers treat their stakeholders with adequate care and fairness, global social and environmental problems should significantly decrease. However, despite many positive exceptions, in the real business world, it is widely believed that there is a significant gap between business ethics theory and actual business practice. In their book *Bridging the Values Gap: How Authentic Organizations Bring Values to Life* authors Freeman and Auster (2015) address the values gap between big business and the general public outside the business sphere. The authors propose introspection and collective reflection as instruments to bridge this gap. They cite the

Zen Buddhist term "a beginner's mind" as a basic attitude that business people should adopt; people should continually question the status quo without pre-judgment or preconceptions. Freeman and Auster (2015) go on to elucidate the need for what they call "outward introspection," by which they mean perceiving and learning from external realities and "tracking and discussing" the impact of decision-making on the environment.

In this chapter, a Vedantic approach toward management is presented as a possible solution to the gap between values and actual business behavior (Parthasarathy, 2014). For instance, a manager might be personally concerned about the wellbeing of the clients *and* the natural environment. At the same time, the manager might be actively involved in greenwashing of the company's products; a recent example of this is the diesel emissions scandal of German car manufacturer Volkswagen.

Vedanta offers a unique model for understanding individual behavior. Human beings are inherently complex, displaying a diverse range of behaviors, such as caring versus uncaring. Uncaring behavior is explained in Vedanta by selfishness, caring behavior with unselfishness and selflessness. Additionally, caring behavior is not only a question of pure emotions such as empathy, but also of rational decision-making and wisdom that is evident in actions. Therefore, individual development of the personality, from selfishness to unselfishness to selflessness, is seen as the prerequisite in order to overcome challenges and for a more caring attitude toward stakeholders. The individual's professional life is an integral part of this transformation. Vedanta teaches concepts and practices for turning objective knowledge into subjective wisdom. Gaining wisdom means that managers will act according to their higher values. In the process of transformation, the level of care toward all beings moves toward the perfect state of Self-realization. For example, in verses 29 to 32, chapter VI of the Bhagavad Gita, the central Indian scripture, the enlightened person is portrayed as seeing Divinity in all beings and all beings in Divinity. Thus, being one with all, the enlightened person displays the highest possible level of love and care to all beings (Parthasarathy, 2011d).

This chapter is organized as follows. First, a short introduction to Stakeholder Theory is given with a focus on the discussion of the need for better stakeholder relationships. Second, the ancient Indian Vedanta philosophy and its historical relevance to management is presented. The main part of the chapter determines the need for individual transformation on the basis of ancient Indian scriptures and describes how transformation can be achieved. The transformation of the individual personality can be seen from four interconnected perspectives: (1) development of the intellect (buddhi), (2) circle of identification, (3) pyramid of desires, and (4) theory of *gunas*. The case study of the South African start-up Dags Labs tells the story of how spiritual practice can be applied to the business environment. In conclusion, the links between Stakeholder Theory and Vedanta philosophy are elucidated.

The Why and How of Managing Stakeholder Relations Carefully

In his seminal book of 1984, *Stakeholder Management: A Stakeholder Approach* R. Edward Freeman sought to support managers in responding to constant change and extreme volatility by creating a strategic framework that goes beyond management capitalism to include the management of relationships between additional groups who have a vested interest in the firm (Freeman & McVea, 2001). Freeman "redefined" the term *stakeholder* in direct reference to the word *stockholder*, a term that is often associated with Milton Friedman and his influential essay of 1970, in which he claimed that the responsibilities of business people do not extend beyond maximizing profits and fulfilling the interests of a selected group of investors, owners, and managers (Friedman, 1970). Freeman however extends the list of stakeholder groups who "really matter," and widens the circle beyond owners, investors, and managers to include groups such as employees, suppliers, customers, and the local community in which a firm operates and of which it is a part.

Justification for this longer list of stakeholders is fiduciary duty, which Freeman claims exists not just between owners–investors and their agents the executive managers, but between many other groups of stakeholders. A fiduciary duty comprises the ethical relationship of trust and loyalty and a duty of care that encompasses reciprocal recognition of interests, rights, expectations, and obligations.

In his Stakeholder Theory Freeman also emphasizes the essential alignment of long-term interests of stakeholder groups (Freeman, 1984) as the prerequisite for the health and ultimately the continued existence of the firm (Freeman, 2001). A business enterprise, says Freeman, must inquire continually, evaluate and re-evaluate the purpose of the business activity, and identify the shared value that the business activity actually creates for the wider spectrum of stakeholder groups.

Risk and accountability are central concepts in business ethics and thus central to Stakeholder Theory. While in business enterprise a certain degree of risk is not only desirable, but also necessary, excessive risk that exposes stakeholder groups to existential crisis is unethical, because the danger to stakeholder groups who stand to lose everything is too great. Another ethical objection is that in most cases the stakeholder groups who are exposed to an inappropriate level of risk are those who do not have enough control over the level of risk they are exposed to because they have no decision-making powers. A good example is the Rana Plaza factory building collapse in Bangladesh in 2013. On a drive for ever cheaper garment production, the health and safety of the employees were neglected, resulting in more than 1000 dead and more than 2000 injured workers.

The term ethical proximity means the intensity of effect that a certain business maneuver, for instance, will have on a certain stakeholder group. The notions of risk level and of accountability are inextricably linked to the concept of ethical proximity. Stakeholder Theory pleads for a leveling of power structures with regard to decision-making and advocates a more even distribution with regard to risk levels and accountability. Sharing risk and assuming responsibility are both behavioral strategies that protect stakeholder groups.

Humility in creating diverse skillsets in teams, thus guardrailing against one's own cognitive biases and weaknesses, fosters oneness and unity and embodies the core values of Stakeholder Theory, because the level of risk is actively recognized with regard to individual stakeholder groups. Risk and accountability are distributed while decisions taken are balanced and consistent with the interests of other groups.

Brower and Mahajan, in their empirical study (2013), emphasize the importance of acknowledging and responding to the needs and demands of stakeholder groups with regard to enhancing the firm's corporate social performance. Their empirical findings indicate that firms which do acknowledge the needs of stakeholders can potentially improve future opportunities.

Finally, Kenneth Goodpaster, in his essay "Corporate Responsibility and its Constituents" (2010) describes the Tripartite Model, a unified concept in comprehensive moral thinking, placing Freeman's stakeholder capitalism model within a seamless background of human dignity on the one hand and the just community on the other.

The Ancient Vedanta Philosophy and Its Link with Business

India has a rich tradition of trade and business as well as a diverse and pluralistic philosophical tradition (see for instance Jayapalan, 2008; Matilal, 1998; Mohanty, 1992; Ramanujan, 1989; Sanyal, 2008; Sen, 2005). India's philosophies comprise orthodox (*astika*) systems (Nyaya, Vaisheshika, Samkhya, Yoga, Purva-Mimamsa, and Vedanta schools of philosophy), and unorthodox (*nastika*) systems (e.g., Charvaka, Buddhism, Jainism). The orthodox systems such as Vedanta accept the authority of the Vedas, ancient scriptures of India, while the unorthodox systems do not accept the ritualistic tracts of the Vedas (Mohanty, 2011).

The Sanskrit word Vedanta is a compound of two words, *veda* and *anta*. *Veda* means knowledge and *anta*, end. Thus, Vedanta may be translated as "culmination of knowledge" (Parthasarathy, 2011d). Its philosophical import is contained in the Upanishads, the last section of the Vedas, where the philosophy is conveyed in the aphoristic style. Since Vedic times Vedanta has been a creative living tradition handed down through preceptor-disciple lineage (*guru-shisya-parampara*). In acknowledgment of this history, a Vedanta philosopher draws on a tradition that started with the Upanishads and continued through Adi Shankara (8th century) up to the philosopher's own personal teacher (*guru pranam mantra*). A modern revival of Vedanta in the second half of the 19th century was sparked by such philosophers as Ramakrishna Paramahamsa (1836–1886), Vivekananda (1863–1902), Rama Tirtha (1873–1906), and Ramana Maharishi (1879–1950). Sri Ramakrishna emphasized that the truths of the Upanishads must be experienced through day-to-day human interaction (Saradananda, 2003). His disciple Swami Vivekanda gave a concrete shape to this insight: selfless service in any field became the core spiritual practice (Vivekananda, 2016). Swami Rama Tirtha's mantra of "work is worship" works along the same lines (Tirtha, 2012). This chapter highlights the contemporary development of Vedanta as presented by A. Parthasarathy (1927–), who is one of the succeeding generation of philosophers.

Notable management academics who have looked to Vedanta for potential insights into contemporary business challenges include S. K. Chakraborty and Peter Pruzan (i.e., Chakraborty, 1998; Pruzan, 2015; Pruzan & Pruzan Mikkelsen, 2007). Other Indian spiritual, religious, and/or philosophical traditions have been discussed in relation to management and leadership, reflecting the diversity of Indian philosophical schools (Chatterji & Zsolnai, 2016; Corner, 2009; Gupta, 2017; Köllen, 2016; for more Vedantic management see also Muniapan, 2017; Satyarupananda, 2004; Sharma, 2004; Sur, 2017).

Selected Vedantic Concepts for Better Stakeholder Relations

The fundamental philosophical concept of Vedanta can be found in *Chandogya Upanishad* in the *Sama Veda: Tat tvam asi*, translated as That Thou Art. *Tat* (That) represents the supreme Reality, Brahman, the one homogeneous Reality that pervades everywhere. *Tvam* (Thou) refers to the supreme Self in all beings, Atman. *Asi* (Art) establishes the oneness of the all-pervasive Reality and the Self within. Hence the aphorism makes a bold declaration of humanity's essential divinity (Parthasarathy, 2011d). Similar statements can be found in *Isavasya Upanishad* (mantra 16) and *Kaivalya Upanishad* (mantra 19), among others (Parthasarathy, 2011b).

Human beings, however, are ignorant of their Divine inner core. This ignorance is described, for instance, in *Mundaka Upanishad* (Parthasarathy, 2011b). Such ignorance breeds the tendency to seek happiness in the world without regard for others. This quest in turn fosters attachment and worldly desire. Chapter III of the *Bhagavad Gita* sets out the criteria of an ideal action (*karma yoga*). In verses 37 to 43, desires are declared as the ultimate barrier between a human being and human perfection. With respect to a leader, therefore, desires are the greatest adversary to good conduct. Conflict and misery in the world are born of ignorant and therefore selfish, egocentric, desire-ridden human behavior. Vedanta traces the root of uncaring and irresponsible behavior as arising from the individual's blindly selfish habits, due to a lack of experience of oneness with the world. A spiritually ignorant individual "lacks the sense of oneness, camaraderie, friendliness with beings. The world is full of rivalry and competition" (Parthasarathy, 2011b, p. 2158).

How can this ignorance of the divine nature within be resolved? The antidote to ignorance is knowledge (*jnanam*). However, Vedanta points out that knowledge of the Divine is qualitatively different from knowledge of the phenomenal world. The Infinite is not an object of perception, emotion, and thought. Therefore, according to Vedanta, the only way for a person to know their divine Self is to become That (*Tat*), to realize one's true Self, to experience "I am That." It is very rare for a human being to reach this Ultimate State.

The path to Self-realization is a gradual, constant process of improving one's personality (Parthasarathy, 2011d). Such self-development already shows benefits for stakeholder relations long before the Ultimate State is reached. For the sake of self-development, the spiritual seeker is encouraged in the *Bhagavad Gita* (chapter III, verse 20) to act "with an eye to the welfare of the world" (Parthasarathy, 2011a, p. 1188). Applied to the business context, self-development will manifest itself in (financially) successful business endeavors, whose success is evaluated on the basis of good conduct rather than profits generated at the expense of other people and the natural environment.

However, merely intending to do good to others is not sufficient; a caring attitude and caring actions toward stakeholders need to become second nature. How can the gap be closed between good intentions and real actions? According to Parthasarathy, it is not theoretical knowledge but wisdom that flows naturally into practice. Knowledge (*jnanam*) is understood here as scholastic, theoretical knowledge. The knowledge that cheap clothes are usually the product of inhuman conditions in sweatshops is one example. A lack of wisdom (*vijnanam*) is established through the inability of persons to act upon the knowledge they have gained. For example, consumers are enraged about the working conditions in textile sweatshops, yet many continue to buy low-priced clothes from companies that source from these factories. Vedanta provides a concrete methodology of bridging the gap between theory and practice through individual reflection (*manana*). Theoretical knowledge is reflected upon by the individual until it is assimilated into the personality and then results in action (Parthasarathy, 2011d). To achieve this, daily exercises are recommended for the practitioner, such as early morning study of scriptural texts and introspection (Parthasarathy, 2011d).

Development of the Intellect (Buddhi)

According to Vedanta, a human being is made up of body, mind, and intellect (BMI). The body (*stula sarira*) performs actions guided either by the mind or the intellect. The mind (*manas*) is defined as the seat of feelings, emotions, impulses, likes, and dislikes. The intellect (*buddhi*) is defined as that which thinks, comprehends, judges, and decides. Parthasarathy sees the task of the intellect (*buddhi*) as guidance and control of the mind's emotions and desires and of the body's actions and perceptions (Parthasarathy, 2011d).

The Vedantic concept of intellect (*buddhi*) versus mind (*manas*) emphasizes the negative consequences of impulsive, emotionally driven behavior. In chapter II of the *Bhagavad Gita*, the conflict between mind (*manas*) and intellect (*buddhi*) is conveyed in verse 44. The effects of an uncontrolled mind are vividly described in the following two famous verses of the same chapter:

> 62. A man musing on objects develops attachment for them, from attachment arises desire, from desire arises anger.
>
> 63. From anger arises delusion, from delusion, confusion of memory, from confusion of memory loss of intellect, from loss of intellect he perishes.
>
> *(Parthasarathy, 2011a, p. 1136)*

Parthasarathy distinguishes intellect (*buddhi*) from intelligence. Intelligence is understood as mere information acquired from external sources such as schools and universities. For instance, a person may acquire extraordinary learning in a professional field as a result of intelligence, and at the same time they may not have a strong intellect (*buddhi*) to control personal, professional, and social actions (Parthasarathy, 2011d).

Emphasis on the Vedantic concept of intellect (*buddhi*) is critical at the present juncture because advancements in areas such as science, welfare, media, and information technology have led to an explosion of choices and temptations, which in turn trigger an uncontrolled increase of desires in the mind (*manas*). These desires are accompanied by a rise in selfishness, anxieties, and other negative emotions such as greed, jealousy, avarice, and hatred. In other words, the disturbed, unhappy mind (*manas*) has become so prevalent in humankind, that an untrained intellect (*buddhi*) cannot handle it anymore. The result is impulsive, often self-destructive and careless behavior (Parthasarathy, 2011c, 2011a).

To regain mental peace individually and social harmony collectively, egocentric, selfish behavior needs to be reduced on the micro level. To achieve this, the intellect (*buddhi*) must be trained to increase rational decision-making and unselfish, even selfless action, while keeping in mind the needs of others. In other words, a strong intellect (*buddhi*) is needed to analyze all the conflicting and potentially selfish emotions and preferences of the mind and to guide caring behavior.

A well-trained intellect (*buddhi*) also means critical, innovative, and creative thinking of a higher order, and is seen as fundamental for human flourishing in times of artificial intelligence and smart machines (Hess & Ludwig, 2017). For instance, a strong intellect (*buddhi*) can control the instinct of the mind (*manas*) to follow the herd. This opens the door for innovative and creative thinking. An entrepreneur with a sharp intellect will quickly identify opportunities for value creation. A clear intellect will assist the manager in the successful handling of complex relationships and tasks.

To train the intellect (*buddhi*), Parthasarathy suggests an attitude of questioning; of not taking anything for granted, and that this attitude should be inculcated from an early age. Two practices are recommended. First, early morning study and reflection (*manana*) of scriptural literature aims at developing the intellect. Second, the practice of daily introspection is intended to make the existing level of intellect (*buddhi*) available (Parthasarathy, 2011d).

Circle of Identification: Who Does the Manager Care About?

The emotions of love and caring about others are the fruition of a person's oneness with the world (Parthasarathy, 2011a). A person perceives self-identification—they recognize themselves in another. Human life is an opportunity for human beings to expand their capacity to identify with larger entities in the world. For example, becoming a parent is the process of expanding an individual's circle of identification from themselves to the family unit. This expansion should continue to grow to include eventually the wider community, the country, all humanity, and all living beings. The love and care of a Self-realized person has no boundaries (Parthasarathy, 2011d). Another assumption of this model is inclusiveness of the inner circles. Caring for the community will benefit the family and the individual. As Freeman et al. (2011) note, many stakeholder networks share common interests.

The level of an individual's transformation can be visualized as a lifelong journey through concentric circles of identification, as depicted in Figure 25.1. The individual experiences harmony, oneness, a sense of belonging, and care within their circle of identification. The zones beyond the individual's circle are experienced as distant formality, otherness, alienation, and

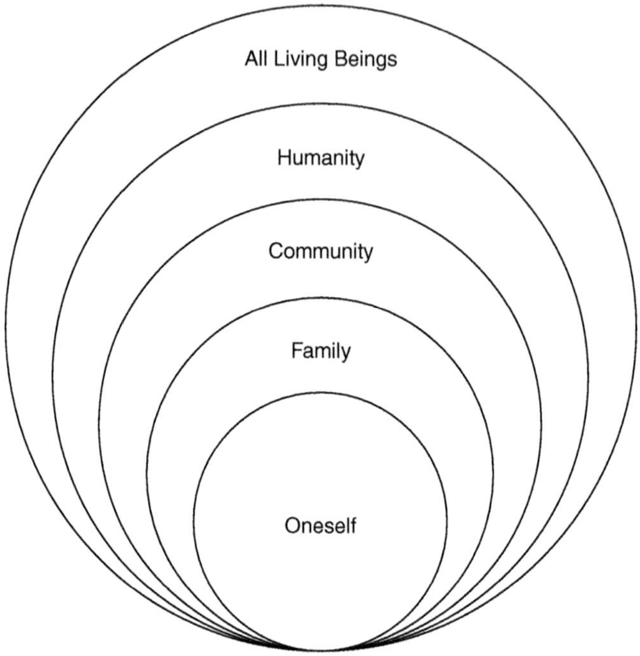

Figure 25.1 Circle of Identification

Source: Adapted from Parthasarathy (2011d, p. 500).

even hostility. Additionally, there is a risk that the individual may develop selfish, possessive attachment to their own circle. Within their circle of identification, managers will demonstrate adequate care as long as they keep in check the tendency to become possessive. By contrast, lack of care toward certain stakeholders can be explained by their relegation to a position outside the manager's circle of identification. Here, conflicts between stakeholder interests arise, as has been widely discussed in Stakeholder Theory.

For the personality to grow, there must be a conscious effort on the part of the individual to identify with a larger circle of identification. Thus, managers will be able to include larger and more complex stakeholder networks within their area of identification. This is a gradual process. It is not realistic for a self-centered person all of a sudden to become caring and loving with all living beings. A person needs to recognize their circle of identification and then gradually aim for the next larger circle (Parthasarathy, 2011d). The importance of continuously aspiring to a higher ideal will be discussed in the next section.

Purifying Desires: The Pyramid of Desires

Another perspective on the transformation of the personality centers around desires. As mentioned before, in Vedanta, uncaring and irresponsible behavior is rooted in desires and attachment. So, the level of development of the personality can be assessed by the quantity and quality of desires. Selfish, egocentric desires are of low quality and, as a rule, they come in large numbers. Nobler desires are usually fewer in number. When the quality of desires is high, and the number of desires is low, the personality becomes purer and behavior becomes more caring, as depicted in Figure 25.2 (Parthasarathy, 2011d). In verse 25 of chapter V in the *Bhagavad Gita*, sages are

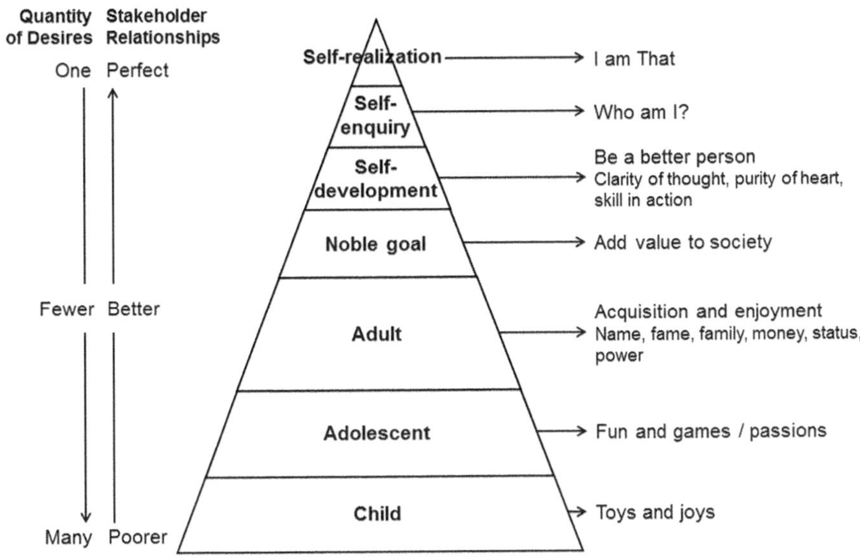

Figure 25.2 Pyramid of Desires

said to be free from sin, which can be understood as mental agitations stemming from impulsive, desire-ridden actions. Such sages "revel in the welfare of all beings" (Parthasarathy, 2011a, p. 1334). So how can a person reduce the number of desires and increase the quality of desires?

Vedanta says that it is not possible to give up desires. It is only by setting themselves higher, nobler goals that desires of lower quality will fall away. Children, on the bottom level of the Pyramid of Desires (Figure 25.2), will not lose their interest in toys. But when as a teen a child develops an interest in video games, the interest in toys will fall away. As an adult, other desires will become important (name, fame, family, status, power) and the passions of the youth will be forgotten (Parthasarathy, 2011d). The next level is the desire to positively contribute to society.

In recent years many researchers have investigated the positive impact in the world of work of having a higher goal and a greater sense of meaning and purpose in life (Ariely, Kamenica, & Prelec, 2008; Berg, 2016; Dik, Byrne, & Steger, 2013). A sense of purpose in life is a predictor of higher income and wealth (Hill, Edmonds, Peterson, Luyckx, & Andrews, 2016). Additionally, there is a lot of evidence that purpose in life has a positive impact on subjective wellbeing, physical and mental health, as well as longevity (Boyle, Buchman, Barnes, & Bennett, 2010; Cotton Bronk, Hill, Lapsley, Talib, & Finch, 2009; Hill & Turiano, 2014; Kim, Sun, Park, Kubzansky, & Peterson, 2013; Kim, Sun, Park, & Peterson, 2013; Lau et al., 2014; McKnight & Kashdan, 2009; Yu et al., 2015). People with purpose in life sleep better (Kim et al., 2015). It mitigates the negative effects of poverty on young people (Machell, Disabato, & Kashdan, 2016).

Self-development aims at refining the personality at all levels. This involves changing the intention that motivates actions from selfish to unselfish to selfless, thus purifying emotions, sharpening the intellect, and redirecting thoughts from the mundane to the Divine. The traditional spiritual practices of *karma yoga* (path of action), *bhakti yoga* (path of devotion), and *jnana yoga* (path of knowledge) are recommended to accomplish these goals. These practices will be illustrated in more detail in the Dags Lab case study. Purifying the personality through self-development will lead to self-enquiry (Who am I?) and ultimately to Self-realization (I Am That.) (Parthasarathy, 2011d, p. 611).

Table 25.1 The Three Gunas

	Tamas (Inactive)	*Rajas (Active)*	*Sattva (Trans-Active)*
Characteristics	State of inertia; lethargic, indifferent, heedless, bereft of emotional or intellectual expression	State of passionate desires and agitated thoughts; highly active; emotionally involved in life's affairs	State of equanimity and serenity Dynamic and relaxed action
State of mind (*manas*)	Inert	Unstable	Perfectly balanced
State of intellect (*buddhi*)	Sees wrong as right	Confused	Clear, sharp, and objective

Source: Adapted from Parthasarathy (2011d, 460–466).

Purifying Thoughts: The Concept of the Three Gunas

The concept of the three temperaments (*gunas*) is an indigenous Indian personality model based on Vedic literature. There are several psychological inventories that measure these temperaments in a person (Murthy & S., 2014; Murthy & Kumar, 2007; Wolf, 1999). According to Vedanta, every individual has aspects of all three *gunas* in the personality. However, the proportions of the three aspects within a person differ widely and this accounts for the immense diversity of personalities. The temperament *tamas* is described as a state of inertia, laziness. A predominately *tamasik* person lives a dull and inactive life. The temperament *rajas* is the state of passionate activity. Predominantly *rajasik* persons are very active and productive, but also highly agitated and involved in their actions, and therefore stressed. The temperament *sattva* is described as a state of equanimity and serenity. A predominantly *sattvik* person is very mature and objective. A *sattvik* person's thoughts and actions are balanced and effective (Parthasarathy, 2011d). A study by Sharma, Singh, and Mehrotra (2016) found the *sattvik* personality was a predictor of wisdom and psychological wellbeing. Stempel, Cheston, Greer, and Gillespie (2006) found a *sattvik* personality to be related to "goodness." Thus, a *sattvik* manager can be expected to show a high degree of care toward stakeholders. In line with the previous discussion of the Circle of Identification, the transformation of the personality aims at developing a predominately *sattvik* personality. The model and related questionnaires can be used to measure the development stage of a person, and to identify areas for improvement. However, Vedanta practitioners should take care not to unintentionally develop even more self-centeredness through constant measurement of their spiritual progress.

Applied Vedantic Stakeholder Management: The Case of Dags Labs, Durban, South Africa

So, how can entrepreneurial and managerial activities be harmonized with this individual, transformational journey? This chapter documents the case of Nikhil Somaru from Durban, South Africa. His entrepreneurial activities started after he graduated from the 3-year residential Vedanta philosophy course at the Vedanta Academy in Malavli, India. Somaru recognized a need in his hometown of Durban, South Africa to bring technological solutions to the burgeoning African economy. His startup, Dags Labs, has operated on a contractual basis in the financial, shipping, events, and legal industries, offering technological solutions to the unique challenges present in the African context. After graduation, Somaru continued to practice daily Vedanta study and reflection early in the morning.

His operating principles, both individually and from the business perspective, follow from the Vedantic standard model of the individual (BMI). This refers to the interplay between body, mind, and intellect as previously discussed. He counts this model as being crucial to prospering in a manner that benefits both business and the community around him.

Vedanta explains that the threefold activity of perception, emotion, and thought are unified by the conception of an ideal—some purpose beyond the immediate selfish needs of the individual, or even the business as a whole. This *raison d'être* forms the basis whence all endeavors emerge and may be likened to the formulation of a mission statement in conventional business parlance, but with a distinctly unselfish flavor.

Somaru mentions that the concept of *karma yoga*, action by the body in service of the ideal, keeps his team focused, despite challenges. When exploring a problem, it enables his team to remain in context, and provides a goal that goes beyond the interests of any one stakeholder, instead unifying them into a cohesive vision that is beneficial to all.

When combating stress within the organization, the concept of *bhakti yoga* has been invaluable to Dags Labs. *Bhakti yoga* is the path of devotion. According to Parthasarathy (2011d, p. 603), "True devotion means faith in good rather than faith in God." A true *bhakta* surrenders his individuality to the Higher, the great plan of nature (Parthasarathy, 2011d).

In addition to standard business practices such as root–cause analysis and post-mortems, *bhakti yoga* allows the team members to recognize the limits of their own activities and confine their expectations to the realms over which they have control. This controlling of expectation, according to Vedanta, is the best way to limit stress at the individual and organizational level. Causation in Vedanta must be respected as the ultimate authority with regard to the success and failure of any endeavor, and the liberation from stress that this perspective offers is invaluable in delivering solutions that address the challenges of the problem domain.

Jnana yoga in Vedanta is defined as an awareness of the distinction between the permanent and the impermanent. All human activity and endeavor is fundamentally limited in its scope. While this might suggest a nihilistic approach to activity, Vedanta is in fact a philosophy that promotes and encourages action. Somaru suggests that instilling this awareness among the team has allowed the team members to avoid becoming attached to activity per se, instead enabling an objective approach to action, which brings success in the business world.

Summary

Vedanta philosophy enhances the business ethics discussion because it provides unique findings about human beings, based on thousands of years of observation of human behavior. Human beings are inherently diverse (theory of *gunas*). Most human beings show limited rationality in their behavior (theory of intellect *buddhi*). Uncaring and irresponsible behavior arises from selfishness. The conclusion Vedanta draws is that it is essential for the individual to actively develop their personality.

While focusing on the individual transformational process, Vedanta practitioners will contribute to the benefit of every generation, society, and environment as much as the respective level of spiritual development allows. The more unselfishly a manager thinks and acts, the higher the contribution to the greater good. With a highly developed intellect (*buddhi*), the Vedanta practitioner will identify opportunities for value creation for a large circle of stakeholders. (Financial) rewards are a consequence of careful consideration of stakeholders' interests.

What is common to both Vedanta and Stakeholder Theory is the perception of other entities as being of equal intrinsic worth, to whom care and respect is due. Despite their different origins, both schools of thought are founded on a worldview that actively perceives in ever-increasing circles of awareness the entities who interact with one another in human life.

Freeman and Auster's (2015) approach to closing the values gap on the organizational level corresponds directly with the individual approach taken by Vedanta. The principles of risk and accountability of Stakeholder Theory resonates with the concept in Vedanta of a *sattvik* manager who can be expected to show a high degree of care toward stakeholders.

References

Ariely, D., Kamenica, E., & Prelec, D. (2008). Man's search for meaning: The case of Legos. *Journal of Economic Behavior and Organization, 67*(3–4), 671–677.

Berg, J. L. (2016). The impact of personal and company purpose on engagement, life satisfaction and commitment. *Academy of Management Annual Meeting Proceedings*, 1. https://doi.org/10.5465/ambpp.2016.12353abstract.

Boyle, P. A., Buchman, A. S., Barnes, L. L., & Bennett, D. A. (2010). Effect of a purpose in life on risk of incident Alzheimer Disease and mild cognitive impairment in community-dwelling older persons. *Archives of General Psychiatry, 67*(3), 304.

Brower, J., & Mahajan, V. (2013). Driven to be good: A stakeholder theory perspective on the drivers of corporate social performance. *Journal of Business Ethics, 117*(2), 313–331.

Chakraborty, S. K. (1998). Ethics for business and management: Explorations in Hindu thought. In B. N. Kumar & H. Steinmann (Eds.), *Ethics in International Management* (1st ed.). Berlin: de Gruyter, 281–307.

Chatterji, M., & Zsolnai, L. (Eds.). (2016). *Ethical Leadership: Indian and European Spiritual Approaches*. London: Palgrave Macmillan.

Corner, P. D. (2009). Workplace spirituality and business ethics: Insights from an Eastern spiritual tradition. *Journal of Business Ethics, 85*(3), 377–389.

Cotton Bronk, K., Hill, P. L., Lapsley, D. K., Talib, T. L., & Finch, H. (2009). Purpose, hope, and life satisfaction in three age groups. *Journal of Positive Psychology, 4*(6), 500–510.

Dik, B. J., Byrne, Z. S., & Steger, M. F. (Eds.). (2013). *Purpose and Meaning in the Workplace* (1st ed.). Washington, DC: American Psychological Association.

Freeman, R. E. (1984). *Strategic Management: A Stakeholder Approach*. Boston: Pitman Publishing.

Freeman, R. E. (2001). A Stakeholder Theory of the modern corporation. *Perspectives in Business Ethics SIE, 3*(144), 38–48.

Freeman, R. E., & Auster, E. R. (2015). *Bridging the Values Gap: How Authentic Organizations Bring Values to Life* (1st ed.). Oakland, CA: Berrett-Koehler Publishers.

Freeman, R. E., & McVea, J. F. (2001). A stakeholder approach to strategic management. Darden Business School Working Paper No. 01-02.

Freeman, R. E., Wicks, A. C., & Parmar, B. (2011). Stakeholder Theory as a basis for capitalism. In L. Sacconi, M. Blair, E. R. Freeman, & A. Vercelli (Eds.), *Corporate Social Responsibility and Corporate Governance*. Basingstoke, UK: Palgrave Macmillan, 52–72.

Friedman, M. (1970, September 13). The social responsibility of business is to increase its profits. *New York Times*, 122–126.

Goodpaster, K. E. (2010). Corporate responsibility and its constituents. In G. G. Brenkert & T. L. Beauchamp (Eds.), *The Oxford Handbook of Business Ethics*. Oxford: Oxford University Press, 43–157.

Gupta, S. (2017). The "Indian philosophy of consciousness" and its relevance to 21st century business management. *Philosophy of Management, 16*, 35–54.

Harrison, J. S., & Wicks, A. C. (2013). Stakeholder Theory, value, and firm performance. *Business Ethics Quarterly, 23*(1), 97–124.

Hess, E. D., & Ludwig, K. (2017). *Humility Is the New Smart: Rethinking Human Excellence in the Smart Machine Age* (1st ed.). Oakland, CA: Berrett-Koehler Publishers.

Hill, P. L., Edmonds, G. W., Peterson, M., Luyckx, K., & Andrews, J. A. (2016). Purpose in life in emerging adulthood: Development and validation of a new brief measure. *Journal of Positive Psychology, 11*(30), 237–245.

Hill, P. L., & Turiano, N. A. (2014). Purpose in life as a predictor of mortality across adulthood. *Psychological Science, 25*(7), 1482–1486.

Jayapalan, N. (2008). *Economic History of India : Ancient to Present Day* (2nd rev. ed.). New Delhi, India: Atlantic Publications.

Kim, E. S., Hershner, S. D., & Strecher, V. J. (2015). Purpose in life and incidence of sleep disturbances. *Journal of Behavioral Medicine, 38*(3), 590–597.
Kim, E. S., Sun, J. K., Park, N., Kubzansky, L. D., & Peterson, C. (2013). Purpose in life and reduced risk of myocardial infarction among older U.S. adults with coronary heart disease: A two-year follow-up. *Journal of Behavioral Medicine, 36*(2), 124–133.
Kim, E. S., Sun, J. K., Park, N., & Peterson, C. (2013). Purpose in life and reduced incidence of stroke in older adults: "The Health and Retirement Study." *Journal of Psychosomatic Research, 74*(5), 427–432.
Köllen, T. (2016). Reconceptualizing profit-orientation in management: A karmic view on "Return on investment" calculations. *Philosophy of Management, 15*(1), 7–20.
Lau, E. Y. Y., Cheung, S. H., Lam, J., Hui, C. H., Cheung, S. F., & Mok, D. S. Y. (2014). Purpose-driven life: Life goals as a predictor of quality of life and psychological health. *Journal of Happiness Studies, 16*(5), 1163–1184.
Machell, K. A., Disabato, D. J., & Kashdan, T. B. (2016). Buffering the negative impact of poverty on youth: The power of purpose in life. *Social Indicators Research, 126*(2), 845–861.
McKnight, P. E., & Kashdan, T. B. (2009). Purpose in life as a system that creates and sustains health and well-being: An integrative, testable theory. *Review of General Psychology, 13*, 242–251.
Matilal, B. K. (1998). *The Character of Logic in India*. Albany: State University of New York Press.
Mohanty, J. M. (1992). *Reason and Tradition in Indian Thought: An Essay on the Nature of Indian Philosophical Thinking*. Oxford, UK: Clarendon Press.
Mohanty, J. M. (2011). Indian philosophy. Retrieved from www.britannica.com/topic/Indian-philosophy#ref20650.
Muniapan, B. (2017). Philosophy and management : The relevance of Vedanta in management. In P. Ordóñez de Pablos (Ed.), *Managerial Strategies and Solutions for Business Success in Asia*. Hershey, PA: Business Science Reference, 124–139.
Murthy, C. G. V., & S., S. (2014). Assessment of traits and types on personality: An Indian psychological perspective. *Indian Journal of Psychology*, 41–57.
Murthy, P. K., & Kumar, S. K. K. (2007). Concept Triguna: A critical analysis and synthesis. *Psychological Studies, 52*(1), 103–113.
Parthasarathy, A. (2011a). Bhagavad Gita. In A. Parthasarathy (Ed.), *The Complete Works of Swami Parthasarathy* (1st ed.). Mumbai, India: A. Parthasarathy, 963–2041.
Parthasarathy, A. (2011b). Choice Upanishads. In A. Parthasarathy (Ed.), *The Complete Works of Swami Parthasarathy* (1st ed.). Mumbai, India: A. Parthasarathy, 2043–2353.
Parthasarathy, A. (2011c). The fall of the human intellect. In A. Parthasarathy (Ed.), *The Complete Works of Swami Parthasarathy* (1st ed.). Mumbai, India: A. Parthasarathy, 9–117.
Parthasarathy, A. (2011d). Vedanta treatise: The eternities. In A. Parthasarathy (Ed.), *The Complete Works of Swami Parthasarathy* (1st ed.). Mumbai, India: A. Parthasarathy, 394–776.
Parthasarathy, A. (2014). *Governing Business & Relationships* (2nd ed.). Mumbai, India: A. Parthasarathy.
Pruzan, P. (2015). The source of ethical competency: Eastern perspectives provided by a westerner. In K. J. Ims & L. J. T. Pedersen (Eds.), *Business and the Greater Good: Rethinking Business Ethics in an Age of Crisis*. Cheltenham, UK: Edward Elgar, 117–148.
Pruzan, P., & Pruzan Mikkelsen, K. (2007). *Leading With Wisdom: Spiritual-based Leadership in Business*. Sheffield, UK: Greenleaf Publishing Limited.
Ramanujan, A. K. (1989). Is there an Indian way of thinking? An informal essay. *Contributions to Indian Sociology, 23*(1), 41–58.
Sanyal, S. (2008). *The Indian Renaissance: India's Rise After a Thousand Years of Decline*. Singapore: World Scientific.
Saradananda, S. (2003). *Sri Ramakrishna and His Divine Play*. St. Louis, MO: Vedanta Society of St. Louis.
Satyarupananda, S. (2004). Life within and life without: A managerial approach to living. In A. Das Gupta (Ed.), *Human Values in Management* (1st ed.). Aldershot, UK: Ashgate, 39–48.
Sen, A. (2005). *The Argumentative Indian: Writings on Indian History, Culture and Identity*. London: Allen Lane.
Sharma, S. (2004). Indian ethics and the spirit of development: The VEDA model of leadership and management. In A. Das Gupta (Ed.), *Human Values in Management* (1st ed.). Aldershot, UK: Ashgate, 49–57.
Sharma, S., Singh, A., & Mehrotra, S. (2016). Sattva Guna as a predictor of wisdom and PWB. *International Journal of Indian Psychology, 4*(1), 158–167.
Stempel, H. S., Cheston, S. E., Greer, J. M., & Gillespie, C. K. (2006). Further exploration of the Vedic personality inventory: Validity, reliability and generalizability. *Psychological Reports, 98*(1), 261–273.

Sur, S. (2017). Beyond the Indus: How Hinduism offers an alternate management paradigm. *Philosophy of Management, 16*(1), 69–89.

Tirtha, R. (2012). *In Woods of God-Realization* (Vol. 1, reprint). Lucknow, India: Swami Rama Tirtha Pratisthan.

Vivekananda, S. (2016). *The Complete Works of Swami Vivekananda* (18th Print, Vol. 2). Kolkata, India: Adhyaksha Advaita Ashrama.

Wicks, A. (2014). Stakeholder Theory and spirituality. *Journal of Management, Spirituality and Religion, 11*(4), 294–306.

Wolf, D. B. (1999). A psychometric analysis of the three gunas. *Psychological Reports, 84*(3 Pt 2), 1379–1390.

Yu, L., Boyle, P. A., Wilson, R. S., Levine, S. R., Schneider, J. A., & Bennett, D. A. (2015). Purpose in life and cerebral infarcts in community-dwelling older people. *Stroke, 46*(4), 1071–1076.

26

SPIRITUALITY AS A REFLECTION OF VALUE-CENTEREDNESS

Sylvia W. Burgess and Karen Martin-Jones

Introduction

In the past 10 years spirituality in the workplace has gained more traction. Historically, all attempts to leave everything spiritual out of the workplace has been the norm. As the workplace has been transformed by the various generations continuously entering the workforce, a look at value systems is critical to the ongoing success of organizations. The introduction of the connection between spirituality and spiritual capital as an asset that everyone possesses and can use in various ways creates a foundation for understanding the meaning and importance of spiritual capital as a means of sustainability for those in leadership roles.

Leaders in organizations need to be able to create a workplace culture that is evolving and sustainable for future generations. Thus, leading to the importance of empowering workers to lead using spiritual capital's intrinsic value system as a moral compass to build relationships, enhance trust, and create organizational change as a tool to support the intergenerational workplace that is forced with knowing how to effectively communicate and build relationships. Spiritual capital while not directly representative of any religion or religious practice is born out of one's personal spirituality. Spirituality is an interconnected duality between a leader's intrinsic value system and the world around them. These intrinsic values are reflective of the leader's spirituality. It is important that leaders understand the importance of spirituality and the role that it plays in assisting us in working together, building trust in our relationships and our fundamental wholeness as individuals. This value-centered approach emphasizes the importance of treating spirituality as a resource in this rapidly changing work environment, with the hopes of bridging any existing conflictual generational gaps.

Spiritual capital is defined as the intrinsic values of an individual that are aligned with trust, culture, and deep commitment to relationship building, to better serve society as well as to satisfy our internal human need to serve. These intrinsic factors are value-based and not focused on religious constructs (Lloyd, 2010). Spiritual capital is dependent upon having faith in one another that is not necessarily bound by traditional contractual agreements for working together. Spiritual capital has nothing to do with one's personal religious practices (Burgess, 2011). Traditionally, the church has played a significant role in helping us develop our value systems, but it does not stop there. When cultivated in the right way, spiritual capital can help individuals go beyond just working together to foster repeatable and sustainable relationships in the workplace.

In 2011, Burgess conducted research examining the relationship between engagement and spiritual capital. The results indicated that as an individual's spiritual capital increases so does their willingness to engage and participate. As such, spiritual capital can be used as an asset to build organizational participation among workers. Spiritual capital is a resource that is not possessed by select leaders, but by all humans. By helping leaders understand that they already possess an intrinsic nature to participate and engage with others can change the organizational climate in very positive ways; especially considering the multiple generations currently in the workplace and the challenges associated with this. As the makeup of organizations continues to rapidly change, leaders will need more tools to bridge the gaps between differences in the workforce.

Currently, there is a great deal of discussion about organizational leadership and generational challenges that exist in the workplace. The topic around generational differences has become an ever-increasing discussion in many arenas. Much of it revolves around the fact that for the first time in history, four generations are in the workplace and a fifth generation (GenZ) is not far behind. Thus, the ability to collaborate effectively is integral for leaders not only in the workplace, but in every environment. With each successive generation, the advancements and access to technology changes the way in which we communicate, engage, and collaborate (Martin-Jones, 2012). Furthermore, technology significantly impacts our values and beliefs. After all, people's values are reflective of what is important to them.

Generational Differences

Historically, generational differences are always at play. However, with multiple generations in the workplace vying for the available leadership roles, the relationship and collaboration gap is more noticeable. Of note is the notion that Millennials are challenging the leadership status quo. But, more importantly, they are challenging the value system exhibited by others in the workplace. In the past, salaries and material rewards were considered measures of success. While these are still important, they rank less important than more intangible values to the Millennial generation (Bottomley & Burgess, 2017). It is important to understand the generational differences and their perspectives on spirituality in the workplace.

According to Mannheim (1972), generation is defined as a group of individuals who are the same age and have experienced similar social events in time. The term generation is most often used to describe ancestral affinity, but it has been adopted into common use to describe broader social trends (Joshi, Dencker, & Gentz, 2011; Pilcher, 1994; Ryder, 1965). However, from a social perspective, it is defined as individuals born during the same time, sharing similar historical and socio-cultural experiences. Thus, relegating them to a specific age group implies that their historical and social experiences are in fact similar. However, much of the literature suggests that this demarcation is indicative of a generational cohort (Sessa, Kabacoff, Deal, & Brown, 2007).

Although there are many inconsistencies in the literature as it relates to the start and end date of these generations, for this chapter generations are defined as follows: Silent (1928–1943), Baby Boomers (1944–1964), Generation X (1965–1980), Generation Y, most commonly referred to as the Millennials (1981–1995), and most recently Generation Z (born after 1996). Each generation has experienced significant events which have shaped who they are and more importantly what they value (Gursoy, Chi, & Karadag, 2013). Many of the generational experiences between Generations X, Y, and Z are not significantly different (Twenge, 2010). After all, many of the experiences parallel events that have transpired over decades (i.e., equality, social, and political movements). Understanding these similar, yet prominent, experiences are key to creating a culture that is inclusive and supportive of all generations.

The largest generational gap exists between the Millennials and Boomers. Millennials have far surpassed Boomers and are the largest living generation in the nation. Millennials number over 75.4 million versus 74.9 million Boomers (Pew Research Center, 2010). As a result, the Millennials are setting the pace of growth and leadership styles in the workplace. This is causing organizations to rethink their operating and leadership strategies. Gone are the days when GenXers and Boomers stay with their organizations until retirement and longer. Along with the Millennial population growth in organizations, they are also the dominant culture in most church organizations. After all, if one is to believe that church is one of the fundamental places where spirituality is cultivated, values are formed, and leaders developed, this is certainly a critical point to examine in terms of how spirituality is impacting the workplace with multiple generations present who no longer worship in the same traditional manners. According to a study conducted by Pew Research, 36% of Americans attend religious services weekly and 61% use streaming services to watch shows. Furthermore, 88% of individuals between ages 18 and 29 use some form of social media (Snapchat, Instagram, YouTube) multiple times a day. This research suggests that technology is being utilized as a key component in shaping values and how intergenerational communication is occurring (Pew Research Center, 2010).

Baby Boomers. High births were prominent during this time, hence the name "baby boomers." As a result, this generation has a strong presence in the workforce. They are described as self-indulgent, entitled, and career oriented. This is a generation who experienced post-war economic prosperity. They believe that hard work pays off and is the key to success and promotion. They are defined as workaholics, who respect hierarchical organizational structures. Some of the literature suggests that this has been a point of contention for baby boomers and younger generations who believe that there should be more flexibility in the workplace (Burke, 2016). In terms of spirituality, the Boomer generation is representative of those who rejected religious institutions at an early age, but later in life sought some spiritual confirmation that may be a result of aging. This generation's approach to spirituality includes both traditional and non-traditional practices for spiritual growth. Interestingly, Boomers may choose to experience several approaches to spirituality in their lifetime.

GenX. Generation X is known as the "latch-key" generation. They are the generation who had to learn to balance work and family life. The generation that saw fewer nuclear families and more single parent and blended families. Many of the salient events that occurred during this time were layoffs, divorce, economic recession, and Watergate. They represent 33% of the workforce. They are known for staying on their job for long periods of time. As a result, they value independence and the potential for advancement at work. They are comfortable with diversity and tend to focus on similarities rather than differences. They compete with Millennials for upper management jobs (Stark & Farner, 2015). Unlike their Boomer parents, GenXers are more likely to stay attached to religious institutions for their spiritual growth. They often change institutions but are likely to keep trying to find the right connection until they land in a place of contentment for their spirituality. GenXers have tended to embrace God, religious beliefs, and spirituality in non-traditional ways which translated into raising their children with a strong sense of right and wrong as well as making decisions for themselves based on examining information critically.

Millennials. Stapleton, Wen, Starrett, and Kilburn (2007) describe Millennials as independent, inclusive, innovative, and instantaneous—wanting things quickly. They value personal development and work–life balance over money and status. They would rather be happy than to stay at a job they dislike. As a result, their résumés reflect a varied work history. This is a generation who appreciates diversity. Thus, a culturally diverse workplace is what they desire. This generation is concerned with making a name for themselves through altruistic acts, and long to have those acts praised and recognized (Stevens, 2010). They have a higher technical skill set than their prior generations. Their access to technology makes them a generation who has changed the way in which we acquire knowledge and access information. They too are a generation who have experienced non-traditional family structures. Contrary to popular belief, just because Millennials are not necessarily attending traditional church does not mean that they have forsaken their spirituality. They are seeking alternative avenues to address their spirituality. Technology has created venues that were not available to Boomers and GenXers in the same way it is for Millennials. Their spirituality is more often expressed through the things that they care deeply about. Traditional religious practices are being replaced with a new way of thinking about spirituality that does not require putting a label on it. Their focus is on doing things for the greater good of the world and respecting the beliefs of others as opposed to focusing on what they should believe based on their parents' traditions.

Generation Z. GenZ makes up approximately 26% of the US population. GenZ is considered a generation that is less focused because they live with constant updates. They must process a lot of information and at a rapid pace. This tags them as great multi-taskers. GenZs are considered to be early starters with most joining the workforce between the ages of 16 and 18. They tend to opt for more non-traditional education such as online. Further, they tend to be more entrepreneurial as they prefer more independent work environments. Lastly, this group tends to be more global with the ever-changing advances in technology (Beal, 2017). This generation is noted to be more anti-religion than any other generation. Does this mean that they are not spiritual? No, but their perspectives on God and religion may be more flexible and non-traditional than any former generations. They often ask spiritual questions and many of them pray, but their views are more liberal than those of their parents. It may be too soon to try and predict the path that this generation will take as they are currently teenagers and still have many choices to make. However, all signs suggest that this is a generation who will use technology and will fight for what they believe is fair and equitable for all people.

One of the major themes that resonates throughout the research on generational differences are the similarities that Generation X and the Millennials possess as it relates to the importance of work–life balance and flexibility. Retention of these generations is contingent upon creating a culture that values work–life balance and flexibility as well as altruistic and social values as key components to their job satisfaction (Twenge, 2010). This culture should include space for individual spirituality. Although the expression of spirituality for each generation may be different, it is important to take note of how individual spirituality will impact the value systems in the workplace.

There are many differences in value systems among generations. These differences in values have often served to widen the gap of understanding between generations. A chief factor to remember is that although value systems may be different, they are all important. Leaders are often defined by their values and the values often emphasize what things are essential to success. It is vital for good leaders to hold on to their values even if they are unpopular, as long as they are helping the organization succeed. However, when the values become outdated or no longer applicable to organizational success, the leader must recognize this and change. When the values of leaders are instilled in the organization this creates an opportunity for others to have a way by which to respond in times of crisis or turbulence that is consistent with the value system of the leaders (Bottomley & Burgess, 2017). Operating from this perspective, it gives credibility to the need to appreciate multiple value systems. It also should encourage relationship building across generations, which encompasses values from all leaders within the workplace. The challenge is in blending these values in such a manner that is more inclusive for those involved and enhances productivity in the work environment. There are many ways to accomplish this, which include being present in the moment, being comfortable in the work community, accepting limits, and building positive relationships even in conflictual situations.

Table 26.1 Overview of the Currently Working Generations

Generation	*Key Characteristics*	*Spirituality*
Baby boomers	• Hard worker • Respect hierarchical structures • Stay on the job for long periods	• Rejected religious institutions at early an age • Seek spiritual growth later in life (traditional and non-traditional) • Experience several approaches to spirituality
GenX	• Latch-key generation • Had to learn to balance work/family life • Seek flexibility in the workplace • Stay on the job for long periods of time • Experienced non-traditional family structures	• More likely to stay attached to their spiritual institutions for spiritual growth • Tend to embrace religious beliefs and God in non-traditional ways • Access to information through technology started
Millennials	• Independent • Instantaneous • Value work–life balance over money • Consistently switch jobs • Appreciates diversity • Altruistic • Experienced non-traditional family structures • Connected to technology	• Seek non-traditional avenues for spirituality • Access to technology provides more non-traditional spiritual opportunities • Spirituality is closely aligned with their altruistic acts
GenZ	• Connected to technology and constantly receiving updates and immediate feedback • Non-traditional family structures • Value diversity and inclusion • Tend to prefer more online non-traditional education • Globally connected • Entrepreneurial	• Noted to be more agnostic than other generations • More flexible in their views on religion and God • Spiritually inquisitive • Liberal

Generational Values and Leadership

Values also play an important role in individual relationships. They serve as guiding principles for decision-making and lifestyle choices. Individuals differ in what constitutes values, but that they are recognizable and universal in some ways (Schwartz, 2012). Spiritual values take different forms for different people. There are some commonalities across spiritual values which include: (a) a connection with God; (b) alignment with nature; (c) less emphasis on material and personal desires; and (d) a social connection with other people. Values are influential in the workplace. Values are often indicative of the decisions we will make (Rokeach, 1973). They can be self-determining, but also provides space for group cooperation within the workplace. Further, values can set the tone for all of an individual's interaction and defines the culture of an organization (Kraemer, 2011). Values promote personal, collective, and relationship building among individuals.

Values are learned within a social context. They are the result of life experiences. Many of the younger generations (X, Y, Z) have grown up with technology as a constant fixture in their lives. As a result, technology has significantly shaped the value system of these generations who use technology as their social medium. A member of GenZ was asked about what she values, and her response was, "technology." I went on to ask, "what about technology do you value?" and she responded by saying, "I value the freedom that technology provides." She went on to say, "It is the medium which our generation (Z) uses to invoke change, both locally and globally" (A. Martin, personal communication, April 2018). In effect, values are what a person believes to be right or wrong. Therefore, these generations choose to be the voice of change that shifts the dynamics from the status quo and realigns the value system to one that is inclusive and equitable from a global perspective. The pervasiveness and freedom that technology provides allows for injustices and inequalities to be exposed.

Values are an intrinsic compass that guide the choices and decisions that one will make. Although values are an eternal component of one's being developed over time, they are in effect malleable (Lyons & Kuron, 2014). Suggesting that they can change over time depending upon their influences. Social scientists propose that every individual possesses a unique set of values that are shaped by culture, life experiences, and family dynamics (Weber, 2017). Thus, a generation who is shaped as mere infants by a culture that is deeply rooted in technology and family, both traditional and non-traditional will likely value similar aspects in the workplace. Additionally, it is important to note that for younger generations the freedom that technology provides is an additional variable that can potentially be used to shape their values. After all, it has been access to technology that the younger generations have used to expose inequalities or injustices that exist. For example, Google's equal pay for women, Black Lives Matter movements and protests, gun laws, and recorded police brutality using social media have all been initiated by younger generations. Baby boomers whose value system may not have aligned with the younger generations are now forced to engage with a generation who did not grow up with segregation. Therefore, it is time for the current leaders to actually consider the values of younger generations who are taking a stand and making a change.

Moreover, it is in fact these differing values, cognitions, and behaviors across generations that have led to many of the intergenerational conflicts (Stark, & Farner, 2015). Furthermore, work values among generations serve as a source of contention in many organizational units (Gursoy et al., 2013). Some research suggests that generations do not exist and that young leaders do not lead any differently from older leaders. This may very well be true, however there is an increase in the number of young people in leadership positions and the conflicts are becoming ever increasing. After all, according to data obtained from the Bureau of Labor Statistics, in 2011 there were 290 individuals between the ages of 16 and 19 in management positions and by 2017 there were 435. This is a 50% increase in just 6 years. Additionally, in 2011 there were 2611 individuals between the ages of 20 and 24 in management positions and in 2017 that number rose to 3275. This is an increase of 25% over the last 6 years (Bureau of Labor Statistics, 2011). These data support the notion that more Millennials and GenZs are entering the workforce. Which leads us to question are generational differences the problem or are the conflicts due in large part to generations who have the power and ability to shift the status quo by using their voices through technology to invoke change? Is the generational conflict due in part to a younger generation whose values are closely aligned with their generational characteristics (altruism, diversity, etc.)? Have our older generations conformed to the norm that they themselves set and now we have a generation who is creating a workplace that challenges the structures that are in place? Disrupting the norm creates an uncomfortable environment for older generations who have become accustomed to the way things have always been. Additionally, Fry (2005) suggests that generations are likely have similar attitudes and values toward leadership and workplace culture. Thus, understanding generational values is integral to addressing the issues that could arise in an intergenerational workplace.

Rokeach (1973) contends that "a value system is an enduring organization of beliefs concerning preferable modes of conduct or end states of existence along a continuum of relative importance" (p. 5). What one believes dictates how one behaves and responds to situations. Along this continuum of life generational experiences shape the value-centered belief systems. Although values are one variable impacting behaviors in organizations, researchers suggest that there are multiple variables that impact a person's decision-making. The new variable impacting and shaping Millennials and GenZ is their access to technology. This is a generation who has used social media as a driving force in shaping and defining their values and self-worth through the number of likes or followers they have. Gursoy et al. (2013) suggests that, for some, values are a measure of their worth. Gehman, Treviño, and Garud (2013) argue that values play an integral role in organization performance and behavior.

The impact of values on leadership is immense. From a leadership perspective, values can take multiple forms. Values help to determine how leaders make decisions. While past theories have promoted the natural innate qualities of leadership, values help shape leaders and their behavior. In addition, a leader's values help determine how the organizational value system is developed. In developing a value system within the organization, leaders help to create the strategy and focus for the workplace. It is important that leaders understand that their values influence organizational strategy which also directs the organizational culture. It is also necessary for leaders to understand the role that their personal value system plays in challenging the status quo. Thus, it is important for leaders to embrace the idea that with the multiple generations in the workplace there will be varied value systems in play as well.

Burgess (2011) noted that the connection between leadership and spiritual capital is one such value system that can shape the values of an organization and impact participation and engagement. When spiritual capital is viewed as an intrinsic value, there are enhanced opportunities to use it to create change through building better relationships, enhancing the trust and faith among individuals, and using it as an intentional resource with the premise that the organization will be better and a more cohesive and collaborative place to work. Incorporating spiritual capital as a tool for effective leadership and recognizing that there are multiple layers depending on which generation is putting it forth can provide leverage for leaders to build the foundation of value-centered culture within the organization that becomes more inclusive while bridging the generational gaps (Burgess, 2011).

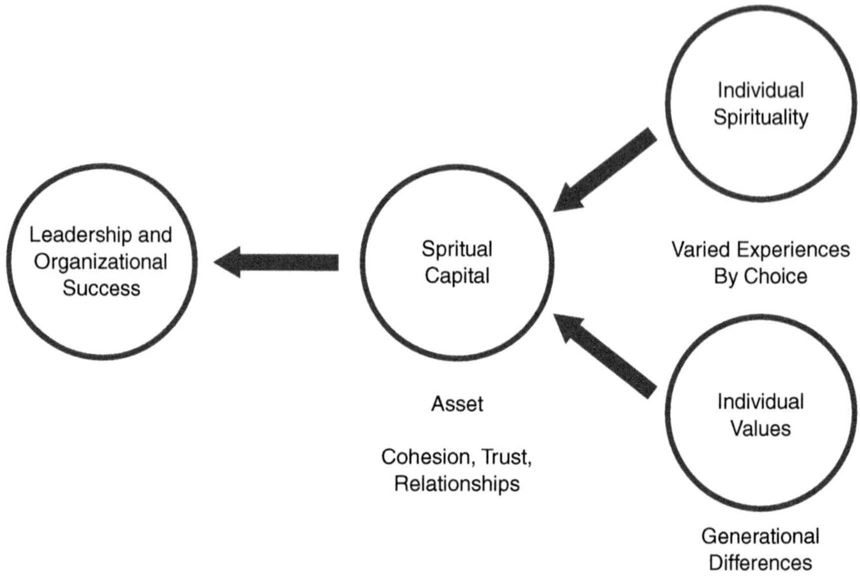

Figure 26.1 Link Between Individual Spirituality and Individual Values

Spiritual capital is universal. It is not something that only a few possess. We all have spiritual capital. The use of this capital should be intentional, as it helps individuals engage and create relationships that extend beyond just being colleagues. It helps us establish connections that give us advantages in situations where material wealth cannot. It raises the common good among individuals. Spiritual capital is a resource that can be used to bridge the gaps between generations in the workplace when used as a relational asset that brings groups together. The ultimate goal of spiritual capital is the utilization of it as an asset to help leaders and their teams understand the importance of their influence and relationship building to create a climate of participation, trust, and harmony. Further, the use of spiritual capital is a method by which leaders can connect to their teams and to other leaders by building the trust and working through faith in others to facilitate better working conditions. It is important for leaders to understand the benefits of spiritual capital and how it can provide space for greater participation among individuals (Burgess, 2011).

Continuing to work from the earlier premise that spiritual capital is born out of one's personal spirituality helps to solidify the relationship between values and spirituality. When the link between individual spirituality and individual values is made it reinforces cohesion, trust, and relationship building, which is the foundation for spiritual capital (see Figure 26.1). The intentional understanding of the connection between values, spirituality, and spiritual capital then creates a process whereby the generational differences can be better managed and subsequently influence leadership behavior and organizational success.

The Future of Leadership in the Workplace

Leadership and generations have been a topic of concern for ages, but as access and the advance of technology become even more pervasive the ability to lead multiple generations is critical to organizational growth and sustainability. Smola and Sutton (2002) propose that "continued enquiry into this field is important to business leaders as they attempt to understand motivate, and successfully lead the individuals in their organizations and function as good corporate citizens" (p. 381). "Leadership is about the growth and positive change that a leader can bring about while working with others" (Kraemer, 2011).

A leader's values are a measure of what they stand for and believe. Transformational leadership is a leader/follower model, in which the leader is able to transfer his/her values and beliefs to an organization creating a following of individuals who respect and value the leader's vision. A leader's value system is clear and transformative throughout the entire organization. The more a leader can transfer their values and beliefs, the better an organization is able to cooperate. Thus, creating an environment that is conducive for multiple generations to work together. The ability to understand a leader's values creates a culture and climate of intergenerational cohesion within the organization, in which collaboration and respect are mutually exclusive. In effect, leadership becomes a seamless process. Regardless of one's values, if there is a clear understanding and respect of the leader's values the more likely an organization is to succeed. Values-centered leadership is undergirded by four main pillars: (1) self-reflection, (2) balance, (3), self-confidence, and (4) humility.

The importance of self-reflection speaks to the need to know yourself. Through self-reflection the leader can navigate through the maze of complexity within organizations. Good leaders will take the time for self-reflection by turning off the noise and looking through their spiritual capital lens to answer what are my values and how will they help me in this situation? Self-reflection should be a daily routine. Second, balance is often spoken of as a necessity. It is difficult to find balance if you do not know what you value. One approach to creating balance is to observe and understand the value systems of those in the workplace and align values with the rules, processes, and procedures. This process begins by ensuring that people in the organization are secure, respected, trusted, and treated fairly. Leaders who have values that guide organizational behavior and are applied consistently increase the chance for balance. Allowing employees to own these guiding values creates a climate of adaptability and responsibility which adds to balance. Establishing organizational values allows for alignment with policies and procedures that are necessary for success. Third, having self-confidence and being clear about your skills and strengths create value alignment. When you lack self-confidence, it is likely that your values are not aligned. Self-confidence helps us see clearly where we are going and helps in our decision-making. It is vital that we do not mistake self-confidence for arrogance and in turn dismiss the value of individuals whom we may misjudge. Lastly, humility is often considered a soft value. Humility does not represent softness and lack of drive. It does represent finding value in the right place in the organization. When individuals exhibit humility, they support the belief that others can have good ideas, minds can be changed, and that old values should be re-examined for current usability. Examining these pillars through one's spiritual capital lens allows for the creation of cohesion, strong relationships, and trust. This is a key component to using values to bridge the generation divide around value-centeredness.

Finally, leaders need to understand the differences of each generation and build upon them and they also need to learn how to take those similarities and differences to create an environment that allows each generation to thrive collectively. After all, Mikitka (2009) posits this is a critical component of organizational success. Studies suggest that understanding workplace values is the first step in understanding how to address generational differences in the workplace. According to a study examining the perceptions of Millennials on value-centered leadership, the study contends that value-centered leadership is the most viable leadership model for addressing the intergenerational organizational structure (Maier, Tavanti, Bombard, Gentile, & Bradford, 2015). The researchers liken the value-centered model to the transformational leadership theory in that it is a leader follower model. The value-centered leadership theory focuses on creating an organizational structure that is inclusive, respects and embraces diversity while supporting common values of all entities (Maier et al., 2015). Values-based leadership is leading by example and creating a culture that is concerned about the organization as a whole, "the greater good" (Kraemer, 2011). The values-based leadership approach speaks to generations, especially a generation rooted in creating change and being change agents. Ultimately, leadership is in and of itself the ability to lead regardless of the challenges, albeit age, generational conflict, or differences, etc. Leaders need to engage in intergenerational dialogue to find out what they would like to see in the workplace. Therefore, the future of leadership must be malleable, flexible, consistent, and equitable. Thus, these aspects resonate with the descriptions of how generations describe their individual spirituality.

Conclusion

Spirituality can produce a synergy that may help bridge intentional or unintentional gaps between generations in the workplace. Value-centeredness approaches are a unique way that spirituality is acceptable in many work environments. We proffer spiritual capital as the mechanism through which this can occur. The effective use of spiritual capital can promote a climate of cohesion, strong relationships, trust, and faith in one another that goes beyond just working together daily. It creates a repeatable and sustainable climate for success through deliberate participation.

Leaders already possess spiritual capital and thus the foundation for focusing on values is in place. Spiritual capital is based on our intrinsic value system that has evolved from our experiences of spirituality and the impact of technology. This coupled with an emphasis on building relationships and understanding that there are multiple value systems operating within any organization at the same time, sets the stage for a more open-minded acceptance of others. It will take leaders that are not afraid to challenge the status quo to create an environment where intergenerational groups can co-exist, and organizational goals are accomplished with less conflict because of differences in values. This will require building mutually beneficial relationships across generations and through leaders who are intentional about incorporating values in the workplace (Burgess, 2011).

As more leaders become engaged in using value-centered approaches within their teams, the use of spiritual capital can rise as an opportunity to focus on creating organizational synergy through building relationships, building trust, and having faith in others to do their part. This is the intentional use of spiritual capital as a resource. This resource can and should yield a high return on the investment required for organizational success. It is necessary for leaders to find a place for their spirituality in the workplace. Just as the knowledge and skills you bring to work are considered a value to the success of the organization, so should your spirituality. We suggest that through the lens of spiritual capital individual spirituality can and does have a place in the work environment. Spiritual capital is an integral part of every person. Individuals should be entitled to bring their "whole" self to work. Highlighting spiritual capital as part of the success factors for organizational outcomes positions it as a resource owned by everyone. This resource along with knowledge and skills can help frame the way leaders perceive spirituality not only as a useful asset, but as a necessary requirement for intergenerational success.

References

Beal, G. (2017). 8 key differences between GenZ and Millennials. Retrieved from www.huffingtonpost.com/george-beall/8-key-differences-between_b_12814200.html.

Bottomley, K., & Burgess, S. (2017, October). Leadership skills for millennials: Challenging the status quo. Presentation at the International Leadership Association 19th Annual Global Conference, Brussels, Belgium.

Bureau of Labor Statistics. (2011). Retrieved from www.bls.gov/.

Burgess, S. W. (2011). *Spiritual capital: Relationship with civic engagement among faith-based leaders.* (Doctoral dissertation), North Carolina Agricultural and Technical State University, Greensboro, NC.

Burke, K. (2016). Millennials and baby boomers have this one thing in common. *MarketWatch.* Retrieved from www.marketwatch.com/story/millennials-and-baby-boomers-have-this-one-thing-in-common-2016-07-21.

Fry, L. W. (2005). Introduction to the Leadership Quarterly special issue: Toward a paradigm of spiritual leadership. *Leadership Quarterly, 16*(5), 619–622.

Gehman, J., Treviño, L. K., & Garud, R. (2013). Values work: A process study of the emergence and performance of organizational values practices. *Academy of Management Journal, 56*(1), 84.

Gursoy, D., Chi, C. G. Q., & Karadag, E. (2013). Generational differences in work values and attitudes among frontline and service contact employees. *International Journal of Hospitality Management, 32*(1), 40–48.

Joshi, A., Dencker, J., & Gentz, F. (2011). Generations in organizations. *Research Organizational Behavior, 31*, 177–205.

Kraemer, H. M. (2011). *From Values to Action: The Four Principles of Values-Based Leadership.* Hoboken, NJ: John Wiley & Sons.

Lloyd, C. M. (2010). *University relations.* (Doctoral dissertation), North Carolina Agricultural and Technical State University, Greensboro, NC.

Lyons, S., & Kuron, L. (2014). Generational differences in the workplace: A review of the evidence and directions for future research. *Journal of Organizational Behavior, 35*(S1), S139–S157.

Maier, T., Tavanti, M., Bombard, P., Gentile, M., & Bradford, B. (2015). Millennial generation perceptions of value-centered leadership principles. *Journal of Human Resources in Hospitality & Tourism, 14*(4), 382.

Mannheim, K. (1972). *Essays on the Sociology of Knowledge.* London: Routledge & Kegan Paul.

Martin-Jones, K. (2012). *Emergent technology and the millennial generation: Examining the perceptions of students and implications for higher education.* (Doctoral dissertation), North Carolina Agricultural and Technical State University, Greensboro, NC.

Mikitka, M. J. (2009). Managing the multi-generational workforce. *Material Handling Management, 64*(8), 11.

Pew Research Center. (2010). Millennials: A portrait of generation next. *Pew Research Center.* Retrieved from www.pewsocialtrends.org/files/2010/10/millennials-confident-connected-open-to-change.pdf.

Pilcher, J. (1994). Mannheim's sociology of generations: An undervalued legacy. *British Journal of Sociology, 45*, 481–495.

Rokeach, M. (1973). *The Nature of Human Values.* New York: Free Press.

Ryder, N. B. (1965). The cohort as a concept in the study of social change. *American Sociological Review*, 30, 843–861.

Schwartz, S. H. (2012). An overview of the Schwartz theory of basic values. *Online Readings in Psychology and Culture, 2*(1).

Sessa, V. I., Kabacoff, R. I., Deal, J., & Brown, H. (2007). Generational differences in leader values and leadership behaviors. *Psychologist-Manager Journal, 10*(1), 47–74.

Smola, K. W., & Sutton, C. D. (2002). Generational differences: Revisiting generational work values for the new millennium. *Journal of Organizational Behavior, 23*(4), 363–382.

Stapleton, J. L., Wen, H. J., Starrett, D., & Kilburn, M. (2007). Generational differences in using online learning systems. *Human Systems Management, 26*(2), 99.

Stark, E., & Farner, S. (2015). Intergenerational warfare in the U.S. workplace, or nothing more than growing pains? *Sam Advanced Management Journal, 80*(1).

Stevens, R. H. (2010). Managing human capital: How to use knowledge management to transfer knowledge in today's multi-generational workforce. *International Business Research, 3*(3) 77–83.

Twenge, J. M. (2010). A review of the empirical evidence on generational differences in work attitudes. *Journal of Business and Psychology, 25*(2), 201–210.

Weber, J. (2017). Discovering the Millennials' personal values orientation: A comparison to two managerial populations. *Journal of Business Ethics, 143*(3), 517–529.

27

INTEGRAL YOGA AS FOUNDATION FOR SOCIAL ENTREPRENEURSHIP LEADING TOWARD SUSTAINABLE WELFARE (*SHUBH LAABH*)

Sharda Nandram and Puneet Bindlish

Introduction

This chapter is based on the relevance of the ancient philosophy of yoga in the development of social entrepreneurship as a manifestation of sustainable welfare (*Shubh Laabh*). Knowledge and value creation is at the heart of entrepreneurship and a key asset for realizing the bottom line of business. In the last decade there are emerging issues in entrepreneurship where scholars address the need to broader this bottom line, by re-addressing the objectives of entrepreneurship and proposing a shift from merely financial driven to social driven objectives and innovations aiming at societal impact and taking responsibility for society's welfare (*Shubh Laabh*). Often these new views are positioned under the umbrella of social entrepreneurship. This upcoming theme requires theory building in order to understand its dynamics and applications in entrepreneurship education. In this chapter the yoga philosophy is being proposed as input for such endeavors. It proposes the eight limbs based on *Ashtaanga Yoga* as possible steps of knowledge creation. Such knowledge creation is in its pure nature about discovering and following human aspirations. Therefore the eight limbs, as paths of discovering and following human aspirations, provide a new lens for the phenomenon of entrepreneurship, more particularly, social entrepreneurship. It furthermore proposes interpretations by Sri Aurobindo in his concept of *Integral Yoga*. Integral yoga is not a step by step approach but a way of life regarding the search and application of knowledge as a main human aspiration. Acquiring knowledge in this respect is about consciousness development. While *Ashtaanga Yoga* provides a systematic framework for consciousness development as the expression of knowledge creation, it does not address a person's motivational differences. By explaining the laws of nature Sri Aurobindo explains how individuals can choose different types of drives in their lives. These insights bring us ideas on individual differences that we see in entrepreneurship. The research question for this chapter is: what is the relationship between aims of life and the inclination to social entrepreneurship. The more the consciousness is developed the closer the entrepreneur enters the law of nature which is represented in the unified field of oneness and harmony. Activities driven by this level of consciousness not only work as a base for intelligence and creativity as input for knowledge creation but also naturally invite societal concerns in the mindset of the entrepreneur. One could say that the entrepreneur automatically gets concerned about a broader bottom line of business as a natural tendency of his entrepreneurial processes. This could be expressed in consequences such as financial impact, social impact, creative intelligence, and concern for others. Attempts in this chapter were made to propose knowledge creation as input for social entrepreneurship. This lens shows how knowledge creation enhances consciousness levels so that behaviors of entrepreneurs naturally tend toward societal concerns as they then become a part of their human aspirations. These entrepreneurs can be labeled social entrepreneurs. While scholars have tried to position these phenomena in several schools of thought in the social entrepreneurship literature it seems that the motivation for social entrepreneurial endeavors has not received much attention so far. This chapter shows how ancient wisdom can be applied to understand contemporary phenomena. In the next sections of the chapter the context of social entrepreneurship will be briefly explained and it will describe what gap can be filled with the concept of *Shubh Laabh*. Furthermore the main part of the chapter will provide building blocks for the determinants and consequences of applying the Yogic Philosophy.

Social Entrepreneurship

Social entrepreneurship is currently at an early stage of knowledge development, both on the European continent, as well as internationally. To a large extent, studies are based on small-scale individual case studies and often with an incomplete definition (Dees, 1998; Weerawardena & Sullivan Mort, 2006; Stevens, 2008). As the existing literature is the contribution of scholars from various fields, professional from not-for-profit, for-profit, governmental organizations, or a combination of the three, a unified definition has not yet emerged (Short, Moss, & Lumpkin, 2009). This creates more confusion and less real focus on the opportunities that the field has to offer. A way to solve this confusion in the area of social entrepreneurship research has been to formalize the existing literature as part of general trends. Such efforts have resulted in descriptions of social entrepreneurship in schools of thought, following geographical criteria. A first classification identifies two major schools, one on each side of the Atlantic: the European and the American Schools. The European School is dominated by works done in the EMES—European Research Network—whereas the American School is divided into the Social Enterprise School of Thought and Social Innovation School of Thought (Bacq & Janssen, 2008). A second classification can be added to the three schools mentioned above. This classification distinguishes on the European continent the UK approach and the EMES approach, which results in a total of four schools of thought in social entrepreneurship research (Hoogendoorn, Pennings, & Thurik, 2010).

In America, the Innovation School values the individual (social entrepreneur) as a person with exceptional traits as well as innovation that is needed to bring social change. The Social Enterprise School is defined by organizations belonging to the non-profit sector, that use earned income (market based) strategies while complying with a non-distribution constraint. On the European continent the EMES School emphasizes the social enterprise and a group rather than individual governance of this type of organization. The UK approach, presents itself as a hybrid between the EMES approach, and the Social Enterprise School, by its community emphasis and the principle of reinvesting the surplus in the business (Bacq & Janssen, 2011; Hoogendoorn et al., 2010, Dees & Battle-Anderson, 2003). However there is one element that both continents share: the focus on a *social enterprise* (European School and Social Enterprise School in America). They differ mainly in the attention given to defining the person behind the concept and the process of social entrepreneurship. The American tradition concerning social entrepreneurship has diverted almost equal attention to all parts, whereas the European School still has to focus on the process or even on the individual behind the concept. They are mainly focusing on defining social enterprise. This may be due to the prominent existing social security systems and social work in the European continent which makes it hard to define social enterprise within the larger context of the role of government and public policy. And each country has its own rules and regulations concerning these systems and social work.

Several authors have tried to explain the phenomenon occurrence into different entities, although it is still largely related to the non-profit sector and civil society organization (Hoogendoorn et al., 2010; Thompson & Doherty, 2006; Ashoka, 2006; Austin, Stevenson, & Wei-Skillern, 2006; Boschee & McClurg, 2003; Dees, 1998).

Adding to the mentioned conclusions in all these schools of thoughts, Mair and Martí consider that:

> Social entrepreneurship research replicated to a certain extent the empirical and theoretical development of entrepreneurship. Researchers focused on the social entrepreneur's personality, the peculiarities of his personality, the particular behaviour in the process involved, or on the social opportunity to highlight its entrepreneurial nature and thus differentiate it from other phenomena.
>
> *(2006, p. 37)*

Such efforts, related to the difference within entrepreneurship also belong to authors like Austin, Stevenson, & Wei-Skillern (2003), Dorado (2006), Mair and Martí (2006), Roberts and Woods (2005), Lasprogata and Cotten (2003), and Cochran (2007). However, recent studies concluded that the difference in social entrepreneurship merely is the motivation, considering social entrepreneurship as a socially motivated venturing action and the social mission as a distinctive "visible" concept (Bacq & Janssen, 2011; Bacq, Hartog, & Hoogendoorn, 2013; Hoogendoorn et al., 2010). Where this motivation comes from has not been questioned so far. This brings us to the basic question of human aspiration. Patanjali's Yoga Philosophy is about human aspiration explaining approaches to search for this human aspiration and how to bring it into practice. The instrument to question our human aspiration is our mind offering us knowledge in different forms and intensities. Why would an entrepreneur not only focus on financial return? Why would an entrepreneur feel concerned for societal improvements, welfare for all, show altruistic behavior, put innovative ideas into the social domain to revitalize society and its citizens' wellbeing? This brings us to the study of the entrepreneur and his motivation. By studying the knowledge creation process we hope to contribute to this perspective of entrepreneurship. We believe that the Yoga Philosophy gives us a universal base which will fill the gap between the different schools of thoughts and their ideas and preferences to study the social entrepreneur. Following such a universal base fuels the thought that social entrepreneurship ideas can be implemented in any given continent.

Yoga for Consciousness Development: A Way to Knowledge Creation

Yoga is widely practiced worldwide today. It is seen as an effective tool for reducing stress and strain in the business environment, for the prevention of illness, and to develop concentration and focus, and thus it is used as a tool for a balanced life and good physical health. The roots of yoga go back more than 5000 years to the Indus Valley civilization. In those times, the techniques were passed on from a teacher or guru to a disciple through direct teaching. This learning system was only accessible to very motivated and able disciples. Yoga is addressed in the ancient

Hindu scriptures of the Upanishads. In modern times we owe Maharishi Patanjali for a systematic presentation of traditional yoga philosophy in his well-known Yoga Sutras which went on to inspire many yogic traditions (Karambelkar, 2011). The word yoga stems from the Sanskrit word *yuj* which means to join. Yoga has been defined in various ways but in essence it means the path inward toward unity or oneness. Various schools of postures and breathing are the main forms of yoga practiced today. These have been given different names according to their dominant characteristics. In a scientific context the most broadly studied form of yoga is the relationship between breathing, wellness, and stress or anxiety reduction.

Patanjali's yoga does not solely involve breathing or yoga postures. It is a psycho-spiritual model that consists of eight limbs (Nandram, 2010) and explained extensively in Ashtaanga Yoga. All eight limbs are connected to the whole. We need all of them to develop and grow (Sri Sri Ravi Shankar, 2007, p. 144). It is in the teachings of Sri Aurobindo where we can find in detail how such a holistic approach could be applied. He labels it integral yoga.

The concept of "integral" was first introduced by the philosopher Sri Aurobindo (1872–1950) in 1993 to describe the multi-dimensional nature of consciousness comprising mainly the physical, vital (emotions, desires, cravings), mental, and psychic (soul) levels of consciousness. Traditional science looks at phenomena in isolation, from a partial perspective, and from a purely material standpoint while the integral approach seeks to develop a holistic view in order to take into account the full spectrum of consciousness and the underlying oneness in which everything participates.

In his book *The Synthesis of Yoga* (1990), Sri Aurobindo explained how all human activity can be understood in terms of the functioning of nature. He talks about the two necessities of nature. First, where a form tends toward harmonized complexity and totality but which again breaks apart into various channels of special effort and tendency. This breaking apart, again, needs to unite and become part of a larger whole. The second is where everything constantly needs to be renewed by fresh streams of Spirit. His integral view is based on these two fundamental aspects of nature when he says that all life is yoga. It is about

> a union of the human individual with the universal and transcendent Existence we see partially expressed in man and in the Cosmos. But all life, when we look behind its appearances, is a vast Yoga of Nature who attempts in the conscious and the subconscious to realise her perfection in an ever-increasing expression of her yet unrealised potentialities and to unite herself with her own divine reality.
>
> *(Sri Aurobindo, 1990, p. 6)*

Furthermore, Sri Aurobindo explains the three steps in nature that reflect the three aspects of our aim in life:

1. A bodily life (or pragmatic): this forms the basis of our existence in the material world.
2. A mental life: this is that into which we emerge. And it is also that by which we engage the body in higher uses and enlarge it into a greater completeness.
3. A spiritual existence: this is at once the goal of the mental and bodily life and returns to them to liberate them to their highest possibilities.

The first two, while part of the evolution of human development, are not the last terms of evolution. They are, instead, instruments of evolution of the consciousness. Sri Aurobindo states that none of these three is beyond our reach or below our nature. According to him it is not necessary to destroy any of the three aspects to attain the ultimate goal of our existence. These aspects can complement each other and can be lived in co-existence. This can be understood by viewing these aspects from another lens of four life goals as per Indian philosophy. According to this philosophy, life is about working for holistic attainment of four life goals—*Dharmā* (righteousness), *Arthā* (means for prosperity), *Kamā* (worldly or material desires), and *Mokshā* (emancipation or liberation). *Dharmā* is a righteous framework of duties toward whom we believe we are related. The fulfillment of these duties requires means or resources. *Arthā* goal is to earn those resources. Further, the duty fulfillment involves the resources being utilized toward some desires or good. The process of experiencing of fulfillment of these desires is *Kamā*. Since, by our own experience, we know none of the material desires can keep us content for life; therefore, the indescribable goal or the ultimate goal with that property of giving us ever-lasting contentment is referred to as *Mokshā*. Now we can relate the above three aspects to these four life goals. These three life aims are based on *Dharmā*, which refers to our duty to live righteously. It infuses how we deal with all the other life goals. The bodily life could be also labeled *Arthā*, the mental life as *Kamā*, and the spiritual life *Mokshā* as aspects of an integral paradigm rooted in Indian philosophy. Just as our capacity for mental life evolves over our lifetime, so does that capacity for consciousness evolve. Sri Aurobindo said that as a whole, mankind has not yet reached the full height of our mental life; our nature has not yet finished evolving. In Sri Aurobindo's teachings mental life consists of three parts: the material mind, the pure intellectual mind, and the divine mind. This means that *Kamā* could be expressed in all these three ways: material, intellectual, and with divine consciousness. This last aspect of mind is liberated from the illusions of the imperfect modes of our reasoning. The three forms of life are available to every human being who has a choice between an ordinary material existence, a life of mental activity and progress, or a spiritual life. In his development he can even choose to combine these three, which according to Sri Aurobindo is the aim of existence (1990, p. 20). If we apply this to entrepreneurship we could assume that commercially driven entrepreneurs choose a bodily life while social entrepreneurs choose a mental life and some may be even choose a spiritual life. A mental and or spiritual life gives them legitimation for achieving a double bottom line of business where they include more drives than merely gains in the material world. This approach of three aspects of life of Sri Aurobindo gives space for the idea that people make deliberate and conscious choices about their lives which is about fulfilling self-determination needs. Probably entrepreneurs strive for self-determination to a larger extent than non-entrepreneurs. And social entrepreneurs tend to include more than one of the three aims of life.

It is possible to give the material man with his bodily (pragmatic) life a moderate mental life with the possibility for progress, the habit of consciousness change. It is possible too for man to adopt a moderate spirituality through exposing him to spiritual practices, texts, and institutions.

Mental life is particular because, being intangible, it encounters the resistance of matter and does not know how to deal with it, for the reason that the mind can develop in exclusion of the physical and withdraw from life to experience a greater sense of freedom.

According to Sri Aurobindo the spiritual being in us has difficulty living in a world that appears to be lacking in truth and love. It sees the evil and ignorance. Therefore saints, in pursuit of their spiritual life, tend to withdraw from material existence and reject the physical either wholly or in spirit. Sri Aurobindo states that spiritual life becomes distinct to us as we go inward in our consciousness and sometimes also physically to go beyond the world's impurities. We can then assert spiritual reality in spotless isolation (1990, p. 26).

Interestingly, Sri Aurobindo says that spiritual life, the expression of the universal force through each individual, can return upon the material and use it as a means toward its own greater fullness. In this path spirit may use the exogenous existence for the benefit of the individual and for the greater good. In terms of behaviors, it pours itself out in good deeds, service, compassion, and sharing of knowledge. It can challenge material life and seek progress in such a way that it transforms material existence into its own image of the spirit. Material life and spiritual life exist side by side, a duality which, unlike some more ascetic spiritual traditions, is accepted as a rule rather than ignorance which needs to be escaped from. But Sri Aurobindo's philosophy for realizing progress and perfection involves integrating all three. He says

> Spirit is the crown of universal existence; Matter is its basis; Mind is the link between the two. Spirit is that which is eternal; Mind and Matter are its workings. Spirit is that which is concealed and has to be revealed; mind and body are the means by which it seeks to reveal itself.
>
> *(2009, p. 29)*

All life is evolving. The process of nature will work toward realizing evolution at its own speed and in its own way. Such input as given by Sri Aurobindo on the laws of nature and how the process of self-determination can influence how we synthesize or move away from these natural paths can explain why some entrepreneurs tend toward material drives while others tend toward social drives next to material drives, trying to serve a double bottom line. Yoga, on the other hand opens the way for a more rapid revolution of the workings of these laws. It impacts the individual by speeding up all the energies of nature.

In the next section we will explain how this can be done by following the limbs of yoga and analyzing how they are expressed when following the three aims of life.

Limbs of Yoga and the Three Aims of Life

If we look at the limbs we can make the following distinction: moral and psychological limbs, psychic limbs, and the spiritual limbs.

The Moral and Psychological Limbs

Limb 1: Yama: Self-Regulation through Moral Code

This is a purification process which requires an attitude of discipline and trusting one's moral code. It consists of five universal principles. The first one stems from the attitude of *Ahimsa*, which refers to friendliness and not doing harm to others. This incorporates the thinking that our behavior should take others into consideration. This leads to kindness to others, cohesiveness between people, happiness, and, therefore, harmony with the environment. The second is *Satya*, which refers to focusing on truthfulness, commitment to what we say, and considering how our words affect others. Those who act truthfully will attract truthful and responsible behavior in return. The third principle is *Asteya*, not taking what does not belong to you. This conveys the principle that we attract opportunities and wealth based on our karma and that we should not create new bad karma by intervening with this by taking what is not ours. The fourth is *Brahmacharya*, which refers to control of the senses. Following *Brahmacharya* involves living a focused life in order to reach the higher truth, wisdom, and infinity. Everything that deviates from this focus should be avoided. Any thoughts, activities, or even relationships that do not contribute to reach the higher truth should be abandoned. It is about seeing oneself as being more than just the body. The fifth is *Aparigraha*, non-wastefulness and not taking what one does not need. This applies to food, material things, work, and money. Cultivating an attitude of gratitude to what one has eliminates restlessness and increases satisfaction.

In the context of social entrepreneurship we can think of *Ahimsa* in the following ways: maintain friendly relationships with customers, suppliers, and employees, actually engaging a good relationship with all parties in the whole chain of the product or service (pragmatic dimension); avoiding competitive tendencies which are harmful; fostering fair competition in the whole chain (mental dimension), and striving for harmony toward the relevant stakeholders in the environment (spiritual). When it comes to *Satya* one can think of the following: be consistent in activities and aligned to the social achievement drive (pragmatic); examine before you speak about expansion (mental); strive for responsible behavior based on truthfulness, commitment, consistency, and careful speaking toward all stakeholders involved (spiritual). From the concept of *Brahmacharya*: focus on what gives satisfaction in past projects and repeating these (pragmatic); focus on learning from and improving own past achievements (mental), and focus of energy on higher goals while avoiding sidetrack issues (spirit). In the view of *Asteya* we can think of the following intentions: formulate conditions that drive your social driven activities in order to minimalize harm to others (pragmatic); keep finding opportunities to improve but formulate principles and values to evaluate the impact of social driven activities (mental); keep finding opportunities to pursue the social goals but looking at them through a holistic perspective endeavoring to avoid harm to anyone including the environment and the universe (Spirit). From the concept of *Aparigraha*: try to do more with less (pragmatic); try to cultivate a long-term perspective to all activities including social related (mental) and avoid wastage in the processes and the whole chain (Spirit).

Limb 2: Niyama

This refers to internal cleansing and preparation of the body and mind for the higher limbs. *Sauca* is the first rule of this limb that advises cleansing and dealing with the body and mind through healthy habits and purity. *Santosha* is the second *Niyama*, which advises modesty and satisfaction with what you have. One should accept what happens as part of one's karma. The rule is to accept and learn from one's experiences. The concept of *Tapas* is about maintaining the body through eliminating sources of toxicity. This involves eating only what you need. Ayurveda, *Asanas* (postures) and *Pranayamas* (breathing exercises) can be used to help eliminate *ama*, waste and toxins, from the body. The fourth rule is *Svadhyaya*, self-observation and meditation. This practice leads to centeredness and reflection and eliminates destructive thoughts or intentions. Mantra repetition is a good tool for this purpose. The fifth rule is *Isvarapranidhana*, surrender to the universe, cosmos, or a higher being. In life, things will not always work as you wish and we should take life's experiences as an opportunity and a responsibility to learn.

The Niyamas are a bit difficult to apply since they refer to intrapersonal aspects while the *Yamas* deal with interpersonal aspects. When we apply the principle *Sauca*, the first of the *Niyamas*, to setting up a social venture we can think of the following intended behaviors: adjust new intentions to social driven activities according to past experiences (pragmatic); reflect on the type of goal being applied, return to the reason for existence (mental); and integrate the social drives with other goals of the venture and, perceiving it from a wholesome perspective (Spirit). In terms of *Santosha* we can think of: setting feasible and modest goals (pragmatic); celebrate success and learn from setbacks (mental); and accept the results of social initiatives as they turn out (Spirit). Regarding the concept of *Tapas* we can think of the following: from time to time one has to think of applying to renew practices (pragmatic); creating coping strategies for growth, success, and failures and removing procedures that do not work (mental); and create an awareness that renewal involves all parts of the venture. When we focus on the *Svadhayaya* concept we can think of the following intentions: observe what has worked best and set similar aims for the future (pragmatic); evaluate past venture activities related to social drives and try to

Table 27.1 Social Entrepreneurial Activities through Integral Yoga: Psychological Limbs

Concept	*Meaning*	*Pragmatic Life*	*Mental Life*	*Spirit Life*
Intention	–	Maintenance Continuing successful activities: seeking social goals through copying successful behavior	Improvement Fostering innovation, creativity, and challenging change	Perfection Working toward self-actualization, developing compassion toward oneself, the environment, and the universe to unite in wholeness
Yama: Ahimsa	Actions that take others into consideration	Maintain friendly relationships with customers, suppliers, and employees	Avoid competitive tendencies which are harmful; foster fair competition	Harmony with environment while developing social aims
Yama: Satya	Speak the truth	Be consistent in your social features	Think before you speak about social activities	Responsible behavior through truth, consistency, and careful speaking
Yama: Asteya	Do not take what does not belong to you/don't harm others	Formulate the conditions that drive your social goals	Keep finding opportunities to improve but formulate principles and values to evaluate their impact	Keep finding opportunities to pursue social goals but evaluate them from a wholeness view (not harming anyone)
Yama: Brahmacharya	Use your energy in a way which involves control of the senses	Repeat that which has produced satisfaction in past projects	Focus on learning from and improving past achievements	Focus energy on higher goals and avoid side track issues
Yama: Aparigraha	Take only what is needed	Try to do more with less	Try to work on long-term social endeavors	Avoid waste in the growth process
Niyama: Sauca	Healthy use of body and mind	Base new intentions on past experiences	Reflecting on type of goals used to developing the business, returning to original reason for existence	Integrating social venture intention with other goals of the venture and evaluating it from a wholesome perspective
Niyama: Santosha	Modesty and satisfaction	Setting feasible and modest goals	Celebrate success and learn from setbacks for future actions	Accept the results of the social initiatives
Niyama: Tapas	Elimination of waste	Periodically apply renewal methods to the venture instead of only focusing on maintaining practices	Creating coping strategies for success and failures; remove procedures that do not work	Create an awareness that renewal is part of the processes in the venture
Niyama: Svadhyaya	Self-observation; meditation	Base goals on past successes	Evaluate and learn from past venture activities	Observe, reflect, and monitor activities
Niyama: Isvaraprani-dhana	Surrender to a higher purposes	Focus on the actions required for maintaining the venture's position in the market	Evaluate duties and make necessary adjustments regarding social policy	Accept duties and outcomes; put continuous effort into the venture from a wholesome perspective including the impact on the universe

generate lessons (mental); and observe, reflect, and monitor social activities (Spirit). The concept of *Isvarapranidhana* can be covered by the following possible intentions: focus on the duties that are required for maintaining the venture position in the market (pragmatic); evaluate duties and make necessary adjustments to the venture policy (mental); and accept duties, outcomes while putting continuous effort into realizing the social goals of the venture from a wholesome perspective taking into consideration the impact on all stakeholders in the whole chain of the process of developing the product or service (Spirit).

The Psychic Limbs 3 and 4

Limb 3: Asana

Integral posture for perfect energetic and postural alignment. *Asana* develops self-control, freeing the mind from stress, mental balance, and comfort. When one applies this to social venture, one can think of aligning the financial driven and social intention to the geographical and physical potentials of the venture; do things that make one steady and comfortable (pragmatic); an intention aligned with the mental capabilities of the entrepreneur and their employees (mental); and an intention with a wholesome perspective including all relevant stakeholders (Spirit).

Limb 4: Pranayama

Prana is the essence of life. It is found in many sources like food, breath, external stimulation, inner source, and the sun. It is circulated through the breath. Advanced yogis can harness *prana* from the sun and temporarily abstain from physical breath. Patanjali's yoga goes beyond hatha yoga by teaching the means to control the circulation and exchange of *prana*. Both *Asanas* and *Pranayamas* help us to harmonize the flow of energy in our body. As a result, it will help us to cope with life's different situations and demands.

Table 27.2 Social Entrepreneurial Activities through Integral Yoga Psychic Limbs

Concept	*Meaning*	*Pragmatic Life*	*Mental Life*	*Spirit Life*
Intention	–	Maintenance	Improvement	Perfection
		Continuing successful activities: seeking social activities through copying successful behavior	Fostering innovation and creativity and challenging change	Working toward self-actualization, developing compassion toward oneself, the environment, and the universe to unite in wholeness
Asanas	Energetic purification	Social and financial intention aligned with geographical and physical capabilities of the venture	Social intention aligned with mental capabilities of entrepreneur and employees of the venture	Social intention aligned with wholesome perspective
Pranayamas	Energetic purification	Expansion is aligned with vitality of the venture	Controlled intention balancing between financial and social aims	Coping with social activities in relationship to others (interpersonal)

Spiritual Limbs 5, 6, 7, and 8

Limb 5: Pratyahara

Inner process or movement. In this limb the yogi withdraws the attention from the senses thereby stilling the mind. This state is achieved in sleep and, yet, *Pratyahara* is not sleep. Instead, all the energy is drawn inward without any distraction from external stimuli. This can be applied to social entrepreneurship by aligning it with the vitality of the venture (pragmatic), a controlled growth intention (mental), and coping with social activities in relationship to others (interpersonal dimension) (Spirit).

Limb 6: Dharana: concentration by focusing on a fixed point.

Limb 7: Dhyana: meditation; the state of pure thought and absorption in the object of meditation. There is still duality in *Dhyana* as we are aware of the subtle distinction between object and subject. Mastering *Dhyana* leads to *Samadhi*.

Limb 8: Samadhi: the superconscious state of non-duality or oneness. This is the deepest and highest state of consciousness where body and mind have been transcended and the yogi is one with the Self. The three limbs, 6, 7, 8, are all meant for spiritual deepening and the subtle levels of their impact cannot be traced from observing the outer behavior. Therefore the social entrepreneurial activities for all these limbs seem similar. For the pragmatic dimension one can think of social activities solely driven by the entrepreneur's preferences. For the mental dimension one can think of social activities driven by the entrepreneur's vision. For the spiritual dimension one can think of social activities driven by a feeling of harmony with the inner Self and with the environment both for *Dharana* and *Dhyana*. For *Samadhi* one goes much deeper expressing it as a blissful state based on harmony with Self, environment, and the Universe (unity in views and wisdom).

Sri Aurobindo's yoga is claiming that there is no one set method or practice that one should follow. In his own words:

> what we propose in our Yoga is nothing less than to break up the whole formation or our past and present which makes up the ordinary material and mental man and to create a new centre of vision and a new universe of activities in ourselves which shall constitute a divine humanity or superhuman nature.
>
> *(Sri Aurobindo, 1990).*

It respects the uniqueness of each individual and says that each will have a specific path. It only provides guidelines. One principle is that guidance and power and action of the Divine Mother, the Consciousness, and Force of the Supreme are required to achieve this form of yoga. And the other principle is that each individual's obstacles, characteristics, and potential are taken into account by the Divine Consciousness. What it requires from the individual are:

1. Aspiration: sustained call of the individual to the Supreme to take possession of his outward being, his ego. This step is associated with the yoga of works where one's actions are to be done as an offering to the Divine and not for personal satisfaction.
2. Rejection: separation and withdrawing from all wrong habits. This step goes together with the yoga of knowledge where the person draws back the True Self from its false identification with the ego.
3. Complete surrender to the Divine Mother. This step is associated with the yoga of love and devotion.

Table 27.3 Social Entrepreneurial Activities through Integral Yoga: Spiritual Limbs

Concept	*Meaning*	*Pragmatic Life*	*Mental Life*	*Spirit Life*
Intention	–	Maintenance Continuing successful activities: seeking social activities through copying successful behavior	Improvement Fostering innovation, creativity	Perfection Working toward self-actualization, developing compassion toward oneself, the environment, and the universe to unite in wholeness
Pratyahara	Withdraw from focus on the environment and go inward	Social activities solely driven by the entrepreneur's preferences	Social activities driven by entrepreneur's vision	Social activities driven by a feeling of harmony with the inner Self
Dharana	Let the mind get focused	Social activities solely driven by the entrepreneur's preferences	Social activities driven by entrepreneur's vision	Social activities driven by a feeling of harmony with the inner Self
Dhyana	Know the difference between the subject and the object	Social activities solely driven by the entrepreneur's preferences	Social activities driven by entrepreneur's vision	Social activities driven by a feeling of harmony with the inner Self and with the environment
Samadhi	Oneness of function and structure	Social activities solely driven by the entrepreneur's preferences	Social activities driven by entrepreneur's vision	Social activities based on harmony with Self, environment and the Universe (Unity in views and wisdom)

4. Then there is a fourth approach which Sri Aurobindo called the yoga of Self-perfection. This requires purification so that one can reach the higher parts of the mind beyond the intellect which is the higher mind, illumined mind, intuition, and Overmind.

The word integral refers to the fact that each of the four approaches is necessary for an inner realization and the outer transformation of the being. Some of the qualities of the "knowledge of the truths, principles, powers and processes that govern the realization," of which Sri Aurobindo speaks are:

- This knowledge is folded up within us.
- This knowledge can't be taught, it is already concealed as potential knowledge.
- We know the Divine; we can become That, because we are That already.
- All teaching is a revealing which comes to us from within.

Enhancing Social Entrepreneurship through Yoga Principles

How can these four approaches be accomplished? The follower (*Sadhaka*) of this path needs to dissolve the central faith and vision in the mind which concentrates it on its development and satisfaction and interests in the old externalized order of things. Then he needs to compel all his lower being to pay homage to this new faith and greater vision. This means an integral surrender by an offer of himself in every part and every movement. It requires a consecration of all its energies from its soul, mind, sense, heart, will, life, body to become a vehicle for the Divine. This path is not easy as he needs to get rid of his daily habits.

This requires concentration as a first condition. The concentration of an enlightened thought, will, and heart will turn in unison toward a vast goal of our knowledge. It should be a flaming concentration of the heart on the seeking of the one Divine. It can be done by an intellectual preparation by reading or philosophic reasoning but that is not enough. It requires the instruments of the heart and the will. In the process the follower is working by means of the instruments of the lower Nature and needs to be aided more and more from above. It makes him available for transformation. Later it will work based on the higher Nature where the consciousness is getting a greater role. At the end it does not require any effort or method. It will become a natural, simple, powerful, and happy disclosing of the flower of the Divine. Thus Yoga is considered a way of life. The beauty of Yoga philosophy is its wholesome view. This makes it possible for application to moral, psychological, psychic, and spiritual development. The presented integral model is based on the three aspects of Nature according to the work of Sri Aurobindo and the eight limbs of Ashtaanga Yoga. These limbs prepare the practitioner for psychological and spiritual development. The *Yamas* are behaviors at the interpersonal level. The *Niyamas* are behaviors on the intrapersonal level in dealing with psychic, body, and mind. *Svadhyaya* is at the cognitive intrapersonal level. *Isvarapranidhana* is on the intra-cosmic level meaning that here the individual relates with a higher power. The *Asanas* and *Pranayamas* are meant to unite the mind and body. The other four limbs: *Pratyahara, Dharana, Dhyana,* and *Samadhi* cannot be practiced directly with specific attitude or behaviors; they are consequences of the other levels.

Therefore, we see limbs 1 and 2 (*Yamas* and *Niyamas*) as ways to prepare the psychology and the physiology to start with Yoga as a way of life. Limbs 3 and 4 (*Asanas* and *Pranayama*) represent psychic preparation. Limbs 5 and 6 are the inward gates that aim to control energy through concentration. Limb 7 is pure focus. All limbs up to this one are coming from duality of consciousness, because there is separation of lower self from Divine or higher self. Limbs 5 up to 8 cover spiritual development. While there is still duality at the limbs up till limb 7 the more one concentrates upon this duality the more potential the practitioner develops to transcend the duality which ultimately leads to limb eight which is *advaita*, non-duality.

Conclusion

While social entrepreneurship is a growing field of interest in management it is still in its infancy stage of understanding. In this chapter we have tried to contribute to the understanding of the aspirations of a social entrepreneur. There are different schools of thought, each with its own emphasis on certain concepts to be explored. One such concept is the motivation of the social entrepreneur. Scholars have claimed that social entrepreneurs differ from commercial entrepreneurs in their motivation to serve a social cause. Why certain individual entrepreneurs tend to such a motivation while others just strive for opportunities to serve a financial bottom line has not received much attention so far. By introducing the Yoga philosophy we have gained additional insights on how individuals apply three types of aims in their lives, following the nature of law. These are a bodily or pragmatic life, a mental life, and a spiritual life. The philosophy has offered us the idea that it is the individual who consciously decides which of these to strive for or even which combination to strive for. This holds for entrepreneurs as well. While it seems that entrepreneurs mainly are driven by a bodily life aiming for material comfort and therefore placing the financial bottom line as top priority, we see a growing interest in entrepreneurs striving for contributing to solve a societal problem and putting a social bottom line as a main or additional priority to the bottom line of their entrepreneurial activities. So far following the mainstream literature we would end up explaining motivation either from intrinsic or extrinsic perspectives. By adding the Yoga perspective it tells us that there are more possibilities. It is a deliberate process of human aspirations to be followed in order to understand why an entrepreneur follows a social entrepreneurial aim and why others do not. It is a universal perspective where a person follows any of the three aims or combinations of it. Even the bodily life dimension turned out to be applicable in the context of social entrepreneurs if he is willing to follow the Yoga philosophical steps. By doing so the entrepreneur chooses for his consciousness development, it is not something that just happens. Such a choice results in knowledge to be used subsequently in entrepreneurial activities. Social entrepreneurship then becomes an expression of a natural individual process of developing one's consciousness as part of the natural human aspiration. It can then become a mainstream phenomenon with several positive side effects such as societal problems being solved which would wait for governmental policy; and personal development of the entrepreneur reaching to higher levels of his consciousness. If we follow the Yoga philosophy we could define a three-fold typology of the social entrepreneur: the pragmatic, the mental, and the spiritual, which legitimizes several types of bottom lines for entrepreneurial activities. In follow-up, studies should examine whether social entrepreneurs fit this typology and what concrete features they use in practice to create sustainable welfare for all (*Shubh Laabh*).

References

Ashoka. (2006). *Leading Social Entrepreneurs*. Arlington, VA: Ashoka Foundation.

Austin, J. E., Stevenson, H. H., & Wei-Skillern, J. (2003). Social entrepreneurship and commercial entrepreneurship: Same, different, or both? Division of Research, Harvard Business School.

Austin, J., Stevenson, H., & Wei-Skillern, J. (2006). Social and commercial entrepreneurship: Same, different or both? *Entrepreneurship: Theory and Practice, 30*(1), 1–22.

Bacq, S., & Janssen, F. (2008). From social entrepreneurship as a practice to legitimate field of research: Literature review and classification. European Summer University Conference on Entrepreneurship. Center for Research in Entrepreneurial Change and Innovative Strategies, Bodø, Norway.

Bacq, S., & Janssen, F. (2011). The multiple faces of social entrepreneurship: A review of definitional issues based on geographical and thematic criteria. *Entrepreneurship and Regional Development, 23*(5–6), 373–403.

Bacq, S., Hartog, C., & Hoogendoorn, B. (2013). A quantitative comparison of social and commercial entrepreneurship: Toward a more nuanced understanding of social entrepreneurship organizations in context. *Journal of Social Entrepreneurship, 4*(1), 40–68.

Boschee, J., & McClurg, J. (2003). Toward a better understanding of social entrepreneurship: Some important directions. Working Chapter. Retrieved from www.sealliance.org/better_understanding.pdf.

Cochran, P. L. (2007). The evolution of corporate social responsibility. *Business Horizons, 50*(6), 449–454.

Dees, J. G. (1998). The meaning of "social entrepreneurship." Stanford University: Draft Report for the Kauffman Center for Entrepreneurial Leadership, 6 pp.

Dees, J., & Battle-Anderson, B. (2003). Sector–bending: Blurring lines between nonprofit and for–profit. *Society, 40*(4), 16–27.

Dorado, S. (2006). Social entrepreneurial ventures: Different values so different processes of creation, no? *Journal of Developmental Entrepreneurship, 11*(4), 319–343.

Hoogendoorn, B., Pennings, E., & Thurik, R. (2010, January). What do we know about social entrepreneurship: An analysis of empirical research. ERIM Report Series Research In Management, 1–39.

Karambelkar, P. V. (2011). *Patanjala Yoga Sutras*. Kaivalyadhama, Lonavala, India.

Lasprogata, G. A., & Cotten, M. N. (2003). Contemplating "enterprise": The business and legal challenges of social entrepreneurship. *American Business Law Journal, 41*(1), 67–114.

Mair, J., & Martí, I. (2006). Social entrepreneurship research: A source of explanation, prediction, and delight. *Journal of World Business, 41*, 36–44.

Nandram, S. S. (2010). Synchronizing leadership style with integral transformational yoga principles. In S. S. Nandram & M. E. Borden (Eds.), *Spirituality and Business: Exploring Possibilities for a New Management Paradigm*. Heidelberg, Germany: Springer, 183–204.

Roberts, D., & Woods, C. (2005). Changing the world on a shoestring: The concept of social entrepreneurship. *University of Auckland Business Review*, 7(1), 45–51.

Short, J. C., Moss, T. W., & Lumpkin, G. T. (2009). Research in social entrepreneurship: Past contributions and future opportunities. *Strategic Entrepreneurship Journal, 3*(2), 161–194.

Sri Aurobindo (1990). *The Synthesis of Yoga*. Pondicherry, India: Sri Aurobindo Ashram Trust.

Sri Aurobindo (1993). *The Integral Yoga: Sri Aurobindo's Teaching and Method of Practice*. Pondicherry, India: Sri Aurobindo Ashram.

Sri Sri Ravi Shankar, H. H. (2007). *The Yoga Sutras of Patanjali*. Stramproy, Netherlands: Shankara Europe.

Stevens, C. E. (2008). *Social entrepreneurship and earned income opportunities: An examination of the importance of institutional factors in predicting entrepreneurial action among nonprofit organizations*. (Doctoral dissertation), Case Western Reserve University, Ohio.

Thompson, J., & Doherty, B. (2006). The diverse world of social enterprise: A collection of social enterprise stories. *International Journal of Social Economics, 33*(5/6), 361–375.

Weerawardena, J., & Sullivan Mort, G. (2006). Investigating social entrepreneurship: A multidimensional model. *Journal of World Business, 41*(1), 21–35.

28

INSTITUTIONALIZING WORKPLACE SPIRITUALITY TO CREATE AN ETHICAL CLIMATE

Bekir Emre Kurtulmuş

Introduction

The modern workplace has become more stressful than ever. Stakeholders pressurize employees and management to meet their demands, even though their demands may be unethical/immoral. Nonetheless, stakeholders, from shareholders to governments, are an important consideration for organizations. There are also other factors that put immense pressure on employees in contemporary workplaces. Considering recent business scandals in different organizations across the globe there is more pressure than ever from governments and societies on the management of organizations to prevent such immoral/unethical behaviors. In response to calls from various stakeholders, organizations are required to provide ethical guidelines, codes of conduct, and official training to employees to prevent unethical behavior. In fact, business ethics has become more popular than ever among scholars (Crane & Matten, 2016) but it is questionable if this is enough to prevent such incidents.

It is difficult to establish the sort of framework that would prevent employees inclining toward unethical/immoral behavior, but the challenge is still there. Furthermore, there are not only ethical problems to solve, but there are also some internal demands from individuals to management to create a peaceful environment within organizations. Studies show that peaceful workplaces contribute positively to employees' wellbeing (Fry, Vitucci, & Cedillo, 2005) and organizational effectiveness (Duchon & Plowman, 2005). Perhaps, above all, engaging in workplace spirituality may positively influence ethical behavior of employees at the workplace (Corner, 2009). Therefore, for many organizations, it has become a necessity to create and establish an ethical climate. However, challenges remain.

Therefore, organizations more and more are trying to establish ethical limitations and guidelines that would create a framework for individuals, which should be also accepted and followed by individuals. Only after this process has been established can consensus ensue and be the framework be institutionalized across the organization. However, the process is difficult to achieve. However, there is a relatively new term in business studies that would immensely help the process. Scholars are slowly embracing a new term, "workplace spirituality." The concept could provide more reasonable ethical values for individuals that could be accepted more easily by members of organizations. Despite that, the term has been neglected by scholars (Danielz, Franz, & Wong, 2000). Nonetheless, for two to three decades the term has gained importance and there are more studies now that discuss the impact of workplace spirituality on various organizational activities both at individual and organizational levels (Houghton, Neck, & Krishnakumar, 2016).

In the same vein, another challenge is that it is a difficult process to institutionalize ethical values and norms. Creating core values for organizations depends on the established values and beliefs. However, in order for new ethical values and beliefs to be institutionalized the first thing is that they should be accepted by the majority of the members of the organizations. The more members who accept the new ethical values and beliefs would mean that that culture would get stronger. This consequently would guide the mission and vision statements and, hence, would be the main reference points for the strategic decision-making processes of organizations. Perhaps organizations would immensely benefit from workplace spirituality/spiritual traditions as they may be utilized to enhance employees' positive organizational attitudes.

The chapter will provide an answer to the question of how organizations/organization members, by practicing workplace spirituality/religion, can create or agree on an ethical climate. In that, this chapter will provide an argument on the positive role that workplace spirituality/spiritual traditions can play. The chapter will also include a discussion of the positive enhancements that workplace spirituality would bring both to individuals and to organizations. The study will provide a comprehensive meta-analysis of the issues.

Workplace Spirituality

Spirituality is one of the emerging areas of business studies and it is addressed as an important trend for organizations (Chen, Yang, & Li, 2012). Interest in workplace spirituality has been accelerated immensely in the last two decades. However, the connection to business and management studies, according to Hicks (2003), can be traced back until the late 1980s. It has become a trend in the last two to three decades because of socio-economic and cultural factors (Hicks, 2003). Historically, the field emerged from the faith at work movement—which initially began in the 19th century in the Western world as a response to the Church's lack of perceived concern toward employees' working conditions in, what can be described as, secular organizations—and workplace spirituality's foundational roots can be found in the Protestant work ethic (Benefiel, Fry, & Geigle, 2014). Even though, initially, the concept seemed irrelevant to management studies, later research showed it to be positively correlated (Benefiel, 2003). In fact, it is shown that workplace spirituality's contribution to organizational reality is more prominent than initially thought (Gotsis & Kortezi, 2008).

In that, the term spirituality could be described as "our inner consciousness" and "that which is spiritual comes from within-beyond our programs beliefs and values" (Guillroy, 2000, p. 33). In addition, Mitroff (2003, p. 377) defines the term spirituality as "spirituality is not the only the intense feeling of being totally integrated as a whole person, but also the feeling of being totally connected with everything else in the universe." It is the holistic infusion of wisdom into the management field (Steingard, 2005). Workplace spirituality was initially considered as a search for God or described as a search for ultimate being (Gupta, Kumar, & Singh, 2014). It could be identified as beliefs and values that eventually influence behavior. It might be observed and influence behavior both at individual and organizational levels (Moore & Casper, 2006). The relationship between spirituality and management encourage us to engage in the metaphysical foundation of our field (Steingard, 2005).

In this vein, research in the related literature found a relationship between workplace spirituality and different organizational activities. The majority of these works focus on positive outcomes of organizational reality (Benefiel, Fry, & Geigle, 2014) with scholars usually focusing on organizational management and organizational leadership issues (Gotsis & Kortezi, 2008). It should be noted that although there are many studies literature on the topic is still limited. Therefore there is a need for more research to be conducted in the field (Gupta et al., 2014).

Studies found that workplace spirituality has a significant influence on employees' work attitudes (Milliman, Czaplewski, & Ferguson, 2003; Garcia-Zamor, 2003), management processes (Steingard, 2005), organizational citizenship behavior (Chen & Yang, 2012), and leadership practices, (Chen et al., 2012), and engaging with workplace spirituality reduces stress and increases organizational commitment (Rego & Pina e Cunha, 2008). An organization that engages in spirituality tends to have better-performing individuals (Gordon, 1996) and there are narrower wage and status differentials between employees (Giacolone & Jurkiewicz, 2003). It is also found that "more spiritual" organizations are significantly more profitable. Therefore, if organizations would like to be "more" successful they need to be engaging more in spirituality. In this way, they could achieve competitive advantage (Mitroff, 2003). Moreover, if managers attempted to understand differing spiritual views and also encouraged all these views in the organization, this would create a positive environment for organizations and contribute to ethical consensus (Krishnakumar & Neck, 2002), which is one of the main requirements for creating an ethical climate (Martin & Cullen, 2006). However, despite these positive effects, there is also an argument that workplace spirituality may cause a negative impact. Moreover, it may be also utilized for control and instrumentality purposes (Lips-Wiersma, Lund Dean, & Fornaciari, 2009) and may also mask manipulation for compliance (Tzouramani & Karakas, 2016).

Moreover, all this argument focuses on two different levels: workplace spirituality's impact can be seen both individual and organizational level. Issues discussed on these two levels are different and have various views and angles. At the individual level within organizations, workplace spirituality includes a sense of community, understanding of inner life, and meaningful work. Whereas at the organization level, workplace spirituality consists of a spiritual climate or culture that consists of the purpose, values, and vision of the organization (Houghton et al., 2016).

Furthermore, the relationship between spirituality and religion could be problematic. Steingard (2005, p. 228) suggests that both terms are categorically different. He argues that "Religion is a form (structure) and spirituality is essence (experience)." Religion is seen dividing people through dogmas and with a strong emphasis on formal structures (Mitroff, 2003). This is because we are far from realizing a consensual religion in the everyday life of the workplace. For example, the two biggest religions in the world, in terms of follower numbers—Christianity and Islam—are monotheistic (believe in only one God), whereas the third biggest—Hinduism—believes in more than one God (Steingard, 2005).

Furthermore, the first two of these religions are portray God as masculine. As such, as Mitroff (2003) discusses, formal, organized religion has little role to play in contemporary and highly diverse workplaces, as certain religions may divide people from one to another. This is despite the fact that religion can add much to employees particularly in regards to high and admired ethical values. Nonetheless, both religion and spirituality are central to individuals' identities. Besides that, there are many different religions and spiritual views. Therefore, the role of management is perhaps not to create a unify environment where one religion/spiritual view dominates, but to create an environment where individuals freely express their own beliefs and practices (Hicks, 2003). Despite the above argument, it is also claimed that broad meanings of spirituality intersect or converge with the world's five big religions—Islam, Christianity, Judaism, Buddhism, and Hinduism (Case & Gosling, 2010). However, it is not necessary to discuss religion and spirituality in the same context. Perhaps, they are more different than initially thought.

There are three different views that strive to identify the meaning of workplace spirituality—religious views, intrinsic origin views, and the existential view (Krishnakumar & Neck, 2002). However, eventually from these views, two distinct camps emerged, spiritually focused and religion focused (Neal, 2013). For the proponent of the first view an individual who is spiritual does not necessarily need to be religious. A person can believe in spirituality but not necessarily to be religious. Whereas, according to the second view, religion and spirituality are so inseparably connected that would be impossible to identify one concept without the other (Houghton et al., 2016).

Business Ethic

Recent ethical scandals from various organizations in different sectors across the world have gained attention from various stakeholders. There has been growing interest in societies across the globe toward the unethical/immoral behavior of organizations. Such organizations' attitudes are not accepted and are disapproved of. However, it still happens. Therefore, it becomes clearer than ever that business ethics is crucial for organizations, not only providing legitimacy but also without which businesses cannot be successful. Studies on business ethics are relatively new.

It was after the 1990s that we started to see an increase in research focused on this topic. In fact, these studies have increased exponentially. It is not arguable any more whether businesses should have business ethics or not. It is a necessity to have ethics in business. It is not only a requirement from stakeholders but also a must for conducting a business. This is because all business activities are based on trust and, without it, there cannot be a healthy market transaction. Therefore, although some unethical business activities have been seen, this does not mean all businesses have unethical/immoral behavior. In fact, more businesses are moral and ethical than otherwise. It should be also noted that without ethics firms could not be successful. Besides, even unethical/immoral decisions are based on a sort of ethics underlying the decision (Crane & Matten, 2016).

In this context, related literature classifies ethics in two different views. First, normative ethics related to theology and philosophy that tell individuals how to behave. The second view is descriptive ethics and focuses on predicting and explaining individuals' behavior during ethical dilemmas (O'Fallon & Butterfield, 2005). Business ethics can be described as a "study of business situations, activities and, decisions where issues of right and wrong are addressed" (Crane & Matten, 2016, p. 5). The question of right or wrong should be answered according to morality. Hence, what should our morality be based on? Should we rely on universal or individual values? Should our company provide all the values? Perhaps, one of the main sources of morality might be an organizational culture. This would be based on values and norms that are accepted by the majority of the organization members. If more members accept the aforementioned values then it forms a stronger organizational culture. However, forming a unified organizational culture is a difficult task. Contemporary large businesses may spread across to the globe and into various departments. Ensuring the same values and norms are shared between different departments and in dispersed geography is a daunting task. There is also an issue of ensuring certain ethical/moral behavior is followed by employees. Perhaps, arguably, the answers to the above questions are ethical which is something that guides individuals' behavior, but is not something that an organization has (Pullen & Rhodes, 2015).

Corporate business ethics provide alignment with the public's request for corporations to improve their ethical standards and behaviors. Despite the fact that such practices are engaged voluntarily, these practices tend to be institutionalized within organizations. Engaging in business ethics not only gains approval from stakeholders but also helps corporations to maximize profit (Metzger, Dalton, & Hill, 1993). Furthermore, implementing and institutionalizing ethical practices regulates ethical behavior and for this purpose an ethical code of conduct can be issued. Ultimately, the idea of engaging in corporate business ethics is that social values and the capitalist corporate system can be complementary to each other (Cederström & Marinetto, 2013). However, there are abundant works in the related literature criticizing such sentiment. Moreover, recent research strongly criticizes this idea and finds it difficult to envisage the capitalist corporate system and business ethics co-existing without any problem: perhaps it is because this is ethics with a pro-business stance (Rhodes, 2016).

Furthermore, discussions in the related literature suggest that ethics be situated and contextual in character (Kjonstad & Willmott, 1995). It is difficult to discuss ethics with a rule-based approach. To illustrate, enforcing individuals to follow moral principles sometimes ensures compliance but may not cause morally sound behavior. What it means is that ethical standards will be followed in cases of ambiguity and when there are ethical dilemmas. In these circumstances, individuals will be far from having the comfort of consensus. The problem is if an ethical decision is being made simply to follow publicly released ethical codes of conduct, then there is no need for individuals to be taking moral responsibility. In response, the argument is that ethics begins when the rule of law cannot apply or there is no established regulation (Clegg, Kornberger, & Rhodes, 2007). There is also the problem of a boundary law. Ethics starts where laws cannot apply. If the law can be applied to a situation than there is no longer ethical argument needed. Thus, organizational reality and ethical certainty may not be matched.

Following from that, one of the difficulties of organizations/individuals being moral/ethical is to be able to meet organizational practices with ethical behavior under the pressure of other needs such as being competitive or achieving profit maximization. In these circumstances, individuals may incline rather toward to the dark side. It would not be surprising to see individuals being immoral/unethical. The problem is how to prevent such behavior. Further complicating the issue is the general acceptance of such behavior into the organizational culture. If immoral/unethical behavior becomes normal, then it would be very difficult to reverse it. Eventually, such behavior would also cause negative performance in many different organizational aspects. So, is there any way to somehow institutionalize ethical/moral standards through informal means?

Ethical Climate

Employees' behavior can be regulated through formal and informal means within organizations. One of the ways of achieving that is through creating a climate that the majority of individuals accept norms, regulations, and values across the organization. More employees accept the aforementioned norms and values then ethical consensus ensues and, consequently, they becomes a framework for individuals. However, this process is complex in nature, as the aforementioned values might be difficult to share by all employees. This is because, eventually, each individual has a unique personality and culture. Besides, changing or implementing a culture/climate can happen slowly.

Scholars define the work climate as "psychologically meaningful molar descriptions that people can agree characterize a system's practices and procedures" (Schneider, 1975, p. 474). Work climate is separated into different sub-types and there are various work climates. However, eventually, these are separated into two main groups. The first one is "aggregated perceptions of organizational conventions regarding forms of structure and procedures for the use of rewards and control"; and the second is "aggregated perceptions of the existence of organizational norms supporting values such as providing warmth and support to peers and subordinates" (Victor & Cullen, 1988, p. 102).

Furthermore, within this group of identification, there is a so-called ethical climate, which is described by Victor and Cullen (1988) as the management's behavior toward ethics within the workplace in a way that is perceived by employees. In other words, the ethical climate is described as "a descriptive map of ethical decision-making and actions within an organization based on philosophical and sociological theory" (Martin & Cullen, 2006, p. 176). Ethical climate theory is one of the strongest theoretical concepts in the business ethics literature that helps scholars to identify ethical challenges within the organizational domain. It created a framework that helps scholars to understand ethical decision-making from the perspective of philosophical and sociological theory (Martin & Cullen, 2006). Victor and Cullen (1988) created a chart that has two axes showing how they created the ethical climate system and to whom it applies. They also created nine theoretical dimensions of ethical climate typology that has, eventually, after series of surveys been reduced to five. The identified dimensions are instrumental, caring, independence, rules, and laws and code. These dimensions most consistently appear in research across the range of disciplines and provide the vast majority of data available to other scholars (Martin & Cullen, 2006).

Furthermore, this typology then created a fundamental base for the ethical climate questionnaire. It is discussed in the related literature that human beings develop moral standards through different ethical criteria and engage in different moral reasoning. This process is multistage and sequential. It begins with a fear of punishment for consequences of actions and progresses toward concern for others and concerns for humanity. Within this context, three standard ethical criteria are identified, and these are caring, self-interest, and principle. The standards also reflect the three major ethical theory school criteria, deontology, utilitarianism, and egoism (Cullen, Victor, & Bronson, 1993).

In this context, each organization and subsystem develop their own normative system and this determines whether the decision or actions taken are appropriate. These normative systems are perceived as ethical systems to employees (Victor & Cullen, 1988). There are determinants of ethical climate. These are organizational form, organization-specific history, and the existing socio-cultural environment (Demirtas & Akdogan, 2015). The ethical climate is a multi-dimensional concept and it is connected to various employee behavior including, but not confined to, ethical and counterproductive working attitudes (Wimbush & Shepard, 1994).

This impact of ethical climate on various organizational outcomes is identified in the related literature. The aforementioned effect is not only related to ethics but also to various organizational research and managerial issues. The relationship is not only limited to individuals but also includes organizational factors. In that, scholars found relationships between ethical climate and strategic orientation of firms (Neubaum, Mitchell, & Schminke, 2004), leadership behavior (Schminke, Ambrose, & Neubaum, 2005), organizational commitment of employees (Cullen, Parboteeah, & Victor, 2003), moral distress intensity (Atabay, Çangarli, & Penbek, 2015), staff compassion in the hotel industry (Zoghbi-Manrique-de-Lara & Guerra-Baez, 2016), customer satisfaction and financial performance (Koo Moon & Kwon Choi, 2014), some type of deviant workplace behavior (Schminke et al., 2005), and business school ethical climate and students' unethical behavior (Birtch & Chiang, 2014).

All these studies lead to a general conclusion that many organizational activities and employee behavior and attitudes are directly and indirectly influenced by the consensus that is created under the name of organizational ethical climate. So, then, how can organizations somehow create a positive consensus that would be shared by the members and would have a positive impact on both organizational outcomes and individuals?

Creating an Ethical Climate through Workplace Spirituality

Ethical scandals in various organizations in different sectors around the world received considerable attention from scholars from a range of disciplines. As more attention has been given, certain understanding is accumulated and researchers identified certain issues causing the unethical/immoral behavior of organizations/individuals. Shreds of evidence show that these misdeeds were not the responsibility of certain individuals but "rather, they emerged from freewheeling, aggressive, entrepreneurial organizational systems and cultures that allowed and even encouraged unethical behavior" (Neubaum et al., 2004, p. 335). In fact, for a certain while, scholars were suspicious that such behavior was the outcome of greedy corporate cultures (Neubaum et al., 2004).

So, then, how can certain norms, values, and perhaps traditions be established? Institutional theory answers these questions from various angles. New institutional economists create the first approach. North (1991) discusses institutions being made of formal and informal institutional frameworks. The first is created and written those who have power, particularly enforcement power. These groups of people receive power through formal ways. Enforcement power means individuals should follow the established system. Disobedience to the rules and regulations would bring formal punishment. The second consists of unwritten rules, norms, and values that are established by the members of the groups. There is no enforcement power if the norms and values are not followed.

However, punishments based on an informal institutional framework would be more severe than those for formal institutional framework. This is because the group may exclude the member who does not follow the established informal system. This could be more difficult for individuals, as humans are social beings. Being excluded from the social environment can be much more difficult for individuals than to be formally punished.

Furthermore, the new institutional theory, from organizational scientists' perspective, discusses the pressures that arise from both the internal and external environments that eventually force organizations to behave and design in similar ways. In his work, Scott (2007) identified three pillars of institutions that influence almost every interaction within an organization. These pillars are regulative pillars, normative pillars, and cognitive-cultural pillars. The first consists of formal institutions where written rules are enforced. The second, normative pillars, is created jointly by the norms and values on which some institutional theorists believe the institutions primarily rest. The third, cognitive-cultural pillars, is based on culture and includes accepted values and beliefs.

So, how could workplace spirituality be utilized to create an ethical climate? According to institutional theory in order for a certain climate to be created, it should be written and then enforced on individuals. For example, a code of conduct can be utilized for this purpose. The key point here is enforcement: to ensure individuals follow the expected behavior there should be some sort of punishment. It does not necessarily have to be harsh but should be a deterrent. This is how formal institutions can be established. The problem here is that it is enforced by the will of the one who has power, and not created by consensus of members. Such methods can be effective and enforced but may not be accepted by the majority of individuals.

The other alternative is to utilize informal means. The approach here should be completely different. There is no enforcement power. Therefore, everything should be voluntarily accepted. There are different methods that could be implemented by managers, such as: ideal and expected behaviors can be explained to employees; special reward systems that emphasize ethical/moral behavior can be implemented; special ceremonies could be announced where the most ethical/moral individual can be appraised; myths and stories can be told to employees; dress and physical outlines can be designed. These are the methods that could be utilized to implement an ethical climate. So why and how can workplace spirituality be used?

One of the main reasons workplace spirituality is used is that it can emphasize ethicality across the organization. It can provide a peaceful environment where harmony between individuals would exist. It provides so many positive advantages. Particularly, norms and values can be based on workplace spirituality and spiritual traditions. This is an important point as these would be based on the ethical climate. It could also provide a framework for individuals. It can also be used to create a consensus. It is clear that ethical consensus requires consensus among employees. If the ethical climate based norms and values come from workplace spirituality it may be easier to accept by the members of an organization.

The problem with that is whether all the members would have similar spiritual/religious beliefs. This is a challenging question. In contemporary and diverse workplaces, employees come from different religious and belief systems. It is quite common now to see people believing in Christian, Islam, Judaism, and Buddhism, or any other religion, and working together in the same workplace. Therefore, it is very unlikely that a certain religion's norms and values could be chosen to create ethical climate. It is only possible to do that in the workplace if people believe in the same religion, even sect.

However, workplace spirituality offers a very tempting alternative. It is not based on any specific religion or belief systems but appreciates the wellbeing of employees. It would be much easier for the individuals to accept certain norms and values which stem from workplace spirituality. It may help management to achieve ethical consensus much easier and, perhaps, with less resistance. Therefore, in order to achieve an ethical climate that is accepted by the majority of individuals, workplace spirituality can be utilized.

Conclusion

To summarize, ethical scandals are more visible than ever. Importantly, ongoing immoral/unethical behavior of organizations has been brought to public attention. In these circumstances, it is more apparent that there is a need for a different approach to the ongoing ethical problems. Yet, making the issue more complicated is that modern workplaces are more diverse than ever. People from the very different cultural backgrounds are working toward reaching certain goals established in organizations. This creates a dynamic environment where establishing certain ethical/moral standards is difficult.

To overcome the aforementioned challenges organizations can engage in workplace spirituality. However, certain problems also exist in this. One of the main problems is considering on which norms and values should our ethical climate be based. Considering that in the contemporary workplaces people come from the very diverse background it is a difficult challenge. Another difficulty is how to institutionalize the ethical climate. The key point here is that consensus to achieve this. This perhaps can more effectively be solved by the utilization of informal institutions, where the punishment is more severe than formal institutions and can be more effectively utilized to institutionalize an ethical climate as a framework within organizations.

References

Atabay, G., Çangarli, B. G., & Penbek, Ş. (2015). Impact of ethical climate on moral distress revisited: Multidimensional view. *Nursing ethics, 22*(1), 103–116.

Benefiel, M. (2003). Irreconcilable foes? The discourse of spirituality and the discourse of organizational science. *Organization, 10*(2), 383–391.

Benefiel, M., Fry, L. W., & Geigle, D. (2014). Spirituality and religion in the workplace: History, theory, and research. *Psychology of Religion and Spirituality, 6*(3), 175–187.
Birtch, T. A., & Chiang, F. F. (2014). The influence of business school's ethical climate on students' unethical behavior. *Journal of Business Ethics, 123*(2), 283–294.
Case, P., & Gosling, J. (2010). The spiritual organization: Critical reflections on the instrumentality of workplace spirituality. *Journal of Management, Spirituality and Religion, 7*(4), 257–282.
Cederström, C., & Marinetto, M. (2013). Corporate social responsibility á la the liberal communist. *Organization, 20*(3), 416–432.
Chen, C. Y., & Yang, C. F. (2012). The impact of spiritual leadership on organizational citizenship behavior: A multi-sample analysis. *Journal of Business Ethics, 105*(1), 107–114.
Chen, C. Y., Yang, C. Y., & Li, C. I. (2012). Spiritual leadership, follower mediators, and organizational outcomes: Evidence from three industries across two major Chinese societies. *Journal of Applied Social Psychology, 42*(4), 890–938.
Clegg, S., Kornberger, M., & Rhodes, C. (2007). Business ethics as practice. *British Journal of Management, 18*(2), 107–122.
Crane, A., & Matten, D. (2016). Business Ethics: Managing Corporate Citizenship and Sustainability in the Age of Globalization. Oxford, UK: Oxford University Press.
Corner, P. D. (2009). Workplace spirituality and business ethics: Insights from an eastern spiritual tradition. *Journal of Business Ethics, 85*(3), 377–389.
Cullen, J. B., Victor, B., & Bronson, J. W. (1993). The ethical climate questionnaire: An assessment of its development and validity. *Psychological Reports, 73*(2), 667–674.
Cullen, J. B., Parboteeah, K. P., & Victor, B. (2003). The effects of ethical climates on organizational commitment: A two-study analysis. *Journal of Business Ethics, 46*(2), 127–141.
Danielz, D., Franz, R. S., & Wong, K. (2000). A classroom with worldview: Making spiritual assumption explicit in management education. *Journal of Management Education, 24*, 540–562.
Demirtas, O., & Akdogan, A. A. (2015). The effect of ethical leadership behavior on ethical climate, turnover intention, and affective commitment. *Journal of Business Ethics, 130*(1), 59–67.
Duchon, D., & Plowman, D. A. (2005). Nurturing the spirit at work: Impact on work unit performance. *Leadership Quarterly, 16*(5), 807–833.
Fry, L. W., Vitucci, S., & Cedillo, M. (2005). Spiritual leadership and army transformation: Theory, measurement, and establishing a baseline. *Leadership Quarterly, 5*, 835.
Garcia-Zamor, J. C. (2003). Workplace spirituality and organizational performance. *Public Administration Review, 63*(3), 355–363.
Giacalone, R. A., & Jurkiewicz, C. L. (2003). *Handbook of Workplace Spirituality and Organizational Performance*. New York: M. E. Sharpe.
Gordon, D. M. (1996). *Fat and Mean: The Corporate Squeeze of Working Americans and the Myth of Managerial "Downsizing."* New York: Simon & Schuster.
Gotsis, G., & Kortezi, Z. (2008). Philosophical foundations of workplace spirituality: A critical approach. *Journal of Business Ethics, 78*(4), 575–600.
Guillroy, W. D. (2000). *The Living Organization: Spirituality in the Workplace*. Salt Lake City, UT: Innovations International Inc.
Gupta, M., Kumar, V., & Singh, M. (2014). Creating satisfied employees through workplace spirituality: A study of the private insurance sector in Punjab (India). *Journal of Business Ethics, 122*(1), 79–88.
Hicks, D. A. (2003). *Religion and the Workplace: Pluralism, Spirituality, Leadership*. Cambridge, UK: Cambridge University Press.
Houghton, J. D., Neck, C. P., & Krishnakumar, S. (2016). The what, why, and how of spirituality in the workplace revisited: A 14-year update and extension. *Journal of Management, Spirituality and Religion, 13*(3), 177–205.
Kjonstad, B., & Willmott, H. (1995). Business ethics: Restrictive or empowering? *Journal of Business Ethics, 14*(6), 445–464.
Koo Moon, H., & Kwon Choi, B. (2014). How an organization's ethical climate contributes to customer satisfaction and financial performance: Perceived organizational innovation perspective. *European Journal of Innovation Management, 17*(1), 85–106.
Krishnakumar, S., & Neck, C. P. (2002). The "what", "why" and "how" of spirituality in the workplace. *Journal of Managerial Psychology, 17*(3), 153–164.
Lips-Wiersma, M., Lund Dean, K., & Fornaciari, C. J. (2009). Theorizing the dark side of the workplace spirituality movement. *Journal of Management Inquiry, 18*(4), 288–300.

Martin, K. D., & Cullen, J. B. (2006). Continuities and extensions of ethical climate theory: A meta-analytic review. *Journal of Business Ethics, 69*(2), 175–194.

Metzger, M., Dalton, D. R., & Hill, J. W. (1993). The organization of ethics and the ethics of organizations: The case for expanded organizational ethics audits. *Business Ethics Quarterly, 3*(1), 27–43.

Milliman, J., Czaplewski, A. J., & Ferguson, J. (2003). Workplace spirituality and employee work attitudes: An exploratory empirical assessment. *Journal of Organizational Change Management, 16*(4), 426–447.

Mitroff, I. I. (2003). Do not promote religion under the guise of spirituality. *Organization, 10*(2), 375–382.

Moore, T. W., & Casper, W. J. (2006). An examination of proxy measures of workplace spirituality: A profile model of multidimensional constructs. *Journal of Leadership and Organisational Studies, 12*, 10–19.

Neal, J. (2013). Faith and spirituality in the workplace: Emerging research and practice. In J. Neal (Ed.), *Handbook of Faith and Spirituality in the Workplace*. New York: Springer, 3–18.

Neubaum, D., Mitchell, M., & Schminke, M. (2004). Firm newness, entrepreneurial orientation, and ethical climate. *Journal of Business Ethics, 52*(4), 335–347.

North, D. C. (1991). Institutions. *Journal of Economic Perspectives, 5*(1), 97–112.

O'Fallon, M. J., & Butterfield, K. D. (2005). A review of the empirical ethical decision-making literature: 1996–2003. *Journal of Business Ethics, 59*(4), 375–413.

Pullen, A., & Rhodes, C. (2015). Ethics, embodiment and organizations. *Organization, 22*(2), 159–165.

Rego, A., & Pina e Cunha, M. (2008). Workplace spirituality and organizational commitment: An empirical study. *Journal of Organizational Change Management, 21*(1), 53–75.

Rhodes, C. (2016). Democratic business ethics: Volkswagen's emissions scandal and the disruption of corporate sovereignty. *Organization Studies, 37*(10), 1501–1518.

Schminke, M., Ambrose, M. L., & Neubaum, D. O. (2005). The effect of leader moral development on ethical climate and employee attitudes. *Organizational Behavior and Human Decision Processes, 97*(2), 135–151.

Schneider, B. (1975). Organizational climates: An essay. *Personnel Psychology, 28*(4), 447–479.

Scott, W. R. (2007). Prefatory chapter: Institutions and social innovation. In T. J. Hämäläinen & R. Heiskala (Eds.), *Social Innovations, Institutional Change and Economic Performance*. Cheltenham, UK: Edward Elgar, viii–xxi.

Steingard, D. S. (2005). Spiritually-informed management theory: Toward profound possibilities for inquiry and transformation. *Journal of Management Inquiry, 14*(3), 227–241.

Tzouramani, E., & Karakas, F. (2016). Spirituality in management. In M. de Souza, J. Bone, & J. Watson (Eds.), *Spirituality across Disciplines: Research and Practice*. Cham, Switzerland: Springer, 273–284.

Victor, B., & Cullen, J. B. (1988). The organizational bases of ethical work climates. *Administrative Science Quarterly, 33*, 101–125.

Wimbush, J. C., & Shepard, J. M. (1994). Toward an understanding of ethical climate: Its relationship to ethical behavior and supervisory influence. *Journal of Business Ethics, 13*(8), 637–647.

Zoghbi-Manrique-de-Lara, P., & Guerra-Baez, R. (2016). Exploring the influence of ethical climate on employee compassion in the hospitality industry. *Journal of Business Ethics, 133*(3), 605–617.

29

LEADING WITH THE FUTURE IN MIND

Giles Hutchins

Introduction

At 46 years old, I have now spent half my life working in business. Formerly as a management consultant for KPMG and more recently as Global Head of Sustainability Solutions for a multinational IT services provider, Atos, with over 50,000 employees internationally, I found myself helping all manner of organizations through various transformations. I left corporate life in 2012 with the imminent birth of our first child, feeling thoroughly spent by corporate-think and management-speak. Yet, not wishing to turn my back on business, and its potential as a force-for-good in the world, I have since specialized on life-affirming conscious business, publishing three specialist books while helping leaders and organizations attune with the logic of life.

It has been for many more years of my life that I have felt, deeply in my heart, that underpinning our plethora of problems—whether it be rising mental illness through to rampant consumerism, or rising climate change through to the widespread destruction of life on Earth—is a root source; a root problem that spawns the downstream effects of consumerism, individualism, rationalism, capitalism, anthropocentrism, and the like. It is a disease of the psyche—one might say a crisis of spirit. It is due to a profound mental dislocation of self-identity from environment. With the risk of trying to *define* something fluid, complex, and inter-relational, which is itself part of the problem, it is commonly described as fragmentation or disconnection: disconnection within ourselves (our deeper sense of selfhood), disconnection from each other (the relational nature of our communality), and disconnection from Nature, Life, and Universe.

This disconnection manifests in our inner and outer worlds in varying ways. In our outer world it manifests in the stories we tell ourselves about how we think the world works and our sense of place and purpose within it. Our mythologies, cosmologies, and worldviews influence our socio-economic narrative, which in turn influences the way we behave in business, politics, and beyond.

In our inner world, this disconnection manifests in how we attend to each evolving moment in our midst, and the perceptual filters and constrictions we habituate and acculturate. These habituations and acculturations are influenced by, and also influence, the outer narrative or worldview we tell ourselves about how the world works. As the philosopher Richard Tarnas so eloquently notes:

> Our world view is not simply the way we look at the world. It reaches inward to constitute our innermost being, and outward to constitute the world. It mirrors but also reinforces and even forges the structures, armorings, and possibilities of our interior life. It deeply configures our psychic and somatic experience, the patterns of our sensing, knowing, and interacting with the world. No less potently, our world view—our beliefs and theories, our maps, our metaphors, our myths, our interpretive assumptions—constellates our outer reality, shaping and working the world's malleable potentials in a thousand ways of subtly reciprocal interaction. World views create worlds.
>
> *(2007, p. 16)*

It seems that we are individually and collectively participating in an inner–outer worldview which—according to the scientific evidence now available to us—is actually undermining our own wellbeing and the very fabric of life on Earth. Something is deeply flawed. This disconnection is wreaking havoc.

The time to address this flawed way of attending and flawed worldview appears to be upon us. We are living through an epochal moment in our human history, what UN ex-Secretary General Ban Ki-Moon refers to as Great Transition where, he says, "the decisions we make will have a deeper and more lasting impact than perhaps any other set of decisions in recent decades" (Ki-Moon, 2013). This is a time of simultaneous breakdown/breakthrough, a supreme moment within which we must act consciously and coherently to avoid catastrophe.

The contemporary philosopher Joseph Milne notes that, "there is a tendency in our age to rush to change the manifest effects of wrong actions without seriously considering the root causes" (Milne, 2010). This tendency is built-in to the disconnected mindset which creates the problems in the first place. We filter our perception of life through a polarizing reductive filter that separates "things" into siloes, objects, and others. We then seek fixes to the problems created by this logic, by applying the same mechanistic perspective that created the problems in the first place. And so we fail to reach beyond the symptoms, often unwittingly exacerbating the very situation we are trying to solve.

Einstein's overly used and heavily hackneyed insight—we cannot change our problems with the same level of consciousness that created them in the first place—is a perfect insight for the manifold problems we face and our way beyond them. Yet, so often we find ourselves doing just this, and we simply don't have time for this anymore. This is humanity's hour of reckoning. It's time to get radical and deal with the root cause, our now pathological disconnectedness.

And this is where leadership comes in. As leadership specialist Joan Marques notes, "we need leadership to move from the here-and-now to the future" (Marques, 2016). Leadership is essentially about creating the conditions conducive for ourselves and others to continually deepen our understanding of how the world works, in so doing deepening our sense of place and purpose within the world, and understanding how best to create and deliver value while shaping a viable future (Jaworski, 2011). This imperative to call forth a viable future for all of humanity and the wider fabric of life on Earth is, I believe, an inherent quality of *Homo sapiens* (wise beings). While we may unwittingly do a great job of distracting ourselves from real wisdom, there is something within our kernel of selfhood that impels us to deepen into this wisdom as we explore life-affirming futures. It reminds me of George Bernard Shaw's insight, "We are made wise not by the recollections of our past but by the responsibility of our future" (Shaw, n.d.).

Before we explore how best to lead with this life-affirming future in mind, let's briefly sense into the epochal threshold that is being crossed in these times of breakdown/breakthrough.

The Journey of Separation and Return

We might see the age-old shamanic journey or hero's quest of departure–separation–return as an arc playing out over the last 5000 years or so in the West, into this moment of arcing back into "return."

The "separation" phase followed our "departure" from *participation mystique* (animist worldview of indigenous communal life, inter-relational self–other–world) into the equalitarian communities of Neolithic Europe and the Patriarchal conquests that overturned this equalitarianism.

Then Pre-Socratic Hellenistic philosophy and cosmology blended with Hebraic monotheism and then developed into Aristotelian Scholastic logic. This gave rise to an increasing sense of separation of self–other–world being woven into the song-lines of the Western worldview.

This sense of separateness peaked with the Enlightenment and its Cartesian, Newtonian, and Darwinian perspectives portraying evolution and Universe as devoid of intrinsic animism. Purpose and consciousness were drained out of Nature. Human consciousness came to be viewed as individualistic, an epiphenomenon of the brain (with an exceptional direct connection into a transcendent God which has been removed from the immanence of Nature).

The human psyche became differentiated and accentuated from the matrix of Nature and Universe to such an extent that it was almost entirely cut-off, sealed into an individualistic sense of self, which drained the vibrancy of our relationality.

The increasingly narrowing-down objectifying lens through which we perceive the world, sees "self" as separate from "other" and "world." Enter Neo-Darwinism which views the organism as separate from and in competition with its environment, and the process of evolution as one of selfish ascendency.

The "me–we" relationality that ought to make *Homo sapiens* so special as communal social-loving beings is compartmentalized, objectified, and rationalized into cause-and-effect individualistic self-agency. This brings individual empowerment, mechanistic advancement, desacralized nature-as-utility to be plundered for human gain, and a heightened sense of self emancipated from the animistic inter-relational communisis of life. This aggrandizement of the "self" has been a defining factor of the modern mind in the 19th and 20th centuries, with all the advancements in modern medicine, transportation, technology, and mod-cons we all enjoy.

While this "separation" phase of the arc has been accompanied by much advancement, it also has a shadow. Our sense of "self" becomes dislocated from any deeper sense of place and purpose in the world. Psychic atrophy sets in, along with self-reflexive magnification, status anxiety, consumerism, and egotism. We create all sorts of problems for ourselves: increasing sense of anxiety, rising mental illness, and narcissistic tendencies. Our relationships struggle under the strain and the fabric of society is worn thin.

Likewise, this disconnection warps our worldview. Our socio-economic narrative is cut adrift from any deeper sense of meaning other than to satisfy egotistic needs and desires. We become dis-eased, desperately pursuing happiness "out there," no longer adequately relating to our deeper selfhood, or able to sense the inter-dependency of life. We get caught up in our own illusions of separateness. Rampant social and ecological degradation amidst a contagion of consumerism becomes our present reality. Our worldview creates our world. We create what Einstein (n.d.) famously referred to as an optical delusion of consciousness.

And yet, it may be argued, this post-modern critical self-awareness and human autonomy prepares us for the "return home," as long as we have the insight and courage to break through the delusion created in our own minds by shifting our consciousness so that we can see our way back into the inter-relational "communisis" of life. This is our journey home.

The "return" arc of this journey from disconnection toward reconnection is the reintegration of this empowered "self" along with the tools, technologies, and developments we have gained from this "journey of separation." Yet, this return requires a remembering of the inter-relational nature of reality.

This return is quite different from the *participation mystique* state of consciousness at "departure," as we are "seeing with new eyes." By example, Clare Graves (2005), the originator of Spiral Dynamics, refers to Tier Two consciousness—Yellow (Teal), Turquoise, Coral—as having an echo of the early Beige and Purple animistic levels of consciousness, and yet being quite different. In fact, Graves went as far as to say that as we move into Tier Two consciousness (our "return" back into inter-connectedness) we become a new human being as our neurology is substantially different from Tier One—a substantial threshold in consciousness is crossed. We "return" with a new level of consciousness, a deeper prehension (as Alfred North Whitehead put it), a deeper perception and cognitive engagement with reality. We embody and experience the self–other–world dynamic in a different and yet similar way: same, same but different, as the Thais might say!

As we return back into connectedness from separateness, we embody both a sense of differentiation and integration. This allows us to hold a deeper perspective of the vitality of diversity-within-unity transcending the polarities of either homogenized we-are-all-one (whether that be clannism, communism, or totalitarianism) or individualistic we-are-all-separate (whether that be individualism, racism, or neo-liberalism).

From the journey of departing, separating, and then returning, we gain perspective on the awesomeness of the diversity-within-unity, and move beyond "isms." We become more fully conscious of the "pattern that connects" inherent within Nature–Life–Universe. This embodied realization expands not only our consciousness but also our human agency—we become more human, and sense more deeply into this more-than-human world of ours, and deepen our sense of place and purpose within it. This shift in consciousness is at once a humbling yet courageous undertaking, as we let go of old ways of seeing ourselves and open up to the awesome responsibility of being a conscious participator in this continuous ocean of inter-being.

Crossing the Threshold

It would seem that as we cross the threshold from separateness back into the reconnectedness of diversity-within-unity, we are remembering something timeless (fresh and yet ancient) within our psyche, and an "ontological and epistemological threshold" is crossed.

This threshold is a shift in our ways of being (ontology) and ways of knowing (epistemology), nothing less than a metamorphosis of our humanity. This metamorphosis shape-shifts our cosmology and worldview, which in turn influences the dominant socio-economic narrative, which in turn influences our behavior in our organizations, conversations, and contemplations.

The shift in our ways of knowing (epistemology) is from our still prevalent "disconnected" rational-analytic and mechanistic way of knowing that separates what it perceives, reducing inter-relational systems down into siloes, taxonomies, and discrete managerial functions, which it then sets about mechanizing in a linear fashion to design and deploy mechanistic services and solutions. This rational-analytic tendency we have is a useful way of navigating that serves us as part of our wider human epistemology, but during our "journey of separation" it has come to dominate our human repertoire to such an extent that our deeper ways of knowing are suppressed. The resultant skewed epistemology undermines our human potential.

Carl Jung referred to our wider repertoire of epistemology as our "four ways of knowing": intuitive, rational, emotional, and somatic/sensorial (Harding, 2006, p. 30). Others have provided a slightly richer "epistemological bandwidth" (for instance: imaginal, archetypal, and symbolic can be differentiated within Jung's intuitive-knowing) but Jung's four ways of knowing suffice for our purposes here.

We shift our sense of self from separateness into a more integrated self–other–world holistic awareness through what Jung referred to as a process of "individuation." As we individuate we find ourselves more readily drawing upon a more integrated knowingness—an integration of intuitive, rational, emotional, and somatic—rather than a dominance of rational-analytic. This integrated knowingness draws upon the conscious/unconscious "Self"—our deeper selfhood which permeates within the *anima mundi*, World Soul, collective unconscious of Nature and the wider Universe.

This process of individuation—which is essentially a psycho-spiritual journey of self-realization—opens up our sense of self. We draw upon more of reality through these different ways of knowing. Our enriched and enlivened inner-knowing becomes more intimately inter-related with our outer senses, perturbations, relations, and activities. The boundary of inner–outer becomes more fluid and permeable, as does our ego–self, psyche, and soul. We are at once more our "Self," more of who we truly are, while simultaneously more vulnerable, receptive, and authentic with others and the world. This is humbling and requires patience, discipline, and courage as ego-masks and hardened habituations begin to loosen around old wounds, self-defenses, and acculturations.

This "epistemological opening" requires discernment as one can be overwhelmed or subsumed by this "thinning of the veil"—our sense of self can either be overwhelmed or over-inflated by this influx of psychic connection.

This discernment is a surrendering or letting-go of the desire to grasp at, define, and analytically know what is now becoming available to our conscious mind through this extended epistemology. As well as a letting-go, it is an opening-up receptively and responsively to this deeper sense of reality. There is a danger of being caught in self-delusion if we project this deeper experience through a superficial self-referential meaning, which only sees self as separate, rather than self as a relational participant within an ocean of inter-being. This is the challenge/opportunity of the "return."

For example, we may experience a "synchronistic" encounter, numinous moment, or epiphany. This is a felt-sense and also an intuitive-sense beyond the bounds of our normal perceptual horizon, which may then inflate the egotistic sense of self as special, or fuel a pleasure-seeking "self-high," rather than a sensing-in to the deeper permeating emergence of "Self" within an interconnected self–other–world matrix.

Hence, this "return" requires an integrative interplay of multiple cognitive faculties—the intuitive and imaginal, the emotional and empirical, the sensorial and symbolic, the relational and rational, the conscious and unconscious—a more integrated and integral consciousness. Therefore, the discernment required is of a more comprehensive (or "higher") level from that of our current dominant consciousness (Tier One) where our knowing is largely skewed toward the rational-analytic and the intuitive and imaginal often deprioritized or inadequately assimilated.

The higher level discernment required with this integral consciousness is a more disciplined body-mindfulness—a deeper quality of being more present to the evolving moments in our midst. It is a "receptive discernment" rather than a rational-analytic discernment. This is why it is simultaneously a threshold in being (ontology) and knowing (epistemology).

We sense into life within the current of "now." As we attend with a more comprehensive attentiveness—an imaginal, intuitive, somatic, empathic receptivity—a wiser responsiveness spawns. Our receptivity enables our responsiveness.

This quality of "beingness" allows for our integral "knowingness" and vice versa. It is a simultaneous beingness-and-knowingness that allows for a wiser receptive-responsiveness to unfold within us. The natural scientist and philosopher Alan Rayner (2017) explores this extensively in his pioneering work on *Natural Inclusion*.

This shift in our way of being-and-knowing is foundational to expanding human consciousness—our journey toward becoming wise-beings, *Homo sapiens*.

Disturbance, dissonance, fatigue, failure, or stress can quite naturally stimulate a closing down, fight–flight aggressiveness-defensiveness, which accentuates a sense of separate-self, and reduces the permeability of our inner–outer boundaries. Our ability for empathy, compassion, and wisdom relates to our epistemological and ontological state. We pull ourselves back from across the threshold into the perceived safety of "self as separate." To paraphrase Pink Floyd, we become comfortable yet numb.

As we learn and develop, we become more masterful at embracing disturbance and dissonance. Challenges may stimulate our learning and contribute to our individuating journey, rather than undermining our vulnerable unfolding into a deeper being-and-knowing. This is the essence of emotional and spiritual development—of being able to love thy neighbor and stranger as thy self.

The work of Jung, James, and Hillman in the 20th century, and the emergence of Depth Psychology helped set the scene for this epochal shift in understanding within Western psychology which is now being enriched further with advances in Ecological Psychology and Transpersonal Psychology.

The work of Heidegger, Merleau-Ponty, Gadamer, and other great 20th century phenomenologists helped set the scene for this epochal shift in understanding within Western philosophy along with Whitehead, Teilhard de Chardin, Bergson, Barfield, Steiner, and others.

Likewise, across all the disciplines in science, the scene has been set for this epochal shift through the pioneering work of so many brilliant minds ranging from Bohm to Prigogine and Bateson to Wheeler (simply too many to list).

Until now though, these emergent trends in psychology, philosophy, biology, sociology, etc. have not been adequately underpinned by a coherent cosmology that supports this more integral and participatory perspective. Only recently has a new coherent cosmology started to emerge amongst pioneering cosmologists—for instance, Jude Currivan, Ervin Laszlo, Bernard Haisch, Brian Swimme, Nassim Haramein, and others. This new cosmology, which portrays the Universe as deeply interconnected and participatory in nature, has the potential to form the new meta-narrative, the new scaffolding (or "relational framing") upon which this journey into a holistic worldview can unfold.

Amongst other things, this new cosmology explains how consciousness pervades not just our human minds but all of life, and all of matter, time, and space across the entire Universe. Consciousness, according to this new cosmology, pervades our entire space–time continuum; it is the plenum in-forming all mind-matter within our Universe. Compelling evidence is emerging of a unified reality pervaded by an informational field that informs all forms. Latest findings indicate this informational field manifests holographically. This proposes that our entire universe exists and evolves as a "cosmic hologram" (Currivan, 2017).

The story we are still telling ourselves, teaching our children, and serving up to our leaders in our business schools today, of a push–pull Newtonian Neo-Darwinist world with randomly mutating separate organisms struggling selfishly in a battle for the survival of the fittest is no longer serving us (if it ever did).

The forefront of scientific understanding is now informing us of what the ancients have long pointed to: mind pervades matter and space. This shape-shifts our worldview and has the potential to change everything, not least the level of consciousness we bring to today's challenges.

The Nested Mind

We are just beginning to unpack what this understanding of the universal field of consciousness means for ourselves as human beings. For instance, our perception of "mind" is metamorphosing before our eyes. We used to assume mind was a product of the brain, but recent scientific findings in embodied cognition show that the brain, the heart, and the gut all have complex neurobiological networks in them capable of memory, learning, and cognition, and that these three neurological centers interconnect with a sensing and responding network spanning our entire body (Claxton, 2015; Childre, Martin, Rozman, & McCraty, 2016).

The areas of cardiology, neuroscience, endocrinology, immunology, physiology, and psychology have tended to be treated as quite separate areas in Western science until now, but it is becoming more and more apparent that our entire body is an inter-relational network of brain, organs, muscles, lymph nodes, hormones, neural networks, and neuropeptides. The body is a physiological network of both mind and matter. It is intelligent, its emotions and body sensations are forms of intelligence. These emotional and somatic intelligences are a blend of physiology and psychology, mind and matter, providing an "embodied intelligence" not just in the brain but throughout our entire body–mind system (Pert, 1997).

During the 1980s and 1990s, the award-winning psychologist Eugene Gendlin published his seminal research on *Focusing* (1996), proving that the mind is pervading the entire body, and that the body engages with the world through ongoing interactivity. Gendlin's research shows that we are inherently inter-relational. We have ongoing body–environment inter-relationality, and our interactive connection with the world continuously regenerates itself. This ongoing inter-relationality provides an "implicit knowing" within us—a source of wisdom—which we can learn to become more conscious of. Through attending to somatic sensations in our body, we unlock the wisdom of the body which is continuous with, not separate from, the world around us. We can learn to sense fluctuations in our local field thus enhance our receptivity and responsiveness to this ongoing inter-relationality of mind–body–environment.

In 1995, Daniel Goleman's work on *Emotional Intelligence* highlighted the importance of emotions and emotional intelligence (EQ) for leadership development and organizational learning. Goleman found that how we cultivate awareness of our own and others' feelings and consciously respond to these feelings in appropriate ways helps our leadership potential. Studies show that EQ outperforms IQ as a predictor of job success and performance capability (Goleman, 1995).

Then, in 1997, the neuroscientist Candace Pert's ground-breaking work *Molecules of Emotion* provided more insight into the integration of body–mind sensations, feelings, and thoughts, in what Pert referred to as the "psychosomatic network"—an integrated system of psyche and soma (p. 185). The psyche comprises the non-material aspects such as mind, emotion, and soul, and the soma comprises the material aspects such as the cells, organs, and tissues. Pert notes:

> we need to start thinking about how the mind manifests itself in various parts of the body and, beyond that, how we can bring that process into [our] consciousness. The concept of a network, stressing the interconnectedness of all systems of the organism, has a variety of paradigm-breaking implications … Mind doesn't dominate body, it becomes body—body and mind are one … Bodymind, a term first proposed by Dianne Connelly reflects the understanding, derived from Chinese medicine, that the body is inseparable from the mind … it could be said that intelligence is located not only in the brain but in the cells that are distributed throughout the body, and that the traditional separation of mental processes, including emotions, from the body is no longer valid.
>
> *(p. 187)*

More recently, in 2012, Wholebody Focusing therapists Glenn Fleisch and Karen Whalen explore how Quantum Field Theory helps explain the bodymind's innate ability to sense subtle changes in the field within and all about us both at local and non-local levels. For clarity—"local" means our immediate surroundings or neighborhood, and "non-local" means places which may be vast distances from our surroundings. Fleisch and Whalen integrate Quantum Consciousness with Gendlin's Focusing, to explore how our bodymind is in continuous dialogue with the local environment and the informational field pervading reality at the quantum level.

It would seem that due to the interconnected nature of sub-atomic vibrations at both local and non-local levels, our bodymind can detect changes in the field locally and non-locally. This helps explain the subtle perturbations we may notice in us due to changes in our local field—like a person's mood changing in a meeting—and also perturbations due to changes in our non-local field—like a loved-one having a car accident and we sense an empathic resonance, likewise when someone phones us at the same time as we are thinking of them. It helps explain intuitions, deep inner-knowings, and hunches that inform us about the rightness of a situation, the right path to take, or dissonance that needs attention.

We are tuning-in to the subconscious conversations in our bodymind, and cultivating an awareness of body-in-environment which senses into the whole field: this is cultivating self-awareness and systemic-awareness simultaneously.

With a more receptive awareness—an epistemological and ontological opening—we can sense into these quantum conversations going on in our bodymind, and so tap into this field within and all around us. Practices such as Wholebody Focusing, Deep Listening, Heart Centering Prayer, Mindful Meditation, Yoga Nidra, and Heart Entrainment help cultivate this "quantum listening" by cultivating our "bodymindfulness."

We can cultivate the collective conditions conducive for our organizations to become more receptive-responsive, by deepening how we attend, listen, converse, hold meetings, and make decisions within our daily organizational culture. For instance, I often practice deep listening exercises, and hold sharing circles or more formal Way of Council circles, for leaders within an organizational setting. In these practices we create a safe space for people to speak and listen from a place of epistemological and ontological openness. This is often referred to as speaking and listening from the heart, as it is a conscious shift out of our ever-grasping analytic head-knowing into a deeper heart-centered yet full-bodied beingness-and-knowingness.

As we shift our beingness through "bodymindfulness" we tune-in to these subtle system fluctuations. Our systemic awareness deepens, not just within ourselves but within the group.

This requires the art of holding space in a welcoming and deep way that invites in, nurtures, and holds a communal sharing-space for the individuals and collective to feel able to vulnerably open up and become bodymindful while speaking and listening receptively and responsively.

Group practices such as Constellations, Social Presencing Theater, Deep Listening, Circles, Applied Improv, help embody this quality of beingness-and-knowingness within teams and across diverse groups. I call this "living systems being," as we are opening up to more of how life really is. Clare Graves (2005) refers to this as opening up to the magnificence of life. This is a threshold crossing, as it shifts our sense of self and our relationality with the world.

The more we can create the conditions conducive for ourselves and others to "cross the threshold," the more we can consciously align ourselves to the field, and become consciously aware of the dynamic interchange of ourselves with life; an ever-unfolding interplay of systemic influences, patterns, emergence, and flow. Our organizations can then become future-fit and life-affirming through how the people and the organization "shows-up" in the world, and in terms of how it authentically contributes to the magnificence of life.

As the pioneering philosopher Owen Barfield foresaw, this comes with an individual and collective "burden of existential responsibility" to participate wisely within the all-pervasive wisdom of this interconnected world (1988, p. 186). Barfield knew this "return" demands our discernment to attend in ways that work with, rather than against, this magnificence of life. Because, as we "return," we begin to realize that our moment-to-moment conscious experience of life influences and is influenced by our intention and attention: we become conscious co-creators within this magnificent tapestry of life.

And now, with all this in "mind", let's explore the future.

Anticipating the Future

Future-orientated strategic thinking, foresight methods, and the use of anticipatory practices aim to help organizations better realize their strategic intent.

There is clearly a need to better guide ourselves in times of increased volatility, and what is sometimes overlooked is that the increased volatility and systemic wicked problems of this "new-norm" context affects the suitability of the tools, techniques, and foresight methods we use.

We can see that over the recent decades, our use of future-orientated thinking has changed. For instance, in the 1960s, Delphi studies and systems modeling were fashionable, and in the 1980s to 2000s scenario planning was popular. With the rise of wicked systemic problems, disruptive innovations, and the multi-dimensional nature of change, often scenario planning is often not enough. Hence, there is rising demand for anticipatory practices that help organizations navigate this uncertainty by improving their capacity to better anticipate and respond to the emerging future.

To date, conventional anticipatory practices have tended to be rooted in a Newtonian cause-and-effect view of complex systems. We learn from past experiences, spot trends from data about what has already happened, and provide models or scenarios about the future. This approach lags behind the scientific discoveries of the 20th century with the arrival of Einstein's Theory of Relativity and subsequent Quantum Theory, as well as Complexity Theory and Systems Theory being enriched by a deeper understanding of living systems' emergence and predictive behavior at both local and non-local levels.

The pioneering biologist Robert Rosen (2005) has explored anticipatory predictive systems within Nature, in terms of how biological organisms respond to their ever-changing environment. It is not just biological systems that use anticipatory systems to survive and thrive, but also the living systems of our organizations and social systems. Rosen's research shows that complex living systems naturally construct internal models which predict pattern changes in their environment. It would seem that all living systems have an innate anticipatory capacity—modeling past experience while involving feedback from the future. This innate anticipatory capacity can be influenced by the strategic intent of the living system—its sense of purpose or intrinsic teleology. Interestingly, this radical idea is now being supported by pioneering findings in Quantum Theory.

In short, how we lead, sense-in, and respond, while creating the conditions for others in the organization to better lead, sense-in, and respond, directly influences the future-fitness of the organization, improving its ability to thrive amid increasing volatility while making good on its strategic intent.

Let's unpack this a bit, as it is important to understanding how we best create the conditions conducive for life-affirming organizations to thrive now and into the uncertain future.

The work of Senge, Scharmer, and others at MIT and the Presencing Institute explores the importance of creating the conducive conditions within ourselves as leaders and within our team dynamics so that we allow the natural capacity of leaders, teams, and organizational systems to sense into the emerging future—to anticipate and respond in ways that allow the organization to flourish. We shall explore this important body of work around "sensing into our emerging future" in a moment. But first, let's explore futurist and cultural change researcher Hardin Tibbs' (2017) insights on the upgrading of anticipatory practices in light of 20th and 21st century findings about living systems, consciousness, Quantum Theory, and non-locality.

Physics shows us that the world we live in is permeated by electromagnetic waves, radiant energy formed by an interweaving of electricity and magnetism—familiar to us as light and radio waves.

According to Quantum Theory, these electromagnetic waves have a dual nature. They travel through space and time as waves and at the point of arrival—or specific observation—they appear to have the characteristics of point particles. This shape-shifting is referred to as wave-particle duality.

In Newtonian causation, particles are like billiard balls—we can know their position throughout their trajectory of travel. Whereas, in Quantum Theory, the state and future possibilities of the wave-energy are determined by probabilities until the moment of arrival, whereupon the wave function collapses into the particle.

To explain this mysterious "collapse of the wave function," physicist John Cramer, at the University of Washington, has proposed that quantum transactions occur between the future and the present (Tibbs, 2017). According to his "transactional interpretation" the transmission of a photon from an emitter to a receiver consists first of an "offer" wave moving forward in time which elicits an "echo" wave back in time (from the future toward the present) that travels back from the receiver to the emitter. This quantum transaction is like a "handshake" wave that rapidly builds up backwards and forwards between the emitter and the receiver, culminating in the transference of a quantum of energy and momentum. There is a buzzing back and forth—but in time not space—a resonance that builds, before the actual transfer takes place. Hence, this "handshake" energy exchange between the present and the future is a two-way present–future, future–present interaction. From the standpoint of this interpretation of quantum theory, no longer can we view our engagement with the future as one-way, a peering out into the future, but instead it is an inter-relation, a two-way resonance. And this two-way resonance, it would seem, is affected by our strategic, goal-directed intention. Our intention helps call forth the future, as it helps set up the resonance with the future which then draws us forward as resonance builds up (Tibbs, 2017).

It is the quality of our beingness-and-knowingness that allows us to be open enough to then sense into our emerging future which we are intentionally co-creating.

This radically recasts the one-way linear notion of cause-and-effect which conventional anticipatory practices and foresight models tend to be based upon.

Cramer's insights could explain how potential futures are actualized through our participatory intention and attentive being-and-knowing. From this we see the importance of the intention and attention held by the leader, and the importance of the intention and attention held by the organization as a goal-directed, purposeful living system.

Big data and analytical modeling crunching past trends of what has already happened and looking for patterns based on these past behaviors is useful and provides part of the picture, and yet it is only part of the puzzle (Tibbs, 2017). To call forth the future we intend to create, we need to create the conditions within our organizational culture for the right resonance—through intention, attention (beingness-and-knowingness), and sense of purpose. Then, we can better call forth the best future possibilities, flexing and adapting as we learn from our ever-changing field conditions. This attunes our future-fitness.

Hardin Tibbs (2017) posits that as well as living systems' anticipatory capacity being based on past experience, there is an intrinsic potential within reality for true anticipatory consciousness: past–present–future. How we "show up": our intention, our attentiveness, and our purposefulness, all contribute to the resonance we create with emerging future possibilities.

Let us now turn to Otto Scharmer's (2016) Theory U work at MIT exploring how as leaders we can best sense into our emerging future. Scharmer highlights the importance of our selves being an instrument of the emerging future (p. 198).

The more we open up, cross the threshold, and access deeper sources of knowing, we sense into the emergent flow of life, its inherent synchronistic currents. The key here is allowing space for generative explorations, what Scharmer refers to as "activating generative social fields" that allow us to open heart, open mind, open will, and cross the epistemological and ontological threshold (p. 251).

We open up these generative social fields by creating space for stillness and connection within ourselves and within our group dynamics. And then we activate the generative fields through the spark of our intentional and attentive awareness (Scharmer, 2016, p. 251). We deepen our self-awareness and systemic-awareness, and deepen the social field, cultivating a deeper source of creativity and consciousness (p. 252). This simultaneous letting-go and opening-up, calls for receptive discernment. We need to be able to discern subtle perturbations within us and within the field, and ensure we are not being distracted or affected by reactivity instead of receptive-responsiveness.

Scharmer highlights the problem of "mindless action or actionless mind": where we are not fully open, integrated, receptive, and responsive, mindless action can creep in; or when we are deeply receptive but lack the impetus to be responsive enough to take action and prototype into the future through small explorations, actionless mind can creep in (p. 213).

We are our own vessels of exploration, forever sensing-into, responding, and learning. It is up to us to discern when we are coming from a place of connectedness, and when we are getting caught up in reactivity, habit, unconscious bias, ego-machination, or projected illusion. The more we practice, the more artful we become at sensing when we are flowing with this self-system-field connectedness, and responding to dissonances, consonances, and synchronistic pathways into our emerging future.

It has been said by many wise folk throughout the ages, that when we stay true to ourselves, the Universe conspires to help us. It is this that we are unpacking here, how to stay in tune and true while holding clear intent toward our life-affirming futures, for ourselves and our organizations. Leadership specialist Joseph Jaworski sets the bar when he notes that true leadership comes through "staying true and connected with that deeper intention all the time, throughout the whole day or week or year, or even longer" (cited in Scharmer, 2016, p. 207).

Scharmer identifies three types of connection (p. 213):

1. Upward connection—connecting to our truer Self, that lies beyond our masks and habituations, and also connecting with our Higher Purpose through intuition and intention.
2. Horizontal connection—deeply listening in to feedback within and beyond ourselves, this is the opening-up to beingness-and-knowingness, sensing system feedback, noticing signs, and mirror-signals from our environment.
3. Downward connection—locally learning through fast-cycle prototypes, embodying and engaging here-in-the-moment, manifesting it, testing it out, learning through doing.

Scharmer speaks of the need for a new social grammar—"the capacity to access the subtler and deeper dimensions of social fields" (p. 299).

My hope is that this chapter contributes to this new social grammar in terms of highlighting the importance of our receptivity and responsiveness, as we deepen our self-awareness and systemic-awareness.

I predict that tools and methods which aid this systemic leadership capacity and organizational responsiveness will become more and more in demand over the coming months and years ahead as the turbulence of our uncertain future increases.

I believe we are living through an epochal moment in our human history where the very concept of what it means to be human is shape-shifting, and this is catalyzed by, and in turn influences, how we lead with the future in mind. In business, this worldview shift is characterized by the organization-as-machine metaphor giving way to the organization-as-living-system. This shift in worldview demands new approaches to leadership development. Enter the rise of leadership methodologies rooted in living systems thinking, such as regenerative leadership, bio-leadership, Teal Evolutionary, and Theory U.

The well-respected business futurist John Naisbitt notes, "The greatest breakthroughs of the twenty-first century will not be because of technology, they will be because of an expanding concept of what it means to be human" (cited in Laloux, 2014, p. 43). I, for one, wish to consciously co-create life-affirming future possibilities through how I show up, and through my leadership development work with leaders across a great variety of sectors. These times ask—demand—that we create the conditions conducive for ourselves and our organizations to become more conscious, more attuned, more human, as we open ourselves up to and re-connect with the magnificence of this more-than-human world and Universe.

References

Barfield, O. (1988). *Saving the Appearances*. Middletown, CT: Wesleyan University Press.

Childre, D., Martin, H., Rozman, D., & McCraty, R. (2016). *Heart Intelligence*. London: HeartMath, Waterfront Press.

Claxton, G. (2015). *Intelligence in the Flesh*. London: Yale University Press.

Currivan, J. (2017). *The Cosmic Hologram*. Rochester, UK: Inner Traditions.

Einstein, A. (n.d.). Retrieved from www.gurteen.com/gurteen/gurteen.nsf/id/X00028F62/.

Fleisch, G., & Whalen, K. (2012). Quantum consciousness: An explanatory model for life forward movement in wholebody focusing. *Folio*, 84–97.

Gendlin, E. (1996). *Focusing-Orientated Psychotherapy*. New York: Guilford Press.

Goleman, D. (1995). *Emotional Intelligence*. London: Bantam Books.

Graves, C. (2005). *The Never Ending Quest*. Eds. Christopher Cowan & Natasha Tordorovic.

Harding, S. (2006). *Animate Earth: Science, Intuition and Gaia*. Totnes, UK: Green Books.

Jaworski, J. (2011). *Synchronicity* San Francisco: Berrett-Koehler.

Ki-Moon, B. (2013). Lecture given to Stanford University, USA. Retrieved from www.un.org/sg/en/content/sg/speeches/2013-01-17/remarks-stanford-university.

Laloux, F. (2014). *Reinventing Organizations*. New York: Nelson Parker.

Marques, J. (2016). TEDx College of the Canyons. Retrieved from www.youtube.com/watch?v=LJPLY-SJakM&feature=youtu.be.

Milne, J. (2010). Ascent to the good. Lecture given to the Henry George Foundation, London.

Pert, C. (1997). *Molecules of Emotion* New York: Pocket Books.

Rayner, A. (2017). *The Origin of Life Patterns in the Natural Inclusion of Space in Flux*. Berlin: Springer.

Rosen, R. (2005). *Life Itself.* New York: Columbia University Press.

Scharmer, O. (2016). *Theory U*. Oakland, CA: Berrett-Koehler Publishers.

Shaw, G. B. (n.d.). Retrieved from www.goodreads.com/quotes/28382-we-are-made-wise-not-by-the-recollection-of-our.

Tarnas, R. (2007). *Cosmos and Psyche*. New York: Plume.

Tibbs, H. (2017). Future anticipatory practices. In R. Poli (Ed.), *Handbook of Anticipation: Theoretical and Applied Aspects of the Use of Future in Decision Making*. Springer International Publishing.

30

A TIME FOR US

Collectively Moving Toward Higher Consciousness

Joan Marques

The Greatest Thing You'll Ever Learn
Is Just To Love And Be Loved In Return.
(Eden Ahbez, "Nature Boy," 1947)

The Power of Love

We don't need a high level of education to understand the statement above. It is a statement that is comprehensible for all human beings, because love is the single emotion that is felt long before other ways of communicating start. And yet, while it may be the topic that most songs and poems have been devoted to over time, it seems to have disappeared from our common, everyday radar. Perhaps not in the romantic sense of passion and desire, but very much so in the humane sense of compassion and acceptance—at work, as well as in other settings.

Still, there are an infinite number of touching stories that attest to the greatness of love, such as Max DePree's (2008) story of Zoe, his granddaughter, who made it through premature birth thanks to love. Born weighing 1 pound and 7 ounces, Zoe had only 5 to 10% chance of making it through 3 days in life. DePree, best known as the successful CEO of Herman Miller, Inc. and currently referring to himself as a student of human nature and life, recalls the orders from the hospital nurse who was aware that Zoe's father had left and was unwilling to take on his role. The nurse explained to Max,

> For the next several months, at least, you're the surrogate father. I want you to come to the hospital every day to visit Zoe, and when you come, I want you to rub her body and her legs and arms with the tip of your finger. While you're caressing her, you should tell her over and over how much you love her, because she has to be able to connect your voice to your touch.

Zoe, which is the Greek word for "life," made it thanks to this love that was shown to her before she could actually comprehend any other verbal communication.

The Cause of Discontentment and the Need for Loving-kindness

> The greatest protection in all the world is Loving-kindness.
>
> *(Buddha)*

> The second half of the twentieth century was characterized by individualism, the desire to do things only for the sake of our separate self. Our society has been dominated by the desire for fame and wealth, material things, and hedonism. As a result, many people have fallen away from their spiritual traditions and their families. We cannot have healthy families if we believe joy can be found only in the pursuit of power, sex, and wealth.
>
> *(Thich, 2003, p. 171)*

As our 21st century world—and therefore our environment—becomes more complicated due to greater diversity, increased speed of actions, accelerated change, and a continuous demand for self-reinvention due to greater job insecurity, many of us find ourselves looking for ways to maintain our inner-balance, and refrain from being overtaken by an unremitting state of disgruntlement. The questions that we oftentimes ask ourselves are, "Is this all there is to it?—Is it really worth my while to continue racing against everyone else?" There is a well-known statement that says, "Even if you win the rat race, you're still a rat." I, personally, have no problem with rats in their symbolic depiction, because they form a rather smart group that we can surely learn a thing or two from. But a *rat race* has something hopeless to it. Dictionary.com (2018) describes "rat race" as "A difficult, tiring, often competitive activity or routine." Wikipedia (2018) even adds a very striking contemporary analogy to the definition:

> A rat race is a term used for an endless, self-defeating or pointless pursuit. It conjures up the image of the futile efforts of a lab rat trying to escape whilst running around a maze or in a wheel. In an analogy to the modern city, many rats in a single maze run around making a lot of noise bumping into each other, but ultimately *achieve nothing (meaningful) either collectively or individually.*

How true! Whether we are masters at playing office politics or not; and regardless if we can play our part in the socializing game well or not, we all wonder at times what it is ultimately good for. A prestigious position? A high salary? Excellent benefits? Gaining a place in the in-group? Should we really define ourselves as such? How long do these so-called privileges stay with us anyway? And what about our self-perception? How much do we like ourselves at the end of the day when we quietly review our actions and get confronted with our conscience? What about the long-term picture? After retirement, for instance?

I know a man—we'll call him Frank—who is now a senior citizen in another country. During his working years, he held a very prestigious position. He was a management member at a large multi-national corporation, and was very proud of his job. So proud, that he would identify himself through his workplace, even when he would answer the phone at home. He would consistently use his last name followed by the name of the company he worked for, as if that were his identity. His family members would chuckle about it, but they never said anything to him in order to spare his feelings, as he was otherwise really a very nice man. Then, two major things happened almost at the same time: Frank's retirement came up, and the economy of his country went down. His local-currency pension, which he had highly anticipated, became practically worthless, and the company that he had so highly admired and faithfully served for over four decades, was unwilling to do anything about it. Frank had been replaced and forgotten, as he was no longer of any use to the corporation. So, the well-to-do, proud man became poor and disillusioned, and instantly dependent upon his children for financial support.

Frank's story illustrates how fickle positions and prestige are, and how rude the awakening can be if we cling too much to status symbols of any kind. While the level of appreciation may have changed for the better in the past years in some workplaces, there are still many organizations that only value their workers for what they can get out of them, and not any further.

On the other hand, if we consider that there is a continuous increase in books, workshops, and organizational leaders that focus on issues related to human wellbeing at work, we may become a little more hopeful about the place of loving-kindness in the workplace. Contrary to what the daily rat race instills within us, loving-kindness is not an obsolete emotion, but one that is very much alive.

Wallace (1993) shares the idea that loving-kindness is still vibrant and very useful in our world today. He states,

> The cultivation of loving-kindness is ideally suited for the bustling world we live in. It generates a quality of mind that wishes for the well-being of others, and at the same time it profoundly enhances our ability to attain well-being in our own lives.
>
> *(p. 119)*

Kornfield (2002) agrees, "Loving-kindness offers care and well-wishing to another without expectation or demand. There is no distance between their well-being and your own" (p. 71).

Understanding Wallace's and Kornfield's statements above requires for us to elevate our level of consciousness in order to transcend the boundaries of "self." Indeed, we are our own person, but even more than that, we are part of the greater whole that is humanity, and an even greater whole that is life on Earth. When we decide to raise our awareness to this level, we start realizing the futility of shortsighted selfishness, excessive profit focus, or discrimination on any basis. And then, loving-kindness becomes possible.

Stepping Up to Higher Consciousness

Increasingly, distinguished authors from various disciplines are referring to the necessity of a higher consciousness for human wellbeing and the wellbeing of all life on earth.

In *Power vs. Force*, David Hawkins (1995) distinguishes between the *self* and the *Self*. He starts out by explaining, "Our vision of consciousness is aligned with our concept of self: The more limited the sense of self, the smaller the parameter of experiencing is" (p. 251). Explaining the narrowness of perceiving ourselves as separate entities from all others, Hawkins continues, "The identification and experience of *self* could be limited to a description of one's physical body" (p. 252). Hawkins then explains how we can move away from limited perspectives of the *self* toward an increased awareness of *consciousness* as the driver in our existence, simply by expanding our thought process from having a body with the mind as its driver, to consciousness as the observer of all subjective and objective phenomena in life. He clarifies, "Consciousness is experienced as beyond all form and time and seen as equally present everywhere" (p. 253). In his continued elaboration Hawkins affirms that consciousness is a state "beyond mind" (p. 253); "it is complete, all-inclusive, with neither need nor want, and beyond the limitation of experiencing the merely individualized, personal self" (p. 254). He also explains that pure consciousness transcends ordinary thoughts or feelings and elicits senses of infinite power, compassion, gentleness, and love (p. 254).

Hawkins is not the only one calling for higher consciousness. In his book *The Universe in a Single Atom*, His Holiness the Dalai Lama also devotes a number of chapters to this topic. Consciousness is of high importance in Buddhist philosophy. "In Buddhism, since the definition of 'living' refers to sentient beings, consciousness is the primary characteristic of 'life'" (Dalai Lama, 2005, p. 106). The Dalai Lama asserts that, while there is still little consensus about what consciousness exactly is, the process of in-depth examination of this phenomenon has significantly intensified in the past decades. He emphasizes, "According to the earliest scriptures, the Buddha saw consciousness as playing a key role in determining the course of human happiness and suffering" (p. 121).

Another authority in the area of consciousness is Wallace (2002), who accentuates in his article "A Science of Consciousness: Buddhism (1), the Modern West (0)" that, while Western civilization has not yet developed a science of consciousness, Buddhist philosophy has traditionally taught its adherents to *observe the mind with the mind* in order to bring about transformations for the better in one's perceptions and behaviors. This is captured in the last of the Four Noble Truths. These Truths are, "[1] the truth of suffering, [2] the source of suffering, [3] the cessation of suffering together with its source, and [4] the path leading to that cessation" (Wallace, 2002, p. 18). So, the fourth truth, the path leading to the end of suffering, is the one where consciousness enters the picture, and it is not difficult to conclude that, if our suffering is caused by office politics, strife, increased job insecurity, or any other source of external stress, we should seek the answer in ourselves, by transcending the boundaries that we have thus far erected in our minds.

Reviewing the current status of consciousness as a research topic, Wallace (2002) does conclude that neither the scientific nor the Buddhist tradition thus far embodies "a rigorous, unbiased, multifaceted science of consciousness" (p. 26).

A Time for Us

Regardless of the current levels of development in examining consciousness as a scientific phenomenon, it seems that an increasing segment of humanity is becoming aware of the flaw in defining one's existence as merely a limited "self," while all contemporary developments and trends lead us into one unified direction: the necessity to realize our one-ness as "life on earth," regardless of our divergent physical or psychological traits. At the largest level, this necessity manifests itself in the serious ecological threats that our planet is facing today. The need to do something about the continuously and increasingly worrying endangerment of various forms of life on Earth—human beings not excluded—is forcing us to rethink our acts, and, with that, our narrow perceptions of "self."

Overcoming the Hurdles: Some Thoughts and Steps

I have known you
For the longest time
Because you are me
And I am you
Yet, I have been blinded
By lessons from blind teachers
Who received their lessons
From blind ones before
But as my eyes are opening,
I see the real essence of this—our existence

We are all in this together
And by lending each other a hand
The journey becomes more enjoyable
For I am you
And you are me

(Joan Marques)

Interconnectedness: that's what this is all about. Yet, it takes time to distinguish that, especially in our fast-paced, aggressive, ever-changing contemporary world. Many people go through the motions of their cultural values and religious beliefs without ever fully integrating loving-kindness in their lives. Yet, if we start pursuing higher consciousness, the realization of loving-kindness becomes a true reward to ourselves and all our stakeholders. Wallace (1993) explains,

> To develop an attitude of loving-kindness, first we must develop a truly loving attitude toward ourselves, compassionately understanding our own desire to be happy and to avoid suffering. As part of that, we must understand the nature of our own ignorance that thwarts this desire for happiness and instead brings suffering. This done, we will have taken an essential first step toward developing loving-kindness toward all beings. *(p. 120)*

Before starting to comment that loving-kindness toward all beings in this turbulent world is an impossible task to achieve, we should consider the following: every major problem started as a small issue, but got escalated into something humongous. Equally, every major solution can begin as a small gesture that can expand into something great. The small gesture in this case, is love or loving-kindness. But this type of love can only be ignited when we become willing to look past our trivial differences, and take these for what they really are: beautification of life on Earth as a multifaceted, multi-colored flower garden. I once saw an advertisement for Denny's, an American restaurant chain, in their campaign toward embracing diversity. It entailed a young man explaining that America is a garden of flowers: some are daisies and some are roses, but they are all in the same garden, contributing to the beauty and colorful view that brightens a day.

The garden we should focus on today is larger than just America: it spans our entire globe. All we need to recognize it, is a higher level of consciousness: a sense where we learn to stimulate the part of our mind (right brain hemisphere) that is aware of interconnectedness and mutuality, and bring that in balance with the part that accentuates our individualism, which forces us into the constant strive with the Joneses and encourages the rat race mentality (left brain hemisphere). When we choose to rise to higher consciousness, we cease to focus on only the short-term outcomes of our actions.

- We start broadening our perspectives and examine the wellbeing of life in general in everything we do.
- We start rethinking our job and its contents, the organization where we work and its mission, and our behavior toward our colleagues, friends, and loved ones.
- We become aware that meaning is crucial in making our life's journey a pleasant one for others and ourselves.
- Consequently, we start engaging in ways to create meaning. In doing so, we reach out. We deviate from positional protectionism, political friction, and selfishness in our daily actions, and evolve toward the things that are really important: a purpose in everything we do, and sustainability for all life on Earth.

Because the process of obtaining higher consciousness in our daily actions has to start small before it can evolve into something larger, we need to begin at the personal level. Some useful reflective questions we might ask ourselves are:

1. Am I *who* I want to be? What part of my actions am I proud of, and what part am I embarrassed about? How can I minimize the latter? What do I need to do to achieve that?
2. Am I *where* I want to be? Do I like my job? Are the rewards I receive meaningful to me and those around me? Am I content with my life at home, and are my loved ones content with me? If not, what can I do to achieve that?
3. Am I living *how* I would like to? Am I living beyond my means? Am I doing things solely to impress others? Why is that? Is it necessary? If it causes too much pressure onto me, what can I do about that?
4. Am I *treating* those around me in a correct manner? Am I honest and truthful toward them? Do I give enough? If something is not right, what can I do to change that?
5. Am I *contributing* to the wellbeing of the planet? Am I participating in the wellbeing of my community? Is it enough? Am I satisfied with it? If not, what can I do about that?

These simple reflective questions can help us focus toward a more meaningful life for ourselves and those around us, but, ultimately, also for those who don't even know us. Living with higher consciousness is beneficial for our own existence as well as those of others. It opens the gate to loving-kindness. And loving-kindness is expressed through compassion. Compassion is an intrinsic element in all religions, but it stands as a pinnacle in Buddhism. The Dalai Lama (2005) confirms this in his statement, "In Buddhism the highest spiritual ideal is to cultivate compassion for all sentient beings and to work for their welfare to the greatest possible extent" (p. 10). In *The Art of Happiness*, the Dalai Lama further explains,

> Compassion can be roughly defined in terms of a state of mind that is non-violent, nonharming, and nonaggressive. It is a mental attitude based on the wish for others to be free of their suffering and is associated with a sense of commitment, responsibility, and respect towards others.
>
> *(Dalai Lama & Cutler, 1998, p. 114)*

Thich Nhat Hanh (1991) wonderfully weaves love and compassion together when he states,

> Love is a mind that brings peace, joy, and happiness to another person. Compassion is a mind that removes the suffering that is present in the other. We all have the seeds of love and compassion in our minds, and we can develop these fine and wonderful sources of energy.
>
> *(p. 81)*

Figure 30.1 illustrates the cycle that can be instigated when replacing *self* with *Self*.
Figure 30.1 should be interpreted as follows:

- Adopting a higher consciousness is a process that happens from the inside out: you have to be willing to re-evaluate your attitudes, actions, and perceptions, in order to attain higher consciousness (see reflective questions above).
- In attaining higher consciousness, the awareness of being interconnected with all others increasingly starts making sense.

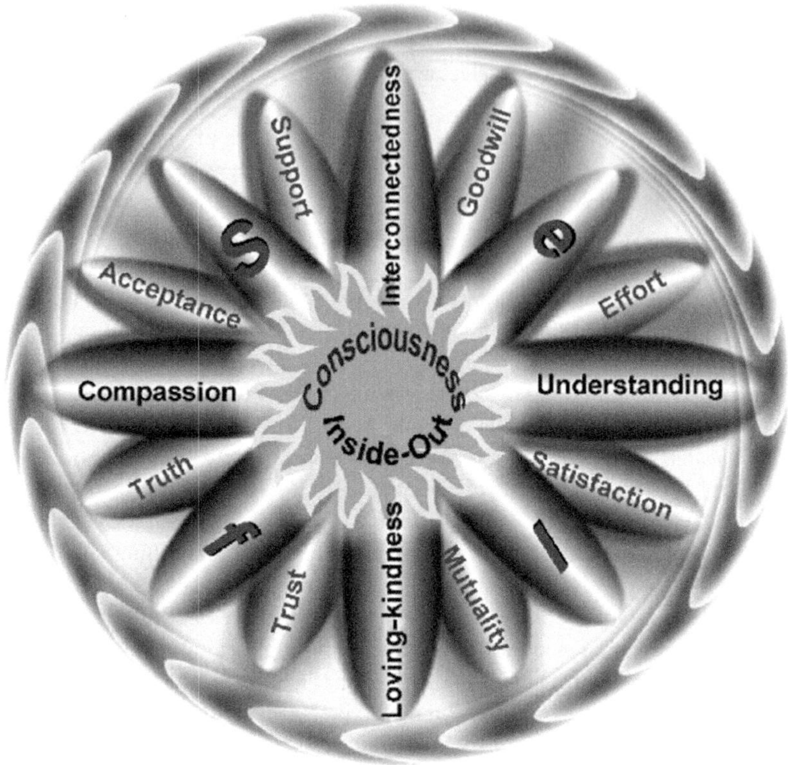

Figure 30.1 Self Through Higher Consciousness

- Your understanding of we-ness augments, and your sense of I-ness decreases.
- Because you learn to see others as part of yourself, you learn to accept and love them, and loving-kindness becomes a part of your life.
- Through love, compassion gets stimulated, and, with that, the will to help others get ahead alongside you instead of continuously competing, striving, backstabbing, and badmouthing. "Mindful observation is the element which nourishes the tree of understanding, and compassion and love are the most beautiful flowers" (Thich, 1991, p. 84).
- With these major realizations, *Self* has started.
- As a consequence of this all-encompassing awareness of *Self*, reciprocal values-based actions such as trust, truth, acceptance, support, goodwill, effort, satisfaction, mutuality, and others become logical petals of the beautiful flower that is life.

When we allow love for all life as part of the *Self* into our existence, the greater picture comes into view. We learn to understand the lesson in everything that happens to us, because we instigated a process of conscious elevation. The world becomes a better place for us, and those around us, and therewith, also for those around them, up till the global level.

> The source of love is deep in us, and we can help others realize a lot of happiness. One word, one action, or one thought can reduce another person's suffering and bring him joy. One word can give comfort and confidence, destroy doubt, help someone avoid

> a mistake, reconcile a conflict, or open the door to liberation. One action can save a person's life or help him take advantage of a rare opportunity. One thought can do the same, because thoughts always lead to words and actions. If love is in our heart, every thought, word, and deed can bring about a miracle. Because understanding is the very foundation of love, words and actions that emerge from our love are always helpful.
>
> *(Thich, 1991, pp. 84–85)*

Toward Wakefulness

Once we can get ourselves in a frame of mind that seeks higher consciousness in order to practice continuously amplified compassion and elevating loving-kindness, we have started our path toward awakening. Thich Nhat Hanh (1998) reviews the seven factors of awakening, which he refers to as limbs of the same tree, and which are:

1. Mindfulness: this involves "remembering, [thus] not forgetting where we are, what we are doing, and who we are with" (p. 215).
2. Investigation: this should not be implemented with a preconceived intention of outcomes, but rather with an open mind in order to "allow things simply to reveal themselves" (p. 216).

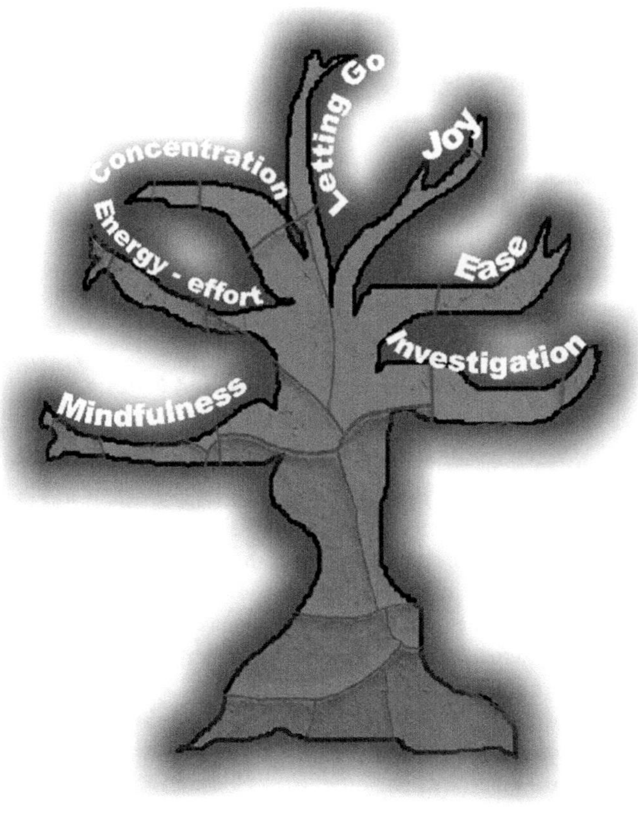

Figure 30.2 Seven Factors of Awakening

3. Energy, effort, diligence, or perseverance: this requires deeper looking into the things that matter, and realizing their essence.

> When we look deeply, we see that life is a miracle beyond our comprehension. But for many young people today, life is meaningless. Many thousands of young people commit suicide every year. [...] We need to help their lives have meaning.
> *(p. 216)*

4. Ease: this is harder to attain and maintain as the standard of our life—and with that the pressure—increases.

> We have to learn ways to bring our energy from our head back to our abdomen. At least once every fifteen minutes, we need to practice letting go [...]. We need to practice resting even when we are not sick.
> *(p. 217)*

5. Joy: this precedes happiness. Thich (1998) explains, "When you are thirsty and a glass of water is being served to you, that is joy. When you are actually able to drink the water, that is happiness" (p. 218). Thich elaborates, "If we can expand our vision and also see what is right, this wider picture always brings joy" (p. 218).
6. Concentration: this only becomes wholesome if we make it beneficial to our wellbeing. Buddha used his concentration "to shine light upon his suffering, and he was able to go deeply into life and develop understanding, compassion, and liberation" (p. 218).
7. Equanimity, or letting go: this is not the same as indifference. Rather, it entails that "we love everyone equally" (p. 218).

Every seed that is planted and nurtured well grows. Why not the seed of loving-kindness? "He who experiences the unity of life sees his own Self in all beings, and all beings in his own Self, and looks on everything with an impartial eye" (Buddha).

As a conclusive note, I am inviting you to read the story below about loving-kindness, and how compassion ultimately gets understood, respected, and rewarded.

The Elephant and His Old Blind Mother

Long ago, in the hills of the Himalayas near a lotus pool, the Buddha was once born as a baby elephant. He was a magnificent elephant, pure white with feet and face the color of coral. His trunk gleamed like a silver rope and his ivory tusks curled up in a long arc.

He followed his mother everywhere. She plucked the tenderest leaves and sweetest mangoes from the tall trees and gave them to him. "First you, then me," she said. She bathed him in the cool lotus pool among the fragrant flowers. Drawing the sparkling water up in her trunk, she sprayed him over the top of his head and back until he shone. Then filling his trunk with water, he took careful aim and squirted a perfect geyser right between his mother's eyes. Without blinking, she squirted him back. And back and forth, they gleefully squirted and splashed each other. Splish! Splash! Then they rested in the soft muck with their trunks curled together. In the deep shadows of afternoon, the mother elephant rested in the shade of a rose-apple tree and watched her son romp and frolic with the other baby elephants.

The little elephant grew and grew until he was the tallest and strongest young bull in the herd. And while he grew taller and stronger, his mother grew older and older. Her tusks were yellow and broken and in time she became blind. The young elephant plucked the tenderest leaves and sweetest mangoes from the tall trees and gave them to his dear old blind mother. "First you, then me," he said.

He bathed her in the cool lotus pool among the fragrant flowers. Drawing the sparkling water up in his trunk, he sprayed her over the top of her head and back until she shone. Then they rested in the soft muck with their trunks curled together. In the deep shadows of afternoon, the young elephant guided his mother to the shade of a rose-apple tree. Then he went roaming with the other elephants. One day a king was hunting and spied the beautiful white elephant. "What a splendid animal! I must have him to ride upon!" So the king captured the elephant and put him in the royal stable. He adorned him with silk and jewels and garlands of lotus flowers. He gave him sweet grass and juicy plums and filled his trough with pure water.

But the young elephant would not eat or drink. He wept and wept, growing thinner each day. "Noble elephant," said the king, "I adorn you with silk and jewels. I give you the finest food and the purest water, yet you do not eat or drink. What will please you?" The young elephant said, "Silk and jewels, food and drink do not make me happy. My blind old mother is alone in the forest with no one to care for her. Though I may die, I will take no food or water until I give some to her first."

The king said, "Never have I seen such kindness, not even among humans. It is not right to keep this young elephant in chains." Free, the young elephant raced through the hills looking for his mother. He found her by the lotus pool. There she lay in the mud, too weak to move. With tears in his eyes, he filled his trunk with water and sprayed the top of her head and back until she shone. "Is it raining?" she asked. "Or has my son returned to me?" "It is your very own son!" he cried. "The king has set me free!" As he washed her eyes, a miracle happened. Her sight returned. "May the king rejoice today as I rejoice at seeing my son again!" she said.

The young elephant then plucked the tenderest leaves and sweetest mangoes from a tree and gave them to her. "First you, then me."

Adapted from Buddhist Stories (2018).

References

Buddhist Stories. (2018). The elephant and his old blind mother. Retrieved from http://viewonbuddhism.org/resources/buddhist_stories.html.

Dalai Lama. (2005). *The Universe in a Single Atom.* New York: Broadway Books.

Dalai Lama, & Cutler, H. (1998). *The Art of Happiness.* New York: Riverhead Books.

DePree, M. (2008). It comes from God. First Presbyterian Church of Crestview and Laurel Hill, Florida. Retrieved from www.firstpresbyterian-crestview.org/080217sermon.htm.

Dictionary.com. (2018). Rat race. Retrieved from http://dictionary.reference.com/browse/rat%20race.

Hawkins, D. R. (1995). *Power vs. Force.* Sedona, AZ: Hay House, Inc.

Kornfield, J. (2002). *The Art of Forgiveness, Loving-kindness, and Peace.* New York: Bantam Books.

Thich, N. H. (1991). *Peace Is Every Step.* New York: Bantam Books.

Thich, N. H. (1998). *The Heart of the Buddha's Teaching.* New York: Broadway Books.

Thich, N. H. (2003). *Creating True Peace.* New York: Free Press.

Wallace, A. (1993). *Tibetan Buddhism from the Ground Up.* Boston: Wisdom Publications.

Wallace, A. (2002). A science of consciousness: Buddhism (1), the modern West (0). *Pacific World: Journal of the Institute of Buddhist Studies, 3*(4), 15–32.

Wikipedia. (2018). Rat race. WIKIMEDIA. Retrieved from http://en.wikipedia.org/wiki/Rat_race.

INDEX

For Product Safety Concerns and Information please contact our EU representative GPSR@taylorandfrancis.com Taylor & Francis Verlag GmbH, Kaufingerstraße 24, 80331 München, Germany

Batch number: 10726294

Printed by Printforce, the Netherlands